Philosophical Questions

Philosophy and the Global Context

General Editor: Michael Krausz, Bryn Mawr College

This new series addresses a range of emerging global concerns. It situates philosophical efforts in their global and cultural contexts, and it offers works from thinkers whose cultures are challenged by globalizing movements. Comparative and intercultural studies address such social and political issues as the environment, poverty, consumerism, civil society, tolerance, colonialism, global ethics, and community in cyberspace. They also address related methodological issues of translation and cross-cultural understanding.

Titles in the Series

Intellectual Property: Moral, Legal, and International Dilemmas (1997)
by Adam D. Moore
Ethics of Consumption: The Good Life, Justice, and Global Stewardship (1998)
edited by David A. Crocker and Toby Linden
Alternative Visions: Paths in the Global Village (1998) by Fred Dallmayr

Philosophical Questions

East and West

Edited by
Bina Gupta
and
J. N. Mohanty

ROWMAN & LITTLEFIELD PUBLISHERS, INC.
Lanham • Boulder • New York • Oxford

ROWMAN & LITTLEFIELD PUBLISHERS, INC.

Published in the United States of America
by Rowman & Littlefield Publishers, Inc.
4720 Boston Way, Lanham, Maryland 20706
http://www.rowmanlittlefield.com

12 Hid's Copse Road
Cumnor Hill, Oxford OX2 9JJ, England

British Library Cataloguing in Publication Information Available

Library of Congress Cataloging-in-Publication Data

Philosophical questions : East and West / edited by Bina Gupta and J.N. Mohanty.
    p. cm.—(Philosophy and the global context)
  Includes bibliographical references and index.
  ISBN 0-8476-9284-1 (alk. paper)—ISBN 0-8476-9285-X (pbk. : alk. paper)
  1. Philosophy, Comparative. 2. East and West. I. Gupta, Bina, 1947– II. Mohanty,
Jitendranath, 1928– III. Series.

B799.P46 1996
100—dc21   99-042372

Printed in the United States of America

♾™ The paper used in this publication meets the minimum requirements of
American National Standard for Information Sciences—Permanence of Paper
for Printed Library Materials, ANSI/NISO Z39.48–1992.

Contents

Preface

This is a new venture on our part. The idea of putting together such a volume arose out of our experience of teaching courses on "Philosophy: East and West." Eastern philosophy represents one of the most ancient intellectual traditions in human culture, yet it is generally ignored by Western philosophers. The neglect may stem from a prevalent bias that philosophy as a systematic inquiry, properly understood, is exclusively a Western phenomenon and hence absent in non-Western traditions. The editors of this anthology, trained in both Western and Eastern philosophy, clearly demonstrate that philosophy is more than a history of Greek and European thought.

In this work, we present the readers with the questions and challenges that philosophers confront today irrespective of their tradition. A dialogue across traditions is both necessary and desirable; perhaps it is inevitable. In order for it to be fruitful, it must begin with a sensitivity to both differences and commonalities, neither ignoring the differences nor attempting to reduce the one to the other. When similarities are uncovered, they are potentially revealing, while differences speak for themselves. And whatever unique insights are offered within one philosophical tradition can and should be grist for other philosophic mills.

Keeping the above in mind, the texts have been selected from different streams within the Eastern and the Western traditions, though the materials selected have been grouped under traditional philosophical categories: metaphysics, epistemology, ethics, and religion. We have also included a section on philosophical anthropology, a central concern of philosophy of the East and the West alike. Selections in each section are preceded by an introduction and followed by study questions and suggestions for further reading.

We welcome suggestions, comments, questions, and responses from the instructors who use this volume for their classes.

Above all, we hope this volume will contribute toward breaking the barriers between the East and the West, which specialists have set up over centuries.

General Introduction:
A Framework
for Comparative Philosophy

In the history of Western thought, there is a strong and influential tendency to look upon "philosophy" as a Western cultural product. The word "philosophy" is Greek in origin. But is the discipline called "philosophy" also Western? Even such an eminent and perceptive philosopher as Edmund Husserl held that the expression "Western philosophy" is tautologous and the idea of "non-Western philosophy" a contradiction in terms. The present anthology could serve as a refutation of that narrow conception of philosophy. Happily, today most serious thinkers have come to accept that there are genuine non-Western systems of thought which deserve to be called philosophy.

If philosophy is a thinking consideration of things, then one cannot a priori restrict such thinking only to the West. If philosophy consists in attempts to answer ultimate questions about the nature of reality, the nature and methods of knowledge, the standards of moral judgment, and the deliverance of religious consciousness, then one unmistakably finds such attempts in Indian, Chinese, and Islamic thought. Metaphysics, epistemology, and logic underwent significantly sophisticated developments in India; metaphysics and ethics developed in China; all of these subdisciplines were cultivated in the Islamic world.

Now that science, technology (especially information technology), trade, and commerce promise to transform the world into a "global village," it would be anachronistic if students of philosophy read only about Western philosophy, thereby acquiring the prejudice that that is all there is to "philosophy." How sad it is that students of philosophy learn about Plato and Aristotle, Kant and Hegel and Nietzsche, and do not learn anything about

Gautama and Confucius, or about Śaṃkara and Nāgārjuna, or about Avicenna and Al Ghazāli.

The editors of the present anthology were inspired by the belief that there are at least three birthplaces of philosophy: India, China, and Greece.

Among those who recognize the undeniable truth that there are non-Western philosophies, there is no agreement as to how different the non-Western philosophies are from the Western. Any attempt to answer this question leads inevitably to a discipline known as "comparative philosophy." In its early phase, comparative philosophy set up certain radical and rigid contrasts between Western and Eastern philosophies. These contrasts may be set down, in a tabular form, as follows:

West	India	China	
Life and World Affirmation	Life and World Negation	Life and World Affirmation	(Albert Schweitzer)
Determinate conception of reality	Indeterminism-cum-perspectivism	Hierarchical	(Charles Moore)
Theoretic/ concepts by postulation	Aesthetic/concepts by intuition	Practical— Concrete Concepts	(F.S.C. Northrop)
Pure theory	Practical-Spiritual	Practical-Ethical	(Husserl)
Concept	Intuition	Action	(Hegel)
Intellectual	Intuitive	Ethical	(Radhakrishnan)
Objectifying	Non-objectifying	Non-objectifying	(Heidegger)
World as artifact, i.e., made	World as drama, i.e., manifested	World as organism	(Alan Watts)
Willfulness	Will-lessness	Willingness	(Archie Bahm)

We have in this table an example of the many different ways the contrasts have been drawn between Eastern and Western philosophies and, within Eastern philosophy, between Chinese and Indian philosophies. Many of these are impressionistic and derive as much from the matters themselves as from the philosophical interests of those who make the comparisons.

Hegel's is an instructive case in point. Hegel has proved most influential in shaping the Western attitude toward Oriental thought. His way of looking at things is characterized by a historical view that considers non-Western modes of thinking as lower phases in a developmental process which leads to Western philosophy; eventually culminating, of course, in the purely conceptual system of Hegel himself. Many early comparativists, working in fields other than philosophy, also adopted this general attitude: other religions and cultures are represented as stages in a process that finds its fulfilment in Christianity and Western culture. Today, this attitude is hardly accepted by anyone, except possibly a few dogmatic defenders of that lost cause.

There is also a tendency among Western scholars who are trying to understand the Oriental culture to look there for an "other," for something that derives its interest from its being so different. Based on the assumption that Western thinking is intellectual, logical, and discursive, it is believed that Oriental thinking must be intuitive, experiential, esoteric, and even mystic. Once this contrast is established, then facts fall into place: texts, rituals, practices, arts, medicine and *yoga*—in short, everything is taken to illustrate this contrast. But these are only selected facts. To maintain the belief in an Oriental "other," one must be ignorant of or shut one's eyes to the presence of theories, thoughts, strictly defined concepts, systems of logic, and even the development of empirical sciences and technologies in other cultures. Let us only recall the masses of data collected in Joseph Needham's *Science and Civilisation in China,* B. N. Seal's *Positive Sciences of the Ancient Hindus,* and P. C. Ray's *Ancient Hindu Chemistry*—not to speak of numerous works on Hindu and Buddhist logics and epistemological theories.

The editors of the present volume reject (1) all attempts to set up rigid lines of distinction between Western and Eastern modes of thinking; (2) all attempts to set up philosophical theories of the East or of the West in a linear series of development culminating or intended to culminate in some one favored theory such as we find in Hegel's system, Advaita Vedānta, and Husserl's transcendental phenomenology; and (3) any attempt by scholars, Eastern or Western, to look for an absolute "other" as a means to genuine self-understanding, recognizing that the "absolute other" may, in fact, be of our own making.

The editors also believe that both "Western philosophy" and "Eastern philosophy" are high-level intellectual constructs. What is designated by each name is not a monolithic theory or even a homogenous, mutually commensurable set of theories. Within Western philosophy belong such disparate philosophies as those of Socrates and Nietzsche, Plato and Quine, Heidegger and Carnap. Although in some respects (e.g., with regard to its discursive and metaphysical character) Indian philosophy seems much closer to

Western than to Chinese philosophy, Eastern philosophy comprehends the great divide between Indian and Chinese philosophy. We should keep in mind that the philosophies of India and China, like Western philosophies, also contain enormous diversity within the confines of their own traditions. In order to see that this is the case one needs only compare the pluralistic realism of the Nyāya with the idealistic monism of the Vedānta, or Confucian ethical humanism with the Taoist esoteric monism. Without denying that there is a sustainable sense in which one can talk about them, we should therefore avoid as far as possible referring to these as global entities.

Ethnocentric thinkers who do not want to commit themselves to essentialism (the thesis that each of these global entities has its own irreducible "essence") inevitably fall back on history. Thus Richard Rorty has maintained that what knits Western philosophy into one thread is its historical development, or rather the history of Western culture and the role philosophy has played in it. There is no a priori guarantee, however, that Western and Eastern philosophies, in the course of their histories, never came into contact with each other. It is quite plausible that they did make contact in antiquity, and we are certain that they have influenced each other beginning with the nineteenth century. If new research brings to light that there indeed were fruitful contacts in the past, would it not lead us to revise our "ethnocentrism"?

Shunning high-level global generalizations, it may be more desirable, at a preliminary stage, to look at problems, questions, and issues discussed in the various traditions piecemeal. Philosophers in every tradition have asked, and variously answered (without agreeing among themselves), the question: what is the ultimate reality? Is it Being, Brahman, or the Tao? Is it Nature or is it Spirit? Various versions of "realism" and "idealism" (meaning respectively "that things exist and have their nature independent of any mind" and "that things derive their existence and nature from some mind or other"), and arguments for and against each, abound in both Western and Indian philosophies. However, as one proceeds in this way, one is struck by the fact that—to give but one example—the issue between rationalism and empiricism (whether knowledge derives from reason or is acquired by experience) is never raised in Indian thought. Theories of truth—the so-called correspondence, coherence, pragmatist, and self-evidence theories—play an important role in Western and Indian epistemologies, but the Indian epistemologists ask questions (such as: is knowledge intrinsically or extrinsically true and/or intrinsically or extrinsically false?) that are not asked by their counterparts in the Western tradition. Likewise, among the so-called sources of knowledge the Indians consider *śabda* ("word") as the decisive one, a concept bearing only a remote resemblance to the idea of "testimony," which did not in any case play a major role in Western thought.

One can pursue similar piecemeal questioning with regard to ethics, religion, art, and social philosophy. One can raise, and try to answer—always on the basis of available textual resources and not merely a priori—such questions as: Did the Indian and Chinese thinkers have concepts of man? Recall that Foucault has held that the concept of "man" appeared only with the coming into being of the "human sciences." Did the Indians and the Chinese develop ethical theories or do they give only lists of duties and virtues? What about the idea of freedom of will? Is freedom of will consistent with the belief in *karma* and rebirth? But note that before the last two questions can be answered, one needs to ask: did the psychological theories of the Indians (and the Chinese) make room for a concept of *will* as distinguished from knowledge and feeling? One should also ask: how is Indian logic different from, or to what extent the same as Western logic? Why is it that a strictly logical theory did not develop in China to the extent that it did in India and in Greece? Has it anything to do with the nearness of Sanskrit to Greek, or with the distance of both from Chinese?

Even when one undertakes such piecemeal questionings, one should be careful to ensure that one is not simply taking a concept out of its original home (i.e., the cultural milieu in which it developed) and "recontextualizing" it in order to score a point. This raises such fundamental questions as: To what extent are Sanskrit and Chinese translatable into English without loss—and, correspondingly, addition—of meaning? Sanskrit, one would expect, is more translatable than Chinese into English. What about German? (Is Hegel's *Wissenschaft der Logik* translatable into English?) In view of Quine's thesis that radical translation is not at all possible, one's skepticism regarding translation of Sanskrit or Chinese texts should be regarded as only a special case of *any* translation. In that case, unless one is willing to court the more radical skepticism, the limited skepticism with regard to other cultures may as well be set aside in favor of trying to come up with the best possible translations.

Once these blind alleys and clichés are set aside, the really fruitful work of comparative philosophy can begin. Philosophy, then, can become a conversation of humankind, and not merely a conversation of the West. Let it be a conversation in which Plato and Śaṃkara, Heidegger and Nāgārjuna, Kant and Confucius, Spinoza and Taoism can take part. Only then will philosophy be able to cope with the speed of worldwide communication that technology and commerce have established in the global village.

With these preliminary remarks, we can now explain to readers and instructors the project undertaken in this volume. We have chosen some fundamental areas of philosophy: metaphysics, epistemology, ethics, religion, and human nature. Among philosophers or philosophical theories, we have included in our selection both classical philosophers (Plato, Aristotle,

Descartes, and Kant from the Western tradition; the Buddha, Nāgārjuna, Śaṃkara, Confucius, Mencius, Lao Tzu, Mo Tzu, and Al-Ghazāli from the Eastern tradition) and more recent ones (Heidegger, Martin Luther King Jr., and de Beauvoir from the Western tradition; Radhakrishnan, Aurobindo, Gandhi, Tagore, and Nishida from the Eastern tradition). It is now necessary that we place these selections in their proper contexts.

THE HISTORICAL TRADITIONS

Mall and Hülsmann have spoken appropriately of *"Die drei Geburtsorte der Philosophie,"* these being China, India, and Greece. In this introductory essay, we shall present brief historical accounts of these traditions.

The Chinese Philosophical Tradition

The earliest records of Chinese thinking are found in the oracle bones of the Shang dynasty (eighteenth–eleventh centuries B.C.E.), and even as early as that we find a developed system of rituals, a diversified economy, division of labor, a bureaucracy, and a hierarchical society. Some of these features continue to characterize the Chinese mind. To the ones listed above may be added emphasis on group rather than on individual ethics of social and family obligation and a lack of a sense of tragedy and irony. All of these lead to a basic humanism as a pervasive feature of Chinese thinking.

By the so-called Spring and Autumn Period (722–481 B.C.E.), there were already the "Hundred Schools," including naturalists, cosmologists, sophists, and humanists. But we should not think that humanism excluded the conception of gods and heavenly beings. On the contrary, there was a sense of unity of the human world and the cosmic order including the heavenly force. Politics and religion were the primary moving forces of Chinese thought.

Scholars have emphasized other features of Chinese thought besides humanism. Some have insisted on its historicist character, on the priority accorded to process and change over form and substance or on the importance of cosmology as against ontology. Equally important is the concreteness of Chinese thinking, deriving from the nature of the Chinese language. This point has been elaborately expounded by Hajime Nakamura in his *Ways of Thinking of Eastern People.* Nakamura draws attention to the fact that Chinese abounds in words expressing bodies and shapes; consequently, the Chinese way of articulating concepts is concrete. Thus, for example, the important philosophical word "*li*," meaning "principle," is a character that originally meant "well-distributed veins or minerals or precious stones." Likewise, the universe or cosmos is expressed as "mountains, rivers, and the great earth." The Zen expression for the human body is "the stinking bag of scum." "Perfection" is expressed as "round." The Chinese also had little interest for abstract universals; connected with all of this is the fact that the Chinese created theory not for its own sake, but only insofar as it was relevant for pracical conduct and practical understanding.

However, in spite of its close connection to politics and morality, and in an important sense to religion, Chinese thinking contains what should be called "philosophy"—if by philosophy we mean a systematic reflective thinking on life. Thus Confucianism, Taoism, Mohism, and Legalism should be regarded as philosophical schools. Unlike much of Western philosophy, however, Chinese philosophical thinking, besides laying down theoretical and practical principles, sought to comprehend all of human life with a view to improving it, both individually and socially.

At the head of Chinese philosophy, of course, stands the figure of Confucius (551–479 B.C.E.), whose actual name was K'ung Ch'iu. First and foremost a teacher, he drew around him a substantial number of students to whom he taught his views on morality in personal, family, and social life. He did not write any book, but his sayings appeared in collections by the first century C.E. His best known collection is the *Lun-yü* or the *Analects*. Since he lived at a time when the state had become corrupt and proper use of words seemed to have disappeared from personal and public life, Confucius placed emphasis on proper education in order to train public officials. In his teachings, he emphasized the importance of learning and following tradition. He taught poetry, history, morals, music, ancestral codes of propriety, and social manners, but did not teach any of the practical skills. Although as a philosopher he did not develop either a metaphysics or an epistemology, he did develop a theory of human nature and an elaborate theory of moral virtues. To these we shall return at appropriate places.

The major Neo-Confucian philosopher Mencius (370–290 B.C.E.) modified and extended the teachings of the Master, and has been taken as belonging to the idealistic wing of Confucianism. He sought to explain why a person should act in the way Confucius recommended—following *jen* (or human-heartedness) and *yi* (righteousness)—by developing a theory of the original goodness of human nature and an account of how the Confucian virtues are rooted in that nature. But Mencius also defended Confucius against the criticism of the Master's first opponent, namely, Mo Tzu, who had developed an ethics of all-embracing love. As a Confucian, Mencius saw that the first obligation to love was to family members, then to one's own community, though eventually one may extend it to include all others. But to love all humankind equally, to begin with, would be impossible.

The other major school of Chinese philosophy is Taoism. Known to have been recluses who "escaped from the world" in their zeal to preserve the purity of their individual selves, the Taoists shied away from taking part in public life. The earliest Taoist is Yang Chu, whose dates are uncertain, but who most probably lived sometime between Mo Tzu (479–381 B.C.E.) and Mencius (371–289 B.C.E.). Yang Chu is reported to have despised things and valued self, and taught that one ought not to allow things to imprison one's self. He is also regarded as having encouraged selfishness.

However, *Chuang Tzu* and *Lao Tzu* are the oldest and most respected classical works on Taoism. Lao Tzu, also taken to be the name of the author of *Lao Tzu,* was a contemporary of Confucius who reportedly had met him. Both works express a discontent with life as it is ordinarily lived. The concern with self-perfection remains. But Taoism also had a later religious tradition, more mystical than the thought found in *Chuang Tzu* and *Lao Tzu.* The mystical Taoism looks upon the individual as a mere element in the cosmos; the religious tradition recognized the localized, historicalized existence of individuals in a community. In both, one is invoked to reconnect with a deeper level of reality.

The crucial term, of course, is "*Tao.*" It is the totality of all things, the stuff out of which all things are made. The Absolute, is indescribable and undefinable; simple and formless; the Force operating in and guiding, Nature. It is sometimes described as being (*yu*), sometimes as non-being (*wu*), the latter being more primordial. Obviously, the concept of *Tao* is close to the Upaniṣadic Brahman.

Realization of the *Tao* leads to a simple life in harmony with nature; a life of "non-action" and quietude, beyond "good and evil"; a life of naturalness and spontaneity, of nonattachment. The Taoist ideal life is clearly opposed to the socially committed, rule- and hierarchy-bound life encouraged by Confucius.

The Chinese philosophical tradition moves between Confucianism and Taoism. Another strand of thought merged with both: namely, Buddhism, which entered China from India around the beginning of the Christian era. Attempts were made to reconcile all of these. Mo Tzu, for example, regarded the Confucian classics as flowers and Buddhism as the fruit; he also compared the Buddhist *nirvāṇa* with the Taoist "*wu wei*" (do nothing). In general, despite intermittent periods of antipathy and rivalry between the three schools, the Chinese, in general, were tolerant enough so as not to see any contradiction between them. Thus, in an important sense, the Chinese thinkers had been engaged in creative comparative philosophy long before Western thought came to China; each of the three schools came to be interpreted anew under the influence of the other two.

The Indian Tradition

The Indian philosophical tradition began in the hymns of the *Ṛg Veda,* the earliest of the four Vedas composed probably around 2000 B.C.E. The word

"Veda," derived from the verbal root *vid* (to know), means "knowledge" (or *Wissenschaft*). The Vedas, though regarded as sacred scriptures of the Hindus, contain not only religious hymns to be chanted in praise of gods and goddesses and accounts of sacrificial rituals to be performed, but also documentation of all that the community of that time knew, including astronomy, agriculture, social practices, magical practices, medicine, and music. The sacred, even infallible, status of this literature probably is due not to its revealed character (as is often misleadingly attributed), but to the fact that it is the source of the Hindu culture and civilization: everything begins there, even philosophy.

The decisive origins of philosophy in India are marked by those places where there is a search, a deep questioning, of the "origin" of all things (whether it is in being or in non-being); where behind the multiplicity of deities (*deva*), such as sun, rain, cloud, fire, wind, dawn, there is posited one Being who is only called by (these) different names; where a natural, and at the same time a moral, law (called *ṛta*) is posited as what even the gods follow. The search for the resulting unity underlying the phenomenal multiplicity of things becomes a search for the Brahman (derived from the root *bṛh*, "to burst forth"), the greatest and the root of all things. To the question, What is Brahman? a decisive answer, superseding all of the various answers proffered by thinkers of the time, was given by the Upaniṣads (a group of highly speculative, esoteric–mystical texts) to the effect that Brahman is none other then the *ātman* (the inner self). Thus, by the age of the Upaniṣads (1000–500 B.C.E.), we arrive at the identification of the cosmic Absolute with the inner self, of object and subject—which continues to remain a great theme, though not entirely unchallenged, of Hindu metaphysical thought.

The challenge came very soon in the form of Buddhism, a religious, ethical, and philosophical school founded by Siddhartha Gautama (born 562 B.C.E.) who rejected the Upaniṣadic concept of *ātman* (understood as an eternal, all-pervasive spirit) while preserving and building upon the already handed down concepts of *karma* and rebirth, *avidyā* or ignorance, and freedom from suffering known as *mokṣa,* now called *nirvāṇa.* The idea of an unchanging substance underlying changing manifestations is replaced by the ideas of an aggregate of constituent elements and/or stream of events. The nonsubstantiality of things leads to the recognition of their utter essencelessness, and in that sense, emptiness (*śūnyatā*). Deprived of any ontological grounding, language becomes a means of conventional, but practically useful, designation—the truth of things (i.e., their emptiness) being ineffable, logic becomes an effective tool for destroying logic.

The controversy between the Vedic-Upaniṣadic and the Buddhist traditions led to the development, refinement, and sophistication of both. Each tradition developed its logic, its epistemology, and its philosophy of language, and, of course, its metaphysics. But none of the traditions was ever a homogenous thought structure. By the beginning of the Christian era, Hindu philosophic tradition had diversified itself—picking up and developing ideas from the Vedic literature—into various systems or *darśanas* among which the most important were Sāṃkhya, Yoga, Vaiśeṣika, Nyāya, Pūrva Mīmāṃsā, Uttara Mīmāṃsā, and Vedānta. Each of these systems appeared, most likely after a long period of gestation, in the form of *sūtras* or aphorisms, and commentaries thereon. The intersystem dialogue—often in the forms of merciless critique as well as generous synthesis—prompted development of each system toward greater precision of theses, formalization of arguments, and extension of scope. Of the six systems listed above, three (Sāṃkhya, Yoga, and Vedānta) remained spiritually inclined (*ādhyātmika*), while the other three developed into logical and analytical systems (*ānvikṣikī*). However, even the most spiritually inclined systems had their logical, epistemological, and analytic foundations, and the most logical systems had their spiritual goals.

Again, of the systems, some remained incurably dualistic (e.g., Sāṃkhya dualism between spirit [*puruṣa*] and nature [*prakṛti*]), some pluralistic and realistic (e.g., Vaiśeṣika and Nyāya), some monistic (as is Vedānta preeminently), some theistic (e.g., Vaiśeṣika and Nyāya and some forms of Vedānta), some others clearly atheistic (Sāṃkhya), and some admitting a provisional theism (e.g., Yoga and Pūrva Mīmāṃsā).

This Hindu philosophical tradition is internally differentiated; so also is the Buddhist tradition. Buddhism in India developed several philosophical schools, the chief among them being Sarvāstivāda (the thesis that everything—both material and mental elements, past, present, and future—exists), Yogācara or Vijñānavāda (that only cognitions exist), and Mādhyamika or Śūnyavāda (the middle path, or the thesis that all things are empty).

Besides Buddhism, we have to include within the Indian tradition several non-Vedic schools, the chief among them being Cārvāka or Lokāyata (a materialistic philosophy that regards sense perception to be the only true knowledge, rejects afterlife and karma, and recommends pleasure as the only good) and Jainism (which considers reality to have infinite aspects and so believes every philosophy to possess an element of truth, denies God but admits perfectibility of humans, and recommends practice of noninjury to all living beings).

The Western Tradition

Unlike Indian thought, which very early in its history developed all its major schools as simultaneous possibilities, Western philosophy exhibits a process of historical development in the strict sense. One may distinguish three main phases in the history of Western thought: the Greek or ancient, the Christian or medieval, and the modern. Each of these phases introduced new themes and concerns, which were superadded to the ancient motifs; the rise of modern science with Galileo and Newton introduced still novel themes and gave rise to new concerns and methodologies making modern philosophy possible.

The fundamental concepts of Western philosophy were laid down by the Greeks: the concept of Being of Parmenides, the Platonic theory of Forms or Ideas, the Aristotelian logic, the idea of "metaphysics" as the first science, and the basic ideas of political thought. The Greeks—Plato, Aristotle, and the Stoics—also founded moral philosophy for the West: the idea of the highest good, the doctrine of virtue as the Golden Mean, and the idea of justice. As far as philosophical method is concerned, Socrates continues to be the paradigm of analytical thinking inspiring all thinkers by his illimitable example.

Judeo-Christianity introduced new themes and concerns, a monotheistic idea of God, the idea of creation out of nothing, the idea of linear time, the idea of sin as constitutive of human nature, the concept of salvation, and the theme of human brotherhood (thereby rejecting slavery as unjust). The task for medieval philosophy was to reconcile Christian theology with Platonic-Aristotelian metaphysics, to justify faith by reason (by proving the existence of God and reconciling human freedom with divine foreknowledge), and to formulate and solve numerous epistemological problems arising from these tasks. This enormous task reaches its high point in Thomas Aquinas's *Summa Theologica.*

If the First Principle for medieval thinking was the Idea of God and his transcendental predicates (Unity, Truth, and Goodness), modern philosophy—whose foundation was laid by Descartes—begins with doubt and arrives at the indubitable existence of the thinking ego as the first principle to start with. This symbolizes the spirit of modern thought—continuous return to the inner subjectivity of the thinking self. Alternately construed as the experiencing self (by Empiricism) and the rational thinker (by Rationalism), as passive receptivity and active spontaneity, modern thinking reached its full self-consciousness in the German philosopher Kant, who argued that the true and the innermost subjectivity is the transcendental self-consciousness which makes possible the order and regularity that characterizes nature. A new concept of self and its relation to the world made its appearance.

Western philosophy, however, did not stop with this insight and its maturity in German idealism. We are today supposedly in the era of postmodernism, which has rejected that recourse to the subject, and which consequently has gone beyond that humanism which characterized the best of modernism. It is at this crucial point that comparative philosophy is of the utmost importance for Western philosophy.

The Islamic Tradition

Islam came into being in the sixth century C.E. Islamic philosophical tradition arose out of an appropriation of the Aristotelian system into Arabic philosophical thinking. At the beginning of the long and complex process of this appropriation stands Al Kindi (d. 873), who interpreted Aristotle's idea of active intelligence, indicated in his *De Anima,* as a single suprahuman intellect, which acts upon individual passive intellects and generates human thought. Al Farabi (d. 950) first made the distinction between essence and existence, regarded existence as an accident of essence, and used Al Kindi's idea of a single active intellect—that is, God's intellect—as the cause of the intelligibility of things. The most famous of all Arabic philosophers, of course, is Ibn Sina or Avicenna (980–1037), who also considerably influenced the course of Western thought by transmitting Aristotelian thought to the medieval world, including St. Thomas. One of his famous distinctions is between the existence of universals *ante res* (originally, in the mind of god), *in rebus* (in the existing individuals, clothed with accidents), and *post res* (abstracted by the thinking mind). He is responsible for the distinction between *intentio prima,* by which we perceive the individual thing as existing outside our minds, and *intentio secunda,* by which we analyze it into essence, accidents, and existence and make it an object of scientific knowledge. The essences, he held, are in themselves proper objects of metaphysics; in our minds, objects of logic; and in existing things, objects of science.

The merging of Aristotelian metaphysics into Islamic theology provides a fascinating chapter of comparative and intercultural philosophy. The rationalist tendency of this Aristotelian-influenced Arabic scholasticism was replaced by the Neoplatonism- and Hindu Upaniṣad-influenced mysticism of Sufism. Al Ghazāli (d. 1111) reconciled the two tendencies and remains the greatest among Muslim theologians.

A TIME LINE

2000–1000 B.C.E.	*Vedas*
1000–500	*Upaniṣads*
1000	*I ching*
722-481	*The Spring and Autumn Annals*
6th century	Lao Tzu
	Chuang Tzu
599–527	Mahāvīra
585	Thales, beginning of Western philosophy
562–?	Gautama, the Buddha

551–479	Confucius
525–?	Pythagoras
479 (?)–381 (?)	Mo Tzu
515–?	Parmenides
469–399	Socrates
470–347	Plato
427–347 B.C.E.	Aristotle
400 B.C.E.–400 C.E. (?)	*Bhagavad Gītā*
370–290 B.C.E.	Mencius
150 B.C.E.–250 C.E.	Nāgārjuna
1st century C.E.	Introduction of Buddhism into China
788–820	Śaṃkara
died 870	Al Kindi
873–950	Al Farabi
980–1037	Avicenna
1058–1111	Al Ghāzali
1130–1200	Chu Hsi (Neo-Confucian)
1139–1193	Lu Hsiang-sham (Neo-Confucian)
1175–1250	Rāmānuja
1225–1274	Aquinas
1569–1650	Descartes
1724–1804	Kant
1771–1831	Hegel

SOME CONCLUDING REFLECTIONS

None of the four traditions represented here have been entirely immune from outside influence at any stage of their development. The origins of Greek thought, prior to Thales, are shrouded in mystery, but it is quite reasonable to surmise some influence of ancient Egyptian culture. Hindu thought reportedly reached Pythagoras, and very probably influenced Neo-Platonism. Hindu mathematics reached the West through the Arabs. Again through the Arabic scholars, Greek philosophy came to the West, just as Platonic, Aristotelian, and Neo-Platonic philosophies shaped Arabic Islamic philosophies. Chinese philosophy is indigenous in origin, but Buddhism reached China around the first century C.E. and had a lasting influence there as much as it was transformed by Chinese thought. Hindu mysticism influenced Islamic sufism as much as Islamic philosophy became a part of the Indian tradition. Confucius's thought influenced the European enlightenment. Indian thought reached the German Romantics, and through them Hegel and Schopenhauer, and, eventually, Nietzsche. Thoreau and Tolstoy influenced Gandhi. Raja Rammohan Roy founded the discipline called "comparative religion."

So we comparativists need not think we are heralding an entirely new discipline. In spite of the mutual contacts between the traditions, the philosophers today have remained isolationists. Never before has the need for a conversation of humankind been greater. The conversation can be fruitful if the partners know, and respect, each other.

The editors hope this textbook will help in this process.

Part 1

Metaphysics

1.1

Introduction: What Is Real or Reality?

The word "metaphysics," meaning "beyond physics," came to be used for a discipline or inquiry simply by a historical accident. When Aristotle's works were compiled, one of his untitled works was called by his compilers "Metaphysics," since this was the one he wrote after writing the "Physics." The name has been used ever since to designate an inquiry and a subject matter; namely, that which is beyond nature, which physics studies. In his book, Aristotle defined his concern (and so "metaphysics") as the science of *being qua being*. This famous definition came to be understood—again following Aristotle's suggestions—in various ways. It was taken to be:

the science of the most general predicates of any being or entity whatsoever;
the science of the primary entity or substance;
the science of the most perfect being (or God); and
the science of the "meaning" of "being."

In the first of the above senses, metaphysics becomes the science of the categories. The categories are the most general concepts that can be predicated of any entity whatsoever. Aristotle's list includes such concepts as substance, quality, rest, motion, one, and many.

Of these, substance is being, in a preeminent sense. It alone is being in the primary sense; it alone is independent. Substance is that on which everything is predicated, but it is not predicated on anything. As the science of the most perfect being, metaphysics becomes the science of God and so theology. It is only in recent times that the question of the meaning of being has come to the forefront in the thought of Heidegger.

Metaphysics seeks to comprehend the beingness (*ousia*) of beings. For Plato, this is "idea"; for Aristotle, it is *energia*.

3

Aristotle's world is one of progress, in which the potential becomes actual. Before Aristotle, Parmenides, who had discovered for Western thought the concept of being, had already denied all change and becoming. In the earliest introduction of the question of being, Parmenides distinguished between: (1) the way of truth which is the way of being, of what is; and (2) the way of becoming which is the way of opinion or *doxa*. According to Parmenides, being necessarily excludes non-being. Non-being cannot possibly be known; to represent non-being is impossible. Whatever is known is known as being, which is changeless; change is mere appearance. Being is also undifferentiated and one; difference and plurality are only names. Things are not what they seem to be. However, Parmenides did not give a good account of why people posit, besides being, a separate world of appearances. Since Aristotle emphasized that "being" has many senses, he could not, like Parmenides, say that "being" stands for one thing. Yet he did see that the different beings did form a unity, by being related to a single primary substance.

By the time Parmenides introduced the question of being in Western thought (fifth century B.C.E.), the *Nāsadīyasūkta* of the *Ṛg Veda* and many of the Upaniṣads had posed the same question. The famous hymn to creation included in this text discusses the origin of the existents. The hymn opens in the time before creation, when there was nothing: neither being nor non-being, no midspace, no trace of air or heaven; even the moon and the sun did not exist so that one could differentiate between the day and night, days and months. The One, which was enveloped by emptiness, came into being by its own fervor, desire arose giving rise to thought; thus, existence somehow arose out of non-existence. At this juncture, the poet realizes that he has gone too far; to claim that existence arises out of non-existence goes against the verdict of experience. Thus, after presumably describing the origin of things, the last two verses ask whether anyone truly knows what is really the origin of the existents. Even the gods cannot answer this question, because they were created along with the world. Thus, the poet concludes that the origin of the existents is inexplicable; it is an enigma, a riddle.

The hymns from the *Atharva Veda,* on the other hand, articulate time as the one ontological reality; it is the creator, preserver, and destroyer of the universe. The Sanskrit term "*kāla,*" derived from the root √*kal,* means "to collect," "to count." Time, in these hymns, is taken to be the collector or the gatherer of everything past, present, and future. Time is compared to a perfectly trained horse upon which a jar filled to the brim with water is placed; time runs like a horse without spilling even a single drop. Everything—earth and the heavens beyond, the shining of the sun, thought, breath, the blowing of the wind—originates in time. It is not an exaggeration to say that time is both the *Prajāpati* and the *brahman* of the *Atharva Veda.* The significance of these hymns must not be minimized; they underscore the fact that conceptions of time in the Indian context date back to the *Atharva Veda,* thereby refuting the general Western perception that Indian philosophy does not take time into account and that the conceptions of time are strictly limited to the Western context.

Some of the Upaniṣads also echo the same concern for the origin of things. Uddālaka Āruṇi in *Chāndogya Upaniṣad* teaches his son Śvetaketu in the following words:

> In the beginning, my dear, this world was just being, one only, without a second. Some say that in the beginning this was non-being alone, one only, without a second. Being was produced from that non-being. But how could being be produced from non-being? (VI. 2. 1–2)

Thus the concept of being oscillates between a purely theoretical concept (the pure is, *asti*) and a practical concept ("from non-being, *asat*, lead me to being, *sat*"). Śaṃkara's nondualistic Vedānta develops the former; the *brahman* is mere being, *sanmātra*—but also consciousness and bliss.

While the question about the origin of all things is raised both in the Vedic hymns and in the Upaniṣads, the latter also provide a definite answer to this question. This answer, it is important to note, determined much of subsequent Indian thought. After raising the question in the above Upaniṣad, Uddālaka Āruṇi informs his son as follows:

> In the beginning there was being alone, one only without a second. . . . He, the One, thought to himself; "let me be many; let me grow forth." Thus, he out of himself projected the universe. And having projected this a universe out of himself; he entered into every being. That being alone is the essence of all beings. All things have being as their abode, being as their support.
>
> That which is the subtle essence, this whole world has that for its self. That is the true self. That thou art, Śvetaketu. (VI. 2. 2; VI. 8. 6–7)

Thus the Upaniṣads identify a single being, a fundamental principle, which underlies everything and explicates everything. The most typical designation for this is the "*brahman.*" This objective principle is also the core of each individual and this core has been designated as the "*ātman,*" the "self," the life-force independent of physical body. In the language of the Upaniṣads, the *brahman,* the first principle, is discovered within the *ātman;* or conversely, the secret of the *ātman,* the foundational reality of the individual self, lies in the first principle, the root of all existence. In other words, the *ātman,* (the subjective) and the *brahman* (the objective) are identical. Through an analysis of the nature of the self, an individual realizes that the *brahman* and the *ātman,* the objective and the subjective, are identical. This theme of identity has been reiterated in the Upaniṣads in different ways. Thus it is not an exaggeration to say that each Upaniṣadic teaching stresses the coherence and final unity of all things.

The selections from the *Īśa Upaniṣad* describe the *brahman* in paradoxical terms. The entire poem employs paradoxes and antinomies to explain the all comprehensiveness of the One reality. For example, verse 4 describes the One, the fundamental principle of things, at once as "unmoving, yet swifter than the mind." It is unmoving insofar as it is eternal; it is swifter than the mind because it is inconceivable. Verse 5 articulates the One as something that moves and does not move, as far and near, and as within and outside of all things. The point that is being made is that the One encompasses everything; it signifies the totality of things. The *brahman* is both the unmanifested beyond and the manifest phenomena, implying it is both one and many; it is also the self, the seer, and the thinker.

The *Kena Upaniṣad,* as the title indicates, raises the question, By whom?—that is, who is the real power behind the universe? Since neither the mind, nor the sense organs, nor speech can perform their roles without (their foundation in) the self; the self is the basis of all knowledge, the single unitary power. It is important to remember that the self, though it makes knowledge possible, is not itself an object of knowledge. The self cannot be known like another physical object—say, a pitcher. It is different from the objects known. Therefore, it cannot be known in the manner in which objects are known. The self is not knowable by any empirical means of knowledge. In fact, it is other than the known and the unknown. *Kena Upaniṣad* II. 3 explains this theme as follows: to whom the self is not known, to him it is known; to whom it is known, he does not know it. It is unknown to those who think they understand it; it is known to those who know they do not understand it. In concrete terms, it amounts to saying that the *brahman* or the self is not an object of knowledge: if one thinks that one knows the self and can describe it as an object perceived in the ordinary world then he does not know it. On the other hand, those who are convinced that the self is not an object of knowledge do indeed know it. The self cannot be comprehended by the senses and logic, but only by intuitive realization. The self, in other words, is other than the known (as an object) and the unknown (*anyad eva tad viditād atho aviditād adhi*).

At this point, the question may be raised, if the self is never an object, how can objects and their properties be superimposed upon it? Śaṃkara states that the self (pure consciousness) is apprehended as an object when one becomes aware of oneself as "I am." The "I" which is the referent of the self-consciousness of the empirical individual is bound by the limitations of the body, the mind, and the senses. Thus, beginningless superimposition, in the form of the multiplicity of names and forms, results, conjuring up the notions of agency and enjoyer which empirical individuals experience. The superimposition of the self on the senses, intellect, and so on endows the empirical individual with consciousness, while the superimposition of the intellect on the *ātman* endows the empirical individual with the notion that he or she is the doer of actions and the enjoyer of the fruits of actions. This notion of superimposition forms the subject matter of the selection contained in this text from Śaṃkara. The selection is taken from Śaṃkara's "Introduction" to his commentary on the *Brahmasūtra* 1.1.1. This introduction is, in the Advaita Vedānta tradition, called "*Adhyāsabhāṣya*" i.e., the (part of the) commentary devoted to the theme of *adhyāsa* or superimposition. However, before we discuss Śaṃkara's notion of superimposition, let us briefly review the fundamental tenets of Śaṃkara's philosophy.

For Śaṃkara, the *brahman* is the only reality. The multiplicity of names and forms experienced at the phenomenal level, the level where philosophical inquiry transpires, is real only from an empirical/practical standpoint. Śaṃkara's realistic epistemology contends that every cognition points to an objective referent, regardless of its veridicality or falsity. So the issue is: how real are the things that we experience in the phenomenal realm? Plurality is real as long as one remains in the empirical world. Reality is never contradicted; it is never sublated (*bādhita*). It *was, is,* and *will be* real. In the order of discovery, in the order of knowing things, appearance comes first. In the order of existence, however, the *brahman* comes first. The former is the epistemic order, which explains why Śaṃkara begins his investigation in his commentary on the *Brahmasūtra* with the idea of superimposition. For Śaṃkara, superimposition gives rise to "I-ness" (*aham*), resulting in a confusion between *this* (*idam*) and *not-this* (*anidam*). Pure consciousness, when superimposed, becomes an "I." Accordingly, one makes a distinction among many "I's" (*ahams*). In fact, the distinctions between the knower, the known, and the means of knowledge are the result of the mutual superimpositions of the self and the not-self. This mutual superimposition is the subject matter of the selection in the text.

The self and the not-self, two fundamental components of human experience, opposed to each other as light and darkness, are yet confused with each other—as a result of which properties of the one are (wrongly) ascribed to the other. The self can never become the not-self and vice versa; nor can the properties of the one be superimposed on the other. However, our everyday experience revolves around a beginningless confounding between the two, in the forms "I am this," and "This is mine." In the first form, the distinction between the self and the body is forgotten. In the latter form, however, the distinction between the self and the body is not forgotten, though the attributes of the two are mixed up. The former can assume either of these two forms: (a) "I am this body," or (b) "This body is I." In (a) the body per se is superimposed on the self, whereas in (b) the self is superimposed on the body.

Śaṃkara adduces numerous examples to demonstrate the varieties of superimposition: it may be the superimposition of (a) the body on the self, e.g., "I am a man," "I am a woman"; (b) the properties of the body on the self, e.g.,

"I am fat," "I am thin"; (c) mental states, such as desires, doubt, pleasure, pain, on the self, e.g., "I am happy," "I am virtuous"; and (d) the properties of the sense organs on the self, e.g., "I am blind," "I am deaf." Thus the superimposition not only assumes the form of the "I" but also of the "mine." The former is the superimposition of the substance (*dharmī*), the latter of the attribute (*dharma*). The reciprocal superimposition of the self and the not-self, and of the properties of the one on the other, results in the bondage of the empirical self. The empirical self acts and enjoys because of erroneous identification of the inner self with the inner sense (*antaḥkarana*). The goal of Vedānta is to remove this ignorance by making knowledge of the self possible.

Lao Tzu's *Tao* is, in many respects, close to the concept of the Brahman of the Upaniṣads. It is beyond name and form, the nameless source of all things, it is beyond all oppositions, it is described in paradoxical terms. Compare Lao Tzu's "We look at it and do not see it. . . . We listen to it and do not hear it" with "That which is not seen by the eye, but by which the eyes are seen. . . . That which is not heard by the ear, but by which this ear is heard." There are, however, differences that the careful reader will not fail to note. The practical consequences of the two metaphysical theories are not far apart: contrast the *Bhagavadgītā's* prescription of "attaining true inaction by acting" with Lao Tzu's "Do nothing."

This hint at a possible comparison between Lao Tzu and the Upaniṣads is only one way of entering into the concept of *Tao*. The enormous complexity of this concept is brought out in the essay by Charles Fu. Most important, *Tao* is not an entity or a substance. One may ask: is Brahman-*Ātman* an entity or a substance? Positively, Fu brings out six aspects of *Tao: Tao* as Reality, as Origin, as Principle, as Function, as Virtue, and as Technique. It may be suggested that while the first three are true of Brahman, the last three are not.

No tradition, it should be emphasized, is monolithic. In the Indian tradition, there are the materialistic and naturalistic philosophies, such as the *Lokāyāta* and the *Ājīvikas*. As contrasted with Confucianism, Taoism, and Buddhism, Chinese philosophy also has a place for Chang Tsai (or Zhang Zai, 1020–1077 C.E.), a neo-Confucian no doubt, but also a materialist. For him the Great Ultimate is material Force. The original material Force is one, although its manifestations are many; it is the unity of nature and consciousness. Clearly, such a position is not reductionist. The selection included is from his work *Hsi Ming* or Western Inscription, which owes its name to the fact that it was inscribed on the west wall of the Hall in which he lectured. The universe is characterized as the Great Harmony of opposites, united as one family; it is the *Tao*. The Great Harmony arises out of the Great Vacuity. *Li* is the principle of its operation. The Confucian virtue of love/humanheartedness (*jen*) is derived from this metaphysical principle.

As an example of a philosophical school that critiques all metaphysical positions and itself claims to be none, one has to read Nāgārjuna's *Mū-*

lamādhyamikakārikā. Born sometime between the first and the second centuries C.E., Nāgārjuna is one of the most famous philosophers of India, and certainly the most famous Buddhist philosopher. Following a middle path, he rejects metaphysical alternatives: no entity arises out of itself, nor from another, nor from both, nor from neither. Things do not have their own essence; they are fully relational. Yet nothing can be explained either in terms of itself or in terms of other things. Identity and Difference, whole and part, cause and effect, rest and motion, permanence and change; each of these implies the other, and cannot be understood without the other. All of this leads Nāgārjuna to the thesis that all things are empty (*śūnya*) i.e., essenceless, all concepts are incoherent; language refers not to things but to itself. This emptiness itself is empty, i.e., need not be reified into an entity. Truth is ineffable. Philosophical wisdom lets things be what they are.

Nāgārjuna's doctrine of *śūnyatā* is the original inspiration for Zen Buddhism, and Kitarō Nishida (1870–1945) is the most famous interpreter of Zen in terms of Western philosophy. Founder of the Kyoto school, Nishida influenced such philosophers as Hajime Tanabe and Keiji Nishitani. Nishida, in "The True Nature of Reality," begins by asking: "What is direct knowledge that we cannot even begin to doubt?" In a Cartesian fashion, he holds that if we free ourselves of all assumptions, we shall find such a firm basis in "intuition" which underlies all of our intellectual constructions. It stands beyond the opposition between subject and object, as the unity of knowledge, feeling, and volition, as what he calls "pure experience," which is then regarded by Nishida as the true reality. Clearly, the exposition is a modern understanding of Zen by one who was well-versed in Western philosophy, and also in Zen practice. This essay represents Nishida's early philosophy. This concept of pure experience is subsequently developed by him into the idea of "self-awakening," which again led him to his idea of "absolute free will." In the final phase, he develops his more well-known concept of *basho* as the "absolute nothingness," which provides the "place" or the "ground" that alone lets everything be itself.

1.2

The Way of Truth

Parmenides

6.5 Come now, and I will tell you (and you, when you have heard my speech shall bear it away with you) the ways of inquiry which alone exist for thought. The one is the way of how it is, and how it is not possible for it not to be; this is the way of persuasion, for it attends to Truth. The other is the way of how it is not, and how it is necessary for it not to be; this, I tell you, is a way wholly unknowable. For you could not know what is not—that is impossible—nor could you express it.

6.6 For thought and being are the same.

6.7 Thinking and the thought that it is are the same; for you will not find thought apart from what is, in relation to which it is uttered.

In all thinking we seem at first sight to be confronted with a choice: we can think about what is, or we can think about what is not. But in fact this choice is illusory; we cannot think about what is not, for it is impossible to think about nothing. You cannot think at all without thinking of something—something which exists as an object *for* thought. Parmenides expresses this idea somewhat awkwardly by saying that thinking and being are "the same," but he does not mean by this that they are identical. They are "the same" in the sense in which, for Heraclitus, day and night are "the same." They are not identical, for they are clearly distinguishable, but they are inseparable; you cannot have one without the other. And this is what Parmenides means when he says that thought and being are "the same." He means, as he goes on to explain, that "you will not find thinking apart from what is"; for thought is *of* what is.

This does not mean that since we are able to think of mermaids, it follows that they exist. But thinking, even about mermaids, involves thinking about *something,* namely, about what is, though it involves thinking something false about what is, namely, that it contains mermaids. The existence of *something* is the presupposition of all thinking whatever. But precisely because it is, we cannot think its nonexistence; it not only is but, as Parmenides puts it, "it is impossible for it not to be."

Nor is not-being a possible object of thought. For to think it would be to make it an object of thought and thus give it an existence which by definition it cannot have. We cannot therefore think what is not; and since we can give utterance only to what passes in thought, it follows also that we cannot say anything about it.

The proposition that all thought is of what is seems harmless enough. But Parmenides immediately proceeds to deduce an important corollary from it:

6.8 It is necessary to speak and to think what is; for being is, but nothing is not. These things I bid you consider. For I hold you back from this first way of inquiry; but also from that way on which mortals knowing nothing wander, of two minds. For helplessness guides the wandering thought in their breasts; they are carried along deaf and blind alike, dazed, beasts without judgment, convinced that to be and not to be are the same and not the same, and that the road of all things is a backward-turning one.

6.9 For never shall this prevail: that things that are not, are. But hold back your thought from this way of inquiry, nor let habit born of long experience force you to ply an aimless eye and droning ear along this road; but judge by reasoning the much-contested argument that I have spoken.

Of the ways of inquiry which exist for thought, then, we must reject the first; for nothing is not. But by the same token we must reject any view which involves the denial of this, and the view which Parmenides attacks in 6.8 clearly does deny it, though what it asserts is much less clear.

The language in which this view is expressed has a familiar ring to it. To say "the same and not the same"—to assert and deny in the same breath—is Heraclitean. To say, for example, that day and night are "the same" is to say that they are inseparable from one another; to say that they are "not the same" is to say (with a shift of sense characteristic of Heraclitus) that they are distinct. They are "the same" and "not the same" both at once. But in "being" and "not-being" we have a similar pair of opposites. Insofar as they are distinct they are "not the same"; but in another sense they *are* "the same," for they are inseparable. They are inseparable because both are involved in all coming into being and passing away.

Wherever we look we are confronted with coming into being and passing away, for this is the essence of process. What is not comes into being, exists for a time, then passes away and exists no longer. In this sense "the road of all things" is indeed a "backward-turning one." But for Parmenides this alternation cannot possibly take place. For all talk of coming into being and passing away rests on the mistaken assumption that it is possible to think not-being. If the argument of 6.5 is sound, we cannot say of a thing that "it no longer exists"; for if it no longer exists it is nothing, and nothing is not a possible object of thought. "Not-being" is not the opposite of "being," as "day" is of "night"; it does not stand for anything at all. But in this case it does not make sense to speak of coming into being and passing away, for if "to pass away" means "to become non-existent," it is obvious that passing away is impossible. But by the same token, if "to come to be" means "to come out of not-being," this too is impossible.

It is useless to protest that both coming into being and passing away are matters of common experience, for Parmenides does not accept the arbitration of experience. He puts this very clearly in 6.9. The question is not one, he says, which is settled by an appeal to sense—the evidence of eyes and ears. It is not "experience" which passes on such questions, but "argument." It is *reason* that shows us, by arguments of inescapable force, that what is not is not a possible object of thought, and therefore that coming into being and passing away cannot take place. If experience teaches us otherwise, so much the worse for experience. We have here the first statement of that uncompromising rationalism which has left its mark on so much of Western philosophy.

That it represented a radical break with the past is obvious enough. The whole Ionian philosophy of nature was based upon observation—not, to be sure, upon the controlled observation which characterizes modern science, but on "experience" in the ordinary sense. The appeal to the senses is so fundamental in the Milesians that it never occurs to them to mention it; but it is quite explicit in Heraclitus. "Those things of which there is sight, hearing, understanding, I esteem most," he says (5.42); the "eyes and ears are bad witnesses to men" only "if they have souls that do not understand their language" (5.43), that is, only if they are unable to grasp the significance of what they see and hear. Parmenides exploits the principle implicit in this unguarded admission. If it is intelligence alone that can make sense of experience, then intelligence is superior to experience. And if it should prove, as in the present case, that the deliverances of sense actually come into conflict with those of intelligence, it is clear which must give way. Whatever experience may have to say to the contrary, there can be neither any coming into being nor passing away. Parmenides proceeds to develop this point in detail:

6.10   One way remains to be spoken of: the way how it is. Along this road
        there are very many indications that what is is unbegotten and imper-

ishable; for it is whole and immovable and complete. Nor was it at any time, nor will it be, since it is now, all at once, one and continuous.

For what begetting of it would you search for? How and whence did it grow? I shall not let you say or think "from what is not"; for it is not possible either to say or to think how it is not. Again, what need would have driven it, if it began from nothing, to grow later rather than sooner? Thus it must exist fully or not at all. Nor will the force of conviction ever allow anything over and above itself to arise out of what is not; wherefore Justice does not loosen her fetters so as to allow it to come into being or pass away, but holds it fast.

Concerning these things the decision lies here: either it is, or it is not. But it has been decided, as was necessary, that the one way is unknowable and unnamable (for it is no true road) and that the other is real and true. How could what is perish? How could it have come to be? For if it came into being, it is not; nor is it if ever it is going to be. Thus coming into being is extinguished, and destruction unknown.

What is is unbegotten and imperishable; for if it had come into being it would have to have come from not-being, and this is impossible. For not-being has not that in it which could enable it to give rise to anything. It is nothing, and something cannot come from nothing; "nor will the force of conviction ever allow anything over and above itself to arise out of what is not." By the same token, it is impossible for what is to pass away and become nothing; for it would have to come to *be* nothing—would have to exchange its existence for non-existence. It is, then, as impossible for what is to cease to be as it is for it to come into being.

It would be better, therefore, if we did not speak of what is in terms having temporal reference. For to say of a thing that it was is to suggest that it no longer is, while to say of something that it will be suggests that it is not yet. This mode of speech is misleading when applied to what is, for what is "is now, all at once." The phrase is awkward only because, strictly speaking, "now" no longer has its ordinary meaning. The now ceases to be a time—the present; for the mode of existence of what is is nontemporal.

THE NATURE OF WHAT IS

Parmenides now turns to the task of deducing those characteristics which must of necessity belong to what is:

6.11 Nor is it divisible, since it is all alike; nor is there any more or less of it in one place which might prevent it from holding together, but all is full of what is.

6.12 Look steadfastly at those things which, though absent, are firmly present to the mind. For it cannot cut off what is from clinging to what is, either scattering it in every direction in order or bringing it together.

What is, says Parmenides, cleaves to what is; and it is easy to see why this must be so. For what is could be separated from what is only by what is not, and what is not has no existence. It has no power to prevent what is from "holding together" so as to be continuous. But if what is is continuous, it follows that "all is full of what is," so that it is impossible for there to be more or less of it in one place than another.

It will be obvious that as Parmenides proceeds he tends to speak of what is in more and more physical terms. In 6.11, for example, being is pictured as everywhere in contact with being, whereas strictly speaking only bodies can be in contact with one another. But in 6.12 this tendency is even more pronounced; for the closing words of this fragment clearly refer to some sort of physical process, and one which is in fact perfectly familiar to us. It is, as the words "in order" indicate, the process of world formation and dissolution.

This double process is implicit from the first in Anaximander's conception of the world-order as coming into being and passing away through the separation of earth, air, fire, and water by the vortex motion and their reunion through its cessation. This conception was central to the Ionian philosophy of nature, and in questioning it Parmenides was questioning the work of his predecessors from Anaximander onwards. Yet his doing so was the inevitable consequence of his calling into question that still more fundamental assumption of the Ionian tradition, the reliability of the senses as sources of information concerning what is.

Parmenides proceeds to drive his point home:

6.13 But motionless in the limits of mighty bonds, it is without beginning or end, since coming into being and passing away have been driven far off, cast out by true belief. Remaining the same, and in the same place, it lies in itself, and so abides firmly where it is. For strong Necessity holds it in the bonds of the limit which shuts it in on every side, because it is not right for what is to be incomplete. For it is not in need of anything, but not-being would stand in need of everything.

All process is change, and all change involves coming into being and passing away. In a world from which these have been cast out there can be no process. What is lies motionless, abiding in itself, for "strong Necessity holds it in the bonds of the limit which shuts it in on every side." Parmenides, it will be observed, does not distinguish between logical and physical necessity. For us the necessity that renders being immovable is a logical one. If what is is everywhere in contact with what is, it *follows* (according to Parmenides) that it can neither scatter nor come together. But Parmenides thinks of Necessity as a kind of *force* which *prevents* being from scattering or coming together, and this mode of thought is typical of the early Greek philosophers. We have seen it already in Heraclitus, who thinks of the *logos* not merely as the order of events but as somehow enforcing that order, much as justice is enforced in the cosmology of Anaximander.

There is a further point to be observed in connection with 6.13. It will be obvious that in certain respects Parmenides' conception of being resembles Anaximander's conception of the infinite. His description of it as unbegotten and imperishable answers to Anaximander's description of the infinite in 2.4. But the infinite is, as the name implies, without limit, whereas Parmenides, as if in deliberate correction of Anaximander, describes the unbegotten and imperishable as "held in the bonds of the limit." Being, then, is limited, and the proof follows immediately. If it were without limit, it would stand in need of one. But if it stood in need of anything, it would be incomplete, which is not the case, for being is complete (6.10) and therefore cannot be without a limit.

Parmenides proceeds to draw certain consequences from this:

6.14 But since there is a furthest limit, it is complete on every side, like the body of a well-rounded sphere, evenly balanced in every direction from the middle; for it cannot be any greater or any less in one place than in another. For neither is there what is not, which would stop it from reaching its like, nor could what is possibly be more in one place and less than another, since it is all inviolable. For being equal to itself in every direction it nevertheless meets with its limits.

Shakespeare speaks of our little life as "rounded" in a sleep. He means, of course, "terminated"; but to set a term to something is to set a limit to it—to bring it to completion. All of these notions are bound up together, and the image of a sphere is well adapted to express them. But it is impossible to draw a sharp line in early Greek philosophy between the metaphorical and the literal. To be sure, Parmenides does not say that what is *is* a well-rounded sphere; he only says that it is *like* one. But he goes on to use language which irresistibly suggests something extended in space, to which the limit stands as a circumference. To this circumference being tends equally from the center, to form a motionless sphere.

The motionlessness of being is asserted again and again, and in the strongest possible terms:

6.15 For there is not, nor will there be, anything other than what is, since indeed Destiny has fettered it to remain whole and immovable.

Therefore those things which mortals have established, believing them to be true, will be mere names: "coming into being and passing away," "being and not-being," "change of place and alteration of bright color."

We can see immediately why it would have to be motionless. In order for a thing to move, it must have a place to move to. But clearly there is no place into which being could move. For as Parmenides has already explained, "all is full of what is" (6.11). There is nothing outside what is, capable of containing it; for what could be outside it? Only nothingness, and the existence of nothingness is inconceivable. It follows that we must not think of being as having location at all. This is not easy to do; Parmenides himself lapses into saying that it remains "in the same place" (6.13). But he immediately adds that "it lies in itself." It "abides firmly where it is" because there is no place for it to go.

So far we have dealt only with local motion or change of place. In 6.15 this is set over against "alteration of bright color," or qualitative change. But the proof that this sort of change, too, is impossible is merely a corollary of the proof of the impossibility of coming into being or passing away. To say of a leaf that it has changed color is to say that something now exists, *i.e.,* a red leaf, which did not exist formerly; for what existed formerly was a green leaf. This would clearly involve a process of becoming, since if it did not exist formerly but does now it must, at some time in between, have come into being. Similarly, before the change took place something existed, *i.e.,* a green leaf, which no longer exists; hence at some time in between it must have passed away. But we have ruled out as impossible both coming into being and passing away; they have been "driven far off, cast out by true belief" (6.13). The alleged change, therefore, cannot have taken place.

Parmenides, then, rejects change as such, whether it takes the form of coming into being, passing away, local motion, or qualitative transformation; all these are "mere names" which mortals, "beasts without judgment," make use of, thinking them to be true (6.8). In denying reality to change, Parmenides was to all intents and purposes cutting the ground out from under all his predecessors. For to study nature is to study process, and no one can set out to investigate nature who does not assume its existence as process. Just as geometers, says Aristotle, must assume the existence of continuous quantity,

6.16 We physicists on the other hand must assume as "given" that the things that exist by nature are, either all or some of them, in motion—which indeed is evident from induction.

Unfortunately, the appeal to induction is useless in this case, for to appeal to induction is to appeal to experience, and in particular to our experience of particulars by means of sense perception. But it is precisely this appeal that Parmenides rejects. Do not, he says, "let habit born of long experience" direct your mind "but judge by argument the much-contested argument that I have spoken" (6.9). It is a reasonable demand, and Aristotle, with some grumbling breaks off his analysis of change long enough to submit Parmenides' logic to some shrewd criticism. But Parmenides' immediate successors were not capable of this sort of criticism. His logic seemed to them unanswerable. Their energies went, instead, into the attempt to save the Ionian philosophy of nature by adjusting it to the requirements of that logic. Indeed, the subsequent history of early Greek philosophy is the history of this attempt.

THE WAY OF OPINION

The goddess has promised to instruct Parmenides in "all things—both the unshakable heart of well-rounded truth and the opinions of mortals in which there is no true belief" (6.3). Of this task the first half is now complete. The truth has been revealed, and it may be seen to bear the marks of being itself. For as being is held fast by the bonds of the limit so as to be "complete on every side like the body of a well rounded sphere" (6.14), so is the "unshakable heart of well-rounded truth" unchanging and self-contained. Hence the goddess can say:

6.17 It is all one to me where I begin, for I shall come back there again.

The truth possesses a unity which is a reflex of the unity of being itself.

The opinions of mortals are another matter, and to these the goddess now turns somewhat abruptly:

6.18 Here I end my trustworthy account and thought concerning truth. Learn henceforth the beliefs of mortals, harkening to the deceitful ordering of my words. For they have made up their minds to name two forms, one of which it is not right to name—here is where they have gone astray and have distinguished them as opposite in bodily form and have assigned to them marks distinguishing them from one another: to one ethereal flame of fire, which is gentle, very light, the same with itself in every direction but not the same with the other. That other too, in itself, is opposite: dark night, dense in bodily form and heavy. The whole arrangement of these I tell to you as it seems likely, so that no thought of mortals shall ever outstrip you.

To this passage a scholiast has added:

6.19 There is further a passage in prose inserted between the verses, as though by Parmenides himself, which runs as follows: "In addition to this fire is called the rare, the hot, the 'illumining,' the 'soft,' and the light, while the dense is called the cold, 'darkness,' 'harsh,' and 'heavy.'"

Where mortals go astray is in breaking up the unity of being, in thinking of it as made up of opposites. That this is true of the Milesians is clear. Anaximander accounted for the diversity of experience in terms of the hot, the cold, the wet, the dry and the other opposites, and in this he was followed by his successors. Down to the time of the Pythagoreans, however, no attempt was made to produce a list of these opposites:

6.20 Alcmaeon . . . says that most things human go in pairs—meaning "by opposites." But his examples—white and black, sweet and bitter, good and bad, large and small—are chosen at random, and about the rest he is indefinite. But the Pythagoreans stated how many the opposites were and what they were.

Aristotle has preserved for us a table showing how many the opposites are, according to the Pythagoreans, and what they are. There are ten pairs:

6.21 limit and absence of limit
 odd and even
 one and many
 right and left
 male and female
 rest and motion
 straight and curved
 light and dark
 good and bad
 square and oblong

Four of these pairs stand out sharply as having a peculiar relevance for Parmenides' thought: limit and absence of limit, one and many, rest and motion, light and dark. In the first part of his poem Parmenides argues that being is one, limited and at rest, and that motion, plurality, and want of limit are not predicable of what is. The first part of his poem, then, is an attack upon the dualism of Pythagorean thought. In 6.18 this attack is extended to the fourth pair of opposites mentioned above: light and dark. Mortals have decided to name both forms of being, and this is where they have gone astray. For being is "all alike" (6.11); there cannot be two forms of it.

So much seems clear. Yet the goddess announces that she will describe to Parmenides "the whole arrangement of these [light and night] as it seems likely," and the few fragments of the second part of the poem which have come down to us indicate that it covered essentially the same ground as that covered by earlier thinkers:

6.22 You shall know the nature of the ether and all the signs in the ether, and the unseen works of the pure torch of the bright sun and whence they came into being And you shall know the wandering works of the round-faced moon and its nature, and you shall know, too, the heaven which surrounds all, whence it grew, and how Necessity, guiding it, fettered it to keep the limits of the stars.

6.23 [And you shall learn] how sun and moon, the ether which is common to all, the Milky Way and outermost Olympos and the burning might of the stars, began to arise.

It is in fact a cosmogony that is announced—an account of the coming into being of the world-order. Yet we have just been told that coming into being is a mere name, signifying nothing real. Moreover, this cosmogony is based (as we shall see) on the very dualism which Parmenides rejects in 6.18 with the words "here is where they have gone astray." Indeed, the goddess herself states that the ordering of her words is deceitful, and that there is in them no true belief. Why, then, does the goddess require Parmenides to learn them?

The goddess herself answers this question in the concluding words of 6.18: ". . . so that no thought of mortals shall ever outstrip you." What, precisely, would be required of any thinker who set out to "outstrip" Parmenides? He would, clearly, have to cover the ground already covered by Parmenides. But in order to outstrip him he would have to go further, and it is hard to see how he could do this without going on to account for the world of experience, using Parmenides' own principles. And this, to all intents and purposes, is what Parmenides himself does.

It is obvious that in the nature of the case no such attempt could be wholly successful. For change can only be dealt with in terms of an opposition between that which effects and that which suffers change. This is why, as early as Hesiod, it is necessary to assume *within* the primordial unity the opposition of male and female. For without the impregnation of the latter by the former the children of Earth could not come into existence. And so with Hesiod's successors: in one form or another all are obliged to assume the existence of opposites. No account of change, therefore, can avoid dualism; and no account of change, therefore, can be true, for being is one. Moreover, the unity of being is reflected in the unity of truth itself, so that no account of change can be *partly* true; it must, if it is false, be altogether false. The goddess herself insists that her words are deceitful, and that there is in them no true belief.

But as Xenophanes had already pointed out, an account which is not true may yet resemble truth (3.48), and one account may resemble it more closely than another. "The whole arrangement of these [light and night] I tell to you as it seems likely," the goddess says, and adds immediately, "so that no thought of mortals shall ever outstrip you" (6.18). The account which she gives, then, is to bear not only a likeness to the truth but the closest likeness which any account short of the truth *could* have to it.

We cannot avoid dualism if we are to give an account of experience at all. We must therefore allow the existence of a minimum of two "forms" of being. But we can insist upon requiring of each of these forms of being that it conform to the requirements which have been laid down as applying to being as such, and this Parmenides proceeds to do:

> 6.24 But now that all things have been named light and night, and their powers have been assigned to each, everything is full at once of light and obscure night, both equally, since neither has a share in noth-ingness.

Light and night are equal because, given dualism as a starting point, both of them *are;* and therefore what is true of one, so far as it is, is true of the other. The fact that everything is full equally of night and light is merely a corollary of this. For "all is full of what is" (6.11), and if night and light are to have an equal share in being they must play an equal part in filling the whole.

The concluding words of 6.24 may also mean "for neither has a share of the other." While this would not be sufficient to explain why night and light are "equal," it is in fact true. For what is is "all alike," and consequently this must be true of light and night. Each must be "all alike"; hence neither can have any share in the other's nature. This in turn implies the unchanging na-ture of both. For change requires opposition, and within light as within night there can be no opposition. Each is all alike; neither partakes of the other. Each is unchanging, and therefore meets the requirement which all that is must meet if it is to be at all.

Thus each has, so far as possible, the character of the one being of the way of truth. And to this extent the account of the visible world which fol-lows, while it is not true, partakes indirectly of the truth insofar as it is pat-terned after it. It is only a likeness of the truth, but it supplies the standpoint from which alone appearances may be made "acceptable" (6.3).

1.3

Metaphysics

Aristotle

BOOK IV

1. There is a science which investigates being as being and the attributes which belong to this in virtue of its own nature. Now this is not the same as any of the so-called special sciences; for none of these others treats universally of being as being. They cut off a part of being and investigate the attribute of this part; this is what the mathematical sciences for instance do. Now since we are seeking the first principles and the highest causes, clearly there must be something to which these belong in virtue of its own nature. If then those who sought the elements of existing things were seeking these same principles, it is necessary that the elements must be elements of being not by accident but just because it *is* being. Therefore it is of being as being that we also must grasp the first causes.

BOOK VII

1. There are several senses in which a thing may be said to 'be', as we pointed out previously in our book on the various senses of words;[1] for in one sense the 'being' meant 'what a thing is' or a 'this', and in another sense it means a quality or quantity or one of the other things that are predicated as these are. While 'being' has all these senses, obviously that which 'is' primarily is the 'what', which indicates the substance of the thing. For when we say of what quality a thing is, we say that it is good or bad, not that it is three cubits long or that it is a man; but when we say *what* it is, we do not say

From *The Basic Works of Aristotle,* edited by Richard McKeon (New York: Random House, 1941), pp. 731–32 & 783–86. Copyright © 1941, Random House, Inc.

'white' or 'hot' or 'three cubits long', but 'a man' or 'a god'. And all other things are said to be because they are, some of them, quantities of that which is in this primary sense, others qualities of it, others affections of it, and others some other determination of it. And so one might even raise the question whether the words 'to walk', 'to be healthy', 'to sit' imply that each of these things is existent, and similarly in any other case of this sort; for none of them is either self-subsistent or capable of being separated from substance, but rather, if anything, it is that which walks or sits or is healthy that is an existent thing. Now these are seen to be more real because there is something definite which underlies them (i.e., the substance or individual), which is implied in such predicate; for we never use the word 'good' or 'sitting' without implying this. Clearly then it is in virtue of this category that each of the others also *is*. Therefore that which is primarily, i.e. not in a qualified sense but without qualification, must be substance.

Now there are several senses in which a thing is said to be first; yet substance is first in every sense—(1) in definition, (2) in order of knowledge, (3) in time. For (3) of the other categories none can exist independently, but only substance. And (1) in definition also this is first; for in the definition of each term the definition of its substance must be present. And (2) we think we know each thing most fully, when we know what it is, e.g., what man is or what fire is, rather than when we know its quality, its quantity, or its place; since we know each of these predicates also, only when we know *what* the quantity or the quality *is*.

And indeed the question which was raised of old and is raised now and always and is always the subject of doubt, viz. what being is, is just the question, what is substance? For it is this that some[2] assert to be one, others more than one, and that some[3] assert to be limited in number, others[4] unlimited. And so we also must consider chiefly and primarily and almost exclusively what that is which is in *this* sense.

2. Substance is thought to belong most obviously to bodies; and so we say that not only animals and plants and their parts are substances, but also natural bodies such as fire and water and earth and everything of the sort, and all things that are either parts of these or composed of these (either of parts or of the whole bodies), e.g., the physical universe and its parts, stars and moon and sun. But whether these alone are substances, or there are also others, or only some of these, or others as well, or none of these but only some other things, are substances, must be considered. Some[5] think the limits of body, i.e., surface, line, point, and unit, are substances, and more so than body or the solid.

Further, some do not think there is anything substantial besides sensible things, but others think there are eternal substances which are more in number and more real; e.g., Plato posited two kinds of substance—the Forms and the objects of mathematics—as well as a third kind, viz. the substance of sensible bodies. And Speusippus made still more kinds of substance, beginning with the One, and assuming principles for each kind of substance, one for numbers, another for spatial magnitudes, and then another for the soul; and by going on in this way he multiplies the kinds of substance. And some[6] say Forms and numbers have the same nature, and the other things come after them—lines and planes—until we come to the substance of the material universe and to sensible bodies.

Regarding these matters, then, we must inquire which of the common statements are right and which are not right, and what substances there are, and whether there are or are not any besides sensible substances, and how sensible substances exist, and whether there is a substance capable of separate existence (and if so why and how) or no such substance, apart from sensible substances; and we must first sketch the nature of substance.

3. The word 'substance' is applied, if not in more senses, still at least to four main objects; for both the essence and the universal and the genus are thought to be the substance of each thing, and fourthly the substratum. Now the substratum is that of which everything else is predicated, while it is itself not predicated of anything else. And so we must first determine the nature of this; for that which underlies a thing primarily is thought to be in the truest sense its substance. And in one sense matter is said to be of the nature of substratum, in another, shape, and in a third, the compound of these. (By the matter I mean, for instance, the bronze, by the shape the pattern of its form, and by the compound of these the statue, the concrete whole.) Therefore if the form is prior to the matter and more real, it will be prior also to the compound of both, for the same reason.

We have now outlined the nature of substance, showing that it is that which is not predicated of a stratum, but of which all else is predicated. But we must not merely state the matter thus; for this is not enough. The statement itself is obscure, and further, on this view, matter becomes substance. For if this is not substance, it baffles us to say what else is. When all else is stripped off evidently nothing but matter remains. For while the rest are affections, products, and potencies of bodies, length, breadth, and depth are quantities and not substances (for a quantity is not a substance), but the substance is rather that to which these belong primarily. But when length and breadth and depth are taken away we see nothing left unless there is something that is bounded by these; so that to those who consider the question thus matter alone must seem to be substance. By matter I mean that which in itself is neither a particular thing nor of a certain quantity nor assigned to any other of the categories by which being is determined. For there is something of which each of these is predicated, whose being is different from that of each of the predicates (for the predicates other than substance are predicated of substance, while substance is predicated of matter). Therefore the ultimate substratum is of itself neither a particular thing nor of a particular quantity nor otherwise positively characterized; nor yet is it the negations of these, for negations also will belong to it only by accident.

If we adopt this point of view, then, it follows that matter is substance. But this is impossible; for both separability and 'thisness' are thought to belong chiefly to substance. And so form and the compound of form and matter would be thought to be substance, rather than matter. The substance compounded of both, i.e., of matter and shape, may be dismissed; for it is posterior and its nature is obvious. And matter also is in a sense manifest. But we must inquire into the third kind of substance; for this is the most perplexing.

Some of the sensible substances are generally admitted to be substances, so that we must look first among these. For it is an advantage to advance to that which is more knowable. For learning proceeds for all in this way—through that which is less knowable by nature to that which is more knowable; and just as in conduct our task is to start from what is good for each and make what is without qualification good good for each, so it is our task to start from what is more knowable to oneself and make what is knowable by nature knowable to oneself. Now what is knowable and primary for particular sets of people is often knowable to a very small extent, and has little or nothing of reality. But yet one must start from that which is barely knowable but knowable to oneself, and try to know what is knowable without qualification, passing, as has been said, by way of those very things which one does know.

NOTES

1. cf. v. 7.
2. The schools of Miletus and Elea.
3. The Pythagoreans and Empedocles.
4. Anaxagoras and the Atomists.
5. The Pythagoreans.
6. The school of Xenocrates.

1.4

Hymn to Creation

Ṛg Veda

1. The non-existent did not exist nor did the existent exist at that time. There existed neither the midspace nor the heaven beyond. What stirred? From where and in whose protection? Did water exist, a deep depth?
2. Death did not exist nor deathlessness then. There existed no sign of night or of day. That One breathed without wind through its inherent force. There existed nothing else beyond that.
3. Darkness existed, hidden by darkness, in the beginning. All this was a signless ocean. The (thing) coming into being, which existed concealed by emptiness—that One was born by the power of heat.
4. Then in the beginning, from thought there developed desire, which existed as the primal semen. Searching in their hearts through inspired thinking, poets found the connection of the existent in the non-existent.
5. Their cord was stretched across: Did (something) exist below (it)? Did (something) exist above? There were placers of semen and there were powers. (There was) inherent force below, offering above.
6. Who really knows? Who shall here proclaim It?—from where was it born, from where this creation? The gods are on this side of the creation of this (world). So then who does know from where it came to be?
7. This creation, from where it came to be, if it was produced or if not—he who is its overseer in the highest heaven, he surely knows. Or if he does not know.

Ṛg Veda 10.129. Translated by Joel Brereton (n.p.).

1.5

Hymn to Time

Atharva Veda

19.53

1. Thousand-eyed, unaging, filled with semen, Time pulls (its chariot) as a horse with seven reins. Inspired poets climb aboard it. Its wheels are all beings.
2. This Time pulls seven wheels: seven are their center pieces; their axle is the immortal. Time has reached (?) [*añjat/añjaṅ ' ṛñjat*/*arñjat*??] all beings. It moves as the foremost deity.
3. A filled jar has been placed upon Time. We see it, although it is manifold. It is turned (upside down?) toward all these beings here. Time—they say that it is in the highest heaven.
4. It alone brought together beings, and it alone encompassed them. Though their father, it became their son. Therefore there is no other higher glory.
5. Time gave rise to the heaven beyond and these earths here. Driven by Time, what has been and what will be stand apart from one another.
6. Time sent forth the existent: within Time the sun shines; within Time are all those things that come to be; within Time the eye sees widely.
7. Within Time is thought, within Time is breath, within Time is name centered. Through Time, when it has come, all these living beings find joy.
8. Within Time is heat, within Time is the foremost, within Time is the sacred truth centered. Time is the master of all, he who was the father of the Lord of Living Beings (*Prajāpati*).

Atharvaveda 19.53–54. Translated by Joel Brereton (n.p.).

9. Sent by it, born by it, and on it that was based. Becoming the sacred truth, Time bears that which stands at the highest.

10. Time sent forth the living beings, and in the beginning, Time (sent forth) the Lord of Living Beings. The self-existent *Kaśyapa* was born from Time; heat was born from Time.

19.54

1. From Time the waters arose; from Time the sacred truth, heat, and the directions. By Time the sun arises, and in Time it goes down again.

2. By Time the wind blows. By Time the great earth, and in Time the great heaven is set in place.

3. (Although) their son, Time long ago gave birth to what has been and what will be. From Time the verses of the *Ṛgveda* arose; from Time, the recitation of the *Yajur Veda* was born.

4. Time gave rise to the sacrifice, the inexhaustible portion for the gods. Within Time, the male and female celestials (*Gandharvas* and *Apsarasas*), within Time the worlds find their foundations.

5. Upon Time this divine Singer (*Aṅgiras*) here and this Fire Priest (*Atharvan*) both stand. Both this world here and the highest world beyond, both the worlds won by merit and the boundaries won by merit—

6. Conquering all these worlds by means of the sacred truth, Time then races on, (for it is) the highest deity.

1.6

Īśa

Upaniṣad

4. Itself unmoving, it is faster than the mind. The gods do not know what was there before them. Itself standing, it overtakes those who run. In it are supported waters and wind.
5. It moves, it does not move. It is far, and yet it is near. It is within all things, it is also outside all this.
6. He who sees all beings in himself and himself in all beings, he does not feel any hatred because of this.
7. One who knows that all beings have become one with self, what delusion, what sorrow can arise in him who experiences the oneness.
8. He pervades all, he is the seed, he is incorporeal, without wounds and without veins, pure, untouched by evil. The seer, the thinker, all-pervading, self-existent, he created the things through the years in accordance with their natures.
9. Those who worship ignorance enter into blinding darkness; those who enjoy knowledge enter into still greater darkness.
10. The result of knowledge is one thing, the result of ignorance is another. We have heard this from those wise persons who have explained to us these matters.
11. One who knows that with the help of both knowledge and ignorance, goes beyond death with the help of ignorance, and reaches immortality through knowledge.
12. Those who worship the manifest enter into blinding darkness; those who enjoy the unmanifest enter into still greater darkness.
13. It is said that which arises from the manifest is different and that which arises from the unmanifest is different. We have heard this from the wise who have explained it to us thus.

Translated by J. N. Mohanty.

14. He who understands both the manifest and the unmanifest, goes beyond death with the help of the unmanifest, and achieves immortality through the manifest.
15. The face of truth is concealed with a golden container. Unconceal it, O Sun, so that it is visible to me who is dedicated to truth.

1.7

Kena

Upaniṣad

I.1. Directed and desired by whom, does the mind fall (on its object)? Ordered by whom does life first move? Willed by whom is this speech uttered? Which god activates the eye and the ear?

2. It is the ear of the ear, mind of the mind, speech of the speech, breath of the breath, the eye of the eye. The wise, renouncing (all) and leaving the world, become immortal.

3. The eye does not go there. The speech does not go (there), nor does the mind. How this can be taught, we do not know, we do not understand.

4. It is other than the known, it is also beyond the unknown. We have heard this from the ancients who explained all this to us.

5. That which is not manifested by speech, by which speech is manifested, know that to be the *brahman*, but not what people worship here.

6. That which is not conceived by the mind, but by which the mind is said to be thought, know that to be the *brahman*, not that which people worship here.

7. That which is not seen by the eye, but by which the eyes are seen, know that to be *brahman*, but not what people here worship.

8. That which is not heard by the ear, but by which this ear is heard, know that to be *brahman*, but not what people here worship.

9. That which is not breathed by breath, but by which breath is breathed, know that to be the *brahman*, but not what people here worship.

II.3. It is known to him, by whom it is not known; he who knows it, does not know. He who does not understand it, understands, he who understands it, does not.

Translated by J. N. Mohanty.

1.8

Superimposition

Śaṃkara

Of the two, subject and object, the former being the referent of the sense of "I" and the latter the referent of the sense of "you" (= "this"), which are as opposed as light and darkness, any sense of identity (between these two) is impossible, therefore any mutual identification of their properties is also impossible. Therefore, the superimposition of the object, which is the referent of the sense of "you," and of its properties, upon the subject, whose nature is consciousness and which is the referent of the sense of "I", and upon its properties, as well as its reverse, namely, the superimposition of the subject and its properties upon the object, ought to be false.

Nevertheless, owing to beginningless non-distinction, the distinction between self and not self, which are radically different, is not apprehended, the other and the others' properties are superimposed upon oneself, just as the self and its properties are superimposed upon the other—as a result of which, because of the false cognition of the things and their properties, the true and the false are coupled together, and one uses such expressions as "this is I" and "this is mine." This "natural" usage is beginningless.

Now, the question arises: what is this superimposition? The reply is: superimposition is an appearance, like memory, of something seen previously in something else. Some say that it is the superimposition on one thing the properties of another, there is an error which is due to non-apprehension of their difference. Still others say, when one thing is superimposed on another, there is an error which is due to non-apprehension of their difference. Still others say, when one thing is superimposed on another, an opposed property is imagined on the latter. All these views agree that one thing appears as another. Thus it is ordinarily experienced that a shell appears as silver, one moon appears as two.

From introduction to Śaṃkara's *Bhāṣya*, I.1.1.

How then can there be superimposition of objects and their properties upon the inner self which is not an object at all ? In all cases, one superimposes another object upon an object before him; you have said that this inner self is beyond the sense of "you" and so is not an object.

(To this objection) we reply: it is not the case that the self is, in all respects, non-object, since it is the object of the sense of "I", it is also immediately known as the inner self. Children ascribe the blue color and the property of curvature of [the bottom of] a pan to the sky which is not itself perceivable. Therefore the superimposition of the not-self on the self is not impossible.

The wise regard this superimposition as "ignorance"; as distinguished from it, the determination of the true nature of things they call "knowledge." This being so, when one thing is superimposed on another, the latter is not in the least touched by the faults or merits of the former. It is as depending on this mutual superimposition between self and not-self, called Ignorance, that all activity, ordinary as well as Vedic, concerning means of knowing and objects of knowing, arise, also all scriptures about injunctions, prohibitions and salvation are possible.

If it be asked, how do you know that means of knowing such as perception and also scriptures have, for their objects, what are the products of ignorance, we reply: if "I" and "mine" are not ascribed to the body and sense organs, the property of being the subject of true cognition and so the activities of the means of knowing would be impossible. Without the use of the sense-organs, uses of perception etc. are not possible. Without a body on which the sense of "I" is superimposed, one cannot do anything. When all these superimpositions are absent, the self is alone, and cannot be a subject of knowing. If there is no subjecthood with regard to knowing, the means of knowledge cannot be active. Therefore, means of knowing such as perception etc. and the scriptures have only objects which are the products of ignorance.

This is not different in the case of animals. Just as animals, when their ears etc. come in contact with sound etc., apprehend sound etc., and finding such knowledge of sound etc. threatening, run away from it while finding it favorable, move towards it; just as when they see a man approaching them with a rod in his hand, they think "he is coming to hit us" and begin to run away, but when they see a person with green grass in his hands, approach him; so do even wise men, when they see a person, with sword in his hand and with eyes red with anger approaching, run away and when they see the opposite, approach toward him. The practical behavior, depending upon means and objects of true cognition are therefore the same with animals and men. That in the case of animals, perception etc. are based upon ignorance, is well-known. Since the behavior of even wise persons is like that of animals, their perceptual behaviour etc. also must be based upon ignorance.

Although without knowing that one's self has an after life, one cannot perform actions recommended by the scriptures, so that only those who have knowledge are qualified to perform scriptural actions, nevertheless the knowledge of the self, which is the proper subject matter of Vedāntic knowledge, who is free from hunger and thirst and from the distinctions between caste and color such as Brahmin etc., and who is one and undifferentiated in his nature, is not required for scriptural action, because of inappropriateness and incompatibility.

For as long as there is no knowledge of the nature of the self, there remains incentive for scriptural actions. Therefore the scriptures cannot go beyond the fact that their objects are products of ignorance. The texts such as "the Brahmin should offer sacrifice" depend, for their efficacy, upon falsely ascribing caste and age distinctions to the self.

Superimposition is apprehending something as what it is not: this we have said before. For example: if one's wife and son etc. are afflicted or are well, one says "I am afflicted or I am well," whereby he superimposes external properties on himself. Likewise with properties of the body: "I am fat, I am thin, I am fair, I am sitting, going, crossing etc."; also properties of sense organs: "I am dumb, I am impotent, I am deaf, I am blind, etc.,"; similarly, with properties of the inner sense such as desire, resolution, discrimination, determination, etc." In this manner, one superimposes upon the inner sense the sense of "I" which is the witness of all things including the inner sense and the inner sense upon the witness of all things which is utterly different from it.

The beginningless, endless, natural superimposition which is a false cognition and is the cause of knowerhood and enjoyerhood, is experienced by everyone.

The Vedānta texts aim at destroying this ignorance which is at the root of all evil and giving rise to the knowledge of the oneness of self. This is the significance of all Vedāntic texts.

1.9

Brahman

Eliot Deutsch

There is a principle of utter simplicity ubiquitous in Nature. The wise realize it as silence divine.

Brahman, the One, is a state of being. It is not a "He," a personal being; nor is it an "It," an impersonal concept. Brahman is that state which *is* when all subject/object distinctions are obliterated. Brahman is ultimately a name for the experience of the timeless plenitude of being.[1]

I

Brahman is designated by Advaitins as *saccidānanda:* as "being" (*sat*), "consciousness" (*cit*) and "bliss" (*ānanda*). These are not so much qualifying attributes of Brahman as they are the terms that express the apprehension of Brahman by man. *Saccidānanda* is a symbol of Brahman as formulated by the mind interpreting its Brahman-experience.[2]

Being—(*sat*) apart from its complex historical-linguistic associations— points to the ontological principle of unity,[3] to the oneness not constituted of parts, to the existential substratum of all subjects and objects. Brahman is experienced as pure unqualified being. In fact it alone truly "exists"—which is to say that its manner of being is not comparable to the supposed existence of anything else. Consciousness (*cit*) points to the principle of awareness which informs being and which is, for the Advaitin, an unchanging witness of our being. Brahman-experience is illuminating experience; it is a state of conscious enlightenment. And it is a

From *Advaita Vedānta: A Philosophical Reconstruction* (Honolulu: East-West Center Press, 1969), chapter 1, pp. 9–14. Copyright © 1969 by East-West Center Press (since 1971, the University Press of Hawaii).

state of joyous being. Bliss (*ānanda*) points to the principle of value; to the fact that Brahman-experience is ecstatic and annuls all partial value in its incomparable splendor.

Phenomenologically, then, Brahman is affirmed by the Advaitin as that fullness of being which enlightens and is joy. It has its basis for him in experience (*anubhava*), not in mere speculation; and the experience, which is enduring for one who attains it, is the goal of human life.

II

And yet Brahman is not *saccidānanda,* if by that designation a positive limiting character is given to Brahman. Brahman, as transcendental being given in spiritual experience, defies all description or characterization. As Yājñavalkya, the Upaniṣadic sage, holds: "There is no other or better description [of Brahman] than this; that it is not-this, not-this (*neti neti*)."[4] And as Śaṃkara notes regarding the definition of Brahman—*satyaṃ jñā nam anantam brahma,* Brahman is truth, knowledge, infinite—words like *satya* (truth, reality) serve to "differentiate Brahman from other entities that possess opposite qualities."[5] Experientially, the role of a positive characterization or definition of Brahman is to direct the mind towards Brahman by affirming essential qualities that are really only denials of their opposites. To say "Brahman is truth" negates the quality of untruth—and this negation, it is believed, serves pragmatically to orient the mind towards Brahman. All characterizations of Brahman, in short, are intended in their experiential dimension to aid those who are searching for Brahman but have not yet realized It.

The *via negativa* of Advaita Vedānta also safeguards the unqualified oneness of that state of being called Brahman and silences all argument that would seek either to demonstrate or to refute it. Human language has its source in phenomenal experience; hence, it is limited in its application to states of being that are beyond that experience; logic is grounded in the mind as it relates to the phenomenal order; hence, it is unable to affirm, without at the same time denying, what extends beyond that order. "All determination is negation"; to apply a predicate to something is to impose a limitation upon it; for, logically, something is being excluded from the subject. The Real is without internal difference and, in essence, is unrelated to the content of any other form of experience. "The Real is thus unthinkable: thought can be brought to it only through negations of what is thinkable."[6]

Advaita Vedānta, then, must labor under this fact, which it explicitly acknowledges, that whatever is expressed is ultimately non-Brahman, is ultimately untrue.

III

Advaita Vedānta thus distinguishes two aspects or modes of Brahman, *nirguṇa* and *saguṇa*. *Nirguṇa* Brahman—Brahman without qualities—is just that transcendent indeterminate state of being about which ultimately nothing can be affirmed. *Saguṇa* Brahman—Brahman with qualities—is Brahman as interpreted and affirmed by the mind from its necessarily limited standpoint; it is that about which something can be said. And it is also a kind of spiritual experience.[7]

Brahman is a state of silent being; it is also a dynamic becoming. Brahman is divine and the Divine is Brahman.

This divine status of Brahman is not to be construed, however, in this context, as a personal deity who responds to prayer, bestows grace, or enters into history; rather, like *nirguṇa* Brahman, *saguṇa* Brahman is a state of being. It is a state of being wherein all distinctions between subject and object are harmonized. In *nirguṇa* Brahman all distinctions are obliterated and are overcome; in *saguṇa* Brahman they are integrated: a duality in unity is present here, and, consequently, the power of love. *Nirguṇa* Brahman is a state of mental-spiritual enlightenment (*jñāna*); *saguṇa* Brahman is a state of vital loving awareness (*bhakti*). *Nirguṇa* is conceptually an objectification of spiritual experience without distinction or determination (*nirvikalpa samādhi*); *saguṇa* Brahman is an objectification of determinate spiritual experience (*savikalpa samādhi*). It is the experience that, although negated by *nirguṇa* Brahman, yet complements *nirguṇa* Brahman-experience and, because it takes up and harmonizes everything within itself, makes possible the affirmation of the spirituality or intrinsic value of all modes of being.

In sum: Brahman, for Advaita Vedānta, is a name for that fullness of being which is the "content" of non-dualistic spiritual experience: an experience in which all distinctions between subject and object are shattered and in which remains only a pure, unqualified "oneness." The characterization of Brahman as *saccidānanda*—as infinite being (*sat*), consciousness (*cit*), and bliss (*ānanda*)—is intended not so much to ascribe attributes to Brahman as it is to describe the primary moments or features of the non-dualistic experience itself. Brahman is not *saccidānanda,* if by designating Brahman as *saccidānanda* one does intend to ascribe a positive character to Brahman. As "oneness," no wholly true affirmations (or negations) can be made about Brahman. Human language is grounded in a phenomenal experience of multiplicity and cannot therefore be used accurately to refer to Brahman; likewise, human logic is based upon phenomenal experience and thus is incapable of "determining," without at the same time "negating," its subject. This condition which the mind finds itself subject to leads to the necessity to distinguish two forms, as it were, of Brahman: Brahman as it is in itself, *nirguṇa* Brahman, or Brahman without quality: and Brahman as it is conceived by man from his limited phenomenal standpoint, *saguṇa,* Brahman, or Brahman with qualities. The affirmation of *saguṇa* Brahman, however, is not merely an acknowledgment of human limitations; it is also the name for that spiritual experience that harmonizes rather than obliterates distinctions. *Saguṇa* Brahman is the "content" of a loving experience of unity; *nirguṇa* Brahman is the "content" of an intuitive experience of identity. *Saguṇa* Brahman is not the highest possible form of experience; nevertheless, it is an extremely valuable experience in that it enables the Advaitin to affirm on one level of being the essential spirituality of everything that has being.

NOTES

1. The term "Brahman" first appears in the *Ṛg Veda* (ca. 1200 B.C.) in close connection with various sacred utterances that were thought to have a special magical power. Originally, then, the term may have meant "spell" or "prayer"; an utterance that was used for the magical attainment of worldly wishes and other worldly desires. Later, in the *Brāhmaṇas,* Brahman comes to signify that which stands behind the gods as their ground and source, and in the Upaniṣads generally it becomes the unitary principle of all being, the knowledge of which liberates one from finitude.

2. Advaitic thinkers refer to this type of designation as "definition with reference to essence" (*svarūpalakṣaṇa*) as distinguished from a "definition with reference to accidents" (*taṭsthalakṣaṇa*). With the designation of Brahman as *saccidānanda,* we have an essential identification of *sat, cit, ānanda* with Brahman rather than an adjectival qualifying of Brahman. In other words, *sat, cit, ānanda* are not intended to be qualifying attributes or accidents of Brahman, i.e., something that is superadded to it; they are intended to be expressions of its essence. Our main contention here, though, is that these terms are really being used properly not so much in a logical as in a phenomenological manner, for the problem is not so much one of defining Brahman as it is one of describing the fundamental features of man's experience of Oneness.

3. Cf. J. A. B. van Buitenen's Introduction to *Rāmānuja's Vedārthasaṃgraha* ("Deccan College Monograph Series," 16 [Poona: 1956]) for an excellent discussion of the historical-philosophical development of *sat.*

4. *Bṛhad-āraṇyaka Upaniṣad,* II, 3.6.

5. Śaṃkara's Commentary on *Taittirīya Upaniṣad,* 11, 1, 1.

6. Cf. Śaṃkara, *Brahmasūtrabhāṣya,* II, 1, 6; II, 1, 11; also his Commentary on *Bṛhad-āraṇyaka Upaniṣad,* I, 4, 6. Advaitins have, nevertheless, proffered arguments, if not "rational proofs," for Brahman. These arguments, as we have suggested, function primarily in a pragmatic context of orienting the mind towards the possibility of Brahman experience. The most common Advaitic argument for Brahman has to do with "necessary existence." Reminiscent of (but differing in many interesting and obvious ways from) Thomas' "third proof," the Advaitin argues that there must be a ground or substratum to experience for otherwise it would be impossible to deny or negate the existence of anything. Śaṃkara puts it this way: "Whenever we deny something unreal, we do so with reference to something real, the unreal snake,

e.g., is negatived with reference to the real rope. But this (denial of something un-real with reference to something real) is possible only if some entity is left. If every-thing is denied, no entity is left, and if no entity is left, the denial of some other which we may wish to undertake, becomes impossible, i.e., that latter entity becomes real and as such cannot be negatived."—*Brahmasūtrabhāṣya*, III, 2, 22, in *The Vedānta-Sūtra with the Commentary of Śaṅkarācarya*, trans. by George Thibaut, vols. 24 and 28 of *Sacred Books of the East*, ed. by Max Müller (Oxford: The Clarendon Press, 1890 and 1896).

This argument will be clearer from the discussion in the next chapter, which pro-vides the ontological distinctions and psychological processes that are presupposed in the argument.

7. This interpretation of *saguṇa* Brahman—as a type of spiritual experience as well as an epistemic transformation of *nirguṇa* Brahman into an object—is justified, we believe, on the grounds that Śaṃkara and other Advaitins insist that *saguṇa* Brahman (also referred to in this type of context as *Īśvara*, the Lord) is a proper ob-ject of devotion and, when realized in experience, is a state of loving bliss (Cf. *Brah-masūtrabhāṣya*, 1, 1, 11; I, 1, 20) and that Advaitins, in their analysis of the self, clearly describe a level of harmony in experience that is associated ontologically with *saguṇa* Brahman.

1.10

Tao Te Ching

Lao Tzu

1. The Tao [Way] that can be told of is not the eternal Tao;
   The name that can be named is not the eternal name.
   The Nameless is the origin of Heaven and Earth;
   The Name is the mother of all things.
   Therefore let there always be nonbeing so we may see their subtlety,
   And let there always be being so we may see their outcome.
   The two are the same,
   But after they are produced, they have different names.
   They both may be called deep and profound.
   Deeper and more profound, The door of all subtleties!

   not straightfoward

2. When the people of the world all know beauty as beauty,
   There arises the recognition of ugliness.
   When they all know the good as good,
   There arises the recognition of evil.
Therefore:
   Being and nonbeing produce each other;
   Difficult and easy complete each other;
   Long and short contrast each other;
   High and low distinguish each other;
   Sound and voice harmonize with each other;
   Front and back follow each other.
   Therefore the sage manages affairs without action [*wu-wei*]
   And spreads doctrines without words.

From *The Great Asian Religions,* edited and compiled by Wing-tsit Chan, Isma'īl Rāgī Fārūqi, Joseph M. Kitagawa, and P. T. Raju (New York: Macmillan, 1969), pp. 151–55. Copyright © Macmillan 1969. Footnotes deleted.

All things arise, and he does not turn away from them.
He produces them, but does not take possession of them.
He acts, but does not rely on his own ability.
He accomplishes his task, but does not claim credit for it.
It is precisely because he does not claim credit that his accomplishment
   remains with him.

6. The spirit of the valley never dies.
   It is called the subtle and profound female.
   The gate of the subtle and profound female
   Is the root of Heaven and Earth.
   It is continuous, and seems to be always existing.
   Use it and you will never wear it out.

7. Heaven is eternal and Earth ever lasting.
   They can be eternal and everlasting because they do not exist for them-
      selves,
   And for this reason can exist forever.
   Therefore the sage places himself in the background, but finds himself
      in the foreground.
   He puts himself away, and yet he always remains.
   Is it not because he has no personal interests?
   This is the reason why his personal interests are fulfilled.

10. Can you keep the spirit and embrace the One without departing from
      them?
    Can you concentrate your vital force [*ch'i*] and achieve the highest de-
       gree of weakness like an infant?
    Can you clean and purify your profound insight so it will be spotless?
    Can you love the people and govern the state without knowledge [cun-
       ning]?
    Can you play the role of the female in the opening and closing of the
       gates of Heaven?
    Can you understand all and penetrate all without taking any action?
       To produce things and to rear them,
       To produce, but not to take possession of them,
       To act, but not to rely on one's own ability,
       To lead them, but not to master them
       This is called profound and secret virtue.

14. We look at it and do not see it; Its name is The Invisible.
    We listen to it and do not hear it; Its name is The Inaudible.
    We touch it and do not find it;

Its name is The Subtle [formless].
These three cannot be further inquired into,
And hence merge into one.
Going up high, it is not bright, and coming down low, it is not dark.
Infinite and boundless, it cannot be given any name;
It reverts to nothingness.
This is called shape without shape,
Form [*hsiang*] without object.
It is The Vague and Elusive.
Meet it and you will not see its head.
Follow it and you will not see its back.
Hold on to the Tao of old in order to master the things of the present.
From this one may know the primeval beginning [of the universe].
This is called the bond of Tao.

16. Attain complete vacuity,
    Maintain steadfast quietude.
    All things come into being,
    And I see thereby their return.
    All things flourish,
    But each one returns to its root.
    The return to its root means tranquillity.
    It is called returning to its destiny.
    To return to destiny is called the eternal [Tao].
    To know the eternal is called enlightenment.
    Not to know the eternal is to act blindly to result in disaster.
    He who knows the eternal is all-embracing.
    Being all-embracing, he is impartial.
    Being impartial, he is kingly [universal].
    Being kingly, he is one with Nature.
    Being one with Nature, he is in accord with Tao.
    Being in accord with Tao, he is ever lasting,
    And is free from danger throughout his lifetime.

19. Abandon sageliness and discard wisdom;
    Then the people will benefit a hundred fold.
    Abandon humanity and discard righteousness;
    Then the people will return to filial piety and deep love.
    Abandon skill and discard profit;
    Then there will be no thieves or robbers. However, these three things
        are ornament [*wen*] and not adequate.
    Therefore let people hold on to these:
        Manifest plainness,

Embrace simplicity,
Reduce selfishness,
Have few desires.

21. The all-embracing quality of the great virtue [*te*] follows alone from the
    Tao.
    The thing that is called Tao is eluding and vague.
    Vague and eluding, there is in it the form.
    Eluding and vague, in it are things.
    Deep and obscure, in it is the essence.
    The essence is very real; in it are evidences.
    From the time of old until now, its name (manifestations) ever remains,
    By which we may see the beginning of all things.
    How do I know that the beginnings of all things are so?
    Through this [Tao].

25. There was something undifferentiated and yet complete,
    Which existed before heaven and earth.
    Soundless and formless, it depends on nothing and does not change.
    It operates everywhere and is free from danger.
    It may be considered the mother of the universe.
    I do not know its name; I call it Tao.
    If forced to give it a name, I shall call it Great.
    Now being great means functioning everywhere.
    Functioning everywhere means far-reaching.
    Being far-reaching means returning to the original point.
    Therefore Tao is great.
    Heaven is great.
    Earth is great.
    And the king is also great.
    There are four great things in the universe, and the king is one of them.
    Man models himself after Earth.
    Earth models itself after Heaven.
    Heaven models itself after Tao.
    And Tao models itself after Nature.

28. He who knows the male [active force] and keeps to the female [the pas-
    sive force or receptive element]
    Becomes the ravine of the world. Being the ravine of the world, He will
        never depart from eternal virtue,
    But returns to the state of infancy.
    He who knows the white [glory] and yet keeps to the black [humility],
    Becomes the model for the world.

Being the model for the world,
He will never deviate from eternal virtue,
But returns to the state of the Ultimate of Nonbeing.
He who knows glory but keeps to humility,
Becomes the valley of the world.
Being the valley of the world,
He will be proficient in eternal virtue,
And returns to the state of simplicity [uncarved wood].
When the uncarved wood is broken up, it is turned into concrete things
    [as Tao is transformed into the myriad things].
But when the sage uses it, he becomes the leading official.
Therefore the great ruler does not cut up.

34. The Great Tao flows everywhere.
    It may go left or right.
All things depend on it for life, and it does not turn away from them.
It accomplishes its task, but does not claim credit for it.
It clothes and feeds all things but does not claim to be master over them.
Always without desires, it may be called The Small.
All things come to it and it does not master them; it may be called The
    Great.
Therefore [the sage] never strives himself for the great, and thereby the
    great is achieved.

40. Reversion is the action of Tao.
Weakness is the function of Tao.
All things in the world come from being.
And being comes from nonbeing.

42. Tao produced the One.
The One produced the two
The two produced the three.
And the three produced the ten thousand things.
The ten thousand things carry the yin [negative cosmic force] and em-
    brace the yang [positive cosmic force], and through the blending of
    the material force [*ch'i*] they achieve harmony.
People hate to be children without parents, lonely people without
    spouses, or men without food to eat,
And yet kings and lords call themselves by these names.
Therefore it is often the case that things gain by losing and lose by gaining.
What others have taught, I teach also:
Violent and fierce people do not die a natural death.
I shall make this the father [basis or starting point] of my teaching.

43. The softest things in the world overcome the hardest things in the
    world.
    Nonbeing penetrates that in which there is no space.
    Through this I know the advantage of taking no action.
    Few in the world can understand teaching without words and the ad-
       vantage of taking no action.

51. Tao produces them [the ten thousand things].
    Virtue fosters them.
    Matter gives them physical form.
    The circumstances and tendencies complete them.
    Therefore the ten thousand things esteem Tao and honor virtue.
    Tao is esteemed and virtue is honored without anyone's order.
    They always come spontaneously.
    Therefore Tao produces them and virtue fosters them.
    They rear them and develop them.
    They give them security and give them peace.
    They nurture them and protect them.
    [Tao] produces them but does not take possession of them.
    It acts, but does not rely on its own ability.
    It leads them but does not master them. This is called profound and se-
       cret virtue.

55. He who possesses virtue in abundance
    May be compared to an infant.
    Poisonous insects will not sting him.
    Fierce beasts will not seize him.
    Birds of prey will not strike him.
    His bones are weak, his sinews tender, but his grasp is firm.
    He does not yet know the union of male and female,
    But his organ is aroused.
    This means that his essence is at its height.
    He may cry all day without becoming hoarse,
    This means that his [natural] harmony is perfect.
    To know harmony means to be in accord with the eternal.
    To be in accord with the eternal means to be enlightened.
    To force the growth of life means ill omen.
    For the mind to employ the vital force without restraint means violence.
    After things reach their prime, they begin to grow old,
    Which means being contrary to Tao.
    Whatever is contrary to Tao will soon perish.

57. Govern the state with correctness.

    Operate the army with surprise tactics. Administer the empire by engaging in no activity.

    How do I know that this should be so? Through this:

    The more taboos and prohibitions there are in the world,

    The poorer the people will be.

    The more sharp weapons the people have,

    The more troubled the state will be.

    The more cunning and skill man possesses,

    The more vicious things will appear.

    The more laws and orders are made prominent,

    The more thieves and robbers there will be.

    Therefore the sage says:

    I take no action and the people of themselves are transformed.

    I love tranquillity and the people of themselves become correct.

    I engage in no activity and the people of themselves become prosperous.

    I have no desires and the people of themselves become simple.

59. To rule people and to serve Heaven there is nothing better than to be frugal.

    Only by being frugal can one recover quickly.

    To recover quickly means to accumulate virtue heavily.

    By heavy accumulation of virtue one can overcome everything.

    If one can overcome everything, then he will acquire a capacity the limit of which is beyond anyone's knowledge.

    When his capacity is beyond anyone's knowledge, he is fit to rule a state.

    He who possesses the Mother Tao of the state will last long.

    This means that the roots are deep and the stalks are firm, which is the way of long life and everlasting existence.

73. He who is brave in daring will be killed.

    He who is brave in not daring will live.

    Of these two, one is advantageous and one is harmful.

    Who knows why Heaven dislikes what it dislikes?

    Even the sage considers it a difficult question.

    The Way of Heaven does not compete, and yet it skillfully achieves victory.

    It does not speak, and yet it skillfully responds to things.

    It comes to you without your invitation. It is not anxious about things and yet it plans well.

    Heaven's net is indeed vast.

    Though its meshes are wide, it misses nothing.

1.11

Lao Tzu's Conception of *Tao*

Charles Wei-Hsun Fu

This article attempts a new interpretation of Lao Tzu's metaphysics of Tao by employing a combined method of linguistic and philosophical analyses. This new methodological approach involves the following basic assumptions: (1) Lao Tzu's metaphysics of Tao can be characterized as a kind of non-dualistic and non-conceptual metaphysics *sub specie aeternitatis;* (2) Tao is not an entity, substance, God, *Idée,* or anything hypostatized or conceptualized, but is rather a metaphysical symbol unifying various dimensions of Nature as the totality of things-as-they-are; (3) there is, generally speaking, no confusion or inconsistency of thought involved in the *Lao-Tzu;* (4) there are two kinds of speech used by Lao Tzu, viz. philosophical (real) speech and figurative (metaphorical) speech; and (5) figurative expressions, which predominate, can be reduced to philosophical expressions for the sake of the clarification of Lao Tzu's thought. In the light of these basic assumptions, a philosophical explication of Lao Tzu's conception of Tao is undertaken by exploring its six dimensions. They are: (i) Tao as Reality, (ii) Tao as Origin, (iii) Tao as Principle, (iv) Tao as Function, (v) Tao as Virtue, and (vi) Tao as Technique; and (ii)–(vi) can he subsumed under Tao as Manifestation (to us). These six dimensions are not "categories" or "attributes" in the Western (conceptual) sense, but are the inseparable aspects or perspectives of Tao reconstructed from the *Lao-Tzu* in order to show the best possible way of understanding Lao Tzu's metaphysical thinking. In the Epilogue, a brief comparison of Lao Tzu and Spinoza is made in order to emphasize the non-conceptual and non-propositional nature of Lao Tzu's metaphysical language. . . .

From *Inquiry* 16 (1973): 367–94. Copyright © by Scandinavian University Press.

II. TAO AS REALITY AND MANIFESTATION

In spite of its linguistic ambiguity and philosophical abstruseness, the opening chapter of the *Tao-têh ching* seems to me to put in a nutshell the essential nature of Lao Tzu's metaphysics of Tao. In accordance with my basic assumptions I attempt a new and philosophical translation of this chapter as follows:

> The Tao that can be tracked [expressed in words] is not the
> invariable Tao;
> The name that can be named [given in concept] is not the
> invariable Name.
> [As] non-being [Tao] is named the origin of heaven-and-
> earth [the universe];
> [As] being [Tao] is named the mother of all things.[1]

Therefore:

> [Under the aspect of its] non-being [as hidden] as ever, One
> may see into the inner wonders of Tao;
> [Under the aspect of its] being [as manifest] as ever, One
> may see into the outer forms of Tao.[2]
> These two [non-being and being] are of the same source,
> though differently named.
> They are both called "deep and profound" [*hsüan*].
> All-deep and all-profound.
> [Here is] the gate to infinite wonders.

Lao Tzu is here warning us that Tao as "the Absolute" cannot, by definition, be described or conceptually manipulated by any human (relative) means; it is indeed nameless and ineffable. In other words, Lao Tzu declares that all our human quest for "the Absolute" by means of conceptual dichotomization is at best an as-if metaphysical adventure about what is ontologically non-differentiated and epistemologically non-differentiatable. To use an analogy, the nameless Tao is likened to the most fastidious and unconquerable woman's heart in the world, or better, to the tail of an eel too slippery for us to grasp. Lao Tzu himself figuratively describes this "slippery" nature of the nameless Tao:

> We gaze at it but see it not; it is called Invisible [*yi*].
> We listen to it but hear it not; it is called Inaudible [*hsi*]. We grasp it but
> find it not; it is called Intangible [*wei*].[3]
> These three all elude our inquiries, and hence merge into One.
> Its rising brings no light; its sinking, no darkness.
> Continuous, unceasing, and unnameable,

It returns to No-[particular-]thingness
This is called the Formless Form, the Imageless Image.
This is called the Vague and Elusive.
We meet it and do not see its face;
We follow it and do not see its back. (14)

However, as soon as Lao Tzu announces that Tao as Reality is nameless and ineffable (ontologically non-differentiated and epistemologically non-differentiatable), Tao immediately manifests itself to us as "something" epistemologically differentiated into non-being ("the nameless Tao" thus-named by Lao Tzu) and being (the nameable Tao conceived by us). This is indeed a metaphysical paradox, and this is why Lao Tzu often emphasizes that "the wise does not speak" (56), or that "the greatest eloquence appears tongue-tied" (45). Once we delve, out of metaphysical curiosity, into the meaning of the nameless Tao, it all of a sudden "reveals" itself in terms of the dichotomy of non-being (*wu*) and being (*yu*). It is in this sense that the nameless Tao which Lao Tzu speaks of is the "ultimate reality" approximately thus-named, and is still at [one] remove from the nameless Tao totally unnameable. This is the only respect in which mysticism is applicable to Lao Tzu's metaphysics of Tao.

This should not, I hope, mislead the reader into considering that the real nameless Tao exists as "the object" of Lao Tzu's metaphysical vision, for it cannot be said to exist or not-exist apart from the nameless Tao thus-named. Both the nameless Tao thus-named and the real nameless Tao are two ways of saying the same thing, namely Tao as Reality; they are not categories but perspectives. But again, Tao as Reality cannot be said to exist or not-exist apart from Tao as Manifestation in terms of the totality of things-as-they-are. In terms of the conceptual elusiveness (epistemological non-differentiatability) and existential no-particular-thingness (ontological non-differentiatedness) of Nature (the totality of things-as-they-are), Lao Tzu names it "non-being" or "the nameless Tao" (Tao as Reality); and in terms of the outwardly manifest forms of Nature itself epistemologically differentiated by us humans, he names it "being" (Tao as Manifestation). Tao as Reality and Tao as Manifestation are two perspectives or aspects of Tao, which is a mere symbol reflecting Lao Tzu's metaphysical way of understanding Nature or the totality of things-as-they-are. Only Nature or the totality of all things can be said to exist, and not "Tao" itself. It is in this sense, therefore, that Lao Tzu's philosophy is characterizable more properly as the natural way rather than the mystical way.

The ontological relationship between non-being and being in the *Lao-Tzu* (as seen from the opening chapter quoted above) is strikingly similar to that between emptiness (*śūnyatā*) and forms (*rūpa*) in Mahāyāna Buddhism, as well as to that between Tao (the metaphysical) and concrete things (the phenomenal) in the *Classic of Changes*,[4] all three being illustrative of the idea of (what Ch'éng Yi calls) "the same source of substance-and-function and the inseparability of hidden and-manifest,"[5] peculiar to the Chinese metaphysical tradition which is basically non-dualistic and non-conceptual. To use a famous Mahāyāna analogy, Lao Tzu's non-being and being are likened to the great ocean and the totality of waves; they are two ways of looking at one and the same ontologically non-differentiated "Tao." . . .

Aside from the two Philosophical names "non-being" and "being," Lao Tzu also gives to Tao several other figurative names. In terms of its being ubiquitous, all-pervading, and infinite, Tao is named "Great" (25, 34); in terms of its being hidden and unseen by the vulgar man, it is named "Small" (34, 52); in terms of its spontaneity or naturalness, it is named "Nature" (23, 25); in terms of its impartiality or lack of private affections, it is named "Way of Heaven" (77, 79, 81); in terms of its being infinitely wondrous, it is called "deep and profound" (1); in terms of its being metaphysically prior to all things "produced and fostered," it is named "mother of the world" (25, 52); in terms of its primordial simplicity, it is named "(nameless) uncarved wood" (32) 37); in terms of its yieldingness and humbleness, it is likened to water (8); in terms of its being tender and inexhaustibly productive *in potentia,* it is likened to "the profound female" (6); and in terms of its vacuity and unceasing creativity, it is also likened to "the Spirit of the valley" (6). Interestingly, even "Tao" itself is a provisional name (*prajñapti*) given to the ontologically non-differentiated aspect of Nature. Lao Tzu's own words as follows prove one of my basic assumptions that "Tao" is simply a metaphysical symbol:

> There is "something" non-differentiated and yet all-complete,
>> Which comes before heaven-and-earth.
> Silent and boundless, it stands alone without change,
>> Yet revolving and pervading without fail.
> It may be considered the mother of the world.
> I know not its name;
> I give it a provisional name "Tao."
> Or, for lack of a proper term, "Great." (25)

This passage is a good example of Lao Tzu's use of figurative expressions to give an approximate description of the nameless Tao. But what is the philosophical meaning conveyed by this passage? The name "the mother of the world" here strongly suggests that Tao manifests itself as (cosmological) origin. Let me now explicate the real meaning of this first dimension of Tao as Manifestation (to us).

III. TAO AS ORIGIN

In addition to the above passage in Chapter 25, we find in five other chapters (1, 4, 40, 42, 52) short sentences or passages dealing with Tao as Origin. The most important appears in Chapter 42:

> Tao produces [*shéng*] One;
> One produces Two;
> Two produces Three;
> Three produces all things.
> All things carry them and embrace the *yang,*
> And attain their harmony through the proper blending of
>   *ch'i* [Ether].

There are two questions with respect to this puzzling passage: (i) What exactly are One, Two, and Three? (ii) What is the real meaning of the verb *shéng* (produce, yield, give birth to)?

In the main, there are two possible hermeneutic versions of Lao Tzu's cosmological thinking. According to the first version, namely the cosmological interpretation *sub specie temporis* (in the literal sense), Tao as Origin is taken to mean the real natural cause of the existence of all things (in the actual time-process). That is why most translators of the *Tao-têh ching* use the past tense in their translation of this passage, e.g., James Legge ("produced"), Arthur Waley ("gave birth"), R. B. Blakney ("begot"), John Wu ("gave birth"), and Chan ("produced").[6]

It is my contention that this first (literal) version involves a contradiction of thought in the *Lao-Tzu* and is therefore unjustifiable. First, those who take this version seem to forget or ignore the fact that Lao Tzu is using figurative expressions when he deals with the cosmological dimension of Tao (as Origin). Since Lao Tzu is primarily engaged, like Spinoza, in metaphysical thinking *sub specie aeternitatis,* there is no actual process of natural causation or evolution involved. Further, Lao Tzu says very clearly in the opening chapter that Tao is not describable or conceptualizable; he also says, "Tao is hidden and nameless" (41). Since Tao is hidden and non-conceptualizable, how can Tao become a real subject and not a mere grammatical subject? Again, Lao Tzu makes it clear that "Tao models itself after Nature" (25) and that "Tao always takes non-action" (37). This simply means that all things run their own courses spontaneously (in accordance with Tao as the principle of reversion). How can Tao then be said to produce or give birth to One, Two, Three, and all things (in the past tense)? The crucial point here is that almost all specialists on the *Lao-Tzu* have not fully understood the nature of Lao Tzu's non-conceptual metaphysical thinking *sub specie aeternitatis,* or the figurative nature of his metaphysical language.

Philosophically speaking, therefore, the second version, namely the ontological interpretation under the form of eternity, is far more acceptable. And the passage about "Tao produces One" should be re-rendered philosophically as "Tao (metaphysically) comes before One . . . Three (metaphysically) comes before all things." Taking the ontological version of Lao Tzu's cosmological thinking, I would maintain that Tao is the ontological ground of all things in the non-conceptual, symbolic sense; and One, Two, and Three can be regarded simply as the ontological symbols pointing to the truth that what is non-differentiated is that upon which what is differentiated is metaphysically dependent. Following this line of interpretation, the sentence about "something non-differentiated," as mentioned at the end of the last section, should be philosophically interpreted as follows:

> The ontologically non-differentiated and yet all-complete is metaphysically prior to the beingness of the universe (which can be perceived through its manifest forms and is therefore incomplete).

That is to say, the ontologically differentiated and incomplete depends metaphysically upon the ontologically non-differentiated and all-complete. Or, to make the point clearer, (i) the ontologically non-differentiated and the ontologically differentiated are but two aspects of the same Tao; (ii) from the metaphysical point of view *sub specie aeternitatis,* Nature (the totality of things-as-they-are) is seen as the ontologically non-differentiated (nameless Tao as Reality), whereas from the vulgar point of view *sub specie temporis,* it is seen as the ontologically differentiated (nameable Tao as Manifestation); (iii) under the form of eternity, the ontologically non-differentiated is metaphysically prior to the ontologically differentiated; (iv) this does not mean that originally there is something called "Tao" and then it is divided up into the non-differentiated and the differentiated, for these two aspects of Tao presuppose the above two different points of view, and Tao itself is not some hypostatized entity or *Idée* that exists independently of these two aspects; therefore, (v) Ockham's razor does not apply to Lao Tzu's conception of Tao.

Lao Tzu also says, "All things in the world are born (*shéng*) from being, and being from non-being" (40). This sentence can again be re-rendered in the above manner. To my present knowledge, Fung Yu-lan has given, in 1947 (before he returned to China), the best philosophical analysis of this sentence. As he holds:

> This saying of Lao Tzu does not mean that there was a time when there was only Non-being, and that then there came a time when Being came into being from Non-being. It simply means that if we analyze the existence of things, we see there must first be Being before there can be any things. *Tao* is the unnameable,

is Non-being, and is that by which all things come to be. Therefore, before the being of Being, there must be Non-being, from which Being comes into being. What is here said belongs to ontology, not to cosmology. It has nothing to do with time and actuality. For in time and actuality, there is no Being; there are only beings.[7]

It might be asked: Doesn't the philosophical analysis proposed in this paper and by Fung make Lao Tzu's cosmology too Western? My answer is definitely, no. If my basic assumption regarding Tao as a symbol is accepted, there will be no misunderstanding of our use of such terms as "non-being," "being," or "cosmology." And one more piece of evidence can be shown to support the ontological interpretation of Tao as Origin. Lao Tzu says also: "Being and non-being produce (*shéng*) each other" (2). The philosophical meaning of this sentence is that non-being and being ontologically depend on each other and constitute two inseparable aspects of Tao, though non-being is much more to be emphasized in so far as Tao is devoid of any specific, positive characterization. Therefore, there is no contradiction between this sentence and the previous one, "All things originate in being, and being in non-being."

That being and non-being ontologically depend on each other implies philosophically that all pairs of opposites in the world, e.g., *yin* and *yang*, male and female, birth and death, etc., are dialectically inseparable from each other. And here we find another dimension of Tao. Indeed, Tao as Origin cannot be properly understood without reference to Tao as Principle, which seems to me the key dimension of Tao.

IV. TAO AS PRINCIPLE

Han Fei Tzu (d. 233 B.C.) of the Legalist school was the first Chinese philosopher who tried to understand Lao Tzu's Tao as Principle or Reason (*Li*). In his "Interpretation of Tao," which constitutes the 20th chapter of the *Han-Fei-Tzu* and is the oldest commentary on the *Lao-Tzu* extant today, he says:

Tao is that whereby all things become what they are; it is that wherewith all principles are in accord. Principles are patterns according to which all things come into being. Tao is the ground upon which all things are formed. It is said therefore that Tao puts things in order [*Li*]. All things have different principles of their own, while Tao brings the principles of all things into single agreement. As far as definite and particular principles are concerned, there are existence and extinction, life and death, flowering and decay. . . . What is invariable has neither change nor definite, particular principles. Having no definite, particular principles, it [Tao] is free from limitation. Hence its being inexpressible.[8]

Based on Han's interpretation of Tao as Principle, we may say that from the standpoint of the differentiation of (the being-aspect of) Tao, all things are governed by different specific principles or reasons by means of which they change and are transformed in different ways. But there is something invariable which functions as the ultimate principle of the change and transformation of all things, and that is Tao (as Principle) itself. To illustrate Lao Tzu's conception of Tao as Principle more clearly, we may borrow from the *Classic of Changes* "the three names (meanings) of *Yi* (Change)," viz. (i) *pien-yi* (change and transformation), (ii) *chien-yi* (simplicity in change), and (iii) *pu-yi* (non-change or invariableness).[9]

(i) Both Taoists and Confucianists agree that all things in the universe perpetually change and transform (*pien-yi*) themselves. As Lao Tzu says: "Nature utters few words. A whirlwind does not last a whole morning, nor does a rainstorm a whole day. What is it that causes these? Heaven-and-earth [Nature]! Even heaven-and-earth [Nature] cannot [blow or pour] for long, how much less should human beings?" (23). Echoing Lao Tzu's words here, Confucius also once sighed, when standing by a stream, "Like this stream, everything is flowing on ceaselessly, day and night."[10] Both of them are in agreement with the Buddha and Heraclitus that nothing can really escape from *pien-yi*. This is indeed the first step toward metaphysical wisdom concerning the ontological nature of all things. And to understand the necessity and significance of metaphysical wisdom, one should realize (*erleben*) very deeply the futility of chasing all the changeable objects in the world, as is touchingly expressed in the opening passages of Spinoza's *On the Improvement of the Understanding*. From the metaphysical point of view *sub specie aeternitatis*, however, it is not enough just to realize that nothing is permanent (*anitya*); one must be able to create a keen ontological insight into something simple, universal, and invariable in the spontaneous and unceasing course of change and transformation of all things.

(ii) The *chien-yi* (principle of simplicity in change) Lao Tzu observes is that all things in the process of *pien-yi* always have their opposites to constitute a dialectical pair. In Nature, Tao manifests itself as the Way of Heaven, which is likened to "the bending of a bow. When the string is high, bring it down; when low, raise it up. . . . The Way of Heaven reduces whatever is excessive, and supplements whatever is insufficient" (77). He also says: "Being and non-being produce each other; difficult and easy contrast with each other; front and back follow each other" (2). Parallel to the Way of Heaven there is the Way of Man: "Misfortune is that upon which fortune leans; fortune is that in which misfortune is latent" (58). Also: "It is because men of the world distinguish beauty as beauty that there appears ugliness; it is because they distinguish good as good that there appears evil" (2).

(iii) This *chien-yi* turns out, in the *Lao-Tzu*, to be the invariable principle (*pu-yi*) of the cyclic reversion of all things in Nature. Lao Tzu mentions the

terms *yin* and *yang* only once (42), and it is not clear whether he shares with
the *Classic of Changes* the same idea of *yin-yang* interaction. In any case the
pu-yi refers to the principle of (cyclic) reversion of all things to their opposites, as is expressed in the words, "Reversing is the movement of Tao" (40).
This Tao as Principle can be illustrated by an age old Chinese proverb, *wu-
chi pi-fan,* meaning "When a thing reaches its (extreme) limit, it reverts to
its opposite." But the ultimate meaning of the reversion of all things to their
opposites lies in the ontological facticity that all things return to their root
(the original Tao or Nature). In other words, Tao as Principle in terms of
cyclic reversion is to be understood, from the higher point of view, in terms
of the returning of all things to Nature itself, wherein is found the real Invariable. The principle of reversion and the principle of returning to the root
are simply two ways of looking at things-as-they-are (in the course of
change and transformation); but the latter expresses Lao Tzu's deeper metaphysical wisdom. He says:

> All things however they flourish return to the root [Tao] from which they
>   grow.
> This return to the root is Repose.
> This is called "fulfilling destiny."
> To fulfill destiny is to become part of the Invariable [Tao].
> To know the Invariable [Tao] is called *ming* [ontological insight].
> Not to know the Invariable [Tao] is to run into disaster. (16)

> To be great [as the Way] is to be passing on;
> To be passing on is to be far-reaching;
> To be far-reaching is to be returning
> [to the original state of things]. (25)

The metaphysical wisdom conveyed by this passage is that only after one
knows the Invariable in terms of the reversion of all things is one able to follow Tao as Principle spontaneously, that is, to participate oneself in the
spontaneous returning of all things back to Nature. From the Taoist point of
view, here is to be found the real emancipation from human bondage: fulfilling one's destiny is to transcend one's "little ego" and totally to identify
oneself with the great Nature (56). All pairs of opposites are thus completely
equalized and merge into one unitary whole, which we may call Nature,
Tao, or Nothingness (*wu*).

As we can see, Lao Tzu's conception of Tao as Principle reflects a very
strong naturalistic tendency. From the Taoist point of view, the ontological
insight into the reversion/returning of all beings is the best metaphysical
way of seeing-things-as-they-are (*yathā-bhūta-darśana*) without any
human distortion of Nature. Here lies Lao Tzu's total disagreement with
Hegel (*Weltgeist* as the infinite synthesis), Marx (the synthesis attained in the

classless society), St. Augustine (City of Jerusalem), Plato (the world of Forms), John Bury (Idea of Progress), or any philosopher who wants to introduce a non-naturalistic ultra-meaning into the context of Nature; for this would be a human distortion of the as-it-is-ness (*tzu-jan*) of the world and man in one way or another. And, despite the similarities between the *Lao-Tzu* and the *Classic of Changes,* the moralistic coloration of the unceasing process of the change and transformation of things in the latter is, from the Taoist point of view, to be rejected. "Tao models itself after Nature" (25) and transcends all value-commitments that are, to quote the title of Nietzsche's book; "*Menschliches, Allzumenschliches"* (human, all-too-human)!

V. TAO AS FUNCTION

While Tao as Principle refers to the invariable law of nature governing the change and transformation of all things, Tao as Function refers to the wondrous operations of (the non-being-aspect of) Tao in terms of spontaneous non-action (*wu-wei*) and softness (*jou-jo*). In his conception of Tao as Principle, Lao Tzu simply accepts the necessary truth of the destiny of all things in terms of their return to the root; in his conception of Tao as Function much emphasis is put on our metaphysical realization of the inner wonders of non-being. When Lao Tzu says that "[Under the aspect of its] being [as manifest] as ever, one may see into the outer forms of Tao" (1), these outer forms reflect the change and transformation of all things in accordance with Tao as Principle; and when he says that "[Under the aspect of its] non-being [as hidden] as ever, one may see into the inner wonders of Tao" (1), these inner wonders reflect the deeper structure of Tao as Principle, that is, the function of Tao as non-being.

Lao Tzu uses three analogies in the following figurative expressions to illustrate the wondrous functioning of non-being:

> Thirty spokes converge upon a single hub [to make a wheel]; but it is on its non-being [the empty space for the axle] that the function of the wheel depends. Clay is fashioned into a vessel; but it is on its non-being [empty hollowness] that its function depends. Doors and windows are pierced to make a room; but it is on its non-being [empty space] that its function depends. Therefore just as we take advantage of being [what-is], we should realize the function of non-being [what-is-not]. (11)

What Lao Tzu means to say here is that while the vulgar man can utilize the particular objects for secular needs, he is metaphysically blind to the greatest usefulness of the unlimited and inexhaustible wonders of non-being (what-is-not) functioning in both Nature and the world of man. As he says: "Tao is like an empty bowl, and its function is inexhaustible" (4); "Between heaven-and-earth there seems to be a bellows: being vacuous, its function is unlimited; the more it is worked, the more it brings forth" (5).

But why is the function of Tao as non-being unlimited and inexhaustible? The answer lies in Lao Tzu's own words: "Tao always takes non-action, and yet nothing is left undone" (37). To take non-action does not mean not to take any action at all, but rather not to take any non-artificial action based on any purposeful motives of (e.g.) gain or striving. More positively, to take non-artificial or unnatural action means to take spontaneous action. But it would be misleading to say that Tao takes spontaneous action, for Tao is not a real agent. In accordance with Lao Tzu's words, "Tao models itself after Nature" (25), we should re-render the sentence "Tao always takes non-action" philosophically as "All things run their courses spontaneously without any interference," and this explains why "nothing is left undone." The philosophical meaning of all previous figurative expressions about the function of Tao as non-being can also be clarified in this light.

Tao as Principle and Tao as Function are indeed two ways of expressing the same spontaneous change and transformation of all things in the world. That all things revert to their opposites (Tao as Principle) and that non-being works wonders in terms of all beings" taking their courses spontaneously (Tao as Function) refer to the same thing, though they mean something different. Tao as Principle expresses the manifestation of Tao more objectively; the invariable principle of reversion is simply and naturally there, and we cannot but accept its truth. Tao as Function expresses the manifestation of Tao more subjectively, for Lao Tzu is here trying to establish a naturalist wisdom out of Tao as Principle. Thus, the inseparability of Tao as Principle and Tao as Function reflects well the inseparability of objective truth (the principle of reversion) and subjective truth (wisdom of spontaneous non-action) in Lao Tzu's metaphysics of Tao.

Lao Tzu also says, "Softness is the function of Tao" (40). In reality, softness and non-action are two different ways of expressing the same Tao as Function. To take non-action is, negatively speaking, not to display one's strength, not to take advantage of others, not to strive and compete, etc.; and is, positively speaking, to let all things take their own courses spontaneously. As Professor Wing-tsit Chan observes, softness (tenderness, or weakness) is often an outward expression of real inner strength and can overcome strength in the long run.[11] "Nothing in the world is softer and weaker than water, yet there is nothing better for conquering the hard and strong" (78). Again: "The softest in the world overrides the hardest. That-which-is-formless penetrates that-which-has-no-crevice. Through this I knew the advantage of non-action" (43). Applying his conception of Tao as Function to human affairs, Lao Tzu leaves us an invaluable pack of Taoist wisdom for the naturalist way of life. As he says, for instance, "The greatest

straight appears crooked; the greatest skill appears clumsy; the greatest eloquence appears stammering" (45). But in order to appreciate fully his naturalist philosophy of life, we need to understand the next dimension of Tao.

VI. TAO AS VIRTUE

Tao as Function refers to the inner wonders of non-being in the change and
transformation of things, while Tao as Virtue (*téh*) is what every individual
being obtains (*téh*) from Tao (Nature). As Chuang Tzu says: "What things
obtain (*téh*) for their existence is called virtue (*téh*).[12] Tao as Function is understood in terms of the dynamic working of Nature as a whole in the spontaneous course of change and transformation of things; Tao as Virtue (Character, or Power) is understood in terms of the individualized natural
characters each particular being receives from Nature in the same spontaneous course of change and transformation. Since non-action, spontaneity,
and softness constitute the way non-being functions, they also become the
natural features or characters every being obtains from Tao. Although Lao
Tzu does not make it clear, he seems to prefer the term *hsüan-(téh)* (profound virtue) to characterize the universal and fundamental virtue or character of Tao. The myriad things can therefore be said to share commonly the
profound virtue of Tao as Function differentiated into softness, spontaneity,
non-action, fostering, benefitting, non-possession, non-interference, etc., as
is figuratively described in the following:

> Tao gives life to all things;
> [Its] Virtue fosters them;
> Matter shapes them [according to their kinds];
> [Natural] tendency perfects them.
> Therefore all things cannot but worship Tao and exalt its Virtue.
> Tao is worshipped and its Virtue is exalted without anyone's order
>   but is always done spontaneously so.
> Therefore Tao gives them life;
> And its Virtue fosters them, grows them, develops them,
>   harbors them, comforts them, feeds them, shelters them.
> Tao gives them life but takes no possession of them;
> Benefits them but lays no claim to them;
> Develops them but does not master them.
> This is called "the profound virtue." (51)

This chapter is a typical example of Lao Tzu's figurative speech, in which lies
hidden a real naturalist wisdom. As far as I know, no translator or interpreter
of the *Lao-Tzu* has ever clarified the real meaning of this chapter by removing
the linguistic confusion arising from "Tao" being used as a grammatical

subject but not to refer to a real subject (agent) in the hypostatic sense. In accordance with my methodological approach, I attempt a philosophical reduction of the above chapter as follows:

> The life of every particular thing is formed through the spontaneous change and transformation of Nature [the totality of all things] itself. The beingness of each individual being is completed through the blending of *ch'i* [Ether] with *yin* and *yang* under a particular natural tendency. All things grow and flourish, decay and perish, without any interference outside Nature itself. The original nature [Tao as Virtue] of all things is such that they cannot be said to be governed or controlled by any sort of non-natural element or power. Their life-and-death simply follows the invariable principle of cyclic reversion naturally and spontaneously [Tao as Principle].

I have to admit, of course, that in the above philosophical reduction I have "killed" much of the deep and profound metaphysical and religious sentiment which Lao Tzu expresses in figurative speech. But there is ample reason, as I have shown, to say that this is the best way of removing any possible confusion or contradiction of thought in this figurative speech. And my linguistic-philosophical analysis can be applied to all other cases where Lao Tzu speaks of Tao as Virtue.

As in the case of other dimensions of Tao, Tao as Virtue is manifested in both Nature and the world of man. Tao as Virtue in Nature, in a sense, a metaphysical mirror reflecting our natural endowment (Taoist virtue) as it is most perfectly cultivated by the Taoist sage. As a man of metaphysical wisdom, Lao Tzu is particularly interested in persuading the vulgar man to accept the Taoist way of life, by advocating the following virtues: non-action (2, 3, 10, 37, 43, 48, 57, 63, 64), non-affairs (48, 57, 63), non-acquisition (2, 10, 22, 34, 51, 81), non-striving (2, 3, 8, 22, 51, 66, 68, 73, 81), non-favoritism (5, 79), non-desire (3, 12, 13, 19, 34, 57), non-knowledge (3, 10, 19, 20, 48, 65, 81), non-self (7, 13, 19, 44), non-word (2, 5, 43, 56, 73, 81), non-morality or non-artifice (18, 19, 38), yieldingness or humbleness (28, 39, 61, 66, 67), vacuity or emptiness (16), tranquility (16, 37, 45, 57, 61), softness (10, 36, 43, 52, 61, 76, 78), contentment (46), naturalness or spontaneity (17, 19, 64), simplicity or primitiveness (15, 19, 28, 37, 57, 80), harmony (4, 55, 56), unity or oneness (4, 22, 39), and profound identity (56). These different natural virtues of men can be regarded as various manifestations of Tao as the Profound Virtue in human society, personally realized by Lao Tzu himself.

Lao Tzu is keenly aware of the mundane fact that most people, lacking ontological insight (*ming*) into "the inner wonders of Tao" (1), tend to act against the invariable, spontaneous course of the change and transformation of things, and "run blindly into disaster" (16). Hence his Taoist advice to the men of the world:

Tao is always nameless. Small as this uncarved wood is in its simplicity, nothing in the world can master it. . . . Once there are human artifices, there appear
different names. Once there are names, know when to stop. To know when to
stop is to be free from danger. (32)

But the vulgar man may still ask: Why does Lao Tzu have to emphasize
those "negative" virtues? The answer lies partly in his conception of Tao as
Principle manifesting itself in the world of men: "Misfortune is that upon
which fortune leans; fortune is that in which misfortune is latent" (58). He
would say to the vulgar man that all Taoist "negative" virtues are paradoxically the greatest virtues exhibiting the inner strength and perfect happiness
of the man of Tao.

To those who are lucky enough not to run into disaster by taking all non-
natural actions, Lao Tzu's instruction as to "the power of negative thinking"[13]
may appear to be useless or senseless. Here human argument ends and
metaphysical wisdom begins. Lao Tzu's final answer would be that only
from the standpoint of Taoist metaphysics *sub specie aeternitatis* is one able
to realize the natural truth of the invariable principle of reversion and therefore face with a great metaphysical courage the natural lot assigned to one
by Nature. To Lao Tzu, Taoist metaphysical wisdom about things-as-they-are
is itself a perfect freedom or emancipation. In short, the best way of life,
from the Taoist point of view, is that of profound identification of one's little self with Tao or Nature, and all Taoist virtues advocated by Lao Tzu are
but different ways of expressing the harmonious unity of Nature and a man
of Taoist wisdom.

VII. TAO AS TECHNIQUE

Tao as Technique is the practical way of the Taoist sage to govern the State,
win the people's hearts, and employ strategy in the time of war; it is the realistic application of Tao as Virtue when occasion or situation demands it in
(what the Taoists call) "the dusty world." Since the vulgar men who constitute the majority of the human race would take no interest in the natural way
of life depicted in Lao Tzu's political utopia (80), he has to effect the best
practicable compromise between his Taoist life-ideal and the great artifices
of the worldlings. Therefore, unlike other dimensions of Tao, Tao as Technique involves much of the Taoist effort to transform the interest-concerned
and profit-centered world of men into that of spontaneity and non-action.

In various places in the *Tao-têh ching,* Lao Tzu describes the best possible way of governing the state as "guiding all things to find their nature without venturing to lead them by the nose" (64). According to his *laissez-faire*
political way, the sage is advised to "take non-action so that the people can

be spontaneously transformed; love tranquility so that the people can be spontaneously rectified; engage in non-affairs (*wu-shih*) so that the people can return spontaneously to primordial simplicity (*p'u*)" (57). In particular, the sage is said to have three treasures, viz. tender love, frugality, and not-daring-to-take-precedence-of-others, by means of which he can be truly courageous, generous, and become the leader of the world (67).

But Lao Tzu is realistic enough to know that in most cases the *laissez-faire* practice of the sage can hardly change the dusty world into that of natural-ness and simplicity. Hence his "tough-minded advice to the sage about how to take a provisional means to gain the power of leadership and win the bat-tle, etc. Lao Tzu is often accused, especially by the Confucianists, of being an artisan of politico-military tricks.[14] This is far from the truth. For, in vari-ous places in the text, Lao Tzu wisely warns the sage who is compelled to use tactics, that one should know when to stop (32), that one should not dominate the world by force of arms (30, 31), that a good soldier should not be oppressive with his military strength (68), that one's conquest of the world by tampering with it is doomed to failure (29). Especially in time of war, he says, one should be able to realize that "Wherever armies are sta-tioned, thorns and brambles grow; after the raising of a great host, years of dearth follow" (30). He may sometimes instruct the sage how to appear fem-ininely yielding and tranquil in order to conquer the masculine (61), how to "nip troubles in the bud and sow the great in the small" (63), how to "be a guest rather than a host, retreat a foot rather than advance an inch" (69) in military actions, as well as how to "operate the army with surprise tactics" (57). But he also advises that the occasion of victory be observed with fu-neral ceremonies for the slaughter of the multitude (31), that hatred or in-juries be requited with virtuous deeds (63). In any case, all possible misun-derstanding of Lao Tzu with respect to his politico-military philosophy must be removed if one properly grasps what he says in the following:

> Achieve your purpose but properly stop,
> And never venture to rely upon your strength;
> Achieve your purpose but never parade your success;
> Achieve your purpose but never boast of your ability;
> Achieve your purpose but never take pride in it;
> Achieve your purpose but only as an unavoidable step;
> Achieve your purpose but never show off your strength.
> For things age and decay after they reach their prime;
> Whatever is against Tao soon ceases to be. (30)

Lao Tzu can therefore be said to be, to borrow a Buddhist term, a Taoist philosopher of the Middle Way (*madhyamāpratipad*): from the higher point of view of Tao as Virtue, spontaneity, non-action, tranquility, simplicity, etc., are the natural virtues in accordance with which one can lead the life of the *summum bonum;* from the point of view of Tao as Technique, it is sometimes necessary even for a philosopher of *wu-wei* to speak of politico-military practices, if only as a regrettable compromise in the world of greed, hate, and stupidity. Lao Tzu's conception of Tao as Technique only proves that there is no inconsistency of thought in the *Lao-Tzu,* and that he is neither a pure political idealist (like Gandhi) nor a ruthless realist (like Hitler). He is indeed a man of great wisdom, understanding quite well the gulf between ideal and actual which is so hard to bridge in human society, yet trying his best to "harmonize all lights and leveling up all dusts" (56) for the attainment to the profound unity of Nature and man.

NOTES

The embryonic form of this article was my visiting lecture on "Lao Tzu's Metaphysics of Tao" at Johns Hopkins University, 2 December 1971.

1. Traditionally, there are two ways of translating these two sentences, depending on two different ways of punctuating the original: (i) "Non-being is named the origin of heaven and earth; being is named the mother of the myriad things," (ii) "The Nameless is the origin of heaven and earth; the Named is the mother of all things." But my new translation here can express more clearly the inseparable relation between non-being and being as two aspects of Tao. As Chuang Tzu says, Lao Tzu "expounded it [the art of Tao] in terms of invariable non-being and [invariable] being, and headed it with the conception of the Great Unity." Cf. Burton Watson *The Complete Works of Chuang Tzu,* Columbia University Press, New York 1968, pp. 371–72.

2. Again, there are two traditional ways of translating these two sentences in accordance with two different ways of punctuating them. For an example of the two different translations, see Wing-tsit Chan's *The Way of Lao Tzu,* Library of Liberal Arts, Indianapolis 1963, p. 97, and Lin Yu-tang's *The Wisdom of Lao Tzu,* Random House, New York 1948, p. 41. My own translation would be more consistent with Lao Tzu's conception of Tao which unifies both non-being and being as two inseparable aspects of it.

3. Lin Yu-tang notes, "Jesuit scholars consider these three words (in ancient Chinese pronounced nearly like *i-hi-vei*) an interesting coincidence with the Hebrew word "Jahve," ibid., p. 101. I should add, however, that this is no more than a linguistic coincidence.

4. "Here . . . form is emptiness and the very emptiness is form." (*The Heart Sutra, The Buddhist Wisdom Book,* trans. by Edward Conze, George Allen & Unwin, London 1958, p. 81). As to the passage concerned in the *Classic of the Changes,* see Wing-tsit Chan, *A Source Book in Chinese Philosophy,* Princeton University Press, Princeton, N.J. 1963, p. 267.

5. See Ch'éng Yi's own *Introduction* to his *Philosophical Commentary on the Classic of Changes,* in *Erh-Ch'éng chüan-shu* (The Complete Works of the Ch'éng Brothers), Vol. II.

6. Chan's translation of the word *shéng* as "produced" is very puzzling, for he seems to agree with Fung Yu-lan that there is no actual time involved in Lao Tzu's

metaphysics of Tao. See ibid., pp. 7 and 176. (Fung's passage in question will be quoted below.)

7. Fung Yu-lan, *A Short History of Chinese Philosophy*, ed. by Derk Bodde, The Macmillan Co., New York 1948, p. 96.

8. See *Han-Fei-Tzu*, Ch. 20.

9. See Preface to *Chon-yi chéng-yi* (The Correct Meaning of the Classic of Changes), by K'ung Ying-ta (574–648) of the T'ang dynasty.

10. *The Analects of Confucius,* 9:16.

11. Wing-tsit Chan, op. cit., p. 15.

12. *Chuang-Tzu,* Ch. 12 ("Heaven and Earth"). See also Burton Watson, op. cit., p. 131.

13. The term "the power of negative thinking" is coined by Holmes Welch of Harvard University. He says, "We believe that a man or a business or a nation can never stand still, that they must either go forward or backward. He [Lao Tzu] teaches that to stand still is the most effective way of dealing with almost every problem and of finding spiritual contentment. We want to be high. He wants to be low. The *Tao Te Ching* might—with apologies to Dr. Peale—be called *The Power of Negative Thinking*. Lao Tzu is not the kind of thinker to whom twentieth century Americans would turn for advice" (*Taoism: The Parting of the Way,* Beacon Press, Boston 1957, pp. 164–5).

14. Wing-tsit Chan, op. cit., pp. 202 and 222.

1.12

The Philosophy of Material Force

Chang Tsai

1. The Great Harmony is called the Way (Tao, Moral Law). It embraces the nature which underlies all counter processes of floating and sinking, rising and falling, and motion and rest. It is the origin of the process of fusion and intermingling, of overcoming and being overcome, and of expansion and contraction. At the commencement, these processes are incipient, subtle, obscure, easy, and simple, but at the end they are extensive, great, strong, and firm. It is *ch'ien* (Heaven) that begins with the knowledge of Change, and *k'un* (Earth) that models after simplicity. That which is dispersed, differentiated, and capable of assuming form becomes material force (*ch'i*), and that which is pure, penetrating, and not capable of assuming form becomes spirit. Unless the whole universe is in the process of fusion and intermingling like fleeting forces moving in all directions, it may not be called Great Harmony. When those who talk about the Way know this, then they really know the Way, and when those who study Change (or the *Book of Changes*) understand this, then they really understand Change. Otherwise, even though they possess the admirable talents of Duke Chou, their wisdom is not praiseworthy.

2. The Great Vacuity (Hsü) has no physical form. It is the original substance of material force. Its integration and disintegration are but objectifications caused by Change. Human nature at its source is absolutely tranquil and unaffected by externality. When it is affected by contact with the external world, consciousness and knowledge emerge. Only those who fully develop their nature can unify the state

of formlessness and unaffectedness, and the state of objectification and affectedness.

3. Although material force in the universe integrates and disintegrates, and attracts and repulses in a hundred ways, nevertheless the principle (*li*) according to which it operates has an order and is unerring.

As an entity, material force simply reverts to its original substance when it disintegrates and becomes formless. When it integrates and assumes form, it does not lose the eternal principle (of Change).

The Great Vacuity of necessity consists of material force. Material force of necessity integrates to become the myriad things. Things of necessity disintegrate and return to the Great Vacuity. Appearance and disappearance following this cycle are a matter of necessity. When, in the midst [of this universal operation] the sage fulfills the Way to the utmost, and identifies himself [with the universal processes of appearance and disappearance] without partiality (i.e., lives the best life and takes life and death objectively), his spirit is preserved in the highest degree. Those (the Buddhists) who believe in annihilation expect departure without returning, and those (the Taoists) who cling to everlasting life and are attached to existence expect things not to change. While they differ, they are the same in failing to understand the Way. Whether integrated or disintegrated, it is my body just the same. One is qualified to discuss the nature of man when he realizes that death is not annihilation.

Comment. As Chang Po-hsing (1651–1725) has noted, to say that death is not annihilation is dangerously close to Buddhist transmigration. He quickly points out, however, that what Chang meant is neither Buddhist transmigration nor Taoist immortality on earth but the indestructibility of material force whether it is integrated or disintegrated. What is not annihilated, then, is not the person but principle, according to which material force operates.

4. When it is understood that the Vacuity, the Void, is nothing but material force, then existence and nonexistence, the hidden and the manifested, spirit and eternal transformation, and human nature and destiny are all one and not a duality. He who apprehends integration and disintegration, appearance and disappearance, form and absence of form, and traces them to their source, penetrates the secret of Change.

If it is argued that material force is produced from the Vacuity, then because the two are completely different, the Vacuity being infinite while material force is finite, the one being substance and the other function, such an argument would fall into the naturalism of Lao Tzu who claimed that being comes from non-being and failed to understand the eternal principle of the undifferentiated unity of being and non-being. If it is argued that all phenomena are but things perceived in the Great Vacuity, then since things and the Vacuity would not be mutually conditioned, since the physical form and the nature of things would be self-contained, and since these, as well as Heaven and man, would not be interdependent, such an argument would fall into the doctrine of the Buddha who taught that mountains, rivers, and the total stretch of land are all subjective illusions. This principle of unity is not understood because ignorant people know superficially that the substance of the nature of things is the Vacuity, the Void, but do not know that function is based on the Way of Heaven (Law of Nature). Instead, they try to explain the universe with limited human knowledge. Since their undertaking is not thorough, they falsely assert that the universal operation of the principles of Heaven and Earth is but illusory. They do not know the essentials of the hidden and the manifest, and jump to erroneous conclusions. They do not understand that the successive movements of the yin and the yang (passive and active cosmic forces) cover the entire universe, penetrate day and night, and form the central standard of Heaven, Earth, and man. Consequently they confuse Confucianism with Buddhism and Taoism. When they discuss the problems of the nature (of man and things) and their destiny or the Way of Heaven, they either fall into the trap of illusionism or are determined that being comes from non-being, and regard these doctrines as the summit of philosophical insight as well as the way to enter into virtue. They do not know how to choose the proper method for their investigation. This clearly shows they are obscured by one-sided doctrines and fall into extremes.

5. As the Great Vacuity, material force is extensive and vague. Yet it ascends and descends and moves in all ways without ever ceasing. This is what is called in the *Book of Changes* "fusion and intermingling" and in the *Chuang Tzu* "fleeting forces moving in all directions while all living beings blow against one another with their breath." Here lies the subtle, incipient activation of reality and unreality, of motion and rest, and the beginning of yin and yang, as well as the elements of strength and weakness. Yang that is clear ascends upward, whereas yin that is turbid sinks downward. As a result of their contact and influence and of their integration and disintegration, winds and rains, snow and frost come into being. Whether it be the countless variety of things in their changing configurations or the mountains and rivers in their fixed forms, the dregs of wine or the ashes of fire, there is nothing (in which the principle) is not revealed.

6. If material force integrates, its visibility becomes effective and physical form appears. If material force does not integrate, its visibility is

not effective and there is no physical form. While material force is integrated, how can one not say that it is temporary? While it is disintegrated, how can one hastily say that it is non-being? For this reason, the sage, having observed phenomena and examined above and below, only claims to know the causes of what is hidden and what is manifest but does not claim to know the causes of being and non-being.

What fills the universe is but molds and forms (copies). With our insight (or clarity of mind), the system and principles of the universe cannot be examined. When there are physical forms, one may trace back to the causes of that which is hidden, and when there is no physical form, one may trace back to the cause of that which is manifested.

7. The integration and disintegration of material force is to the Great Vacuity as the freezing and melting of ice is to water. If we realize that the Great Vacuity is identical with material force, we know that there is no such thing as non-being. Therefore, when discussing the ultimate problems of the nature of things and the Way of Heaven, the sage limits himself to the marvelous changes and transformations of yin and yang and the Five Agents (of Metal, Wood, Water, Fire, and Earth). The doctrine of those superficial and mistaken philosophers who draw the distinction between being and non-being is not the way to investigate principle to the utmost.

Comment. Chang's theory of material force exercised considerable influence on Wang Fu-chih (Wang Ch'uan-shan, 1619–1692), whose philosophy of principle as inherent in material force is as materialistic as the philosophy of Chang. It is easily understandable why Wang was an admirer of Chang but a severe critic of Chu Hsi and Ch'eng I, who contrasted principle and material force too sharply to suit him. As to Chang's own theory of material force, he has never explained why some is clear and some is turbid. Neither has he made his idea of the nature clear. For these, we have to wait till Ch'eng and Chu.

8. The Great Vacuity is clear. Being clear, it cannot be obstructed. Not being obstructed, it is therefore spirit. The opposite of clearness is turbidity. Turbidity leads to obstruction. And obstruction leads to physical form. When material force is clear, it penetrates; and when it is turbid, it obstructs. When clearness reaches its limit, there is spirit. When spirit concentrates, it penetrates like the breeze going through the holes (of musical instruments), producing tones and carrying them to great distances. This is the evidence of clearness. As if arriving at the destination without the necessity of going there, penetration reaches the highest degree.

9. From the Great Vacuity, there is Heaven. From the transformation of material force, there is the Way. In the unity of the Great Vacuity and material force, there is the nature (of man and things). And in the unity of the nature and consciousness, there is the mind.

   Comment. Although Chang made it quite clear that the Great Vacuity is identical with material force (before its integration) and is nothing like the Taoist non-being, still the concept is too Taoistic to be acceptable to Neo-Confucianists, for vacuity is a typical and prominent Taoist concept. Ch'eng I thought that reality should not be described simply as clear and vacuous, but should also be considered turbid and substantial.Chu Hsi thought that to describe reality purely as integration and disintegration of material force would be to view it as a great process of transmigration. These criticisms are by no means unfair. There is no doubt that Chang's materialistic philosophy tends to be one-sided and mechanical. At any rate, his philosophy of vacuity has never been propagated by any later Neo-Confucianist.

10. The negative and positive spiritual forces (*kuei-shen*) are the spontaneous activity of the two material forces (yin and yang). Sage-hood means absolute sincerity forming a unity with Heaven, and spirit means the Great Vacuity in its wondrous operation and response. All molds and forms in the universe are but dregs of this spiritual transformation.

   Comment. This is a completely new interpretation of *kuei* and *shen.* The rationalistic approach to *kuei-shen,* which had meant spiritual beings, is evident in the *Book of Changes,* but no one before Chang had understood *kuei-shen* as the spontaneous activity of material force and incorporated the concept into a coherent metaphysical system.

11. The Way of Heaven is infinite but does not go beyond the succession of summer and winter [for example]. The activities of things are infinite but do not go beyond expansion and contraction. The reality of the negative and positive spiritual forces does not go beyond these two fundamental elements (of yin and yang).

12. If yin and yang do not exist, the One (the Great Ultimate) cannot be revealed. If the One cannot be revealed, then the function of the two forces will cease. Reality and unreality, motion and rest, integration and disintegration, and clearness and turbidity are two different substances. In the final analysis, however, they are one.

13. Only after [the One] is acted upon will it begin to penetrate [through yin and yang]. Without the two forces there cannot be the One. Hence the sage establishes the two principles of strength and weakness as the foundation of things. "If *ch'en* and *k'un* are obliterated, there would be no means of seeing the system of Change."

14. Material force moves and flows in all directions and in all manners. Its two elements unite and give rise to the concrete. Thus the multiplicity of things and human beings is produced. In their ceaseless successions the two elements of yin and yang constitute the great principles of the universe.

15. "The sun and moon push each other in their course and thus light appears. The winter and summer push each other and thus the year is completed." Spirit has no spatial restrictions and Change has no physical form. "The successive movement of yin and yang" and "unfathomable is the movement of yin and yang." These describe the way in which day and night are penetrated.

16. Day and night are but a moment of the universe, and winter and summer but its day and night. According to the Way of Heaven, material force changes as spring and autumn succeed each other, just as man's soul exists in different states between waking and sleeping hours. In such alternating states, dreams are completed and a great variety of feelings are expressed in utter confusion. This and the contrasting waking hours constitute the day and night of a person. Material force enters into a new state in the spring and the myriad things flourish in profusion. This and its contrasting autumn constitute the day and night of Heaven. In its original state of Great Vacuity, material force is absolutely tranquil and formless. As it is acted upon, it engenders the two fundamental elements of yin and yang, and through integration gives rise to forms. As there are forms, there are their opposites. These opposites necessarily stand in opposition to what they do. Opposition leads to conflict, which will necessarily be reconciled and resolved. Thus the feelings of love and hate are both derived from the Great Vacuity, and they ultimately result in material desires. Suddenly to bring into existence and promptly to bring to completion without a moment's interruption—this is indeed the wonderful operation of spirit.

17. No two of the products of creation are alike. From this we know that although the number of things is infinite, at bottom there is nothing without yin or yang [which differentiate them]. From this we know also that the transformations and changes in the universe are due to these two fundamental forces.

18. The multiple forms and appearances of the myriad things are the dregs of spirit. The nature and the Way of Heaven are but Change.

The mind varies and differs in a thousand ways because it is acted on by the external world in various ways. Heaven is vast and there is nothing outside of it. What acts on the mind are the two fundamental processes of fusion and intermingling.

19. In the mutual interaction of things, it is impossible to know the directions of their operation and of their appearance and disappearance. This is the wonder that lies in all things. These are principles by which material force and the will, as well as Heaven and man, overcome each other. When the sage-ruler reigns above, all his subjects follow his good example. This demonstrates the principle that when material force is concentrated and acts, it moves the will. When the male and female phoenix arrive and perform their ceremonial dance (peace and order prevail). This demonstrates the principle that when the will concentrates and acts, it moves material force. . . . (sppy, 2: lb–Sb)

29. There has never been any substance which is non-existent. Nature means examining and practising the substance. . . .

63. It is according to one's nature that being and non-being, and reality and unreality pervade a thing. If they are not united as one, nature cannot be developed fully. Food and sex are both nature. How can they be obliterated? Thus being and non-being are both nature. How can there be no opposition? The Taoists and Buddhists have for long maintained that there is none. Do they really understand truth? (ch. 17, sppy, 3:21b)

1.13

Conditioning Causes and *Nirvāṇa*

Nāgārjuna

I. AN EXAMINATION OF CONDITIONING CAUSES (*PRATYAYA*)

1. Never are any existing things found to originate from themselves, from something else, from both, or from no cause.
2. There are four conditioning causes: A cause (*hetu*), objects of sensations, "immediately preceding condition," and of course the predominant influence—there is no fifth.
3. Certainly there is no self-existence (*svabhava*) of existing things in conditioning causes, etc.; and if no self-existence exists, neither does "other-existence" (*parabhāva*).
4. The efficient cause (*kriyā*) does not exist possessing a conditioning cause, nor does the efficient cause exist without possessing a conditioning cause. Conditioning causes are not without efficient causes, nor are there [conditioning causes] which possess efficient causes.
5. Certainly those things are called "conditioning causes" whereby something originates after having come upon them; as long as something has not originated, why are they not so long "*non*-conditioning causes"?
6. There can be a conditioning cause neither of a non-real thing nor of a real thing. Of what non-real thing is there a conditioning cause? And if it is [already] real, what use is a cause?
7. If an element (*dharma*) occurs which is neither real nor non-real nor both real-and-non-real, how can there be a cause which is effective in this situation?

From *Mūlamadhyamakakārika* (Fundamentals of the Middle Way), translated by Fred Streng (Nashville, TN: Abingdon press, 1967). Copyright © Abingdon Press, 1967. Text edited.

8. Just that which is without an object of sensation is accepted as a real element. Then if there is an element having no object of sensation, how is it possible to have an object of sensation?

9. When no elements have originated, [their] disappearance is not possible. Therefore it is not proper to speak of an "immediately preceding condition"; for if something has already ceased, what cause is there for it?

10. Since existing things which have no self-existence are not real, it is not possible at all that: "This thing 'becomes' upon the existence of that other one."

11. The product does not reside in the conditioning causes, individually or collectively, so how can that which does not reside in the conditioning cause result from conditioning causes?

12. Then the "non-real" would result from those conditioning-causes. Why then would a product not proceed also from non-causes?

13. On the one hand, the product [consists in its] conditioning causes; on the other hand, the causes do not consist of themselves. How can a product [resulting] from [conditioning causes] not consisting of themselves be consisting of those causes?

14. Therefore, that product does not consist in those causes; [yet] it is agreed that a product does not consist of non-causes. How [can there be] a conditioning cause or non-cause when a product is not produced?

XXV. AN ANALYSIS OF *NIRVĀṆA*

1. [An opponent says:] If all existence is empty, there is no origination nor destruction. Then whose *nirvāṇa* through elimination [of suffering] and destruction [of illusion] would be postulated?

2. [Nāgārjuna replies:] If all existence is non-empty, there is no origination nor destruction. Then whose *nirvāṇa* through elimination [of suffering] and destruction [of illusion] would be postulated?

3. *Nirvāṇa* has been said to be neither eliminated nor attained, neither annihilated nor eternal, neither disappeared nor originated.

4. *Nirvāṇa* is certainly not an existing thing, for then it would be characterized *by* old age and death. In consequence it would involve the error that an existing thing would not become old and be without death.

5. And if *nirvāṇa* is an existing thing, *nirvāṇa* would be a constructed product (*saṃskṛta*), since never ever has an existing thing been found to be a non-constructed-product (*asaṃskṛta*).

6. But if *nirvāṇa is* an existing thing, how could (*nirvāṇa*) exist without dependence [on something else]? Certainly *nirvāṇa* does not exist as something without dependence.

7. If *nirvāṇa* is not an existing thing, will *nirvāṇa* become a non-existing thing? Wherever there is no existing thing, neither is there a non-existing thing.

8. But if *nirvāṇa* is a non-existing thing, how could (*nirvāṇa*) exist without dependence [on something else]? Certainly *nirvāṇa* is not a non-existing thing which exists without dependence.

9. That state which is the rushing in and out [of existence] when dependent or conditioned—this [state], when not dependent or not conditioned, is seen to be *nirvāṇa*.

10. The teacher [Gautama] has taught that a "becoming" and a "non-becoming" (*vibhava*) are destroyed; therefore it obtains that: *nirvāṇa* is neither an existent thing nor a non-existent thing.

11. If *nirvāṇa* were both an existent and a non-existent thing, final release (*mokṣa*) would be [both] an existent and a non-existent thing; but that is not possible.

12. If *nirvāṇa* were both an existent and a non-existent thing, there would be no *nirvāṇa* without conditions, for these both [operate with] conditions.

13. How can *nirvāṇa* exist as both an existent thing and a non-existent thing, for *nirvāṇa* is a non-composite-product (*asaṃskṛta*), while both an existent thing and a non-existent thing are composite products (*saṃskṛta*).

14. How can *nirvāṇa* exist as both an existent and a non-existent thing? There is no existence of both at one and the same place, as in the case of both darkness and light.

15. The assertion: *"nirvāṇa,* is neither an existent thing nor a non-existent thing" is proved if [the assertion]: "It is an existent thing and a non-existent thing" were proved.

16. If *nirvāṇa* is neither an existent thing nor a non-existent thing, who can really arrive at [the assertion]: "neither an existent thing nor a non-existent thing"?

17. It is not expressed if the Glorious One [the Buddha] exists after his death, or does not exist, or both or neither.

18. Also, it is not expressed if the Glorious One exists while remaining [in the world], or does not exist, or both or neither.

19. There is nothing whatever which differentiates the existence-in-flux (*saṃsāra*) from *nirvāṇa;* and there is nothing whatever which differentiates *nirvāṇa* from existence-in-flux.

20. The extreme limit (*koṭi*) of *nirvāṇa* is also the extreme limit of existence-in-flux; there is not the slightest bit of difference between these two.

21. The views [regarding] whether that which is beyond death is limited by a beginning or an end or some other alternative depend on a *nirvāṇa* limited by a beginning (*pūrvānta*) and an end (*aparānta*).

22. Since all *dharmas* are empty, what is finite? What is infinite? What is both finite and infinite? What is neither finite nor infinite?

23. Is there anything which is this or something else, which is permanent or impermanent, which is both permanent and impermanent, or which is neither?

24. The cessation of accepting everything [as real] is a salutary (*śiva*) cessation of phenomenal development (*prapañca*); no *dharma* anywhere has been taught by the Buddha of anything.

1.14

The True Nature of Reality

Kitarō Nishida

THE STARTING POINT OF THE INQUIRY

Philosophical views of the world and of human life relate closely to the practical demands of morality and religion, which dictate how people should act and where they can find peace of mind. People are never satisfied with intellectual convictions and practical demands that contradict each other. Those with high spiritual demands fail to find satisfaction in materialism, and those who believe in materialism come to harbor doubts about spiritual demands. Fundamentally, truth is singular. Intellectual truth and practical truth must be one and the same. Those who think deeply or are genuinely serious inevitably seek congruence between knowledge and the practical realm of feeling and willing. We must now investigate what we ought to do and where we ought to find peace of mind, but this calls first for clarification of the nature of the universe, human life, and true reality.

The Indian religio-philosophical tradition, which provides the most highly developed congruence of philosophy and religion, holds that knowledge is good and delusion is evil. The fundamental reality of the universe is Brahman, which is our soul, our Ātman. Knowledge of this identity of Brahman and Ātman is the culmination of Indian philosophy and religion. Christianity was entirely practical at its inception, but because the human mind insistently demands intellectual satisfaction, Christian philosophy was developed in the Middle Ages. In the Chinese tradition, the system of morality at first lacked philosophical elaboration, but since the Sung period this dimension has predominated. Such historical trends in the Indian, Christian, and Chinese traditions attest to the basic human demand for congruence between our knowledge and our feeling and will.

In classical Western philosophy beginning with Socrates and Plato, didactic goals were central, whereas in modern times knowledge has assumed a prominent position, making the unity of the intellectual and the emotional-volitional aspects more difficult. In fact, the two dimensions now tend to diverge, and this in no way satisfies the fundamental demands of the human mind.

To understand true reality and to know the true nature of the universe and human life, we must discard all artificial assumptions, doubt whatever can be doubted, and proceed on the basis of direct and indubitable knowledge. From the perspective of common sense, we think that things exist in the external world apart from consciousness and that in the back of consciousness there is something called the mind, which performs various functions. Our assumption that mind and matter exist independently constitutes the basis of our conduct and is itself based on the demands posed by our thinking. This assumption leaves much room for doubt. Science, which does not take the most profound explanation of reality as its goal, is constructed on such hypothetical knowledge. But insufficiently critical thinking is also found in philosophy, which does take that explanation as its goal. Many philosophers base their thinking on existing assumptions and hence fail to engage in penetrating doubt.

The independent existence of mind and matter is generally considered an intuitive fact, but on reflection we realize that this clearly is not the case. What is the desk before me right now? Its color and shape are sensations of the eye; the feeling of resistance when I touch it is a sensation of the hand. The form, size, position, and movement of a thing—that which we intuit—are not the objective state of the thing in itself. To intuit things in themselves apart from our consciousness is impossible. This holds true for our minds as well. What we know is not the mind itself but the *activity* of knowing, feeling, and willing. When viewed psychologically, that which we think of as a self functioning through time is nothing more than the continuation of a sensation or feeling; the mind and matter that we take to be intuitive facts are merely unchanging combinations of similar phenomena of consciousness. We are led to believe in the existence of mind and matter by the requirements of the law of causality. But can we infer existence apart from consciousness by this law? Let us now address this question.

What is direct knowledge that we cannot even begin to doubt? It is knowledge of facts in our intuitive experience, knowledge of phenomena of consciousness. A present phenomenon of consciousness and our being conscious of it are identical; they cannot be divided into subject and object. Since facts are not separated even a hair's breadth from knowing, we cannot doubt this knowledge. Of course we can err when we judge or recollect a phenomenon of consciousness, but at such a time we are no longer engaged in intuition, for we have shifted to inference. The later consciousness—which is engaged in judgment or recollection—and the original consciousness are different phenomena of consciousness: intuition is not the judging of the original consciousness by the later one, but simply knowledge of facts just as they are. Accordingly, in intuition, erring or not erring is out of the question. All of our knowledge must be constructed upon such intuitive experience.

Philosophy returns to such direct knowledge whenever it rids itself of all existing assumptions and seeks anew a firm base. Bacon, at the dawn of modern philosophy, considered experience the basis of all knowledge; Descartes took as his philosophical starting point the proposition "I think, therefore I am" (*cogito ergo sum*) and considered anything equally clear to be truth. Nevertheless, experience in Bacon's framework was not pure experience but experience accompanied by the arbitrary assumption that we are able, by means of it, to intuit facts outside of consciousness. And when Descartes said, "I think, therefore I am," his statement was no longer a fact of immediate experience, for he was already inferring "I am." Moreover, to hold that clear thinking can know noumena is an arbitrary assumption; Kant and philosophers after him did not accept this assumption as an indubitable truth. Accordingly, what I term direct knowledge consists of the intuitive facts that are discerned when we abandon all such arbitrary assumptions. If I were to follow the lead of Hegel and succeeding historians of philosophy and to assume that Descartes's "I think, therefore I am" is not an inference but an expression of the intuitive certainty that links reality and thinking, then of course Descartes's starting point would be the same as mine.

Thinking and intuition are usually considered to be totally different activities, but when we view them as facts of consciousness we realize that they are the same kind of activity. Many people hold that intuition and experience are purely passive activities in which we realize individual things just as they are irrespective of other things; in contrast, they regard thinking as an active function that compares and judges things and determines their relations. When we survey the range of actual activities of consciousness, however, we find no totally passive activity. Intuition is a direct judgment, and for this reason I stated before that intuition is the starting point of knowledge that is free from arbitrary assumptions.

"Intuition" thus does not refer simply to the activity of sensation. At the base of thinking there is always a certain unifying reality that we can know only through intuition. Judgment arises from the analysis of this intuition.

THE TRUE FEATURES OF REALITY

What is immediate reality before we have added the fabrications of thinking? In other words, what is a fact of truly pure experience? At the time of pure experience, there is still no opposition between subject and object and no separation of knowledge, feeling, and volition; there is only an independent, self-sufficient, pure activity.

Intellectualist psychologists regard sensations and ideas as the requisite elements of mental phenomena and hold that all mental phenomena are constituted by their union. From this perspective, they construe a fact of pure experience to be the most passive state of consciousness, namely, sensation. But this approach confuses the results of academic analysis with the facts of direct experience. In facts of direct experience, there is no pure sensation. What we term pure sensation is already a simple perception, but no matter how simple, perception is not at all passive: it necessarily includes active—constructive—elements. (This is obvious when we consider examples of spatial perception.)

The characterization of pure experience as active becomes clearer when we examine such complex cognitive activities as association and thinking. Though association is usually deemed passive, the direction of the linkage of ideas in association is determined not only by circumstances in the external world, but also by the internal qualities of consciousness. Association and thinking thus differ only in degree. Moreover, people divide the phenomena of consciousness into knowledge, but in actuality we do not find these three types of phenomena. In fact, each and every phenomenon of consciousness possesses all three aspects. (For instance, although academic research is considered a purely intellectual activity, it can never exist apart from feeling and the will.) Of these three aspects the will is the most fundamental form of consciousness. As voluntarist psychologists assert, our consciousness is always active: it begins with an impulse and ends with the will. However simple, the most direct phenomena of consciousness take the form of the will—that is, the will is a fact of pure experience. . . .

In pure experience, our thinking, feeling, and willing are still undivided; there is a single activity, with no opposition between subject and object. Such opposition arises from the demands of thinking, so it is not a fact of direct experience. In direct experience there is only an independent, self-sufficient event, with neither a subject that sees nor an object that is seen. Just like when we become enraptured by exquisite music, forget ourselves and everything around us, and experience the universe as one melodious sound, true reality presents itself in the moment of direct experience. Should the thought arise that the music is the vibration of air or that one is listening to music, at that point one has already separated oneself from true reality because that thought derives from reflection and thinking divorced from the true state of the reality of the music.

It is usually thought that subject and object are realities that can exist independently of each other and that phenomena of consciousness arise through their activity, which leads to the idea that there are two realities:

mind and matter. This is a total mistake. The notions of subject and object derive from two different ways of looking at a single fact, as does the distinction between mind and matter. But these dichotomies are not inherent in the fact itself. As a concrete fact, a flower is not at all like the purely material flower of scientists; it is pleasing, with a beauty of color, shape, and scent. Heine[1] gazed at the stars in a quiet night sky and called them golden tacks in the azure. Though astronomers would laugh at his words as the folly of a poet, the true nature of stars may very well be expressed in his phrase.

In the independent, self-sufficient true reality prior to the separation of subject and object, our knowledge, feeling, and volition are one. Contrary to popular belief, true reality is not the subject matter of dispassionate knowledge; it is established through our feeling and willing. It is not simply an existence but something with meaning. If we were to remove our feelings and the will from this world of actuality, it would no longer be a concrete fact— it would become an abstract concept. The world described by physicists, like a line without width and a plane without thickness, is not something that actually exists. In this respect, it is the artist, not the scholar, who arrives at the true nature of reality. Each and everything we see or hear contains our individuality. Though we might speak of identical consciousness, our consciousnesses are not truly the same. When viewing a cow, for example, farmers, zoologists, and artists have different mental images. Depending on one's feeling at the moment, the same scenery can appear resplendently beautiful or depressingly gloomy. Buddhist thought holds that according to one's mood the world becomes either heaven or hell. Thus our world is constructed upon our feeling and volition. However much we talk about the objective world as the subject matter of pure knowledge, it cannot escape its relation to our feelings.

People think that the world seen scientifically is most objective in that it exists independently of our feeling and volition. But it is in no way divorced from the demands of feeling and the will because scientific inquiry derives from actual demands in our struggle for survival. As especially Jerusalem has said, the idea that a power in the external world performs various activities—this idea being the fundamental principle of the scientific world view—is generated by analogical inference from one's will.[2] Ancient explanations of things in the universe were anthropomorphic, and they are the springboard from which contemporary scientific explanations developed.

Taking the distinction between subject and object as fundamental, some think that objective elements are included only in knowledge and that idiosyncratic, subjective events constitute feeling and volition. This view is mistaken in its basic assumptions. If we argue that phenomena arise by means of the mutual activity of subject and object, then even such content of knowledge as color or form can be seen as subjective or individual. If we argue further that there is a quality in the external world that gives rise to feeling and volition, then they come to possess an objective base, and it is therefore an error to say they are totally individual. Our feeling and volition allow for communication and sympathy between individuals; they have a trans-individual element.

Because we think that such emotional and volitional entities as joy, anger, love, and desire arise in individual people, we also think that feeling and the will are purely individual. Yet it is not that the individual possesses feeling and the will, but rather that feeling and the will create the individual. Feeling and the will are facts of direct experience.

The anthropomorphic explanation of the myriad things in the universe is the way of explanation used by ancient people and naive children in all eras. Although scientists might laugh it away—indeed, it is infantile—from a certain perspective this is the true way of explaining reality. A scientist's way of explanation is slanted toward just one aspect of knowledge, whereas in a complete explanation of reality we must satisfy intellectual demands as well as the demands of feeling and the will.

To the Greeks, all of nature was alive. Thunder and lightning were the wrath of Zeus on Mount Olympus, the voice of the cuckoo was Philamela's lament of the past.[3] To the natural eye of a Greek, the true meaning of the present appeared just as it was. Contemporary art, religion, and philosophy all strive to express this true meaning.

NOTES

1. Heinrich Heine (1797–1856) was a German poet and critic who was heavily influenced by German romanticism.

2. K. W. Jerusalem, *Einleitung in die Philosophie*, 6, Auf. section 27.

3. Nishida's note is from Friedrich Schiller, *Die Götter Griechenlands* Schiller's poem, "The Gods of Greece," includes the verse: "yonder Laurel once imploring wound, / Tantal's daughter slumbers in this stone; / From yon rose Syrinx' mournful sound, / From this thicket, Philomela's moan." *Schiller's Works*, vol. 1, ed., J. G. Fischer (Philadelphia: George Barrie, 1883), p. 36.

STUDY QUESTIONS

1. Discuss the distinction that Parmenides makes between the Way of Truth and the Way of Being. He argues that the two are necessarily mutually exclusive. Evaluate this claim and give reasons for your position.
2. Discuss the account of being given in the *Ṛg Veda*. Is Vedic account of the *brahman* as the origin of all things defensible? Argue for your position.
3. Discuss the *Ṛg Vedic* concept of time as that which encompasses past, present, and the future.
4. Discuss the Upaniṣadic concept of being. Do you agree with the Upaniṣadic claim that the original being, the creator of the universe, was the self in the form of a person? Do you find the Upaniṣadic account satisfactory? Give reasons.
5. Discuss the Upaniṣadic notion of the identity of *ātman* and the *brahman*.
6. Discuss the concept of being after Aristotle. What is the most primary sense of being according to Aristotle?
7. Discuss superimposition. What is the significance of this notion for Śaṃkara's philosophy?
8. Explain clearly the Advaita conception of Brahman. Be sure to include in your answer a discussion of the distinction between *nirguṇa* and *saguṇa* Brahman.
9. What is *māyā?* Discuss its characteristics. Critically discuss the Advaitic conceptions of appearance, causation, self, and *mokṣa*.
10. Can the Advaitin analysis of the relation between Brahman and *māyā* be vindicated? If yes, discuss some of the strongest objections to the doctrine and why they do not constitute good reasons for rejecting the doctrine. If no, discuss some of the strongest reasons for accepting the doctrine and why they do not constitute good reasons for the acceptance of the doctrine.
11. What is *Tao?* What are its main characteristics?
12. Taoism uses various analogies to explain the nature of *tao*. Select three analogies and discuss their significance.
13. Explain the significance of *wu wei*.
14. Lao Tzu argues that *tao* is nameless, invisible, formless, etc. How does one know *tao?*
15. Taoists repeatedly emphasize harmony between one's life with the movement of the *tao*. Why is this harmony essential?
16. Explain the nature of the Great Ultimate as the material force. Is it one or many?
17. Is Chang Tsai a reductionist materialist? How does he ground the moral virtues on his materialism?

18. Discuss Nāgārjuna's position regarding metaphysical entities. Do you agree with his thesis? Argue pro or con.
19. Discuss Nāgārjuna's notion of emptiness. Does it make sense to you? If yes, why yes? If not, why not?
20. Discuss Nishida's notion of immediate reality. How does one gain an access to immediate reality?
21. Nishida maintains that knowledge must not be divorced from feeling and will. Do you agree? Explain your position clearly.
22. Nishida uses the example of the person engrossed in music to demonstrate the existence of immediate reality. Do you think that he substantiates his position.
23. Formulate and discuss the important metaphysical issues that the reading assignments raise. Listed below are possible areas of discussion, although you may formulate your discussion in any manner you wish.
    (i) Is reality one or many?
    (ii) Is it material or spiritual?
    (iii) What is the relationship between reality and its manifestations?
    (iv) Is reality permanent or change?
24. Compare and contrast the *brahman, tao,* and immediate reality. Which account of these concepts seems plausible and why?

SUGGESTIONS FOR FURTHER READING

A Source Book in Chinese Philosophy translated and compiled by Wing-tsit Chan (Princeton: Princeton University Press, 1963), contains an excellent translation of the most important Chinese philosophical texts. Students might wish to consult this work for both Lao Tzu and Chu Hsi.

Chu Hsi: New Studies by Wing-tsit Chan (Hawaii: University of Hawaii Press, 1973) is an in-depth study of Chu as a person and philosopher.

Plato and Parmenides by F.M. Cornford (London: Kegan & Paul, 1939) contains a chapter entitled "Parmenides' Way of Truth." It is a clear and precise account of the main tenets of Parmenides' philosophy.

Advaita Vedānta: A Philosophical Introduction by Eliot Deutsch (Hawaii: University of Hawaii Press, 1973) is one of the best introductions available on the philosophy of Śaṃkara, the founder of Advaita Vedānta. This book is a must for any beginner of Vedānta.

A Source Book of Advaita Vedānta compiled by Eliot Deutsch and J.A.B. Van Buitenen (Honolulu: University of Hawaii Press, 1971) will help students of Advaita Vedānta to study this school through an examination of its primary sources.

History of Greek Philosophy by W.K.C. Guthrie (Cambridge: Cambridge University Press, 1962–81) provides a good general introduction to important Greek philosophers. Students might wish to consult this work for both Parmenides as well as Aristotle.

The Essentials of Indian Philosophy by Mysore Hiriyanna (London: George Allen & Unwin, 1932) provides a good overview of the nine schools of Indian philosophy.

Nāgārjuna: A Translation of His Mūlamādhyamikakārikā with an Introductory Essay by Kenneth Inada (Tokyo: Hokuseido Press, 1970) is a lucid translation of this basic Mādhyamika text. The introductory essay explains the main issues of Nāgārjuna's philosophy in the context of the basic teachings of the historical Buddha. Each chapter contains explanatory notes.

Buddhist Philosophy: An Historical Analysis by David J. Kalupahana (Honolulu: University of Hawaii Press, 1976) is a clearly written account of early Buddhism and its development in the Therāvāda and Mahāyāna traditions. The appendices on metaphysics and Zen provide useful introductions.

Three Pillars of Zen by Philip Kapleau (New York: Harper & Row, 1969) is one of the best introductions to the thought and the practice of Zen.

Nishida Kitaro by Nishitani Keiji, translated by Yamaoto Seisaku and James W. Heisig (Berkeley: University of California Press, 1991), is the best available account of Nishida's thoughts.

Fundamentals of Indian Philosophy by R. Puligandla (New York: Abingdon Press, 1975) is a good introduction to the main schools of Indian philosophical systems. It contains a very useful essay on Advaita Vedānta.

A Sourcebook of Indian Philosophy by S. Radhakrishnan and C.A. Moore (Princeton: University of Princeton, 1957) introduces Indian philosophy through primary sources. The general introduction as well as introductions to selections make this volume very helpful.

The Way of Lao Tzu (Tao-te Ching) translated by Wing-tsit Chan (Indianapolis: Bobbs-Merrill, Library of Liberal Arts, 1963), provides a clear translation. It also contains very helpful introductory essays, comments, and notes.

Tao: A New Way of Thinking by Chang Chung-yuan (New York: Harper & Row, 1975) is a reliable translation of the *Tao Te Ching* with an introduction and Commentary. It will be of special interest to the students of comparative philosophy.

The Ṛg Veda: An Anthology translated and annotated by Wendy Doniger O'Flaherty (New York: Penguin Books, 1981), contains a modern translation of 108 *Ṛg Vedic* hymns.

Upaniṣads by Patrick Ollivelle (Oxford: Oxford University Press, 1996) contains a lucid translation of the major Upaniṣads. An excellent introduction precedes the translations.

Superimposition in Advaita Vedānta by T. M. P. Mahadevan (New Delhi: Sterling Publishers Private Ltd., 1985) is a very clear account of Śaṃkara's idea that the world, as an appearance of the real, is a superimposition on the Self.

The Vedic Experience: Mantramañjarī by Raimundo Panikkar (Los Angeles: University of California Press, 1977), is a collection of teachings from the Vedas, *Brāhmaṇas,* and Upaniṣads. No other anthology comes close in choice of material and clarity of translation. Each section contains a very helpful introduction.

The Principal Upaniṣads edited and translated by Sarvapalli Radhakrishnan (London: George Allen & Unwin, 1953), includes the Sanskrit texts and translations of all the early Upaniṣads. It also contains a good introductory essay from the perspective of Advaita Vedānta.

What the Buddha Taught, 2nd ed., by Walpola Rahula (New York: Grove Press, 1978) provides an excellent introduction to Buddhism by a practising Buddhist monk.

Aristotle by W.D. Ross (New York: University Paperbacks, 1923) has a chapter on Aristotle's metaphysics. It provides a very good account of the key ideas of Aristotle's metaphysics.

For a readable translation of Śaṃkara's *Brahma-Sūtra-Śhānkara-Bhāṣya,* students might wish to consult V. M. Apte's translation (Bombay: Popular Book Depot, 1960).

Metaphysics, 2nd ed., by Richard Taylor (Engelwood Cliffs, N.J.: Prentice Hall, 1974) is a very useful introduction to Aristotle's metaphysics. It is one of the best single-volume treatments by one of the editors of Aristotle's writings in English.

Part 2

Epistemology

2.1

Introduction: What Are the Nature and Sources of Knowledge?

One of the major concerns of philosophy has been with "knowledge" as contrasted with "Being," the subject matter of metaphysics. The part of philosophy that tries to answer such questions as What is knowledge? What are the different kinds of knowledge? What are the means or sources of knowing? What is truth? What is the test of truth? How is truth apprehended? is called "epistemology" (the science of *episteme*) or the theory of knowledge. This part of philosophy, as far as Western thought is concerned, was placed on a scientific path by Socrates and Plato, and, following them, by Aristotle. Many of the great Scholastic philosophers of the Middle Ages, such as Thomas Aquinas and Duns Scotus, made important contributions. In modern times, Descartes laid the foundation for a rationalist epistemology, just as Locke, Berkeley, and Hume developed an empiricist theory. The rationalists held that the human mind has "innate" or "a priori" knowledge; that reason, unaided by sense-experience, can be the source of our most significant knowledge such as mathematics; and that true knowledge must be universally and necessarily true. The empiricists rejected innate or a priori ideas; held that the human mind at birth is like an empty slate, tabula rasa, acquiring all of its knowledge by means of sensory experience; and believed that universal and necessary cognitions can be had only in the case of such purely "analytic" (and so "trivial," "tautologous") sciences as logic and mathematics, whereas all knowledge about "matters of fact," derived as it is from sensory experience, is only "probable" and so defeasible. This opposition between rationalism and empiricism determines a large part of Western philosophy, and the story predates modern times; were not Socrates and Plato rationalists, and wasn't Aristotle an empiricist? But attempts were made to combine or synthesize both: notably, at the earliest, by Aristotle (who held that knowledge requires human intellect exercising upon sensory experience), but more famously, in modern times, by Kant (who held that sensory experience provides only new data, which needs to be processed, that is to say, ordered in space and time, and brought under a whole range of a priori concepts in order that knowledge, exemplified in ordinary perception, but also in mathematics and physics, may be possible). It is only in our times, during the very last decades of this century, that this whole issue—discussed in terms of "reason" and "experience," "form" and "content," "concepts" and "data"—has been radically called into question by such philosophers as Karl Popper, Wilfred Sellars, and the new brand of American Pragmatists, although more than a century earlier Hegel had raised the same questions.

In this collection, we have included not only extracts from two dialogues by Plato, which have been seminal for Western epistemology, but also pieces from influential Sanskrit texts, an essay by the Islamic mystic philosopher Al Ghazāli, as well as selections from Descartes's *Meditations,* and as the concluding chapter, an essay by Huston Smith, comparing the Western and the Eastern perspectives on truth. We want to emphasize that it is not accurate to say—as many philosophers do—that epistemology is a typically Western pursuit. It may be argued that Chinese philosophy did not raise dominantly epistemological questions, but even that claim is only partly true. Indian philosophy, however, has had a dominant epistemological strand, so that every philosophical school in India developed its own theory of knowledge or theory of *pramāṇa* (or, the means of true cognition).

Now, to begin with the Platonic dialogues. In *Theaetetus,* Socrates relentlessly pursues the question as to what knowledge is (as distinguished from what are the possible objects of knowledge and from what are the different sorts of knowledge), shows the absurd consequences of Protagoras's doctrine that man is the measure of all things, argues that knowledge does not reside in mere sense-impressions and cannot be the same as perception, and finally focuses upon the nature of judgment. He then goes on to raise very difficult questions about "false judgment," especially about its object. How, he asks, can a person take one thing for another? (see Śaṃkara on *Adhyāsa* in the Metaphysics section of this work). He takes thinking to be an inner discourse; but if that is so, he wonders, can a man say to himself that a thing is what it is not? From this problem, Socrates moves on to make sense of the locution "x possesses knowledge." Is knowledge a thing one can possess as one possesses birds one has caught? Maybe this last analogy itself is misleading. Eventually, Socrates comes to present a famous and much-discussed theory that knowledge is justified true belief. In recent times, philosophers have pointed out that even if one has a justified true judgment, one may not be said to know. So they inquire about additional factors needed to make a justified true judgment knowledge. In response, there are those who argue that a true belief (or judgment) must be caused in the right way. But what is this right way? For an answer, we may have to turn to the Indian theories of *pramāṇas.*

Before we turn to Indian theories, let us note what Plato does in the *Meno*. Beginning with a rather tricky question, how inquiry is possible (for a man cannot inquire into what he already knows, nor into what he does not know), Socrates introduces the theory that all learning is a process of recollection (for the soul already knows all things). This theory, he argues, explains how a slave boy can possibly be taught geometry. What the soul already knows is only awakened through the Socratic method of asking and answering questions. In this way, Plato introduces into Western thought the very important concept of a priori knowledge which, in its later embodiments, is freed from the idea of "recollection."

As regards Indian philosophy, we have selected three pieces: one from Gautama's *Nyāyasūtra* (1.1.3) and Vātsyāyan's Commentary on it, another from Dharmarāja's widely used text on Advaita Vedānta epistemology, and the third from the Buddhist logician Dharmakirti's *Nyāyabindu*. Common to all of them is the concept of *pramāṇa* or "means of true cognition." Correspondingly we can speak of *pramā* or true cognition as cognition that arises from or is acquired through a *pramāṇa*. Each of the words "perception" and "inference" is then ambiguous as between "a means of acquiring true knowledge" and "a kind of true knowledge," namely, "a true knowledge that is acquired in the appropriate manner."

Indian philosophers held different views regarding the number of *pramāṇa*s as well as their natures and definitions. Thus, while Gautama admits four *pramāṇa*s (perception, inference, comparison, and verbal utterance), Dharmakirti recognizes only two (perception and inference), and Dharmarāja six (the above four and, in addition, "postulation" and "non-perception"). Even regarding those that are admitted in common, philosophers belonging to different schools defined them differently. These differences are deeply grounded in some fundamental tenets of the schools.

Perception as such can be defined either by pointing out some feature intrinsic to the perceptual cognition, by insisting upon any peculiar object of such cognition, or by how the cognition is caused. The Buddhist definition is of the first kind: perception is a cognition that is free from imagination (by which Dharmakirti means all conceptual constructions) and so is not linguistic, and is unerring. The Nyāya definition is in terms of how perceptual cognition is generated: it is that cognition which arises from the contact of a sense organ with its object. Vātsyāyana further adds: it is nondeviant with regard to its object, hence it is true and it is a cognition that is not a state of doubt (for a doubt may also be generated by contact of a sense organ with its object). Dharmarāja also gives a causal account (in a rather complicated manner: the inner sense assumes the form of the object, etc.), but supplements the causal with a cognitive account. A cognition is *pramā* if it is not contradicted by a subsequent *pramā*.

There are other differences between the epistemologies of these schools, to which we can hardly do justice in this introduction. One such difference concerns, with regard to perception, its different types. Dharmakīrti recognizes three types: sensory perception, mental perception, and self-cognition (of each state of consciousness). The object of perception, on this view, is always a unique particular, which therefore is ineffable. All cognitions of universal objects are inferential.

The Nyāya philosophers, however, distinguished between two phases of the unfolding of perceptual cognition: the first is nonconceptual and non-judgmental and so nonlinguistic, the second is judgmental and linguistic. They also distinguished between inner perception and outer perception, and took the objects of perception to include both particulars and universals.

The selection from Dharmarāja focuses upon another kind of true cognition: cognition that is produced by words alone. When one hears a competent (intellectually as well as morally) speaker, and if one understands the meanings of the words uttered, and if the sequence of utterances is syntactically and semantically well formed, then one acquires a true cognition of what the speaker is talking about. This is what is called *śabda* knowledge, and recognition of it is an important feature of the Indian epistemologies— although not all of them recognize it as true cognition, and even if some others recognize its truth, they reduce it to inference.

From the Indian epistemologies, we pass on to Descartes, who in his relentless search for certainty passes through a radical but methodological skepticism before he discusses the absolute indubitability of the existence of the thinking ego. Descartes argues that this apodictic truth, encapsulated in the celebrated dictum "*cogito ergo sum*," is the foundation upon which the edifice of knowledge needs to be built.

Descartes's ideas have influenced several major Western philosophers, but have also given rise, especially in more recent times, to several lines of criticism. The most important—influential as well as controversial—elements of Cartesian epistemology are: a foundationalism that seeks to ground scientific knowledge on the indubitable foundation of self-knowledge ("I think, therefore I am"), the claim that mind is more certain than matter and that I know my own occurrent mental states with infallible certainty; and finally, the true must be evident (or, rather, self-evident). With regard to the first, Descartes has influenced all transcendental philosophers, notably Kant and Husserl, though both Kant and Husserl tried to radicalize Descartes's claim by making the foundational "I" a transcendental and not a mundane ego. As regards the second, a large number of epistemologists tried to show how, starting with my own mental experience which is allegedly directly known, I could inferentially know of the existence and nature of material things; but it must be said that they have failed to overcome the possibility of skepticism with regard to knowledge of an external world. The third Cartesian doctrine has been revised in more recent times by Brentano and Husserl, but the thesis that the true must be evident has generally been taken to be either not clear enough or just plainly wrong. Descartes's critics are too many to be listed here. His foundationalism has fallen into disrepute. His claim to apodictic self-knowledge, dubbed as the theory of the "privileged access" (by a person into his or her own mental life), has been revised by many, and taken by others to have been falsified by the phenomena of self-deception about one's own mental states. It has also been pointed out that Descartes's epistemology both supports and is supported by his dubious metaphysical dualism between mind and matter. The Cartesian soul has been mocked as being a "ghost in a machine." Despite these challenges, Cartesianism holds out an alternative for many thinkers.

But almost four hundred years before Descartes, Al Ghazāli asked the same questions as Descartes did and traversed the same path of doubt in search for certainty. He raises the same Cartesian doubt based on inability to distinguish waking from dreaming. But the certainty that he finds is along the way of mysticism culminating in a mystical state realized in immediate experience. Western thought, even if it knew of such a state, excluded it from philosophy.

Although in this section on epistemology we have included only one piece on Islamic epistemology, the one by Al-Ghazāli, it is important for instructors and students to bear in mind that Islamic epistemology had a long history and much internal sophistication, in its attempt to keep together Aristotelian logic and theory of knowledge and Islamic mysticism as well as the testimony of scriptures. Different cognitive powers were distinguished, such as Aristotelian potential and active intellects, and acquired intellect and demonstrative intellect (Al-Kindi). Distinction was made between knowledge acquired through logic and direct intuitive knowledge such as one's knowledge of one's ego (Ibn Sina). Not unlike some Indian epistemologists, al-Suhrawardi regarded knowledge as making manifest what is previously unknown, and described the highest knowledge of the truth as "illumination of the soul." The idea of causality played an important role in some of the Islamic epistemological theories. While Al-Ghazāli regarded the cause–effect relationship as a matter of habit, Averros regarded true knowledge of a thing as knowing what caused the knowledge of it. A most fascinating theory of knowledge is to be found in the Ismail philosopher Al-Kitmāni who regarded everything as belonging to some universal structure or other (of the four: metaphysical, the religious community, the natural order, and the human order), and true knowledge as knowledge of the place of a thing in that order.

Truth is the goal of knowledge. All theories of knowledge have to have a theory of truth. Huston Smith advances a large, globally oriented, and comparative theory of truth in the Western, Chinese, and Indian traditions. Any such global theory has to be examined in the light of actual historical data and philosophical texts, but it certainly provides an initial perspective for sorting out a large mass of data.

2.2

The Nature of Knowledge (*Theaetetus*)

Plato

(146–147C)

Socrates: Well, that is precisely what I am puzzled about. I cannot make out to my own satisfaction what knowledge is. Can we answer that question? What do you all say? Which of us will speak first? Everyone who misses shall "sit down and be donkey," as children say when they are playing at ball; anyone who gets through without missing shall be king and have the right to make us answer any question he likes. Why are you all silent? I hope, Theodorus, that my passion for argument is not making me ill-mannered, in my eagerness to start a conversation and set us all at ease with one another like friends?

Theodorus: Not at all, Socrates; there is nothing ill-mannered in that. But please ask one of these young people to answer your questions; I am not at home in an abstract discussion of this sort, nor likely to become so at my age. But it is just the thing for them, and they have a far better prospect of improvement; youth, indeed, is capable of improving at anything. So do not let Theaetetus off; go on putting your questions to him.

Soc.: You hear what Theodorus says, Theaetetus. I do not think you will want to disobey him, and it would be wrong for you not to do what an older and wiser man bids you. So tell me, in a generous spirit, what you think knowledge is.

Theaetetus: Well, Socrates, I cannot refuse, since you and Theodorus ask me. Anyhow, if I do make a mistake, you will set me right.

Soc.: By all means, if we can.

The.: Then I think the things one can learn from Theodorus are knowledge—geometry and all the sciences you mentioned just now, and then there are the crafts of the cobbler and other workmen. Each and all of these are knowledge and nothing else.

From *The Collected Dialogues of Plato,* edited by E. Hamilton and H. Cairns, Bollingen Series 71 (New York: Pantheon Books, 1966) pp. 850–906.

Soc.: You are generous indeed, my dear Theaetetus—so openhanded that, when you are asked for one simple thing, you offer a whole variety.

The.: What do you mean, Socrates?

Soc.: There may be nothing in it, but I will explain what my notion is. When you speak of cobbling, you mean by that word precisely a knowledge of shoemaking?

The.: Precisely.

Soc.: And when you speak of carpentry, you mean just a knowledge of how to make wooden furniture?

The.: Yes.

Soc.: In both cases, then, you are defining what the craft is a knowledge of?

The.: Yes.

Soc.: But the question you were asked, Theaetetus, was not, what are the objects of knowledge, nor yet how many sorts of knowledge there are. We did not want to count them, but to find out what the thing itself—knowledge—is. Is there nothing in that?

The.: No, you are quite right.

Soc.: Take another example. Suppose we were asked about some obvious common thing, for instance, what clay is; it would be absurd to answer: potter's clay, and ovenmaker's clay, and brickmaker's clay.

The.: No doubt.

Soc.: To begin with, it is absurd to imagine that our answer conveys any meaning to the questioner, when we use the word 'clay,' no matter whose clay we call it—the dollmaker's or any other craftsman's. You do not suppose a man can understand the name of a thing, when he does not know what the thing is?

The.: Certainly not.

Soc.: Then, if he has no idea of knowledge, 'knowledge about shoes' conveys nothing to him?

The.: No.

Soc.: 'Cobblery,' in fact, or the name of any other art has no meaning for anyone who has no conception of knowledge.

The.: That is so.

Soc.: Then, when we are asked what knowledge is, it is absurd to reply by giving the name of some art. The answer is 'knowledge of so-and-so,' but that was not what the question called for.

The.: So it seems.

(170–171C)

Soc.: Let us, then, as briefly as possible, obtain his agreement, not through any third person, but from his own statement.

Theodorus: How?

Soc.: In this way. He says, doesn't he, that what seems true to anyone is true for him to whom it seems so?

Theodorus: He does.

Soc.: Well now, Protagoras, we are expressing what seems true to a man, or rather to all men, when we say that everyone without exception holds that in some respects he is wiser than his neighbors and in others they are wiser than he. For instance, in moments of great danger and distress, whether in war or in sickness or at sea, men regard as a god anyone who can take control of the situation and look to him as a savior, when his only point of superiority is his knowledge. Indeed, the world is full of people looking for those who can instruct and govern men and animals and direct their doings, and on the other hand of people who think themselves quite competent to undertake the teaching and governing. In all these cases what can we say, if not that men do hold that wisdom and ignorance exist among them?

Theodorus: We must say that.

Soc.: And they hold that wisdom lies in thinking truly, and ignorance in false belief?

Theodorus: Of course.

Soc.: In that case, Protagoras, what are we to make of your doctrine? Are we to say that what men think is always true, or that it is sometimes true and sometimes false? From either supposition it results that their thoughts are not always true, but both true and false. For consider, Theodorus. Are you, or is any Protagorean, prepared to maintain that no one regards anyone else as ignorant or as making false judgments?

Theodorus: That is incredible, Socrates.

Soc.: That, however, is the inevitable consequence of the doctrine which makes man the measure of all things.

Theodorus: How so?

Soc.: When you have formed a judgment on some matter in your own mind and express an opinion about it to me, let us grant that, as Protagoras' theory says, it is true for you, but are we to understand that it is impossible for us, the rest of the company, to pronounce any judgment upon your judgment, or, if we can, that we always pronounce your opinion to be true? Do you not rather find thousands of opponents who set their opinion against yours on every occasion and hold that your judgment and belief are false?

Theodorus: I should just think so, Socrates—thousands and tens of thousands, as Homer says, and they give me all the trouble in the world.

Soc.: And what then? Would you have us say that in such a case the opinion you hold is true for yourself and false for these tens of thousands?

Theodorus: The doctrine certainly seems to imply that.

Soc.: And what is the consequence for Protagoras himself? Is it not this? Supposing that not even he believed in man being the measure and the world in general did not believe it either—as in fact it doesn't—then this *Truth* which he wrote would not be true for anyone. If, on the other hand, he did believe it, but the mass of mankind does not agree with him, then, you see, it is more false than true by just so much as the unbelievers outnumber the believers.

Theodorus: That follows, if its truth or falsity varies with each individual opinion.

Soc.: Yes, and besides that it involves a really exquisite conclusion. Protagoras, for his part, admitting as he does that everybody's opinion is true, must acknowledge the truth of his opponents' belief about his own belief, where they think he is wrong.

Theodorus: Certainly.

Soc.: That is to say, he would acknowledge his own belief to be false, if he admits that the belief of those who think him wrong is true?

Theodorus: Necessarily.

Soc.: But the others, on their side, do not admit to themselves that they are wrong.

Theodorus: No.

Soc.: Whereas Protagoras, once more, according to what he has written, admits that this opinion of theirs is as true as any other.

Theodorus: Evidently.

Soc.: On all hands, then, Protagoras included, his opinion will be disputed, or rather Protagoras will join in the general consent—when he admits to an opponent the truth of his contrary Opinion, from that moment Protagoras himself will be admitting that a dog or the man in the street is not a measure of anything whatever that he does not understand. Isn't that so?

Theodorus: Yes.

Soc.: Then, since it is disputed by everyone, the *Truth* of Protagoras is true to nobody—to himself no more than to anyone else.

Theodorus: We are running my old friend too hard, Socrates.

(186–190E)

Soc.: Under which head, then, do you place existence? For that is, above all, a thing that belongs to everything.

The.: I should put it among the things that the mind apprehends by itself.

Soc.: And also likeness and unlikeness and sameness and difference?

The.: Yes.

Soc.: And how about 'honorable' and 'dishonorable' and 'good' and 'bad'?

The.: Those again seem to me, above all, to be things whose being is considered, one in comparison with another, by the mind, when it reflects within itself upon the past and the present with an eye to the future.

Soc.: Wait a moment. The hardness of something hard and the softness of something soft will be perceived by the mind through touch, will they not?

The.: Yes.

Soc.: But their existence and the fact that they both exist, and their contrariety to one another and again the existence of this contrariety are things which the mind itself undertakes to judge for us, when it reflects upon them and compares one with another.

The.: Certainly.

Soc.: Is it not true, then, that whereas all the impressions which penetrate to the mind through the body are things which men and animals alike are naturally constituted to perceive from the moment of birth, reflections about them with respect to their existence and usefulness only come, if they come at all, with difficulty through a long and troublesome process of education?

The.: Assuredly.

Soc.: Is it possible, then, to reach truth when one cannot reach existence?

The.: It is impossible.

Soc.: But if a man cannot reach the truth of a thing, can he possibly know that thing?

The.: No, Socrates, how could he?

Soc.: If that is so, knowledge does not reside in the impressions, but in our reflection upon them. It is there, seemingly, and not in the impressions, that it is possible to grasp existence and truth.

The.: Evidently.

Soc.: Then are you going to give the same name to two things which differ so widely?

The.: Surely that would not be right.

Soc.: Well then, what name do you give to the first one—to seeing, hearing, smelling, feeling cold and feeling warm?

The.: Perceiving. What other name is there for it?

Soc.: Taking it all together, then, you call this perception?

The.: Necessarily.

Soc.: A thing which, we agree, has no part in apprehending truth, since it has none in apprehending existence.

The.: No, it has none.

Soc.: Nor, consequently, in knowledge either.

The.: No.

Soc.: Then, Theaetetus, perception and knowledge cannot possibly be the same thing.

The.: Evidently not, Socrates. Indeed, it is now perfectly plain that knowledge is something different from perception.

Soc.: But when we began our talk it was certainly not our object to find out what knowledge is not, but what it is. Still, we have advanced so far as to see that we must not look for it in sense perception at all, but in what goes on when the mind is occupied with things by itself, whatever name you give to that.

The.: Well, Socrates, the name for that, I imagine, is 'making judgments.'

Soc.: You are right, my friend. Now begin all over again. Blot out all we have been saying, and see if you can get a clearer view from the position you have now reached. Tell us once more what knowledge is.

The.: I cannot say it is judgment as a whole, because there is false judgment, but perhaps true judgment is knowledge. You may take that as my answer. If, as we go further, it turns out to be less convincing than it seems now, I will try to find another.

Soc.: Good, Theaetetus. This promptness is much better than hanging back as you did at first. If we go on like this, either we shall find what we are after, or we shall be less inclined to imagine we know something of which we know nothing whatever, and that surely is a reward not to be despised. And now, what is this you say—that there are two sorts of judgment, one true, the other false, and you define knowledge as judgment that is true?

The.: Yes, that is the view I have come to now.

Soc.: Then, had we better go back to a point that came up about judgment?

The.: What point do you mean?

Soc.: A question that worries me now, as often before, and has much perplexed me in my own mind and also in talking to others. I cannot explain the nature of this experience we have, or how it can arise in our minds.

The.: What experience?

Soc.: Making a false judgment. At this moment I am still in doubt and wondering whether to let that question alone or to follow it further, not as we did a while ago, but in a new way.

The.: Why not, Socrates, if it seems to be in the least necessary? Only just now, when you and Theodorus were speaking of leisure, you said very rightly that there is no pressing hurry in a discussion of this sort.

Soc.: A good reminder, for this may be the right moment to go back upon our track. It is better to carry through a small task well than make a bad job of a big one.

The.: Certainly it is.

Soc.: How shall we set about it, then? What is it that we do mean? Do we assert that there is in every case a false judgment, and that one of us thinks what is false, another what is true, such being the nature of things?

The.: Certainly we do.

Soc.: And, in each and all cases, it is possible for us either to know a thing or not to know it? I leave out of account for the moment becoming acquainted with things and forgetting, considered as falling between the two. Our argument is not concerned with them just now.

The.: Well then, Socrates, there is no third alternative left in any case, besides knowing and not-knowing.

Soc.: And it follows at once that when one is thinking he must be thinking either of something he knows or of something he does not know?

The.: Necessarily.

Soc.: And further, if you know a thing, you cannot also not know it, and if you do not know it, you cannot also know it?

The.: Of course.

Soc.: Then is the man who thinks what is false supposing that things he knows are not those things but other things he knows, so that, while he knows both, he fails to recognize either?

The.: No, that is impossible, Socrates.

Soc.: Well then, is he supposing that things he does *not* know are other things he does not know? Is this possible—that a man who knows neither Theaetetus nor Socrates should take it into his head that Socrates is Theaetetus or Theaetetus Socrates?

The.: No. How could he?

Soc.: But surely a man does not imagine that things he does know are things he does not know, or that things he does not know are things he knows?

The.: No, that would be a miracle.

Soc.: What other way is there, then, of judging falsely? There is, presumably, no possibility of judging outside these alternatives, granted that everything is either known by us or not known, and inside them there seems to be no room for a false judgment.

The.: Quite true.

Soc.: Perhaps, then, we had better approach what we are looking for by way of another alternative. Instead of 'knowing or not-knowing,' let us take 'being or not-being.'

The.: How do you mean?

Soc.: May it not simply be that one who thinks *what is not* about anything cannot but be thinking what is false, whatever his state of mind may be in other respects?

The.: There is some likelihood in that, Socrates.

Soc.: Then what shall we say, Theaetetus, if we are asked, 'But is what you describe possible for anyone? Can any man think what is not, either about something that is or absolutely?' I suppose we must answer to that, Yes, when he believes something and what he believes is not true.' Or what are we to say?

The.: We must say that.

Soc.: Then is the same sort of thing possible in any other case?

The.: What sort of thing?

Soc.: That a man should see something, and yet what he sees should be nothing.

The.: No. How could that be?

Soc.: Yet surely if what he sees is something, it must be a thing that is. Or do you suppose that 'something' can be reckoned among things that have no being at all?

The.: No, I don't.

Soc.: Then, if he sees something, he sees a thing that is.

The.: Evidently.

Soc.: And if he hears a thing, he hears something and hears a thing that is.

The.: Yes.

Soc.: And if he touches a thing, he touches something, and if something, then a thing that is.

The.: That also is true.

Soc.: And if he thinks, he thinks something, doesn't he?

The.: Necessarily.

Soc.: And when he thinks something, he thinks a thing that is?

The.: I agree.

Soc.: So to think what is not is to think nothing.

The.: Clearly.

Soc.: But surely to think nothing is the same as not to think at all.

The.: That seems plain.

Soc.: If so, it is impossible to think what is not, either about anything that is, or absolutely.

The.: Evidently.

Soc.: Then thinking falsely must be something different from thinking what is not.

The.: So it seems.

Soc.: False judgment, then, is no more possible for us on these lines than on those we were following just now.

The.: No, it certainly is not.

Soc.: Well, does the thing we call false judgment arise in this way?

The.: How?

Soc.: We do recognize the existence of false judgment as a sort of misjudgment that occurs when a person interchanges in his mind two things, both of which are, and asserts that the one is the other. In this way he is always thinking of something which is, but of one thing in place of another, and since he misses the mark he may fairly be said to be judging falsely.

The.: I believe you have got it quite right now. When a person thinks 'ugly' in place of 'beautiful' or 'beautiful' in place of 'ugly,' he is really and truly thinking what is false.

Soc.: I can see that you are no longer in awe of me, Theaetetus, but beginning to despise me.

The.: Why, precisely?

Soc.: I believe you think I shall miss the opening you give me by speaking of '*truly* thinking what is *false,*' and not ask you whether a thing can be slowly quick or heavily light or whether any contrary can desert its own nature and behave like its opposite. However, I will justify your boldness by letting that pass. So you like this notion that false judgment is mistaking.

The.: I do.

Soc.: According to you, then, it is possible for the mind to take one thing for another, and not for itself.

The.: Yes, it is.

Soc.: And when the mind does that, must it not be thinking either of both things or of one of the two?

The.: Certainly it must, either at the same time or one after the other.

Soc.: Excellent. And do you accept my description of the process of thinking?

The.: How do you describe it?

Soc.: As a discourse that the mind carries on with itself about any subject it is considering. You must take this explanation as coming from an ignoramus, but I have a notion that, when the mind is thinking, it is simply talking to itself, asking questions and answering them, and saying yes or no. When it reaches a decision—which may come slowly or in a sudden rush—when doubt is over and the two voices affirm the same thing, then we call that its 'judgment.' So I should describe thinking as discourse, and judgment as a statement pronounced, not aloud to someone else, but silently to oneself.

The.: I agree.

Soc.: It seems, then, that when a person thinks of one thing as another, he is affirming to himself that the one is the other.

The.: Of course.

Soc.: Now search your memory and see, if you have ever said to yourself, 'Certainly, what is beautiful is ugly,' or 'What is unjust is just.' To put it generally, consider if you have ever set about convincing yourself that any one thing is certainly another thing, or whether, on the contrary, you have never, even in a dream, gone so far as to say to yourself that odd numbers must be even, or anything of that sort.

The.: That is true.

Soc.: Do you suppose anyone else, mad or sane, ever goes so far as to talk himself over, in his own mind, into stating seriously that an ox must be a horse or that two must be one?

The.: Certainly not.

Soc.: So, if making a statement to oneself is the same as judging, then, so long as a man is making a statement or judgment about both things at once and his mind has hold of both, he cannot say or judge that one of them is the other. You, in your turn, must not cavil at my language; I mean it in the sense that no one thinks 'the ugly is beautiful' or anything of that kind.

The.: I will not cavil, Socrates. I agree with you.

Soc.: So long, then, as a person is thinking of both, he cannot think of the one as the other.

The.: So it appears.

Soc.: On the other hand, if he is thinking of one only and not of the other at all, he will never think that the one is the other.

The.: True, for then he would have to have before his mind the thing he was not thinking of.

Soc.: It follows, then, that 'mistaking' is impossible, whether he thinks of both things or of one only. So there will be no sense in defining false judgment as 'misjudgment.' It does not appear that false judgment exists in us in this form any more than in those we dismissed earlier.

The.: So it seems.

(197B–199E)

Soc.: They say it is 'having knowledge.'

The.: True.

Soc.: Let us make a slight amendment and say, 'possessing knowledge.'

The.: What difference would you say that makes?

Soc.: None, perhaps, but let me tell you my idea and you shall help me test it.

The.: I will if I can.

Soc.: 'Having' seems to me different from 'possessing.' If a man has bought a coat and owns it, but is not wearing it, we should say he possesses it without having it about him.

The.: True.

Soc.: Now consider whether knowledge is a thing you can possess in that way without having it about you, like a man who has caught some wild birds—pigeons or what not—and keeps them in an aviary he has made for them at home. In a sense, of course, we might say he 'has' them all the time inasmuch as he possesses them, mightn't we?

The.: Yes.

Soc.: But in another sense he 'has' none of them, though he has got control of them, now that he has made them captive in an enclosure of his own; he can take and have hold of them whenever he likes by catching any bird he chooses, and let them go again, and it is open to him to do that as often as he pleases.

The.: That is so.

Soc.: Once more then, just as a while ago we imagined a sort of waxen block in our minds, so now let us suppose that every mind contains a kind of aviary stocked with birds of every sort, some in flocks apart from the rest, some in small groups, and some solitary, flying in any direction among them all.

The.: Be it so. What follows?

Soc.: When we are babies we must suppose this receptacle empty, and take the birds to stand for pieces of knowledge. Whenever a person acquires any piece of knowledge and shuts it up in his enclosure, we must say he has learned or discovered the thing of which this is the knowledge, and that is what 'knowing' means.

The.: Be it so.

Soc.: Now think of him hunting once more for any piece of knowledge that he wants, catching and holding it, and letting it go again. In what terms are we to describe that—the same that we used of the original process of acquisition, or different ones? An illustration may help you to see what I mean. There is a science you call 'arithmetic.'

The.: Yes.

Soc.: Conceive that, then, as a chase after pieces of knowledge about all the numbers, odd or even.

The.: I will.

Soc.: That, I take it, is the science in virtue of which a man has in his control pieces of knowledge about numbers and can hand them over to someone else.

The.: Yes.

Soc.: And when he hands them over, we call it 'teaching,' and when the other takes them from him, that is 'learning,' and when he has them in the sense of possessing them in that aviary of his, that is 'knowing.'

The.: Certainly.

Soc.: Now observe what follows. The finished arithmetician knows all numbers, doesn't he? There is no number the knowledge of which is not in his mind.

The.: Naturally.

Soc.: And such a person may sometimes count either the numbers themselves in his own head or some set of external things that have a number.

The.: Of course.

Soc.: And by counting we shall mean simply trying to find out what some particular number amounts to?

The.: Yes.

Soc.: It appears, then, that the man who, as we admitted, knows every number, is trying to find out what he knows as if he had no knowledge of it. No doubt you sometimes hear puzzles of that sort debated.

The.: Indeed I do.

Soc.: Well, our illustration from hunting pigeons and getting possession of them will enable us to explain that the hunting occurs in two ways—first, before you possess your pigeon in order to have possession of it; secondly, after getting possession of it, in order to catch and hold in your hand what you have already possessed for some time. In the same way, if you have long possessed pieces of knowledge about things you have learned and know, it is still possible to get to know the same things again, by the process of recovering the knowledge of some particular thing and getting hold of it. It is knowledge you have possessed for some time, but you had not got it handy in your mind.

The.: True.

Soc.: That, then, was the drift of my question—what terms should be used to describe the arithmetician who sets about counting or the literate person who sets about reading—because it seemed as if, in such a case, the man was setting about learning again from himself what he already knew.

The.: That sounds odd, Socrates.

Soc.: Well, but can we say he is going to read or count something he does *not* know, when we have already granted that he knows all the letters or all the numbers?

The.: No, that is absurd too.

Soc.: Shall we say, then, that we care nothing about words, if it amuses anyone to turn and twist the expressions 'knowing' and 'learning'? Having drawn a distinction between possessing knowledge and having it about one, we agree that it is impossible not to possess what one does possess, and so we avoid the result that a man should not know what he does know, but we say that it is possible for him to get hold of a false judgment about it. For he may not have about him the knowledge of that thing but a different piece of knowledge instead, if it so happens that, in hunting for some particular piece of knowledge, among those that are fluttering about, he misses it and catches hold of a different one. In that case, you see, he mistakes eleven for twelve, because he has caught hold of the knowledge of eleven that is inside him, instead of his knowledge of twelve, as he might catch a dove in place of a pigeon.

The.: That seems reasonable.

Soc.: Whereas, when he catches the piece of knowledge he is trying to catch, he is not mistaken but thinks what is true. In this way both true and false judgments can exist, and the obstacles that were troubling us are removed. You will agree to this, perhaps? Or will you not?

The.: I will.

Soc.: Yes, for now we are rid of the contradiction about people not knowing what they do know. That no longer implies our not possessing what we do possess, whether we are mistaken about something or not. But it strikes me that a still stranger consequence is coming in sight.

The.: What is that?

Soc.: That the interchange of pieces of knowledge should ever result in a judgment that is false.

The.: How do you mean?

Soc.: In the first place, that a man should have knowledge of something and at the same time fail to recognize that very thing, not for want of knowing it but by reason of his own knowledge, and next that he should judge that thing to be something else and vice versa—isn't that very unreasonable, that when a piece of knowledge presents itself, the mind should fail to recognize anything and know nothing? On this showing, the presence of ignorance might just as well make us know something, or the presence of blindness make us see—if knowledge can ever make us fail to know.

The.: Perhaps, Socrates, we were wrong in making the birds stand for pieces of knowledge only, and we ought to have imagined pieces of ignorance flying about with them in the mind. Then, in chasing them, our man would lay hold sometimes of a piece of knowledge, sometimes of a piece of ignorance, and the ignorance would make him judge falsely, the knowledge truly, about the same thing.

Soc.: It is not easy to disapprove of anything you say, Theaetetus. . . .

2.3

Theory of Recollection (*Meno*)

Plato

Socrates. . . . What, according to you and your friend, is the definition of virtue?

Meno. O Socrates; I used to be told, before I knew you, that you are always puzzling yourself and others; and now you are casting your spells over me, and I am simply getting bewitched and enchanted, and am at my wits' end. And if I may venture to make a jest upon you, you seem to me both in your appearance and in your power over others to be very like the flat torpedo fish, who torpifies those who come near him with the touch, as you have now torpified me, I think. For my soul and my tongue are really torpid, and I do not know how to answer you; and though I have been delivered of an infinite variety of speeches about virtue before now, and to many persons—and very good ones they were, as I thought—now I can not even say what virtue is. And I think that you are very wise in not voyaging and going away from home, for if you did in other places as you do in Athens, you would be cast into prison as a magician.

Soc. You are a rogue, Meno, and had all but caught me. . . . As to my being a torpedo, if the torpedo is torpid as well as the cause of torpidity in others, then indeed I am a torpedo, but not otherwise; for I perplex others, not because I am clear, but because I am utterly perplexed myself. And now I know not what virtue is, and you seem to be in the same case, although you did once know before you touched me. However, I have no objection to join with you in the inquiry.

Men. And how will you inquire, Socrates, into that which you know not? What will you put forth as the subject of inquiry? And if you find what you want, how will you ever know that this is what you did not know?

Soc. I know, Meno, what you mean; but just see what a tiresome dispute you are introducing. You argue that a man cannot inquire either about that which he knows, or about that which he does not know; for he knows, and therefore has no need to inquire about that—nor about that which he does not know; for he does not know that about which he is to inquire.

From *Meno*, translated by Benjamin Jowett, pp. 25–36, Tudor Publishing Company, New York. First appeared in 1896.

Men. Well, Socrates, and is not the argument sound?

Soc. I think not.

Men. Why not?

Soc. I will tell you why. I have heard from certain wise men and women who spoke of things divine that—

Men. What did they say?

Soc. They spoke of a glorious truth, as I conceive.

Men. What was that? and who were they?

Soc. Some of them were priests and priestesses, who have studied how they might be able to give a reason of their profession: there have been poets also, such as the poet Pindar and other inspired men. And what they say is—mark, now, and see whether their words are true—they say that the soul of man is immortal, and at one time has an end, which is termed dying, and at another time is born again, but is never destroyed. And the moral is, that a man ought to live always in perfect holiness. For in the ninth year Persephone sends the souls of those from whom she has received the penalty of ancient crime back again into the light of this world, and these are they who become noble kings and mighty men and great in wisdom and are called saintly heroes in after ages. The soul, then, as being immortal, and having been born again many times, and having seen all things that there are, whether in this world or in the world below, has knowledge of them all; and it is no wonder that she should be able to call to remembrance all that she ever knew about virtue, and about everything; for as all nature is akin, and the soul has learned all things, there is no difficulty in her eliciting, or as men say learning, all out of a single recollection, if a man is strenuous and does not faint; for all inquiry and all learning is but recollection. And therefore we ought not to listen to this sophistical argument about the impossibility of inquiry that is a saying which will make us idle, and is sweet only to the sluggard; but the other saying will make us active and enterprising. In that confiding, I will gladly inquire with you into the nature of virtue.

Meno. Yes, Socrates; but what do you mean by saying that we do not learn, and that what we call learning is only a process of recollection? Can you teach me that?

Soc. I told you, Meno, that you were a rogue, and now you ask whether I can teach you, when I am saying that there is no teaching, but only recollection; and thus you imagine that you will involve me in a contradiction.

Men. Indeed, Socrates, I protest that I had no such intention. I only asked the question from habit; but if you can prove to me that what you say is true, I wish that you would.

Soc. That is no easy matter, but I will try to please you to the utmost of my power. Suppose that you call one of your numerous attendants, that I may demonstrate on him.

Men. Certainly. Come hither, boy.

Soc. He is Greek; and speaks Greek, does he not?

Men. Yes; he was born in the house.

Soc. Attend now to the questions which I ask him, and observe whether he learns of me or only remembers.

Men. I will.

Soc. Tell me, boy, do you know that a figure like this is a square?

Boy. I do.

Soc. And you know that a square figure has these four lines equal?

Boy. Certainly.

Soc. And these lines which I have drawn through the middle of the square are also equal?

Boy. Yes.

Soc. A square may be of any size?

Boy. Certainly.

Soc. And if one side of the figure be of two feet, and the other side be of two feet, how much will the whole be? Let me explain: if in one direction the space was of two feet, and in the other direction of one foot, the whole would be of two feet taken once?

Boy. Yes.

Soc. But since this side is also of two feet, there are twice two feet?

Boy. There are.

Soc. Then the square is of twice two feet?

Boy. Yes.

Soc. And how many are twice two feet? count and tell me.

Boy. Four, Socrates.

Soc. And might there not be another square twice as large as this, and having like this the lines equal?

Boy. Yes.

Soc. And of how many feet will that be?

Boy. Of eight feet.

Soc. And now try and tell me the length of the line which forms the side of that double square: this is two feet—what will that be?

Boy. Clearly, Socrates, that will be double.

Soc. Do you observe, Meno, that I am not teaching the boy anything, but only asking him questions; and now he fancies that he knows how long a line is necessary in order to produce a figure of eight square feet; does he not?

Men. Yes.

Soc. And does he really know?

Men. Certainly not.

Soc. He only guesses that [because the square is double], the line is double.

Men. True.

Soc. Observe him while he recalls the steps in regular order. (*To the Boy.*) Tell me, boy, do you assert that a double space comes from a double line? Remember that I am not speaking of an oblong, but of a square, and of a square twice the size of this one—that is to say of eight feet; and I want to know whether you still say that a double square comes from a double line?

Boy. Yes.

Soc. But does not this line become doubled if we add another such line here?

Boy. Certainly.

Soc. And four such lines will make a space containing eight feet?

Boy. Yes.

Soc. Let us describe such a figure: is not that what you would say is the figure of eight feet?

Boy. Yes.

Soc. And are there not these four divisions in the figure, each of which is equal to the figure of four feet?

Boy. True.

Soc. And is not that four times four?

Boy. Certainly.

Soc. And four times is not double.

Boy. No, indeed.

Soc. But how much?

Boy. Four times as much.

Soc. Therefore the double line, boy, has formed a space, not twice, but four times as much.

Boy. True.

Soc. And four times four are sixteen—are they not?

Boy. Yes.

Soc. What line would give you a space of eight feet, as this gives one of sixteen feet;—do you see?

Boy. Yes.

Soc. And the space of four feet is made from this half line?

Boy. Yes.

Soc. Good; and is not a space of eight feet twice the size of this, and half the size of the other?

Boy. Certainly.

Soc. Such a space, then, will be made out of a line greater than this one, and less than that one?

Boy. Yes, that is what I think.

Soc. Very good; I like to hear you say what you think. And now tell me, is not this a line of two feet and that of four?

Boy. Yes.

Soc. Then the line which forms the side of eight feet ought to be more than this line of two feet, and less than the other of four feet?

Boy. It ought.

Soc. Try and see if you can tell me how much it will be.

Boy. Three feet.

Soc. Then if we add a half to this line of two, that will be the line of three. Here are two and there is one; and on the other side here are two also and there is one: and that makes the figure of which you speak?

Boy. Yes.

Soc. But if there are three feet this way and three feet that way, the whole space will be three times three feet?

Boy. That is evident.

Soc. And how much are three times three feet?

Boy. Nine.

Soc. And how much is the double of four?

Boy. Eight.

Soc. Then the figure of eight is not made out of a line of three?

Boy. No.

Soc. But from what line?—tell me exactly; and if you would rather not reckon, try and show me the line.

Boy. Indeed, Socrates, I do not know.

Soc. Do you see, Meno, what advances he has made in his power of recollection? He did not know at first, and he does not know now, what is the side of a figure of eight feet but then he thought that he knew, and answered confidently as if he knew, and had no difficulty; but now he has a difficulty, and neither knows nor fancies that he knows.

Men. True.

Soc. Is he not better off in knowing his ignorance?

Men. I think that he is.

Soc. If we have made him doubt, and given him the "torpedo's shock," have we done him any harm?

Men. I think not.

Soc. We have certainly done something that may assist him in finding out the truth of the matter; and now he will wish to remedy his ignorance, but then he would have been ready to tell all the world that the double space should have a double side.

Men. True.

Soc. But do you suppose that he would ever have inquired or learned what he fancied that he knew and did not know, until he had fallen into perplexity under the idea that he did not know, and had desired to know?

Men. I think not, Socrates.

Soc. Then he was the better for the torpedo's touch?

Men. I think that he was.

Soc. Mark now the farther development. I shall only ask him, and not teach him, and he shall share the inquiry with me: and do you watch and see if you find me telling or explaining anything to him, instead of eliciting his opinion. Tell me, boy, is not this a square of four feet which I have drawn?

Boy. Yes.

Soc. And now I add another square equal to the former one?

Boy. Yes.

Soc. And a third, which is equal to either of them?

Boy. Yes.

Soc. Suppose that we fill up the vacant corner.

Boy. Very good.

Soc. Here, then, there are four equal spaces?

Boy. Yes.

Soc. And how many times is this space larger than this?

Boy. Four times.

Soc. But it ought to have been twice only, as you will remember.

Boy. True.

Soc. And does not this line, reaching from corner to corner, bisect each of these spaces?

Boy. Yes.

Soc. And are there not here four equal lines which contain this space?

Boy. There are.

Soc. Look and see how much this space is.

Boy. I do not understand.

Soc. Has not each interior line cut off half of the four spaces?

Boy. Yes.

Soc. And how many such spaces are there in this division?

Boy. Four.

Soc. And how many in this?

Boy. Two.

Soc. And four is how many times two?

Boy. Twice.

Soc. And this space is of how many feet?

Boy. Of eight feet.

Soc. And from what line do you get this figure?

Boy. From this.

Soc. That is, from the line which extends from corner to corner?

Boy. Yes.

Soc. And that is the line which the learned call the diagonal. And if this is the proper name, then you, Meno's slave, are prepared to affirm that the double space is the square of the diagonal?

Boy. Certainly, Socrates.

Soc. What do you say of him, Meno? Were not all these answers given out of his own head?

Men. Yes, they were all his own.

Soc. And yet, as we were just now saying, he did not know?

Men. True.

Soc. And yet he had those notions in him?

Men. Yes.

Soc. Then he who does not know still has true notions of that which he does not know?

Men. He has.

Soc. And at present these notions are just wakening up in him, as in a dream; but if he were frequently asked the same questions, in different forms, he would know as well as anyone at last?

Men. I dare say.

Soc. Without anyone teaching him he will recover his knowledge *for* himself, if he is only asked questions?

Men. Yes.

Soc. And this spontaneous recovery in him is recollection?

Men. True.

Soc. And this knowledge which he now has must he not either have acquired or always possessed?

Men. Yes.

Soc. But if he always possessed this knowledge he would always have known; or if he has acquired the knowledge, he could not have acquired it in this life, unless he has been taught geometry; for he may be made to do the same with all geometry and every other branch of knowledge. Now, has any one ever taught him? You must know that, if, as you say, he was born and bred in your house.

Men. And I am certain that no one ever did teach him.

Soc. And yet has he not the knowledge?

Men. That, Socrates, is most certain.

Soc. But if he did not acquire this knowledge in this life, then clearly he must have had and learned it at some other time?

Men. That is evident.

Soc. And that must have been the time when he was not a man?

Men. Yes.

Soc. And if there have been always true thoughts in him, both at the time when he was and was not a man, which only need to be awakened into knowledge by putting questions to him, his soul must have always possessed this knowledge, for he always either was or was not a man?

Men. That is clear.

Soc. And if the truth of all things always existed in the soul, then the soul is immortal. Wherefore be of good cheer, and try to recollect what you do not know, or rather do not remember.

Men. I feel, somehow, that I like what you are saying.

Soc. And I, Meno, like what I am saying. Some things I have said of which I am not altogether confident. But that we shall be better and braver and less helpless if we think that we ought to inquire, than we should have been if we indulged in the idle fancy that there was no knowing and no use in searching after what we know not;—that is a theme upon which I am ready to light, in word and deed, to the utmost of my power.

Men. That again, Socrates, appears to me to be well said.

2.4

Means of True Cognition

Gautama and Vātsyāyana

Nyāyasūtra:
The means of true cognition are: perception, inference, comparison, verbal utterance. (N.S. 1.1.3)

Commentary:
"*Pratyakṣa*" (perception) is the *vṛtti* of each sense organ to its object. The word "*vṛtti*" here means either contact or cognition. Wherever there is contact, there arises true cognition, where there is cognition, the result is the determination that the object is to be shunned or acquired.

Inference is: cognition of an object through an ascertained mark and after perception.

Comparison is: cognition of similarity as in "Gavaya is like a cow." Here similarity is relatedness to a universal property.

Verbal utterance is: that by which an object is spoken about, designated and made known.

The *pramāṇa*s are means for producing knowledge. The word "*pramāṇa*" is to be understood in the instrumental sense.

PERCEPTION (*PRATYAKṢA*): DEFINITION AND TYPES

Nyāyasūtra:
Perception is the knowledge which arises from the contact of a sense organ with its object and which is non-linguistic,[1] non-deviant with regard to its object and of the nature of certainty.[2] (N.S. 1.1.4)

From Gautama's Nyāyasūtra and Vātsyāyana's Commentary, chapter 1. Translated by J.N. Mohanty.

Commentary:

Perception is that knowledge which arises from the contact of sense organ with object. It may be objected that this is not so. (For) the self comes in contact with mind (*manas*), mind (*manas*) comes in contact with the sense organ, the sense organ with the object. (The first two contacts are not stated in the definition.). (We reply that) this is not intended to be a determination that this alone causes perception, it only states the specific cause (of perception). What however is a common cause of all cognitions such as inference etc., has not been denied. (The objector may retort.) Then the contact of mind with sense organ should be mentioned. (We reply that) this (contact) does not serve to distinguish the different distinguishable kinds of perceptual knowledge from each other.

All things have their own (respective) names; things are apprehended along with their names. Correct apprehension of a thing gives rise to (linguistic) behavior. Now, this knowledge of object arising from contact of a sense organ with its object, is either "this is color" or "this is taste." Words like "color" and "taste" are names for objects of such knowledge. With the help of these names, the knowledge is expressed as "I am knowing this (as) color," "I am knowing this (as) taste." Since the knowledge is thus expressed by name, let it be linguistic knowledge! Because of this, the author (of the *sūtra*) said "non-verbal" (*avyapadeśya*). If the relation between word and thing is not known, the knowledge of the thing is not expressed by the name. If the relation between word and the thing is known the knowledge that arises is (of the form): "This word is the name of this thing." When, however, that thing is known, that knowledge is not different from the preceding knowledge of that thing. That knowledge of the thing is exactly like the preceding one. The latter is not related to any name which being apprehended, it will be capable of being linguistically expressed. Nor is expression made possible by something that is not known. That is why, the knowledge of the thing is expressed by adding the word "*iti*" to the name of the thing known—as for example, "the knowledge '*rūpam iti*,' '*rasam iti*.'" Therefore, at the time of knowledge of the thing, the name does not come into operation. It comes into operation only during expressing the knowledge. Therefore, the knowledge of the thing that arises from contact of sense organ with the thing is non-linguistic.

During the summer, the moving sun rays in contact with the heat of the earth, come in contact with the eyes of a person in the distance. From this contact of sense organ with the thing, there arises a knowledge "water" whose object is the sunray. This knowledge also may be regarded as perception. Therefore (in order to exclude this case of hallucination), the author (of the *sūtra*) said "non-deviant." A knowledge is deviant if it is knowledge as such-and-such (*tat*) of an object which is not such-and-such (*tat*). Seeing a thing with the eyes from a distance, one does not ascertain if it is smoke or dust. This non-ascertaining cognition, arising from contact of sense organ with the thing, may be regarded as perception. Therefore (i.e., in order to exclude this), the author (of the *sūtra*) said "of the nature of certainty."

It cannot be held that the non-ascertaining knowledge is caused by the contact of the self with the mind (*manas*). For, this person, while seeing the thing with his eyes, fails to ascertain the thing. Furthermore, just as a thing that is apprehended by a sense organ, is (also) apprehended by the mind (*manas*), so also when a thing is not ascertained by the sense organ it is also not ascertained by the mind (*manas*). This non-ascertainment by the mind (*manas*) (which is) consequent upon non-ascertainment by the sense organ, and which presupposes cognition of the specific (alternatives)—this cognition (of two incompatible properties in one and the same thing) is doubt (and this is what the author of the *sūtra* has in mind), not the former one (i.e., the doubt which arises only from the contact of the self with *manas*). In every case of perception, the knower ascertains the object by means of the sense organ; for, persons whose sense organ has been destroyed do not have the (appropriate) secondary (mental) perception (of the putative perceptual cognition.)

(It may be said that) a (different) definition of perception is needed in the case of (perception of) self etc.[3] and pleasure etc.,[4] for such perception is not a result of contact of sense organ with the thing (being perceived). (The reply to this is that) although mind (*manas*) is a sense organ, it is enumerated as different from sense organs because of its distinctive properties. The sense organs are made of the (five) elements, each of them has a determinate object, they have qualities with regard to which they function as sense-organs. Mind, however, is not made out of the elements and it can have everything as its object, its being a sense organ is not determined by its having a determinate quality. We shall say that given contact of sense organs with things, the non-emergence of simultaneous cognitions (of many objects) is due to the conjunction or absence of conjunction of the mind (*manas*) with some sense organ (or other). Since *manas* is a sense organ, a separate definition need not be given. That mind (*manas*) is a sense organ can be ascertained from (the author's) not contradicting agreement (i.e., lack of critique) of other views. The principle (*tantrayuktiḥ*) is: when the other's view is not contradicted or opposed, it is (to be taken as) one's own view. With this perception is explained.

NOTES

1. This refers to the Nyāya view that perception at the initial stage is non-linguistic or *nirvikalpaka,* then becomes linguistic or *savikalpaka.*

2. This distinguishes perception from doubt that may arise from contact of a sense organ with an object.

3. Here "etc." refers to such universals as "knowledge-ness."

4. Here "etc." refers to non-eternal cognitions, desire, hatred, effort, and pain.

2.5

Cognition Generated by a Sentence

Dharmarāja

Now, *āgama*[1] or *śabda*[2] as a *pramāṇa*[3] is being determined.

A sentence is a *pramāṇa*, if its relatedness to what has become its object by its significative intention is not contradicted by any other *pramāṇa*.

There are four causes of a cognition generated by a sentence: expectation, appropriateness, contiguity, and knowledge of intention.

"Expectation"[4] is (defined as) the appropriateness of the designated entities to be objects of enquiry of each other. On hearing a (word designating a) verb, the idea of the noun to which the verb relates becomes the object of desire to know; on hearing the noun with a case-ending, one wants to know the verb; on hearing what is to be done, one desires to know "how to be done?" . . .

"Appropriateness"[5] is (defined as) absence of contradiction of the relatedness amongst the purported (intended) meanings. Thus, since in the case of "He sprinkles with fire" there is such a contradiction of relatedness (between "sprinkling" and "fire"), there is no appropriateness. . . . In the case of sentences like "thou art that,"[6] although identity between the designated entities is contradicted, there is non-difference amongst the mediate meanings and so no contradiction, and therefore there is appropriateness.

"Contiguity" is the presentation of the object brought about by a word in immediate succession.[7] Here "brought about by a word" is inserted in order to exclude cases where an object is presented by other *pramāṇas* (such as perception or inference). When a word is not mentioned (as in "the door"), the appropriate word has to be assumed ("close").

Meanings (or meant entities)[8] are of two kinds: the immediate designation and the mediate designation. The immediate relation of a word to an object is called "*śakti*," as in the case of the application of the word "pot" to something having the shape of fat belly.

From *Vedānta Paribhāṣā*, chapter 4. Translated by J.N. Mohanty.

This power or *śakti* is a separate entity.[9] According to us, the power in a cause to produce its effect is a distinct entity. A word's power produces knowledge of its meaning. The existence of such a power is to be inferred from the effect, i.e., the appropriate cognition. To be the object of such power is to be a *śakya*.

This property of being the *śakya* (i.e., the immediate or [primary] meaning) resides in the universal, not in particulars. Particulars are infinite in number, hence (if particular cows are taken to be the primary meaning of the word "cow"), there would be multiplication of entities (i.e., a power corresponding to each particular). How then is cognition of particulars made possible by words such as "cow"? (To this question) we reply: on our view, the universal and particulars (coming under it) are known (together) by the same knowledge, or (alternately, we can reply), the words such as "cow" possess the power which by itself, not as known, signifies the particulars, whereas in the case of universal, the power must be known in order to signify it. To suppose that also in the case of particulars, knowledge of power is required, would be unnecessary, for knowledge of particulars immediately follows from knowledge of a word's power to designate the universal.

Whatever is the object of known power, is the direct referent of a word. That is why the particular is not a direct referent, only the universal is. Alternately, the particular is known by mediate meaning, just as in "blue pot." The word "blue" indirectly signifies "having the blue color." Likewise, a word directly refers to a universal but may be regarded as mediately signifying particulars who are qualified by that universal. What cannot be known by mediate signification is the direct referent, such is the universal.

Now, the mediate designation is being determined. The object of mediate designation is called the *lakṣya*. The meaning is of two kinds: "meremediate meaning" and "mediately mediate meaning." The former is the case when there is a direct relation to the primary meaning, as in the case of "the village on the Ganges." The word "Ganges" mediately designates the bank of the river which is directly related to the stream of water (which is the primary meaning of the word).

The second i.e., "mediately mediate meaning" obtains where a quite different object is presented by relatedness to the primary meaning through a chain of relations. For example, the word "*dvirepha*" primarily means a word which has two occurrences of "r," mediately designates the word "*bhramara*" (which has two occurrences of "r"), and mediately—mediately designates the honey-bee (primarily designated by the last mentioned word "*bhramara*").

Considered in another way, mediate meaning is of three kinds: first, where the mediate designation gives up the primary meaning; secondly, where the mediate designation does not give up the primary meaning; and, finally, where the mediate designation partly retains and partly gives up the primary meaning. In the first case, the object that is mediately meant does not include the primary meaning, just as the sentence "take poison" drops its primary meaning and mediately means "do not eat in your enemy's house." The second occurs where the mediate designation is presented inclusive of the primary meaning, just as in the expression "white jar," the word "white" relates to the white substance while still including its primary meaning, i.e., white color. The third occurs where a word primarily designating a qualified entity refers to one part of it while giving up the other part. as in the case of "He is this Devadatta," where, since identity between the two qualified entities is not possible, the identity holds good only between the two substantives. Or, in cases such as "That art Thou" since identity between the referent of "that" i.e., the being which possesses such qualities as omniscience and the referent of "thou" i.e., being which is qualified by the inner sense, is impossible, in order to establish identity, the mediate designation (in each case) is the own nature (of the entity under consideration). Such is the view of some.

[The last cause of cognition generated by a sentence is knowledge of intention. Here intention (*tātparya*) is to be understood as: The ability of a sentence to generate knowledge of that, where the speaker does not intend, by uttering the sentence, to generate cognition of something else. The latter clause "where. . ." is meant to exclude cases of ambiguous or equivocal words such as "*saindhava*" which, in Sanskrit means, both horse (of a certain kind) and salt.

NOTES

1. "*Āgama*" means tradition, also scriptures.

2. "*Śabda*" is sound; in the present context, it means sentence or text.

3. "*Pramāṇa*" means source or instrument of true cognition.

4. This is the requirement that the succeeding word must satisfy the expectations aroused by the preceding word.

5. Words must be semantically appropriate. In the example given in the text, fire is not appropriate for sprinkling, water is.

6. This is a sentence from the Upaniṣads asserting the identity of the finite individual and the universal self. We get the mediate meanings by abstracting from the individuating features of the individual self.

7. An utterance is not utterance of a sentence, if the word-utterances are not contiguous in time, i.e., if a minute, for example lapses between two word-utterances.

8. Meanings, on the great majority of Indian philosophies, are but meant entities—although there is a difference of opinion as to whether these entities are universal or particulars.

9. The Mīmāṃsā philosophers recognize "power" as a separate type of entity. The Nyāya school rejects this contention.

2.6

Cognition

Śrī Dharmakīrti

All human ends are reached after true knowledge. Therefore, in this work, true knowledge is being expounded.

True knowledge is of two kinds: perception and inference.

Of these, perception is the knowledge that is free from imagination and is unerring.

It is free from imagination, which is the appearance of an object that is capable of being related to a name.

It is [also] such cognition that does not contain error that is due to such causes as darkness,[1] quick movement,[2] moving on a boat [on a river][3] and aggravation of biles and cough[4] etc.

Perception [so defined] is of four kinds:

(1) Cognition by means of the senses.
(2) Mental cognition [which] follows sense-cognition which is its immediate homogenous cause, in cooperation with the object, which immediately follows the object of sense-cognition.[5]
(3) Self-cognition[6] is manifestation of every consciousness and every mental phenomena to itself.
(4) The cognition of the Yogin,[7] which arises from repeated thinking of the reality, when such thinking reaches a perfection that cannot be exceeded.

Its object is the particular having its own unique nature.[8] This object, with its own unique nature, is that whose nearness or not-nearness gives rise to differences in the manifestation of cognition.[9] That is ultimately real, for it alone gives rise to the power of causal efficacy of things.[10]

From *Nyāyabindu,* chapter 1. Translated by J.N. Mohanty.

What is other than it is universal object,[11] which is the object of inferential cognition.

Perceptual cognition is the result of *pramāṇa*,[12] being of the nature of cognition of the object.

Pramāṇa consists in a cognition's similarity to the object.[13]

Because of it, cognition of object is possible.

NOTES

1. Darkness makes one mistake a rope for a snake.
2. Quick circular motion of a stick on fire looks like a circular band of fire.
3. Being on a moving boat, one perceives things on the bank as if they are moving
4. These aggravations of the bodily chemicals make one's eyes jaundiced so that one sees all things as yellow.
5. The Buddhist view is that mental cognition follows the sense-cognition of an object.
6. On the Buddhist view, every mental state is self-manifesting, it apprehends itself.
7. The *yogis* know a thing as a result of repeated thinking about it.
8. Here "its object" is the object of perception. The object of perception is the pure particular, the unique particular (not instantiating any universal).
9. This is a definition of the unique particular.
10. The Buddhist here defines the real as what is capable of being causally efficacious.
11. Contrasted with the unique particular is the universal object.
12. Perception as a means of knowing produces perception as a true cognition.
13. Here "*pramāṇa*" means "truth." Truth is "similarity" between cognition and its object.

2.7

Deliverance from Error

Al-Ghazāli

To thirst after a comprehension of things as they really are was my habit and custom from a very early age. It was instinctive with me, a part of my God-given nature, a matter of temperament and not of my choice or contriving. Consequently as I drew near the age of adolescence the bonds of mere authority (*taqlīd*) ceased to hold me and inherited beliefs lost their grip upon me, for I saw that Christian youths always grew up to be Christians, Jewish youths to be Jews and Muslim youths to be Muslims. I heard, too, the Tradition related of the Prophet of God according to which he said: "Everyone who is born is born with a sound nature; it is his parents who make him a Jew or a Christian or a Magian." My inmost being was moved to discover what this original nature really was and what the beliefs derived from the authority of parents and teachers really were. The attempt to distinguish between these authority-based opinions and their principles developed the mind, for in distinguishing the true in them from the false differences appeared.

I therefore said within myself: "To begin with, what I am looking for is knowledge of what things really are, so I must undoubtedly try to find what knowledge really is." It was plain to me that sure and certain knowledge is that knowledge in which the object is disclosed in such a fashion that no doubt remains along with it, that no possibility of error or illusion accompanies it, and that the mind cannot even entertain such a supposition. Certain knowledge must also be infallible; and this infallibility or security from error is such that no attempt to show the falsity of the knowledge can occasion doubt or denial, even though the attempt is made by someone who turns stones into gold or a rod into a serpent. Thus, I know that ten is more

---

From chapters 2, 3, & 4 of *The Faith and Practice of Al-Ghazāli*, translated by W. Montgomery Watt, pp. 21–68. Copyright © by George Allen and Unwin, Oct. 1953. Footnotes have been deleted.

than three. Let us suppose that someone says to me: "No, three is more than ten, and in proof of that I shall change this rod into a serpent"; and let us suppose that he actually changes the rod into a serpent and that I witness him doing so. No doubts about what I know are raised in me because of this. The only result is that I wonder precisely how he is able to produce this change. Of doubt about my knowledge there is no trace.

After these reflections I knew that whatever I do not know in this fashion and with this mode of certainty is not reliable and infallible knowledge; and knowledge that is not infallible is not certain knowledge.

PRELIMINARIES:
SKEPTICISM AND THE DENIAL OF ALL KNOWLEDGE

Thereupon I investigated the various kinds of knowledge I had, and found myself destitute of all knowledge with this characteristic of infallibility except in the case of sense-perception and necessary truths. So I said: "Now that despair has come over me, there is no point in studying any problems except on the basis of what is self-evident, namely, necessary truths and the affirmations of the senses. I must first bring these to be judged in order that I may be certain on this matter. Is my reliance on sense-perception and my trust in the soundness of necessary truths of the same kind as my previous trust in the beliefs I had merely taken over from others and as the trust most men have in the results of thinking? Or is it a justified trust that is in no danger of being betrayed or destroyed?"

I proceeded therefore with extreme earnestness to reflect on sense-perception and on necessary truths, to see whether I could make myself doubt them. The outcome of this protracted effort to induce doubt was that I could no longer trust sense-perception either. Doubt began to spread here and say: "From where does this reliance on sense-perception come? The most powerful sense is that of sight. Yet when it looks at the shadow (*Sc.* of a stick or the gnomon of a sun dial), it sees it standing still, and judges that there is no motion. Then by experiment and observation after an hour it knows that the shadow is moving and, moreover, that it is moving not by fits and starts but gradually and steadily by infinitely small distances in such a way that it is never in a state of rest. Again, it looks at the heavenly body (*sc.* the sun) and sees it small, the size of a shilling; yet geometrical computations show that it is greater than the earth in size."

In this and similar cases of sense-perception the sense as judge forms his judgments, but another judge, the intellect, shows him repeatedly to be wrong; and the charge of falsity cannot be rebutted.

To this I said: "My reliance on sense-perception also has been destroyed. Perhaps only those intellectual truths which are first principles (or derived from first principles) are to be relied upon, such as the assertion that ten are more than three, that the same thing cannot be both affirmed and denied at one time, that one thing is not both generated in time and eternal, nor both existent and non-existent, nor both necessary and impossible."

Sense-perception replied: "Do you not expect that your reliance on intellectual truths will fare like your reliance on sense-perception? You used to trust in me; then along came the intellect-judge and proved me wrong; if it were not for the intellect-judge you would have continued to regard me as true. Perhaps behind intellectual apprehension there is another judge who, if he manifests himself, will show the falsity of intellect in its judging, just as, when intellect manifested itself, it showed the falsity of sense in its judging. The fact that such a supra-intellectual apprehension has not manifested itself is no proof that it is impossible."

My ego hesitated a little about the reply to that, and sense-perception heightened the difficulty by referring to dreams. "Do you not see," it said, "how, when you are asleep, you believe things and imagine circumstances, holding them to be stable and enduring, and, so long as you are in that dream-condition, have no doubts about them? And is it not the case that when you awake you know that all you have imagined and believed is unfounded and ineffectual? Why then are you confident that all your waking beliefs, whether from sense or intellect, are genuine? They are true in respect of your present state; but it is possible that a state will come upon you whose relation to your waking consciousness is analogous to the relation of the latter to dreaming. In comparison with this state your waking consciousness would be like dreaming! When you have entered into this state, you will be certain that all the suppositions of your intellect are empty imaginings. It may be that that state is what the Sufis claim as their special 'state' (*sc.* mystic union or ecstasy), for they consider that in their 'states' (or ecstasies), which occur when they have withdrawn into themselves and are absent from their senses, they witness states (or circumstances) which do not tally with these principles of the intellect. Perhaps that 'state' is death; for the Messenger of God (God bless and preserve him) says: 'The people are dreaming; when they die, they become awake.' So perhaps life in this world is a dream by comparison with the world to come; and when a man dies, things come to appear differently to him from what he now beholds, and at the same time the words are addressed to him: 'We have taken off thee thy covering, and thy sight today is sharp'" (Q. 50, 21).

When these thoughts had occurred to me and penetrated my being, I tried to find some way of treating my unhealthy condition; but it was not easy. Such ideas can only be repelled by demonstration; but a demonstration requires a knowledge of first principles; since this is not admitted, however, it is impossible to make the demonstration. The disease was baffling, and lasted almost two months, during which I was a skeptic in fact though not in theory nor in outward expression. At length God cured me of the malady; my being was restored to health and an even balance; the necessary truths of the intellect became once more accepted, as I regained confidence in their certain and trustworthy character.

This did not come about by systematic demonstration or marshalled argument, but by a light which God most high cast into my breast. That light is the key to the greater part of knowledge. Whoever thinks that the understanding of things Divine rests upon strict proofs has in his thought narrowed down the wideness of God's mercy. When the Messenger of God (peace be upon him) was asked about "enlarging" (*sharhy*) and its meaning in the verse, "Whenever God wills to guide a man, He enlarges his breast for *islām* (i.e., surrender to God)" (Q. 6, 125), he said, "It is a light which God most high casts into the heart." When asked, "What is the sign of it?" he said, "Withdrawal from the mansion of deception and return to the mansion of eternity." It was about this light that Muhammad (peace be upon him) said, "God created the creatures in darkness, and then sprinkled upon them some of His light." From that light must be sought an intuitive understanding of things Divine. That light at certain times gushes from the spring of Divine generosity, and for it one must watch and wait—as Muhammad (peace be upon him) said: "In the days of your age your Lord has gusts of favor; then place yourselves in the way of them."

The point of these accounts is that the task is perfectly fulfilled when the quest is prosecuted up to the stage of seeking what is not sought (but stops short of that). For first principles are not sought, since they are present and to hand; and if what is present is sought for, it becomes hidden and lost. When, however, a man seeks what is sought (and that only), he is not accused of falling short in the seeking of what is sought.

THE WAYS OF MYSTICISM

I knew that the complete mystic "way" includes both intellectual belief and practical activity; the latter consists in getting rid of the obstacles in the self and in stripping off its base characteristics and vicious morals, so that the heart may attain to freedom from what is not God and to constant recollection of Him.

The intellectual belief was easier to me than the practical activity. I began to acquaint myself with their belief by reading their books, such as *The Food of the Hearts* by Abū Ṭālib al-Makkī (God have mercy upon him), the works of al-Ḥārith al-Muḥāsibī, the various anecdotes about al-Junayd, ash-Shiblī and Abū Yazīd al-Bisṭāmī (may God sanctify their spirits), and other discourses of their leading men. I thus comprehended their fundamental teachings on the intellectual side, and progressed, as far as is possible by study and oral instruction, in the knowledge of mysticism. It became clear to me, however, that what is most distinctive of mysticism is something which cannot be apprehended by study, but only by immediate experience (*dhawq*— literally "tasting"), by ecstasy and by a moral change. What a difference there is between *knowing* the definition of health and satiety, together with their causes and presuppositions, and *being* healthy and satisfied! What a difference between being acquainted with the definition of drunkenness— namely, that it designates a state arising from the domination of the seat of the intellect by vapours arising from the stomach—and being drunk! Indeed, the drunken man while in that condition does not know the definition of drunkenness nor the scientific account of it; he has not the very least scientific knowledge of it. The sober man, on the other hand, knows the definition of drunkenness and its basis, yet he is not drunk in the very least. Again the doctor, when he is himself ill, knows the definition and causes of health and the remedies which restore it, and yet is lacking in health. Similarly there is a difference between knowing the true nature and causes and conditions of the ascetic life and actually leading such a life and forsaking the world.

I apprehended clearly that the mystics were men who had real experiences, not men of words, and that I had already progressed as far as was possible by way of intellectual apprehension. What remained for me was not to be attained by oral instruction and study but only by immediate experience and by walking in the mystic way.

Now from the sciences I had labored at and the paths I had traversed in my investigation of the revelational and rational sciences (that is, presumably, theology and philosophy), there had come to me a sure faith in God most high, in prophethood (or revelation), and in the Last Day. These three creedal principles were firmly rooted in my being, not through any carefully argued proofs, but by reason of various causes, coincidences and experiences which are not capable of being stated in detail.

It had already become clear to me that I had no hope of the bliss of the world to come save through a God-fearing life and the withdrawal of myself from vain desire. It was clear to me too that the key to all this was to sever the attachment of the heart to worldly things by leaving the mansion of deception and returning to that of eternity, and to advance towards God most high with all earnestness. It was also clear that this was only to be achieved by turning away from wealth and position and fleeing from all time-consuming entanglements.

Next I considered the circumstances of my life, and realized that I was caught in a veritable thicket of attachments. I also considered my activities, of which the best was my teaching and lecturing, and realized that in them I was dealing with sciences that were unimportant and contributed nothing to the attainment of eternal life.

After that I examined my motive in my work of teaching, and realized that it was not a pure desire for the things of God, but that the impulse moving me was the desire for an influential position and public recognition. I saw for certain that I was on the brink of a crumbling bank of sand and in imminent danger of hell-fire unless I set about to mend my ways.

I reflected on this continuously for a time, while the choice still remained open to me. One day I would form the resolution to quit Baghdad and get rid of these adverse circumstances; the next day I would abandon my resolution. I put one foot forward and drew the other back. If in the morning I had a genuine longing to seek eternal life, by the evening the attack of a whole host of desires had reduced it to impotence. Worldly desires were striving to keep me by their chains just where I was, while the voice of faith was calling, "To the road! to the road! What is left of life is but little and the journey before you is long. All that keeps you busy, both intellectually and practically, is but hypocrisy and delusion. If you do not prepare *now* for eternal life, when will you prepare? If you do not now sever these attachments, when will you sever them?" On hearing that, the impulse would be stirred and the resolution made to take to flight. . . .

I left Baghdad, then. I distributed what wealth I had, retaining only as much as would suffice myself and provide sustenance for my children. This I could easily manage, as the wealth of Iraq was available for good works, since it constitutes a trust fund for the benefit of the Muslims. No where in the world have I seen better financial arrangements to assist a scholar to provide for his children.

In general, then, how is a mystic "way" (*tariqah*) described? The purity which is the first condition of it (*sc.* as bodily purity is the prior condition of formal Worship for Muslims) is the purification of the heart completely from what is other than God most high; the key to it, which corresponds to the opening act of adoration in prayer, is the sinking of the heart completely in the recollection of God; and the end of it is complete absorption (*fanā'*) in God. At least this is its end relatively to those first steps which almost come within the sphere of choice and personal responsibility; but in reality in the actual mystic "way" it is the first step, what comes before it being, as it were, the ante-chamber for those who are journeying towards it.

With this first stage of the "way" there begin the revelations and visions. The mystics in their waking state now behold angels and the spirits of the prophets; they hear these speaking to them and are instructed by them. Later, a higher state is reached; instead of beholding forms and figures, they come to stages in the "way" which it is hard to describe in language; if a man attempts to express these, his words inevitably contain what is clearly erroneous.

In general what they manage to achieve is nearness to God; some, however, would conceive of this as "inherence" (*ḥulūl*), some as "union" (*ittiḥad*), and some as "connection" (*wuṣūl*). All that is erroneous. In my book, *The Noblest Aim,* I have explained the nature of the error here. Yet he who has attained the mystic state" need do no more than say:

> Of the things I do not remember, what was, was;
> Think it good; do not ask an account of it

(Ibn al-Mu'tazz)

In general the man to whom He has granted no immediate experience at all, apprehends no more of what prophetic revelation really is than the name. The miraculous graces given to the saints are in truth the beginnings of the prophets; and that was the first "state" of the Messenger of God (peace be upon him) when he went out to Mount Ḥirā', and was given up entirely to his Lord, and worshipped, so that the bedouin said, "Muhammad loves his Lord passionately."

Now this is a mystical "state" which is realized in immediate experience by those who walk in the way leading to it. Those to whom it is not granted to have immediate experience can become assured of it by trial (*sc.* contact with mystics or observation of them) and by hearsay, if they have sufficiently numerous opportunities of associating with mystics to understand that (*sc.* ecstasy) with certainty by means of what accompanies the "states." Whoever sits in their company derives from them this faith; and none who sits in their company is pained.

Those to whom it is not even granted to have contacts with mystics may know with certainty the possibility of ecstasy by the evidence of demonstration, as I have remarked in the section entitled *The Wonders of the Heart* of my *Revival of the Religious Sciences.*

Certainty reached by demonstration is *knowledge* (*'ilm*); actual acquaintance with that "state" is *immediate experience* (*dhawq*); the acceptance of it as probable from hearsay and trial (or observation) is *faith* (*īmān*). These are three degrees. "God will raise those of you who have faith and those who have been given knowledge in degrees (*sc.* of honor)" (Q. 58, 12).

Behind the mystics, however, there is a crowd of ignorant people. They deny this fundamentally, they are astonished at this line of thought, they listen and mock. "Amazing," they say. "What nonsense they talk!" About such people God most high has said: "Some of them listen to you, until, upon going out from you, they say to those to whom knowledge has been given, 'What did he say just now?' These are the people on whose hearts God sets a seal and they follow their passions" (Q. 47, 18). He makes them deaf, and blinds their sight.

Among the things that necessarily became clear to me from my practice of the mystic "way" was the true nature and special characteristics of prophetic revelation. The basis of that must undoubtedly be indicated in view of the urgent need for it.

THE TRUE NATURE OF PROPHECY AND THE
COMPELLING NEED OF ALL CREATION FOR IT

You must know that the substance of man in his original condition was created in bareness and simplicity without any information about the worlds of God most high. These worlds are many, not to be reckoned save by God most high Himself. As He said, "None knows the hosts of thy Lord save He" (Q. 74, 34). Man's information about the world is by means of perception; and every perception of perceptibles is created so that thereby man may have some acquaintance with a world (or sphere) from among existents. By "worlds (or spheres)" we simply mean "classes of existents."

The first thing created in man was the sense of *touch,* and by it he perceives certain classes of existents, such as heat and cold, moisture and dryness, smoothness and roughness. Touch is completely unable to apprehend colors and noises. These might be non-existent so far as concerns touch.

Next there is created in him the sense of *sight* and by it he apprehends colors and shapes. This is the most extensive of the worlds of sensibles. Next *hearing* is implanted in him, so that he hears sounds of various kinds. After that *taste* is created in him; and so on until he has completed the world of sensibles.

Next, when he is about seven years old, there is created in him *discernment* (or the power of distinguishing—*tamyīz*). This is a fresh stage in his development. He now apprehends more than the world of sensibles; and none of these additional factors (*sc.* relations, etc.) exists in the world of sense.

From this he ascends to another stage, and *intellect* (or reason) (*'aql*) is created in him. He apprehends things necessary, possible, impossible, things which do not occur in the previous stages.

Beyond intellect there is yet another stage. In this another eye is opened, by which he beholds the unseen, what is to be in the future, and other things which are beyond the ken of intellect in the same way as the objects of intellect are beyond the ken of the faculty of discernment and the objects of discernment are beyond the ken of sense. Moreover, just as the man at the stage of discernment would reject and disregard the objects of intellect were these to be presented to him, so some intellectuals reject and disregard the objects of prophetic revelation. That is sheer ignorance. They have no ground for their view except that this is a stage which they have not reached and which for them does not exist; yet they suppose that it is non-existent in itself. When a man blind from birth, who has not learnt about colors and shapes by listening to people's talk, is told about these things for the first time, he does not understand them nor admit their existence.

God most high, however, has favored His creatures by giving them something analogous to the special faculty of prophecy, namely dreams. In the dream-state a man apprehends what is to be in the future, which is something of the unseen; he does so either explicitly or else clothed in a symbolic form whose interpretation is disclosed.

Suppose a man has not experienced this himself, and suppose that he is told how some people fall into a dead faint, in which hearing, sight and the other senses no longer function, and in this condition perceive the unseen. He would deny that this is so and demonstrate its impossibility. "The sensible powers," he would say, "are the causes of perception (or apprehension); if a man does not perceive things (*sc.* the unseen) when these powers are actively present, much less will he do so when the senses are not functioning." This is a form of analogy which is shown to be false by what actually occurs and is observed. Just as intellect is one of the stages of human development in which there is an "eye" which sees the various types of intelligible objects, which are beyond the ken of the senses, so prophecy also is the description of a stage in which there is an eye endowed with light such that in that light the unseen and other supra-intellectual objects become visible.

Doubt about prophetic revelation is either (a) doubt of its possibility in general, or (b) doubt of its actual occurrence, or (c) doubt of the attainment of it by a specific individual.

The proof of the possibility of there being prophecy and the proof that there has been prophecy is that there is knowledge in the world the attainment of which by reason is inconceivable; for example, in medical science and astronomy. Whoever researches in such matters knows of necessity that this knowledge is attained only by Divine inspiration and by assistance from God most high. It cannot be reached by observation. For instance there are some astronomical laws based on phenomena which occur only once in a thousand years; how can these be arrived at by personal observation? It is the same with the properties of drugs.

This argument shows that it is possible for there to be a way of apprehending these matters which are not apprehended by the intellect. This is the meaning of prophetic revelation. That is not to say that prophecy is merely an expression for such knowledge. Rather, the apprehending of this class of extra-intellectual objects is *one* of the properties of prophecy; but it has many other properties as well. The said property is but a drop in the ocean of prophecy. It has been singled out for mention because you have something analogous to it in what you apprehend in dreaming, and because you have medical and astronomical knowledge belonging to the same class, namely, the miracles of the prophets, for the intellectuals cannot arrive at these at all by any intellectual efforts.

The other properties of prophetic revelation are apprehended only by immediate experience (*dhawq*) from the practice of the mystic way, but this property of prophecy you can understand by an analogy granted you, namely, the dream-state. If it were not for the latter you would not believe in that. If the prophet possessed a faculty to which you had nothing analogous and which you did not understand, how could you believe in it? Believing presupposes understanding. Now that analogous experience comes to a man in the early stages of the mystic way. Thereby he attains to a kind of immediate experience, extending as far as that to which he has attained, and by analogy to a kind of belief (or assent) in respect of that to which he has not attained. Thus this single property is a sufficient basis for one's faith in the principle of prophecy.

If you come to doubt whether a specific person is a prophet or not, certainty can only be reached by acquaintance with his conduct, either by personal observation, or by hearsay as a matter of common knowledge. For example, if you are familiar with medicine and law, you can recognize lawyers and doctors by observing what they are, or, where observation is impossible, by hearing what they have to say. Thus you are not unable to recognize that al-Shāfi'ī (God have mercy upon him) is a lawyer and Galen a doctor; and your recognition is based on the facts and not on the judgment of someone else. Indeed, just because you have some knowledge of law and medicine, and examine their books and writings, you arrive at a necessary knowledge of what these men are.

Similarly, if you understand what it is to be a prophet, and have devoted much time to the study of the Qur'ān and the Traditions, you will arrive at a necessary knowledge of the fact that Muhammad (God bless and preserve him) is in the highest grades of the prophetic calling. Convince yourself of that by trying out what he said about the influence of devotional practices on the purification of the heart—how truly he asserted that "whoever lives out what he knows will receive from God what he does not know"; how truly he asserted that "if anyone aids an evil-doer, God will give that man power over him"; how truly he asserted that "if a man rises up in the morning with but a single care (*sc.* to please God), God most high will preserve him from all cares in this world and the next." When you have made trial of these in a thousand or several thousand instances, you will arrive at a necessary knowledge beyond all doubt.

By this method, then, seek certainty about the prophetic office, and not from the transformation of a rod into a serpent or the cleaving of the moon. For if you consider such an event by itself, without taking account of the numerous circumstances accompanying it—circumstances readily eluding the grasp of the intellect—then you might perhaps suppose that it was magic and deception and that it came from God to lead men astray; for "He leads astray whom He will, and guides whom He will." Thus the topic of miracles will be thrown back upon you; for if your faith is based on a reasoned argument involving the probative force of the miracle, then your faith is destroyed by an ordered argument showing the difficulty and ambiguity of the miracle.

Admit, then, that wonders of this sort are one of the proofs and accompanying circumstances out of the totality of your thought on the matter; and that you attain necessary knowledge and yet are unable to say specifically on what it is based. The case is similar to that of a man who receives from a multitude of people a piece of information which is a matter of common belief. . . . He is unable to say that the certainty is derived from the remark of a single specific person; rather, its source is unknown to him; it is neither from outside the whole, nor is it from specific individuals. This is strong, intellectual faith. Immediate experience, on the other hand, is like actually witnessing a thing and taking it in one's hand. It is only found in the way of mysticism.

2.8

Meditations

René Descartes

MEDITATION ON FIRST PHILOSOPHY—

in which are demonstrated the existence of God and the distinction between the human soul and the body

FIRST MEDITATION: WHAT CAN BE CALLED INTO DOUBT

Some years ago I was struck by the large number of falsehoods that I had accepted as true in my childhood, and by the highly doubtful nature of the whole edifice that I had subsequently based on them. I realized that it was necessary, once in the course of my life, to demolish everything completely and start again right from the foundations if I wanted to establish anything at all in the sciences that was stable and likely to last. But the task looked an enormous one, and I began to wait until I should reach a mature enough age to ensure that no subsequent time of life would be more suitable for tackling such inquiries. This led me to put the project off for so long that I would now be to blame if by pondering over it any further I wasted the time still left for carrying it out. So today I have expressly rid my mind of all worries and arranged for myself a clear stretch of free time. I am here quite alone, and at last I will devote myself sincerely and without reservation to the general demolition of my opinions. But to accomplish this, it will not be necessary for me to show that all my opinions are false, which is something I could perhaps never manage. Reason now leads me to think that I should hold back my assent from opinions which are not completely certain and indubitable

just as carefully as I do from those which are patently false. So, for the purpose of rejecting all my opinions, it will be enough if I find in each of them
at least some reason for doubt. And to do this I will not need to run through
them all individually, which would be an endless task. Once the foundations
of a building are undermined, anything built on them collapses of its own
accord; so I will go straight for the basic principles on which all my former
beliefs rested.

Whatever I have up till now accepted as most true I have acquired either
from the senses or through the senses. But from time to time I have found
that the senses deceive, and it is prudent never to trust completely those
who have deceived us even once.

Yet although the senses occasionally deceive us with respect to objects
which are very small or in the distance, there are many other beliefs about
which doubt is quite impossible, even though they are derived from the
senses—for example, that I am here, sitting by the fire, wearing a winter
dressing-gown, holding this piece of paper in my hands, and so on. Again,
how could it be denied that these hands or this whole body are mine? Unless perhaps I were to liken myself to madmen, whose brains are so damaged by the persistent vapours of melancholia that they firmly maintain they
are kings when they are paupers, or say they are dressed in purple when
they are naked, or that their heads are made of earthenware, or that they are
pumpkins, or made of glass. But such people are insane, and I would be
thought equally mad if I took anything from them as a model for myself.

A brilliant piece of reasoning! As if I were not a man who sleeps at night,
and regularly has all the same experiences[1] while asleep as madmen do
when awake—indeed sometimes even more improbable ones. How often,
asleep at night, am I convinced of just such familiar events—that I am here
in my dressing-gown, sitting by the fire—when in fact I am lying undressed
in bed! Yet at the moment my eyes are certainly wide awake when I look at
this piece of paper; I shake my head and it is not asleep; as I stretch out and
feel my hand I do so deliberately, and I know what I am doing, All this
would not happen with such distinctness to someone asleep. Indeed! As if I
did not remember other occasions when I have been tricked by exactly similar thoughts while asleep! As I think about this more carefully, I see plainly
that there are never any sure signs by means of which being awake can be
distinguished from being asleep. The result is that I begin to feel dazed, and
this very feeling only reinforces the notion that I may be asleep.

Suppose then that I am dreaming, and that these particulars—that my
eyes are open, that I am moving my head and stretching out my hands—are
not true. Perhaps, indeed, I do not even have such hands or such a body at
all. Nonetheless, it must surely be admitted that the visions which come in
sleep are like paintings, which must have been fashioned in the likeness of
things that are real, and hence that at least these general kinds of things—

eyes, head, hands and the body as a whole—are things which are not imaginary but are real and exist. For even when painters try to create sirens and satyrs with the most extraordinary bodies, they cannot give them natures which are new in all respects; they simply jumble up the limbs of different animals. Or if perhaps they manage to think up something so new that nothing remotely similar has ever been seen before—something which is therefore completely fictitious and unreal—at least the colours used in the composition must be real. By similar reasoning, although these general kinds of things—eyes, head, hands and so on—could be imaginary, it must at least be admitted that certain other even simpler and more universal things are real. These are as it were the real colours from which we form all the images of things, whether true or false, that occur in our thought.

This class appears to include corporeal nature in general, and its extension; the shape of extended things; the quantity, or size and number of these things; the place in which they may exist, the time through which they may endure,[2] and so on. So a reasonable conclusion from this might be that physics, astronomy, medicine, and all other disciplines which depend on the study of composite things, are doubtful; while arithmetic, geometry and other subjects of this kind, which deal only with the simplest and most general things, regardless of whether they really exist in nature or not, contain something certain and indubitable. For whether I am awake or asleep, two and three added together are five, and a square has no more than four sides. It seems impossible that such transparent truths should incur any suspicion of being false.

And yet firmly rooted in my mind is the long-standing opinion that there is an omnipotent God who made me the kind of creature that I am. How do I know that he has not brought it about that there is no earth, no sky, no extended thing, no shape, no size, no place, while at the same time ensuring that all these things appear to me to exist just as they do now? What is more, since I sometimes believe that others go astray in cases where they think they have the most perfect knowledge, may I not similarly go wrong every time I add two and three or count the sides of a square, or in some even simpler matter, if that is imaginable? But perhaps God would not have allowed me to be deceived in this way, since he is said to be supremely good. But if it were inconsistent with his goodness to have created me such that I am deceived all the time, it would seem equally foreign to his goodness to allow me to be deceived even occasionally; yet this last assertion cannot be made.[3]

Perhaps there may be some who would prefer to deny the existence of so powerful a God rather than believe that everything else is uncertain. Let us not argue with them, but grant them that everything said about God is a fiction. According to their supposition, then, I have arrived at my present state by fate or chance or a continuous chain of events, or by some other means; yet since deception and error seem to be imperfections, the less powerful they make my original cause, the more likely it is that I am so imperfect as to be deceived all the time. I have no answer to these arguments, but am finally compelled to admit that there is not one of my former beliefs about which a doubt may not properly be raised; and this is not a flippant or ill-considered conclusion, but is based on powerful and well thought-out reasons. So in future I must withhold my assent from these former beliefs just as carefully as I would from obvious falsehoods, if I want to discover any certainty.[4]

But it is not enough merely to have noticed this; I must make an effort to remember it. My habitual opinions keep coming back, and, despite my wishes, they capture my belief, which is as it were bound over to them as a result of long occupation and the law of custom. I shall never get out of the habit of confidently assenting to these opinions, so long as I suppose them to be what in fact they are, namely highly probable opinions—opinions which, despite the fact that they are in a sense doubtful, as has just been shown, it is still much more reasonable to believe than to deny. In view of this, I think it will be a good plan to turn my will in completely the opposite direction and deceive myself, by pretending for a time that these former opinions are utterly false and imaginary. I shall do this until the weight of preconceived opinion is counter-balanced and the distorting influence of habit no longer prevents my judgement from perceiving things correctly. In the meantime, I know that no danger or error will result from my plan, and that I cannot possibly go too far in my distrustful attitude. This is because the task now in hand does not involve action but merely the acquisition of knowledge.

I will suppose therefore that not God, who is supremely good and the source of truth, but rather some malicious demon of the utmost power and cunning has employed all his energies in order to deceive me. I shall think that the sky, the air, the earth, colours, shapes, sounds and all external things are merely the delusions of dreams which he has devised to ensnare my judgement. I shall consider myself as not having hands or eyes, or flesh, or blood or senses, but as falsely believing that I have all these things. I shall stubbornly and firmly persist in this meditation; and, even if it is not in my power to know any truth, I shall at least do what is in my power,[5] that is, resolutely guard against assenting to any falsehoods, so that the deceiver, however powerful and cunning he may be, will be unable to impose on me in the slightest degree. But this is an arduous undertaking, and a kind of laziness brings me back to normal life. I am like a prisoner who is enjoying an imaginary freedom while asleep; as he begins to suspect that he is asleep, he dreads being woken up, and goes along with the pleasant illusion as long as he can. In the same way, I happily slide back into my old opinions and dread being shaken out of them, for fear that my peaceful sleep may be followed by hard labour when I wake, and that I shall have to toil not in the light, but amid the inextricable darkness of the problems I have now raised.

SECOND MEDITATION: THE NATURE OF THE HUMAN MIND, AND HOW IT IS BETTER KNOWN THAN THE BODY

So serious are the doubts into which I have been thrown as a result of yesterday's meditation that I can neither put them out of my mind nor see any way of resolving them. It feels as if I have fallen unexpectedly into a deep whirlpool which tumbles me around so that I can neither stand on the bottom nor swim up to the top. Nevertheless I will make an effort and once more attempt the same path which I started on yesterday. Anything which admits of the slightest doubt I will set aside just as if I had found it to be wholly false; and I will proceed in this way until I recognize something certain, or, if nothing else, until I at least recognize for certain that there is no certainty. Archimedes used to demand just one firm and immovable point in order to shift the entire earth; so I too can hope for great things if I manage to find just one thing, however slight, that is certain and unshakeable.

I will suppose then, that everything I see is spurious. I will believe that my memory tells me lies, and that none of the things that it reports ever happened. I have no senses. Body, shape, extension, movement and place are chimeras. So what remains true? Perhaps just the one fact that nothing is certain.

Yet apart from everything I have just listed, how do I know that there is not something else which does not allow even the slightest occasion for doubt? Is there not a God, or whatever I may call him, who puts into me[6] the thoughts I am now having? But why do I think this, since I myself may perhaps be the author of these thoughts? In that case am not I, at least, something? But I have just said that I have no senses and no body. This is the sticking point: what follows from this? Am I not so bound up with a body and with senses that I cannot exist without them? But I have convinced myself that there is absolutely nothing in the world, no sky, no earth, no minds, no bodies. Does it now follow that I too do not exist? No: if I convinced myself of something[7] then I certainly existed. But there is a deceiver of supreme power and cunning who is deliberately and constantly deceiving me. In that case I too undoubtedly exist, if he is deceiving me; and let him deceive me as much as he can, he will never bring it about that I am nothing so long as I think that I am something. So after considering everything very thoroughly, I must finally conclude that this proposition, *I am, I exist,* is necessarily true whenever it is put forward by me or conceived in my mind.

But I do not yet have a sufficient understanding of what this 'I' is, that now necessarily exists. So I must be on my guard against carelessly taking something else to be this 'I', and so making a mistake in the very item of knowledge that I maintain is the most certain and evident of all. I will therefore go back and meditate on what I originally believed myself to be, before I embarked on this present train of thought. I will then subtract anything capable of being weakened, even minimally, by the arguments now introduced, so that what is left at the end may be exactly and only what is certain and unshakeable.

What then did I formerly think I was? A man. But what is a man? Shall I say 'a rational animal'? No; for then I should have to inquire what an animal is, what rationality is, and in this way one question would lead me down the slope to other harder ones, and I do not now have the time to waste on subtleties of this kind. Instead I propose to concentrate on what came into my thoughts spontaneously and quite naturally whenever I used to consider what I was. Well, the first thought to come to mind was that I had a face, hands, arms and the whole mechanical structure of limbs which can be seen in a corpse, and which I called the body. The next thought was that I was nourished, that I moved about, and that I engaged in sense-perception and thinking; and these actions I attributed to the soul. But as to the nature of this soul, either I did not think about this or else I imagined it to be something tenuous, like a wind or fire or ether, which permeated my more solid parts. As to the body, however, I had no doubts about it, but thought I knew its nature distinctly. If I had tried to describe the mental conception I had of it, I would have expressed it as follows: by a body I understand whatever has a determinable shape and a definable location and can occupy a space in such a way as to exclude any other body; it can be perceived by touch, sight, hearing, taste or smell, and can be moved in various ways, not by itself but by whatever else comes into contact with it. For, according to my judgement, the power of self-movement, like the power of sensation or of thought, was quite foreign to the nature of a body; indeed, it was a source of wonder to me that certain bodies were found to contain faculties of this kind.

But what shall I now say that I am, when I am supposing that there is some supremely powerful and, if it is permissible to say so, malicious deceiver, who is deliberately trying to trick me in every way he can? Can I now assert that I possess even the most insignificant of all the attributes which I have just said belong to the nature of a body? I scrutinize them, think about them, go over them again, but nothing suggests itself; it is tiresome and pointless to go through the list once more. But what about the attributes I assigned to the soul? Nutrition or movement? Since now I do not have a body, these are mere fabrications. Sense-perception? This surely does not occur without a body, and besides, when asleep I have appeared to perceive through the senses many things which I afterwards realized I did not perceive through the senses at all. Thinking? At last I have discovered it— thought; this alone is inseparable from me. I am, I exist—that is certain. But for how long? For as long as I am thinking. For it could be that were I totally to cease from thinking, I should totally cease to exist. At present I am not admitting anything except what is necessarily true. I am, then, in the strict sense only a thing that thinks;[8] that is, I am a mind, or intelligence, or intellect, or reason—words whose meaning I have been ignorant of until now. But for all that I am a thing which is real and which truly exists. But what kind of a thing? As I have just said—a thinking thing.

What else am I? I will use my imagination.[9] I am not that structure of limbs which is called a human body. I am not even some thin vapour which permeates the limbs—a wind, fire, air, breath, or whatever I depict in my imagination; for these are things which I have supposed to be nothing. Let this supposition stand;[10] for all that I am still something. And yet may it not perhaps be the case that these very things which I am supposing to be nothing, because they are unknown to me, are in reality identical with the 'I' of which I am aware? I do not know, and for the moment I shall not argue the point, since I can make judgements only about things which are known to me. I know that I exist; the question is, what is this 'I' that I know? If the 'I' is understood strictly as we have been taking it, then it is quite certain that knowledge of it does not depend on things of whose existence I am as yet unaware; so it cannot depend on any of the things which I invent in my imagination. And this very word 'invent' shows me my mistake. It would indeed be a case of fictitious invention if I used my imagination to establish that I was something or other; for imagining is simply contemplating the shape or image of a corporeal thing. Yet now I know for certain both that I exist and at the same time that all such images and, in general, everything relating to the nature of body, could be mere dreams <and chimeras>. Once this point has been grasped, to say 'I' will use my imagination to get to know more distinctly what 'I am' would seem to be as silly as saying 'I am now awake, and see some truth; but since my vision is not yet clear enough, I will deliberately fall asleep so that my dreams may provide a truer and clearer representation.' I thus realize that none of the things that the imagination enables me to grasp is at all relevant to this knowledge of myself which I possess, and that the mind must therefore be most carefully diverted from such things[11] if it is to perceive its own nature as distinctly as possible.

But what then am I? A thing that thinks. What is that? A thing that doubts, understands, affirms, denies, is willing, is unwilling, and also imagines and has sensory perceptions.

This is a considerable list, if everything on it belongs to me. But does it? Is it not one and the same 'I' who is now doubting almost everything, who nonetheless understands some things, who affirms that this one thing is true, denies everything else, desires to know more, is unwilling to be deceived, imagines many things even involuntarily, and is aware of many things which apparently come from the senses? Are not all these things just as true as the fact that I exist, even if I am asleep all the time, and even if he who created me is doing all he can to deceive me? Which of all these activities is distinct from my thinking? Which of them can be said to be separate from myself? The fact that it is I who am doubting and understanding and willing is so evident that I see no way of making it any clearer. But it is also the case that the 'I' who imagines is the same 'I'. For even if, as I have supposed, none of the objects of imagination are real, the power of imagination is something which really exists and is part of my thinking. Lastly, it is also the same 'I' who has sensory perceptions, or is aware of bodily things as it were through the senses. For example, I am now seeing light, hearing a noise, feeling heat. But I am asleep, so all this is false. Yet I certainly seem to see, to hear, and to be warmed. This cannot be false; what is called 'having a sensory perception' is strictly just this, and in this restricted sense of the term it is simply thinking.

From all this I am beginning to have a rather better understanding of what I am. But it still appears—and I cannot stop thinking this—that the corporeal things of which images are formed in my thought, and which the senses investigate, are known with much more distinctness than this puzzling 'I' which cannot be pictured in the imagination. And yet it is surely surprising that I should have a more distinct grasp of things which I realize are doubtful, unknown and foreign to me, than I have of that which is true and known—my own self. But I see what it is: my mind enjoys wandering off and will not yet submit to being restrained within the bounds of truth. Very well then; just this once let us give it a completely free rein, so that after a while, when it is time to tighten the reins, it may more readily submit to being curbed.

Let us consider the things which people commonly think they understand most distinctly of all; that is, the bodies which we touch and see. I do not mean bodies in general—for general perceptions are apt to be somewhat more confused—but one particular body. Let us take, for example, this piece of wax. It has just been taken from the honeycomb; it has not yet quite lost the taste of the honey; it retains some of the scent of the flowers from which it was gathered; its colour, shape and size are plain to see; it is hard, cold and can be handled without difficulty; if you rap it with your knuckle it makes a sound. In short, it has everything which appears necessary to enable a body to be known as distinctly as possible. But even as I speak, I put the wax by the fire, and look: the residual taste is eliminated, the smell goes away, the colour changes, the shape is lost, the size increases; it becomes liquid and hot; you can hardly touch it, and if you strike it, it no longer makes a sound. But does the same wax remain? It must be admitted that it does; no one denies it, no one thinks otherwise. So what was it in the wax that I understood with such distinctness? Evidently none of the features which I arrived at by means of the senses; for whatever came under taste, smell, sight, touch or hearing has now altered—yet the wax remains.

Perhaps the answer lies in the thought which now comes to my mind; namely, the wax was not after all the sweetness of the honey, or the fragrance of the flowers, or the whiteness, or the shape, or the sound, but was rather a body which presented itself to me in these various forms a little while ago, but which now exhibits different ones. But what exactly is it that I am now imagining? Let us concentrate, take away everything which does not belong to the wax, and see what is left: merely something extended, flexible and changeable. But what is meant here by 'flexible' and 'changeable'? Is it what I picture in my imagination: that this piece of wax is capable of changing from a round shape to a square shape, or from a square shape to a triangular shape? Not at all; for I can grasp that the wax is capable of countless changes of this kind, yet I am unable to run through this immeasurable number from which it follows that it is not the faculty of imagination that gives me my grasp of the wax as flexible and changeable. And what is meant by 'extended'? Is the extension of the wax also unknown? For it increases if the wax melts, increases again if it boils, and is greater still if the heat is increased. I would not be making a correct judgement about the nature of wax unless I believed it capable of being extended in many more different ways than I will ever encompass in my imagination. I must therefore admit that the nature of this piece of wax is in no way revealed by my imagination, but is perceived by the mind alone. (I am speaking of this particular piece of wax; the point is even clearer with regard to wax in general.) But what is this wax which is perceived by the mind alone?[12] It is of course the same wax which I see, which I touch, which I picture in my imagination, in short the same wax which I thought it to be from the start. And yet, and here is the point the perception I have of it[13] is a case not of vision or touch or imagination nor has it ever been, despite previous appearances—but of purely mental scrutiny; and this can be imperfect and confused, as it was before, or clear and distinct as it is now, depending on how carefully I concentrate on what the wax consists in.

But as I reach this conclusion I am amazed at how weak and prone to error my mind is. For although I am thinking about these matters within myself, silently and without speaking, nonetheless the actual words bring me up short, and I am almost tricked by ordinary ways of talking. We say that we see the wax itself, if it is there before us, not that we judge it to be there from its colour or shape; and this might lead me to conclude without more ado that knowledge of the wax comes from what the eye sees, and not from the scrutiny of the mind alone. But then if I look out of the window and see men crossing the square, as I just happen to have done, I normally say that I see the men themselves, just as I say that I see the wax. Yet do I see any more than hats and coats which could conceal automatons? I judge that they are men. And so something which I thought I was seeing with my eyes is in fact grasped solely by the faculty of judgement which is in my mind.

However, one who wants to achieve knowledge above the ordinary level should feel ashamed at having taken ordinary ways of talking as a basis for doubt. So let us proceed, and consider on which occasion my perception of the nature of the wax was more perfect and evident. Was it when I first looked at it, and believed I knew it by my external senses, or at least by what they call the 'common' sense—that is, the power of imagination? Or is my knowledge more perfect now, after a more careful investigation of the nature of the wax and of the means by which it is known? Any doubt on this issue would clearly be foolish; for what distinctness was there in my earlier perception? Was there anything in it which an animal could not possess? But when I distinguish the wax from its outward forms—take the clothes off, as it were, and consider it naked—then although my judgement may still contain errors, at least my perception now requires a human mind.

But what am I to say about this mind, or about myself? (So far, remember, I am not admitting that there is anything else in me except a mind.) What, I ask, is this 'I' which seems to perceive the wax so distinctly? Surely my awareness of my own self is not merely much truer and more certain than my awareness of the wax, but also much more distinct and evident. For if I judge that the wax exists from the fact that I see it, clearly this same fact entails much more evidently that I myself also exist. It is possible that what I see is not really the wax; it is possible that I do not even have eyes with which to see anything. But when I see, or think I see (I am not here distinguishing the two), it is simply not possible that I who am now thinking am not something. By the same token, if I judge that the wax exists from the fact that I touch it, the same result follows, namely that I exist. If I judge that it exists from the fact that I imagine it, or for any other reason, exactly the same thing follows. And the result that I have grasped in the case of the wax may be applied to everything else located outside me. Moreover, if my perception of the wax seemed more distinct[14] after it was established not just by sight or touch but by many other considerations, it must be admitted that I now know myself even more distinctly. This is because every consideration whatsoever which contributes to my perception of the wax, or of any other body, cannot but establish even more effectively the nature of my own mind. But besides this, there is so much else in the mind itself which can serve to make my knowledge of it more distinct, that it scarcely seems worth going through the contributions made by considering bodily things.

I see that without any effort I have now finally got back to where I wanted. I now know that even bodies are not strictly perceived by the senses or the faculty of imagination but by the intellect alone, and that this perception derives not from their being touched or seen but from their being understood; and in view of this I know plainly that I can achieve an easier and more evident perception of my own mind than of anything else. But since the habit of holding on to old opinions cannot be set aside so quickly, I should like to stop here and meditate for some time on this new knowledge I have gained, so as to fix it more deeply in my memory.

NOTES

1. ". . . and in my dreams regularly represent to myself the same things" (French version).

2. ". . . the place where they are, the time which measures their duration" (French version).

3. ". . . I cannot doubt that he does allow this" (French version).

4. ". . . in the sciences" (added in French version).

5. "nevertheless it is in my power to suspend my judgement" (French version).

6. ". . . puts into my mind" (French version).

7. ". . . Or thought anything at all" (French version).

8. The word "only" is most naturally taken as going with "a thing that thinks," and this interpretation is followed in the French version. When discussing this passage with Gassendi, however, Descartes suggests that he meant the "only" to govern "in the strict sense."

9. ". . . to see if I am not something more" (added in French version).

10. Lat. *maneat* ("let it stand"), first edition. The second edition has the indicative *manet:* "The proposition still stands, viz., that I am nonetheless something." The French version reads: "without changing this supposition, I find that I am still certain that I am something."

11. ". . . from this manner of conceiving things" (French version).

12. ". . . which can only be conceived by the understanding or the mind" (French version).

13. ". . . or rather the act whereby it is perceived" (added in French version).

14. The French version has "more clear and distinct" and, at the end of this sentence, "more evidently, distinctly and clearly."

2.9

Western and Comparative Perspectives on Truth

Huston Smith

My article consists of four parts. Beginning with the comparative side of our symposium theme, I divide this into a temporal, historical comparison (Part I) and a geographical, spatial comparison (Part II). In Part III, I turn expressly to our Western handling of the truth issue, reserving Part IV for pulling these various strands together.

I. TRUTH IN TIME

There was a time, lasting roughly up to the European Renaissance, when we were one in our view of truth, though, of course, we did not know that fact. Not only did we not know that we were one, which is to say, alike; we were barely aware that we were multiple—Indian, Chinese, Western, and so on— while sharing, in our notion of truth, a view that was essentially the same. What this original, shared view of truth was, I shall say in a moment, but let me make sure that the strategy for this first section of my article is clear. I am saying that the basic comparison, in this matter of truth, is not geographical or spatial, but temporal: we need to contrast an original, primordial time when our views of truth were virtually alike, with a later (let us call it modern) time in which they diverge. The essential point about our original, shared view of truth is that it gathered three things into its single corral: things, assertions, and persons; the last bridging the other two inasmuch as persons are those unique kinds of things that are capable of making asser-

Philosophy East and West 30, no. 4 (October, 1980). Copyright by The University Press of Hawaii.

tions. In every civilization at its start, truth had this triple reference: to things, to statements, and to persons.

If this sounds surprising, I claim that fact as itself a support for my thesis. The surprise stems, I assume, from our assumption that only propositions are *really* true or false, so that in suggesting (as I just did) that these properties might also apply to persons and things, I must have been using the word loosely if not metaphorically, the way I would be using "crooked" if I applied it to a politician. I was not. I was not speaking metaphorically or even loosely; I was speaking universally. To lift from the pool of truth's total, undifferentiated meaning a single referent—propositions—and develop its meaning in that direction is our Western contribution to the subject.[1] Part III will be devoted to that contribution. Here our task is to see that it was a selective move. It involved, however unconsciously, a choice.

Let me back into my claim about truth's original, threefold referent. Though as Western philosophers we tend now to restrict truth to propositions,[2] if we widen our gaze to note the way the word functions in our language at large, we find clear signs that its earlier referent was much broader. In the category of truth as a property of things, we still speak of "true north" and "a true tone." Were a carpenter to validate that a "tabletop is true," we would understand that he meant that it is level. We speak of "true friendships," or "a true university." Statesmen tell us that "NATO must try to effect a true unity," and for some time we have been apprised that "beauty is truth, truth beauty." As for truth as a property of persons, we have Christ's claim that he was the truth ("I am the way, the truth, and the life," John 14:6) and that truth can be enacted ("He that doeth truth cometh to the light," John 3:21). We refer to so-and-so as being "a true gentleman (statesman, friend, whatever)"; there is "true bravery" and "false modesty"; and since the rise of existentialism, authenticity has become a way of talking about being "true to oneself."

These may be residues in our language. If so, they hark back to a time when truth had a wider referent than it has in Western philosophy today. Nietzsche noted that when "members of the Greek aristocracy [spoke] . . . of themselves as 'the truthful' . . . the word they used was *esthlos,* meaning one who *is,* who has true reality, who is true; [only] by a subjective turn [did] the *true* later become the *truthful.*"[3] The Latin *verus* means true; it also means real, genuine, and authentic—properties that obviously are not restricted to statements. The same holds for the key terms in other civilizations. In Sanskrit *satya* doubles for both truth and reality, as the famous *sat-cit-ānanda* (being-awareness-bliss) discloses immediately. "Etymologically, the Chinese character *chen[a]* in its original seal form denotes a loaded scale standing on a stool which implies full, real, solid, and therefore the meaning of true, as opposed to empty and unreal, i.e. *chia[b].*"[4] Arabic has three basic terms that deal with truth: *ḥaqqa,* which leans toward the truth of things; *ṣadaqa,* which points toward the truth of persons; and *saḥḥa* which stresses the truth of statements. To elaborate only the first of these, *ḥaqq* denotes what is true in and of itself by dint of its metaphysical or cosmic status. This makes it supremely applicable to God: when Manṣūr al-Hallāj proclaimed in a moment of ecstasy "*anā'l-Ḥaqq,*" "I am the Truth," he was crucified, it being taken for granted by those who heard him that in so saying he had claimed that he was Allāh. As Wilfred Smith points out:

> *Al-Ḥaqq* is a name of God not merely as an attribute but as a denotation. *Al-Ḥaqq Al-Ḥaqq:* He is reality as such. Yet every other thing that is genuine is also *ḥaqq* and, some of the mystics went on to say, is therefore divine. Yet the word means reality first, and then God, for those who equate him with reality.[5]

To sum up this first section, originally truth was triple. Yet even then there were differences.

II. TRUTH IN SPACE

As far back as our historical eyes can see we find different emphases in peoples' notions of truth. At first these differences were small, but as the civilizations worked out their distinctive identities—or discovered their respective destinies, however you wish to put the matter—the differences became more pronounced. If we confine ourselves to the three civilizations that are being considered in this symposium—East Asia (China and Japan), South Asia (India), and the West—we can risk the generalization that more than did either of the other two, India tied truth to things, East Asia to persons, and the West to statements.

India

"To the knower of Truth, all things have verily become the Self," the *Īśa Upaniṣad* tells us. "What delusion, what sorrow can there be for him who realizes that oneness" (verse 7)? It is that oneness carried to its absolute, logical limit that gives India no alternative but to lodge truth primarily in things, for if "That One Thing"[6] is truly the only thing that exists, everything else, persons and propositions included, must be *māyā*. These latter are real in the empirical order (*vyāvahārika sattva*), but in absolute existence (*pāramārthika sattva*) they do not figure at all. Professor K. L. Seshagiri makes this point explicitly in the "Dialogue on Truth" that appeared between him and Father Peter Riga in *Philosophy East and West:*

> The Hindu view is . . . that truth is not an abstract, intellectual formulation or proposition. . . . Truth . . . is not that which is . . . understood by the intellect. It is prior to all knowledge. . . . Being [and] truth . . . are interchangeable. . . . Rea-

soning is posterior and secondary to the fundamental experience of being. (20, no. 4 [October, 1970]: 377, 379)

Buddhism's substitution of a process vocabulary (verbs) for Hinduism's nouns does not affect the point at issue: it, too, makes a state-of-affairs truth's basic home, as Nāgārjuna's twofold theory of truth (practical, conventional, world-ensconced *samvrtti-satya* versus ultimate, highest *paramārtha-satya*) makes plain. "As long as 'truth' is regarded as an idea," it is at best inferior truth that we are dealing with; at worst such truth "can destroy a person 'like a snake wrongly grasped or magical knowledge incorrectly applied' (*Kārikās* 24. 11). . . . 'Emptiness' should not be regarded as another 'viewpoint.'"[7] This basic Indian association of truth with being continues to the present. When Mahatma Gandhi turned *satyāgraha* into an international word which, among other things, was to play an important part in the Black Liberation movement in America, it was truth-*force* he was talking about. Truth as veridical concept and utterance were secondary.

East Asia

My suggestion that East Asia lodges truth basically in persons should come as no surprise, given the social emphasis of its orientation as a whole. I assume that this social emphasis is generally recognized, but I shall cite several witnesses to it anyway, to bring it to our direct attention. The following characterizations all focus on China, but they could easily be extended to cover Japan as well:

Wei-ming Tu: "Étienne Balazs, the brilliant sinologist, once characterized all Chinese philosophy as preeminently social philosophy."[8]

Arthur Waley: "All Chinese philosophy is essentially the study of how men can best be helped to live together in harmony and good order."[9]

Fung Yu-Lan: "Chinese philosophy . . . is directly or indirectly concerned with government and ethics. . . . All [its branches] are connected with political thought in one way or another."[10]

Wing-tsit Chan: "Chinese philosophers . . . have been interested primarily in ethical, social, and political problems."[11]

How this social preoccupation affected the East Asian notion of truth can be briefly summarized as follows: To begin with a negative point, the Chinese language does not appear to have been devised with an eye for dealing with abstract, intangible entities; absence of definite grammatical rules in ancient China and the ambiguity of individual ideograms and pictograms make it awkward for it to do so.[12] To cite but a single example, the closest Chinese comes to the Sanskrit *sat* and the English "being" or "existence" is *yu,* which basically means "to have" or "to possess." Possession implies a possessor, of course, and as persons are the kinds of possessors we tend to think of first, the word *yu* gives a personal flavor to even metaphysics' final generality and abstraction—I am thinking of Aristotle's definition of metaphysics as the study of being *qua* being.

As we turn from the notion of being to the notion of truth itself, that flavor increases.[13] I shall soon be arguing that our Western tendency has been to regard truth as the correspondence of an idea or utterance with an objective state of affairs which ideally could be captured on videotape. Using this criterion, Westerners have given Orientals bad marks for veracity. The following nineteenth-century missionary reports amount to outright condemnation:

> More uneradicable than the sins of the flesh is the falsity of the Chinese; . . . their disregard of truth has perhaps done more to lower their character than any other fault.[14]

> The ordinary speech of the Chinese is so full of insincerity . . . that it is very difficult to learn the truth in almost every case. In China it is literally true that a fact is the hardest thing in the world to get at.[15]

We would not expect Jacob Bronowski to be as biased as those missionaries were, but even he does not conceal his frustration:

> Anyone who has worked in the East knows how hard it is there to get an answer to a question of fact. When I had to study the casualties from the atomic bombs in Japan at the end of the war, I was dogged and perplexed by this difficulty. . . . Whatever man one asks, [he] does not really understand what one wants to know. . . . At bottom he does not know the facts because they are not his language. These cultures of the East . . . lack the language and the very habit of fact. [16]

Pearl Buck knew East Asia well enough to see that it is different views of truth working against each other that give rise to criticisms like these. She writes,

> We are often puzzled by the lack of what we consider truth-telling on the part of Asians. It seems at times impossible to get facts from Asian persons. The difference here is that [we have come] to consider truth as factual . . . whereas for the Asian truth is contained in an ethic. When we inquire of an Asian as to what may have happened in a specific incident, we grow impatient because we cannot get from him a clear and simple statement of fact. But for him . . . human feelings and intentions are more important than mere material fact.[17]

William Haas, whose neglected *Destiny of the Mind in East and West* I consider a minor classic in comparative philosophy, echoes Pearl Buck's point, which is also my point here:

> Facts are sacred to the Westerner; they are less so to the Oriental, who has always been more interested in the psychological and human aspects of phe-

nomena. What to him is important, what, as a matter of fact, is real, is not the object in its supposed "objectivity," but its significance for man. So in dealing with the Oriental there arise continually situations for which the Westerner finds himself wholly unprepared and for which he may propose all-too-simple interpretations. . . . The readiness with which the Oriental gives erroneous information instead of confessing his ignorance is motivated by reluctance to disappoint; this motive often makes him give an answer which he considers agreeable to the questioner. In such cases and many others the desire to please and to feel obliging has a tendency to make one ignore plain facts. [18]

There is not the slightest reason to suppose that virtue is unequally distributed around our globe. If Asians have seemed unreliable to Westerners, that is because we have judged them by our Western standards. *We* think their utterances should conform to objective facts; *they* think it more important that they be tuned to the sentiments of the persons their words will affect. In both civilizations there are referents to which utterances should be responsible; in both, there can be strong temptations not to honor those referents and to become, thereby, untruthful. The difference lies in the nature of the referents themselves.

In saying that East Asia adopted a basically personal view of truth we should not, of course, read "personal" in our Western, individualistic sense. "To thine own self be true" is strictly Western advice; its East Asian counterpart might read, "To the selves of others—all whom your words and actions will affect—be true." This social rendering of "personal" gives the key Oriental virtue, "sincerity," a twist that comes close to being the opposite of that which the word carries in the West. In the West sincerity bespeaks fidelity to one's own, individually-arrived-at conscience and principles. In East Asia it involves bracketing these private preferences in favor of the outward-oriented social standards I have noted; to repeat, it involves optimizing the feelings of all interested parties, in accord with guidelines (we could go on to add) that have been impounded in ritualized customs (*li*). Bertrand Russell failed to see the difference between East Asian and Western meanings of truth, when he wrote in his essay on "The Chinese Character": "Chinese life . . . is far more polite than anything to which we are accustomed. This, of course, interferes . . . with sincerity and truth in personal relations."[19]

Even a sinologist as on top of the issues as Donald Munro bows to the Western definition of truth when he writes in the Preface to his *Concept of Man in Early China:* "What were important to the Chinese philosophers, *where questions of truth* and falsity *were not,* were the behavioral implications of the statement of belief in question."[20] Later in his book, he raises by implication the possibility of an alternative, Chinese definition of the word when he writes that "in China, truth and falsity *in the Greek sense* have rarely been important considerations" (p. 55, italics mine), but he does not go on to develop that alternative. What we need to see is that, as someone has put the matter, for Confucius the important thing was not to call a spade a spade (that is, make statements conform to impersonal realities), but rather to *cheng ming;* for example, make (primarily personal) realities conform to their (normative) names—to have a father speak as a "father" should speak, his words governed by the sensitivities a father should possess or be working to acquire.

To summarize: truth for China is personal in a dual or twofold sense. Outwardly it takes into consideration the feelings of the persons an act or utterance will affect (one thinks of the normality of white lies and keeping one's mouth shut when appropriate). Meanwhile, inwardly it aligns the speaker to the self he ought to be; invoking a word dear to the correspondence theorists we can say that truth "adequates" its possessor to his normative self.[21] The external and internal referents of the notion are tightly fused, of course, for it is primarily by identifying with the feelings of others (developing *jen*) that one becomes a *chun tzu* (the self one shoud be). If we are getting the feeling that the Chinese sense of truth opens onto her entire ethical system, this is as it should be, but I cannot exploit that virtue further here. There is space only to round off this section with a short, *staccato* coda. With truth as personally oriented as it was in East Asia, we should not be surprised to find *ad hominem* arguments counting for more there than they have in the West where they tend to be waived as logically irrelevant. As Henry Rosemont once put this point to me, if someone were to argue that the ideal form of marriage is monogamy while himself having three wives, the Chinese would consider this the best reason in the world not to take him seriously.

Against the background of these South Asian and East Asian notions of truth I proceed now to our Western vision.

III. OUR WESTERN ODYSSEY

I am not a Heideggerian, but I agree with Heidegger that the West's view of truth has been, distinctively, correspondence. Of the three theories of truth the Western-oriented *Encyclopedia of Philosophy* lists in addition to correspondence—coherence, pragmatic, and performative—the last is too recent and episodic to warrant space in an overview article like this one. It burst on the scene in Strawson's essay on "Truth" less than thirty years ago, and since he himself softened its original claim that to say that a statement is true is not to make a statement about a statement but to perform the act of agreeing with, accepting, or endorsing a statement—it seems to be receiving decreasing notice. I do not think it will last as more than a footnote. The pragmatic theory has more substance, but it is shaking down into an epistemological *emphasis*. It continues, in Quine, for example, as a broad reminder that theorizing over experience is fundamentally motivated and justified by conditions of efficacy and utility in servicing our aims and needs, but as a theory that claims to say what truth as such is, I would say of it, as the *Encyclopedia of Philosophy* says of the pragmatic movement in general, that it "cannot be said to be alive today" (VI, 435). For one thing, it never did succeed in doing justice to aesthetic and disinterested truth, as William James himself recognized by introducing his "mechanical wife"—would the fact that she serviced me flawlessly show that she loved me? Edwin Bevyn argues the deficiencies of the pragmatic theory conclusively, and as his objection is aimed at the coherence theory as well, I quote it at some length.

> It may be that everything which has been said to show that the unsatisfactoriness of the correspondence theory of truth . . . holds good in regard to inanimate nature. But the moment one comes to the world of conscious Spirit, every theory of truth except the correspondence theory becomes absurd. If one thinks of the anxiety of the lover to know whether the person he aspires to win really loves him, it is precisely the question whether an idea in his mind, the image of the other person's state of mind, really corresponds with fact existing independently of his mind which torments him. What would the lover say if we told him not to be so concerned about reality apart from his mind; it would be enough for him to act as if the person in question loved him? . . . Does she really—really, apart from anything I may think—care for me? What really are her thoughts in themselves, her way of regarding me in herself?—that is his insistent cry. My belief about another human spirit, about what that spirit now thinks or feels or has experienced in the past is essentially belief about a reality existing apart from my own mind. . . . The desire to know the truth in this sense is raised to its greatest intensity in love.[22]

As I said, Bevyn's point is aimed as much against the coherence theory of truth as against the pragmatic, and it is this coherence theory which, in the West, has been the correspondence theory's major rival. But rival only to the extent of constituting its loyal opposition, we may add, which obviates my needing to deal with it further here. Chronologically the coherence theory emerges only in *modern* philosophy, and even here it has been confined to such metaphysicians as Leibniz, Spinoza, Hegel, and Bradley (all rationalists and idealists in the West's predominantly empiricist, realist tradition) and a few logical positivists (notably Neurath and Hempel) who have been attracted by its resemblance to theoretical physics and pure mathematics.

So I come out agreeing with Heidegger that the West has settled primarily into a correspondence theory of truth. In fixing on the way things are, this theory retains traces of the ontological emphasis India pushed to the hilt, while at the same time its concern for the way things appear *to man* aligns it to some extent with China's humanistic interests. But now the differences.

Against India, correspondence exempts truth from concern with the ontological status of things in themselves—the question of their genuineness. It brings the question down to whether we see a bed, say, as it actually is; the ontological status of the bed—if that phrase has meaning; I shall return to this question as a separate issue. As for East Asia, though the correspondence theory sides with it (as I just said) in lodging truth in man, it does so with two restrictions—constrictions, I am tempted to say.

First, correspondence denies that truth pertains to persons in their entirety; it is imprecise, it holds, to speak of "true persons." (In holding that it *is* appropriate to do so, the Chinese perspective overlaps India's at this one point, in principle subscribing to a graded ontology of selfhood.) Rather than a predicate of selves, truth as defined by correspondence theorists is a predicate of *parts* of selves, their conceptual parts.

Second, these mental parts—I am using the phrase to cover images, ideas, propositions, statements, sentences, the entire corpus—are related (by the correspondence theory) to their referents *passively*. This elicited in the West the pragmatic theory of truth and notion of performative speech-acts as correctives, but these have neither unhorsed the correspondence theory nor (per impossible) been incorporated within it. The correspondence view does not say that thoughts must mirror things (the discredited 'camera theory' of naive realism), but however we conceive of "represent," it should represent them accurately. This puts the referent in the driver's seat; the job of true thought, we might say, is to settle down quietly in the seat beside it; that is, conform itself as fully as possible to the referent's nature. The East Asian view is more dynamic; pragmatic elements are built right into it, for it holds an act or utterance to be true to the extent that it 'gestalts' (composes, resolves) the ingredients of a situation in a way that furthers a desired outcome—in China's case, social harmony. Truth thus conceived is a kind of performative: it is speech or deed aimed at effecting an intended consequence.

Having devoted the first half of this section to agreeing with Heidegger that our Western view of truth is primarily that of correspondence, I shall devote its second half to disagreeing with him on when we settled into this position. I think we gravitated toward it more gradually than Heidegger would have us think. Heidegger sees the die as having been cast by Plato,[23] whereas it seems to me unlikely that we would continue to sign our letters, "'Yours truly," speak of lovers as being "true to each other," or refer to jurors as "twelve good men and true" if we had turned our backs on truth's personal and ontological referents twenty-five hundred years ago. Right down through the Middle Ages, "goodness, truth and being are convertible."[24] As for Plato, I side with Paul Friedlander in his criticism of Heidegger's handling of that fount of Western philosophy. Plato did not, as Heidegger claims, subordinate truth's ontological to its epistemological referent. "Truth in Plato's system," Friedlander writes,

> is always both: reality of being and correctness of apprehension and assertion. . . . Plato's allegory of the cave [which Heidegger rightly focuses on] is

characterized by the dual meaning of the hierarchical ascent: the ascent of being and the ascent of knowledge, both exactly related to each other.[25]

Nor was truth's third, or personal, referent lacking in Plato:

> As witness for these thoughts he chose Socrates, facing death for the sake of truth and reality. Thus, the dual meaning of the hierarchical ascent becomes three-fold if it is kept in mind that the allegory of unbidden and revealing truth is told by the truthful man.[26]

In sum, "in Plato . . . the ontological, the epistemological, and the existential . . . facets of the Greek *alētheia* . . . are intimately united."[27] If Plato had narrowed truth to its epistemological referent, as Heidegger claims, we would have to assume that the move escaped his pupil Aristotle, for to him too *alētheia* means, as in Plato, both the nature of the real and the nature of a true statement.[28] Freidlander thinks that in passing to Aristotle, *alētheia* suffered some constriction- "the 'existential' aspect . . . represented in Plato through the figure of Socrates, has disappeared"[29]—but I do not see that even this is the case. For, as Thomas Kasulis points out in his contribution to this symposium, though correspondence theorists regularly take as their point of departure Aristotle's assertion that "to say of what is that it is not, or what is not that it is, is false, while to say of what is that it is, and of what is not that it is not, is true,"[30] Aristotle himself "goes on to speak in two further ways about truth. In the lexiconical section of the *Metaphysics* (1024b), he analyzes three senses of 'false': false as thing, false as an account and false as a man" ("The Zen View of Truth," first page). The last of these seems to correspond to what Friedlander calls the existential meaning of *alētheia*. In Aristotle's description,

> a false *man* is one who is ready at and fond of (false) accounts, not for any other reason but for their own sake, and one who is good at impressing such accounts on other people, just as we say *things* are false, which produce a false appearance.[31]

And again, in the *Nicomachean Ethics:* "The man who observes the mean [between 'boastfulness' and 'false modesty'] is true both in word and in life because his character is such" (1127a).

Professor Kasulis notes that Thomas says this also,[32] but this is not the place to go further into history. I hope that I have been clear. I do not deny that the seeds of our Western move—the extraction of truth from its original, threefold reference to lodge it in intellectual judgments that correspond with things outside themselves—can, with wisdom of hindsight, be found in Greek philosophy.[33] But I want to insist that these seeds matured slowly. It seems to me that there is a huge and precise block of evidence for this point that is so clear as to amount, virtually, to proof; it is not often in philosophy

that one comes upon evidence that is so palpable as to feel crisp, but in the
present case the feel (for me, at least) pertains. Right "down to the late eighteenth century," Arthur Lovejoy tells us,

> most educated men were to accept without question the conception of the uni-
> verse as a "Great Chain of Being," composed of an immense, or . . . infinite,
> number of links ranging in hierarchical order from the meagerest kind of exis-
> tents . . . through "every possible" grade up to the *ens perfectissimum.*[34]

And what was the gradient for these grades to which Lovejoy refers? Can it
be doubted that in last resort it was ontological; does not the very name,
"Great Chain of *Being*" make this claim clear? Given truth's original involve-
ment with ontology, I do not see how the word *could* have withdrawn its
ontological claims as long as the Chain of Being held firm. Or to transpose
the wording, I do not see how that chain could have remained what it was,
had it not been possible—natural, even—to regard its higher links as more
genuine and real; in a word, more true.

IV. RETURN TO THE CENTER

It was not Plato, it was modern science that caused the West to contract its
notion of truth until in philosophy it is now thought to refer strictly and properly only to judgments (or statements, or propositions). For in science the
notion of degrees of reality (and its correlate, degrees of ontological truth)
are meaningless: a state-of-affairs is a state-of-affairs, and that is the end of
the matter. And with the demise of ontological truth was it Eddington who
proposed that "Reality" capitalized means nothing more than "reality followed by loud cheers"?—personal truth collapses as well. (In a last minute
move, Kierkegaard tries to save it by proposing his notion of "subjective
truth," but we know how little this influenced subsequent philosophy.) For
persons, too, are ontological in the sense that they are beings; they are built
of substance. I do not see how one can do anything but trivialize the notion
of a "true *mensch*" if one undercuts the possibility that there is more to him,
as we say, than there is to most men—that he is more substantial.

I think that we have been onto important things in this symposium.

> Little is more important about a culture, a century, a person, than its (or his) no-
> tion of truth. Pilate's unanswered question, What is Truth? whether expressed
> or latent, haunts every civilization, and finally . . . every man.

That statement comes from Wilfred Cantwell Smith, whose essays on "Ori-
entalism and Truth"[35] and "A Human View of Truth"[36] have influenced this
article in major ways. As the title of the second essay suggests, Professor

Smith is primarily concerned with the depersonalization of truth in the contemporary West:

> Natural scientists deliberately and with success strive to construct impersonal statements, sentences whose meaning and whose truth are both independent of who makes them; and they see the truth of a statement as in large measure precisely a function of its impersonality. In the natural sciences this seems to do not only much good, but concomitantly little harm: elsewhere this is not clear. . . . There are some extremely important statements . . . whose meaning and whose truth depend, and properly depend, on the moral integrity of who makes them, and who hears them (statements such as "I refuse to fight in Vietnam").

> For a university or a civilization to set up impersonal propositions as the model of all propositions, and then to make these the primary locus of truth and falsity, is to exercise, wittingly or otherwise, a remarkably decisive option in one's orientation to the world ("Orientalism and Truth," p. 11).

It is indeed! And it is no less decisive to strip truth of its ontological reference, I would add, reducing thereby the Great Chain of Being to its single, ground-floor level. How far the West has gone down this road is shown by the fact that there are now Platonic scholars, presidents of the American Philosophical Association, no less, who can no longer comprehend how Plato could have been serious in arguing that there are things more real (and hence more true) than physical objects: Plato must have been linguistically confused.[37]

If, in broad outline at least, my paper is correct, its moral, I should think, is plain:

- No theory of truth works as well in the natural sciences as does our Western, correspondence theory.
- Only a profoundly personal theory of truth, such as was developed in East Asia, can do justice to man.
- Only a theory, like the Indian, that lodges truth in being, can be metaphysically adequate.

I feel that our Society for Asian and Comparative Philosophy has a message here for the philosophical community at large. All three perspectives on truth are important. They need to be sounded as a common chord.

NOTES

1. Confer the opening page of Eliot Deutsch's *On Truth: An Ontological Theory* (Honolulu, Hawaii: The University Press of Hawaii, 1979): "In recent decades, especially under the impact of positivism, which led philosophers to make a sharp division

between cognitive meaning . . . and emotive meaning . . . 'truth' has come more and more to be narrowly restricted to . . . propositions, with all other forms and usages of 'truth' taken to be metaphorical."

Deutsch's book appeared after my article was written and is constructive rather than historical in intent, but as its subtitle indicates, it shares the concern I register at the close of my article to return truth to its original ontological base. The statement I just quoted is followed by Deutsch's contention that "this restriction of the application and narrowing of the meaning, of 'truth' [to the truth-value of propositions] is wrong and unfortunate: for it robs the concept of some of its richest possible meaning" (ibid.).

2. This seems self-evident to me, but to nail it down I shall add to Deutsch's confirming opinion (cited in note 1) another one which can be taken as typical. Nicholas Rescher's *The Coherence Theory of Truth* (Oxford: Clarendon Press, 1973) opens by saying that "Philosophical theories in general deal exclusively with the truth of statements or propositions or, derivatively, such complexes thereof as accounts, narrations, and stories. Other uses of 'true' in ordinary language . . . are beside the point" (p. 1. Also Deutsch, *On Truth,* p. 121).

3. *The Genealogy of Morals,* trans. Francis Golffing (Garden City, N.Y.: Doubleday Anchor Book, 1956), p. 163.

4. From Professor Siu-chi Huang's paper, "Truth in the Chinese Tradition," which formed a part of the Washington Symposium but which, for reasons of space, unfortunately could not be included among the papers herein.

5. "A Human View of Truth," *Studies in Religion/Sciences religieuses* 1, no. 1(1971): 7.

6. From what has come to be called the Hymn to Creation in the *Ṛg-Veda* (X, 129) which goes on to say explicitly that "apart from it was nothing whatsoever." R. T. H. Griffith (trans.), *The Hymns of the Ṛg-veda,* 2 vols. (Benares: F. L. Lazarus, 1920).

7. Frederick Streng, "Buddhist Doctrine of Two Truths as Religious Philosophy," *Journal of Indian Philosophy* 1, no. 3 (November, 1971): 263.

8. *Philosophy East and West* 21, no. 1 (January, 1971): 79.

9. *The Way and Its Power* (New York: Grove Press. 1958), p. 64.

10. *A Short History of Chinese Philosophy* (New York: Collier-Macmillan, the Free Press, 1966), pp. 7, 9.

11. Charles Moore, ed., *Essays in East-West Philosophy* (Honolulu, Hawaii: University of Hawaii Press, 1951), p. 163.

12. I do not think that this statement and the example that follows take issue with Henry Rosemont's point that too much has been made of the constraints archaic written Chinese is alleged to have imposed on Chinese thinking, see his "On Representing Abstractions in Archaic Chinese," *Philosophy East and West* 24, no. 1 (January, 1974): 71–88. In the end, people develop languages that enable them to do what they want to do, rather than being forced to do what their languages require.

13. One thinks of Confucius' statement, "It is not truth which makes man great, but man that makes truth great."

14. S. Wells Williams, *The Middle Kingdom* (New York: Scribner's, 1882; revised edition, 1907), 1:834.

15. Both cited in Derke Bodde, *China's Cultural Tradition* (New York: Holt, Rinehart & Winston, 1963), p. 8.

16. *Science and Human Values* (New York: Harper & Row, 1959), p. 43.

17. Friend to Friend (New York: John Day, 1958), pp. 121–122.

18. (New York: Columbia University Press, 1946), pp. 127–128.

19. *Selected Papers of Bertrand Russell* (New York: Modern Library, 1927), p. 232. Japanese politicians find it difficult to persuade voters to be sincere in the Western sense of voting by principle instead of by *giri,* which means, roughly, obligation as arising from *ninjo* or human feelings. On the eve of a national election in the 1960s, a prominent law professor pleaded the virtues of principle in a newspaper article which was strategically titled, "Private Giri and Public Giri" (J. O. Gauntlett, "Undercurrents in Japanese Social Behaviour," *Journal, College of Literature* 6 (1962): 15–16, Tokyo: Aoyama Gakuin University).

20. (Stanford, California: Stanford University Press, 1969), p. ix, emphasis added.

21. I am adapting to China the standard medieval formulation of the correspondence theory, *veritas est adequatio rei et intellectus* (truth is the adequation of a thing and intellect).

22. *Symbolism and Belief* (New York: Macmillan Co., 1938), p. 300.

23. "Plato's Doctrine of Truth," trans. John Barlow, in ed. Henry Aiken and William Barrett, *Philosophy in the Twentieth Century,* vol. 3 (New York: Random House, 1962), pp. 251–270.

24. Frederick Copleston, *A History of Philosophy,* vol. 2, part 2, p. 63. Copleston is describing St. Thomas' position.

It is worth noting, though, that in the Platonic tradition ontological truth itself has a correspondence aspect where the created world is concerned. "Creatures have ontological truth in so far as they embody or exemplify [correspond to] the model in the divine mind" (ibid. 2, 1, p. 88, a propos St. Augustine.)

25. *Plato: An Introduction* (Princeton, New Jersey: Princeton University Press, 1958), pp. 225, 227.

26. Ibid., p. 225.

27. Ibid., p. 229.

28. Ibid.

29. Ibid.

30. *Metaphysics,* 101b.

31. *Metaphysics,* 1025a.

32. *Summa Theologica,* Pt. 2–2 Z 109, Art. 3 Reply Obj. 3.

33. *Why* the West moved in this direction, lies beyond this article, as do the questions of why India and East Asia moved in their distinctive directions regarding truth. I have toyed with answers in my "Accents of the World's Philosophies," *Philosophy East and West* 7, nos. 1 and 2 (1957); "Accents of the World's Religions," in John Bowman, ed., *Comparative Religion* (Leiden: E. J. Brill, 1972); "Valid Materialism: A Western Offering to Hocking's 'Civilization in the Singular,'" in Leroy Rouner, ed., *Philosophy, Religion, and the Coming World Civilization* (The Hague: Martinus Nijhoff, 1966); "Tao Now: An Ecological Testament," in Ian Barbour, ed., *Earth Might Be Fair* (Englewood Cliffs, New Jersey: Prentice-Hall, 1972); and "Man's Western Way: An Essay on Reason and the Given," *Philosophy East and West* 22, no. 4 (October, 1972). I remain far from satisfied with my inroads on the problem, however.

34. *The Great Chain of Being* (Cambridge: Harvard University Press, 1936), p. 59.

35. (Princeton University: Program in Near Eastern Studies, 1969), privately distributed.

36. Op. cit.

37. I am referring, may he forgive me, to a friend, Gregory Vlastos, and his 1965 Presidential Address to the Eastern Division of the American Philosophical Association. An elaboration of his earlier "Degrees of Reality in Plato," appears in his *Platonic Studies* (Princeton, New Jersey: University Press, 1973). Take, he writes, "the 'real' bed in the *Republic,* which turns out to be not the one we sleep on. . . . How could a man who had so little patience with loose talk want to say in all seriousness an abstract Form is 'more real' than wood and glue?" (vii).

STUDY QUESTIONS

1. What is knowledge according to Theaetetus? Where does it reside? In sense-impressions? In perception? In judgment? Give reasons for your answer.
2. Analyze the different sorts of knowledge outlined in *Theaetetus.*
3. Evaluate the claim that knowledge is justified true judgment.
4. In *Theaetetus,* Socrates argues against the Protagrean thesis that man is the measure of all things. Do you find his arguments convincing?
5. Explain Meno's puzzle about learning. What does it demonstrate? Why and how is learning possible?
6. Explain the process by which the boy slave arrives at the right answer. Does he have innate knowledge of geometry? Do you find Socrates' answers convincing? Give reasons for your answer.
7. Explain the concept of innate ideas. Are these ideas a priori or are they implanted in us by God? Argue for your position.
8. What are the means of valid knowledge discussed in Indian philosophy?
9. What is perception? Discuss the distinction between indeterminate and determinate perception that Indian epistemologists make?
10. Discuss the main features of Dharmarāja's account of cognition generated by words alone.
11. Compare and contrast the Nyāya and the Buddhist accounts of perception.
12. What is truth? How is it apprehended?
13. Discuss Al-Ghazāli's conception of knowledge. He challenges the accuracy of the beliefs that are based on sense-perception and intellect. Do you find his arguments defensible? Explain clearly.
14. Discuss what Al-Ghazāli means by prophetic revelation? Do you consider prophetic revelation a reliable source of knowledge? If yes, why yes? If not, why, not?
15. Discuss the distinction that Al-Ghazāli makes among knowledge, immediate experience, and faith?
16. How do we know that someone is a prophet? Are Al-Ghazāli's arguments persuasive? Explain clearly.
17. Descartes says, "I think therefore I am." What arguments does Descartes give to substantiate his thesis? What are these arguments intended to demonstrate? Does he succeed in his efforts? Give reasons for your answer.
18. Both Descartes and Al-Ghazāli begin with doubt to reach certainty. Compare and contrast the two. Which one makes more sense and why?

19. Explain in your words the central issues that surround epistemology? Which issue do you find most fascinating? Why? Select one of the epistemological theories discussed in this section and analyze how this theory will answer the issue that you have selected.

20. Huston Smith in his article discusses truth from a global perspective ,that encompasses India, China, and the West. Which account do you find more persuasive and why?

21. Is knowledge a thing that one can possess? Discuss the issue from an Indian, a Chinese, or a Western perspective. Argue for the perspective that seems most plausible.

SUGGESTIONS FOR FURTHER READING

The Nyāya Theory of Knowledge, 2nd ed., by Satischandra Chatterjee (Calcutta: University of Calcutta Press, 1950) contains lucid discussions of each of the four valid means of true cognition and compares Nyāya theories to other Indian theories of knowledge. It gives a reliable exposition of the epistemological theories of Indian systems of thought.

Plato's Theory of Knowledge by F.M. Cornford (Indianapolis: Bobbs-Merrill, 1957) provides a translation of the *Theaetetus* with a running commentary.

Six Ways of Knowing by D.M. Datta (Calcutta: University of Calcutta, 1972) discusses Advaita Vedānta epistemology critically and compares it with that of other schools of Indian philosophy.

An Introduction to Śaṅkara's Theory of Knowledge by N. K. Devaraja (Delhi: Motilal Banarsidass, 1962) is a good summary of the epistemological issues surrounding Śaṃkara's philosophy.

Dharmarāja's *Vedānta Paribhāṣā* translated by Swami Madhavananda (Calcutta: The Ramakrishna Mission, 1972) is a readable translation of the entire *Vedānta Paribhāṣā*.

Demons, Dreamers, and Madmen by Harry Frankfurt (Indianapolis: Bobbs-Merrill, 1970) contains a careful examination of Descartes's theory of knowledge found in the *Meditations*.

The Central Philosophy of Buddhism by T. R. V. Murti (London: George Allen & Unwin, 1960) gives a very good idea of the key points in Buddhism and its development. The book might be somewhat difficult for beginners.

Philosophy East and West, October 1980 (vol. 30, no. 4), contains very useful articles on truth by contemporary scholars from the Indian, Chinese, and Zen perspectives.

History of Indian Epistemology by Jwala Prasad (Delhi: Munshi Ram Manoharlal, 1958) introduces the students to the basic issues that surround Indian epistemology.

Methods of Knowledge by Swami Satprakashananda (Calcutta: Advaita Ashram, 1974) presents important issues surrounding Advaita epistemology in relation to that of other schools of Indian and Western thought.

Plato—the Man and His Ideas by A.E. Taylor (London: Methuen, 1963) gives a detailed analysis of Plato's dialogues with an excellent commentary. This is a very useful book on Plato's thoughts.

Part 3

Ethics

3.1

Introduction: On What Principles Do I Judge Things Right and Wrong?

The central theme of the discipline known as ethics is captured in Kant's well-known formulation, "what we ought to do." This way of tying ethics to the two concepts of "doing" or action and "ought" has determined the concerns of moral philosophy in the Western tradition since Kant. But at the same time many philosophers within the Western tradition have rejected this restriction, and would rather expand the domain of ethics to include problems of being (as opposed to doing). In Nicolai Hartmann's words, this would put squarely within ethics the question of ought-to-be as much as the question of ought-to-do. For this view of things, we have to return, within the Western tradition, to Aristotle. As regards the other Kantian concept, namely, that of "ought," many moral philosophers have begun to question whether we should restrict ethics to the ought (the ought-to-do as well as the ought-to-be), and should also consider the way people and communities are. In other words, philosophers have begun to question the importance and finality of the distinction between the "is" and the "ought." For this sort of questioning, we turn as well to Aristotle and Hegel, as to Confucius and Gautama, the Buddha.

Plato gives a classic formulation to the ethical questions by distinguishing, in Euthyphro, between giving different instances of piety, for example (or, of justice) and explaining the general idea which makes all pious things pious (or, just acts just). The latter, i.e, piety as such (or justice as such) must be the same in all pious (or, just) acts. Further, nothing can be both pious and impious (or, both just and unjust). The gods and men, Socrates argues, may differ as to which particular men or their acts are pious or impious, just or unjust, but they all should agree as to what is meant by piety or justice. Euthyphro then proceeds to advance various definitions of piety, one of

159

which, as amended by Socrates, is: what all the gods love is pious. But soon Socrates confronts Euthyphro with the question: Is something pious because it is loved by the gods, or do the Gods love it because it is pious? Euthyphro chooses the second alternative as the more reasonable, but then that implies that being holy and being loved by the Gods are quite different properties, which shows that the proposed definitions of being pious or being holy would not do. Similar difficulties arise with regard to the relation between the idea of piety and the idea of justice. In a typically Socratic fashion, the dialog ends abruptly and the central question remains undecided. But we owe it to Socrates that he has sharpened the question, and shown us how to determine if an answer is satisfactory or not. But he has left us with a difficult conceptual question concerning the definition of a concept.; it would seem that the definition would be either analytic and so trivial or synthetic in which case it would be false. The situation led the contemporary philosopher G.E. Moore to hold that goodness is an indefinable property.

The Kantian question of "what we ought to do" may be taken either distributively to mean, What are the actions we ought to do? or in the criteriological sense to mean, What are the criteria, standards and principles by which to decide what to do? When Socrates asked Euthyphro, "What is piety?" he did not ask for examples of piety but for the general idea that makes all pious things to be pious, or for the standard by which one may judge that an action is pious. This search for principles and standards continues through the history of Western thought. In this sense, Kant takes up the Socratic enquiry.

Aristotle, on the other hand, initiated what in our time is called virtue ethics. Some important features of Aristotle's ethics are: first of all, it is not based upon a complete separation between the "is" and the "ought." "It seems not unreasonable," he writes, "that people should derive their conception of the good or happiness from men's lives." Secondly, the theory of virtue is pluralistic, which means that although Aristotle does give definitions of virtue as a general concept, he gives us a whole list of virtues. Along with presenting us with a plethora of virtues, he does not leave them as a chaotic multiplicity, but arranges them in a hierarchy with a conception of the highest good at the apex. He also seeks to tie virtue with happiness closely—not by way of regarding happiness as the dessert to which a virtuous person is entitled, but rather as an intrinsic component of the very idea of a virtuous life. His theory is also "naturalistic" in the sense that the overall concept of "good life" derives from a conception of "the function of human beings," by which he means the specific function of human life. This function he comes to regard as being the life of action in conformity with reason, which is also a life in accordance with the best virtue. To lead a virtuous life is to fulfil the specific function of a human *quā* human. While he thus connects the idea of virtue with the specific function of human life,

Aristotle recognizes that man is not by nature virtuous, nor is his nature contrary to pursuit of virtue. Cultivation of virtue is a matter of habit, just as one loses that excellence by not continuing to do virtuous acts.

In this brief introduction, we will draw attention to two other components of his thoughts on "virtue": one of these is that virtue is a mean between extremes, the other concerns the relation between virtue and happiness. If a virtue is an excellence of a rational person, it must be—as the idea of rationality itself suggests—a mean between extremes. Thus indulgence in sensuous pleasures and ascetic self-denial are extremes between whom temperance is the mean, and so a virtue. Likewise, courage is a virtue, being the mean between foolhardiness and cowardice. The other important idea of Aristotle is that the virtuous person in performing acts of virtue should also feel happy, that virtue and happiness go together, and also that happiness is a necessary component of good life. Both these ideas came to be rejected under the influence of Christianity. Some of the Aristotelian virtues, such as "courage," ceased to be a part of the later conception of good life, and although it continued to be thought that the virtuous ought to be happy, it was also emphasized that as a matter of fact the virtuous quite often suffer. These changes are best reflected in the moral philosophy of Kant. Happiness is construed as a "reward" of virtuous life, and not as a component of it; the relation between virtue and happiness came to be seen as synthetic (needing God to join them together) and not as analytic.

Besides Aristotle's ethics of virtue, Western ethics is dominated by two other philosophical conceptions. One of them is best represented by Kant, the other by utilitarianism. Kant insisted that what is good in itself is good will, everything else derives its moral worth from good will, that consequences are of no value in ascribing moral worth to an action or its agent, and that what is of sole importance is not an external authority but reason itself, so that the rational agent is autonomous, and the principle according to which he acts must be universalizable without contradiction.

As opposed to the Kantian ethics—known as deontological theory—utilitarianism lays exclusive value on the consequences of an action. The principle of utility judges an action by its ability to produce "the greatest happiness of the greatest number." Of two or more alternative courses of action, that ought to be done which brings about greater happiness of the greatest number.

It should be noted that both Kantian and utilitarian ethics recognize a highest principle of morality, for both moral judgment is an application of this principle to a concrete case, both accept something that is intrinsically good, and not merely good as a means (for Kantianism, that is good will; for utilitarianism, it is "the greatest happiness of the greatest number"). Kantianism, in addition, places absolute moral worth on each person as a rational being; utilitarianism regards a person only as the *recipient* of utility, which tends to deprive her of intrinsic worth. Both moral theories involve an impersonal standpoint from which alone moral judgments can be made: for a Kantian, the standpoint requires universalizability, for utilitarianism I am in no more privileged position than any other in calculation of utility. Both theories require the moral judge to be a rational judge: for the Kantian he has to judge self-consistency and universalizability, for the utilitarian he has to calculate maximal happiness.

Contemporary Western moral theory in many respects is a reaction against these two dominant alternatives. Virtue ethics in reaction turns toward an Aristotelian theory of plurality of virtues, i.e., excellences that persons within a tradition may pursue without subjecting themselves to a moral law. Existentialist ethics, on the other hand, warns against making human beings objects of rational investigation, because use of rational dichotomies such as freedom/responsibility, being/non-being, existence/essence precludes human beings from facing reality. They argue for human conditions in which human beings are radically free; "freedom" taken as a condition of human existence, rather than a characteristic of human nature which finds expression in our making decisions. Thus what we are as human beings is a function of the choices we make, but not the other way around, i.e., that choices we make are not a function of what we are as human beings. So they argue that an individual has to make decisions by staking her entire life, the situations that could not be generalized and could not be taken as examples of a law. If Kantian ethics said, "Do not act as if you are an exception," the latter becomes in the words of Simone de Beauvoir, "an ethics of ambiguity."

In her writings, de Beauvoir attempts to bring together the salient features of existentialist ethics to demonstrate its plausibility. Although an individual person is the sole source of values, that does not imply that she or he is free to create values arbitrarily. In no uncertain terms, she points out that the existialist ethics supports human responsibility. "Willing oneself free" is an absolute precondition of morality. She contrasts "willing oneself not free" with "choosing not to will oneself free." The former is self-contradictory and if one chooses not to be free one is not thereby relieved from moral responsibility. With no absolute value to guide her choice, and with no external justifications in terms of utility, the ethical agent chooses, and by her choice, makes herself into what she is. But since human nature is not, unlike with Kant, pure rationality, but rather "to be what one is not," that is to say negativity, existentialism has an explanation of the possibility of evil will which Kantian conception of rational will cannot account for. On de Beauvoir's account, freedom is the capacity to will evil as well as good.

Whereas in the classical Western moral philosophy the task of ethics is to legitimize and ground our moral beliefs on the basis of fundamental principles (e.g., Kant's principle of universalization without self-contradiction,

Mill's principle of utility, etc.), ethics in the non-Western context parallels Hegel's concept of *Sittlichkeit,* the actual order of norms, duties, virtues that a society cherishes. During its formative stage, i.e., during the Classical period of Chinese schools, Chinese philosophers very seldom discussed issues of morality in their own rights. Such questions were generally discussed in the context of rulership and government. Likewise, in the Indian context, ethics was taken to be a means to proper living; the attempt to ground moral judgment on a principle was not there. Finally, in the Islamic philosophy, ethical questions concerned the elaboration and clarification of moral imperatives grounded in the scripture, which was taken to be authoritative. The point that we are trying to make is as follows: non-Western ethics does not provide a full-fledged ethical theory to legitimize all ethical choices but rather covers a large spectrum of issues encompassing within its fold a theory of virtues, a theory of rules, social ethics, and the doctrine of duty for duty's sake.

In reviewing the Chinese thought, we find that a tension, very similar to the one in Western ethics between an ethics of universality and a concrete ethics of virtues, exists. The list of Confucian virtues is well known. However, before we discuss these virtues in abstract, let us briefly review the Confucian ideal of *chün-tzu,* the type of person that Confucius wanted his disciples to become. The term *"chün-tzu"* (meaning the authentic or profound person) did not have moral connotations initially; it was a social term meaning "the sons of the nobles." Confucius extended the meaning of the term to include morality. A profound person was a person of high moral values, not simply a person who was respected socially. Since Confucius believed that the leaders of society—in theory, the potential rulers—should embody traditional moral values, his interpretaion of the term does not come as a surprise.

An authentic person lives his life according to certain virtues. At the top is *jen* (or ren), meaning magnanimity, human-heartedness, compassion for the other. This has a positive and a negative aspect. The positive aspect is *chung* or "doing one's best," conscientiousness; the negative aspect is *shu* or not to impose on others what you yourself do not desire or discarding what other people do not want done to them. Then there are *li* and *yi: li* meaning propriety, appropriate or socially right actions, rituals and ceremonies (compare Hegel's *Sittlichkeit*); and *yi* being dutifulness and oughtness (compare Hegel's *Moralität*). Without *li, yi* is empty; without *yi, li* is just raw stuff. As raw stuff, *li* has to be perfected with *yi* (Fingarette). *Li* is external, *yi* is internal. Alternately, *li* is the action of the lower self, to be overcome by *yi,* the higher self. Or again, *li* is non-moral social conformity, *yi* represents "personal investment of moral meaning" (Ames), such that, in the words of Tuan Yü-t́sai, each person achieves his appropriateness in the performance of social norms. The Confucian idea is that you cannot dispense with *li* altogether, without *li,* morality—as Hegel said of Kantian morality—would be abstract. Finally, in the Confucian list of major virtues, stands *chi* or properly informed intelligence or judgment, judgment about particular situations, which is not merely applying rules, but more like Aristotelian *phronesis.* Besides these four, there are other Confucian virtues of which two need mention: filiality or devotion and obedience to one's ruler.

It is easy to find in these Confucian thoughts several remarkable, though controversial features: a reverence for an idealized past, an emphasis upon ritual, familial pattern as model for a hierarchical society. But a deeper appreciation and closer textual study has led to philosophically more exciting layers of thought. Thus one commentator finds in the concept of *li* a layer of sacredness much akin to that characterizing a sacred ceremony (Fingarette); another takes Confucian ethics to center around the project of learning to be human, to become "good, true, beautiful, great, sagely, and spiritual" (Tu Wei-Ming). A third commentator detects in *li* as liturgy, art as drama, and finds in Confucius three grades of aesthetic experience (symbolic poem, liturgical drama, and musical ecstasy), leading to two sorts of moral creation (creation of personality for each self, and creation of possibility for the others through education) (Imamichi).

Mo Tzu (470–391 B.C.E.?), a rival of Confucius, was the founder of Mohism. Until approximately 200 B.C.E., Mohism and Confucianism were two important schools in Chinese thought. Peace, welfare of all, and impartial love for humankind characterized Mo Tzu's ethical teachings. He opposed Confucius on almost every point. Whereas Confucius emphasized rituals, ceremonies, and veneration of the past, Mo Tzu ridiculed rituals and ceremonies and focused on the future. Confucius argued for the intrinsic goodness of good life based on *jen,* Mo Tzu's emphasis was on *yi* and he articulated goodness of life in terms of its good consequences. In this respect, one finds his teachings to be very similar to utilitarianism: actions were taken to be good to the extent that they maximize the good. Anything that is good for only a few should be rejected, what benefits all on an impartial basis should be accepted. Confucius makes human relations to be the source of moral obligations, Mo Tzu articulates obligations as universal and in this respect echoes Kant's idea of universality. Mo Tzu argues that immoral actions involve making exceptions and morality demands equality. However, equality, for Mo Tzu, implies treating everyone with equal love. The Confucians found this an impractical ideal, and would rather start with filiality and brotherly love as the point of departure. Thus, if Confucius is the Chinese Aristotle, Mo Tzu could be characterized as combining Kant and Mill: partiality is to be replaced by universality, regard others as one's self, the highest ideal is universal love, the good cannot be separated from the useful, universal love would lead to universal happiness.

Buddhism is essentially an ethical religion. With no use for the idea of God, Buddhism encourages a good life for which the Buddha laid down the Noble Eight-fold Path. It is a religion insofar as the large soteriological goal of *nirvāṇa* as freedom from suffering looms large before the Buddhist, but *nirvāṇa* is to be attained only through the Noble Eight-fold Path which, in its essentials, consists in purging the mind of evil passions and thoughts, cultivating noble feelings and thoughts, knowing that things are impermanent and that there is no substantial, eternal self, reaching, as a consequence of that knowledge, desirelessness, and a state of compassion for all human beings. The compassionate wise man is much like the Confucian *chün-tzu*. The Buddhist wise man also avoids extremes and follows the middle path— an idea that found expression also in the Aristotelian "Golden Mean." Cultivating it required unceasing practice, including right knowledge, right concentration, and right meditation.

The ethics of the Hindus interacts at various points with that of Buddhism. The idea of *dharma* (very much like Confucian *li*)—which includes both rules of action pertaining to a person's position in society and virtues as human excellences—comprehends the Hindu *Sittlichkeit,* a large part of which, including the caste (*varṇa*) ethics, was rejected by Gautama, but others, especially what are called *sādhārana dharmas* or *dharmas* holding good of all persons universally (such as truthfulness, noninjury, nonstealing, charity, compassion) were taken into Buddhism. The question whether the *dharmas* have to be practiced in order that the soul may go to heaven, or because they are conducive to other kinds of usefulness, or whether they are to be done simply out of a sense of duty without any consideration of any consequences for the agent was long debated in the early history of Hindu thought until the *Bhagavadagītā,* which gave a decisive and highly influential formulation to the Kantian type of non-consequentialist morality: "Do your duty for its own sake without consideration of, and attachment to, thoughts about likely consequences." The idea of non-attachment remains since then an important component of Hindu ethical tradition. During the time of the *Bhagavadagītā,* there were two prevalent: *pravṛtti* and *nivṛtti.* The first advocated undertaking all obligations with a view to attaining results; the second was the negative ideal of renunciation. The doctrine of renunciation assumed great importance during those days. It was considered a step to pursuing higher life. The rationale was as follows: if any action that one does produces a binding effect, than it is better not to act than to act. The *Bhagavadagītā* puts forward a life of activity while at the same time preserving the spirit of renunciation. It tells one not to renounce actions per se but rather the attitudes that cause attachments to actions. The key to right action is non-attachment to the consequences of the actions. The proper way to perform an act is to dissociate one's mind from pleasure, pain, victory, defeat, fear, and anger and perform the act from a pure sense of duty. This explains why, although the *Bhagavadagītā* begins with *why* one should do one's duty, most of the *Bhagavadagītā* is a discussion of *how* one should do one's duty, i.e., the motive with which one ought to do one's duty. It shows how one can lead a normal life and not accumulate any *karmas* and in so prescribing puts before us a golden mean between the two extremes of *pravṛtti* and *nivṛtti.*

There are several possible answers to the question, Who is the law-giver? What is the source of the moral law? Christianity, and more pointedly Islām, recognized only one source of absolute moral law, and that is God. Contrary to the widespread belief that Islāmic moral philosophy has been monolithically and rigidly God-centered in the sense that all moral rules are divine commands, the history of Islāmic thought shows considerable diversity of views and controversies among Islāmic philosophers on this and related issues. Possibly, the central question has been, whether human reason, independently of revelation, could know what is good and what is not. The Mutazillites held that human reason can determine, by its own powers, the distinctions between good and evil, which are intrinsically objective. Others such as al-Ghazāli reject this view and regard God's revelation as the sole source of our moral knowledge. Attempts were also made to rank all goods in a hierarchical order, with the absolute good often identified as wisdom at the top. Utility, pleasure, and beauty were regarded as three marks of goodness. Ibn Sina identified pure good with pure perfection. Averroes secularized and politicized the idea of the good as being realizable within a political community: like Al Farabi, he could say that the good is the political good.

Kant took the law giver to be none other than the reason that is present in all rational beings. If reason was given to human beings by God who created humans, then Kantian theory may be regarded as a modern conceptualization of the Christian theory. The *Bhagavadagītā* made the scriptures to be the source of *dharma.* In general, however, for both Hinduism and Buddhism, the *dharma* is rooted in the metaphysical nature of things, though disseminated by the Vedas or by the teaching of the Buddha. For Chinese thinking, which does not admit of any eternal law, *li* is essentially historically and socially constituted, as also *yi,* by which one gives moral meaning to one's social actions.

Two pieces included in this volume show how the classical—Indian and Chinese—ethical ideal of non-violence has been extended in our time by Mahatma Gandhi, and following him, by Martin Luther King Jr., to social action and social philosophy. Gandhi transformed non-violence from being a value to be cultivated by an individual in his life to a social ideal, such that a society may be regarded as "non-violent." Such a society he called "*sarvodaya,*" i.e., one in which everyone flourishes. The Gandhian ideal is non-utilitarian, that is to say it does not aim at promoting the greatest happiness of the greatest number. It aims at providing *everyone* with opportunities for flourishing. For this purpose, Gandhi devised an economic plan (based on decentralized, small-scale industry and village-centered organization) and a political setup where the democracy will be party-less and in which everyone would be able to participate at the level of grass-roots. Martin Luther King Jr. used the Gandhian method of non-violent non-cooperation with certain American conditions, and, like Gandhi, he fell victim to the bullets of an assassin who thought his ideology to be dangerous. It is important to keep in mind that the Gandhian idea of non-violence, in spite of its deep roots in the Indian tradition, was also moulded by influences from the West, especially the ideas of Tolstoy and Thoreau: in Gandhi, the East and the West had already met, before he himself became a major influence from the East on the West.

3.2

The First Sermon

Gautama Buddha

. . . the Blessed One that now, having solved the mystery, his work is done, and that the time had arrived for him to pass away without attempting to proclaim to others the glad tidings of the Noble Way.

But he rejected the thought, veiled under this figure of a suggestion from without, and resolved to preach his gospel to the world. First he sought out and proclaimed it to the five recluses who had been till lately his companions. In the oldest account of this episode it is stated that when they saw him coming, they concerted with each other, saying:

"Friends, there comes the Samana Gotama, who lives in abundance, who has given up his exertions, and has turned back to a life of ease. Let us not salute him, nor rise from our seats when he approaches, nor take his bowl and his robe from his hands. But let us just put there a seat. If he likes, let him sit down."

But when the Blessed One gradually approached nigh unto those five recluses, the five could not keep their agreement. They went forth to meet the Blessed One. One took his bowl and his robe, another prepared a seat; a third brought water wherewith to wash his feet, and a footstool thereto and a towel. Then the Blessed One sat down on the seat they had prepared.

Now they addressed the Blessed One by his name, and with the appellation "Friend." But he said to them: "Do not address the Tathagata by his name, or by the appellation 'Friend.' The Tathagata has become an Arahat, the supreme Buddha. Give ear, O recluses. The ambrosia has been won by me. I will teach you. To you I preach the Dharma (the Law, the Norm). If you walk in the way that I will show, you will ere long, having yourselves known it and seen it face to face, live in the possession of that highest goal

From *The History and Literature of Buddhism,* by T.W. Rhys Davids (Varanasi: Bhartiya Publishing House, first appeared in 1896), pp. 68–90. The text edited and Footnotes deleted.

of the holy life, for the sake of which clansmen give up the world and go forth into the homeless state."

They then object that, having given up his austerities, how can he claim to have gained the insight he had been seeking. But he repeats to them his assurance of knowledge; and when they again object, he says : "Do you admit that I have never unburdened myself to you in this way before this day?"

"You have never spoken so, lord," is the reply. He then sets out to them his view of life in a discourse called the *Dhamma-cakka-ppavattana-sutta,* or the "Foundation of the Kingdom of Righteousness.". . .

"There are two extremes, O recluses, which he who has gone forth ought not to follow The habitual practice, on the one hand, of those things whose attraction depends upon the pleasures of sense, and especially of sensuality (a practice low and pagan, fit only for the worldly-minded, unworthy, of no abiding profit); and the habitual practice, on the other hand, of self-mortification (a practice painful, unworthy, and equally of no abiding profit).

"There is a Middle Way, O recluses, avoiding these two extremes, discovered by the Tathagata—a path which opens the eyes and bestows understanding, which leads to peace of mind, to the higher wisdom to full enlightenment, to Nirvana."

"And which is that Middle Way? Verily, it is the Noble Eightfold Path. That is to say
Right Views (free from superstition or delusion)—
Right Aspirations (high, and worthy of the intelligent, worthy man)—
Right Speech (kindly, open, truthful)—
Right Conduct (peaceful, honest, pure)—
Right Livelihood (bringing hurt or danger to no living thing)—
Right Effort (in self-training and in self-control)—
Right Mindfulness (the active, watchful mind)—
Right Rapture (in deep meditation on the realities of life)."

"Now this, O recluses, is the noble truth concerning suffering."

"Birth is painful and so is old age; disease is painful and so is death. Union with the unpleasant is painful, painful is separation from the pleasant; and any craving that is unsatisfied, that too is painful. In brief, the five aggregates which spring from attachment (the conditions of individuality and its cause), they are painful.

"Now this, O recluses, is the noble truth concerning the origin of suffering. Verily, it originates in that craving thirst which causes the renewal of becomings, is accompanied by sensual delight, and seeks satisfaction now here, . . . that is to say, the craving for the gratification of the passions, or the craving for a future life, or the craving for success in this present life (the lust of the flesh, the lust of life, or the pride of life)."

"Now this, O recluses, is the noble truth concerning the destruction of suffering.

Verily, it is the destruction, in which no craving remains over, of this very thirst; the laying aside of, the getting rid of, the being free from, the harbouring no longer of, this thirst."

"And this, O recluses, is the noble truth concerning the way which leads to the destruction of suffering.

"Verily, it is this Noble Eightfold Path; that is to say:

Right Views (free from superstition and delusion)—

Right Aspirations (high and worthy of the intelligent, earnest man)—

Right Speech (kindly, open, truthful)—

Right Conduct (peaceful, honest, pure)—

Right Livelihood (bringing hurt or danger to no living thing)—

Right Effort (in self-training and in self-control)—

Right Mindfulness (the active, watchful mind)—

Right Rapture (in deep meditation on the realities of life)."

Then with regard to each of the Four Truths, the Teacher declared that it was not among the doctrines handed down; but that there arose within him the eye firstly to see it, then to know that he would understand it, and thirdly, to know that he had grasped it; there arose within him the knowledge (of its nature), the understanding (of its cause), the wisdom (to guide in the path of tranquillity), and the light (to dispel darkness from it). And he said

"So long, O recluses, as my knowledge and insight were not quite clear regarding each of these four noble truths in this triple order, in this twelvefold manner—so long I knew that I had not attained to the full insight of that wisdom which is unsurpassed in the heavens or on earth, among the whole race of recluses and Brahmins, gods or men. But now I have attained it. This knowledge and insight have arisen within me. Immovable is the emancipation of my heart. This is my last existence. There will be no rebirth for me."

Thus spoke the Blessed One. The five ascetics glad at heart, exalted the words of the Blessed One.

3.3

Euthyphro

Plato

Euthyphro. Why have you left the Lyceum, Socrates? and what are you doing in the porch of the King Archon? Surely you cannot be engaged in an action before the king, as I am.

Socrates. Not in an action, Euthyphro; impeachment is the word which the Athenians use.

Euth. What! I suppose that someone has been prosecuting you, for I cannot believe that you are the prosecutor of another.

Soc. Certainly not.

Euth. Then someone else has been prosecuting you?

Soc. Yes.

Euth. And who is he?

Soc. A young man who is little known, Euthyphro; and I hardly know him: his name is Meletus, and he is of the deme of Pitthis. Perhaps you may remember his appearance; he has a beak, and long straight hair, and a beard which is ill grown.

Euth. No, I do not remember him, Socrates. And what is the charge which he brings against you?

Soc. What is the charge? Well, a very serious charge, which shows a good deal of character in the young man, and for which he is certainly not to be despised. He says he knows how the youth are corrupted and who are their corruptors. I fancy that he must be a wise man, and seeing that I am anything but a wise man, he has found me out, and is going to accuse me of corrupting his young friends. And of this our mother the state is to be the judge. Of all our political men he is the only one who seems to me to begin in the right way, with the cultivation of virtue in youth; he is a good husbandman, and takes care of the shoots first, and clears away us who are the destroyers of them. That is the first step; he will afterwards attend to the elder branches; and if he goes on as he has begun, he will be a very great public benefactor.

From *Euthyphro,* translated by Benjamin Jowett, Tudor Publishing Company, New York, pp. 57–88. First appeared in 1896.

Euth. I hope that he may; but I rather fear, Socrates, that the reverse will turn out to be the truth. My opinion is that in attacking you he is simply aiming a blow at the state in a sacred place. But in what way does he say that you corrupt the young?

Soc. He brings a wonderful accusation against me, which at first hearing excites surprise: he says that I am a poet or maker of gods, and that I make new gods and deny the existence of old ones; this is the ground of his indictment.

Euth. I understand, Socrates; he means to attack you about the familiar sign which occasionally, as you say, comes to you. He thinks that you are a neologian, and he is going to have you up before the court for this. He knows that such a charge is readily received, for the world is always jealous of novelties in religion. And I know that when I myself speak in the assembly about divine things, and foretell the future to them they laugh at me as a madman; and yet every word that I say is true. But they are jealous of all of us. I suppose that we must be brave and not mind them.

Soc. Their laughter, friend Euthyphro, is not a matter of much consequence. For a man may be thought wise; but the Athenians, I suspect, do not care much about this, until he begins to make other men wise; and then for some reason or other, perhaps, as you say, from jealousy, they are angry.

Euth. I have no desire to try conclusions with them about this.

Soc. I dare say that you don't make yourself common, and are not apt to impart your wisdom. But I have a benevolent habit of pouring out myself to every body, and would even pay for a listener, and I am afraid that the Athenians know this; and therefore, as I was saying, if the Athenians would only laugh at me as you say that they laugh at you, the time might pass gaily enough in the court; but perhaps they may be in earnest, and then what the end will be you soothsayers only can predict.

Euth. I dare say that the affair will end in nothing, Socrates, and that you will win your cause; and I think that I shall win mine.

Soc. And what is your suit? and are you the pursuer or defendant, Euthyphro?

Euth. I am pursuer.

Soc. Of whom?

Euth. You will think me mad when I tell you whom I am pursuing.

Soc. Why, has the fugitive wings?

Euth. Nay, he is not very volatile at his time of life.

Soc. Who is he?

Euth. My father.

Soc. Your father! good heavens, you don't mean that?

Euth. Yes.

Soc. And of what is he accused?

Euth. Murder, Socrates.

Soc. By the powers, Euthyphro! how little does the common herd know of the nature of right and truth. A man must be an extraordinary man and have made great strides in wisdom, before he could have seen his way to this.

Euth. Indeed, Socrates, he must have made great strides.

Soc. I suppose that the man whom your father murdered was one of your relatives; if he had been a stranger you would never have thought of prosecuting him.

Euth. I am amused, Socrates, at your making a distinction between one who is a relation and one who is not a relation; for surely the pollution is the same in either case, if you knowingly associate with the murderer when you ought to clear yourself by proceeding against him. The real question is whether the murdered man has been justly slain. If justly, then your duty is to let the matter alone; but if unjustly, then even if the murderer is under the same roof with you and eats at the same table, proceed against him. Now the man who is dead was a poor dependent of mine who worked for us as a field laborer at Naxos, and one day in a fit of drunken passion he got into a quarrel with one of our domestic servants and slew him. My father bound him hand and foot and threw him into a ditch, and then sent to Athens to ask of a diviner what he should do with him. Meantime he had no care or thought of him, being under the impression that he was a murderer; and that even if he did die there would be no great harm. And this was just what happened. For such was the effect of cold and hunger and chains upon him, that before the messenger returned from the diviner, he was dead. And my father and family are angry with me for taking the part of the murderer and prosecuting my father. They say that he did not kill him, and if he did, that dead man was but a murderer, and I ought not to take any notice, for that a son is impious who prosecutes a father. That shows, Socrates, how little they know of the opinions of the gods about piety and impiety.

Soc. Good heavens, Euthyphro! and have you such a precise knowledge of piety and impiety and of divine things in general, that, supposing the circumstances to be as you state, you are not afraid that you too may be doing an impious thing in bringing an action against your father?

Euth. The best of Euthyphro, and that which distinguishes him, Socrates, from other men, is his exact knowledge of all these matters. What should I be good for without that?

Soc. Rare friend! I think that I cannot do better than be your disciple, before the trial with Meletus comes on. Then I shall challenge him, and say that I have always had a great interest in religious questions and now, as he charges me with rash imaginations and innovations in religion, I have become your disciple. Now you, Meletus, as I shall say to him, acknowledge Euthyphro to be a great theologian, and sound in his opinions; and if you think that of him you ought to think the same of me, and not have me into court; you should begin by indicting him who is my teacher; and who is the real corruptor, not of the young, but of the old; that is to say, of myself whom he instructs, and of his old father whom he admonishes and chastises. And if Meletus refuses to listen to me, but will go on and will not shift the indictment from me to you, I cannot do better than say in the court that I challenged him in this way.

Euth. Yes, Socrates; and if he attempts to indict me I am mistaken if I don't find a flaw in him the court shall have a great deal more to say to him than to me.

Soc. I know that, dear friend; and that is the reason why I desire to be your disciple. For I observe that no one, not even Meletus, appears to notice you; but his sharp eyes have found me out at once, and he has indicted me for impiety. And therefore, I adjure you to tell me the nature of piety and impiety, which you said that you knew so well, and of murder, and the rest of them. What are they? Is not piety in every action always the same? and impiety, again, is not that always the opposite of piety, and also the same with itself, having, as impiety, one notion which includes whatever is impious?

Euth. To be sure, Socrates.

Soc. And what is piety, and what is impiety?

Euth. Piety is doing as I am doing; that is to say, prosecuting anyone who is guilty of murder, sacrilege, or of any other similar crime whether he be your father or mother, or some other person, that makes no difference—and not prosecuting them is impiety. And please to consider, Socrates, what a notable proof I will give you of the truth of what I am saying, which I have already given to others:—of the truth, I mean, of the principle that the impious, whoever he may be, ought not to go unpunished. For do not men regard Zeus as the best and most righteous of the gods?—and even they admit that he bound his father (Cronos) because he wickedly devoured his sons, and that he too had punished his own father (Uranus) for a similar reason, in a nameless manner. And yet when I proceed against my father, they are angry with me. This is their inconsistent way of talking when the gods are concerned, and when I am concerned.

Soc. May not this be the reason, Euthyphro, why I am charged with impiety—that I cannot away with these stories about the gods? and therefore I suppose that people think me wrong. But as you who are well informed about them approve of them, I cannot do better than assent to your superior wisdom. For what else can I say, confessing as I do, that I know nothing of them, I wish you would tell me whether you really believe that they are true?

Euth. Yes, Socrates; and things more wonderful still, of which the world is in ignorance.

Soc. And do you really believe that the gods fought with one another, and had dire quarrels, battles, and the like, as the poets say, and as you may see represented in the works of great artists? The temples are full of them; and notably the robe of Athene, which is carried up to the Acropolis at the great Panathenaea, is embroidered with them. Are all these tales of the gods true, Euthyphro?

Euth. Yes, Socrates; and, as I was saying, I can tell you, if you would like to hear them, may other things about the gods which would quite amaze you.

Soc. I dare say; and you shall tell me them at some other time when I have leisure. But just at present I would rather hear from you a more precise answer, which you have not as yet given, my friend, to the question, What is "piety?" In reply, you only say that piety is, doing, as you do, charging your father with murder?

Euth. And that is true, Socrates.

Soc. I dare say, Euthyphro, but there are many other pious acts.

Euth. There are.

Soc. Remember that I did not *ask* you to give *me* two or three examples of piety, but to explain the general idea which makes all pious things to be pious. Do you not recollect that there was one idea which made impious impious, and the pious pious?

Euth. I remember.

Soc. Tell me what this is, and then I shall have a standard to which I may look, and by which I may measure the nature of actions, whether yours or anyone else's, and say that this action is pious, and that impious?

Euth. I will tell you, if you like.

Soc. I should very much like.

Euth. Piety, then, is that which is dear to the gods, and impiety is that which is not dear to them.

Soc. Very good, Euthyphro; you have now given me just the sort of answer which I wanted. But whether it is true or not I cannot as yet tell, although I make no doubt that you will prove the truth of your words.

Euth. Of course.

Soc. Come, then, and let us examine what we are saying. That thing or person which is dear to the gods is pious, and that thing or person which is hateful to the gods is impious. Was not that said?

Euth. Yes, that was said.

Soc. And that seems to have been very well said too?

Euth. Yes, Socrates, I think that; it was certainly said.

Soc. And further, Euthyphro, the gods were admitted to have enmities and hatreds and differences—that was also said?

Euth. Yes, that was said.

Soc. And what sort of difference creates enmity and anger? Suppose for example that you and I, my good friend, differ about a number; do differences of this sort make us enemies and set us at variance with one another? Do we not go at once to calculation, and end them by a sum?

Euth. True.

Soc. Or suppose that we differ about magnitudes, do we not quickly put an end to that difference by measuring?

Euth. That is true.

Soc. And we end a controversy about heavy and light by resorting to a weighing-machine?

Euth. To be sure.

Soc. But what differences are those which because they cannot be thus decided make us angry and set us at enmity with one another? I dare say the answer does not occur to you at the moment, and therefore I will suggest that this happens when the matters of difference are the just and unjust, good and evil, honorable and dishonorable. Are not these the points about which, when differing, and unable satisfactorily to decide our differences, we quarrel, when we do quarrel, as you and I and all men experience?

Euth. Yes, Socrates, that is the nature of the differences about which we quarrel.

Soc. And the quarrels of the gods, noble Euthyphro, when they occur, are of a like nature?

Euth. They are.

Soc. They have differences of opinion, as you say about good and evil, just and unjust, honorable and dishonorable: there would have been no quarrels among them, if there had been no such differences, would there now?

Euth. You are quite right.

Soc. Does not every man love that which he deems noble and just and good, and hate the opposite of them?

Euth. Very true.

Soc. But then, as you say, people regard the same things, some as just and others as unjust; and they dispute about this, and there arise war and fightings among them.

Euth. Yes, that is true.

Soc. Then the same things, as appears, are hated by the gods and loved by the gods, and are both hateful and dear to them?

Euth. True.

Soc. Then upon this view the same things, Euthyphro, will be pious and also impious?

Euth. That, I suppose, is true.

Soc. Then, my friend, I remark with surprise that you have not answered what I asked. For I certainly did not ask what was that which is at once pious and impious: and that which is loved by the gods appears also to be hated by them. And therefore, Euthyphro, in thus chastising your father you may very likely be doing what is agreeable to Zeus but disagreeable to Cronos or Uranus, and what is acceptable to Hephaestus but unacceptable to Hera, and there may be other gods who have similar differences of opinion.

Euth. But I believe, Socrates, that all the gods would be agreed as to the propriety of punishing a murderer: there would be no difference of opinion about that.

Soc. Well, but speaking of men, Euthyphro, did you ever hear anyone arguing that a murderer or any sort of evil-doer ought to be let off?

Euth. I should rather say that they are always arguing this, especially in courts of law: they commit all sorts of crimes, and there is nothing that they will not do or say in order to escape punishment.

Soc. But do they admit their guilt, Euthyphro, and yet say that they ought not to be punished?

Euth. No; they do not.

Soc. Then there are some things which they do not venture to say and do: for they do not venture to argue that the guilty are to be unpunished, but they deny their guilt, do they not?

Euth. Yes.

Soc. Then they do not argue that the evil-doer should not be punished, but they argue about the fact of who the evil-doer is, and what he did and when?

Euth. True.

Soc. And the gods are in the same case, if as you imply they quarrel about just and unjust, and some of them say that they wrong one another, and others of them deny this. For surely neither God nor man will ever venture to say that the doer of evil is not to be punished:—you don't mean to tell me that?

Euth. That is true, Socrates, in the main.

Soc. But they join issue about particulars; and this applies not only to men but to the gods; if they dispute at all they dispute about some act which is called in question, and which some affirm to be just others to be unjust. Is not that true?

Euth. Quite true.

Soc. Well then, my dear friend Euthyphro, do tell me, for my better instruction and information, what proof have you that in the opinion of all the gods a servant who is guilty of murder, and is put in chains by the master of the dead man, and dies because he is put in chains before his corrector can learn from the interpreters what he ought to do with him, dies unjustly; and that on behalf of such an one a son ought to proceed against his father and accuse him of murder. How would you show that all the gods absolutely agree in approving of his act? Prove to me that, and I will applaud your wisdom as long as you live.

Euth. That would not be an easy task, although I could make the matter very clear indeed to you.

Soc. I understand; you mean to say that I am not so quick of apprehension as the judges: for to them you will be sure to prove that the act is unjust, and hateful to the gods.

Euth.Yes indeed, Socrates; at least if they will listen to me.

Soc. But they will be sure to listen if they find that you are a good speaker. There was a notion that came into my mind while you were speaking; I said to myself: "Well, and what if Euthyphro does prove to me that all the gods regarded the death of the serf as unjust, how do I know anything more of the nature of piety and impiety? for granting that this action may be hateful to the gods, still these distinctions have no bearing on the definition of piety and impiety, for that which is hateful to the gods has been shown to be also pleasing and dear to them." And therefore, Euthyphro, I don't ask you to prove this; I will suppose, if you like, that all the gods condemn and abominate such an action. But I will amend the definition so far as to say that what all the gods hate is impious, and what they love pious or holy; and what some of them love and others hate is both or neither. Shall this be our definition of piety and impiety?

Euth. Why not, Socrates?

Soc. Why not! certainly, as far as I am concerned, Euthyphro. But whether this admission will greatly assist you in the task of instructing me as you promised, is a matter for you to consider.

Euth. Yes, I should say that what all the gods love is pious and holy, and the opposite which they all hate, impious.

Soc. Ought we to inquire into the truth of this, Euthyphro, or simply to accept the mere statement on our own authority and that of others?

Euth. We should inquire; and I believe that the statement will stand the test of inquiry.

Soc. That, my good friend, we shall know better in a little while. The point which I should first wish to understand is whether the pious or holy is beloved by the gods because it is holy, or holy because it is beloved of the gods.

Euth. I don't understand your meaning, Socrates.

Soc. I will endeavor to explain: we speak of carrying and we speak of being carried, of leading and being led, seeing and being seen. And here is a difference, the nature of which you understand.

Euth. I think that I understand.

Soc. And is not that which is beloved distinct from that which loves?

Euth. Certainly.

Soc. Well; and now tell me, is that which is carried in this state of carrying because it is carried, or for some other reason?

Euth. No; that is the reason.

Soc. And the same is true of that which is led and of that which is seen?

Euth. True.

Soc. And a thing is not seen because it is visible, but conversely, visible because it is seen; nor is a thing in the state of being led because it is led, or in the state of being carried because it is carried, but the converse of this. And now I think, Euthyphro, that my meaning will be intelligible; and my meaning is, that any state of action or passion implies previous action or passion. It does not become because it is becoming, but it is becoming because it becomes; neither does it suffer? because it is in a state of suffering, but it is in a state of suffering because it suffers. Do you admit that?

Euth. Yes.

Soc. Is not that which is loved in some state either of becoming or suffering?

Euth. Yes.

Soc. And the same holds as in the previous instances; the state of being loved follows the act of being loved, and not the act the state.

Euth. That is certain.

Soc. And what do you say of piety, Euthyphro: is not piety, according to your definition, loved by all the gods?

Euth. Yes.

Soc. Because it is pious or holy, or for some other reason?

Euth. No, that is the reason.

Soc. It is loved because it is holy, not holy because it is loved?

Euth. Yes.

Soc. And that which is in a state to be loved of the gods, and is dear to them, is in a state to be loved of them because it is loved of them?

Euth. Certainly.

Soc. Then that which is loved of God, Euthyphro, is not holy, nor is that which is holy loved of God, as you affirm; but they are two different things.

Euth. How do you mean, Socrates?

Soc. I mean to say that the holy has been acknowledged by us to be loved of God because it is holy, not to be holy because it is loved.

Euth. Yes.

Soc. But that which is dear to the gods is dear to them because it is loved by them, not loved by them because it is dear to them.

Euth. True.

Soc. But, friend Euthyphro, if that which is holy is the same as that which is dear to God, and that which is holy is loved as being holy, then that which is dear to God would have been loved as being dear to God; but if that which is dear to God is dear to him because loved by him, then that which is holy would have been holy because loved by him. But now you see that the reverse is the case, and that they are quite different from one another. For one is of a kind to be loved because it is loved, and the other . . . is loved because it is of a kind to be loved. Thus you appear to me, Euthyphro, when I ask you what is the essence of holiness, to offer an attribute only, and not the essence, the attribute of being loved by all the gods. But you still refuse to explain to me the nature of piety. And therefore if you please, I will ask you not to hide your treasure, but to tell me once more what piety or holiness really is, whether dear to the gods or not (for that is a matter about which we will not quarrel). And what is impiety?

Euth. I really do not know, Socrates, how to say what I mean. For somehow or other our arguments on whatever ground we rest them, seem to turn round and walk away.

Soc. Your words, Euthyphro are like the handiwork of my ancestor Daedalus; and if I were the sayer or propounder of them, you might say that this comes of my being his relation; and that this is the reason why my arguments walk away and won't remain fixed where they are placed. But now, as the notions are your own, you must find some other gibe, for they certainly, as you yourself allow, show an inclination to be on the move.

Euth. Nay, Socrates, I shall still say that you are the Daedalus who sets arguments in motion; not I, certainly, make them move or go round, for they would never have stirred, as far as I am concerned.

Soc. Then I must be greater than Daedalus for whereas he only made his own inventions to move I move those of other people as well. And the beauty of it is, that I would rather not. For I would give the wisdom of Daedalus, and the wealth of Tantalus to be able to detain them and keep them fixed. But enough of this. As I perceive that you are indolent, I will myself endeavor to show you how you might instruct me in the nature of piety; and I hope that you will not grudge our labor. Tell me, then,—Is not that which is pious necessarily just?

Euth. Yes.

Soc. And is, then, all which is just pious? or, is that which is pious all just, but that which is just only in part and not all pious?

Euth. I don't understand you, Socrates.

Soc. And yet I know that you are as much wiser than I am, as you are younger. But, as I was saying, revered friend, the abundance of your wisdom makes you indolent. Please to exert yourself, for there is no real difficulty in understanding me. What I mean I may explain by an illustration of what I do not mean. The poet (Stasinus) sings—

> "Of Zeus, the author and creator of all these things,
> You will not tell: for where there is fear there is also reverence."

And I disagree with this poet. Shall I tell you in what I disagree?

Euth. By all means.

Soc. I should not say that where there is fear there is also reverence; for I am sure that many persons fear poverty and disease, and the like evils, but I do not perceive that they revere the objects of their fear.

Euth. Very true.

Soc. But where reverence is, there is fear; for he who has a feeling of reverence and shame about the commission of any action, fears and is afraid of an ill reputation.

Euth. No doubt.

Soc. Then we are wrong in saying that where there is fear there is also reverence; and we should say, where there is reverence there is also fear. But there is not always reverence where there is fear; for fear is a more extended notion, and reverence is a part of fear, just as the odd is a part of number, and number is a more extended notion than the odd. I Suppose that you follow me now?

Euth. Quite well.

Soc. That was the sort of question which I meant to raise when asking whether the just is the pious, or the pious the just; and whether there may not be justice where there is not always piety; for justice is the more extended notion of which piety is only a part. Do you agree in that?

Euth. Yes; that, I think, is correct.

Soc. Then, now, if piety is a part of justice, I suppose that we inquire what part? If you had pursued the injury in the previous cases; for instance, if you had asked me what is an even number, and what part of number the even is, I should have had no difficulty in replying, a number which represents a figure having two equal sides. Do you agree?

Euth. Yes.

Soc. In like manner, I want you to tell me what part of justice is piety or holiness; that I may be able to tell Meletus not to do me injustice, or indict me for impiety; as I am now adequately instructed by you in the nature of piety or holiness, and their opposites.

Euth. Piety or holiness, Socrates, appears to me to be that part of justice which attends to the gods, as there is the other part of justice which attends to men.

Soc. That is good, Euthyphro; yet still there is a little point about which I should like to have further information, What is the meaning of "attention?" For attention can hardly be used in the same sense when applied to the gods as when applied to other things. For instance, horses are said to require attention, and not every person is able to attend to them, but only a person skilled in horsemanship. Is not that true?

Euth. Quite true.

Soc. I should suppose that the art of horsemanship is the art of attending to horses?

Euth. Yes.

Soc. Nor is every one qualified to attend to dogs, but only the huntsman.

Euth. True.

Soc. And I should also conceive that the art of the huntsman is the art of attending to dogs?

Euth. Yes.

Soc. As the art of the oxherd is the art of attending to oxen?

Euth. Very true.

Soc. And as holiness or piety is the art of attending to the gods?—that would be your meaning, Euthyphro?

Euth. Yes.

Soc. And is not attention always designed for the good or benefit of that to which the attention is given? As in the case of horses, you may observe that when attended to by the horseman's art they are benefited and improved, are they not?

Euth. True.

Soc. As the dogs are benefited by the huntsman's art, and the oxen by the art of the oxherd, and all other things are tended or attended for their good and not for their hurt?

Euth. Certainly, not for their hurt.

Soc. But for their good?

Euth. Of course.

Soc. And does piety or holiness, which has been defined as the art of attending to the gods, benefit or improve them? Would you say that when you do a holy act you make any of the gods better?

Euth. No, no; that is certainly not my meaning.

Soc. Indeed, Euthyphro, I did not suppose that this was your meaning. And that was the reason why I asked you the nature of this attention, because I thought that this was not your meaning.

Euth. You do me justice, Socrates; for that is not my meaning.

Soc. Good: but I must still ask what is this attention to the gods which is called piety?

Euth. It is such, Socrates, as servants show to their masters.

Soc. I understand—a sort of ministration to the gods.

Euth. Exactly.

Soc. Medicine is also a sort of ministration or service, tending to the attainment of some object would you not say health?

Euth. Yes.

Soc. Again, there is an art which ministers to the ship-builder with a view to the attainment of some result?

Euth. Yes, Socrates, with a view to the building of a ship.

Soc. As there is an art which ministers to the housebuilder with a view to the building of a house?

Euth. Yes.

Soc. And now tell me, my good friend, about this art which ministers to the gods: what work does that help to accomplish? For you must surely know if, as you say, you are of all men living the one who is best instructed in religion.

Euth. And that is true, Socrates.

Soc. Tell me then, oh tell me —what is that fair work which the gods do by the help of us as their ministers?

Euth. Many and fair, Socrates, are the works which they do.

Soc. Why, my friend, and so are those of a general. But the chief of them is easily told. Would you not say that victory in war is the chief of them?

Euth. Certainly.

Soc. Many and fair, too, are the works of the husbandman, if I am not mistaken; but his chief work is the production of food from the earth?

Euth. Exactly.

Soc. And of the many and fair things which the gods do, which is the chief and principal one?

Euth. I have told you already, Socrates, that to learn all these things accurately will be very tiresome. Let me simply say that piety is learning how to please the gods in word and deed, by prayers and sacrifices. That is piety, which is the salvation of families and states, just as the impious, which is unpleasing to the gods, is their ruin and destruction.

Soc. I think that you could have answered in much fewer words the chief question which I asked, Euthyphro, if you had chosen. But I see plainly that you are not disposed to instruct me: else why, when we had reached the point, did you turn aside? Had you only answered me I should have learned of you by this time the nature of piety. Now, as the asker of a question is necessarily dependent on the answerer, whither he leads I must follow; and can only ask again, what is the pious, and what is piety? Do you mean that they are a sort of science of praying and sacrificing?

Euth. Yes, I do.

Soc. And sacrificing is giving to the gods, and prayer is asking of the gods?

Euth. Yes, Socrates.

Soc. Upon this view, then, piety is a science of asking and giving?

Euth. You understand me capitally, Socrates.

Soc. Yes, my friend; the reason is that I am a Votary of your science, and give my mind to it, and therefore nothing which you say will be thrown away upon me. Please then to tell me, what is the nature of this service to the gods? Do you mean that we prefer requests and give gifts to them?

Euth. Yes, I do.

Soc. Is not the right way of asking to ask of them what we want?

Euth. Certainly.

Soc. And the right way of giving is to give to them in return what they want of us. There would be no meaning in an art which gives to anyone that which he does not want,

Euth. Very true, Socrates.

Soc. Then piety, Euthyphro, is an art which gods and men have of doing business with one another?

Euth. That is an expression which you may use, if you like.

Soc. But I have no particular liking for anything but the truth. I wish, however, that you would tell me what benefit accrues to the gods from our gifts. That they are the givers of every good to us is clear; but how we can give any good thing to them in return is far from being equally clear. If they give everything and we give nothing, that must be an affair of business in which we have very greatly the advantage of them.

Euth. And do you imagine, Socrates, that any benefit accrues to the gods from what they receive of us?

Soc. But if not, Euthyphro, what sort of gifts do we confer upon the gods?

Euth. What should we confer upon them, but tributes of honor; and, as I was just now saying, what is pleasing to them?

Soc. Piety, then, is pleasing to the gods, but not beneficial or dear to them?

Euth. I should say that nothing could be dearer.

Soc. Then once more the assertion is repeated that piety is dear to the gods?

Euth. No doubt.

Soc. And when you say this, can you wonder at your words not standing firm, but walking away? Will you accuse me of being the Daedalus who makes them walk away, not perceiving that there is another and far greater artist than Daedalus who makes them go round in a circle; and that is yourself: for the argument, as you will perceive, comes round to the same point. I think that you must remember our saying that the holy or pious was not the same as that which is loved of the gods. Do you remember that?

Euth. I do.

Soc. And do you not see that what is loved of the gods is holy, and that this is the same as what is dear to them?

Euth. True.

Soc. Then either we were wrong in that admission; or, if we were right then, we are wrong now.

Euth. I suppose that is the case.

Soc. Then we must begin again and ask, What is piety? That is an inquiry which I shall never be weary of pursuing as far as in me lies; and I entreat you not to scorn me, but to apply your mind to the utmost and tell me the truth. For, if any man knows, you are he; and therefore I shall detain you, like Proteus, until you tell. For if you had not certainly known the nature of piety and impiety I am confident that you would never, on behalf of a serf, have charged your aged father with murder. You would not have run such a risk of doing wrong in the sight of the gods, and you would have had too much respect for the opinions of men. I am sure therefore, that you know the nature of piety and impiety. Speak out then, my dear Euthyphro, and do not hide your knowledge.

Euth. Another time, Socrates; for I am in a hurry, and must go now.

Soc. Alas! my companion, and will you leave me in despair? I was hoping that you would instruct me in the nature of piety and impiety, so that I might have cleared myself of Meletus and his indictment. Then I might have proved to him that I had been converted by Euthyphro, and had done with rash innovations and speculations, in which I had indulged through ignorance, and was about to lead a better life.

3.4

Nichomachean Ethics

Aristotle

BOOK I

Chapter I

Every art and every scientific inquiry, and similarly every action and purpose, may be said to aim at some good. Hence the good has been well defined as that at which all things aim. But it is clear that there is a difference in the ends; for the ends are sometimes activities, and sometimes results beyond the mere activities. Also, where there are certain ends beyond the actions, the results are naturally superior to the activities.

As there are various actions, arts, and sciences, it follows that the ends are also various. Thus health is the end of medicine, a vessel of shipbuilding, victory of strategy, and wealth of domestic economy. It often happens that there are a number of such arts or sciences which fall under a single faculty, as the art of making bridles, and all such other arts as make the instruments of horsemanship, under horsemanship, and this again as well as every military action under strategy, and in the same way other arts or sciences under other faculties. But in all these cases the ends of the architectonic arts or sciences, whatever they may be, are more desirable than those of the subordinate arts or sciences, as it is for the sake of the former that the latter are themselves sought after. It makes no difference to the argument whether the activities themselves are the ends of the actions, or something else beyond the activities as in the above mentioned sciences.

If it is true that in the sphere of action there is an end which we wish for its own sake, and for the sake of which we wish everything else, and that we do not desire all things for the sake of is of something else (for, if that is

From Aristotle's *Nichomachean Ethics*, translated by James E. C. Welldon, Macmillan, 1906, pp. 1–57.

so, the process will go on *ad infinitum* and our desire will be idle and futile) it is clear that this will be the good or the supreme good. Does it not follow then that the knowledge of this supreme good is of great importance for the conduct of life, and that, *if we know* it, we shall be like archers who have a mark at which to aim, we shall have a better chance of attaining what we want? But, if this is the case, we must endeavour to comprehend, at least in outline, its nature, and the science or faculty to which it belongs.

It would seem that this is the most authoritative or architectonic science or faculty of science, and such is evidently the political; for it is the political science or faculty which determines what sciences are necessary in states, and what kind of sciences should be learnt, and how far they should be learnt by particular people. We perceive too that the faculties which are held in the highest esteem, e.g. strategy, domestic economy, and rhetoric, are subordinate to it. But as it makes use of the other practical sciences, and also legislates upon the things to be done and the things to be left undone, it follows that its end will comprehend the ends of all the other sciences, and will therefore be the true good of mankind. For although the good of an individual is identical with the good of a state, yet the good of the state, whether in attainment or in preservation, is evidently greater and more perfect. For while in an individual by himself it is something to be thankful for, it is nobler and more divine in a nation or state.

These then are the objects at which the present inquiry aims, and it is in a sense a political inquiry. . . .

Chapter II

As every knowledge and moral purpose aspires to some good, what is in our view the good at which the political science aims, and what is the highest of all practical goods? As to its name there is, I may say, a general agreement. The masses and the cultured classes agree ill calling it happiness, and conceive that "to live well" or "to do well" is the same thing as "to be happy." But as to the nature of happiness they do not agree, nor do the masses give the same account of it as the philosophers. The former define it as something visible and palpable, e.g. pleasure, wealth, or honour; different people give different definitions of it, and often the same person gives different definitions at different times; for when a person has been ill, it is health, when he is poor, it is wealth, and, if he is conscious of his own ignorance, he envies people who use grand language above his own comprehension. Some *philosophers* on the other hand have held that, besides these various goods, there is an absolute good which is the cause of goodness in them all. It would perhaps be a waste of time to examine all these opinions, it will be enough to examine such as are most popular or as seem to be more or less reasonable. . . .

Chapter III

. . . It seems not unreasonable that people should derive their conception of the good or of happiness from men's lives. Thus ordinary or vulgar people conceive it to be pleasure, and accordingly approve a life of enjoyment. For there are practically three prominent lives, the sensual, the political, and, thirdly, the speculative. Now the mass of men present an absolutely slavish appearance, as choosing the life of brute beasts, but they meet with consideration because so many persons in authority share the tastes of Sardanapalus. Cultivated and practical people, on the other hand, identify happiness with honour, as honour is the general end of political life. But this appears too superficial for our present purpose; for honour seems to depend more upon the people who pay it than upon the person to whom it is paid, and we have an intuitive feeling that the good is something which is proper to a man himself and cannot easily be taken away from him. It seems too that the reason why men seek honour is that they may be confident of their own goodness. Accordingly they seek it at the hands of the wise and of those who know them well, and they seek it on the ground of virtue; hence it is clear that in their judgment at any rate virtue is superior to honour. It would perhaps be right then to look upon virtue rather than honour as being the end of the political life. Yet virtue again, it appears, lacks completeness; for it seems that a man may posses virtue and yet be asleep or inactive throughout life, and, not only so but may experience the greatest calamities and misfortunes. But nobody would call such a life a life of happiness, unless he were maintaining a paradox. It is not necessary to dwell further on this subject, as it is sufficiently discussed in the popular philosophical treatises. The third life is the speculative which we will investigate hereafter.

The life of money-making is in a sense a life of constraint, and it is clear that wealth is not the good of which we are in quest; for it is useful in part as a means to something else. It would be a more reasonable view therefore that the things mentioned before, viz. *sensual pleasure, honour and virtue,* are ends than that wealth is, as they are things which are desired on their own account. Yet these too are apparently not ends, although much argument has been employed to show that they are. . . .

Chapter V

But leaving this subject for the present let us revert to the good of which we are in quest and consider what its nature may be. For it is clearly different in different actions or arts; it is one thing in medicine, another in strategy, and so on. What then is the good in each of these instances? It is presumably that for the sake of which all else is done. This in medicine is health, in strategy, victory, in domestic architecture, a house, and so on. But in every action and purpose it is the end, as it is for the sake of the end that people all do everything else. If then there is a certain end of all action, it will be this which is the practicable good, and if there are several such ends it will be these.

Our argument has arrived by a different path at the same conclusion as before; but we must endeavour to elucidate it still further. As it appears that there are more ends than one and some of these, e.g. wealth, flutes, and instruments generally we desire as means to something else, it is evident that they are not all final ends. But the highest good is clearly something final. Hence if there is only one final end, this will be the object of which we are in search, and if there are more than one, it will be the most final of them. We speak of that which is sought after for its own sake as more final than that which is sought after as a means to something else; we speak of that which is never desired as a means to something else as more final than the things which are desired both in themselves and as means to something else; and we speak of a thing as absolutely final, if it is always desired in itself and never as a means to something else.

It seems that happiness preeminently answers to this description, as we always desire happiness for its own sake and never as a means to something else, whereas we desire honour, pleasure, intellect, and every virtue, partly for their own sakes (for we should desire them independently of what might result from them) but partly also as being means to happiness, because we suppose they will prove the instruments of happiness. Unhappiness, on the other hand, nobody desires for the sake of these things, nor indeed as a means to anything else at all.

We come to the same conclusion if we start from the consideration of self-sufficiency, if it may be assumed that the final good is self-sufficient. But when we speak of self-sufficiency, we do not mean that a person leads a solitary life all by himself, but that he has parents, children, wife, and friends, and fellow-citizens in general, as man is naturally a social being. But here it is necessary to prescribe some limit; for if the circle be extended so as to include parents, descendants, and friends' friends, it will go on indefinitely. Leaving this point, however, for future investigation, we define the self-sufficient as that which, taken by itself, makes life desirable, and wholly free from want, and this is our conception of happiness.

Again, we conceive happiness to be the most desirable of all things, and that not merely as one among other good things. If it were one among other good things, the addition of the smallest good would increase its desirableness; for the accession makes a superiority of goods, and the greater of two goods is always the more desirable. It appears then that happiness is something final and self-sufficient, being the end of all action.

Chapter VI

Perhaps, however, it seems a truth which is generally admitted, that happiness is the supreme good; what is wanted is to define its nature a little more clearly. The best way of arriving at such a definition will probably be to ascertain the function of Man. For, as with a flute-player, a statuary, or any artisan, or in fact anybody who has a definite function and action, his goodness or excellence seems to lie in his function, so it would seem to be with Man, if indeed he has a definite function. Can it be said then that, while a carpenter and a cobbler have definite functions and actions, Man, unlike them, is naturally functionless? The reasonable view is that, as the eye, the hand, the foot, and similarly each several part of the body has a definite function, so Man may be regarded as having a definite function apart from all these. What then can this function be? It is not life; for life is apparently something which man shares with the plants; and it is some thing peculiar to him that we are looking for. We must exclude therefore the life of nutrition and increase. There is next what may be called the life of sensation. But this too, is apparently shared by Man with horses, cattle, and all other animals. There remains what I may call the practical life of the rational part of *Man's being.* But the rational part is twofold; it is rational partly in the sense of being obedient to reason, and partly in the sense of possessing reason and intelligence. The practical life too may be conceived of in two ways, *viz., either as a moral state,* or as a moral *activity;* but we must understand by it the life of activity, as this seems to be the truer form of the conception.

The function of Man then is an activity of soul in accordance with reason, or not independently of reason. Again the functions of a person of a certain kind, and of such a person who is good of his kind e.g. of a harpist and a good harpist, are in our view generically the same, and this view is trite of people of all kinds without exception, the superior excellence being only an addition to the function; for it is the function of a harpist to play the harp, and of a good harpist to play the harp well. This being so, if we define the function of Man as a kind of life, and this life as an activity of soul, or a course of action in conformity with reason, if the function of a good man is such activity or action of a good and noble kind, and if everything is successfully performed when it is performed in accordance with its proper excellence, it follows that the good of Man is an activity of soul in accordance with virtue or, if there are more virtues than one, in accordance with the best and most complete virtue. But it is necessary to add the words "in a complete life." For as one swallow or one day does not make a spring, so one day or a short time does not make a fortunate or happy man.

BOOK II

Chapter I

Virtue or excellence being twofold, partly intellectual and partly moral, intellectual virtue is both originated and fostered by teaching; it therefore demands experience and time. Moral virtue on the other hand is the outcome of habit, and accordingly its name . . . is derived by a single deflexion from habit. . . . From this fact it is clear that no moral virtue is implanted in us by nature; a law of nature cannot be altered by habituation. Thus a stone naturally tends to fall downwards, and it cannot be habituated or trained to rise upwards, even if we were to habituate it by throwing it upwards ten thousand times; nor again can fire be trained to sink downwards, nor anything else that follows one natural law be habituated or trained to follow another. It is neither by nature then nor in defiance of nature that virtues are implanted in us. Nature gives us the capacity of receiving them, and that capacity is perfected by habit.

Again, if we take the various natural powers which belong to us, we first acquire the proper faculties and afterwards display the activities. It is clearly so with the senses. It was not by seeing frequently or hearing frequently that we acquired the senses of seeing or hearing; on the contrary it was because we possessed the senses that we made use of them, not by making use of them that we obtained them. But the virtues we acquire by first exercising them, as is the case with all the arts, for it is by doing what we ought to do when we have learnt the arts that we learn the arts themselves; we become e.g. builders by building and harpists by playing the harp. Similarly it is by doing just acts that we become just, by doing temperate acts that we become temperate, by doing courageous acts that we become courageous. The experience of states is a witness to this truth, for it is by training the habits that legislators make the citizens good. This is the object which all legislators have at heart; if a legislator does not succeed in it, he fails of his purpose, and it constitutes the distinction between a good polity and a bad one.

Again, the causes and means by which any virtue is produced and by which it is destroyed are the same; and it is equally so with any art; for it is by playing the harp that both good and bad harpists are produced and the case of builders and all other *artisans* is similar, as it is by building well that they will be good builders and by building badly that they will be bad builders. If it were not so, there would be no need of anybody to teach them; they would all be born good or bad *in their several trades*. The case of the virtues is the same. It is by acting in such transactions as take place between man and man that we become either just or unjust. It is by acting in the face of danger and by habituating ourselves to fear or courage that we become either cowardly or courageous. It is much the same with our desires and angry passions. Some people become temperate and gentle, others become licentious and passionate, according as they conduct themselves in one way or another way in particular circumstances. In a word moral states are the results of activities corresponding to the moral states themselves. It is our duty therefore to give a certain character to the activities, as the moral states depend upon the differences of the activities. Accordingly the difference between one training of the habits and another from early days is not a light matter, but is serious or rather all-important.

Chapter II

Our present study is not, like other studies, purely speculative in its intention; for the object of our enquiry is not to know the nature of virtue but to become ourselves virtuous, as that is the sole benefit which it conveys. It is necessary therefore to consider the right way of performing actions, for it is actions as we have said that determine the character of the resulting moral states.

That we should act in accordance with right reason is a common general principle, which may here be taken for granted. The nature of right reason, and its relation to the virtues generally, will be subjects of discussion hereafter. But it must be admitted at the outset that all reasoning upon practical matters must be like a sketch in outline, it cannot be scientifically exact. We began by laying down the principle that the kind of reasoning demanded in any subject must be such as the subject-matter itself allows; and questions of practice and expediency no more admit of invariable rules than questions of health.

But if this is true of general reasoning upon Ethics, still more true is it that scientific exactitude is impossible in reasoning upon particular ethical cases. They do not fall under any art or any law, but the agents themselves are always bound to pay regard to the circumstances of the moment as much as in medicine or navigation.

Still, although such is the nature of the present argument, we must try to make the best of it. The first point to be observed then is that in such matters as we are considering deficiency and excess are equally fatal. It is so, as we observe, in regard to health and strength; for we must judge of what we cannot see by the evidence of what we do see.

Excess or deficiency of gymnastic exercise is fatal to strength. Similarly an excess or deficiency of meat and drink is fatal to health, whereas a suitable amount produces, augments and sustains it. It is the same then with temperance, courage, and the other virtues. A person who avoids and is afraid of everything and faces nothing becomes a coward; a person who is not afraid of anything but is ready to face everything becomes foolhardy. Similarly he who enjoys every pleasure and never abstains from any pleasure is licentious; he who eschews all pleasures like a boor is an insensible sort of person. For temperance and courage are destroyed by excess and deficiency but preserved by the mean state.

Again, not only are the causes and the agencies of production, increase and destruction in the moral states the same, but the sphere of their activity will be proved to be the same also. It is so in other instances which are more conspicuous, e.g. in strength; for strength is produced by taking a great deal of food and undergoing a great deal of labour, and it is the strong man who is able to take most food and to undergo most labour. The same is the case with the virtues. It is by abstinence from pleasures that we become temperate, and, when we have become temperate, we are best able to abstain from them. So too with courage; it is by habituating ourselves to despise and face alarms that we become courageous, and, when we have become courageous, we shall be best able to face them.

The pleasure or pain which follows upon actions may be regarded as a test of a person's moral state. He who abstains from physical pleasures and feels delight in so doing is temperate; but he who feels pain at so doing is licentious. He who faces dangers with pleasure, or at least without pain, is courageous; but he who feels pain at facing them is a coward. For moral virtue is concerned with pleasures and pains. It is pleasure which makes us do what is base, and pain which makes us abstain from doing what is noble. Hence the importance of having had a certain training from very early days. . . .

Chapter IV

We have next to consider the nature of virtue. Now, as the qualities of the soul are three, viz. emotions, faculties and moral states, it follows that virtue must be one of the three. By the emotions I mean desire, anger, fear, courage, envy, joy, love, hatred, regret, emulation, pity, in a word whatever is attended by pleasure or pain. I call those faculties in respect of which we are said to be capable of experiencing these emotions, e.g. capable of getting angry or being pained or feeling pity. And I call those faculties in respect of which which we are well or ill-disposed towards the emotions, ill-disposed e.g. towards the passion of anger, if our anger be too violent or too feeble, and well-disposed, if it be duly moderated, and similarly towards the other emotions.

Now neither the virtues nor the vices are emotions; for we are not called good or evil in respect of our emotions but in respect of our virtues or vices. Again, we are not praised or blamed in respect of our emotions; a person is not praised for being afraid or being angry, nor blamed for being angry in an absolute sense, but only for being angry in a certain way; but we are praised or blamed in respect of our virtues or vices. Again, whereas we are angry or afraid without deliberate purpose, the virtues are in some sense deliberate purposes, or do not exist in the absence of deliberate purpose. It may be added that while we are said to be moved in respect of our emotions, in respect of our virtues or vices we are not said to be moved but to have a certain disposition.

These reasons also prove that the virtues are not faculties. For we are not called either good or bad, nor are we praised or blamed, as having an abstract capacity for emotion. Also while nature gives us our faculties, it is not nature that makes us good or bad. . . . If then the virtues are neither emotions nor faculties, it remains that they must be moral states.

Chapter V

The nature of virtue has been now generically described. But it is not enough to state merely that virtue is a moral state, we must also describe the character of that moral state.

It must be laid down then that every virtue or excellence has the effect of producing a good condition of that of which it is a virtue or excellence, and of enabling it to perform its function well. Thus the excellence of the eye makes the eye good and its function good, as it is by the excellence of the eye that we see well. Similarly, the excellence of the horse makes a horse excellent and good at racing, at carrying its rider and at facing the enemy.

If then this is universally true, the virtue or excellence of man will be such a moral state as makes a man good and able to perform his proper function well. . . .

Now in everything, whether it be continuous or discrete, it is possible to take a greater, a smaller, or an equal amount, and this either absolutely or in relation to ourselves, the equal being a mean between excess and deficiency. By the mean in respect of the thing itself, or the absolute mean, I understand that which is equally distinct from both extremes; and this is one and the same thing for everybody. By the mean considered relatively to ourselves I understand that which is neither too much nor too little; but this is not one thing, nor is it the same for everybody. Thus if 10 be too much and 2 too little we take 6 as a mean in respect of the thing itself; for 6 is as much greater than 2 as it is less than 10, and this is a mean in arithmetical proportion. But the mean considered relatively to ourselves must not be ascertained in this way. It does not follow that if 10 pounds *of meat* be too much and 2 be too little for a man to eat, a trainer will order him 6 pounds, as this may itself be too much or too little for the person who is to take it; it will be too little e.g. for Milo, but too much for a beginner in gymnastics. It will be the same with running and wrestling; *the right amount will vary with the individual.* This being so, everybody who understands his business avoids alike excess and deficiency; he seeks and chooses the mean, not the absolute mean, but the mean considered relatively to ourselves.

Every science then performs its function well, if it regards the mean and refers the works which it produces to the mean. This is the reason why it is usually said of successful works that it is impossible to take anything from them or to add anything to them, which implies that excess or deficiency is fatal to excellence but that the mean state ensures it. Good artists too, as we say, have an eye to the mean in their works. But virtue, like Nature herself, is more accurate and better than any art; virtue therefore will aim at the mean;—I speak of moral virtue, as it is moral virtue which is concerned with emotions and actions, and it is these which admit of excess and deficiency and the mean. Thus it is possible to go too far, or not to go far enough, in respect of fear, courage, desire, anger, pity, and pleasure and pain generally, and the excess and the deficiency are alike wrong; but to experience these emotions at the right times and on the right occasions and towards the right persons and for the right causes and in the right manner is the mean or the supreme good, which is characteristic of virtue. Similarly there may be excess, deficiency, or the mean, in regard to actions. But virtue is concerned with emotions and actions, and here excess is an error and deficiency a fault, whereas the mean is successful and laudable, and success and merit are both characteristics of virtue.

It appears then that virtue is a mean state, so far at least as it aims at the mean.

Again, there are many different ways of going wrong; for evil is in its nature infinite, to use the Pythagorean figure, but good is finite. But there is only one possible way of going right. Accordingly the former is easy and the latter difficult; it is easy to miss the mark but difficult to hit it. This again is a reason why excess and deficiency are characteristics of vice and the mean state a characteristic of virtue. "For good is simple, evil manifold."

Chapter VI

Virtue then is a state of deliberate moral purpose consisting in a mean that is relative to ourselves, the mean being determined by reason, or as prudent man would determine it.

It is a mean state *firstly as lying* between two vices, the vice of excess on the one hand, and the vice of deficiency on the other, and secondly because, whereas the vices either fall short of or go beyond what is proper in the emotions and actions, virtue not only discovers but embraces the mean.

Accordingly, virtue, if regarded in its essence or theoretical conception, is a mean state, but, if regarded from the point of view of the highest good, or of excellence, it is an extreme.

But it is not every action or every emotion that admits of a mean state. There are some whose very name implies wickedness, as e.g. malice, shamelessness, and envy, among emotions, or adultery, theft, and murder, among actions. All these, and others like them, are censured as being intrinsically wicked, not merely the excesses or deficiencies of them. It is never possible then to be right in respect of them; they are always sinful. Right or wrong in such actions as adultery does not depend on our committing them with the right person, at the right time or in the right manner; on the contrary it is sinful to do anything of the kind at alL It would be equally wrong then to suppose that there can be a mean state or an excess or deficiency in unjust, cowardly or licentious conduct; for, if it were so, there would be a mean state of an excess or of a deficiency, an excess of an excess and a deficiency of a deficiency. But as in temperance and courage there can be no excess or deficiency because the mean is, in a sense, an extreme, so too in these cases there cannot be a mean or an excess or deficiency, but, however the acts may be done, they are wrong. For it is a general rule that an excess or deficiency does not admit of a mean state, nor a mean state of an excess or deficiency.

Chapter VII

But it is not enough to lay down this as a general rule; it is necessary to apply it to particular cases, as in reasonings upon actions, general statements, although they are broader, are less exact than particular statements. For all action refers to particulars, and it is essential that our theories should harmonize with the particular cases to which they apply.

We must take particular virtues then from the catalogue *of virtues*.

In regard to feelings of fear and confidence, courage is a mean state. On the side of excess, he whose fearlessness is excessive has no name, as often happens, but he whose confidence is excessive is foolhardy, while he whose timidity is excessive and whose confidence is deficient is a coward.

In respect of pleasures and pains, although not indeed of all pleasures and pains, and to a less extent in respect of pains than of pleasures, the mean state is temperance, the excess is licentiousness. We never find people who are deficient in regard to pleasures; accordingly such people again have not received a name, but we may call them insensible.

As regards the giving and taking of money, the mean state is liberality, the excess and deficiency are prodigality and illiberality. Here the excess and deficiency take opposite forms; for while the prodigal man is excessive in spending and deficient in taking, the illiberal man is excessive in taking and deficient in spending. . . .

Chapter VIII

There are then three dispositions, two being vices, viz. one the vice of excess and the other that of deficiency, and one virtue, which is the mean state between them; and they are all in a sense mutually opposed. For the extremes are opposed both to the mean and to each other, and the mean is opposed to the extremes. For as the equal if compared with the less is greater but if compared with the greater is less, so the mean states, whether in the emotions or in actions, if compared with the deficiencies, are excessive, but if compared with the excesses are deficient. Thus the courageous man appears foolhardy as compared with the coward, but cowardly as compared with the foolhardy. Similarly, the temperate man appears licentious as compared with the insensible but insensible as compared with the licentious, and the liberal man appears prodigal as compared with the illiberal, but illiberal as compared with the prodigal. The result is that the extremes mutually repel and reject the mean; the coward calls the courageous man foolhardy, but the foolhardy man calls him cowardly, and so on in the other cases.

But while there is this mutual opposition between the extremes and the mean, there is greater opposition between the two extremes than between either extreme and the mean; for they are further removed from each other than from the mean, as the great from the small and the small from the great than both from the equal. Again, while some extremes exhibit more or less similarity to the mean, as foolhardiness to courage and prodigality to liberality, there is the greatest possible dissimilarity between the extremes. But things which are furthest removed from each other are defined to be opposites; hence the further things are removed, the greater is the opposition between them.

It is in some cases the deficiency and in others the excess which is the more opposed to the mean. Thus it is not foolhardiness the excess, but cowardice the deficiency which is the more opposed to courage, nor is it insensibility the deficiency, but licentiousness the excess which is the more opposed to temperance. There are two reasons why this should be so. One lies in the nature of the thing itself; for as one of the two extremes is the nearer and more similar to the mean, it is not this extreme, but its opposite, that we chiefly set against the mean. For instance, as it appears that foolhardiness is more similar and nearer to courage than cowardice, it is cowardice that we chiefly set against courage; for things which are further removed from the mean seem to be more opposite to it. This being one reason which lies in the nature of the thing itself, there is a second which lies in our own nature. It is the things to which we ourselves are naturally more inclined that appear more opposed to the mean. Thus we are ourselves naturally more inclined to pleasures *than to their opposites,* and are more prone therefore to licentiousness than to decorum. Accordingly we speak of those things, in which we are more likely to run to great results, as being more opposed to the mean. Hence it follows that licentiousness which is an excess is more opposed to temperance than insensibility.

Chapter IX

It has now been sufficiently shown that moral virtue is a mean state, and in what sense it is a mean state; it is a mean state as lying between two vices, a vice of excess on the one side and a vice of deficiency on the other, and as aiming at the mean in the emotions and actions.

That is the reason why it is so hard to be virtuous; for it is always hard work to find the mean in anything, e.g. it is not everybody, but only a man of science, who can find the mean or centre of a circle. So too anybody can get angry—that is an easy matter—and anybody can give or spend money, but to give it to the right persons, to give the right amount of it and to give it at the right time and for the right cause and in the right way, this is not what anybody can do, nor is it easy. That is the reason why it is rare and laudable and noble to do well. Accordingly one who aims at the mean must begin by departing from that extreme which is the more contrary to the mean; he must act in the spirit of Calypso's advice, "Far from this smoke and swell keep thou thy bark," for of the two extremes one is more sinful than the other. As it is difficult then to hit the mean exactly, we must take the second best course, as the saying is, and choose the lesser of two evils, and this we shall best do in the way that we have described, i.e. by steering clear of the evil which is further from the mean. We must also observe the things to which we are ourselves particularly prone, as different natures have different inclinations, and we may ascertain what these are by a consideration of our feelings of pleasure and pain. And then we must drag ourselves in the direction opposite to them; for it is by removing ourselves as far as possible from what is wrong that we shall arrive at the mean, as we do when we pull a crooked stick straight.

But in all cases we must especially be on our guard against what is pleasant and against pleasure, as we are not impartial judges of pleasure. Hence our attitude towards pleasure must be like that of the elders of the people in the *Iliad* towards Helen, and we must never be afraid of applying the words they use; for if we dismiss pleasure as they dismissed Helen, we shall be less likely to go wrong. It is by action of this kind, to put it summarily, that we shall best succeed in hitting the mean.

It may be admitted that this is a difficult task, especially in particular cases. It is not easy to determine e.g. the right manner, objects, occasions, and duration of anger. There are times when we ourselves praise people who are deficient in anger, and call them gentle, and there are other times when we speak of people who exhibit a savage temper as spirited. It is not however one who deviates a little from what is right, but one who deviates a great deal, whether on the side of excess or of deficiency, that is censured; for he is sure to be found out. Again, it is not easy to decide theoretically how far and to what extent a man may go before he becomes censurable, but neither is it easy to define theoretically anything else within the region of perception; such things fall under the head of particulars, and our judgment of them depends upon our perception.

So much then is plain, that the mean state is everywhere laudable, but that we ought to incline at one time towards the excess and at another towards the deficiency; for this will be our easiest manner of hitting the mean, or in other words of attaining excellence.

3.5

The Analects

Confucius

BOOK I

Chapter I

(1) The Master said, "Is it not pleasant to learn with a constant perseverance and application?"

(2) "Is it not delightful to have friends coming from distant quarters?"

(3) "Is he not a man of complete virtue, who feels no discomposure though men may take no note of him?"

Chapter II

(1) The philosopher Yū said, "They are few who, being filial and fraternal, are fond of offending against their superiors. There have been none who, not liking to offend against their superiors, have been fond of stirring up confusion."

(2) "The superior man bends his attention to what is radical. That being established, all practical courses naturally grow up. Filial piety and fraternal submission!—are they not the root of all benevolent actions?"

Chapter IV

The philosopher Tsāng said, "I daily examine myself on three points:—whether in transacting business for others, I may have been not faithful;—whether, in intercourse with friends I may have been not sincere;—whether I may have not mastered and practiced the instructions of my teacher."

From *The Analects, edited and translated by James Legge* in *The Chinese Classics,* Volume I (Oxford: Clarendon, 1893), pp. 137–354.

Chapter VI

The master said, "A youth, when at home, should be filial, and, abroad, respectful to his elders. He should be earnest and truthful. He should overflow in love to all, and cultivate the friendship of the good. When he has time and opportunity, after the performance of these things, he should employ them in polite studies."

Chapter VII

Tsze-hsia said, "If a man withdraws his mind from the love of beauty, and applies it as sincerely to the love of the virtuous; if, in serving his parents, he can exert his utmost strength; if, in serving his prince, he can devote his life; if, in his intercourse with his friends, his words are sincere:—although men say that he has not learned, I will certainly say that he has."

Chapter VIII

(1) The Master said, "If the scholar be not grave, he will not call forth any veneration and his learning will not be solid."

(2) "Hold faithfulness and sincerity as first principles."

(3) "Have no friends not equal to yourself."

(4) "When you have faults, do not fear to abandon them."

Chapter XI

The Master said, "While a man's father is alive, look at the bent of his will; when his father is dead, look at his conduct. If for three years he does not alter from the way of his father, he may be called filial."

Chapter XII

(1) The philosopher Yū said, "In practicing the rules of propriety, a natural ease is to be prized. In the ways prescribed by the ancient kings, this is the excellent quality, and in things small and great we follow them.

(2) "Yet it is not to be observed in all cases. If one, knowing how such ease should be prized, manifests it, without regulating it by the rules of propriety, this likewise is not to be done."

Chapter XIV

The Master said, "He who aims to be a man of complete virtue in his food does not seek to gratify his appetite, nor in his dwelling place does he seek the appliances of ease; he is earnest in what he is doing, and careful in his speech; he frequents the company of men of principle that he may be rectified;—such a person may be said indeed to love to learn."

Chapter XVI

The Master said, "I will not be afflicted at men's not knowing me; I will be afflicted that I do not know men."

BOOK II

Chapter I

(1) The Master said, "He who exercises government by means of his virtue may be compared to the north polar star, which keeps its place and all the stars turn towards it."

(2) The Master said, "In the Book of Poetry are three hundred pieces, but the design of them all may be embraced in one sentence—Having no depraved thoughts."

(3) The Master said, "If the people be led by laws, and uniformity sought to be given them by punishments, they will try to avoid the punishment, but have no sense of shame."

(4) "If they be led by virtue, and uniformity sought to be given them by the rules of propriety, they will have the sense of shame, and moreover will become good."

Chapter IV

(1) The Master said, "At fifteen, I had my mind bent on learning."

(2) "At thirty, I stood firm."

(3) "At forty, I had no doubts."

(4) "At fifty, I knew the decrees of Heaven."

(5) "At sixty, my ear was an obedient organ *for the reception of truth.*"

(6) "At seventy, I could follow what my heart desired, without transgressing what was right."

Chapter V

(1) Māng Ī asked what filial piety was. The Master said, "It is not being disobedient."

(2) Soon after, as Fan Ch'ih was driving him, the Master told him, saying, "Māng sun asked me what filial piety was, and I answered him,—not being disobedient."

(3) Fan Ch'ih said, "What did you mean?" The Master replied, "That parents, when alive, should be served according to propriety; that, when dead, they should he buried according to propriety; and that they should be sacrificed according to propriety."

Chapter VI

(1) Māng Wŭ asked what filial piety was. The Master said, "Parents are anxious lest their children should be sick."

Chapter X

(1) The Master said, "See what a man does."
(2) "Mark his motives."
(3) "Examine in what things he rests."
(4) "How can a man conceal his character?"
(5) "How can a man conceal his character?"

Chapter XIII

Tsze-kung asked what constituted the superior man. The Master said, "He acts before he speaks, and afterwards speaks according to his actions."

Chapter XIV

The Master said, "The superior man is catholic and not partisan. The mean man is a partisan and not catholic."

Chapter XV

The Master said, "learning without thought is labor lost; thought without learning is perilous."

Chapter XVI

The Master said, "The study of strange doctrines is injurious indeed!"

Chapter XVII

The Master said, "Yŭ, shall I teach you what knowledge is? When you know a thing, to hold that you know it; and when you do not know a thing, to allow that you do not know it;—this is knowledge."

Chapter XIX

The duke Ai asked, saying, "What should be done in order to secure the submission of the people?" Confucius replied, "Advance the upright and set aside the crooked, then the people will submit. Advance the crooked and set aside the upright, then the people will not submit."

Chapter XX

Chi K'ang asked how to cause the people to reverence their ruler, to be faithful to him, and to go on to nerve themselves to virtue. The Master said, "let him preside over them with gravity;—then they will reverence him. Let him be filial and kind to all;—then they will be faithful to him. Let him advance the good and teach the incompetent;—then they will eagerly seek to be virtuous."

Chapter XXIV

(1) The Master said, "For a man to sacrifice to a spirit which does not belong to him is flattery."

(2) "To see what is right and not to do it is want of courage."

BOOK IV

Chapter II

The Master said, "Those who are without virtue cannot abide long either in a condition of poverty and hardship, or in a condition of enjoyment. The virtuous rest in virtue; the wise desire virtue."

Chapter III

The Master said, "It is only the (truly) virtuous man, who can love, or who can hate, others."

Chapter IV

The Master said, "If the will be set on virtue, there will be no practice of wickedness."

Chapter V

(1) The Master said, "Riches and honors are what men desire. If they cannot be obtained in the proper way, they should not be held. Poverty and

meanness are what men dislike. If they cannot be obtained in the proper way, they should not be avoided."

(2) "If a superior man abandons virtue, how can he fulfill the requirements of that name?"

(3) "The superior man does not, even for the space of a single meal, act contrary to virtue. In moments of haste, he cleaves to it. In seasons of danger, he cleaves to it."

Chapter VI

(1) The Master said, "I have not seen a person who loved virtue, or one who hated what was not virtuous. He who loved virtue, would esteem nothing above it. He who hated what is not virtuous would practice virtue in such a way that he would not allow anything that is not virtuous to approach his person."

(2) "Is anyone able for one day to apply his strength to virtue? I have not seen the case in which his strength would be insufficient."

(3) "Should there possibly be any such case, I have not seen it."

Chapter VII

The Master said, "The faults of men are characteristic of the class to which they belong. By observing a man's faults, it may be known that he is virtuous."

Chapter X

The Master said, "The superior man in the world does not set his mind either for anything or against anything; what is right he will follow."

Chapter XI

The Master said, "The superior man thinks of virtue; the small man thinks of comfort. The superior man thinks of the sanctions of law; the small man thinks of favors which he may receive."

Chapter XII

The Master said, "He who acts with a constant view to his own advantage will be much murmured against."

Chapter XIV

The Master said, "A man should say, I am not concerned that I have no place, I am concerned how I may fit myself for one. I am not concerned that I am not known, I seek to be worthy to be known."

Chapter XV

(1) The Master said, "Shān, my doctrine is that of an all-pervading unity." The disciple Tsāng replied, "Yes."

(2) The Master went out, and the other disciples asked, saying, "What do his words mean?" Tsāng said, "The doctrine of our master is to be true to the principles of our nature and the benevolent exercise of them to others,—this and nothing more."

Chapter XVI

The Master said, "The mind of the superior man is conversant with righteousness; the mind of the mean man is conversant with gain."

Chapter XVII

The Master said, "When we see men of worth, we should think of equaling them; when we see men of a contrary character, we should turn inwards and examine ourselves."

Chapter XVIII

The Master said, "In serving his parents, a son may demonstrate with them, but gently; when he sees that they do not incline to follow his advice, he shows an increased degree of reverence, but does not abandon his purpose; and should they punish him, he does not allow himself to murmur."

Chapter XIX

The Master said, "While his parents are alive, the son may not go abroad to a distance. If he does go abroad, he must have a fixed place to which he goes."

Chapter XX

The Master said, "If the son for three years does not alter from the way of his father, he may be called filial."

Chapter XXI

The Master said, "The years of parents may by no means not be kept in the memory as an occasion at once for joy and for *fear.*"

Chapter XXII

The Master said, "The reason why the ancients did not readily give utterance to their words, was that they feared lest their actions should not come up to them."

Chapter XXIII

The Master said, "The cautious seldom err."

Chapter XXIV

The Master said, "The superior man wishes to be slow in his speech and earnest in his conduct."

Chapter XXV

The Master said, "Virtue is not left to stand alone. He who practices it will have neighbors."

BOOK V

Chapter X

The Master said, "I have not seen a firm and unbending man." Someone replied, "There is Shān Ch'ang." "Ch'ang," said the Master, "is under the influence of his passions; how can he be pronounced firm and unbending?"

Chapter XI

Tsze-kung said, "What I do not wish men to do to me, I also wish not to do to men." The Master said, "Tsze, you have not attained that."

Chapter XII

Tsze-kung said, "The Master's *personal* displays of his principles and ordinary descriptions of them may be heard. His discourses about man's nature, and the way of Heaven, cannot be heard."

BOOK VI

Chapter XVIII

The Master said, "They who know the truth are not equal to those who love it, and they who love it are not equal to those who delight in it."

Chapter XX

Fan Ch'ih asked what constituted wisdom. The Master said, "To give one's self earnestly to the duties due to men, and, while respecting spiritual beings, to keep aloof from them, may be called wisdom." He asked about perfect virtue. The Master said, "The man of virtue makes the difficulty to be overcome his first business, and success only a subsequent consideration;—this may be called perfect virtue."

Chapter XXIII

The Master said: "A cornered vessel without corners;—A strange cornered vessel! A strange cornered vessel!"

Chapter XXIV

Tsâi Wo asked, saying, "A benevolent man, though it be told him, 'There is a man in the well,' will go in after him I suppose." Confucius said, "Why should he do so? A superior man may be made to go to the well, but he cannot be made to go down into it. He may be imposed upon, but he cannot be fooled."

Chapter XXV

The Master said, "The superior man, extensively studying all learning, and keeping himself under the restraint of the rules of propriety may thus likewise not overstep what is right."

Chapter XXVII

The Master said, "Perfect is the virtue which is according to the Constant Mean! Rare for a long time has been its practice among the people."

Chapter XXVIII

(1) Tsze-kung said, "Suppose the case of a man extensively conferring benefits on the people, and able to assist all, what would you say of him? Might he be called perfectly virtuous?" The Master said, "Why speak only of virtue in connection with him? Must he not have the qualities of a sage? Even Yao and Shun were still solicitous about this."

(2) "Now the man of perfect virtue, wishing to be established himself, seeks also to establish others; wishing to be enlarged himself he seeks also to enlarge others."

(3) "To be able to judge of others by what is nigh in ourselves;—this may be called the art of virtue."

BOOK VII

Chapter XXVII

The Master said, "There may be those who act without knowing why. I do not do so. Hearing much and selecting what is good and following it; seeing much and keeping it in memory—this is the second style of knowledge."

Chapter XXXVI

The Master said, "The superior man is satisfied and composed; the mean man is always full of distress."

Chapter XXXVII

The Master was mild, and yet dignified; majestic, and yet not fierce; respectful, and yet easy.

BOOK VIII

Chapter II

(1) The Master said, "Respectfulness, without the rules of propriety, becomes laborious bustle; carefulness, without the rules of propriety, becomes timidity; boldness, without the rules of propriety, becomes insubordination; straightforwardness, without the rules of propriety, becomes rudeness."

(2) "When those who are in high stations perform well all their duties to their relations, the people are aroused to virtue. When old friends are not neglected by them, the people are preserved from meanness."

Chapter VIII

(1) The Master said, "It is by Odes that the mind is aroused."

(2) "It is by the Rules of Propriety that the character is established."

(3) "It is from Music that the finish is received."

Chapter XIII

(1) The Master said, "With sincere faith he unites the love of learning; holding firm to death, he is perfecting the excellence of his course."

(2) "*Such an one* will not enter a tottering state, nor dwell in a disorganized one. When right principles of government prevail in the kingdom, he will show himself; when they are prostrated, he will keep concealed."

(3) "When a country is well governed, poverty and a mean condition are things to be ashamed of. When a country is ill-governed, riches and honor are things to be ashamed of."

BOOK IX

Chapter IV

There were four things from which the Master was entirely free. He had no foregone conclusions, no arbitrary predetermination, no obstinacy and no egoism.

Chapter XXIV

The Master said, "Hold faithfulness and sincerity as first principles. Have no friends not equal to yourself. When you have faults, do not fear to abandon them."

BOOK XI

Chapter XI

Chī Lū asked about serving the spirits of the dead. The Master said, "While you are not able to serve men, how can you serve their spirits?" Chī Lū added, "I venture to ask about death?" He was answered, "While you do not know life, how can you know about death?"

BOOK XII

Chapter I

(1) Yen Yūan asked about perfect virtue. The Master said, "To subdue one's self and return to propriety, is perfect virtue. If a man can for one day subdue himself and return to propriety, all under heaven will ascribe perfect virtue to him. Is the practice of perfect virtue from a man himself, or is it from others?"

(2) Yen Yūan said, "I beg to ask the steps of that process." The Master replied, "Look not at what is contrary to propriety; listen not to what is contrary to propriety; speak not what is contrary to propriety; make no movement which is contrary to propriety." Yen Yūan then said, "Though I am deficient in intelligence and vigor, I will make it my business to practice this lesson."

Chapter II

Chung-kung asked about perfect virtue. The Master said, "It is, when you go abroad, to behave to every one as if you were receiving a great guest; to employ the people as if you were assisting at a great sacrifice; not to do to others as you would not wish done to yourself; to have no murmuring against you in the country, and none in the family." Chung-kung said, "Though I am deficient in intelligence and vigor, I will make it my business to practice this lesson."

Chapter IX

(1) The duke Aī inquired of Yū Zo, saying, "The year is one of scarcity, and the returns for expenditure are not sufficient;—what is to be done?"

(2) Yū Zo replied to him, "Why not simply tithe the people?"

(3) "With two tenths" said the duke, "I find them not enough;—how could I do with that system of one tenth?"

(4) Yū Zo answered, "If the people have plenty, their prince will not be left to want alone. If the people are in want, their prince cannot enjoy plenty alone."

Chapter XV

The Master said, "By extensively studying all learning, and keeping himself under the restraint of the rules of propriety, one may thus likewise not err from what is right."

Chapter XVII

Chi K'ang asked Confucius about government. Confucius replied, "To govern means to rectify. If you lead on the people with correctness, who will dare not to be correct?"

BOOK XIII

Chapter III

(4) The Master said, "How uncultivated you are, Yū! A superior man, in regard to what he does not know, shows a cautious reserve."

Chapter VI

The Master said, "When a prince's personal conduct is correct, his government is effective without the issuing of orders. If his personal conduct is not correct, he may issue orders, but they will not be followed."

Chapter XI

The Master said, "If good men were to govern a country in succession for a hundred years, they would be able to transform the violently bad, and dispense with capital punishments. True indeed is this saying!"

Chapter XIII

The Master said, "If a minister make his own conduct correct, what difficulty will he have in assisting in government? If he cannot rectify himself, what has he to do with rectifying others?"

Chapter XVI

The duke of Sheb asked about government. The Master said, "Good government obtains when those who are near are made happy, and those who are far off are attracted."

Chapter XVII

Tsze-hsiā, being governor of Chü-fū, asked about government. The Master said, "Do not be desirous to have things done quickly; do not look at small advantages. Desire to have things done quickly prevents their being done thoroughly. Looking at small advantages prevents great affairs from being accomplished."

Chapter XIX

Fan Ch'ih asked about perfect virtue. The Master said, "It is, in retirement, to be sedately grave; in the management of business, to be reverently attentive; in intercourse with others, to be strictly sincere. Though a man go among rude, uncultivated tribes, these qualities may not be neglected."

BOOK XIV

Chapter XXIV

The Master said, "The progress of the superior man is upwards; the progress of the mean man is downwards."

Chapter XXV

The Master said, "In ancient times, men learned with a view to their own improvement. Nowadays, men learn with a view to the approbation of others."

Chapter XXX

(1) The Master said, "The way of the superior man is threefold, but I am not equal to it. Virtuous, he is free from anxieties; wise, he is free from perplexities; bold, he is free from fear."

(2) Tsze-kung said, "Master, that is what you yourself say."

Chapter XXXVI

(1) Someone said, "What do you say concerning the principle that injury should be recompensed with kindness?"

(2) The Master said, "With what then will you recompense kindness?"

(3) "Recompense injury with justice, and recompense kindness with kindness."

BOOK XV

Chapter II

(1) The Master said, "Tsze, you think, I suppose, that I am one who learns many things and keeps them in memory?"

(2) Tsze-kung replied, "Yes, but perhaps it is not so?"

(3) "No" was the answer, "I seek a unity all-pervading."

Chapter XVII

The Master said, "The superior man in everything considers righteousness to be essential. He performs it according to the rules of propriety. He brings it forth in humility. He completes it with sincerity. This is indeed a superior man."

Chapter XVIII

The Master said, "The superior man is distressed by his want of ability. He is not distressed by men's not knowing him."

Chapter XIX

The Master said, "The superior man dislikes the thought of his name not being mentioned afrer his death."

Chapter XX

The Master said, "What the superior man seeks, is in himself. What the mean man seeks, is in others."

Chapter XXI

The Master said, "The superior man is dignified, but does not wrangle. He is sociable, but not a partisan."

Chapter XXII

The Master said, "The superior man does not promote a man simply on account of his words, nor does he put aside good words because of the man."

Chapter XXIII

Tsze-kung asked, saying, "Is there one word which may serve as a rule of practice for all one's life?" The Master said, "Is not reciprocity such a word? What you do not want done to yourself, do not do to others."

Chapter XXXVIII

The Master said, "In teaching there should be no distinction of classes."

Chapter XXXIX

The Master said, "Those whose courses are different cannot lay plans for one another."

Chapter XL

The Master said, "In language it is simply required that it convey the meaning."

BOOK XVI

Chapter X

Confucius said, "The superior man has nine things which are subjects with him of thoughtful consideration. In regard to the use of his eyes, he is anxious to see clearly. In regard to his countenance, he is anxious that it should be benign. In regard to his demeanor, he is anxious that it should be respectful. In regard to his speech, he is anxious that it should be sincere. In regard to his doing of business, he is anxious that it should be reverently careful. In regard to what he doubts about, he is anxious to question others. When he is angry, he thinks of the difficulties (his anger may involve him in). When he sees gain to be got, he thinks of righteousness."

BOOK XVII

Chapter II

The Master said, "By nature, men are nearly alike; by practice, they get to be wide apart."

Chapter VI

Tsze-chang asked Confucius about perfect virtue. Confucius said, "To be able to practice five things everywhere under heaven constitutes perfect virtue." He begged to ask what they were, and was told, "Gravity, generosity of soul, sincerity, earnestness, and kindness. If you are grave, you will not be treated with disrespect. If you are generous, you will win all. If you are sincere, people will repose trust in you. If you are earnest, you will accomplish much. If you are kind, this will enable you to employ the services of others."

Chapter VIII

(1) The Master said, "Yū, have you heard the six words to which are attached six becloudings?" Yū replied, "I have not."

(2) "Sit down, and I will tell them to you."

(3) "There is the love of being benevolent without the love of learning;—the beclouding here leads to a foolish simplicity. There is the love of knowing without the love of learning;—the beclouding here leads to dissipation of mind. There is the love of being sincere without the love of learning;—the beclouding here leads to an injurious disregard of consequences. There is the love of straightforwardness without the love of learning;—the beclouding here leads to rudeness. There is the love of boldness without the love of learning;—the beclouding here leads to insubordination. There is the love of firmness without the love of learning;—the beclouding here leads to extravagant conduct."

BOOK XX

Chapter III

(1) The Master said, "Without recognizing the ordinances of *Heaven,* it is impossible to be a superior man."

(2) "Without an acquaintance with the rules of Propriety, it is impossible for the character to be established."

(3) "Without knowing the force of words, it is impossible to know men."

3.6

Universal Love

Mo Tzu

PART I

It is the business of the sages to effect the good government of the world. They must know, therefore, whence disorder and confusion arise, for without this knowledge their object cannot be effected. We may compare them to a physician who undertakes to cure men's diseases:—he must ascertain whence a disease has arisen, and then he can assail it with effect, while, without such knowledge, his endeavors will be in vain. Why should we except the case of those who have to regulate disorder from this rule? They must know whence it has arisen, and then they can regulate it.

It is the business of the sages to effect the good government of the world. They must examine therefore into the cause of disorder; and when they do so they will find that it arises from the want of mutual love. When a minister and a son are not filial to their sovereign and their father, this is what is called disorder. A son loves himself, and does not love his father;—he therefore wrongs his father, and seeks his own advantage: a younger brother loves himself and does not love his elder brother;—he therefore wrongs his elder brother, and seeks his own advantage: a minister loves himself, and does not love his sovereign;—he therefore wrongs his sovereign, and seeks his own advantage:—all these are cases of what is called disorder. Though it be the father who is not kind to his son, or the elder brother who is not kind to his younger brother, or the sovereign who is not gracious to his minister:—the case comes equally under the general name of disorder. The father loves himself, and does not love his son:—he therefore wrongs his son, and seeks his own advantage: the elder brother loves himself, and does not

From *The Works of Mencius, edited and translated by James Legge* in *The Chinese Classics,* Volume II (Oxford: Clarendon, 1895), pp. 101–16.

love his younger brother—he therefore wrongs his younger brother; and seeks his own advantage: the sovereign loves himself, and does not love his minister;—he therefore wrongs his minister, and seeks his own advantage. How do these things come to pass? They all arise from the want of mutual love. Take the case of any thief or robber:—it is just the same with him. The thief loves his own house, and does not love his neighbor's house:—he therefore steals from his neighbour's house to benefit his own: the robber loves his own person, and does not love his neighbour;—he therefore does violence to his neighbour to benefit himself. How is this? It all arises from the want of mutual love. Come to the case of great officers throwing each other's Families into confusion, and of princes attacking one another's States:—it is just the same with them. The great officer loves his own Family, and does not love his neighbour's;—he therefore throws the neighbour's Family into disorder to benefit his own: the prince loves his own State, and does not love his neighbour's:—he therefore attacks his neighbour's State to benefit his own. All disorder in the kingdom has the same explanation. When we examine into the cause of it, it is found to be the want of mutual love.

Suppose that universal, mutual love prevailed throughout the kingdom;—if men loved others as they love themselves, disliking to exhibit what was unfilial. . . . And moreover would there be those who were unkind? Looking on their sons, younger brothers, and ministers as themselves, and disliking to exhibit what was unkind . . . the want of filial duty would disappear. And would there be thieves and robbers? When every man regarded his neighbour's house as his own, who would be found to steal? When everyone regarded his neighbour's person as his own, who would be found to rob? Thieves and robbers would disappear. And would there be great officers throwing one another's Families into confusion, and princes attacking one another's States? When officers regarded the Families of others as their own, what one would make confusion? When princes regarded other States as their own, what one would begin an attack? Great officers throwing one another's Families into confusion, and princes attacking one another's States, would disappear.

If, indeed, universal, mutual love prevailed throughout the kingdom; one State not attacking another, and one Family not throwing another into confusion; thieves and robbers nowhere existing; rulers and ministers, fathers and sons, all being filial and kind:—in such a condition the nation would be well governed. On this account, how many sages, whose business it is to effect the good government of the kingdom, do but prohibit hatred and advise to love? On this account it is affirmed that universal mutual love throughout the country will lead to its happy order, and that mutual hatred leads to confusion. This was what our master, the philosopher Mo, meant, when he said, "We must above all inculcate the love of others."

PART II

Our Master, the philosopher Mo, said, "That which benevolent men consider to be incumbent on them as their business, is to stimulate and promote all that will be advantageous to the nation, and to take away all that is injurious to it. This is what they consider to be their business."

And what are the things advantageous to the nation, and the things injurious to it? Our master said, "The mutual attacks of State on State; the mutual usurpations of Family on Family; the mutual robberies of man on man; the want of kindness on the part of the ruler and of loyalty on the part of the minister; the want of tenderness and filial duty between father and son and of harmony between brothers:—these, and such as these, are the things injurious to the kingdom."

And from what do we find, on examination, that these injurious things are produced? Is it not from the want of mutual love?

Our Master said, "Yes, they are produced by the want of mutual love. Here is a prince who only knows to love his own State, and does not love his neighbour's;—he therefore does not shrink from raising all the power of his State to attack his neighbour. Here is the chief of a Family who only knows to love it, and does not love his neighbour's;—he therefore does not shrink from raising all his powers to seize on that other Family. Here is a man who only knows to love his own person, and does not love his neighbour's;—he therefore does not shrink from using all his resources to rob his neighbour. Thus it happens, that the princes, not loving one another, have their battle-fields; and the chiefs of Families, not loving one another, have their mutual usurpations; and men, not loving one another, have their mutual robberies; and rulers and ministers, not loving one another, become unkind and disloyal; and fathers and sons, not loving one another, lose their affection and filial duty; and brothers, not loving one another, contract irreconcilable enmities. Yea, men in general not loving one another, the strong make prey of the weak; the rich do despite to the poor; the noble are insolent to the mean; and the deceitful impose upon the stupid. All the miseries, usurpations, enmities, and hatreds in the world, when traced to their origin, will be found to arise from the want of mutual love. On this account, the benevolent condemn it."

They may condemn it; but how shall they change it?

Our Master said, "They may change it by the law of universal mutual love and by the interchange of mutual benefits."

How will this law of universal mutual love and the interchange of mutual benefits accomplish this?

Our Master said, "It would lead to the regarding another's kingdom as one's own: another's family as one's own: another's person as one's own. That being the case, the princes, loving one another, would have no battle-fields; the chiefs of families, loving one another, would attempt no usurpations; men, loving one another, would commit no robberies; rulers and ministers, loving one another, would be gracious and loyal; fathers and sons, loving one another, would be kind and filial; brothers, loving one another, would be harmonious and easily reconciled. Yea, men in general loving one another, the strong would not make prey of the weak; the many would not plunder the few; the rich would not insult the poor; the noble would not be insolent to the mean; and the deceitful would not impose upon the simple. The way in which all the miseries, usurpations, enmities, and hatreds in the world, may be made not to arise, is universal mutual love. On this account, the benevolent value and praise it."

Yes; but the scholars of the kingdom and superior men say, "True; if there were this universal love, it would be good. It is, however, the most difficult thing in the world."

Our Master said, "This is because the scholars and superior men simply do not understand the advantageousness of the law, and to conduct their reasonings upon that. Take the case of assaulting a city, or of a battle-field, or of the sacrificing one's life for the sake of fame:—this is felt by the people everywhere to be a difficult thing. Yet, if the ruler be pleased with it, both officers and people are able to do it:—how much more might they attain to universal mutual love, and the interchange of mutual benefits, which is different from this! When a man loves others, they respond to and love him; when a man benefits others, they respond to and benefit him; when a man injures others, they respond to and injure him; when a man hates others, they respond to and hate him:—what difficulty is there in the matter? It is only that rulers will not carry on the government on this principle, and so officers do not carry it out in their practice.

Yes; but now the officers and superior men say, "Granted; the universal practice of mutual love would be good; but it is an impracticable thing. It is like taking up the T'ai mountain, and leaping with it over the Ho or the Chi."

Our Master said, "That is not the proper comparison for it. To take up the T'ai mountain and leap with it over the Ho or the Chi, may be called an exercise of most extraordinary strength; it is, in fact, what no one, from antiquity to the present time, has ever been able to do. But how widely different from this is the practice of universal mutual love, and the interchange of mutual benefits!

"Anciently, the sage kings practised this. . . ."

If, now, the rulers of the kingdom truly and sincerely wish all in it to be rich, and dislike any being poor; if they desire its good government, and dislike disorder; they ought to practise universal mutual love, and the interchange of mutual benefits. This was the law of the sage kings; it is the way to effect the good government of the nation; it may not but be striven after.

PART III

Our Master, the philosopher Mo, said, "The business of benevolent men requires that they should strive to stimulate and promote what is advantageous to the kingdom, and to take away what is injurious to it."

Speaking, now, of the present time, what are to be accounted the most injurious things to the kingdom? They are such as the attacking of small States
by great ones; the inroads on small Families by great ones; the plunder of
the weak by the strong; the oppression of the few by the many; the schem-
ing of the crafty against the simple; the insolence of the noble to the mean.
To the same class belong the ungraciousness of rulers, and the disloyalty of
ministers; the unkindness of fathers, and the want of filial duty on the part
of sons. Yea, there is to be added to these the conduct of the mean men,
who employ their edged weapons and poisoned stuff, water and fire, to rob
and injure one another.

Pushing on the inquiry now, let us ask whence all these injurious things
arise. Is it from loving others and advantaging others? It must be answered
"No" and it must likewise be said, "They arise clearly from hating others and
doing violence to others." If it be further asked whether those who hate and
do violence to others hold the principle of loving all, or that of making distinctions, it must be replied, "They make distinctions." So then, it is this principle of making distinctions between man and man, which gives rise to all
that is most injurious in the kingdom. On this account we conclude that that
principle is wrong.

Our Master said, "He who condemns others must have whereby to change
them." To condemn men, and have no means of changing them, is like sav-
ing them from fire by plunging them in water. A man's language in such a
case must be improper. On this account our Master said, "There is the principle of loving all, to take the place of that which makes distinctions." If,
now, we ask, "And how is it that universal love can change the consequences of that other principle which makes distinctions?" the answer is, "If
princes were as much for the States of others as for their own, what one
among them would raise the forces of his State to attack that of another?—
he is for that other as much as for himself. If they were for the capitals of others as much as for their own, what one would raise the forces of his capital
to attack that of another?—he is for that as much as for his own. If chiefs regarded the families of others as their own, what one would lead the power
of his Family to throw that of another into confusion?—he is for that other
as much as for himself. If, now; States did not attack, nor holders of capitals
smite, one another, and if Families were guilty of no mutual aggressions,
would this be injurious to the kingdom, or its benefit?" It must be replied,
"This would be advantageous to the kingdom." Pushing on the inquiry,
now, let us ask whence all these benefits arise. Is it from hating others and

doing violence to others? It must be answered, "No"; and it must likewise be said, "They arise clearly from loving others and doing good to others." If it be further asked whether those who love others and do good to others hold the principle of making distinctions between man and man, or that of loving all, it must be replied, "They love all." So then it is this principle of universal mutual love which really gives rise to all that is most beneficial to the nation. On this account we conclude that that principle is right.

Our Master said, a little while ago, "The business of benevolent men requires that they should strive to stimulate and promote what is advantageous to the kingdom, and to take away what is injurious to it." We have now traced the subject up, and found that it is the principle of universal love which produces all that is most beneficial to the kingdom, and the principle of making distinctions which produces all that is injurious to it. On this account what our Master said, "The principle of making distinctions between man and man is wrong, and the principle of universal love is right," turns out to be correct as the sides of a square.

If, now, we just desire to promote the benefit of the kingdom, and select for that purpose the principle of universal love, then the acute ears and piercing eyes of people will hear and see for one another; and the strong limbs of people will move and be ruled for one another; and men of principle will instruct one another. It will come about that the old, who have neither wife nor children, will get supporters who will enable them to complete their years; and the young and weak, who have no parents, will yet find helpers that shall bring them up. On the contrary, if this principle of universal love is held not to be correct, what benefits will arise from such a view? What can be the reason that the scholars of the kingdom, whenever they hear of this principle of universal love, go on to condemn it? Plain as the case is, their words in condemnation of this principle do not stop;—they say, "It may be good, but how can it be carried into practice?"

Our Master said, "Supposing that it could not be practiced, it seems hard to go on likewise to condemn it. But how can it be good, and yet incapable of being put into practice?"

Let us bring forward two instances to test the matter:—let any one suppose the case of two individuals, the one of whom shall hold the principle of making distinctions, and the other shall hold the principle of universal love. The former of these will say, "How can I be for the person of my friend as much as for my own person? how can I be for the parents of my friend as much as for my own parents?" Reasoning in this way, he may see his friend hungry, but he will not feed him; cold, but he will not clothe him; sick, but he will not nurse him; dead, but he will not bury him. Such will be the language of the individual holding the principle of distinction, and such will be his conduct. He will say, "I have heard that he who wishes to play a lofty part among men, will be for the person of his friend as much as for his own person, and for the parents of his friend as much as for his own parents. It is only thus that he can attain his distinction?" Reasoning in this way, when he sees his friend hungry, he will feed him; cold, he will clothe him; sick, he will nurse him; dead, he will bury him. Such will be the language of him who holds the principle of universal love, and such will be his conduct.

The words of the one of these individuals are a condemnation of those of the other, and their conduct is directly contrary. Suppose now that their words are perfectly sincere, and that their conduct will be carried out,—that their words and actions will correspond like the parts of a token, every word being carried into effect; and let us proceed to put the following questions on the case:—Here is a plain in the open country, and an officer, with coat of mail, gorget, and helmet, is about to take part in a battle to be fought in it, where the issue, whether for life or death, cannot be foreknown; or here is an officer about to be dispatched on a distant commission from Pa to Yüeh, or from Ch'i to Ching, where the issue of the journey, going and coming, is quite uncertain:—on either of these suppositions, to whom will the officer entrust the charge of his house, the support of his parents, and the care of his wife and children?—to one who holds the principle of universal love? or to one who holds that which makes distinctions? I apprehend there is no one under heaven, man or woman, however stupid, though he may condemn the principle of universal love, but would at such a time make one who holds it the subject of his trust. This is in words to condemn the principle, and when there is occasion to choose between it and the opposite, to approve it;—words and conduct are here in contradiction. I do not know how it is that throughout the kingdom scholars condemn the principle of universal love, whenever they hear it.

Plain as the case is, their words in condemnation of it do not cease, but they say, "This principle may suffice perhaps to guide in the choice of an officer, but it will not guide in the choice of a sovereign."

Let us test this by taking two illustrations:—let anyone suppose the case of two sovereigns, the one of whom shall hold the principle of mutual love, and the other shall hold the principle which makes distinctions. In this case, the latter of them will say, "How can I be as much for the persons of all my people as for my own? This is much opposed to human feelings. The life of man upon the earth is but a very brief space; it may be compared to the rapid movement of a team of horses whirling past a small chink." Reasoning in this way, he may see his people hungry, but he will not feed them; cold, but he will not clothe them; sick, but he will not nurse them; dead, but he will not bury them. Such will be the language of the sovereign who holds the principle of distinctions, and such will be his conduct. Different will be the language and conduct of the other who holds the principle of universal love. He will say, "I have heard that he who would show himself a virtuous and intelligent sovereign, ought to make his people the first consideration, and think of himself only after them." Reasoning in this way, when he sees any of the people hungry, he will feed them; cold, he will clothe them; sick, he will nurse them; dead, he will bury them. Such will be the language of the sovereign who holds the principle of universal love, and such his conduct. If we compare the two sovereigns, the words of the one are condemnatory of those of the other, and their actions are opposite. Let us suppose that their words are equally sincere, and that their actions will make them good,—that their words and actions will correspond like the parts of a token, every word being carried into effect; and let us proceed to put the following questions on the case:—Here is a year when a pestilence walks abroad among the people; many of them suffer from cold and famine; multitudes die in the ditches and water channels. If at such a time they might make an election between the two sovereigns whom we have supposed, which would they prefer? I apprehend there is no one under heaven, however stupid, though he may condemn the principle of universal love, but would at such a time prefer to be under the sovereign who holds it. This is in words to condemn the principle, and, when there is occasion to choose between it and the opposite, to approve it;—words and conduct are here in contradiction. I do not know how it is that throughout the kingdom scholars condemn the principle of universal love, whenever they hear it.

How is it that the scholars throughout the kingdom condemn this universal love, whenever they hear of it? Plain as the case is, the words of those who condemn the principle of universal love do not cease. They say, "It is not advantageous to the entire devotion to parents which is required:—it is injurious to filial piety." Our Master said, "let us bring this objection to the test:—A filial son, having the happiness of his parents at heart, considers how it is to be secured. Now, does he, so considering, wish men to love and benefit his parents? or does he wish them to hate and injure his parents?" On this view of the question, it must be evident that he wishes men to love and benefit his parents. And what must he himself first do in order to gain this object? If I first address myself to love and benefit men's parents, will they for that return love and benefit to my parents? or if I first address myself to hate men's parents, will they for that return love and benefit to my parents? It is clear that I must first address myself to love and benefit men's parents, and they will return to me love and benefit to my parents. The conclusion is that a filial son has no alternative.—He must address himself in the first place to love and do good to the parents of others. If it be supposed that this is an accidental course, to be followed on emergency by a filial son, and not sufficient to be regarded as a general rule, let us bring it to the test of what we find in the Books of the ancient kings.—It is said in the Ta Ya,

Every word finds its answer;
Every action its recompense
He threw me a peach;
I returned him a plum.

These words show that he who loves others will be loved, and that he who hates others will be hated. How is it that the scholars throughout the kingdom condemn the principle of universal love, when they hear it?

And now, as to universal mutual love, it is an advantageous thing and easily practiced,—beyond all calculation. The only reason why it is not practised is, in my opinion, because superiors do not take pleasure in it. If superiors were to take pleasure in it, stimulating men to it by rewards and praise, and awing them from opposition to it by punishments and fines, they would, in my opinion, move to it,—the practice of universal mutual love, and the interchange of mutual benefits,—as fire rises upwards, and as water flows downwards:—nothing would be able to check them. This universal love was the way of the sage kings; it is the principle to secure peace for kings, dukes, and great men; it is the means to secure plenty of food and clothes for the myriads of the people. The best course for the superior man is to well understand the principle of universal love, and to exert himself to practise it. It requires the sovereign to be gracious, and the minister to be loyal; the father to be kind, and the son to be filial; the elder brother to be friendly, and the younger to be obedient. Therefore the superior man,— with whom the chief desire is to see gracious sovereigns and loyal ministers; kind fathers and filial sons; friendly elder brothers and obedient younger ones,—ought to insist on the indispensableness of the practice of universal love. It was the way of the sage kings; it would be the most advantageous thing for the myriads of the people.

3.7

Action, Knowledge, and Devotion

The Bhagavad Gītā

THE WAY OF ACTION (*KARMA*)

Chapter II

47. You have right only to [your] actions, not to [their] fruits. Never become the cause of the fruits of actions. [Also] do not have the desire for renouncing [all] action.

48. Being settled in *yoga,* perform actions while giving up [all] attachment, Oh! Dhananjaya, perform actions with a spirit of equanimity for success and failure. [This] equanimity is called *yoga.*

49. Oh! Dhananjay, since action [with desire] is utterly inferior to the *yoga* of *buddhi,*[1] search for taking refuge in [the equanimity of] *buddhi.* Those who desire fruits are depraved.

50. He who is connected with *buddhi* gives up both merit and demerit in this world. Therefore, be settled in *yoga. Yoga* is efficiency in action.

51. The wise who are connected with *buddhi* give up the fruits of actions, (consequently) are freed from the bondage of (re-)birth, and reach the place that is without any suffering.

Chapter III

4. Without performing action, one cannot reach freedom from action. One cannot reach that goal merely by renouncing action.

5. No one can exist even for a moment without performing some action or other. Every one, born of nature, is forced to act, subject to the power of the (three) *guṇas.*[2]

From *The Bhagavad Gītā* Translated by J.N. Mohanty.

6. The ignorant person who, controlling the organs of action,[3] thinks of the objects of the sense organs, is called "one who practises lies."

7. Oh! Arjuna, however, one who, controlling the (cognitive) sense organs with the help of mind,[4] undertakes the *yoga* of action, being non-attached and with the organs of action,—such a person becomes the most distinguished.

8. You do recommended duties, since action is superior to inaction, (and also because) the pilgrimage of your body would be impossible if you renounce all action.

9. All action other than that which is performed for the sake of sacrifice[5] becomes cause of bondage. Therefore, Oh! Sun of Kunti, be free from attachment and perform action for that purpose.

20. Men like Janaka had reached *mokṣa*[6] by means of action. Keeping the goal of good of humankind, you ought to perform your action.

21. Whatever is practised by the best amongst men, that is done by inferior persons. Whatever the wise perform as required by the scriptures, is followed by others.

22. Oh! Pārtha, I do not have to do anything in the three worlds.[7] There is nothing that I have not reached or I need to attain. Nevertheless, I am always engaged in action.

23. Oh! Pārtha, if I am not busied with action instead of being lazy, then human beings will follow my path.

24. (Therefore) If I did not perform any action, all these worlds would be destroyed; I would be responsible for mixture of *varnas*.[8] I will be the cause of the destruction of all living beings.

25. Oh! Bhārata, The wise men, remaining non-attached but with the purpose of rendering good to humankind,[9] shall act in the same way as the ignorant do, with attachment.

26. The wise should not cause confusion in the minds of the ignorant who are attached to their actions; (Rather) by performing all actions with a clear mind they must keep the ignorant engaged in their duties.

27. All actions are performed by the (three) *guṇas* of *prakṛti*.[10] One whose *buddhi* is clouded by the "I"-sense, thinks "I am the agent."

30. Offering all actions to me[11] with a spiritually illuminated mind, be free from desire, without a sense of "mine" and freed from sorrow, and fight.

WAY OF KNOWLEDGE (*JÑĀNA*)

Chapter IV

19. The wise call him learned, all whose efforts to act are free from desire and sense of "ego" and whose actions have been (purified by being) burnt in the fire of knowledge.

23. Freed from attachment, free from sense of ego, with his mind settled in self-knowledge—such a person, even if he performs actions for sacrifice has all his actions destroyed (i.e., without producing any "fruits").

33. Oh! Vanquisher of enemies, Sacrifice in the form of knowledge is superior to sacrifice that is performed with things. Oh! Pārtha, all action culminates in knowledge.

34. Learn that path to knowledge by obeisance, by humble enquiry and by service. Being pleased with you, wise knower of the truth will instruct you about knowledge.

35. Oh! Pandava, when you acquire that knowledge by being instructed by me, you will not again be overtaken by confusion. That knowledge will enable you to see all beings in the self and in me.

36. You will be able to cross the ocean of bondage by the ship of (Brahman) knowledge, even if your are the worst sinner of all.

37. Oh! Arjuna, just as lighted fire reduces a heap of wood to ashes, so does the fire of knowledge reduce all action to ashes.

38. There is nothing in this world as pure (or, purifying) as knowledge. After a long period of purification through *yoga,* one receives this knowledge of the self.

39. One who has faith, and who is attached to knowledge and has controlled his senses, attains knowledge. Achieving knowledge, he immediately afterwards reaches the highest peace.

41. Oh! Dhananjaya, one who has renounced (the fruits of) actions by *Yoga* and whose doubts have been destroyed by knowledge, such a person, in possession of his self, is not bound by actions.

THE WAY OF DEVOTION (BHAKTI)

Chapter XII

6–7. Oh! Pārtha, those who, offering all their actions to me, being devoted to me, by the *yoga* of sole dependence on me, worship and contemplate me, are in no time saved by me—those devotees, wholly thoughtful of me—from the ocean of *Samsāra* infested with death.

8. Place your mind only in me, direct your intellect towards me, in that case after death you will live in me. There is no doubt about this.

9. Oh! Dhananjaya, in case you are not able to concentrate on me with undisturbed mind, then aspire after reaching me by means of repeated practice of *yoga.*

10. If you are unable to perform this repeated practice, then perform such actions which please me. You will reach *mokṣa* by performing all actions for my sake.

11. If you are unable even to do this, then, controlling your senses, taking recourse to the *yoga* of offering all action to me, renounce the fruits of all actions.

12. Knowledge is better than mere practice; meditation is better than knowledge; renouncing the fruits of action is superior to meditation; peace follows immediately after renouncing the fruits of action.

13–14. He who has no aversion for any living being, is friendly, compassionate, ego-less, free from pride, free from attachment to pleasure and aversion to pain, forgiving, ever content, fixed in yoga, self-controlled, with unwavering thought of the Self, who has offered his mind and intellect in me, also is my devotee, he is dear to me.

NOTES

1. "*Buddhi*" means intellect, discernment, reflection.

2. This refers to the Sāṃkhya view that all nature consists of, and is determined by the three "qualities": "*sattva*," "*rajas*," and "*tamas*."

3. The five organs of action are: hands feet, the organ of speaking, the ejecting sense, and the reproductive organ.

4. Here "mind" translates the Sanskrit cognate word "*manas*" meaning the internal organs having the functions of thinking, conception, desire and will.

5. Here "sacrifice" meaning fire sacrifices is used symbolically.

6. "*Mokṣa*" means "spiritual freedom" (from bondage, ignorance, suffering).

7. The three worlds are: earth, heaven, and underworld.

8. "*Varṇa*" means "color" referring to the four castes.

9. This one motive, namely, good of humankind, is permitted in *karmayoga*.

10. "*Prakṛti*" means "nature" as opposed to the spirit or *puruṣa*.

11. Here Kṛṣṇa refers to himself as the incarnation of Godhead.

3.8

Political Theory of Islam

Abul A'la Maududi

With certain people it has become a sort of fashion to somehow identify Islam with one or the other system of life in vogue at the time. So at this time also there are people who say that Islam is a democracy, and by this they mean to imply that there is no difference between Islam and the democracy as in vogue in the West. Some others suggest that Communism is but the latest and revised version of Islam and it is in the fitness of things that Muslims imitate the Communist experiment of Soviet Russia. Still some others whisper that Islam has the elements of dictatorship in it and we should revive the cult of "obedience to the *Amīr*" (the leader). All these people, in this misinformed and misguided zeal to serve what they hold to be the cause of Islam, are always at great pains to prove that Islam contains within itself the elements of all types of contemporary social and political thought and action. Most of the people who indulge in this prattle have no clear idea of the Islamic way of life. They have never made nor try to make a systematic study of the Islamic political order—the place and nature of democracy, social justice, and equality in it. Instead they behave like the proverbial blind men who gave altogether contradictory descriptions of an elephant because one had been able to touch only its tail, the other its legs, the third its belly and the fourth its ears only. Or perhaps they look upon Islam as an orphan whose sole hope for survival lies in winning the patronage and the sheltering care of some dominant creed. That is why some people have begun to present apologies on Islam's behalf As a matter of fact, this attitude emerges from an inferiority complex, from the belief that we as Muslims can earn no honor or respect unless we are able to show that our religion resembles the modern creeds and it is in agreement with most

From *The Islamic Law and Constitution,* translated by Khurshid Ahmad. Copyright © 1955; 1960 by Abul A'la Maududi, pp. 131–32; 145–61.

of the contemporary ideologies. These people have done a great disservice to Islam; they have reduced the political theory of Islam to a puzzle, a hotchpotch. They have turned Islam into a juggler's bag out of which can be produced anything that holds a demand! Such is the intellectual plight in which we are engulfed. Perhaps it is a result of this sorry state of affairs that some people have even begun to say that Islam has no political or economic system of its own and anything can fit into its scheme.

In these circumstances it has become essential that a careful study of the political theory of Islam should be made in a scientific way, with a view to grasp its real meaning, nature, purpose and significance. Such a systematic study alone can put an end to this confusion of thought and silence those who out of ignorance proclaim that there is nothing like Islamic political theory, Islamic social order and Islamic culture. I hope it will also bring to the world groping in darkness the light that it urgently needs, although it is not yet completely conscious of such a need.

FIRST PRINCIPLE OF ISLAMIC POLITICAL THEORY

The belief in the Unity and the sovereignty of Allah is the foundation of the social and moral system propounded by the Prophets. It is the very starting-point of the Islamic political philosophy. The basic principle of Islam is that human beings must, individually and collectively, surrender all rights of overlordship, legislation and exercising of authority over others. No one should be allowed to pass orders or make commands *in his own right* and no one ought to accept the obligation to carry out such commands and obey such orders. None is entitled to make laws on his own authority and none is obliged to abide by them. This right vests in Allah alone:

> The Authority rests with none but Allah. He commands you not to surrender to anyone save Him. This is the right way [of life]. (Qur'ān 12:40)
> They ask: "have we also got some authority?" Say: "all authority belongs to God alone." (3:154)
> Do not say wrongly with your tongues that this is lawful and that is unlawful. (16:116)
> Whoso does not establish and decide by that which Allah has revealed, such are disbelievers. (5:44)

According to this theory, sovereignty belongs to Allah. He alone is the law-giver. No man, even if he be a Prophet, has the right to order others *in his own right* to do or not to do certain things. The Prophet himself is subject to God's commands:

> I do not follow anything except what is revealed to me. (6:50)

Other people are required to obey the Prophet because he enunciates not his own but God's commands:

> We sent no messenger save that he should be obeyed by Allah's command. (4:64)
>
> They are the people to whom We gave the Scripture and Command and Prophethood. (6:90)
>
> It is not [possible] for any human being to whom Allah has given the Scripture and the Wisdom and the Prophethood that he should say to people: Obey me instead of Allah. Such a one [could only say]: be solely devoted to the Lord. (3:79)

Thus the main characteristics of an Islamic state that can be deduced from these express statements of the Holy Qur'ān are as follows:

1. No person, class or group, not even the entire population of the state as a whole, can lay claim to sovereignty. God alone is the real sovereign; all others are merely His subjects.
2. God is the real law-giver and the authority of absolute legislation vests in Him. The believers cannot resort to totally independent legislation nor can they modify any law which God has laid down, even if the desire to effect such legislation or change in Divine laws is unanimous.
3. An Islamic state must, in all respects, be founded upon the law laid down by God through His Prophet. The government which runs such a state will be entitled to obedience in its capacity as a political agency set up to enforce the laws of God and only in so far as it acts in that capacity. If it disregards the law revealed by God, its commands will not be binding on the believers.

THE ISLAMIC STATE: ITS NATURE AND CHARACTERISTICS

The preceding discussion makes it quite clear that Islam, speaking from the view-point of political philosophy, is the very antithesis of secular Western democracy. The philosophical foundation of Western democracy is the sovereignty of the people. In it, this type of absolute powers of legislation—of the determination of values and of the norms of behavior—rests in the hands of the people. Law-making is their prerogative and legislation must correspond to the mood and temper of their opinion. If a particular piece of legislation is desired by the masses, howsoever ill-conceived it may be from a religious and moral viewpoint, steps have to be taken to place it on the statute book; if the people dislike any law and demand its abrogation, howsoever just and rightful it might be, it has to be expunged forthwith. This is not the case in Islam. On this count, Islam has no trace of Western democracy. Islam, as already explained, altogether repudiates the philosophy of popular sovereignty and rears its polity on the foundations of the sovereignty of God and the vicegerency (*Khilāfah*) of man.

A more apt name for the Islamic polity would be the "kingdom of God" which is described in English as a "theocracy." But Islamic theocracy is something altogether different from the theocracy of which Europe has had a bitter experience wherein a priestly class, sharply marked off from the rest of the population, exercises unchecked domination and enforces laws of its own making in the name of God, thus virtually imposing its own divinity and godhood upon the common people. Such a system of government is satanic rather than divine. Contrary to this, the theocracy built up by Islam is not ruled by any particular religious class but by the whole community of Muslims including the rank and file. The entire Muslim population runs the state in accordance with the Book of God and the practice of His Prophet. If I were permitted to coin a new term, I would describe this system of government as a "theo-democracy," that is to say a divine democratic government, because under it the Muslims have been given a limited popular sovereignty under the suzerainty of God. The executive under this system of government is constituted by the general will of the Muslims who have also the right to depose it. All administrative matters and all questions about which no explicit injunction is to be found in the *sharī'ah* are settled by the consensus of opinion among the Muslims. Every Muslim who is capable and qualified to give a sound Opinion on matters of Islamic law, is entitled to interpret the law of God when such interpretation becomes necessary. In this sense the Islamic polity is a democracy. But, as has been explained above, it is a theocracy in the sense that where an explicit command of God or His Prophet already exists, no Muslim leader or legislature, or any religious scholar can form an independent judgment, not even all the Muslims of the world put together have any right to make the least alteration in it.

Before proceeding further, I feel that I should put in a word of explanation as to why these limitations and restrictions have been placed upon popular sovereignty in Islam, and what is the nature of these limitations and restrictions. It may be said that God has, in this manner, taken away the liberty of the human mind and intellect instead of safeguarding it as I was trying to prove. My reply is that God has retained the right of legislation in His own hand not in order to deprive man of his natural freedom but to safeguard that very freedom. His purpose is to save man from going astray and inviting his own ruin.

One can easily understand this point by attempting a little analysis of the so-called Western secular democracy. It is claimed that this democracy is founded on popular sovereignty. But everybody knows that the people who constitute a state do not all of them take part either in legislation or in its administration. They have to delegate their sovereignty to their elected representatives so that the latter may make and enforce laws on their behalf. For this purpose, an electoral system is set up. But a divorce has been effected between politics and religion, and as a result of this secularization, the society and particularly its politically active elements have ceased to attach much or any importance to morality and ethics. And this is also a fact that only those persons generally come to the top who can dupe the masses by their wealth, power, and deceptive propaganda. Although these representatives come into power by the votes of the common people, they soon set themselves up as an independent authority and assume the position of overlords (*ilāhs*). They often make laws not in the best interest of the people who raised them to power but to further their own sectional and class interests. They impose their will on the people by virtue of the authority delegated to them by those over whom they rule. This is the situation which besets people in England, America and in all those countries which claim to be the haven of secular democracy.

Even if we overlook this aspect of the matter and admit that in these countries laws are made according to the wishes of the common people, it has been established by experience that the great mass of the common people are incapable of perceiving their own true interests. It is the natural weakness of man that in most of the affairs concerning his life he takes into consideration only some one aspect of reality and loses sight of other aspects. His judgments are usually one-sided and he is swayed by emotions and desires to such an extent that rarely, if ever, can he judge important matters with the impartiality and objectivity of scientific reason. Quite often he rejects the plea of reason simply because it conflicts with his passions and desires. I can cite many instances in support of this contention but to avoid prolixity I shall content myself with giving only one example: the Prohibition Law of America. It had been rationally and logically established that drinking is injurious to health, produces deleterious effects on mental and intellectual faculties and leads to disorder in human society. The American public accepted these facts and agreed to the enactment of the Prohibition Law. Accordingly the law was passed by the majority vote. But when it was put into effect, the very same people by whose vote it had been passed, revolted against it. The worst kinds of wine were illicitly manufactured and consumed, and their use and consumption became more widespread than before. Crimes increased in number, and eventually drinking was legalized by the vote of the same people who had previously voted for its prohibition. This sudden change in public opinion was not the result of any fresh scientific discovery or the revelation of new facts providing evidence against the advantages of prohibition, but because the people had been completely enslaved by their habit and could not forgo the pleasures of self-indulgence. They delegated their own sovereignty to the evil spirit in them and set up their own desires and passions as their *ilāhs* (gods) at whose call they all went in for the repeal of the very law they had passed after having been convinced of its rationality and correctness. There are many other similar instances which go to prove that man is not competent to become an absolute legislator. Even if he secures deliverance from the service of other *ilāhs*, he becomes a slave to his own petty passions and exalts the devil in him to the position of a supreme Lord. Limitations on human freedom, provided they are appropriate and do not deprive him of all initiative are absolutely necessary in the interest of man himself.

That is why God has laid down those limits which, in Islamic phraseology, are termed "divine limits." These limits consist of certain principles, checks and balances and specific injunctions in different spheres of life and activity, and they have been prescribed in order that man may be trained to lead a balanced and moderate life. They are intended to lay down the broad framework within which man is free to legislate, decide his own affairs and frame subsidiary laws and regulations for his conduct. These limits he is not permitted to overstep and if he does so, the whole scheme of his life will go awry.

Take for example man's economic life. In this sphere God has placed certain restrictions on human freedom. The right to private property has been recognized, but it is qualified by the obligation to pay *Zakāh* (poor dues) and the prohibition of interest, gambling and speculation. A specific law of inheritance for the distribution of property among the largest number of surviving relations on the death of its owner has been laid down and certain forms of acquiring, accumulating and spending wealth have been declared unlawful. If people observe these just limits and regulate their affairs within these boundary walls, on the one hand their personal liberty is adequately safeguarded and, on the other, the possibility of class war and domination of one class over another, which begins with capitalist oppression and ends in working-class dictatorship, is safely and conveniently eliminated.

Similarly in the sphere of family life, God has prohibited the unrestricted intermingling of the sexes and has prescribed *Pardāh*, recognized man's guardianship of woman, and clearly defined the rights and duties of husband, wife and children. The laws of divorce and separation have been clearly set forth, conditional polygamy has been permitted and penalties for fornication and false accusations of adultery have been prescribed. He has thus laid down limits which, if observed by a man, would stabilize his family life and make it a haven of peace and happiness. There would remain neither that tyranny of male over female which makes family life an inferno of cruelty and oppression, nor that satanic flood of female liberty and license which threatens to destroy human civilization in the West.

In like manner, for the preservation of human culture and society God has, by formulating the law of *Qisyāsy* (Retaliation) commanding to cut off the hands for theft, prohibiting wine-drinking, placing limitations on uncovering of one's private parts and by laying down a few similar permanent rules and regulations, closed the door of social disorder forever. I have no time to present to you a complete list of all the divine limits and show in detail how essential each one of them is for maintaining equilibrium and poise in life. What I want to bring home to you here is that through these injunctions God has provided a permanent and immutable code of behavior for man, and that it does not deprive him of any essential liberty nor does it dull the edge of his mental faculties. On the contrary, it sets a straight and clear path before him, so that he may not, owing to his ignorance and weaknesses which he inherently possesses, lose himself in the maze of destruction and instead of wasting his faculties in the pursuit of wrong ends, he may follow the road that leads to success and progress in this world and the hereafter. If you have ever happened to visit a mountainous region, you must have noticed that in the winding mountain paths which are bounded by deep caves on the one side and lofty rocks on the other, the border of the road is barricaded and protected in such a way as to prevent travellers from straying towards the abyss by mistake. Are these barricades intended to deprive the wayfarer of his liberty? No, as a matter of fact, they are meant to protect him from destruction; to warn him at every bend of the dangers ahead and to show him the path leading to his destination. That precisely is the purpose of the restrictions which God has laid down in His revealed Code. These limits determine what direction man should take in life's journey and they guide him at every turn and pass and point out to him the path of safety which he should steadfastly follow.

As I have already stated, this code, enacted as it is by God, is unchangeable. You can, if you like, rebel against it, as some Muslim countries have done. But you cannot alter it. It will continue to be unalterable till the last day. It has its own avenues of growth and evolution, but no human being has any right to tamper with it. Whenever an Islamic State comes into existence, this code would form its fundamental law and will constitute the mainspring of all its legislation. Every one who desires to remain a Muslim is under an obligation to follow the Qur'ān and the Sunnah which must constitute the basic law of an Islamic State.

THE PURPOSE OF THE ISLAMIC STATE

The purpose of the state that may be formed on the basis of the Qur'ān and the *Sunnah* has also been laid down by God. The Qur'ān says:

> We verily sent Our messengers with clear proofs, and revealed with them the Scripture and the Balance, that mankind may observe right measure; and We revealed iron, wherein is mighty power and (many) uses for mankind. (57:25)

In this verse steel symbolizes political power and the verse also makes it clear that the mission of the Prophets is to create conditions in which the mass of people will be assured of social justice in accordance with the standards enunciated by God in His Book which gives explicit instructions for a well-disciplined mode of life. In another place God has said:

> [Muslims are] those who, if We give them power in the land, establish the system of *Ṣalāh* [worship] and *Zakāh* [poor dues] and enjoin virtue and forbid evil and inequity. (22:41)
>
> You are the best community sent forth to mankind; you enjoin the right conduct and forbid the wrong; and you believe in Allah. (3:110)

It will readily become manifest to anyone who reflects upon these verses that the purpose of the state visualized by the Holy Qur'ān is not negative but positive. The object of the state is not merely to prevent people from exploiting each other, to safeguard their liberty and to protect its subjects from foreign invasion. It also aims at evolving and developing that well-balanced system of social justice which has been set forth by God in His Holy Book. Its object is to eradicate all forms of evil and to encourage all types of virtue and excellence expressly mentioned by God in the Holy Qur'ān. For this purpose political power will be made use of as and when the occasion demands; all means of propaganda and peaceful persuasion will be employed; the moral education of the people will also be undertaken; and social influence as well as the force of public opinion will be harnessed to the task.

ISLAMIC STATE IS UNIVERSAL AND ALL-EMBRACING

A state of this sort cannot evidently restrict the scope of its activities. Its approach is universal and all-embracing. Its sphere of activity is coextensive with the whole of human life. It seeks to mould every aspect of life and activity in consonance with its moral norms and program of social reform. In such a state no one can regard any field of his affairs as personal and private. Considered from this aspect the Islamic state bears a kind of resemblance to the Fascist and Communist states. But you will find later on that, despite its all-inclusiveness, it is something vastly and basically different from the modern totalitarian and authoritarian states. Individual liberty is not suppressed under it nor is there any trace of dictatorship in it. It presents the middle course and embodies the best that the human society has ever evolved. The excellent balance and moderation that characterize the Islamic system of government and the precise distinctions made in it between right and wrong—elicit from all men of honesty and intelligence the admiration and the admission that such a balanced system could not have been framed by anyone but the Omniscient and All-Wise God.

ISLAMIC STATE IS AN IDEOLOGICAL STATE

Another characteristic of the Islamic State is that it is an ideological state. It is clear from a careful consideration of the Qur'ān and the *Sunnah* that the state in Islam is based on an ideology and its objective is to establish that ideology. The state is an instrument of reform and must act likewise. It is a dictate of this very nature of the Islamic State that such a state should be run only by those who believe in the ideology on which it is based and in the Divine Law which it is assigned to administer. The administrators of the Islamic state must be those whose whole life is devoted to the observance and enforcement of this Law, who not only agree with its reformatory program and fully believe in it but thoroughly comprehend its spirit and are acquainted with its details. Islam does not recognize any geographical, linguistic or colour bars in this respect. It puts forward its code of guidance and the scheme of its reform before all men. Whoever accepts this program, no matter to what race, nation or country he may belong, can join the community that runs the Islamic state. But those who do not accept it are not entitled to have any hand in shaping the fundamental policy of the State. They can live within the confines of the State as non-Muslim citizens (*Dhimmīs*). Specific rights and privileges have been accorded to them in the Islamic Law. A *Dhimmī's* life, property and honor will be fully protected, and if he is capable of any service, his services will also be made use of. He will not, however, be allowed to influence the basic policy of this ideological state. The Islamic state is based on a particular ideology and it is the community which believes in the Islamic ideology which pilots it. Here again, we notice some sort of resemblance between the Islamic and the Communist states. But the treatment meted out by the Communist states to persons holding creeds and ideologies other than its own bears no comparison with the attitude of the Islamic state. Unlike the Communist state, Islam does not impose its social principles on others by force, nor does it confiscate their properties or unleash a reign of terror by mass executions of the people and their transportation to the slave camps of Siberia. Islam does not want to eliminate its minorities, it wants to protect them and give them the freedom to live according to their own culture. The generous and just treatment which Islam has accorded to non-Muslims in an Islamic state and the fine distinction drawn by it between justice and injustice and good and evil will convince all those who are not prejudiced against it, that the prophets sent by

God accomplish their task in an altogether different manner—something radically different and diametrically opposed to the way of the false reformers who strut about here and there on the stage of history.

THE THEORY OF THE CALIPHATE AND THE NATURE OF DEMOCRACY IN ISLAM

I will now try to give a brief exposition of the composition and structure of the Islamic state. I have already stated that in Islam, God alone is the real sovereign. Keeping this cardinal principle in mind, if we consider the position of those persons who set out to enforce God's law on earth, it is but natural to say that they should be regarded as representatives of the Supreme Ruler. Islam has assigned precisely this very position to them. Accordingly the Holy Qur'ān says:

> Allah has promised to those among you who believe and do righteous deeds that He will assuredly make them to succeed (the present rulers) and grant them vicegerency in the land just as He made those before them to succeed (others).

The verse illustrates very clearly the Islamic theory of state. Two fundamental points emerge from it.

1. The first point is that Islam uses the term "vicegerency" (*Khilāfah*) instead of sovereignty. Since, according to Islam, sovereignty belongs to God alone, anyone who holds power and rules in accordance with the laws of God would undoubtedly be the vicegerent of the Supreme Ruler and would not be authorized to exercise any powers other than those delegated to him.

2. The second point stated in the verse is that the power to rule over the earth has been promised to *the whole community of believers;* it has not been stated that any particular person or class among them will be raised to that position. From this it follows that all believers are repositories of the Caliphate. The Caliphate granted by God to the faithful is the popular vicegerency and not a limited one. There is no reservation in favor of any family, class or race. Every believer is a Caliph of God in his individual capacity. By virtue of this position he is individually responsible to God. The Holy Prophet has said: "Everyone of you is a ruler and everyone is answerable for his subjects." Thus one Caliph is in no way inferior to another.

This is the real foundation of democracy in Islam. The following points emerge from an analysis of this conception of popular vicegerency:

(a) A society in which everyone is a Caliph of God and an equal participant in this Caliphate, cannot tolerate any class divisions based on distinctions of birth and social position. All men enjoy equal status and position in such a society. The only criterion of superiority in this social order is personal ability and character. This is what has been repeatedly and explicitly asserted by the Holy Prophet:

> No one is superior to another except in point of faith and piety. All men are descended from Adam and Adam was made of clay.
>
> An Arab has no superiority over a non-Arab nor a non-Arab over an Arab; neither does a white man possess any superiority over a black man nor a black man over a white one, except in point of piety.

After the conquest of Mekka, when the whole of Arabia came under the domination of the Islamic state, the Holy Prophet addressing the members of his own clan, who in the days before Islam enjoyed the same status in Arabia as the Brahmins did in ancient India, said:

> O people of Quraysh! Allah has rooted out your haughtiness of the days of ignorance and the pride of ancestry. O men, all of you are descended from Adam and Adam was made of clay. There is no pride whatever in ancestry; there is no merit in an Arab as against a non-Arab nor in a non-Arab against an Arab. Verily the most meritorious among you in the eyes of God is he who is the most pious.

(b) In such a society no individual or group of individuals will suffer any disability on account of birth, social status, or profession that may in any way impede the growth of his faculties or hamper the development of his personality.

Every one would enjoy equal opportunities of progress. The way would be left open for him to make as much progress as possible according to his inborn capacity and personal merits without prejudice to similar rights of other people. Thus, unrestricted scope for personal achievement has always been the hallmark of Islamic society. Slaves and their descendants were appointed as military officers and governors of provinces, and noble men belonging to the highest families did not feel ashamed to serve under them. Those who used to stitch and mend shoes rose in the social scale and became leaders of highest order (*imāms*); weavers and cloth-sellers became judges (*muftūs*) and jurists and to this day they are reckoned as the heroes of Islam. The Holy Prophet has said:

> Listen and obey even if a negro is appointed as a ruler over you.

(c) There is no room in such a society for the dictatorship of any person or group of persons since everyone is a Caliph of God herein. No person or group of persons is entitled to become an absolute ruler by depriving the rank and file of their inherent right of Caliphate. The position of a man who is selected to conduct the affairs of the state is no more than this; that all Muslims (or, technically speaking, all Caliphs of God) delegate their Caliphate to him for administrative purposes. *He is answerable to God on the one hand and on the other to his fellow "Caliphs" who have delegated their authority to him.* Now, if he raises himself to the position of an irresponsible absolute ruler, that is to say a dictator, he assumes the character of a usurper rather than a Caliph, because dictatorship is the negation of popular vicegerency. No doubt the Islamic state is an all-embracing state and comprises within its sphere all departments of life, but this all-inclusiveness and universality are based upon the universality of Divine Law which an Islamic ruler has to observe and enforce. The guidance given by God about every aspect of life will certainly be enforced in its entirety. But an Islamic ruler cannot depart from these instructions and adopt a policy of regimentation on his own. He cannot force people to follow or not to follow a particular profession; to learn or not to learn a special art; to use or not to use a certain script; to wear or not to wear a certain dress and to educate or not to educate their children in a certain manner. The powers which the dictators of Russia, Germany and Italy have appropriated or which Ataturk has exercised in Turkey have not been granted by Islam to its *Amīr* (leader). Besides this, another important point is that in Islam *every individual is held personally answerable to God*. This personal responsibility cannot be shared by anyone else. Hence, an individual enjoys full liberty to choose whichever path he likes and to develop his faculties in any direction that suits his natural gifts. If the leader obstructs him or obstructs the growth of his personality, he will himself be punished by God for this tyranny. That is precisely the reason why there is not the slightest trace of regimentation in the rule of the Holy Prophet and of his Rightly-Guided Caliphs; and

(d) In such a society every sane and adult Muslim, male or female, is entitled to express his or her opinion, for each one of them is the repository of the Caliphate. God has made this Caliphate conditional, not upon any particular standard of wealth or competence but only upon faith and good conduct. Therefore all Muslims have equal freedom to express their opinions.

EQUILIBRIUM BETWEEN INDIVIDUALISM AND COLLECTIVISM

Islam seeks to set up, on the one hand, this superlative democracy and on the other it has put an end to that individualism which militates against the health of the body politic. The relations between the individual and the society have been regulated in such a manner that neither the personality of the individual suffers any diminution, or corrosion as it does in the Communist and Fascist social system, nor is the individual allowed to exceed his bounds to such an extent as to become harmful to the community, as happens in the Western democracies. In Islam, the purpose of an individual's life is the same as that of the life of the community, namely, the execution and enforcement of Divine Law and the acquisition of God's pleasure. Moreover, Islam has, after safeguarding the rights of the individual, imposed upon him certain duties towards the community. In this way requirements of individualism and collectivism have been so well harmonized that the individual is afforded the fullest opportunity to develop his potentialities and is thus enabled to employ his developed faculties in the service of the community at large.

These are, briefly, the basic principles and essential features of the Islamic political theory.

3.9

The Categorical Imperative

Immanuel Kant

As my concern here is with moral philosophy, I limit the question suggested to this: Whether it is not of the utmost necessity to construct a pure moral philosophy, perfectly cleared of everything which is only empirical, and which belongs to anthropology? for that such a philosophy must be possible is evident from the common idea of duty and of the moral laws. Everyone must admit that if a law is to have moral force, *i.e.* to be the basis of an obligation, it must carry with it absolute necessity; that, for example, the precept, "Thou shall not lie," is not valid for men alone, as if other rational beings had no need to observe it; and so with all the other moral laws properly so called; that, therefore, the basis of obligation must not be sought in the nature of man, or in the circumstances in the world in which he is placed, but a priori simply in the conception of pure reason; and although any other precept which is founded on principles of mere experience may be in certain respects universal, yet in as far as it rests even in the least degree on an empirical basis, perhaps only as to a motive, such a precept, while it may be a practical rule, can never be called a moral law.

Nothing can possibly be conceived in the world, or even out of it, which can be called good, without qualification, except a *good will*. Intelligence, wit, judgment, and the other *talents* of the mind, however they may be named, or courage, resolution, perseverance, as qualities of temperament, are undoubtedly good and desirable in many respects; but these gifts of nature may also become extremely bad and mischievous if the will which is to make use of them, and which, therefore, constitutes what is called *character* is not good. It is the same with the *gifts of fortune*. Power, riches, hon-

---

From the preface, chapters 1 and 2 of *The Fundamental Principles of the Metaphysic of Morals,* translated by T. K. Abbott (first published in 1873), pp. 5–41. Footnotes deleted.

our, even health, and the general well-being and contentment with one's conditions which is called *happiness,* inspire pride, and often presumption, if there is not a good will to correct the influence of these on the mind, and with this also to rectify the whole principle of acting, and adapt it to its end. The sight of a being who is not adorned with a single feature of a pure and good will, enjoying unbroken prosperity, can never give pleasure to an imperial rational spectator. Thus a good will appears to constitute the indispensable condition even of being worthy of happiness.

There are even some qualities which are of service to this good will itself, and may facilitate its action, yet which have no intrinsic unconditional value, but always presuppose a good will, and this qualifies the esteem that we justly have for them, and does not permit us to regard them as absolutely good. Moderation in the affections and passions, self-control, and calm deliberation are not only good in many respects, but even seem to constitute part of the intrinsic worth of the person; but they are far from deserving to be called good without qualification, although they have been so unconditionally praised by the ancients. For without the principles of a good will, they may become extremely bad; and the coolness of a villain not only makes him far more dangerous, but also directly makes him more abominable in our eyes than he would have been without it.

A good will is good not because of what it performs or effects, not by its aptness for the attainment of some proposed end, but simply by virtue of the volition, that is, it is good in itself and considered by itself to be esteemed much higher than all that can be brought about by it in favour of any inclination, nay, even of the sum-total of all inclinations. Even if it should happen that, owing to special disfavour of fortune, or the niggardly provision of a step-motherly nature, this will should wholly lack power to accomplish its purpose, if with its greatest efforts it should yet achieve nothing, and there should remain only the good will (not, to be sure, a mere wish, but the summoning of all means in our power), then, like a jewel, it would still shine by its own light, as a thing which has its whole value in itself. Its usefulness or fruitlessness can neither add to nor take away anything from this value. It would be, as it were, only the setting to enable us to handle it the more conveniently in common commerce, or to attract to it the attention of those who are not yet connoisseurs, but not to recommend it to true connoisseurs, or to determine its value.

There is, however, something so strange in this idea of the absolute value of the mere will, in which no account is taken of its utility, that notwithstanding the thorough assent of even common reason to the idea, yet a suspicion must arise that it may perhaps really be the product of mere highblown fancy, and that we may have misunderstood the purpose of nature in assigning reason as the governor of our will. Therefore we will examine this idea from this point of view.

In the physical constitution of an organized being, that is, a being adapted suitably to the purposes of life, we assume it as a fundamental principle that no organ for any purpose will be found but what is also the fittest and best adapted for that purpose. Now in a being which has reason and a will, if the proper object of nature were its *conservatism,* its *welfare,* in a word, its *happiness,* then nature would have hit upon a very bad arrangement in selecting the reason of the creature to carry out this purpose. For all the actions which the creature has to perform with a view to this purpose, and the whole rule of its conduct, would be far more surely prescribed to it by instinct, and that end would have been attained thereby much more certainly than it ever can be by reason. Should reason have been communicated to this favoured creature over and above, it must only have served it to contemplate the happy constitution of its nature, to admire it, to congratulate itself thereon, and to feel thankful for it to the beneficient cause, but not that it should subject its desires to that weak and delusive guidance, and meddle bunglingly with the purpose of nature. In a word, nature would have taken care that reason should not break forth into *practical exercise,* nor have the presumption, with its weak insight, to think out for itself the plan of happiness, and of the means of attaining it. Nature would not only have taken on herself the choice of the ends, but also of the means, and with wise foresight would have entrusted both to instinct.

And, in fact, we find that the more a cultivated reason applies itself with deliberate purpose to the enjoyment of life and happiness, so much the more does the man fail of true satisfaction. And from this circumstance there arises in many, if they are candid enough to confess it, a certain degree of *misology, that is, hatred of reason*, especially in the case of those who are most experienced in the use of it, because after calculating all the advantages they derive, I do not say from the invention of all the arts of common luxury, but even from the sciences (which seem to them to be after all only a luxury of the understanding), they find that they have, in fact, only brought more trouble on their shoulders, rather than gained in happiness; and they end by envying, rather than despising, the more common stamp of men who keep closer to the guidance of mere instinct, and do not allow their reason much influence on their conduct. And this we must admit, that the judgment of those who would very much lower the lofty eulogies of the advantages which reason gives us in regard to the happiness and satisfaction of life, or who would even reduce them below zero, is by no means morose or ungrateful to the goodness with which the world is governed, but that there lies at the root of these judgments the idea that our existence has a different and far nobler end, for which, and not for happiness, reason is properly intended, and which must, therefore, be regarded as the supreme condition to which the private ends of man must, for the most part, be postponed.

For as reason is not competent to guide the will with certainty in regard to its objects and the satisfaction of all our wants (which it to some extent even multiplies), this being an end to which an implanted instinct would have led with much greater certainty; and since, nevertheless, reason is imparted to us as a practical faculty, *i.e.* as one which is to have influence on the *will,* therefore, admitting that nature generally in the distribution of her capacities has adapted the means to the end, its true destination must be to produce a *will,* not merely good as a *means* to something else, but *good in itself,* for which reason was absolutely necessary. This will then, though not indeed the sole and complete good, must be the supreme good and the condition of every other, even of the desire of happiness. Under these circumstances, there is nothing inconsistent with the wisdom of nature in the fact that the cultivation of the reason, which is requisite for the first and unconditional purpose, does in many ways interfere, at least in this life, with the attainment of the second, which is always conditional, namely, happiness. Nay, it may even reduce it to nothing, without nature thereby failing in her purpose. For reason recognizes the establishment of a good will as its highest practical destination, and in attaining this purpose is capable only of a satisfaction of its own proper kind, namely, that from the attainment of an end, which end again is determined by reason only, notwithstanding that this may involve many a disappointment to the ends of inclination.

We have then to develop the notion of a will which deserves to be highly esteemed for itself, and is good without a view to anything further, a notion which exists already in the sound natural understanding, requiring rather to be cleared up than to be taught, and which in estimating the value of our actions always takes the first place, and constitutes the condition of all the rest. In order to do this, we will take the notion of duty, which includes that of a good will, although implying certain subjective restrictions and hindrances. These, however, far from concealing it, or rendering it unrecognizable, rather bring it out by contrast, and make it shine forth so much the brighter.

I omit here all actions which are already recognized as inconsistent with duty although they may be useful for this or that purpose, for with these the question whether they are done *from duty* cannot arise at all, since they even conflict with it. I also set aside those actions which really conform to duty, but to which men have *no* direct *inclination,* performing them because they are impelled thereto by some other inclination. For in this case we can readily distinguish whether the action which agrees with duty is done from *duty,* or from a selfish view. It is much harder to make this distinction when the action accords with duty, and the subject has besides a *direct* inclination to it. For example, it is always a matter of duty that a dealer should not overcharge an inexperienced purchaser; and wherever there is much commerce the prudent tradesman does not overcharge, but keeps a fixed price for everyone, so that a child buys of him as well as any other.

Men are thus *honestly* served; but this is not enough to make us believe that the tradesman has so acted from duty and from principles of honesty: his own advantage required it; it is out of the question in this case to suppose that he might besides have a direct inclination in favour of the buyers, so that, as it were, from love he should give no advantage to one over another. Accordingly the action was done neither from duty nor from direct inclination, but merely with a selfish view.

On the other hand, it is a duty to maintain one's life; and, in addition, everyone has also a direct inclination to do so. But on this account the often anxious care which most men take for it has no intrinsic worth, and their maxim has no moral import. They preserve their life *as duty requires,* no doubt, but not *because duty requires.* On the other hand, if adversity and hopeless sorrow have completely taken away the relish for life; if the unfortunate one, strong in mind, indignant at his fate rather than desponding or dejected, wishes for death, and yet preserves his life without loving it—not from inclination or fear, but from duty—then his maxim has a moral worth.

To be beneficent when we can is a duty; and besides this, there are many minds so sympathetically constituted that, without any other motive of vanity or self-interest, they find a pleasure in spreading joy around them, and can take delight in the satisfaction of others so far as it is their own work. But I maintain that in such a case an action of this kind, however proper, however amiable it may be, has nevertheless no true moral worth, but is on a level with other inclinations, *e.g.* the inclination to honour, which, if it is happily directed to that which is in fact of public utility and accordant with duty, and consequently honourable, deserves praise and encouragement, but not esteem. For the maxim lacks the moral import, namely, that such actions be done *from duty,* not from inclination. Put the case that the mind of that philanthropist was clouded by sorrow of his own, extinguishing all sympathy with the lot of others, and that while he still has the power to benefit others in distress, he is not touched by their trouble because he is absorbed with his own; and now suppose that he tears himself out of this dead insensibility, and performs the action without any inclination to it, but simply from duty, then first has his action its genuine moral worth. Further still; if nature has put little sympathy in the heart of this or that man; if he, supposed to be an upright man, is by temperament cold and indifferent to the sufferings of others, perhaps because in respect of his own he is provided with the special gift of patience and fortitude, and supposes, or even requires, that others should have the same—and such a man would certainly not be the meanest product of nature—but if nature had not specially framed him for a philanthropist, would he not still find in himself a source from whence to give himself a far higher worth than that of a good-natured temperament could be? Unquestionably. It is just in this that the moral worth of the character is brought out which is incomparably the highest of all, namely, that he is beneficent, not from inclination, but from duty.

To secure one's own happiness is a duty, at least indirectly; for discontent with one's condition, under a pressure of many anxieties and amidst unsatisfied wants, might easily become a great temptation to transgression of duty. But here again, without looking to duty, all men have already the strongest and most intimate inclination to happiness, because it is just in this idea that all inclinations are combined in one total. But the precept of happiness is often of such a sort that it greatly interferes with some inclinations, and yet a man cannot form any definite and certain conception of the sum of satisfaction of all of them which is called happiness. It is not then to be wondered at that a single inclination, definite both as to what it promises and as to the time within which it can be gratified, is often able to overcome such a fluctuating idea, and that a gouty patient, for instance, can choose to enjoy what he likes, and to suffer what he may, since, according to his calculation, on this occasion at least, he has [only] not sacrificed the enjoyment of the present moment to a possibly mistaken expectation of a happiness which is supposed to be found in health. But even in this case, if the general desire for happiness did not influence his will, and supposing that in his particular case health was not a necessary element in this calculation, there yet remains in this, as in all other cases, this law, namely, that he should promote his happiness not from inclination but from duty, and by this would his conduct first acquire true moral worth.

It is in this manner, undoubtedly, that we are to understand those passages of Scripture also in which we are commanded to love our neighbour, even our enemy. For love, as an affection, cannot be commanded, but beneficence for duty's sake may; even though we are not impelled to it by any inclination—nay, are even repelled by a natural and unconquerable aversion. This is *practical* love, and not *pathological*—a love which is seated in the will, and not in the propensions of sense—in principles of action and not of tender sympathy; and it is this love alone which can be commanded.

The second proposition is: That an action done from duty derives its moral worth, *not from the purpose* which is to be attained by it, but from the maxim by which it is determined, and therefore does not depend on the realization of the object of the action, but merely on the *principle of volition* by which the action has taken place, without regard to any object of desire. It is clear from what precedes that the purposes which we may have in view in our actions, or their effects regarded as ends and springs of the will, cannot give to actions any unconditional or moral worth. In what, then, can their worth lie, if it is not to consist in the will and in reference to its expected effect? It cannot lie anywhere but in the *principle of the will* without regard to the ends which can be attained by the action. For the will stands between its *a priori principle,* which is formal, and its *a posteriori* spring, which is material, as between two roads, and as it must be determined by something, it follows that it must be determined by the formal principle of volition when an action is done from duty, in which case every material principle has been withdrawn from it.

The third proposition, which is a consequence of the two preceding, I would express thus: *Duty is the necessity of acting from respect for the law.* I may have *inclination* for an object as the effect of my proposed action, but I cannot have *respect* for it, just for this reason, that it is an effect and not an energy of will. Similarly, I cannot have respect for inclination, whether my own or another's; I can at most, if my own, approve it; if another's, sometimes even love it; *i.e.* look on it as favourable to my own interest. It is only what is connected with my will as a principle, by no means as an effect—what does not subserve my inclination, but overpowers it, or at least in case of choice excludes it from its calculation—in other words, simply the law of itself, which can be an object of respect, and hence a command. Now an action done from duty must wholly exclude the influence of inclination, and with it every object of the will, so that nothing remains which can determine the will except objectively the *law,* and subjectively *pure respect* for this practical law, and consequently the maxim that I should follow this law even to the thwarting of all my inclinations.

Thus the moral worth of an action does not lie in the effect expected from it, nor in any principle of action which requires to borrow its motive from this expected effect. For all these effects—agreeableness of one's condition, and even the promotion of the happiness of other—could have been also brought about by other causes, so that for this there would have been no need of the will of a rational being; whereas it is in this alone that the supreme and unconditional good can be found. The pre-eminent good which we call moral can therefore consist in nothing else than *the conception of law* in itself, *which certainly is only possible in a rational being,* in so far as this conception, and not the expected effect, determines the will. This is a good which is already present in the person who acts accordingly, and we have not to wait for it to appear first in the result.

But what sort of law can that be, the conception of which must determine the will, even without paying any regard to the effect expected from it, in order that this will may be called good absolutely and without qualification? As I have deprived the will of every impulse which could arise to it from obedience to any law, there remains nothing but the universal conformity of its actions to law in general, which alone is to serve the will as a principle, *i.e.* I am never to act otherwise than so *that I could also will that my maxim should become a universal law.* Here, now, it is the simple conformity to law in general, without assuming any particular law applicable to certain actions, that serves the will as its principle, and must so serve it, if duty is not to be a vain delusion and a chimerical notion. The common reason of men in its practical judgments perfectly coincides with this, and always has in view the principle here suggested. Let the question be, for example: May I when in distress make a promise with the intention not to keep it? I readily distinguish here between the two significations which the question may have: Whether it is prudent, or whether it is right, to make a false promise? The former may undoubtedly often be the case. I see clearly indeed that it is not enough to extricate myself from a present difficulty by means of this subterfuge, but it must be well considered whether there may not hereafter spring from this lie much greater inconvenience than that from which I now free myself, and as, with all my supposed *cunning,* the consequences cannot be so easily foreseen but that credit once lost may be much more injurious to me than any mischief which I seek to avoid at present, it should be considered whether it would not be more *prudent* to act herein according to a universal maxim, and to make it a habit to promise nothing except with the intention of keeping it. But it is soon clear to me that such a maxim will still only be based on the fear of consequences. Now it is a wholly different thing to be truthful from duty, and to be so from apprehension of injurious consequences. In the first case, the very notion of the action already implies a law for me; in the second case, I must first look about elsewhere to see what results may be combined with it which would affect myself. For to deviate from the principle of duty is beyond all doubt wicked; but to be unfaithful to my maxim of prudence may often be very advantageous to me, although to abide by it is certainly safer. The shortest way, however, and an unerring one, to discover the answer to this question whether a lying promise is consistent with duty, is to ask myself, should I be content that my maxim (to extricate myself from difficulty by a false promise) should hold good as a universal law, for myself as well as for others? and should I be able to say to myself, "Everyone may make a deceitful promise when he finds himself in a difficulty from which he cannot otherwise extricate himself"? Then I presently become aware that while I can will the lie, I can by no means will that lying should be a universal law. For with such a law there would be no promises at all, since it would be in vain to allege my intention in regard to my future actions to those who would not believe this allegation, or if they over-hastily did so, would pay me back in my own coin. Hence my maxim, as soon as it should be made a universal law, would necessarily destroy itself.

I do not, therefore, need any far-reaching penetration to discern what I have to do in order that my will may be morally good. Inexperienced in the course of the world, incapable of being prepared for all its contingencies, I only ask myself: Canst thou also will that thy maxim should be a universal law? If not, then it must be rejected, and that not because of a disadvantage accruing from myself or even to others, but because it cannot enter as a principle into a possible universal legislation, and reason extorts from me immediate respect for such legislation. I do not indeed as yet *discern* on what this respect is based (this the philosopher may inquire), but at least I understand this, that it is an estimation of the worth which far outweighs all worth of what is recommended by inclination, and that the necessity of acting from *pure* respect for the practical law is what constitutes duty, to which every other motive must give place, because it is the condition of a will being good *in itself,* and the worth of such a will is above everything.

Thus, then, without quitting the moral knowledge of common human reason, we have arrived at its principle. And although, no doubt, common men do not conceive it in such an abstract and universal form, yet they always have it really before their eyes, and use it as the standard of their decision. . . .

. . . Nor could anything be more fatal to morality than that we should wish to derive it from examples. For every example of it that is set before me must be first itself tested by principles of morality, whether it is worthy to serve as an original example, *i.e.* as a pattern, but by no means can it authoritatively furnish the conception of morality. Even the Holy One of the Gospels must first be compared with our ideal of moral perfection before we can recognize Him as such; and so He says of Himself, "Why call ye Me [whom you see] good; none is good [the model of good] but God only [whom ye do not see]." But whence have we the conception of God as the supreme good? Simply from the *idea* of moral perfection, which reason frames a priori, and connects inseparably with the notion of a free will. Imitation finds no place at all in morality, and examples serve only for encouragement, *i.e.* they put beyond doubt the feasibility of what the law commands, they make visible that which the practical rule expresses more generally, but they can never authorize us to set aside the true original which lies in reason, and to guide ourselves by examples. . . .

From what has been said, it is clear that all moral conceptions have their seat and origin completely a priori in the reason, and that, moreover, in the commonest reason just as truly as in that which is in the highest degree speculative; that they cannot be obtained by abstraction from any empirical, and therefore merely contingent knowledge; that it is just this purity of their origin that makes them worthy to serve as our supreme practical principle, and that just in proportion as we add anything empirical, we detract from their genuine influence, and from the absolute value of actions; that it is not only of the greatest necessity, in a purely speculative point of view, but is also of the greatest practical importance, to derive these notions and laws from pure reason, to present them pure and unmixed, and even to determine the compass of this practical or pure rational knowledge, *i.e.* to determine the whole faculty of pure practical reason; and, in doing so, we must not make its principles dependent on the particular nature of human reason, though in speculative philosophy this may be permitted, or may even at times be necessary; but since moral laws ought to hold good for every rational creature, we must derive them from the general concept of a rational being. In this way, although for its *application* to man morality has need of anthropology, yet, in the first instance, we must treat it independently as pure philosophy, *i.e.* as metaphysic, complete in itself (a thing which in such distinct branches of science is easily done); knowing well that unless we are in possession of this, it would not only be vain to determine the moral element of duty in right actions for purposes of speculative criticism, but it would be impossible to base morals on their genuine principles, even for common practical purposes, especially of moral instruction, so as to produce pure moral dispositions, and to engraft them on men's minds to the promotion of the greatest possible good in the world. . . .

. . . The question, how the imperative of *morality* is possible, is undoubtedly one, the only one, demanding a solution, as this is not at all hypothetical, and the objective necessity which it presents cannot rest on any hypothesis, as is the case with the hypothetical imperatives. Only here we must never leave out of consideration that we *cannot* make out *by any example,* in other words empirically, whether there is such an imperative at all; but it is rather to be feared that all those which seem to be categorical may yet be at bottom hypothetical. For instance, when the precept is: Thou shalt not promise deceitfully; and it is assumed that the necessity of this is not a mere counsel to avoid some other evil, so that it should mean: Thou shalt not make a lying promise, lest if it become known thou shouldst destroy thy credit, but that an action of this kind must be regarded as evil in itself, so that the imperative of the prohibition is categorical; then we cannot show with certainty in any example that the will was determined merely by the law, without any other spring of action, although it may appear to be so. For it is always possible that fear of disgrace, perhaps also obscure dread of other dangers, may have a secret influence on the will. Who can prove by experience the nonexistence of a cause when all that experience tells us is that we do not perceive it? But in such a case the so-called moral imperative, which as such appears to be categorical and unconditional, would in reality be only a pragmatic precept, drawing our attention to our own interests, and merely teaching us to take these into consideration.

We shall therefore have to investigate a priori the possibility of a categorical imperative, as we have not in this case the advantage of its reality being given in experience, so that [the elucidation of] its possibility should be requisite only for its explanation, not for its establishment. In the meantime it may be discerned beforehand that the categorical imperative alone has the purport of a practical law: all the rest may indeed be called principles of the will but not laws, since whatever is only necessary for the attainment of some arbitrary purpose may be considered as in itself contingent, and we can at any time be free from the precept if we give up the purpose: on the contrary, the unconditional command leaves the will no liberty to choose the opposite; consequently it alone carries with it that necessity which we require in a law.

Secondly, in the case of this categorical imperative or law of morality, the difficulty (of discerning its possibility) is a very profound one. It is an a priori synthetical practical proposition; and as there is so much difficulty in discerning the possibility of speculative propositions of this kind, it may readily be supposed that the difficulty will be no less with the practical.

. . . We will first inquire whether the mere conception of a categorical imperative may not perhaps supply us also with the formula of it, containing the proposition which alone can be a categorical imperative; for even if we know the tenor of such an absolute command, yet how it is possible will require further special and laborious study, which we postpone to the last section.

When I conceive a hypothetical imperative, in general I do not know beforehand what it will contain until I am given the condition. But when I conceive a categorical imperative, I know at once what it contains. For as the imperative contains besides the law only the necessity that the maxims shall conform to this law, while the law contain no conditions restricting it, there remains nothing but the general statement that the maxim of the action should conform to a universal law, and it is this conformity alone that the imperative properly represents as necessary.

There is therefore but one categorical imperative, namely, this: *Act only on that maxim whereby thou canst at the same time will that it should become a universal law.*

Now if all imperatives of duty can be deduced from this one imperative as from their principle, then, although it should remain undecided whether what is called duty is not merely a vain notion, yet at least we shall be able to show what we understand by it and what this notion means.

Since the universality of the law according to which effects are produced constitutes what is properly called *nature* in the most general sense (as to form), that is the existence of things so far as it is determined by general laws, the imperative of duty may be expressed thus: *Act as if the maxim of thy action were to become by thy will a universal law of nature.*

FOUR ILLUSTRATIONS

We will now enumerate a few duties, adopting the usual division of them into duties to ourselves and to others, and into perfect and imperfect duties.

I. A man reduced to despair by a series of misfortunes feels wearied of life, but is still so far in possession of his reason that he can ask himself whether it would not be contrary to his duty to himself to take his own life. Now he inquires whether the maxim of his action could become a universal law of nature. His maxim is: From self-love I adopt it as a principle to shorten my life when its longer duration is likely to bring more evil than satisfaction. It is asked then simply whether this principle founded on self-love can become a universal law of nature. Now we see at once that a system of nature of which it should be a law to destroy life by means of the very feeling whose special nature it is to impel to the improvement of life would contradict itself, and therefore could not exist as a system of nature; hence that maxim cannot possibly exist as a universal law of nature, and consequently would be wholly inconsistent with the supreme principle of all duty.

2. Another finds himself forced by necessity to borrow money. He knows that he will not be able to repay it, but sees also that nothing will be lent to him, unless he promises stoutly to repay it in a definite time. He desires to make this promise, but he has still so much conscience as to ask himself: Is it not unlawful and inconsistent with duty to get out of a difficulty in this way? Suppose, however, that he resolves to do so, then the maxim of his action would be expressed thus: When I think myself in want of money, I will borrow money and promise to repay it, although I know that I never can do so. Now this principle of self-love or of one's own advantage may perhaps be consistent with my whole future welfare; but the question is, Is it right? I change then the suggestion of self-love into a universal law, and state the question thus: How would it be if my maxim were a universal law? Then I see at once that it could never hold as a universal law of nature, but would necessarily contradict itself. For supposing it to be a universal law that everyone when he thinks himself in a difficulty should be able to promise whatever he pleases, with the purpose of not keeping his promise, the promise itself would become impossible, as well as the end that one might have in view in it, since no one would consider that anything was promised to him, but would ridicule all such statements as vain pretenses.

3. A third finds in himself a talent which with the help of some culture might make him a useful man in many respects. But he finds himself in comfortable circumstances, and prefers to indulge in pleasure rather than to take pains in enlarging and improving his happy natural capacities. He asks, however, whether his maxim of neglect of his natural gifts, besides agreeing with his inclination to indulgence, agrees also with what is called duty. He sees then that a system of nature could indeed subsist with such a universal law although men (like the South Sea islanders) should let their talents rest, and resolve to devote their lives merely to idleness, amusement, and propagation of their species—in a word, to enjoyment; but he cannot possibly *will* that this should be a universal law of nature, or be implanted in us as such by a natural instinct. For, as a rational being, he necessarily wills that his faculties be developed, since they serve him, and have been given him, for all sorts of possible purposes.

4. A fourth, who is in prosperity, while he sees that others have to contend with great wretchedness and that he could help them, thinks: What

concern is it of mine? Let everyone be as happy as Heaven pleases, or as he can make himself; I will take nothing from him nor even envy him, only I do not wish to contribute anything to his welfare or to his assistance in distress! Now no doubt if such a mode of thinking were a universal law, the human race might very well subsist, and doubtless even better than in a state in which everyone talks of sympathy and good-will, or even takes care occasionally to put it into practice, but, on the other side, also cheats when he can, betrays the rights of men, or other when he can, betrays the rights of men, or otherwise violates them. But although it is possible that a universal law of nature might exist in accordance with that maxim, it is impossible to *will* that such a principle should have the universal validity of a law of nature. For a will which resolved this would contradict itself, inasmuch as many cases might occur in which one would have need of the love and sympathy of others, and in which, by such a law of nature, sprung from his own will, he would deprive himself of all hope of the aid he desires.

These are a few of the many actual duties, or at least what we regard as such, which obviously fall into two classes on the one principle that we have laid down. We must be able to will that a maxim of our action should be a universal law. This is the canon of the moral appreciation of the action generally. Some actions are of such a character that their maxim cannot without contradiction be even conceived as a universal law of nature, far from it being possible that we should will that it should be so. In others this intrinsic impossibility is not found, but still it is impossible to will that their maxim should be raised to the universality of a law of nature, since such a will would contradict itself. It is easily seen that the former violate strict or rigorous (inflexible) duty; the latter only laxer (meritorious) duty. Thus it has been completely shown by these examples how all duties depend as regards the nature of the obligation (not the object of the action) on the same principle.

3.10

Utilitarianism

John Stuart Mill

. . . The creed which accepts as the foundation of morals, Utility, or the Greatest Happiness Principle, holds that actions are right in proportion as they tend to promote happiness, wrong as they tend to produce the reverse of happiness. By happiness is intended pleasure, and the absence of pain; by unhappiness, pain, and the privation of pleasure. To give a clear view of the moral standard set up by the theory, much more requires to be said; in particular, what things it includes in the ideas of pain and pleasure; and to what extent this is left an open question. But these supplementary explanations do not affect the theory of life on which this theory of morality is grounded—namely, that pleasure, and freedom from pain, are the only things desirable as ends; and that all desirable things (which are as numerous in the utilitarian as in any other scheme) are desirable either for the pleasure inherent in themselves, or as means to the promotion of pleasure and the prevention of pain.

Now, such a theory of life excites in many minds, and among them in some of the most estimable in feeling and purpose, inveterate dislike. To suppose that life has (as they express it) no higher end than pleasure—no better and nobler object of desire and pursuit—they designate as utterly mean and groveling; as a doctrine worthy only of swine, to whom the followers of Epicurus were, at a very early period, contemptuously likened; and modern holders of the doctrine are occasionally made the subject of equally polite comparisons by its German, French, and English assailants.

When thus attacked, the Epicureans have always answered, that it is not they, but their accusers, who represent human nature in a degrading light; since the accusation supposes human beings to be capable of no pleasures

From chapters 2, 3, and 4 of *Utilitarianism* (London: J.M. Dent & Sons, 1910), pp. 6–35.

except those of which swine are capable. If this supposition were true, the charge could not be gainsaid, but would then be no longer an imputation; for if the sources of pleasure were precisely the same to human beings and to swine, the rule of life which is good enough for the one would be good enough for the other. The comparison of the Epicurean life to that of beasts is felt as degrading, precisely because a beast's pleasures do not satisfy a human being's conceptions of happiness. Human beings have faculties more elevated than the animal appetites, and when once made conscious of them, do not regard anything as happiness which does not include their gratification. I do not, indeed, consider the Epicureans to have been by any means faultless in drawing out their scheme of consequences from the utilitarian principle. To do this in any sufficient manner, many Stoic, as well as Christian elements require to be included. But there is no known Epicurean theory of life which does not assign to the pleasures of the intellect, of the feelings and imagination, and of the moral sentiments, a much higher value as pleasures than to those of mere sensation. It must be admitted, however, that utilitarian writers in general have placed the superiority of mental over bodily pleasures chiefly in the greater permanency, safety, uncostliness, etc., of the former—that is, in their circumstantial advantages rather than in their intrinsic nature. And on all these points utilitarians have fully proved their case; but they might have taken the other, and, as it may be called, higher ground, with entire consistency. It is quite compatible with the principle of utility to recognize the fact, that some *kinds* of pleasure are more desirable and more valuable than others. It would be absurd that while, in estimating all other things, quality is considered as well as quantity, the estimation of pleasures should be supposed to depend on quantity alone.

If I am asked, what I mean by difference of quality in pleasures, or what makes one pleasure more valuable than another, merely as a pleasure, except its being greater in amount, there is but one possible answer. Of two pleasures, if there be one to which all or almost all who have experience of both give a decided preference, irrespective of any feeling of moral obligation to prefer it, that is the more desirable pleasure. If one of the two is, by those who are competently acquainted with both, placed so far above the other that they prefer it, even though knowing it to be attended with a greater amount of discontent, and would not resign it for any quantity of the other pleasure which their nature is capable of, we are justified in ascribing to the preferred enjoyment a superiority in quality, so far outweighing quantity as to render it, in comparison, of small account.

Now it is an unquestionable fact that those who are equally acquainted with, and equally capable of appreciating and enjoying, both, do give a most marked preference to the manner of existence which employs their higher faculties. Few human creatures would consent to be changed into any of the lower animals, for a promise of the fullest allowance of a beast's pleasures;

no intelligent human being would consent to be a fool, no instructed person would be an ignoramus, no person of feeling and conscience would be self-ish and base, even though they should be persuaded that the fool, the dunce, or the rascal is better satisfied with his lot than they are with theirs. They would not resign what they possess more than he, for the most complete satisfaction of all the desires which they have in common with him. If they ever fancy they would, it is only in cases of unhappiness so extreme, that to escape from it they would exchange their lot for almost any other, however undesirable in their own eyes. A being of higher faculties requires more to make him happy, is capable probably of more acute suffering, and is certainly accessible to it at more points, than one of an inferior type; but in spite of these liabilities, he can never really wish to sink into what he feels to be a lower grade of existence. We may give what explanation we please of this unwillingness; we may attribute it to pride, a name which is given in-discriminately to some of the most and to some of the least estimable feelings of which mankind are capable; we may refer it to the love of liberty and personal independence, an appeal to which was with the Stoics one of the most effective means for the inculcation of it; to the love of power, or to the love of excitement, both of which do really enter into and contribute to it: but its most appropriate appellation is a sense of dignity, which all human beings possess in one form or other, and in some, though by no means in exact, proportion to their higher faculties, and which is so essential a part of the happiness of those in whom it is strong, that nothing which conflicts with it could be, otherwise than momentarily, an object of desire to them. Whoever supposes that this preference takes place at a sacrifice of happi-ness—that the superior being, in anything like the equal circumstances, is not happier than the inferior—confounds the two very different ideas, of happiness, and content. It is indisputable that the being whose capacities of enjoyment are low, has the greatest chance of having them fully satisfied; and a highly-endowed being will always feel that any happiness which he can look for, as the world is constituted, is imperfect. But he can learn to bear its imperfections, if they are at all bearable; and they will not make him envy the being who is indeed unconscious of the imperfections, but only because he feels not at all the good which those imperfections qualify. It is better to be a human being dissatisfied than a pig satisfied; better to be Socrates dissatisfied than a fool satisfied. And if the fool, or the pig, is of a different opinion, it is because they only know their own side of the question. The other party to the comparison knows both sides.

It may be objected, that many who are capable of the higher pleasures, occasionally, under the influence of temptation, postpone them to the lower. But this is quite compatible with a full appreciation of the intrinsic su-periority of the higher. Men often, from infirmity of character, make their election for the nearer good, though they know it to be the less valuable;

and this no less when the choice is between two bodily pleasures, than when it is between bodily and mental. They pursue sensual indulgences to the injury of health, though perfectly aware that health is the greater good. It may be further objected, that many who begin with youthful enthusiasm for everything noble, as they advance in years sink into indolence and self-ishness. But I do not believe that those who undergo this very common change, voluntarily choose the lower description of pleasures in preference to the higher. I believe that before they devote themselves exclusively to the one, they have already become incapable of the other. Capacity for the no-bler feelings is in most natures a very tender plant, easily killed, not only by hostile influences, but by mere want of sustenance; and in the majority of young persons it speedily dies away if the occupations to which their posi-tion in life has devoted them, and the society into which it has thrown them, are not favorable to keeping that higher capacity in exercise. Men lose their high aspirations as they lose their intellectual tastes, because they have not time or opportunity for indulging them; and they addict themselves to infe-rior pleasures, not because they deliberately prefer them, but because they are either the only ones to which they have access, or the only ones which they are any longer capable of enjoying. It may be questioned whether any-one who has remained equally susceptible to both classes of pleasures, ever knowingly and calmly preferred the lower, though many, in all ages, have broken down in an ineffectual attempt to combine both.

From this verdict of the only competent judges, I apprehend there can be no appeal. On a question which is the best worth having of two pleasures, or which of two modes of existence is the most grateful to the feelings, apart from its moral attributes and from its consequences, the judgment of those who are qualified by knowledge of both, or, if they differ, that of the major-ity among them, must be admitted as final. And there needs be the less hes-itation to accept this judgment respecting the quality of pleasures, since there is no other tribunal to be referred to even on the question of quantity. What means are there of determining which is the acutest of two pains, or the intensest of two pleasurable sensations, except the general suffrage of those who are familiar with both? Neither pains nor pleasures are homoge-neous, and pain is always heterogeneous with pleasure. What is there to de-cide whether a particular pleasure is worth purchasing at the cost of a par-ticular pain, except the feelings and judgment of the experienced? When, therefore, those feelings and judgment declare the pleasures derived from the higher faculties to be preferable *in kind,* apart from the question of in-tensity, to those of which the animal nature, disjoined from the higher fac-ulties, is susceptible, they are entitled on this subject to the same regard.

I have dwelt on this point, as being a necessary part of a perfectly just con-ception of Utility or Happiness, considered as the directive rule of human conduct. But it is by no means an indispensable condition to the acceptance of the utilitarian standard; for that standard is not the agent's own greatest happiness, but the greatest amount of happiness altogether; and if it may possibly be doubted whether a noble character is always the happier for its nobleness, there can be no doubt that it makes other people happier, and that the world in general is immensely a gainer by it. Utilitarianism, therefore, could only attain its end by the general cultivation of nobleness of character, even if each individual were only benefitted by the nobleness of others, and his own, so far as happiness is concerned, were a sheer deduction from the benefit. But the bare enunciation of such an absurdity as this last, renders refutation superfluous.

According to the Greatest Happiness Principle, as above explained, the ultimate end, with reference to and for the sake of which all other things are desirable (whether we are considering our own good or that of other people), is an existence exempt as far as possible from pain, and as rich as possible in enjoyments, both in point of quantity and quality; the test of quality, and the rule for measuring it against quantity, being the preference felt by those who, in their opportunities of experience, to which must be added their habits of self-consciousness and self-observation, are best furnished with the means of comparison. This, being, according to the utilitarian opinion, the end of human action, is necessarily also the standard of morality; which may accordingly be defined, the rules and precepts for human conduct, by the observance of which an existence such as has been described might be, to the greatest extent possible, secured to all mankind; and not to them only, but, so far as the nature of things admits, to the whole sentient creation. . . .

I must again repeat, what the assailants of utilitarianism seldom have the justice to acknowledge, that the happiness which forms the utilitarian standard of what is right in conduct, is not the agent's own happiness, but that of all concerned. As between his own happiness and that of others, utilitarianism requires him to be as strictly impartial as a disinterested and benevolent spectator. In the golden rule of Jesus of Nazareth, we read the complete spirit of the ethics of utility. To do as one would be done by, and to love one's neighbor as oneself, constitute the ideal perfection of utilitarian morality. As the means of making the nearest approach to this ideal, utility would enjoin, first, that laws and social arrangements should place the happiness, or (as speaking practically it may be called) the interest, of every individual, as nearly as possible in harmony with the interest of the whole; and secondly, that education and opinion, which have so vast a power over human character, should so use that power as to establish in the mind of every individual an indissoluble association between his own happiness and the good of the whole; especially between his own happiness and the practice of such modes of conduct, negative and positive, as regard for the universal happiness prescribes: so that not only he may be unable to conceive the possibility of happiness to himself, consistently with conduct opposed to the general good, but also that a direct impulse to promote the general good may be in every individual one of the habitual motives of action, and the sentiments connected therewith may fill a large and prominent place in every human being's sentient existence. If the impugners of the utilitarian morality represented it to their own minds in this its true character, I know not what recommendation possessed by any other morality they could possibly affirm to be wanting to it: what more beautiful or more exalted developments of human nature any other ethical system can be supposed to foster, or what springs of action, not accessible to the utilitarian, such systems rely on for giving effect to their mandates.

OF THE ULTIMATE SANCTION OF THE PRINCIPLE OF UTILITY

The question is often asked, and properly so, in regard to any supposed moral standard, What is its sanction? what are the motives to obey? or, more specifically, what is the source of its obligation? whence does it derive its binding force? It is a necessary part of moral philosophy to provide the answer to this question, which, though frequently assuming the shape of an objection to the utilitarian morality, as if it had some special applicability to that above others, really arises in regard to all standards. It arises, in fact, whenever a person is called on to *adopt* a standard, or refer morality to any basis on which he has not been accustomed to rest it. For the customary morality, that which education and opinion have consecrated, is the only one which presents itself to the mind with the feeling of being *in itself* obligatory; and when a person is asked to believe that this morality *derives* its obligation from some general principle round which custom has not thrown the same halo, the assertion is to him a paradox; the supposed corollaries seem to have a more binding force than the original theorem; the superstructure seems to stand better without than with what is represented as its foundation. He says to himself, I feel that I am bound not to rob or murder, betray or deceive; but why am I bound to promote the general happiness? If my own happiness lies in something else, why may I not give that the preference?

If the view adopted by the utilitarian philosophy of the nature of the moral sense be correct, this difficulty will always present itself until the influences which form moral character have taken the same hold of the principle which they have taken of some of the consequences—until, by the improvement of education, the feeling of unity with our fellow creatures shall be (what it cannot be denied that Christ intended it to be) as deeply rooted in our character, and to our own consciousness as completely a part of our nature, as the horror of crime is in an ordinarily well brought up young person. In the meantime, however, the difficulty has no peculiar application to the doctrine of utility, but is inherent in every attempt to analyze morality and reduce it to principles; which, unless the principle is already in men's minds invested with as much sacredness as any of its applications, always seems to divest them of a part of their sanctity.

The principle of utility either has, or there is no reason why it might not have, all the sanctions which belong to any other system of morals. Those sanctions are either external or internal. Of the external sanctions it is not necessary to speak at any length. They are the hope of favor and the fear of displeasure from our fellow creatures or from the Ruler of the universe, along with whatever we may have of sympathy or affection for them, or of love and awe of Him, inclining us to do His will independently of selfish consequences. There is evidently no reason why all these motives for observance should not attach themselves to the utilitarian morality as completely and as powerfully as to any other. Indeed, those of them which refer to our fellow creatures are sure to do so, in proportion to the amount of general intelligence; for whether there be any other ground of moral obligation than the general happiness or not, men do desire happiness; and however imperfect may be their own practice, they desire and commend all conduct in others toward themselves by which they think their happiness is promoted. With regard to the religious motive, if men believe, as most profess to do, in the goodness of God, those who think that conduciveness to the general happiness is the essence or even only the criterion of good must necessarily believe that it is also that which God approves. The whole force therefore of external reward and punishment, whether physical or moral, whether proceeding from God or from our fellow men, together with all that the capacities of human nature admit of disinterested devotion to either, become available to enforce the utilitarian morality, in proportion as that morality is recognized; and the more powerfully, the more the appliances of education and general cultivation are bent to the purpose.

So far as to external sanctions. The internal sanction of duty, whatever our standard of duty may be, is one and the same—a feeling in our own mind; a pain, more or less intense, attendant on violation of duty, which in properly cultivated moral natures rises, in the more serious cases, into shrinking from it as an impossibility. This feeling, when disinterested and connecting itself with the pure idea of duty, and not with some particular form of it, or with any of the merely accessory circumstances, is the essence of conscience; though in that complex phenomenon as it actually exists, the simple fact is in general all encrusted over with collateral associations derived from sympathy, from love, and still more from fear; from all the forms of religious feeling; from the recollections of childhood and of all our past life; from self-esteem, desire of the esteem of others, and occasionally even self-abasement. This extreme complication is, I apprehend, the origin of the sort of mystical character which, by a tendency of the human mind of which there are many other examples, is apt to be attributed to the idea of moral obligation, and which leads people to believe that the idea cannot possibly attach itself to any other objects than those which, by a supposed mysterious law, are found in our present experience to excite it. Its binding force, however, consists in the existence of a mass of feeling which must be broken through in order to do what violates our standard of right, and which, if we do nevertheless violate that standard, will probably have to be encountered afterwards in the form of remorse. Whatever theory we have of the nature or origin of conscience, this is what essentially constitutes it.

The ultimate sanction, therefore, of all morality (external motives apart) being a subjective feeling in our own minds, I see nothing embarrassing to those whose standard is utility in the question, What is the sanction of that particular standard? We may answer, the same as of all other moral standards—the conscientious feelings of mankind. Undoubtedly this sanction has no binding efficacy on those who do not possess the feelings it appeals to; but neither will these persons be more obedient to any other moral principle than to the utilitarian one. On them morality of any kind has no hold but through the external sanctions. Meanwhile the feelings exist, a fact in human nature, the reality of which, and the great power with which they are capable of acting on those in whom they have been duly cultivated, are proved by experience. No reason has ever been shown why they may not be cultivated to as great intensity in connection with the utilitarian as with any other rule of morals.

OF WHAT SORT OF PROOF
THE PRINCIPLE OF UTILITY IS SUSCEPTIBLE

It has already been remarked, that questions of ultimate ends do not admit of proof, in the ordinary acceptation of the term. To be incapable of proof by reasoning is common to all first principles; to the first premises of our knowledge, as well as to those of our conduct. But the former, being matters of fact, may be the subject of a direct appeal to the faculties which judge of fact—namely, our senses, and our internal consciousness. Can an appeal be made to the same faculties on questions of practical ends? Or by what other faculty is cognizance taken of them?

Questions about ends are, in other words, questions about what things are desirable. The utilitarian doctrine is, that happiness is desirable, and the only thing desirable, as an end; all other things being only desirable as means to that end. What ought to be required of this doctrine—what conditions is it requisite that the doctrine should fulfill—to make good its claim to be believed?

The only proof capable of being given that an object is visible, is that people actually see it. The only proof that a sound is audible, is that people hear it: and so of the other sources of our experience. In like manner, I apprehend, the sole evidence it is possible to produce that anything is desirable, is that people do actually desire it. If the end which the utilitarian doctrine proposes to itself were not, in theory and in practice, acknowledged to be an end, nothing could ever convince any person that it was so. No reason can be given why the general happiness is desirable, except that each person, so far as he believes it to be attainable, desires his own happiness. This, however, being a fact, we have not only all the proof which the case admits of, but all which it is possible to require, that happiness is a good: that each person's happiness is a good to that person, and the general happiness, therefore, a good to the aggregate of all persons. Happiness has made out its title as *one* of the ends of conduct, and consequently one of the criteria of morality.

But it has not, by this alone, proved itself to be the sole criterion. To do that, it would seem, by the same rule, necessary to show, not only that people desire happiness, but that they never desire anything else. Now it is palpable that they do desire things which, in common language, are decidedly distinguished from happiness. They desire, for example, virtue, and the absence of vice, no less really than pleasure and the absence of pain. The desire of virtue is not as universal, but it is as authentic a fact, as the desire of happiness. And hence the opponents of the utilitarian standard deem that they have a right to infer that there are other ends of human action besides happiness, and that happiness is not the standard of approbation and disapprobation.

But does the utilitarian doctrine deny that people desire virtue, or maintain that virtue is not a thing to be desired? The very reverse. It maintains not only that virtue is to be desired, but that it is to be desired disinterestedly, for itself. Whatever may be the opinion of utilitarian moralists as to the original conditions by which virtue is made virtue; however they may believe (as they do) that actions and dispositions are only virtuous because they promote another end than virtue; yet this being granted, and it having been decided, from considerations of this description, what is virtuous, they not only place virtue at the very head of the things which are good as means to the ultimate end, but they also recognize as a psychological fact the possibility of its being, to the individual, a good in itself, without looking to any end beyond it; and hold, that the mind is not in a right state, not in a state comfortable to Utility, not in the state most conducive to the general happiness, unless it does love virtue in this manner—as a thing desirable in itself, even although, in the individual instance, it should not produce those other desirable consequences which it tends to produce, and on account of which it is held to be virtue. This opinion is not, in the smallest degree, a departure from the Happiness principle. The ingredients of happiness are very various, and each of them is desirable in itself, and not merely when considered as swelling an aggregate. The principle of utility does not mean that any given pleasure, as music, for instance, or any given exemption from pain, as for example health, are to be looked upon as a means to a collective something termed happiness, and to be desired on that account. They are desired and desirable in and for themselves; besides being means, they are a part of the end. Virtue, according to the utilitarian doctrine, is not naturally and originally part of the end, but it is capable of becoming so; and in those who love it disinterestedly it has become so, and is desired and cherished, not as a means to happiness, but as a part of their happiness.

To illustrate this further, we may remember that virtue is not the only thing, originally a means, and which if it were not a means to anything else, would be and remain indifferent, but which by association with what it is a means to, comes to be desired for itself, and that too with the utmost intensity. What, for example, shall we say of the love of money? There is nothing originally more desirable about money than about any heap of glittering pebbles. Its worth is solely that of the things which it will buy; the desires for other things than itself, which it is a means of gratifying. Yet the love of money is not only one of the strongest moving forces of human life, but money is, in many cases, desired in and for itself; the desire to possess it is often stronger than the desire to use it, and goes on increasing when all the desires which point to ends beyond it, to be encompassed by it, are falling off. It may be then said truly, that money is desired not for the sake of an end, but as part of the end. From being a means to happiness, it has come to be itself a principal ingredient of the individual's conception of happiness. The same may be said of the majority of the great objects of human life—power, for example, or fame; except that to each of these there is a certain amount of immediate pleasure annexed, which has at least the semblance of being naturally inherent in them; a thing which cannot be said of money. Still, however, the strongest natural attraction, both of power and of fame, is the immense aid they give to the attainment of our other wishes; and it is the strong association thus generated between them and all our objects of desire, which gives to the direct desire of them the intensity it often assumes, so as in some characters to surpass in strength all other desires. In these cases the means have become a part of the end, and a more important part of it than any of the things which they are means to. What was once desired as an instrument for the attainment of happiness, has come to be desired for its own sake. In being desired for its own sake it is, however, desired as *part* of happiness. The person is made, or thinks he would be made, happy by its mere possession; and is made unhappy by failure to obtain it. The desire of it is not a different thing from the desire of happiness, any more than the love of music, or the desire of health. They are included in happiness. They are some of the elements of which the desire of happiness is made up. Happiness is not an abstract idea, but a concrete whole; and these are some of its parts. And the utilitarian standard sanctions and approves their being so. Life would be a poor thing, very ill provided with sources of happiness, if there were not this provision of nature, by which things originally indifferent, but conducive to, or otherwise associated with, the satisfaction of our primitive desires, become in themselves sources of pleasure more valuable than the primitive pleasures, both in permanency, in the space of human existence that they are capable of covering, and even in intensity.

Virtue, according to the utilitarian conception, is a good of this description. There was no original desire of it, or motive to it, save its conduciveness to pleasure, and especially to protection from pain. But through the association thus formed, it may be felt a good in itself, and desired as such with as great intensity as any other good; and with this difference between it and the love of money, of power, or of fame, that all of these may, and often do, render the individual noxious to the other members of the society to which he belongs, whereas there is nothing which makes him so much a blessing to them as the cultivation of the disinterested love of virtue. And consequently, the utilitarian standard, while it tolerates and approves those other acquired desires, up to the point beyond which they would be more injurious to the general happiness than promotive of it, enjoins and requires the cultivation of the love of virtue up to the greatest strength possible, as being above all things important to the general happiness.

It results from the preceding considerations, that there is in reality nothing desired except happiness. Whatever is desired otherwise than as a means to some end beyond itself, and ultimately to happiness, is desired as itself a part of happiness, and is not desired for itself until it has become so.

3.11

Ambiguity and Freedom

Simone de Beauvoir

I

"The continuous work of our life," says Montaigne, "is to build death." He quotes the Latin poets: *Prima, quae vitam dedit, hora corpsit.* And again: *Nascentes morimur.* Man knows and thinks this tragic ambivalence which the animal and the plant merely undergo. A new paradox is hereby introduced into his destiny. "Rational animal," "thinking reed," he escapes from his natural condition without, however, freeing himself from it. He is still a part of this world of which he is a consciousness. He asserts himself as a pure internality against which no external power can take hold, and he also experiences himself as a thing crushed by the dark weight of other things. At every moment he can grasp the nontemporal truth of his existence. But between the past which no longer is and the future which is not yet, this moment when he exists is nothing. This privilege, which he alone possesses, of being a sovereign and unique subject amidst a universe of objects, is what he shares with all his fellow men. In turn an object for others, he is nothing more than an individual in the collectivity on which he depends.

As long as there have been men and they have lived, they have all felt this tragic ambiguity of their condition, but as long as there have been philosophers and they have thought, most of them have tried to mask it. They have striven to reduce mind to matter, or to reabsorb matter into mind, or to merge them within a single substance. Those who have accepted the dualism have established a hierarchy between body and soul which permits of considering as negligible the part of the self which cannot be saved. They

From *The Ethics of Ambiguity.* Translated by Bernard Frechtman, pp. 7–34. Copyright © 1948 by Philosophical Library. Text edited.

have denied death, either by integrating it with life or by promising to man immortality. Or, again they have denied life, considering it as a veil of illusion beneath which is hidden the truth of *nirvāṇa*.

And the ethics which they have proposed to their disciples has always pursued the same goal. It has been a matter of eliminating the ambiguity by making oneself pure inwardness or pure externality, by escaping from the sensible world or by being engulfed in it, by yielding to eternity or enclosing oneself in the pure moment. Hegel, with more ingenuity, tried to reject none of the aspects of man's condition and to reconcile them all. According to his system, the moment is preserved in the development of time; Nature asserts itself in the face of Spirit which denies it while assuming it; the individual is again found in the collectivity within which he is lost; and each man's death is fulfilled by being canceled out into the Life of Mankind. One can thus repose in a marvelous optimism where even the bloody wars simply express the fertile restlessness of the Spirit. . . . Let us try to assume our fundamental ambiguity. It is in the knowledge of the genuine conditions of our life that we must draw our strength to live and our reason for acting.

From the very beginning, existentialism defined itself as a philosophy of ambiguity. It was by affirming the irreducible character of ambiguity that Kierkegaard opposed himself to Hegel, and it is by ambiguity that, in our own generation, Sartre, in *Being and Nothingness,* fundamentally defined man, that being whose being is not to be, that subjectivity which realizes itself only as a presence in the world, that engaged freedom, that surging of the for-oneself which is immediately given for others. But it is also claimed that existentialism is a philosophy of the absurd and of despair. It encloses man in a sterile anguish, in an empty subjectivity. It is incapable of furnishing him with any principle for making choices. Let him do as he pleases. In any case, the game is lost. Does not Sartre declare, in effect, that man is a "useless passion," that he tries in vain to realize the synthesis of the for-oneself and the in-oneself, to make himself God? It is true. But it is also true that the most optimistic ethics have all begun by emphasizing the element of failure involved in the condition of man; without failure, no ethics; for a being who, from the very start, would be an exact coincidence with himself, in a perfect plenitude, the notion of having-to-be would have no meaning. One does not offer an ethics to a God. It is impossible to propose any to man if one defines him as nature, as something given. The so-called psychological or empirical ethics manage to establish themselves only by introducing surreptitiously some flaw within the man-thing which they have first defined. . . .

. . . Man, Sartre tells us, is "a being who *makes himself* a lack of being in *order that there might be* being." That means, first of all, that his passion is not inflicted upon him from without. He chooses it. It is his very being and, as such, does not imply the idea of unhappiness. If this advice is considered as useless, it is because there exists no absolute value before the passion of man, outside of it, in relation to which one might distinguish the useless from the useful. The word "useful" has not yet received a meaning on the level of description where *Being and Nothingness* is situated. It can be defined only in the human world established by man's projects and the ends he sets up. In the original helplessness from which man surges up, nothing is useful, nothing is useless. It must therefore be understood that the passion to which man has acquiesced finds no external justification. No outside appeal, no objective necessity permits of its being called useful. It has no reason to will itself. But this does not mean that it cannot justify itself, that it cannot *give itself* reasons for being that it does not have. And indeed Sartre tells us that man makes himself this lack of being *in* order *that* there might be being. The term *in order that* clearly indicates an intentionality. It is not in vain that man nullifies being. Thanks to him, being is disclosed and he desires this disclosure. There is an original type of attachment to being which is not "the relationship waiting to be" but rather "wanting to disclose being." Now, here there is not failure, but rather success. This end, which man proposes to himself by making himself lack of being, is, in effect, realized by him. By uprooting himself from the world, man makes himself present to the world and makes the world present to him. I should like to be the landscape which I am contemplating, I should like this sky this quiet water to think themselves within me, that it might be I whom they express in flesh and bone, and I remain at a distance. But it is also by this distance that the sky and the water exist before me. My contemplation is an excruciation only because it is also a joy. I cannot appropriate the snow field where I slide. It remains foreign, forbidden, but I take delight in this very effort toward an impossible possession. I experience it as a triumph, not as a defeat. This means that man, in his vain attempt to *be* God, makes himself exist as man, and if he is satisfied with this existence, he coincides exactly with himself. It is not granted him to exist without tending toward this being which he will never be. But it is possible for him to want this tension even with the failure which it involves. His being is lack of being, but this lack has a way of being which is precisely existence. . . .

The first implication of such an attitude is that the genuine man will not agree to recognize any foreign absolute. When a man projects into an ideal heaven that impossible synthesis of the for-itself and the in-itself that is called God, it is because he wishes the regard of this existing Being to change his existence into being; but if he agrees not to be in order to exist genuinely, he will abandon the dream of an inhuman objectivity. He will understand that it is not a matter of being right in the eyes of a God, but of being right in his own eyes. Renouncing the thought of seeking the guarantee for his existence outside of himself, he will also refuse to believe in unconditioned values which would set themselves up athwart his freedom like things. Value is this lacking-being of which freedom makes itself a lack; and it is because the latter makes itself a lack that value appears. It is desire which creates the desirable, and the project which sets up the end. It is human existence which makes values spring up in the world on the basis of which it will be able to judge the enterprise in which it will be engaged. But first it locates itself beyond any pessimism, as beyond any optimism, for the fact of its original springing forth is a pure contingency. Before existence there is no more reason to exist than not to exist. The lack of existence cannot be evaluated since it is the fact on the basis of which all evaluation is defined. It cannot be compared to anything for there is nothing outside of it to serve as a term of comparison. This rejection of any extrinsic justification also confirms the rejection of an original pessimism which we posited at the beginning. Since it is unjustifiable from without, to declare from without that it is unjustifiable is not to condemn it. And the truth is that outside of existence there is nobody. Man exists. For him it is not a question of wondering whether his presence in the world is useful, whether life is worth the trouble of being lived. These questions make no sense. It is a matter of knowing whether he wants to live and under what conditions.

But if man is free to define for himself the conditions of a life which is valid in his own eyes, can he not choose whatever he likes and act however he likes? Dostoievski asserted, "If God does not exist, every thing is permitted." Today's believers use this formula for their own advantage. To reestablish man at the heart of his destiny is, they claim to repudiate all ethics. However, far from God's absence authorizing all license, the contrary is the case, because man is abandoned on the earth because his acts are definitive, absolute engagements. He bears the responsibility for a world which is not the work of a strange power, but of himself, where his defeats are inscribed, and his victories as well. A God can pardon, efface, and compensate. But if God does not exist, man's faults are inexpiable. If it is claimed that, whatever the case may be, this earthly stake has no importance, this is precisely because one invokes that inhuman objectivity which we declined at the start. One cannot start by saying that our earthly destiny *has* or *has not* importance, for it depends upon us to give it importance. It is up to man to make it important to be a man, and he alone can feel his success or failure. And if it is again said that nothing forces him to try to justify his being in this way, then one is playing upon the notion of freedom in a dishonest way. The believer is also free to sin. The divine law is imposed upon him only from the moment he decides to save his soul. In the Christian religion, though one speaks very little about them today, there are also the damned. Thus, on the earthly plane, a life which does not seek to ground itself will be a pure contingency. But it is permitted to wish to give itself a meaning and a truth and it then meets rigorous demands within its own heart.

However, even among the proponents of secular ethics, there are many who charge existentialism with offering no objective content to the moral act. It is said that this philosophy is subjective, even solipsistic. If he is once enclosed within himself, how can man get out? But there too we have a great deal of dishonesty. It is rather well known that the fact of being a subject is a universal fact and that the Cartesian *cogito* expresses both the most individual experience and the most objective truth. By affirming that the source of all values resides in the freedom of man, existentialism merely carries on the tradition of Kant, Fichte, and Hegel, who, in the words of Hegel himself, "have taken for their point of departure the principle according to which the essence of right and duty and the essence of the thinking and willing subject are absolutely identical." The idea that defines all humanism is that the world is not a given world, foreign to man, one to which he has to force himself to yield from without. It is the world willed by man, insofar as his will expresses his genuine reality. . . .

And, indeed, we are coming to the real situation of the problem. But to state it is not to demonstrate that it cannot be resolved. On the contrary, we must here again invoke the notion of Hegelian "displacement." There is an ethics only if there is a problem to solve. And it can be said, by inverting the preceding line of argument, that the ethics which have given solutions by effacing the fact of the separation of men are not valid precisely because there is this separation. An ethics of ambiguity will be one which will refuse to deny *a priori* that separate existents can, at the same time, be bound to each other, that their individual freedoms can forge laws valid for all.

As for us, whatever the case may be, we believe in freedom. Is it true that this belief must lead us to despair? Must we grant this curious paradox: that from the moment a man recognizes himself as free, he is prohibited from wishing for anything?

On the contrary, it appears to us that by turning toward this freedom we are going to discover a principle of action whose range will be universal. The characteristic feature of all ethics is to consider human life as a game that can be won or lost and to teach man the means of winning. Now, we have seen that the original scheme of man is ambiguous: he wants to be, and to the extent that he coincides with this wish, he fails. All the plans in which this will to be is actualized are condemned; and the ends circumscribed by these plans remain mirages. Human transcendence is vainly engulfed in those miscarried attempts. But man also wills himself to be a disclosure of being, and if he coincides with this wish, he wins, for the fact is that the world becomes present by his presence in it. But the disclosure implies a perpetual tension to keep being at a certain distance, to tear oneself from the world, and to assert oneself as freedom. To wish for the disclosure of the world and to assert oneself as freedom are one and the same movement. Freedom is the source from which all significations and all values spring. It is the original condition of all justification of existence. The man who seeks to justify his life must want freedom itself absolutely and above everything else. At the same time that it requires the realization of concrete ends, of particular projects, it requires itself universally. It is not a ready-made value which offers itself from the outside to my abstract adherence, but it appears (not on the plane of facility, but on the moral plane) as a cause of itself. It is necessarily summoned up by the values which it sets up and through which it sets itself up. It cannot establish a denial of itself, for in denying itself, it would deny the possibility of any foundation. To will oneself moral and to will oneself free are one and the same decision. . . . To will oneself free is to effect the transition from nature to morality by establishing a genuine freedom on the original upsurge of our existence.

Every man is originally free, in the sense that he spontaneously casts himself into the world. But if we consider this spontaneity in its facticity, it appears to us only as a pure contingency, an upsurging as stupid as the clinamen of the Epicurean atom which turned up at any moment whatsoever from any direction whatsoever. And it was quite necessary for the atom to arrive somewhere. But its movement was not justified by this result which had not been chosen. It remained absurd. Thus, human spontaneity always projects itself toward something. The psychoanalyst discovers a meaning even in abortive acts and attacks of hysteria. But in order for this meaning to justify the transcendence which discloses it, it must itself be founded, which it will never be if I do not choose to found it myself. Now, I can evade this choice. We have said that it would be contradictory deliberately to will oneself not free. But one can choose not to will himself free. In laziness, heedlessness, capriciousness, cowardice, impatience, one contests the meaning of the project at the very moment that one defines it. The spontaneity of the subject is then merely a vain living palpitation, its movement toward the object is a flight, and itself is an absence. To convert the absence into presence, to convert my flight into will, I must assume my project positively. It is not a matter of retiring into the completely inner and, moreover, abstract movement of a given spontaneity, but of adhering to the concrete and particular movement by which this spontaneity defines itself by thrusting itself toward an end. It is through this end that it sets up that my spontaneity confirms itself by reflecting upon itself. Then, by a single movement, my will, establishing the content of the act, is legitimized by it. I realize my escape toward the other as a freedom when, assuming the presence of the object, I thereby assume myself before it as a presence. But this justification requires a constant tension. My project is never founded; it founds itself. To avoid the anguish of this permanent choice, one may attempt to flee into the object itself, to engulf one's own presence in it. In the servitude of the serious, the original spontaneity strives to deny itself. It strives in vain, and meanwhile it then fails to fulfill itself as moral freedom. . . .

It can be seen that, on the one hand, freedom can always save itself, for it is realized as a disclosure of existence through its very failures, and it can again confirm itself by a death freely chosen. But, on the other hand, the situations which it discloses through its project toward itself do not appear as equivalents. It regards as privileged situations those which permit it to realize itself as indefinite movement; that is, it wishes to pass beyond everything which limits its power; and yet, this power is always limited. Thus, just as life is identified with the will to live, freedom always appears as a movement of liberation. It is only by prolonging itself through the freedom of others that it manages to surpass death itself and to realize itself as an indefinite unity. Later on we shall see what problems such a relationship raises. For the time being it is enough for us to have established the fact that the words "to will oneself free" have a positive and concrete meaning. If man wishes to save his existence, as only he himself can do, his original spontaneity must be raised to the height of moral freedom by taking itself as an end through the disclosure of a particular content.

But a new question is immediately raised. If man has one and only one way to save his existence, how can he choose not to choose it in all cases? How is a bad willing possible? We meet with this problem in all ethics, since it is precisely the possibility of a perverted willing which gives a meaning to the idea of virtue. We know the answer of Socrates, of Plato, of Spinoza: "No one is willfully bad." And if Good is a transcendent thing which is more or less foreign to man, one imagines that the mistake can be explained by error. But if one grants that the moral world is the world genuinely willed by man, all possibility of error is eliminated. Moreover, in Kantian ethics, which is at the origin of all ethics of autonomy, it is very difficult to account for an evil will. As the choice of his character which the subject makes is achieved in the intelligible world by a purely rational will, one cannot understand how the latter expressly rejects the law which it gives to itself. But this is because Kantism defined man as a pure positivity, and it therefore recognized no other possibility in him than coincidence with himself. We, too, define morality by this adhesion to the self; and this is why we say that man cannot positively decide between the negation and the assumption of his freedom, for as soon as he decides, he assumes it. He cannot positively will not to be free for such a willing would be self-destructive. Only, unlike Kant, we do not see man as being essentially a positive will. On the contrary, he is first defined as a negativity. He is first at a distance from himself. He can coincide with himself only by agreeing never to rejoin himself. There is within him a perpetual playing with the negative, and he thereby escapes himself, he escapes his freedom. And it is precisely because an evil will is here possible that the words "to will oneself free" have a meaning. Therefore, not only do we assert that the existentialist doctrine permits the elaboration of an ethics but it even appears to us as the only philosophy in which an ethics has its place. For, in a metaphysics of transcendence, in the classical sense of the term, evil is reduced to error; and in humanistic philosophies it is impossible to account for it, man being defined as complete in a complete world. Existentialism alone gives—like religion—a real role to evil, and it is this, perhaps, which makes its judgments so gloomy. Men do not like to feel themselves in danger. Yet, it is because there are real dangers, real failures and real earthly damnation that words like victory, wisdom, or joy have meaning. Nothing is decided in advance, and it is because man has something to lose and because he can lose that he can also win.

Therefore, in the very condition of man there enters the possibility of not fulfilling this condition. In order to fulfill it he must assume himself as a being who "makes himself a lack of being so that there might be being." But the trick of dishonesty permits stopping at any moment whatsoever. One may hesitate to make oneself a lack of being, one may withdraw before existence, or one may falsely assert oneself as being, or assert oneself as nothingness. One may realize his freedom only as an abstract independence, or, on the contrary, reject with despair the distance which separates us from being. All errors are possible since man is a negativity, and they are motivated by the anguish he feels in the face of his freedom. Concretely, men slide incoherently from one attitude to another. . . .

CONCLUSION

Is this kind of ethics individualistic or not? Yes, if one means by that that it accords to the individual an absolute value and that it recognizes in him alone the power of laying the foundations of his own existence. It is individualism in the sense in which the wisdom of the ancients, the Christian ethics of salvation, and the Kantian ideal of virtue also merit this name; it is opposed to the totalitarian doctrines which raise up beyond man the mirage of mankind. But it is not solipsistic, since the individual is defined only by his relationship to the world and to other individuals; he exists only by transcending himself, and his freedom can be achieved only through the freedom of others. He justifies his existence by a movement which, like freedom, springs from his heart but which leads outside of him.

This individualism does not lead to the anarchy of personal whim. Man is free; but he finds his law in his very freedom. First, he must assume his freedom and not flee it; he assumes it by a constructive movement: one does not exist without doing something; and also by a negative movement which rejects oppression for oneself and others. In construction, as in rejection, it is a matter of reconquering freedom on the contingent facticity of existence, that is, of taking the given, which, at the start, is *there* without any reason, as something willed by man. A conquest of this kind is never finished; the contingency remains, and, so that he may assert his will, man is even obliged to stir up in the world the outrage he does not want. But this element of failure is a very condition of his life; one can never dream of eliminating it without immediately dreaming of death. This does not mean that one should consent to failure, but rather one must consent to struggle against it without respite.

Yet, isn't this battle without victory pure gullibility? It will be argued that this is only a ruse of transcendence projecting before itself a goal which constantly recedes, running after itself on an endless treadmill; to exist for mankind is to remain where one is, and it fools itself by calling this turbulent stagnation progress; our whole ethics does nothing but encourage it in this lying enterprise since we are asking each one to confirm existence as a value for all others; isn't it simply a matter of organizing among men a complicity which allows them to substitute a game of illusions for the given world?

We have already attempted to answer this objection. One can formulate it only by placing himself on the grounds of an inhuman and consequently false objectivity; within mankind men may be fooled; the word "lie" has a meaning by opposition to the truth established by men themselves, but mankind cannot fool itself completely since it is precisely mankind which creates the criteria of true and false. In Plato, art is mystification because there is the heaven of Ideas; but in the earthly domain all glorification of the earth is true as soon as it is realized. Let men attach value to words, forms, colors, mathematical theorems, physical laws, and athletic prowess; let them accord value to one another in love and friendship, and the objects, the events, and the men immediately *have* this value; they have it absolutely. It is possible that a man may refuse to love anything on earth; he will prove this refusal and he will carry it out by suicide. If he lives, the reason is that, whatever he may say, there still remains in him some attachment to existence; his life will be commensurate with this attachment; it will justify itself to the extent that it genuinely justifies the world.

This justification, though open upon the entire universe through time and space, will always be finite. Whatever one may do, one never realizes anything but a limited work like existence itself which tries to establish itself through that work and which death also limits. It is the assertion of our finiteness which doubtless gives the doctrine which we have just evoked its austerity and, in some eyes its sadness. As soon as one considers a system abstractly and theoretically, one puts himself, in effect, on the plane of the universal, thus, of the infinite. That is why reading the Hegelian system is so comforting. I remember having experienced a great feeling of calm on reading Hegel in the impersonal framework of the Bibliotheque Nationale in August 1940. But once I got into the street again, into my life, out of the system, beneath a real sky, the system was no longer of any use to me: what it had offered me, under a show of the infinite, was the consolations of death; and I again wanted to live in the midst of living men. I think that, inversely, existentialism does not offer to the reader the consolations of an abstract evasion: existentialism proposes no evasion. On the contrary, its ethics is experienced in the truth of life, and it then appears as the only proposition of salvation which one can address to men. Taking on its own account Descartes's revolt against the evil genius, the pride of the thinking reed in the face of the universe which crushes him, it asserts that, despite his limits, through them, it is up to each one to fulfill his existence as an absolute. Regardless of the staggering dimensions of the world about us, the density of our ignorance, the risks of catastrophes to come, and our individual weakness within the immense collectivity, the fact remains that we are absolutely free today if we choose to will our existence in its finiteness, a finiteness which is open on the infinite. And in fact, any man who has known real loves, real revolts, real desires, and real will knows quite well that he has no need of any outside guarantee to be sure of his goals; their certitude comes from his own drive. There is a very old saying which goes: "Do what you must, come what may." That amounts to saying in a different way that the result is not external to the good will which fulfills itself in aiming at it. If it came to be that each man did what he must, existence would be saved in each one without there being any need of dreaming of a paradise where all would be reconciled in death.

3.12

Letter from Birmingham Jail

Martin Luther King, Jr.

My dear Fellow Clergymen,

While confined here in the Birmingham city jail, I came across your recent statement calling our present activities "unwise and untimely." Seldom, if ever, do I pause to answer criticism of my work and ideas. If I sought to answer all of the criticisms that cross my desk, my secretaries would be engaged in little else in the course of the day, and I would have no time for constructive work. But since I feel that you are men of genuine good will and your criticisms are sincerely set forth, I would like to answer your statement in what I hope will be patient and reasonable terms.

I think I should give the reason for my being in Birmingham, since you have been influenced by the argument of "outsiders coming in." I have the honor of serving as president of the Southern Christian Leadership Conference, an organization operating in every southern state, with headquarters in Atlanta, Georgia. We have some 85 affiliate organizations all across the South—one being the Alabama Christian Movement for Human Rights. Whenever necessary and possible we share staff, educational and financial resources with our affiliates. Several months ago our local affiliate here in Birmingham invited us to be on call to engage in a nonviolent direct-action program if such were deemed necessary. We readily consented and when the hour came we lived up to our promises. So I am here, along with several members of my staff, because we were invited here. I am here because I have basic organizational ties here. Beyond this, I am in Birmingham because injustice is here. Just as the eighth century prophets left their little villages and carried their "thus saith the Lord" far beyond the boundaries of their hometowns; and just as the Apostle Paul left his little village of Tarsus and carried the gospel of Jesus Christ to practically every hamlet and city of the Graeco-Roman world, I too am compelled to carry the gospel of freedom beyond my particular hometown. Like Paul, I must constantly respond to the Macedonian call for aid.

Moreover, I am cognizant of the interrelatedness of all communities and states. I cannot sit idly by in Atlanta and not be concerned about what happens in Birmingham. Injustice anywhere is a threat to justice everywhere. We are caught in an inescapable network of mutuality, tied in a single garment of destiny. Whatever affects one directly affects all indirectly. Never again can we afford to live with the narrow, provincial "outside agitator" idea. Anyone who lives in the United States can never be considered an outsider anywhere in this country.

You deplore the demonstrations that are presently taking place in Birmingham. But I am sorry that your statement did not express a similar concern for the conditions that brought the demonstrations into being. I am sure that each of you would want to go beyond the superficial social analyst who looks merely at effects, and does not grapple with underlying causes. I would not hesitate to say that it is unfortunate that so-called demonstrations are taking place in Birmingham at this time, but I would say in more emphatic terms that it is even more unfortunate that the white power structure of this city left the Negro community with no other alternative.

In any nonviolent campaign there are four basic steps: (1) collection of the facts to determine whether injustices are alive, (2) negotiation, (3) self-purification, and (4) direct action. We have gone through all of these steps in Birmingham. There can be no gainsaying of the fact that racial injustice engulfs this community.

Birmingham is probably the most thoroughly segregated city in the United States. Its ugly record of police brutality is known in every section of this country. Its unjust treatment of Negroes in the courts is a notorious reality. There have been more unsolved bombings of Negro homes and churches in Birmingham than any city in this nation. These are the hard, brutal and unbelievable facts. On the basis of these conditions Negro leaders sought to negotiate with the city fathers. But the political leaders consistently refused to engage in good faith negotiation.

Then came the opportunity last September to talk with some of the leaders of the economic community. In these negotiating sessions certain promises were made by the merchants—such as the promise to remove the humiliating racial signs from the stores. On the basis of these promises Rev. Shuttlesworth and the leaders of the Alabama Christian Movement for Human Rights agreed to call a moratorium on any type of demonstrations. As the weeks and months unfolded we realized that we were the victims of a broken promise. The signs remained. Like so many experiences of the past we were confronted with blasted hopes, and the dark shadow of a deep disappointment settled upon us. So we had no alternative except that of preparing for direct action, whereby we would present our very bodies as a means of laying our case before the conscience of the local and national community. We were not unmindful of the difficulties involved. So we decided to go through a process of self-purification. We started having workshops on nonviolence and repeatedly asked ourselves the questions, "Are you able to accept blows without retaliating?" "Are you able to endure the ordeals of jail?" We decided to set our direct-action program around the Easter season, realizing that with the exception of Christmas, this was the largest shopping period of the year. Knowing that a strong economic withdrawal program would be the by-product of direct action, we felt that this was the best time to bring pressure on the merchants for the needed changes. Then it occurred to us that the March election was ahead and so we speedily decided to postpone action until after election day. When we discovered that Mr. Connor was in the run-off, we decided again to postpone action so that the demonstrations could not be used to cloud the issues. At this time we agreed to begin our nonviolent witness the day after the run-off.

This reveals that we did not move irresponsibly into direct action. We, too, wanted to see Mr. Connor defeated; so we went through postponement after postponement to aid in this community need. After this we felt that direct action could be delayed no longer.

You may well ask, "Why direct action? Why sit-ins, marches, etc.? Isn't negotiation a better path?" You are exactly right in your call for negotiation. Indeed, this is the purpose of direct action. Nonviolent direct action seeks to create such a crisis and establish such creative tension that a community that has constantly refused to negotiate is forced to confront the issue. It seeks so to dramatize the issue that it can no longer be ignored. I just referred to the creation of tension as a part of the work of the nonviolent resister. This may sound rather shocking. But I must confess that I am not afraid of the word tension. I have earnestly worked and preached against violent tension, but there is a type of constructive nonviolent tension that is necessary for growth. Just as Socrates felt that it was necessary to create a tension in the mind so that individuals could rise from the bondage of myths and half-truths to the unfettered realm of creative analysis and objective appraisal, we must see the need of having nonviolent gadflies to create the kind of tension in society that will help men to rise from the dark depths of prejudice and racism to the majestic heights of understanding and brotherhood. So the purpose of the direct action is to create a situation so crisis-packed that it will inevitably open the door to negotiation. We, therefore, concur with you in your call for negotiation. Too long has our beloved Southland been bogged down in the tragic attempt to live in monologue rather than dialogue.

One of the basic points in your statement is that our acts are untimely. Some have asked, "Why didn't you give the new administration time to act?" The only answer that I can give to this inquiry is that the new administration must be prodded about as much as the outgoing one before it acts. We will be sadly mistaken if we feel that the election of Mr. Boutwell will bring the millennium to Birmingham. While Mr. Boutwell is much more articulate and gentle than Mr. Connor, they are both segregationists, dedicated to the task of maintaining the status quo. The hope I see in Mr. Boutwell is that he will be reasonable enough to see the futility of massive resistance to desegregation. But he will not see this without pressure from the devotees of civil rights. My friends, I must say to you that we have not made a single gain in civil rights without determined legal and nonviolent pressure. History is the long and tragic story of the fact that privileged groups seldom give up their privileges voluntarily. Individuals may see the moral light and voluntarily give up their unjust posture; but as Reinhold Niebuhr has reminded us, groups are more immoral than individuals.

We know through painful experience that freedom is never voluntarily given by the oppressor; it must be demanded by the oppressed. Frankly, I have never yet engaged in a direct action movement that was "well-timed," according to the timetable of those who have not suffered unduly from the disease of segregation. For years now I have heard the words "Wait!" It rings in the ear of every Negro with a piercing familiarity. This "Wait" has almost always meant "Never." It has been a tranquilizing thalidomide, relieving the emotional stress for a moment, only to give birth to an ill-formed infant of frustration. We must come to see with the distinguished jurist of yesterday that "justice too long delayed is justice denied." We have waited for more than 340 years for our constitutional and God-given rights. The nations of Asia and Africa are moving with jetlike speed toward the goal of political independence, and we still creep at horse and buggy pace toward the gaining of a cup of coffee at a lunch counter. I guess it is easy for those who have never felt the stinging darts of segregation to say, "Wait." But when you have seen vicious mobs lynch your mothers and fathers at will and drown your sisters and brothers at whim; when you have seen hate-filled policemen curse, kick, brutalize and even kill your black brothers and sisters with impunity; when you see the vast majority of your twenty million Negro brothers smothering in an airtight cage of poverty in the midst of an affluent society; when you suddenly find your tongue twisted and your speech stammering as you seek to explain to your six-year-old daughter why she can't go to the public amusement park that has just been advertised on television, and see tears welling up in her little eyes when she is told that Funtown is closed to colored children, and see the depressing clouds of inferiority begin to form in her little mental sky, and see her begin to distort her little personality by unconsciously developing a bitterness toward white people; when you have to concoct an answer for a five-year-old son asking in agonizing pathos: "Daddy, why do white people treat colored people so mean?"; when you take a cross-country drive and find it necessary to sleep night after night in the uncomfortable corners of your automobile because no motel will accept you; when you are humiliated day in and day out by nagging signs reading "white" and "colored"; when your first name becomes "nigger" and your middle name becomes "boy" (however old you are) and your last name becomes "John," and when your wife and mother are never given the respected title "Mrs."; when you are harried by day and haunted by night by the fact that you are a Negro, living constantly at tiptoe stance never quite knowing what to expect next, and plagued with inner fears and outer resentments; when you are forever fighting a degenerating sense of "nobodiness"; then you will understand why we find it difficult to wait. There comes a time when the cup of endurance runs over, and men are no longer willing to be plunged into an abyss of injustice where they experience the blackness of corroding despair. I hope, sirs, you can understand our legitimate and unavoidable impatience. You express a great deal of anxiety over our willingness to break laws. This is certainly a legitimate concern. Since we so diligently urge people to obey the Supreme Court's decision of 1954 outlawing segregation in the public schools, it is rather strange and paradoxical to find us consciously breaking laws. One may well ask, "How can you advocate breaking some laws and obeying others?" The answer is found in the fact that there are two types of laws: there are *just* and there are *unjust* laws. I would agree with Saint Augustine that "An unjust law is no law at all."

Now what is the difference between the two? How does one determine when a law is just or unjust? A just law is a man-made code that squares with the moral law or the law of God. An unjust law is a code that is out of harmony with the moral law. To put it in the terms of Saint Thomas Aquinas, an unjust law is a human law that is not rooted in eternal and natural law. Any law that uplifts human personality is just. Any law that degrades human personality is unjust. All segregation statutes are unjust because segregation distorts the soul and damages the personality. It gives the segregator a false sense of superiority, and the segregated a false sense of inferiority. To use the words of Martin Buber, the great Jewish philosopher, segregation substitutes an "I-it" relationship for the "I-thou" relationship, and ends up relegating persons to the status of things. So segregation is not only politically, economically and sociologically unsound, but it is morally wrong and sinful. Paul Tillich has said that sin is separation. Isn't segregation an existential expression of man's tragic separation, an expression of his awful estrangement, his terrible sinfulness? So I can urge men to disobey segregation ordinances because they are morally wrong.

Let us turn to a more concrete example of just and unjust laws. An unjust law is a code that a majority inflicts on a minority that is not binding on itself. This is difference made legal. On the other hand a just law is a code that a majority compels a minority to follow that it is willing to follow itself. This is sameness made legal.

Let me give another explanation. An unjust law is a code inflicted upon a minority which that minority had no part in enacting or creating because they did not have the unhampered right to vote. Who can say that the legislature of Alabama which set up the segregation laws was democratically elected? Throughout the state of Alabama all types of conniving methods are used to prevent Negroes from becoming registered voters and there are some counties without a single Negro registered to vote despite the fact that the Negro constitutes a majority of the population. Can any law set up in such a state be considered democratically structured?

These are just a few examples of unjust and just laws. There are some instances when a law is just on its face and unjust in its application. For instance, I was arrested Friday on a charge of parading without a permit. Now there is nothing wrong with an ordinance which requires a permit for a parade, but when the ordinance is used to preserve segregation and to deny citizens the First Amendment privilege of peaceful assembly and peaceful protest, then it becomes unjust.

I hope you can see the distinction I am trying to point out. In no sense do I advocate evading or defying the law as the rabid segregationist would do. This would lead to anarchy. One who breaks an unjust law must do it openly, lovingly (not hatefully as the white mothers did in New Orleans when they were seen on television screaming, "nigger, nigger, nigger"), and with a willingness to accept the penalty. I submit that an individual who breaks a law that conscience tells him is unjust, and willingly accepts the penalty by staying in jail to arouse the conscience of the community over its injustice, is in reality expressing the very highest respect for law.

Of course, there is nothing new about this kind of civil disobedience. It was seen sublimely in the refusal of Shadrach, Meshach and Abednego to obey the laws of Nebuchadnezzar because a higher moral law was involved. It was practiced superbly by the early Christians who were willing to face hungry lions and the excruciating pain of chopping blocks, before submitting to certain unjust laws of the Roman Empire. To a degree academic freedom is a reality today because Socrates practiced civil disobedience.

We can never forget that everything Hitler did in Germany was "legal" and everything the Hungarian freedom fighters did in Hungary was "illegal." It was "illegal" to aid and comfort a Jew in Hitler's Germany. But I am sure that if I had lived in Germany during that time I would have aided and comforted my Jewish brothers even though it was illegal. If I lived in a Communist country today where certain principles dear to the Christian faith are suppressed, I believe I would openly advocate disobeying these antireligious laws. I must make two honest confessions to you, my Christian and Jewish brothers. First, I must confess that over the last few years I have been gravely disappointed with the white moderate. I have almost reached the regrettable conclusion that the Negro's great stumbling block in the stride toward freedom is not the White Citizen's Counciler or the Ku Klux KIanner, but the white moderate who is more devoted to "order" than to justice; who prefers a negative peace which is the absence of tension to a positive peace which is the presence of justice; who constantly says, "I agree with you in the goal you seek, but I can't agree with your methods of direct action"; who paternalistically feels that he can set the timetable for another man's freedom; who lives by the myth of time and who constantly advised the Negro to wait until a "more convenient season." Shallow understanding from people of good will is more frustrating than absolute misunderstanding from people of ill will. Lukewarm acceptance is much more bewildering than outright rejection.

I had hoped that the white moderate would understand that law and order exist for the purpose of establishing justice, and that when they fail to do this they become dangerously structured dams that block the flow of social progress. I had hoped that the white moderate would understand that the present tension of the South is merely a necessary phase of the transition from an obnoxious negative peace, where the Negro passively accepted his unjust plight, to a substance-filled positive peace, where all men will respect the dignity and worth of human personality. Actually, we who engage in nonviolent direct action are not the creators of tension. We merely bring to the surface the hidden tension that is already alive. We bring it out in the open where it can be seen and dealt with. Like a boil that can never be cured as long as it is covered up but must be opened with all its pus-flowing ugliness to the natural medicines of air and light, injustice must likewise be exposed, with all of the tension its exposing creates, to the light of human conscience and the air of national opinion before it can be cured.

In your statement you asserted that our actions, even though peaceful, must be condemned because they precipitate violence. But can this assertion be logically made? Isn't this like condemning the robbed man because his possession of money precipitated the evil act of robbery? Isn't this like condemning Socrates because his unswerving commitment to truth and his philosophical delvings precipitated the misguided popular mind to make him drink the hemlock? Isn't this like condemning Jesus because His unique God-consciousness and never-ceasing devotion to His will precipitated the evil act of crucifixion? We must come to see, as federal courts have consistently affirmed, that it is immoral to urge an individual to withdraw his efforts to gain his basic constitutional rights because the quest precipitates violence. Society must protect the robbed and punish the robber.

I had also hoped that the white moderate would reject the myth of time. I received a letter this morning from a white brother in Texas which said: "All Christians know that the colored people will receive equal rights eventually, but it is possible that you are in too great of a religious hurry. It has taken Christianity almost two thousand years to accomplish what it has. The teachings of Christ take time to come to earth." All that is said here grows out of a tragic misconception of time. It is the strangely irrational notion that there is something in the very flow of time that will inevitably cure all ills. Actually time is neutral. It can be used either destructively or constructively. I am coming to feel that the people of ill will have used time much more effectively than the people of good will. We will have to repent in this generation not merely for the vitriolic words and actions of the bad people, but for the appalling silence of the good people. We must come to see that human progress never rolls in on wheels of inevitability. It comes through the tireless efforts and persistent work of men willing to be co-workers with God, and without this hard work time itself becomes an ally of the forces of social stagnation. We must use time creatively, and forever realize that the time is always ripe to do right. Now is the time to make real the promise of democracy, and transform our pending national elegy into a creative psalm of brotherhood. Now is the time to lift our national policy from the quicksand of racial injustice to the solid rock of human dignity.

You spoke of our activity in Birmingham as extreme. At first I was rather disappointed that fellow clergymen would see my nonviolent efforts as those of the extremist. I started thinking about the fact that I stand in the middle of two opposing forces in the Negro community. One is a force of complacency made up of Negroes who, as a result of long years of oppression, have been so completely drained of self-respect and a sense of "somebodiness" that they have adjusted to segregation, and, of a few Negroes in the middle class who, because of a degree of academic and economic security, and because at points they profit by segregation, have unconsciously become insensitive to the problems of the masses. The other force is one of bitterness and hatred, and comes perilously close to advocating violence. It is expressed in the various black nationalist groups that are springing up over the nation, the largest and best known being Elijah Muhammad's Muslim movement. This movement is nourished by the contemporary frustration over the continued existence of racial discrimination. It is made up of people who have lost faith in America, who have absolutely repudiated Christianity, and who have concluded that the white man is an incurable "devil." I have tried to stand between these two forces, saying that we need not follow the "do-nothingism" of the complacent or the hatred and despair of the black nationalist. There is the more excellent way of love and nonviolent protest. I'm grateful to God that, through the Negro church, the dimension of nonviolence entered our struggle. If this philosophy had not emerged, I am convinced that by now many streets of the South would be flowing with floods of blood. And I am further convinced that if our white brothers dismiss us as "rabble-rousers" and "outside agitators" those of us who are working through the channels of nonviolent direct action and refuse to support our nonviolent efforts, millions of Negroes, out of frustration and despair, will seek solace and security in black nationalist ideologies, a development that will lead inevitably to a frightening racial nightmare.

Oppressed people cannot remain oppressed forever. The urge for freedom will eventually come. This is what happened to the American Negro. Something within has reminded him of his birthright of freedom; something without has reminded him that he can gain it. Consciously and unconsciously, he has been swept in by what the Germans call the *Zeitgeist,* and with his black brothers of Africa, and his brown and yellow brothers of Asia, South America and the Caribbean, he is moving with a sense of cosmic urgency toward the promised land of racial justice. Recognizing this vital urge that has engulfed the Negro community, one should readily understand public demonstrations. The Negro has many pent-up resentments and latent frustrations. He has to get them out. So let him march sometime; let him have his prayer pilgrimages to the city hall; understand why he must have sit-ins and freedom rides. If his repressed emotions do not come out in these nonviolent ways, they will come out in ominous expressions of violence. This is not a threat; it is a fact of history. So I have not said to my people "get rid of your discontent." But I have tried to say that this normal and healthy discontent can be channelized through the creative outlet of nonviolent direct action. Now this approach is being dismissed as extremist. I must admit that I was initially disappointed in being so categorized.

But as I continued to think about the matter, I gradually gained a bit of satisfaction from being considered an extremist. Was not Jesus an extremist in love—"Love your enemies, bless them that curse you, pray for them that despitefully use you." Was not Amos an extremist for justice—"Let justice roll down like waters and righteousness like a mighty stream." Was not Paul an extremist for the gospel of Jesus Christ—"I bear in my body the marks of the Lord Jesus." Was not Martin Luther an extremist—"Here I stand; I can do none other so help me God." Was not John Bunyan an extremist—"I will stay in jail to the end of my days before I make a butchery of my conscience." Was not Abraham Lincoln an extremist—"This nation cannot survive half slave and half free." Was not Thomas Jefferson an extremist—"We hold these truths to be self-evident, that all men are created equal." So the question is not whether we will be extremist but what kind of extremist will we be. Will we be extremists for hate or will we be extremists for love? Will we be extremists for the preservation of injustice—or will we be extremists for the cause of justice? In that dramatic scene on Calvary's hill, three men were crucified. We must not forget that all three were crucified for the same crime—the crime of extremism. Two were extremists for immorality, and thusly fell below their environment. The other, Jesus Christ, was an extremist for love, truth and goodness, and thereby rose above his environment. So, after all, maybe the South, the nation and the world are in dire need of creative extremists.

I had hoped that the white moderate would see this. Maybe I was too optimistic. Maybe I expected too much. I guess I should have realized that few members of a race that has oppressed another race can understand or appreciate the deep groans and passionate yearnings of those that have been oppressed and still fewer have the vision to see that injustice must be rooted out by strong, persistent and determined action. I am thankful, however, that some of our white brothers have grasped the meaning of this social revolution and committed themselves to it. They are still all too small in quantity, but they are big in quality. Some like Ralph McGill, Lillian Smith, Harry Golden and James Dabbs have written about our struggle in eloquent, prophetic and understanding terms. Others have marched with us down nameless streets of the South. They have languished in filthy roach-infested jails, suffering the abuse and brutality of angry policemen who see them as "dirty nigger-lovers." They, unlike so many of their moderate brothers and sisters, have recognized the urgency of the moment and sensed the need for powerful "action" antidotes to combat the disease of segregation.

Let me rush on to mention my other disappointment. I have been so greatly disappointed with the white church and its leadership. Of course, there are some notable exceptions. I am not unmindful of the fact that each of you has taken some significant stands on this issue. I commend you, Rev. Stallings, for your Christian stance on this past Sunday, in welcoming Negroes to your worship service on a nonsegregated basis. I commend the Catholic leaders of this state for integrating Springhill College several years ago.

But despite these notable exceptions I must honestly reiterate that I have been disappointed with the church. I do not say that as one of the negative critics who can always find something wrong with the church. I say it as a minister of the gospel, who loves the church; who was nurtured in its bosom; who has been sustained by its spiritual blessings and who will remain true to it as long as the cord of life shall lengthen.

I had the strange feeling when I was suddenly catapulted into the leadership of the bus protest in Montgomery several years ago that we would have the support of the white church. I felt that the white ministers, priests and rabbis of the South would be some of our strongest allies. Instead, some have been outright opponents, refusing to understand the freedom movement and misrepresenting its leaders; all too many others have been more cautious than courageous and have remained silent behind the anesthetizing security of the stained-glass windows.

In spite of my shattered dreams of the past, I came to Birmingham with the hope that the white religious leadership of this community would see the justice of our cause, and with deep moral concern, serve as the channel through which our just grievances would get to the power structure. I had hoped that each of you would understand. But again I have been disappointed. I have heard numerous religious leaders of the South call upon their worshippers to comply with a desegregation decision because it is the *law,* but I have longed to hear white ministers say, "Follow this decree because integration is morally *right* and the Negro is your brother." In the midst of blatant injustices inflicted upon the Negro, I have watched white churches stand on the sideline and merely mouth pious irrelevancies and sanctimonious trivialities. In the midst of a mighty struggle to rid our nation of racial and economic injustice, I have heard so many ministers say, "Those are social issues with which the gospel has no real concern," and I have watched so many churches commit themselves to a completely other-worldly religion which made a strange distinction between body and soul, the sacred and the secular.

So here we are moving toward the exit of the twentieth century with a religious community largely adjusted to the status quo, standing as a taillight behind other community agencies rather than a headlight leading men to higher levels of justice.

I have traveled the length and breadth of Alabama, Mississippi and all the other southern states. On sweltering summer days and crisp autumn mornings I have looked at her beautiful churches with their lofty spires pointing heaven-ward. I have beheld the impressive outlay of her massive religious education buildings. Over and over again I have found myself asking: "What kind of people worship here? Who is their God? Where were their voices when the lips of Governor Barnett dripped with words of interposition and nullification? Where were they when Governor Wallace gave the clarion call for defiance and hatred? Where were their voices of support when tired, bruised and weary Negro men and women decided to rise from the dark dungeons of complacency to the bright hills of creative protest?"

Yes, these questions are still in my mind. In deep disappointment, I have wept over the laxity of the church. But be assured that my tears have been tears of love. There can be no deep disappointment where there is not deep love. Yes, I love the church; I love her sacred walls. How could I do otherwise? I am in the rather unique position of being the son, the grandson and the great-grandson of preachers. Yes, I see the church as the body of Christ. But, oh! How we have blemished and scarred that body through social neglect and fear of being nonconformists.

There was a time when the church was very powerful. It was during that period when the early Christians rejoiced when they were deemed worthy to suffer for what they believed. In those days the church was not merely a thermometer that recorded the ideas and principles of popular opinion; it was a thermostat that transformed the mores of society. Wherever the early Christians entered a town the power structure got disturbed and immediately sought to convict them for being "disturbers of the peace" and "outside agitators." But they went on with the conviction that they were "a colony of heaven," and had to obey God rather than man. They were small in number but big in commitment. They were too God-intoxicated to be "astronomically intimidated." They brought an end to such ancient evils as infanticide and gladiatorial contest.

Things are different now. The contemporary church is often a weak, ineffectual voice with an uncertain sound. It is so often the arch-supporter of the status quo. Far from being disturbed by the presence of the church, the power structure of the average community is consoled by the church's silent and often vocal sanction of things as they are.

But the judgment of God is upon the church as never before. If the church of today does not recapture the sacrificial spirit of the early church, it will lose its authentic ring, forfeit the loyalty of millions, and be dismissed as an irrelevant social club with no meaning for the twentieth century. I am meeting young people every day whose disappointment with the church has risen to outright disgust.

Maybe again, I have been too optimistic. Is organized religion too inextricably bound to the status quo to save our nation and the world? Maybe I must turn my faith to the inner spiritual church, the church within the church, as the true *ecclesia* and the hope of the world. But again I am thankful to God that some noble souls from the ranks of organized religion have broken loose from the paralyzing chains of conformity and joined us as active partners in the struggle for freedom. They have left their secure congregations and walked the streets of Albany, Georgia, with us. They have gone through the highways of the South on tortuous rides for freedom. Yes, they have gone to jail with us. Some have been kicked out of their churches, and lost support of their bishops and fellow ministers. But they have gone with the faith that right defeated is stronger than evil triumphant. These men have been the leaven in the lump of the race. Their witness has been the spiritual salt that has preserved the true meaning of the gospel in these troubled times. They have carved a tunnel of hope through the dark mountain of disappointment.

I hope the church as a whole will meet the challenge of this decisive hour. But even if the church does not come to the aid of justice, I have no despair about the future. I have no fear about the outcome of our struggle in Birmingham, even if our motives are presently misunderstood. We will reach the goal of freedom in Birmingham and all over the nation, because the goal of America is freedom. Abused and scorned though we may be, our destiny is tied up with the destiny of America. Before the Pilgrims landed at Plymouth we were here. Before the pen of Jefferson etched across the pages of history the majestic words of the Declaration of Independence, we were here. For more than two centuries our fore-parents labored in this country without wages; they made cotton king; and they built the homes of their masters in the midst of brutal injustice and shameful humiliation—and yet out of a bottomless vitality they continued to thrive and develop. If the inexpressible cruelties of slavery could not stop us, the opposition we now face will surely fail. We will win our freedom because the sacred heritage of our nation and the eternal will of God are embodied in our echoing demands.

I must close now. But before closing I am impelled to mention one other point in your statement that troubled me profoundly. You warmly commended the Birmingham police force for keeping "order" and "preventing violence." I don't believe you would have so warmly commended the police force if you had seen its angry violent dogs literally biting six unarmed, nonviolent Negroes. I don't believe you would so quickly commend the policemen if you would observe their ugly and inhuman treatment of Negroes here in the city jail; if you would watch them push and curse old Negro women and young Negro girls; if you would see them slap and kick old Negro men and young boys; if you will observe them, as they did on two occasions, refuse to give us food because we wanted to sing our grace together. I'm sorry that I can't join you in your praise for the police department.

It is true that they have been rather disciplined in their public handling of the demonstrators. In this sense they have been rather publicly "nonviolent." But for what purpose? To preserve the evil system of segregation. Over the last few years I have consistently preached that nonviolence demands that the means we use must be as pure as the ends we seek. So I have tried to make it clear that it is wrong to use immoral means to attain moral ends. But now I must affirm that it is just as wrong, or even more so, to use moral means to preserve immoral ends. Maybe Mr. Connor and his policemen have been rather publicly nonviolent, as Chief Pritchett was in Albany, Georgia, but they have used the moral means of nonviolence to maintain the immoral end of flagrant racial injustice. T. S. Eliot has said that there is no greater treason than to do the right deed for the wrong reason.

I wish you had commended the Negro sit-inners and demonstrators of Birmingham for their sublime courage, their willingness to suffer and their amazing discipline in the midst of the most inhuman provocation. One day the South will recognize its real heroes. They will be the James Merediths, courageously and with a majestic sense of purpose facing jeering and hostile mobs and the agonizing loneliness that characterizes the life of the pioneer. They will be old, oppressed, battered Negro women, symbolized in a seventy-two-year-old woman of Montgomery, Alabama, who rose up with a sense of dignity and with her people decided not to ride the segregated buses, and responded to one who inquired about her tiredness with un-grammatical profundity: "My feet is tired, but my soul is rested." They will be the young high school and college students, young ministers of the gospel and a host of their elders courageously and nonviolently sitting-in at lunch counters and willingly going to jail for conscience's sake. One day the South will know that when these disinherited children of God sat down at lunch counters they were in reality standing up for the best in the American dream and the most sacred values in our Judeo-Christian heritage, and thusly, carrying our whole nation back to those great wells of democracy which were dug deep by the Founding Fathers in the formulation of the Constitution and the Declaration of Independence. Never before have I writ-ten a letter this long (or should I say a book?). I'm afraid that it is much too long to take your precious time. I can assure you that it would have been much shorter if I had been writing from a comfortable desk, but what else is there to do when you are alone for days in the dull monotony of a narrow jail cell other than write long letters, think strange thoughts, and pray long prayers?

If I have said anything in this letter that is an overstatement of the truth and is indicative of an unreasonable impatience, I beg you to forgive me. If I have said anything in this letter that is an understatement of the truth and is indicative of my having a patience that makes me patient with anything less than brotherhood, I beg God to forgive me.

I hope this letter finds you strong in the faith. I also hope that circum-stances will soon make it possible for me to meet each of you, not as an in-tegrationist or a civil rights leader, but as a fellow clergyman and a Christian brother. Let us all hope that the dark clouds of racial prejudice will soon pass away and the deep fog of misunderstanding will be lifted from our fear-drenched communities and in some not too distant tomorrow the radiant stars of love and brotherhood will shine over our great nation with all of their scintillating beauty.

Yours for the cause of Peace and Brotherhood,
Martin Luther King, Jr.

3.13

Ahiṃsā

Mahatma Gandhi

CHAPTER 3: MEANS AND ENDS

Means and end are convertible terms in my philosophy of life.[1]

They say "means are after all means," I would say "means are after all everything." As the means so the end. There is no wall of separation between means and end. Indeed the Creator has given us control (and that too very limited) over means, none over the end. Realization of the goal is in exact proportion to that of the means. This is a proposition that admits of no exception.[2]

Ahiṃsā and Truth are so intertwined that it is practically impossible to disentangle and separate them. They are like the two sides of a coin, or rather a smooth unstamped metallic disc. Who can say, which is the obverse, and which the reverse? Nevertheless, *ahiṃsā* is the means; Truth is the end. Means to be means must always be within our reach, and so *ahiṃsā* is our supreme duty. If we take care of the means, we are bound to reach the end sooner or later. When once we have grasped this point final victory is beyond question. Whatever difficulties we encounter, whatever apparent reverses we sustain we may not give up the quest for Truth which alone is, being God Himself.[3]

I do not believe in short-violent-cuts to success. . . . However much I may sympathize with and admire worthy motives, I am an uncompromising opponent of violent methods even to serve the noblest of causes. There is, therefore, really no meeting-ground between the school of violence and my-

From *All Men Are Brothers,* pp. 81–101. Copyright © 1958 by UNESCO and Columbia University Press.

self. But my creed of non-violence not only does not preclude me but compels me even to associate with anarchists and all those who believe in violence. But that association is always with the sole object of weaning them from what appears to me their error. For experience convinces me that permanent good can never be the outcome of untruth and violence. Even if my belief is a fond delusion, it will be admitted that it is a fascinating delusion.[4]

Your belief that there is no connexion between the means and the end is a great mistake. Through that mistake even men who have been considered religious have committed grievous crimes. Your reasoning is the same as saying that we can get a rose through planting a noxious weed. If I want to cross the ocean, I can do so only by means of a vessel; if I were to use a cart for that purpose, both the cart and I would soon find the bottom. 'As is the God, so is the votary' is a maxim worth considering. Its meaning has been distorted and men have gone astray. The means may be likened to a seed, the end to a tree; and there is just the same inviolable connexion between the means and the end as there is between the seed and the tree. I am not likely to obtain the result flowing from the worship of God by laying myself prostrate before Satan. If, therefore, anyone were to say: 'I want to worship God; it does not matter that I do so by means of Satan', it would be set down as ignorant folly. We reap exactly as we sow.[5]

Socialism is a beautiful word and, so far as I am aware, in socialism all the members of society are equal—none low, none high. In the individual body, the head is not high because it is the top of the body, nor are the soles of the feet low because they touch the earth. Even as members of the individual body are equal, so are the members of society. This is socialism.

In it the prince and the peasant, the wealthy and the poor, the employer and the employee are all on the same level. In terms of religion, there is no duality in socialism. It is all unity. Looking at society all the world over, there is nothing but duality or plurality. Unity is conspicuous by its absence.

In the unity of my conception there is perfect unity in the plurality of designs.

In order to reach this state, we may not look on things philosophically and say that we need not make a move until all are converted to socialism. Without changing our life we may go on giving addresses, forming parties and hawk-like seize the game when it comes our way. This is not socialism. The more we treat it as game to be seized, the farther it must recede from us.

Socialism begins with the first convert. If there is one such you can add zeros to the one and the first zero will account for ten and every addition will account for ten times the previous number. If, however, the beginner is a zero, in other words, no one makes the beginning, multiplicity of zeros will also produce zero value. Time and paper occupied in writing zeros will be so much waste.

This socialism is as pure as crystal. It, therefore, requires crystal-like means to achieve it. Impure means result in an impure end. Hence the prince and the peasant will not be equalled by cutting off the prince's head, nor can the process of cutting off equalize the employer and the employed. One cannot reach truth by untruthfulness. Truthful conduct alone can reach truth. Are not non-violence and truth twins? The answer is an emphatic 'No'. Non-violence is embedded in truth and vice versa. Hence has it been said that they are faces of the same coin. Either is inseparable from the other. Read the coin either way—the spelling of words will be different; the value is the same. This blessed state is unattainable without perfect purity. Harbour impurity of mind or body and you have untruth and violence in you.

Therefore only truthful, non-violent and pure-hearted socialists will be able to establish a socialistic society in India and the world.[6]

The spiritual weapon of self-purification, intangible as it seems, is the most potent means of revolutionizing one's environment and loosening external shackles. It works subtly and invisibly; it is an intense process though it might often seem a weary and long-drawn process, it is the straightest way to liberation, the surest and quickest and no effort can be too great for it. What it requires is faith—an unshakable mountain-like faith that flinches from nothing.[7]

I am more concerned in preventing the brutalization of human nature than in the prevention of the sufferings of my own people. I know that people who voluntarily undergo a course of suffering raise themselves and the whole of humanity; but I also know that people who become brutalized in their desperate efforts to get victory over their opponents or to exploit weaker nations or weaker men, not only drag down themselves but mankind also. And it cannot be a matter of pleasure to me or anyone else to see human nature dragged to the mire. If we are all sons of the same God and partake of the same divine essence, we must partake of the sin of every person whether he belongs to us or to another race. You can understand how repugnant it must be to invoke the beast in any human being, how much more so in Englishmen, among whom I count numerous friends.[8]

The method of passive resistance is the clearest and safest, because, if the cause is not true, it is the resisters, and they alone, who suffer.[9]

CHAPTER 4: *AHIMSĀ* OR THE WAY OF NON-VIOLENCE

Non-violence is the greatest force at the disposal of mankind. It is mightier than the mightiest weapon of destruction devised by the ingenuity of man.

Destruction is not the law of the humans. Man lives freely by his readiness to die, if need be, at the hands of his brother, never by killing him. Every murder or other injury, no matter for what cause, committed or inflicted on another is a crime against humanity.[1]

The first condition of non-violence is justice all round in every department of life. Perhaps, it is too much to expect of human nature. I do not, however, think so. No one should dogmatize about the capacity of human nature for degradation or exhaltation.[2]

In the application of *Satyāgraha,* I discovered in the earliest stages that pursuit of truth did not admit of violence being inflicted on one's opponent but that he must be weaned from error by patience and sympathy. For, what appears to be truth to the one may appear to be error to another. And patience means self-suffering. So the doctrine came to mean vindication of truth, not by infliction of suffering on the opponent, but on one's self.[3]

Man and his deed are two distinct things. It is quite proper to resist and attack a system, but to resist and attack its author is tantamount to resisting and attacking oneself. For we are all tarred with the same brush, and are children of one and the same Creator, and as such the divine powers within us are infinite. To slight a single human being is to slight those divine powers, and thus to harm not only that being but with him the whole world.[4]

Non-violence is a universal principle and its operation is not limited by a hostile environment. Indeed, its efficacy can be tested only when it acts in the midst of and in spite of opposition. Our non-violence would be a hollow thing and worth nothing, if it depended for its success on the goodwill of the authorities.[5]

The only condition of a successful use of this force is a recognition of the existence of the soul as apart from the body and its permanent nature. And this recognition must amount to a living faith and not mere intellectual grasp.[6]

No man could be actively non-violent and not rise against social injustice no matter where it occurred.[7]

Passive resistance is a method of securing rights by personal suffering; it is the reverse of resistance by arms. When I refuse to do a thing that is repugnant to my conscience, I use soul-force. For instance, the government of the day has passed a law which is applicable to me. I do not like it. If by using violence I force the government to repeal the law, I am employing what may be termed body-force. If I do not obey the law and accept the penalty for its breach, I use soul-force. It involves sacrifice of self.

Everybody admits that sacrifice of self is infinitely superior to sacrifice of others. Moreover, if this kind of force is used in a cause that is unjust, only the person using it suffers. He does not make others suffer for his mistakes. Men have before now done many things which were subsequently found to have been wrong. No man can claim that he is absolutely in the right or that a particular thing is wrong because he thinks so, but it is wrong for him so long as that is his deliberate judgement. It is therefore meet that he should not do that which he knows to be wrong, and suffer the consequence whatever it may be. This is the key to the use of soul-force.[8]

A votary of *ahiṃsā* cannot subscribe to the utilitarian formula (of the greatest good of the greatest number). He will strive for the greatest good of all and die in the attempt to realize the ideal. He will therefore be willing to die, so that the others may live. He will serve himself with the rest, by himself dying. The greatest good of all inevitably includes the good of the greatest number, and, therefore, he and the utilitarian will converge in many points in their career but there does come a time when they must part company, and even work in opposite directions. The utilitarian to be logical will never sacrifice himself. The absolutist will even sacrifice himself.[9]

If we are to be non-violent, we must then not wish for anything on this earth which the meanest or the lowest of human beings cannot have.[10]

The principle of non-violence necessitates complete abstention from exploitation in any form.[11]

My resistance to war does not carry me to the point of thwarting those who wish to take part in it. I reason with them. I put before them the better way and leave them to make the choice.[12]

Taking life may be a duty. We do destroy as much life as we think necessary for sustaining our body. Thus for food we take life, vegetable and other, and for health we destroy mosquitoes and the like by the use of disinfectants, etc., and we do not think that we are guilty of irreligion in doing so . . . for the benefit of the species, we kill carnivorous beasts. . . . Even manslaughter may be necessary in certain cases. Suppose a man runs amuck and goes furiously about, sword in hand, and killing anyone that comes in his way, and no one dares to capture him alive. Anyone who despatches this lunatic will earn the gratitude of the community and be regarded as a benevolent man.[13]

I see that there is an instinctive horror of killing living beings under any circumstances whatever. For instance, an alternative has been suggested in the shape of confining even rabid dogs in a certain place and allowing them to die a slow death. Now my idea of compassion makes this thing impossible for me. I cannot for a moment bear to see a dog, or for that matter any other living being, helplessly suffering the torture of a slow death. I do not kill a human being thus circumstanced because I have more hopeful remedies. I should kill a dog similarly situated because in its case I am without a remedy. Should my child be attacked with rabies and there was no helpful remedy to relieve his agony, I should consider it my duty to take his life. Fatalism has its limits. We leave things to fate after exhausting all the remedies. One of the remedies and the final one to relieve the agony of a tortured child is to take his life.[14]

Ahiṃsā is a comprehensive principle. We are helpless mortals caught in the conflagration of *hiṃsā*. The saying that life lives on life has a deep meaning in it. Man cannot for a moment live without consciously or unconsciously committing outward *hiṃsā*. The very fact of his living—eating, drinking and moving about—necessarily involves some *hiṃsā*, destruction of life, be it ever so minute. A votary of *ahiṃsā* therefore remains true to his faith if the spring of all his actions is compassion, if he shuns to the best of his ability the destruction of the tiniest creature, tries to save it, and thus incessantly strives to be free from the deadly coil of *hiṃsā*. He will be constantly growing in self-restraint and compassion, but he can never become entirely free from outward *hiṃsā*.

Then again, because underlying *ahiṃsā* is the unity of all life, the error of one cannot but affect all, and hence man cannot be wholly free from *hiṃsā*. So long as he continues to be a social being, he cannot but participate in the *hiṃsā* that the very existence involves. When two nations are fighting, the duty of a votary of *ahiṃsā* is to stop the war. He who is not equal to that duty, he who has no power of resisting war, he who is not qualified to resist war, may take part in war, and yet whole-heartedly try to free himself, his nation and the world from war.[15]

I make no distinction, from the point of view of *ahiṃsā* between combatants and non-combatants. He who volunteers to serve a band of dacoits, by working as their carrier, or their watchman while they are about their business, or their nurse when they are wounded, is as much guilty of dacoity as the dacoits themselves. In the same way those who confine themselves to attending to the wounded in battle cannot be absolved from the guilt of war.[16]

I object to violence because when it appears to do good, the good is only temporary; the evil it does is permanent. I do not believe that the killing of even every Englishman can do the slightest good to India. The millions will be just as badly off as they are today, if someone made it possible to kill off every Englishman tomorrow. The responsibility is more ours than that of the English for the present state of things. The English will be powerless to do evil if we will but be good. Hence my incessant emphasis on reform from within.[17]

In life, it is impossible to eschew violence completely. Now the question arises, where is one to draw the line? The line cannot be the same for everyone. For, although, essentially the principle is the same, yet everyone applies it in his or her own way What is one man's food can be another's poison. Meat-eating is a sin for me. Yet, for another person, who has always lived on meat and never seen any thing wrong in it, to give it up, simply in order to copy me, will be a sin.

If I wish to be an agriculturist and stay in a jungle, I will have to use the minimum unavoidable violence, in order to protect my fields. I will have to kill monkeys, birds and insects, which eat up my crops. If I do not wish to do so myself, I will have to engage someone to do it for me. There is not much difference between the two. To allow crops to be eaten up by animals, in the name of *ahiṃsā,* while there is a famine in the land, is certainly a sin. Evil and good are relative terms. What is good under certain conditions can become an evil or a sin, under a different set of conditions.

Man is not to drown himself in the well of the *shastras,* but he is to dive in their broad ocean and bring out pearl. At every step he has to use his discrimination as to what is *ahiṃsā* and what is *himsa.* In this, there is no room for shame or cowardice. The poet had said that the road leading up to God is for the brave, never for the cowardly. . . .[18]

CHAPTER 8: POVERTY IN THE MIDST OF PLENTY

That economics is untrue which ignores or disregards moral values. The extension of the law of non-violence in the domain of economics means nothing less than the introduction of moral values as a factor to be considered in regulating international commerce.[1]

According to me the economic constitution of India and for that matter of the world, should be such that no one under it should suffer from want of food and clothing. In other words, everybody should be able to get sufficient work to enable him to make the two ends meet. And this ideal can be universally realized only if the means of production of the elementary necessities of life remain in the control of the masses. These should be freely available to all as God's air and water are or ought to be; they should not be made a vehicle of traffic for the exploitation of others. Their monopolization by any country, nation or group of persons would be unjust. The neglect of this simple principle is the cause of the destitution that we witness today not only in this unhappy land but in other parts of the world too.[2]

My ideal is equal distribution, but so far as I can see, it is not to be realized. I therefore work for equitable distribution.[3]

I suggest that we are thieves in a way. If I take anything that I do not need for my own immediate use, and keep it, I thieve it from somebody else. I venture to suggest that it is the fundamental law of Nature, without exception, that Nature produces enough for our wants from day to day, and if only everybody took enough for himself and nothing more, there would be no pauperism in this world, there would be no man dying of starvation in this world. But so long as we have got this inequality, so long we are thieving. I am no socialist and I do not want to dispossess those who have got possessions; but I do say that, personally, those of us who want to see light out of darkness have to follow this rule. I do not want to dispossess anybody. I should then be departing from the rule of *ahiṃsā*. If somebody else possesses more than I do, let him. But so far as my own life has to be regulated, I do say that I dare not possess anything which I do not want. In India we have got three millions of people having to be satisfied with one meal a day, and that meal consisting of a *chapāti* containing no fat in it, and a pinch of salt. You and I have no right to anything that we really have until these three millions are clothed—and fed better. You and I, who ought to know better, must adjust our wants, and even undergo voluntary starvation in order that they may be nursed, fed and clothed.[4]

Non-possession is allied to non-stealing. A thing not originally stolen must nevertheless be classified stolen property, if one possesses it without needing it. Possession implies provision for the future. A seeker after Truth, a follower of the Law of Love cannot hold anything against tomorrow. God never stores for tomorrow; He never creates more than what is strictly needed for the moment. If, therefore, we repose faith in His providence, we should rest assured, that He will give us everything that we require. Saints and devotees, who have lived in such faith, have always derived a justification for it from their experience. Our ignorance or negligence of the Divine Law, which gives to man from day to day his daily bread and no more, has given rise to inequalities with all the miseries attendant upon them. The rich have a superfluous store of things which they do not need, and which are therefore neglected and wasted, while millions are starved to death for want of sustenance. If each retained possession only of what he needed, no one would be in want, and all would live in contentment. As it is, the rich are discontented no less than the poor. The poor man would fain become a millionaire, and the millionaire a multimillionaire. The rich should take the initiative in dispossession with a view to a universal diffusion of the spirit of contentment. If only they keep their own property within moderate limits, the starving will be easily fed, and will learn the lesson of contentment along with the rich.[5]

Economic equality is the master key to non-violent independence. Working for economic equality means abolishing the eternal conflict between capital and labour. It means the levelling down of the few rich in whose hands is concentrated the bulk of the nation's wealth on the one hand, and a levelling up of the semi-starved naked millions on the other. A non-violent system of government is clearly an impossibility so long as the wide gulf between the rich and the hungry millions persists. The contrast between the palaces of New Delhi and the miserable hovels of the poor, labouring class cannot last one day in a free India in which the poor will enjoy the same power as the richest in the land. A violent and bloody revolution is a certainty one day unless there is a voluntary abdication of riches and the power that riches give and sharing them for the common good. I adhere to my doctrine of trusteeship in spite of the ridicule that has been poured upon it. It is true that it is difficult to reach. So is non-violence difficult to attain.[6]

The real implication of equal distribution is that each man shall have the wherewithal to supply all his natural wants and more. For example, if one man has a weak digestion and requires only a quarter of a pound of flour for his bread and another needs a pound, both should be in a position to satisfy their wants. To bring this ideal into being the entire social order has got to be reconstructed. A society based on non-violence cannot nurture any other ideal. We may not perhaps be able to realize the goal but we must bear it in mind and work unceasingly to near it. To the same extent as we progress towards our goal we shall find contentment and happiness, and to that extent too, shall we have contributed towards the bringing into being of a non-violent society.

Now let us consider how equal distribution can be brought about through non-violence. The first step towards it is for him who has made this ideal part of his being to bring about the necessary changes in his personal life. He would reduce his wants to a minimum, bearing in mind the poverty of India. His earnings would be free of dishonesty. The desire for speculation would be renounced. His habitation would be in keeping with his new mode of life. There would be self-restraint exercised in every sphere of life. When he has done all that is possible in his own life, then only will he be in a position to preach this ideal among his associates and neighbours.

Indeed at the root of this doctrine of equal distribution must lie that of the trusteeship of the wealthy for superfluous wealth possessed by them. For according to the doctrine they may not possess a rupee more than their neighbours. How is this to be brought about? Non-violently? Or should the wealthy be dispossessed of their possessions? To do this we would naturally have to resort to violence. This violent action cannot benefit the society. Society will be the poorer, for it will lose the gifts of a man who knows how to accumulate wealth. Therefore the non-violent way is evidently superior. The rich man will be left in possession of his wealth, of which he will use what he reasonably requires for his personal needs and will act as a trustee for the remainder to be used for the society. In this argument honesty on the part of the trustee is assumed.

If however, in spite of the utmost effort, the rich do not become guardians of the poor in the true sense of the term and the latter are more and more crushed and die of hunger, what is to be done? In trying to find out the solution of this riddle I have lighted on non-violent non-co-operation and civil disobedience as the right and infallible means. The rich cannot accumulate wealth without the cooperation of the poor in society. If this knowledge were to penetrate to and spread amongst the poor, they would become strong and would learn how to free themselves by means of non-violence from the crushing inequalities which have brought them to the verge of starvation.[7]

We should be ashamed of resting or having a square meal so long as there is one able-bodied man or woman without work or food.[8]

I hate privilege and monopoly. Whatever cannot be shared with the masses is taboo to me.[9]

No one has ever suggested that grinding pauperism can lead to anything else than moral degradation. Every human being has a right to live and therefore to find the wherewithal to feed himself and where necessary to clothe and house himself. But for this very simple performance we need no assistance from economists or their laws.

"Take no thought for the morrow" is an injunction which finds an echo in almost all the religious scriptures of the world. In a well-ordered society the securing of one's livelihood should be and is found to be the easiest thing in the world. Indeed the test of orderliness in a country is not the number of millionaires it owns, but the absence of starvation among its masses.[10]

My *ahiṃsā* would not tolerate the idea of giving a free meal to a healthy person who has not worked for it in some honest way and if I had the power, I would stop every *sadāvrata* where free meals are given. It has degraded the nation and it has encouraged laziness, idleness, hypocrisy and even crime.[11]

Every man has an equal right to the necessaries of life even as birds and beasts have. And since every right carries with it a corresponding duty and the corresponding remedy for resisting any attack upon it, it is merely a matter of finding out the corresponding duties and remedies to vindicate the elementary fundamental equality. The corresponding duty is to labour with my limbs and the corresponding remedy is to non-co-operate with him who deprives me of the fruit of my labour. And if I would recognize the fundamental equality, as I must, of the capitalist and the labourer, I must not aim at his destruction. I must strive for his conversion. My non-cooperation with him will open his eyes to the wrong he may be doing.[12]

Complete renunciation of one's possessions is a thing which very few even among ordinary folk are capable of. All that can legitimately be expected of the wealthy class is that they should hold their riches and talents in trust and use them for the service of the society. To insist on more would be to kill the goose that laid the golden eggs.[13]

NOTES

Chapter 3
1. SB, p. 13.
2. *Ibid.,* p. 37.
3. *Ibid.,* p. 37.
4. MM, p. 126.
5. HS, p. 37.
6. MGP, II, pp. 140–41.
7. SB, 160–61.
8. *Ibid.,* p. 161.
9. *Ibid.,* p. 162.
Chapter 4
1. MM, p. 49.
2. MT, V, p. 344.
3. SB, pp. 17–18.
4. *Ibid.,* pp. 27–28.
5. *Ibid.,* p. 33.
6. *Ibid.,* p. 32.
7. *Ibid.,* p. 33.
8. *Ibid.,* p. 34.
9. *Ibid.,* pp. 38-39.
10. *Ibid.,* p. 16.
11. *Ibid.,* p. 33.
12. *Ibid.,* p. 144.
13. *Ibid.,* p. 145.
14. *Ibid.,* p. 147.
15. AMG, pp. 427–28.
16. *Ibid.,* p. 429.
17. SB, p. 157.
18. MT, VII, 152–53.

Chapter 8
1. SB, p. 41.
2. *Ibid.,* p. 40.
3. *Ibid.,* p. 77.
4. *Ibid.,* p. 17.
5. *Ibid.,* p. 75.
6. *Ibid.,* pp. 75–76.
7. *Ibid.,* pp. 77–78.
8. *Ibid.,* p. 49.
9. MM, p. 11.
10. SB, p. 76.
11. *Ibid.,* p. 49.
12. MM, p. 117.
13. MGP, Vol. I, p. 66.

The abbreviations used above refer to the following books:

AMG *An Autobiography or the Story of my Experiments with Truth,* M. K. Gandhi. Ahmedabad, India: Navajivan Publishing House, 1948.

MGP *Mahatma Gandhi, the Last Phase,* Pyarelal. Ahmedabad, India: Navajivan Publishing House, Vol. I, 1956; Vol. II 1958.

MT *Mahatma, Life of Mohandas Karamchand Gandhi,* D. G. Tendulkar. Bombay, India: Vithalbhai K. Jhaveri & D. G. Tendulkar, in eight volumes, Vol. I, 1951; Vol. II, 1995; Vol. III, 1952; Vol. IV, 1952; Vol. V, 1952; Vol. VI, 1953; Vol. VII, 1953, and Vol. VIII, 1954.

HS *Hind Swaraj or Indian Home Rule,* M. K. Gandhi. Ahmedabad, India: Navajivan Publishing House, 1946.

MM *The Mind of Mahatma Gandhi,* compiled by R. K. Prabhu and U. R. Rao. London: Oxford University Press, 1945.

SB *Selections from Gandhi,* Nirmal Kumar Bose. Ahmedabad, India: Navajivan Publishing House, 1948.

3.14

Chinese and Western Interpretations of *Jen* (Humanity)

Wing-tsit Chan

The concept of *jen* (humanity, love, humaneness; pronounced *ren*) is a central concept of Confucian thought and has gone through a long evolution of more than 2000 years. The story of that evolution has been told elsewhere.[1] The purpose here is to see how the Chinese have understood the concept and how the West has interpreted it. We shall discuss the Chinese understanding under seven headings.

(1) *Confucius (551–479 B.C.) the First to Conceive of* Jen *as the General Virtue*. The word *jen* is not prominent in pre-Confucian Classics. It does not appear in the 'Book of Yü' or the 'Book of Hsia' in the *Book of History* and only twice in its 'Book of Shang' where the word was originally *JEN* (man) and three times in its 'Book of Chou'. It is not found in the three 'Eulogies' of the *Book of Odes* and only twice elsewhere in the book besides once written *JEN*.[2] It is found in eight passages in the *Book of Changes,* all in the Appendixes which are generally regarded as post-Confucian and none in the text itself which is believed to be pre-Confucian. In sharp contrast to these pre-Confucian Classics, the Confucian *Analects* mentions *jen* 105 times in 58 out of 499 chapters. Thus more than ten percent of the *Analects* is devoted to the discussion of *jen,* more than those on filial piety, Heaven, or rules of propriety.[3]

What is more important, Confucius looked at *jen* in a new light. In pre-Confucian Classics, whether the word is written *jen* or *JEN,* it means benevolence, a particular virtue, along with other particular virtues like wisdom,

From the *Journal of Chinese Philosophy,* vol. 2 (1975) 107–129. Copyright © by D. Reidel Publishing Company, Dodrecht-Holland.

liberality, etc. Until the time of Confucius, the Chinese had not developed a concept of the general virtue which is universal and fundamental from which all particular virtues ensue. But Confucius was propagating a comprehensive ethical doctrine which must have a basic virtue on which all particular virtues are rooted. In this respect Confucius not only took a great step forward but also built Chinese ethics on a solid foundation. It is true that in a number of cases Confucius still treated *jen* as a particular virtue. When he said, "The man *of jen* is naturally at ease with *jen:* the man of wisdom cultivates *jen* for its advantage" (*Analects,* 4:2) and "The man of wisdom delights in water; the man *of jen* delights in mountains," (6:12), *jen* is coupled with wisdom. When he said, "A man of *jen* necessarily possesses courage but a man of courage does not necessarily have *jen*", (14:5) *jen* and courage are considered as two separate virtues. In his famous saying, "The man of wisdom has no perplexity; the man of *jen* has no worry; the man of courage has no fear", (9:28, 14: 30) *jen* is one of three 'great virtues'. And in talking about the six virtues and six obscurations, (17:8) *jen* is one of the six. In all these cases, Confucius was following tradition in understanding *jen* as a specific virtue. In this sense, *jen* may be translated as 'benevolence', 'kindness', or even 'love' or 'humanity' so long as it is understood as a particular virtue.

The great majority of Confucius' sayings *on jen* in the *Analects,* however, goes beyond this idea of particularity. When he said, "A man who is strong, resolute, simple, and slow to speak is near to *jen*", (13:27) he obviously meant that *jen* involves many moral qualities. The same is true of his utterance, "One who can practice five things wherever he may be is a man *of jen*—earnestness, liberality, truthfulness, diligence, and generosity", (17:6) or "When one has avoided aggressiveness, pride, resentment, and greed, he may be called a man of *jen*", (14:2) or "To study extensively, to be steadfast in one's purpose, to inquire earnestly, and to reflect on what is at hand—*jen* consists in these". (19:6) In saying that "A man of *jen* is respectful in private life, is serious in handling affairs, and is loyal in dealing with orders" (13:19) he clearly thought of *jen* as the moral standard governing one's entire life. He also said, "If a man is not *jen,* what has he to do with ceremonies? If he is not *jen,* what has he to do with music?" (3:3) Thus *jen* even embraces ceremonies and music. The most important sayings on *jen,* however, are these: When a pupil asked about *jen,* Confucius answered, "Do not do to others what you do not want them to do to you". (12:2) When another pupil asked about *jen,* he said, "To master oneself and to return to propriety is *jen*". (12:1) And when a third pupil asked him about *jen,* he replied, "A man of *jen,* wishing to establish his own character, also establishes the character of others, and wishing to be prominent himself, also helps others to be prominent". (6:28) To master oneself and to establish one's character means self-perfection, and to return to (or restore) propriety and to establish the character of others mean to bring about a perfect society. Undoubtedly the virtue of *jen* involves the perfection of others as well of oneself. Significantly the word *jen* is written in two parts, one a figure of a human being, meaning oneself, and the other with two horizontal strokes, meaning human relations. *Jen* is therefore the moral ideal whether the self or society is concerned. In fact, one involves the other. In short, *jen* is the general virtue which is basic, universal, and the source of all specific virtues. "If you set your mind on *jen*", Confucius said, "you will be free from evil". (4:4) "Only the man of *jen* knows how to love people and hate people", (4:3) for he has reached the highest level of morality. Needless to say that 'hate' here does not mean ill will but the refusal to tolerate evil. With the general virtue established, Chinese ethics entered upon a higher stage, for virtue as a whole can now be understood and particular virtues can now have a foundation.

(2) Jen *as Love.* Although Confucius' concept of *jen* as the general virtue is unmistakable, he never defined it. This responsibility fell upon his followers. In the *Doctrine of the Mean* traditionally attributed to his grandson Tzu-ssu (492–431 B.C.), it is said, *"Jen* is *JEN",* (Ch. 20) that is, *jen* is simply man, or rather the distinguishing characteristic of man. Mencius (372–289 B.C.?) expanded it by saying, *"Jen* is *JEN.* When embodied in man's conduct, it is the Way (Tao)" (*Mencius,* 7B: 16). He also said, *"Jen* is man's mind" (6A: 11). Commentators generally agree that by the mind of man he meant man's feeling of love.

The idea that *jen* means love began with Confucius. When a pupil asked him about *jen,* Confucius answered by saying that "It is to love men". (*Analects,* 12:22) This line of thought was continued by Mencius who said, "The man *jen* loves others". (*Mencius,* 4B: 28) He said further, "A man of *jen* extends his love from those he loves to those he does not love". (7B: 1) Again, "The man of *jen* loves all". (7A:46) Generally speaking, from the time of Confucius through the Han Dynasty (206 B.C.–A.D. 220), *jen* was understood in the sense of love. According to Mo Tzu (468–376 B.C.?), *"Jen* is to love" and to "embody love".[4] To Chuang Tzu (c. 369–286 B.C.), "To love people and benefit things is called *jen".*[5] According to Hsün Tzu (313–238 B.C.?), *"Jen* is love".[6] In the words of Han Fei Tzu (d. 233 B.C.), *"Jen* means that in one's heart one joyously loves others".[7] In the *Book of Rites,* it is said, *"Jen* is to love".[8] In the *Kuo-yü* (Conservations of the states), it is said, "To love people is to be able to be *jen".*[9] Tung Chung-shu (176–104 B.C.) was more explicit when he said, *"Jen* is the name for loving people" and *"Jen* is to love mankind".[10] A little later, Yang Hsiung (53 B.C.–A.D. 18) said, *"Jen* is to see and love" and "To love universally is called *jen".*[11] From all these it is clear that the interpretation of *jen* as love was a consistent tradition in ancient Confucianism. It is for this reason, no doubt, that the *Shou-wen* (Explanation of words) of A.D. 100 equated *jen* with *ch'in* (affection, endearing).

The above quotations show that not only the Confucian School understood *jen* as love but the Moist, Taoist, and Legalist Schools as well. However, love to Mo Tzu was universal love, whereas love in the Confucian School meant love with distinctions, degree, or grades. On this score the two schools stood diametrically opposed and engaged in one of the most bitter debates in the history of Chinese thought. In Mencius' eyes, the Moist doctrine was "a great flood and ferocious animals". He cried, "Mo Tzu advocated universal love, which means a denial of the special relationship with the father". (3B:9) To the Confucianists, *jen* must rest on the foundation of affection to relatives. According to a Confucian pupil, "Filial piety and brotherly respect are roots *of jen*". (*Analects,* 1:20) After the *Doctrine of the Mean* describes *jen* as the distinguishing characteristic of man, it immediately continues to say that "The greatest application of it is in being affectionate toward relatives". (Ch. 20) This is why Mencius said, "The actuality (or substance) of *jen* consists in serving one's parents". (4A:27) The result is his well-known formula:

> In regard to [inferior] creatures, the superior man loves them but is not humane (*jen*) to them (that is, showing them the feeling due human beings). In regard to people generally, he is humane to them but not affectionate. He is affectionate to his parents and humane to all people. He is humane to all people and feels love for all. (7A:45)

Put briefly, this is the Confucian doctrine of love with distinctions or grades. From Mencius' point of view, when the Moists regarded people's parents as their own parents, they had two foundations (3A:45), for he believed that "Heaven produced creatures" in such a way as to provide them with one foundation (such as parents being the foundation of men) but the Moists would have two foundations, that is, parents and other people. He argued that "It is the nature of things to be unequal". (3A:4) Applied to human relations, some are close and others are remote, and therefore the intensity of feeling varies. From the one foundation, that is, one's parents, one's love extends to other relatives, other people, and finally to all creatures. The point is that love is the same for all but its application varies with different relations. Confucianists start with parents because the relationship with parents is the first relationship in human life and the indispensable one, for one could be without other relations. From the practical point of view, it is also the nearest. As a matter of common practice, although one should have good will toward all, one greets first of all those nearest to him. It is the application that has degrees or grades, not love itself, for it is unthinkable to have half love or quarter love. The repeated sayings by the Confucianists that *jen* is to love all should make the all-embracing character of *jen* perfectly clear.

Partly because Mencius had to clarify why application must vary while love is the same, he advocated the doctrine of righteousness (*i*), or what is correct and proper, along with *jen*. He spoke of *jen* and *i* together many times.[12] He said, "Humanity is man's mind and righteousness is man's path". (6A: 11) He also said, "Humanity is the peaceful abode of man and righteousness is his straight path". (4A: 10) In other words, the general virtue of humanity has to be carried out in a proper way. This does not mean that humanity is internal whereas righteousness is external, an issue on which Mencius debated vigorously with Kao Tzu. (6A:4) Rather, humanity is the substance while righteousness is the function. In the functioning of anything, there is necessarily priority in time or degree in intensity. The substance does not vary but its operations differ in different situations. The major conflict between Moist universal love and Confucian love for all does not lie in the substance of love but in whether or not there should be differences in application. For the Moists there should be none, but the Confucianists insisted that there should and must be. This has been a persistent theme in the Confucian tradition. The upshot of Moist universal love is universalism in which no distinction is made between one's own parents and other people's parents, thus denying any special relationship with one's own parents. When Mencius attacked Mo Tzu and his followers as having no parents he was not merely rhetorical. Instead, he was defending a central Confucian doctrine on human relations.

(3) Jen *as Universal Love.* As a result of the Burning of Books by the Ch'in rulers in 213 B.C., the Moist School virtually disappeared. After Buddhism entered China, its doctrine of universal salvation for all eventually became prevalent. It reached its climax in the T'ang Dynasty (618–907). Scholars who talked about Tao, virtue, humanity, and righteousness followed either the Taoists or the Buddhists. Being greatly alarmed, the most outstanding Confucianist of the dynasty, Han Yü (768–824), took it upon himself to "clarify the Way of ancient kings". In his *Inquiry on the Way* he loudly declared, "Universal love is called humanity". And he advocated 'burning the books' of the Taoists and Buddhists and "made their lodgings (monasteries) human abodes again".[13] Some writers have claimed that Han Yü's doctrine of universal love is the same as the universal love of the Moists and the doctrine of universal salvation of the Buddhists. If so, what is the difference and why did Han Yu¨ feel he had to attack them?

It should be made clear that the translation of 'universal love' in the case of Han Yü is from the Chinese term *po-ai*. The Moist term is *chien-ai*, literally 'mutual love'. Since the Moist concept is intended to cover all mankind, the translation 'universal love' is perfectly proper. However, although the translation 'universal love' has been used by practically all translators for both Han Yu's *po-ai* and Mo Tzu's *chien-ai*, Mo Tzu repeatedly emphasized the idea of "mutual love and mutual benefit".[14] There is no question that for Mo Tzu the practical benefit is a key factor in mutual love. This utilitarian motive is utterly different from that of Confucianism where humanity is the natural unfolding of man's nature.

The term *po-ai* comes from the *Kuo-yu* where a note to the 'Conversations of Chou' says, *"Jen* is universal love for men".[15] It also appears in the *Classic of Filial Piety* (Ch. 7). It is also found in the *Chung-lun* (Treatise on the Mean) by Hsit Kan (170–217), where it is said, "By the exercise of humanity the superior man loves universally".[16] Thus the concept of universal love is originally Confucian and there was no need to borrow from the outside. Han Yü did not attack the Buddhists and Taoists only but also Mo Tzu and Yang Chu (440–360 B.C.?). The reason he attacked them is that while they taught humanity, they neglected righteousness. This is why he began his *Inquiry on the Way* by saying, "Universal love is called humanity. To practice this in the proper manner is called righteousness". What is proper involves the question of method, a sense of propriety, and a relative degree of intensity. Han Yü granted the Taoists and the Buddhists the feeling of love but he insisted that the lack of righteousness led to the neglect of specific human relations and culminated in neglecting society in favor of a life of quietude and inactivity with the result that economic production was undermined and life itself was endangered. In his view, the Buddhist doctrine of universal salvation is empty and therefore negative whereas the Confucian doctrine is concrete and therefore positive. Actually Han Yü did not contribute much to the development of the Confucian concept of *jen,* but in affirming both the universal and particular aspects of *jen* and in stressing its solid and active character, he did much to strengthen the tradition.

(4) *The Identification of Jen with Nature and Principle and the Doctrine of 'Principle Is One but Its Manifestations Are Many'* (*li-i fen-shu*). Both Mencius and Han Yü spoke of humanity and righteousness together because they wanted it to be clear that while humanity is universal in nature, being extended to the entire human race, its applications in different relations and circumstances require specific expressions. However, they did not provide a philosophical basis for this doctrine. For this we have to wait for the Neo-Confucian philosopher Chang Tsai (1020–1077). The philosophical basis of *jen* may be traced to the saying in the *Doctrine of the Mean,* "Humanity is [the distinguishing characteristic of] man" (20) and Mencius' saying, "Humanity is the mind of man". (6A:11) Mencius also described humanity as "The mind that cannot bear [to see the suffering of] others", that is, "the feeling of commiseration" which is "the beginning of humanity". (2A:6) Here humanity is identified with the nature of man. Han Dynasty Confucianists generally considered humanity to belong to the nature of man and love to belong to man's feeling. For example, in the *Po-hu* (The comprehensive discussion in the White Tiger Hall), it is said that "In man's nature there is humanity", but love is considered as one of six feelings.[17] In his *Inquiry on Human Nature,* Han Yü also considers humanity as nature and love as feeling.[18] To Neo-Confucianists of the Sung Dynasty (960-1279), Humanity, principle, and nature are three in one.

The relationship among these three as well as between them and the doc-trine of principle being one but its manifestations being many is best ex-pressed, though only implicitly, in Chang Tsai's *Western Inscription*. It reads:

> Heaven is my father and Earth is my mother. . . . Therefore that which fills the universe I regard as my body and that which directs the universe I consider as my nature. All people are my brothers and sisters and all things are my com-panions. . . . The sage identifies his character with that of Heaven and Earth. . . . He who disobeys [the Principle of Nature] violates virtue. He who destroys hu-manity is a robber. . . . One who knows the principle of transformation will skill-fully carry forward the undertakings [of Heaven and Earth]. . . . [19]

Though a short essay, the *Western Inscription* is one of the most important writings in Neo-Confucianism. As Yang Shih (1053–1135) told us, Chang Tsai's purpose in writing the essay was to urge us to seek humanity.[20] Yang Shih said,

> The meaning of the *Western Inscription* is that principle is one but its manifes-tations are many. If we know that principle is one, we understand why there is humanity and if we know manifestations are many, we understand why there is righteousness. By manifestations being many is meant, as Mencius has said, to extend affection for relatives to humaneness for people and love for all crea-tures. Since functions are different, the application [of humanity] cannot be without distinctions. Some may say that in this case substance (one principle) and function (many manifestations) are two different things. My answer is that function is never separate from substance. Take the case of the body. When all members of the body are complete, that is substance. In its operation, shoes cannot be put on the head and a hat cannot be worn by the feet. Thus when we speak of substance, functions are already involved in it.[21]

Chu Hsi (1113–1200) made it clearer. He said:

> There is nothing in the entire realm of creatures that does not regard Heaven as the father and Earth as the mother. This means that the principle is one. . . . Each regards his parents as his own parents and his son as his own son. This being the case, how can the principle not be manifested as the many? When the in-tense affection for parents is extended to broaden the impartiality that knows no ego, and when sincerity in serving one's parents leads to the understanding of the way to serve Heaven, then everywhere there is the operation that the principle is one but its manifestations are many.[22]

(5) *The Man of Humanity Regards Heaven and Earth and the Ten Thou-sand Things as One Body.* Chang Tsai said in his *Western Inscription*, "That which fills the universe I regard as my body and that which directs the uni-verse I consider as my nature". The meaning of this is that one extends his

affection for parents and relatives to all things until one, Heaven, Earth, and all things form one body. In his essay *On Understanding the Nature of* Jen, Ch'eng Hao (1032–1085) said, "The student must first of all understand the nature *of jen*. The man of *jen* forms one body with all things without any differentiation".[23] Elsewhere he said,

> A book on medicine describes paralysis of the four limbs as absence of *jen*.[24] This is an excellent description. The man of *jen* regards Heaven and Earth and all things as one body. To him there is nothing that is not himself. Since he has recognized all things as himself, can there be any limit to his humanity? If things are not parts of the self, naturally they have nothing to do with it. As in the case of paralysis of the four limbs, the vital force no longer penetrates them, and therefore they are no longer parts of the self. . . . Therefore, to be charitable and to assist all things is the function of the sage. It is most difficult to describe *jen*. Hence Confucius merely said that the man of *jen,* "wishing to establish his own character, also establishes the character of others, and wishing to be prominent himself, also helps others to be prominent."[25]

This doctrine of forming one body with all things is a cardinal one in the Neo-Confucianism of the Sung and Ming (1368–1644) Dynasties. From Ch'eng Hao, his brother Ch'eng I (1033–1107), to Chu Hsi, Lu Hsiang shan (1139–1193) and Wang Yang-ming (1472–1529), they all advocated it. In Wang Yang-ming, the relationship between the concept of *jen* and this doctrine is the most direct. He said,

> The great man regards Heaven and Earth and the myriad things as one body. . . . That the great man can regard Heaven, Earth, and the myriad things as one body is not because he deliberately wants to do so, but because it is natural to the humane nature of his mind that he does so. . . . Therefore when he sees a child about to fall into a well, he cannot help a feeling of alarm and commiseration.[26] This shows that his humanity forms one body with the child. . . . Even when he sees tiles and stones shattered and crushed, he cannot help a feeling of regret. This shows that his humanity forms one body with tiles and stones. This means that even the mind of the small man necessarily has the humanity that forms one body with all. Such a mind is rooted in his Heaven-endowed nature and is naturally intelligent, clear, and not beclouded.[27]

In Ch'eng Hao's thinking, *jen* is similar to the vital power of the body which penetrates the entire body while in the thinking of Wang Yang-ming, in the clear character of *jen* there is neither division nor obstruction. In both cases, there is in *jen* the natural power of spontaneous flowing to the point of filling the entire universe. Implicit in this idea is that *jen* is a creative force, a power to grow and to give life.

(6) *Jen and the Process of Production and Reproduction (Recreation and Re-creation, sheng-sheng).* The principle of production and reproduction is

a long tradition in the history of Chinese thought. The idea of production goes back to the *Book of Changes* where it is said, "The great virtue of Heaven and Earth is production".[28] In the *Comprehensive Discussion on the White Tiger Hall,* productivity is ascribed to *jen.* "The man *of jen* loves productions", it says.[29] Chou Tun-i said, "To grow things is *jen".*[30] However, the Ch'eng brothers were the ones who definitely interpreted *jen* as the power to produce. To Ch'eng Hao, "The will to grow in all things is most impressive. . . . This is *jen".*[31] And according to his brother Ch'eng I, "The mind is like seeds. Their characteristic of growth is *jen".*[32] And Here the interpretation of *jen* is based on its common meaning as seeds. It is not to be taken as merely a pun. Rather, it is an extension of the meaning of *jen* as love or commiseration to include the characteristic of growth, for only with the creative force of growth can one gradually embrace all things and form one body with the universe. Hence their pupil Hsieh Liang-tso (1050–1103) said, "The seeds of peaches and apricots that can grow are called *jen.* It means that there is the will to grow. If we infer from this, we will understand what *jen* is".[33] For this reason, Ch'eng I said,

> Origination in the Four Characters (of Origination, Flourishing, Advantage, and Firmness in the process of Change) is comparable to humanity in the Five Constant Virtues (of humanity, righteousness, propriety, wisdom, and faithfulness). Separately speaking, it is one of the several, but collectively speaking, it embraces all the four.[34]

Jen naturally gives rise to the other Constant Virtues just as Origination in the spring naturally leads to the successive stages of Flourishing in the summer, Advantage in the autumn, and Firmness in the winter. Hence philosopher Ch'eng said, *"Jen* is the whole body whereas the other four Constant Virtues are the four limbs".[35] Because of the characteristic to grow and to produce, there is the sense of commiseration that cannot bear the suffering of others, the desire to establish the character of others as well as that of oneself, the extension of affection for parents to the love of all creatures, and the goal to form one body with Heaven, Earth, and all things. This is why Wang Yang-ming said that the man of *jen* does not deliberately form one body but it is because of the nature of his *jen* that he does so. From this, it is clear that *jen* is creative and as such is active.

Jen was interpreted as impartiality by Chou Tun-i (1017–1073)[36] but impartiality is merely an attitude; its nature is passive. For this reason, Ch'eng I said,

> Essentially speaking, the way of *jen* may he expressed in one word, namely, impartiality. However, impartiality is but the principle of *jen;* it should not be equated with *jen* itself. When one makes impartiality the substance of his person, that is *jen.* Because of his impartiality, there will be no distinction between him and others.[37]

Hsieh Liang-tso understood *jen* as consciousness or awareness. He said, "When there is the consciousness of pain in the case of illness, we call it *jen*".[38] This theory sounds like that of Ch'eng Hao who considered the paralysis of the four limbs as an absence on *jen*. However, Hsieh's emphasis is on the state of mind. This can be seen from his saying, *"Jen* is the awareness of pain (in case of illness). The Confucianists call it *jen* while the Buddhists call it consciousness."[39] By equating *jen* with Buddhist consciousness, it is obvious that Hsieh's emphasis is on tranquility. Such a Buddhistic doctrine can hardly be attractive to Neo-Confucianists. In criticism of it, Ch'eng I said, "One who is not *jen* is not conscious of anything. But it is incorrect to consider consciousness as *jen*."[40] Later Chu Hsi frankly stated, "In over-emphasizing the concept of consciousness, Hsieh Liang-tso seems to be expounding the doctrine of the Buddhist Meditation School".[41] The main defect of the interpretation of *jen* as impartiality or consciousness is that it lacks the creative character of *jen* as the process of production and reproduction.

(7) *Jen* as 'the Character of the Mind and the Principle of Love'. As to how *jen* can produce and reproduce, the answer has been provided by Chu Hsi. This is what he said:

> The mind of Heaven and Earth is to produce things.[42] In the production of man and things, they receive the mind of Heaven and Earth as their mind.[43] Therefore with reference to the character of the mind although it embraces and penetrates all and leaves nothing to be desired, nevertheless one word will cover all namely, *jen.* In discussing the excellence of man's mind it is said *"Jen* is man's mind. . . ."[44] What mind is this? In Heaven and Earth it is the mind to produce things infinitely. In man it is the mind to love people gently and to benefit things. In my theory, *jen* is described as the principle of love.[45]

What Chu Hsi meant by the 'character of the mind' and 'principle of love' is that the human mind is endowed with the principle of production and reproduction. That is its nature and its substance. When that principle is expressed in love, respect, etc., these are the feelings and the function of the mind. When the mind to produce things is extended throughout the universe, one will form one body with Heaven, Earth, and all things. The various concepts of *jen* are here synthesized and the Neo-Confucian doctrine of *jen* reaches its climax.

From the survey above, it can readily be seen that the concept of *jen* is very profound and extensive. Western studies of it may be said to have begun in 1662 when the *Great Learning* was translated. The Doctrine of the Mean was translated in 1667 and the *Analects* in 1687, all in Latin. The three Classics were rendered into English in 1688 and into French three years later. When in 1711 the *Book of Mencius* was translated into Latin, the Four Books began to attract the attention of Western intellectuals. In 1881, the English missionary James Legge translated the Four Books into English and published them in Hong Kong. He secured the help of Confucian scholar Wang T'ao (1828–1897) and consulted the commentaries of Chu Hsi. Inevitably Chu Hsi's interpretation of the Confucian Classics dominated the translation. Legge's work is scholarly and generally accurate and after a hundred years is still considered as a standard work. Its influence in England and America has been great. In other words, the West has been reading and studying to some extent the Confucian doctrine of *jen* for some three hundred years. What has been its understanding? What has been its appraisal? And what is its tendency? From the survey above, we may roughly draw these conclusions: (1) Although *jen* as the general virtue was understood from the very early days, the fact that *jen* is a central concept in Confucianism is beginning to be appreciated only recently. (2) The West had always considered the Confucian Golden Rule as negative, contrasted with that of Christianity which is considered to be positive. There has been a turnaround but not quite complete. (3) The West has been favorable to the Moist doctrine of universal love and critical of the Confucian doctrine of love with distinctions. The reason for this is that the West has not studied the Neo-Confucian doctrine of principle being one and manifestations being many. (4) In the last thirty years, Western scholars have gradually analyzed the concept of *jen* in its various meanings. This is a most encouraging development. Nevertheless, because Western study of Neo-Confucianism developed only after World War II, there are still misunderstandings that need to be corrected and important aspects of *jen* that need to be expounded.

NOTES

Adapted from my *Jen ti kai-nien chih k'ai-chan yü Ou-Mei chih ch'ün-shih* (The development of the concept of *jen* and its interpretation in Europe and America), *Ju-hsüeh tsai cchih-chieh lwi-wen chi.* (Collection of essays on Confucianism in the world), The Humanist Society, Hong Kong, 1966, pp. 271–285; reprinted in *Neo-Confucianism, Etc., Essays by Wing-tsit Chan,* comp. by Charles H. K. Chen, New Hampshire, Hanover, Oriental Society, 1969, Chinese section, pp. 1–19.

1. Wing-tsit Chan, "The Evolution of the Confucian Concept *Jen,*" *Philosophy East and West* 4 (1955), 295–319; reprinted in *Neo-Confucianism, Etc.,* pp. 144.

2. *Book of Odes,* odes Nos. 77, 103, 204.

3. On whether Confucius really "seldom talked about *jen,*" see my discussion in work cited in Note 2, pp. 296–297.

4. *Mo Tzu,* Ch. 40 and 42, *Ssu-pu ts'ung-k'an* (Four Libraries series), ed., 10: 1a, 6b.

5. *Chuang Tzu,* Ch. 12, *Ssu-pu pei-yao* (Essentials of the Four Libraries series) ed. entitled *Nan-hua chen-ching* (True classic of Nan-hua), 5: 2b.

6. *Hsün Tzu,* Ch. 27, *Ssu-pu pei-yao* ed., 19: 5a.

7. *Han Fei-Tzu,* Ch. 20, *Ssu-pu pei-yao* ed., 6: 1a.

8. *Book of Rites,* Ch. 19.

9. *Kuo-yü,* 'Conversations of Chou,' *Ssu-pu pei-yao* ed., 3:3b.

10. Tung Chung-shu, *Ch'un-ch'iu fan-lu* (Luxuriant gems of the *Spring and Autumn*), Ch. 29 and 30, *Ssu-pu pei-yao* ed., 8: 9a, 12b.

11. Yang Hsiung, *T'ai-hsüan ching* (Classic of the supremely profound principle), Ch. 9, *Ssu-pu ts'ung-k'an* ed., 7: 8b, 9a.

12. In the *Analects, jen* and *i* are not spoken together. However, Confucius is quoted in many ancient works as speaking of *jen* and *i* together.

13. Han Yü, *Yüan tao* (Inquiry on the Way), in *Han Ch'ang-li ch'üan-chi* (Complete works of Han Yü), *Ssu-pu pei-yao* ed., 11:1A 5a. For a translation of the essay, see Wing-tsit Chan. *A Source Book in Chinese Philosophy,* Princeton University Press, Princeton, New Jersey, 1973, pp. 454–456.

14. *Mo Tsu,* Ch. 15.

15. *Kuo-yü;* Ch. 3 (3:3b).

16. Hsü Kan, *Chung-lun,* Ch. 9, *Ssu-pu ts'ung-k'an* ed., 1: 34a.

17. Pan Ku (32–92), *Po-hu t'ung, Ssu-pu ts'ung-k'an ed.,* 8: 1a–b.

18. Han Yü, *op cit.,* 11 : 6a. For a translation, see Chan, *Source Book,* pp. 451–453.

19. *Chang Tzu ch'üan-shu* (Complete works of Master Chang), Ch. 1. For a translation, see Chan, *Source Book,* pp. 497–498.

20. *Kuei-shan yü-lu* (Recorded sayings of Yang Shih), *Ssu-pu ts'ung-k'an* ed., 2: 18a, 3: 28a.

21. *Ibid.*

22. Commentary on the *Western Inscription* in the *Chang Tzu ch'üan-shu.*

23. *I-shu* (Surviving works), 2A : 3a, in Ch'eng Hao and Ch'eng I, *Erh-Ch'eng ch'üan* shu (Complete works of the two Ch'engs), *Ssu Pu pei-yao* ed.

24. *Su-wen* (Questions on original simplicity), Sec. 42.

25. *I-shu,* 2: 2a–b.

26. Referring to the *Book of Mencius,* 2A: 6.

27. *Wang Wen-ch'eng Kung ch'üan-shu,* (Complete works of Wang Yang-ming), *Ssu-pu ts'ung-k'an* ed., 26:1b–3a.

28. Hsi-tz'u (Appended remarks), Pt. 2, Ch. 1.

29. *Po-hu t'ung,* 8: 2a.

30. *T'ung-shu* (Penetrating the *Book of Changes*), Ch. 11.

31. *I-shu,* 11:3a–b.

32. Ts' ui-yen (Pure words), 1: 4b, in the *Erh-Ch'eng ch'üan-shu.*

33. *Shang-ts'ai yu-lu* (Recorded sayings of Hsieh Liang-tso), Pt. I, p. 2b.

34. *I chuan* (Commentary on the *Book of Changes*), 1: 2b, in the *Erh-Ch'eng ch'ün-shu.*

35. *I-shu,* 2A : 2a. It is not known which brother said this. The two brothers shared many ideas in common.

36. *T'ung-shu,* Ch. 21 and 37.

37. *I-shu,* 15: 8b.

38. *Shang-ts'ai yü-lu,* Pt. 1, ha.

39. Ibid., Pt. 2, p. 1a.

40. *Ts'ui-yen,* 1:4a.

41. *Chu Tzu Yü-lui* (Recorded conversations of Master Chu), 1880 edn., 6: 19b.

42. Quoting the Ch'eng brothers, *Wai-shu* (Additional works), 3: 1a, in the *Erh Ch'eng ch'üan-shu.*

43. *Chu Tzu-yü-lei,* 1:4a.

44. *Book of Mencius,* 6A:11.

45. *Chu Tzu wen-chi* (Collection of literary works by Master Chu), *Ssu-pu pei-yao,* ed. entitled *Chu Tzu ta-ch'üan* (Complete works of Master Chu), 67: 20a–21a.

STUDY QUESTIONS

1. Discuss the meaning and the significance of the following passage from the *Gītā:*

   > Removing all attachments to the fruits of action, ever content, independent—such a person even if engaged in action, does not do anything whatsoever.

   Do you think that the notion of *karma yoga* has any relevance for the culture you live in today? Explain why or why not?

2. Discuss the paths of knowledge, action, and devotion. Which path appeals to you more and why?

3. Discuss the relationship among the paths of knowledge, action, and devotion. Do these paths contradict one another, or is there a way in which the three can be synthesized? Give reasons for your answer.

4. What is good and what are its characteristics according to Aristotle?

5. Define virtue. Explain the distinction that Aristotle makes between intellectual and moral virtues.

6. Discuss Aristotle's concept of happiness? Is it a subjective (which takes one to be as happy as one feels) or objective (which implies having certain characteristics regardless of how one feels) notion? Argue pro or con.

7. What is virtue ethics? Some might argue that Aristotle's ethics is circular: If one asks what should one do in a particular situation, Aristotle would seem to say, "Do what a virtuous person would do"; But if one asks how one recognizes a virtuous person, he would seem to say, "a virtuous person is one who acts justly." Do you see the circularity here? Give reasons for your answer.

8. Discuss the aim of Kant's moral philosophy? Why does he reject empirical data in constructing a "pure moral philosophy"?

9. Why is a good will good without qualification? Analyze Kant's arguments here. Are they cogent?

10. Discuss the relationship between duty and inclination? Explain the distinction that Kant makes between actions done in accordance with duty and actions done for the sake of duty. Do you agree with Kant that acts done out of inclination have no moral worth?

11. What is the difference between a maxim and a principle of universal law? What is Categorical Imperative? How does it differ from hypothetical imperatives? Discuss the three formulations of Categorical Imperative. Are Kant's examples given to support his formulations convincing? Which formulation seems most defensible and why?

12. Critically discuss Kant's first formulation of the Categorical Imperative. Would the first formulation of the categorical imperative effectively

rule out the following: (a) cheating on a quiz, (b) betraying a secret, (c) misleading a very sick friend about the condition of his health. Give reasons for your answer.

13. Do you attach the same moral value to the conduct of a soldier who fights because he loves adventures and that of the one who, without this impulse, fights because he thinks he ought to do so? On the basis of your reading of the *Gītā* and Kant, where do you think these two would stand on the question? Discuss various similarities and the differences between the two. Which one appeals to you more and why?

14. How does Mill define utilitarianism?

15. Is utilitarianism a pig philosophy?

16. Do you agree with Mill that it is better to be Socrates dissatisfied than a pig satisfied?

17. Critically discuss the four noble truths of Buddha. Do you agree with Buddha that life is full of suffering?

18. Would you call Buddhism a pessimistic philosophy? Give reasons for your answer.

19. What is *dukkha?* What is the relationship between *dukkha* and craving? Do you agree with Buddha that the cessation of craving is cessation of *dukkha?* Why or why not?

20. Discuss the main characteristics and purpose of an Islamic state? Do you agree with Maududi that Allāh (God) should have the authority to rule? Argue for your position.

21. What makes a society just according to Maududi? Discuss the central tenets of his philosophy.

22. King maintains that injustice is a threat to justice anywhere. Do you agree with him? Give reasons for your answer. Would King allow you to break the law under some conditions? If so, why so? If not, why not?

23. Discuss King's central thesis and argue either for or against it.

24. Outline the essential differences between a just and an unjust law. Do we have the right to disobey unjust laws and take corrective measures? Why or why not?

25. Do you think King was an extremist? Give reasons for your answer.

26. Discuss Mo Tzu's conception of universal love. What are some of its main features?

27. Some might argue that universal love remains an attractive theoretical ideal, however, it is not possible in practice. Argue for or against this claim.

28. Summarize the main arguments given in *Euthyphro*. Who is more convincing, Socrates or Euthyphro? Explain why?

29. Discuss the nature of piety and impiety. Is God necessary for ethics? Give reasons.

30. Clearly outline the six Confucian virtues. How are they interrelated?
31. Discuss Chan's understanding of *jen*. Do you agree with his understanding? Is *jen* as "profound" as Chan makes it out to be?
32. What are the main theses of the *Ethics of Ambiguity* as outlined in the reading assignments? Is Simon de Beauvoir consistent in her claims? Argue for or against her position.
33. What makes a human being a moral being according to de Beauvoir? Discuss the significance of the distinction between "willing oneself not free" and "not willing oneself free"?
34. What is de Beauvoir's account of evil? Do you find her account convincing? Give reasons for your answer.
35. Discuss the concept of *ahiṃsā*. Is complete adherence to *ahiṃsā* possible in practice? Is there any Western concept that comes close to the Gandhian concept of *ahiṃsā*?
36. What is *satyāgraha*? Is this an effective tool to bring about social change? Give reasons for your answer.
37. You are the president of the United States and the nation is gearing up for war. There is much controversy over whether it is justified or not. You've become convinced, contrary to your initial belief, that the war would not be justified. Do you carry through with your initial plans to go to war because of the economic and political ramifications of backing down? or de-escalate the war preparation and withdraw your backing for it based on your newfound convictions? How would Mill decide, and why? How would Kant decide and why? What would the *Gītā* have to say on the topic? What would be King's response?
38. Formulate and discuss the important issues between deontologists and teleologists. What problems can the one solve that the other cannot, and why are these problems significant? You may, to make your answer more specific, choose a deontologist (Kant), and a teleologist (Mill), although you are free to formulate your comparison in any manner you wish.
39. Suppose a hedonist is to argue, "I believe that everyone should strive to achieve the greatest possible amount of pleasure. In other words, whenever I seek pleasure I am entirely willing that the motive from which I act (that is, the Greatest Happiness Principle) should be a universal law governing the actions of everyone. I am therefore a good Kantian at the same time that I am a good Utilitarian." How would Kant have been likely to reply to this argument?
40. Select one of the moral philosophies discussed above. What are its main tenets? Give the reasons for your selection. Will the moral philosophy that you have selected help you in making decisions? Will it tell you how to live? Answer in detail.

41. "Unlike Confucius, Buddha was neither interested in the mysteries of the universe nor in the foretelling of the future." Compare and contrast Confucius and Buddha as ethical teachers and reformers. Indicate clearly specific points of similarity and difference. Explain which one appeals to you the most—and why.

42. Do you see any parallels between the Gandhian philosophy and that of Martin Luther King? Discuss the similarities as well as the differences.

SUGGESTIONS FOR FURTHER READING

Kant's Moral Philosophy by H.B. Acton (London: Macmillan, 1970) is a good brief account of Kant.

Probably the best way to begin your study of Gandhi is to see the 1982 film *Gāndhi,* directed by Richard A. Attenborough. It does a very good job of highlighting the key issues that India was facing during that time.

Black Power by S. Carmichael and C. Hamilton (New York: Vintage Press, 1967) gives a good account of King's general philosophy.

The Analects of Confucius by D.C. Lau (England: Penguin Classic, 1979) is a readable translation of the *Analects* with an introduction and notes.

Confucius and the Chinese Way by H.G. Creel (New York: Harper & Row, 1960, first published in 1949 by John Day Co.) is still, thirty-nine years since its publication, one of the best books available to begin the study of Confucius.

The Philosophy of Mahatma Gandhi, by Dhirendra Mohan Datta (Madison: University of Wisconsin Press, 1953) is a good introduction to the philosophy of Gandhi.

Sources of Chinese Tradition, 2 vols., compiled by William Theodore de Bary, Wing-tsit Chan, and Burton Watson (New York: Columbia University Press, 1964), is a good source for any facet of Chinese civilization. It contains extremely useful introductions as well as clear translations.

Islam in Transition: Muslim Perspectives edited by John J. Donohue and John L. Esposito (New York: Oxford University Press, 1982), contains an excellent selection of articles on Islamic political and social theory from a modern perspective.

The Beginnings of Indian Philosophy by Franklin Edgerton (Cambridge, Mass.: Harvard University Press, 1965) provides an excellent thirty-page introduction to early Indian thought followed by careful translations from the Vedas, the Upaniṣads, the *Gītā,* and the Mahābhārata.

The Wretched of the Earth by Franz Fanon (New York: Grove Press, 1965) provides an excellent account of racism and black liberation.

Confucius—The Secular as Sacred by Herbert Fingarette (New York: Harper & Row, 1972) is a classic philosophical interpretation of ceremony and ritual (*li*) in the thought of Confucius.

Story of My Experiments with Truth, Gandhi's autobiography, is available in many editions.

Dreadful Freedom: A Critique of Existentialism by M. Grene (Chicago: University of Chicago Press, 1948) is a critical examination of the basic existentialist issues.

The Bhagavad Gītā translated by Franklin Edgerton (Cambridge, Mass: Harvard University Press, 1944) is a readable translation with helpful commentary and index.

Plato: The Collected Dialogues edited by Edith Hamilton and Huntington Cairns (New York: Pantheon Books, 1961), contains a chapter on Euthyphro. The introductory essay on Plato's philosophy is quite good; the book also contains a comprehensive index.

Chinese Language Thought and Culture edited by P. J. Ivanhoe (Chicago: Open Court, 1990), is an excellent collection of articles by present-day scholars that gives a good sense of the interaction of the Chinese thought with the Western intellectual world.

Ethics in the Confucian Tradition by P. J. Ivanhoe (Atlanta, Ga.: Scholars Press, 1990) provides a good account of the development of ethical issues in the writings of Mencius and Wang Yang-ming.

The Moral and Political Thought of Mahatma Gandhi by R. Iyer (New York: Oxford University Press) provides an excellent account of the subject matter.

The Nichomachean Ethics by H.H. Joachim (London: Oxford University Press, 1954) contains a good discussion of basic issues of Aristotle's ethics.

Foundations of the Metaphysics of Morals translated by Lewis White Beck (Indianapolis: Bobbs Merrill, 1959), is one of the best translations in English of Kant's major ethical writings.

Ethical and Political Works of Mo-Tzu translated by Yi-Pao Mei, is a good translation of Mo-Tzu's writings.

What the Buddha Taught by Walpola Rahula contains a very clear analysis of the Four Noble Truths and the Noble Eightfold Path of Buddha from the Therāvāda perspective.

Aristotle by W.D. Ross (New York: University Paperbacks, 1923) has a chapter on Aristotle's ethics. It provides a very good account of the key ideas of Aristotle's ethics.

The Right and the Good by W. D. Ross presents an uncompromising attack on Utilitarianism: (Oxford: Oxford University Press, 1930).

Concept of Islam by Mahmoud Abu-Saud (Indianapolis: American Trust Publications, 1983) is a good introduction to the basic ideas of Islam.

Mill's Ethical Writings edited by J. B. Schneewind (New York: Collier, 1965) is a good collection of several of Mill's writings.

Utilitarianism and Beyond edited by Amartya Sen and Bernard Williams (Cambridge: Cambridge University Press, 1982) is an anthology of more recent articles on the subject.

Plato—the Man and His Works by A. E. Taylor gives a detailed analysis of Plato's dialogues with an excellent commentary. This is a very useful book on Plato's thoughts.

Mo-Tzu: The Basic Writings translated by Burton Watson (New York: Columbia University Press, 1963), is an excellent translation that beginning students should consult.

Kant: Foundations of the Metaphysics of Morals: Text and Critical Essays edited by Robert Paul Wolff (Indianapolis: Bobbs-Merrill, 1969), is a helpful collection of writings on Kant's ethics.

Part 4

Religion

4.1

Introduction: Does God Exist? What Is the Nature of God?

If ethics is concerned with the relation of persons to other persons (and, arguably, to other sentient beings), religion is principally either (1) a person's relation to God (conceived as the creator of the universe) or to what is the innermost spirit deep within one's being (understood as *ātman* or self), as well as in all beings, or (2) concerned with the ultimate destiny and goal of human existence conceived as "salvation," "liberation," "*mokṣa*" or "*nirvāṇa*." While it is common to regard God as the central theme of religious thought, that certainly is not acceptable in view of the fact that there are religions such as Buddhism (at least in its earliest formulation) which are atheistic, and there are religions, such as Advaita Vedānta, which look upon the God of the theist to be an appearance of the universal spirit or *Brahman* to the finite individual. But whatever religion one takes into account, there is no denying the fact that the ultimate concern of every religion is a higher form of human existence freed from the frailties of mundane existence and marked by freedom from suffering and blessedness. It is in this sense that we have to understand Kant's formulation of the central question of religion as "what can we hope for?"

Philosophy of religion is either revealed theology (in which case it is a conceptual articulation of a body of revealed texts) *or* purely philosophical (in which case it establishes the truth of a religion by independent arguments). Thus, the "five ways" given by Aquinas are purely philosophical arguments inasmuch as they do not make use of the scriptural texts at all. Sri Aurobindo's "Reality Omnipresent" is an exposition of the metaphysical position of Advaita Vedānta as interpreted by him, an idea that he thought would have far-reaching implications for transformation of the life of an individual as well as for humankind. The Islamic conception of God is based upon the scriptural text *Qur'ān,* of which al Qāsimī gives a modern exposition. The Zen stands at the other end of the spectrum of the range of religions: it is, or claims to be, purely experiential.

The theistic arguments for proving the existence of God have played an important role in the history of Western philosophy during the past sixteen hundred years. St. Augustine (354–430), in his writings, took the existence of God for granted. The existence of God was taken to be so self-evident that proof to demonstrate his existence was taken to be superfluous. Like St. Augustine, whom he sought to emulate, St. Anselm of Canterbury (1225–1275) perceived his role to be that of an apologist for Christian orthodoxy. He formulated the ontological argument to demonstrate that God truly exists, that there is a supreme good which requires nothing else and which all other things require for their existence.

The argument begins with the concept of the most perfect being and argues that such a being cannot be conceived not to exist. The thrust of the argument is as follows: "By the term 'God' is meant being than which none greater can be conceived; such a God exists in understanding; existing in both understanding and reality is greater than merely existing in understanding; therefore, God exists." Accordingly St. Anselm argues that God is an all-perfect being which contains all conceivable perfections. However, if in addition to possessing omnipotence, omniscience, etc., if this being did not possess existence then it would be less perfect than if it possessed the attribute of existence. Since God by definition is all-perfect, he must exist. St. Anselm tries to demonstrate that the concept of a non-existent God is logically self-contradictory. He tries to prove the existence of God by drawing our attention, not to some observed feature of the world, but entirely from the idea of God that we human beings entertain. It is an a priori proof, which means that it is based on principles that can be known independently of one's experience of the world.

Thomas Aquinas (1225–1275), one of the greatest medieval philosopher-theologians, sought to reconcile Augustinian Christianity with the teachings of Aristotle by arguing that the existence of God can be proved in "five ways." None of the "five ways" originated with Aquinas, nor did he claim that they did. Historically, these ways can be traced to the writings of Plato and Aristotle.

Aquinas rejected St. Anselm's ontological argument on the ground that one cannot prove the existence of God merely by considering the meaning of the term "God." Unlike the ontological argument, which begins with the idea of God and then proceeds to unfold its implications, Thomas Aquinas's cosmological argument rests on a premise or principle that can be known only with the help of our experience of the world. In his "five ways" to prove the existence of God, Thomas Aquinas argues that there cannot be a world with some particular feature unless there were also the reality we call "God." The first argues from the fact of motion to a first mover, which is moved by no other. Things are in motion. A's motion is caused by B's and B's by C's and so on. Either there is some unmoved mover or we must suppose an infinite regress of motions, which is absurd. This unmoved mover who starts the first movement and is responsible for all subsequent motion is none other than God. The second argues from the nature of efficient cause to a first efficient cause. We know that material things do not come into existence by themselves. Either there is an infinite series of causes or there is a first uncaused cause. An infinity of causes is impossible, so there must be a first uncaused cause and that cause is none other than God. The third argues that if everything were contingent (that is, may have not existed), then at one time nothing existed, from which it would follow that even now nothing exists, which is not the case. So there must be something that necessarily exists and does not derive its necessity from something else. The fourth argument starts from the fact that things can be ordered as having more or less of goodness, truth, and nobility, and that there must be something which possesses these qualities in the highest degree (and which, for that reason, causes other things to possess these qualities in whatever degree they do). The fifth and the last way is to argue that the things in the world show a design, such that they achieve an end in the best possible way, and that such a design would not have been possible on the part of unconscious things unless they were guided by an intelligent being. All these "ways" prove the existence of the same being which is called by the name "God."

Both ontological and cosmological arguments have been subjected to severe critical examinations. One of the basic objections against the ontological argument tries to demonstrate that one cannot prove the existence of a thing merely from the idea of it. The most devastating attack upon this argument comes from Kant, who argues that existence is not a quality or characteristic or property, that is, it has a very different function from property words like "red" or "blue" or "green." "My shirt is blue" resembles the proposition "My shirt exists"; however, to attribute "blueness" to a shirt is different from attributing "existence" to it. Kant points out that existence is not a real predicate, insofar as it is not a property which may be predicated on the concept of a thing (and so cannot analytically follow from a concept). If it were a real predicate, and not simply a grammatical predicate, it would form part of the definition of the term "God." It might well be the case that God exists; however, one cannot prove it from the idea of God.

The logical structure of each of the "five ways" of Aquinas has been very much debated by Western and non-Western scholars alike. In this Introduction, however, we are not concerned with the logical formulations of these arguments. The first three ways are very similar. They make use of a premise that is not obviously true. For many thinkers—the premise, namely, that "this cannot go on to infinity," and the way Thomas Aquinas justifies this premise has the appearance of begging the issue. The search for the cause of the motion cannot go on to infinity, we are told, "because then there would be no first mover"; likewise, the search for efficient causes cannot go on to infinity, "for there will be no first efficient cause"; and finally, the search for the necessary thing cannot go on to infinity in necessary things that have their necessity caused by another "for there will be no uncaused necessity." In each of these cases, the argument is intended to prove that there is a first mover, a first efficient cause, and an uncaused necessary cause. Arguments 1 and 2 make use of the idea of causality, especially of efficient causation. Arguments 1 and 3 make use of the "modal" concepts of potentiality-actuality and contingency-necessity.

One of the strongest criticisms against the cosmological argument attempts to demonstrate that the conclusion of the first three arguments i.e., unmoved mover, uncaused cause, and uncaused necessary cause contradicts its premise that for everything there is a cause. Kant, in his attack on this argument, points out that these arguments do not logically yield the theistic conclusion, and that for every such theistic argument, an argument yielding the opposite conclusion is possible. This criticism not only applies to the ontological and cosmological arguments, but also to other arguments, i.e., the moral and the teleological, as well. However, the moral argument (that God is the source of the moral law) and the teleological argument (that nature, despite its mathematical structure, can still be looked upon as if it were also purposive) remain, for Kant, the strongest among all theistic proofs.

We should like to add here that it would be wrong to suppose that the the theistic arguments belong only to the Judeo-Christian tradition. The Hindu theists, especially of the Nyāya-Vaiśeṣika school, advanced several arguments to prove—against the Buddhists who denied the existence of God—that the world was created by an omniscient, omnipotent, and wise being who is also the source of the moral laws enjoined in the Vedic scriptures and whose wisdom accounts for the purposiveness to be found in nature. However, for the Hindu theists, the souls, even the finite souls, are immortal, and even God cannot act against the law of *karma,* so that God creates in accordance with the laws of *karma.* The absolute power of creation, which is ascribed to God in Islam, whereby everything is a new creation which he produces by his power from non-existence, is not to be found in Hinduism.

Very early in the history of Hinduism, as noted in the *Nāsadīyasūkta* of the *Ṛg Veda,* the idea of creation out of nothing was rejected in favor of the origin of the universe out of one primal being, which later in the Upaniṣads was characterized as *Brahman* or *ātman.* Originally the process of creation was conceived as emanation, on the analogy of the spiderweb emerging out of the spider's body (*Muṇḍaka Upaniṣads,* I.1.7); it seemed as if *brahman-ātman* was immanent in the universe as its indwelling spirit exactly in the same way as a lump of salt dissolved in a bucket of water that pervades it. In course of time, however, creativity was ascribed to *māyāśakti,* the power of Brahman to produce the world of names and forms and this creation was sought to be understood with the analogy of an illusory, false appearance superimposed on reality owing to one's ignorance of the nature of reality. In Śaṃkara's Vedānta, the world is reduced to the status of illusory phenomena. The chapter from Śrī Aurobindo included in this volume claims to return to the original intention of the Vedic texts and to conceive of *Brahman* as "Reality Omnipresent." The chapter is taken from Śrī Aurobindo's *magnum opus The Life Divine,* in which he propounds what he calls "Integral Advaita" or integral nondualism as opposed to Śaṃkara's pure nondualism. What Śrī Aurobindo proposes is to break down the oppositions between matter and spirit, between the one and the many, between the immutable being and the dynamic creativity, between withdrawal and active engagement. The integral *Brahman,* on his view, according to the Upaniṣads, comprehends all of these aspects within its unity.

What is the place of religion in Chinese thought? The interpretation of Chinese thought that exclusively emphasizes its anthropocentric nature is rejected by many scholars today. Thus Tu Wei Ming finds in it cosmological inspiration as well as an anthropological vision. Politics and religion, rather than economy and technology, provide the original impetus. According to Tu Wei Ming, even Confucian thought is deeply religious; human self-creation is brought about through poetry, ritual, and music. Mencius recognizes six stages of human development: goodness, truth, beauty, greatness, sageliness, and spirituality. The Taoists ask us to attend to the cosmic process and to live in attunement with it. Thus Chinese religiosity fundamentally consists in living in accordance with the cosmos or the Way. The idea of a personal creator God that dominates Western religious thinking is replaced by a conception of divinity that is formless, holistic, and impersonal, which, like Spinoza's substance, is the cosmos. Thus what we have is "divinity without theology," "religiosity without theistic belief"—in Whitehead's inimitable words religion as "world-loyalty."

It is in light of this brief characterization of Chinese religiosity that we should read Wang Ch'ung's (27–100? C.E.) essay "On Spontaneity." Wang Ch'ung was an independent thinker who was not attached to any school. Skepticism, critical spirit, scientific method, revolt against the past beliefs and dogmas characterize his thinking. His goal was to rid Chinese thought of superstitions that had beset the Chinese thinking of his times and reinforce the critical and rational spirit among human beings. Among the many important Chinese beliefs that he rejected, the most severe was his attack on the existence of a conscious life after death. The Chinese in the ancient times believed that souls of the dead assumed human form and appeared among humans to hurt them. His rejection of conscious life after death is one of the earliest and most exhaustive accounts of the issue, which assumed great significance in Chinese thought after the introduction of Buddhism in China.

He rejects any belief in a personal deity, and defends the spontaneity of the natural order. Like Taoists, he argues that the natural order is without any consciousness and purpose and that such an order is pure and functions spontaneously. He defends non-intentional action on the part of nature which amounts to "action without acting," that it is this generative and re-generative process that is the Way in accordance with which we should orient our lives.

Recall the Sāṃkhya ascription of an unconscious teleology to *prakṛti* (or nature), explained analogically to a rain cloud bursting forth into rain to serve human needs on earth, without any guidance from a conscious deity. Also recall the *Bhagavad Gītā's* statement that all actions belong to nature as if ruled by a machine. Or the Buddhist theories of dependent origination, by knowing which one recognizes the emptiness and essencelessness of all things, and becomes free and compassionate and egoless.

Earlier in the introductory essay, we have referred to Buddhism as a religion that has no need of a concept of God. But it does have other marks of a religion: it is guided by the soteriological idea of *nirvāṇa,* it has a conception of selfhood that is deeper and more profound than the ordinary belief in an undying soul, it has an awareness of an inner relation between the individual and the cosmos, and it teaches an ethic of virtues culminating in the virtue of compassion. The essay on Buddhism as an experiential religion is, in this volume, devoted to "Zen Enlightenment" written by a Japanese scholar and practitioner of Zen. The Japanese name "Zen" is derived from the Chinese "Ch'an" and the latter from Indian "*dhyāna*" meaning "meditation." The school of Yogācāra Buddhism had already emphasized *yogic* practices; in China, it came under Taoist influence and led to the rise of Ch'an. The belief that everything possesses a Buddha-nature, taken to be in accordance with Nāgārjuna's teaching of "emptiness" (*śūnyatā*), led to the goal of experiencing the emptiness in a state of enlightenment. Around the ninth century C.E., two branches of Ch'an developed in Japan: the Rinzai and the Sōtō. The Rinzai used a paradoxical question or statement in answer to a question, known as *Koan,* to deconceptualize the mind and to bring about enlightenment instantaneously. The Sōtō school, founded by Dōgen in the thirteenth century C.E., emphasized sitting in meditation and studying the scripture.

The essay by Kaiten Nukariya brings out several interesting features of Zen enlightenment. Zen, like classical Buddhism, denies an immortal soul, does not sharply separate the body and the mind (the body is mind observed outwardly, the mind is the body experienced inwardly), asserts the unity of all selves, takes nature to be the root cause of all things, and takes the real self to be present in all sentient beings. Enlightenment consists in realizing the real self, purifying the mind, and experiencing the emptiness of all things and the presence of the Buddha-nature everywhere, even in the apparently most insignificant of things. The author also shows how Zen understands the relation between appearance and reality: the two cannot be separated. The reality is in the appearances and the appearances are the real as presented to the human mind. The Zen philosophy becomes a mixture of the Taoist metaphysics, Upaniṣadic concept of *ātman,* Mādhyamika idea of emptiness—all to be experienced in an instant of enlightenment here and now on this earth. The experience is closer to aesthetic experience in which mundane objects and things around acquire a new and ineffable significance.

If belief in God or even belief in a transcendent reality (as Zen illustrates), is not the essence of religion, what then constitutes religion? Or, what constitutes the essence of religious experience? Shall we say religious experience must be experience of sacredness? Shall we say, "the sacred" is the ultimate, further unanalyzable and irreducible category of the religious domain, just as beauty is the central category of aesthetics?

4.2

The Ontological Argument

St. Anselm

. . . Lord, I acknowledge and I thank thee that thou hast created me in this, thine image, in order that I may be mindful of thee, may conceive of thee, and love thee; but that image has been so consumed and wasted away by vices, and obscured by the smoke of wrong-doing, that it cannot achieve that for which it was made, except thou renew it, and create it anew. I do not endeavor, Lord, to penetrate thy sublimity, for in no wise do I compare my understanding with that; but I long to understand in some degree thy truth, which my heart believes and loves. For I do not seek to understand that I may believe, but I believe in order to understand. For this also I believe—that unless I believed, I should not understand.

CHAPTER 2

Truly there is a God, although the fool hath said in his heart, there is no God.

And so, Lord, do thou, who dost give understanding to faith, give me, so far as thou knowest it to be profitable, to understand that thou art as we believe; and that thou art that which we believe. And, indeed, we believe that thou art a being than which nothing greater can be conceived. Or is there no such nature, since the fool hath said in his heart, there is no God? . . . But, at any rate, this very fool, when he hears of this being of which I speak—a being than which nothing greater can be conceived—understands what he hears, and what he understands is in his understanding; although he does

From Chapters 1, 2, 3, and 4 of *Proslogium,* trans. by Sidney Norton Deane, pp. 6–10 (La Salle, Ill.: The Open Court Publishing Co., 1903).

not understand it to exist. For, it is one thing for an object to be in the understanding, and another to understand that the object exists. When a painter first conceives of what he will afterwards perform, he has it in his understanding, but he does not yet understand it to be, because he has not yet performed it. But after he has made the painting, he both has it in his understanding, and he understands that it exists, because he has made it.

Hence, even the fool is convinced that something exists in the understanding, at least, than which nothing greater can be conceived. For, when he hears of this, he understands it. And whatever is understood exists in the understanding. And assuredly that than which nothing greater can be conceived cannot exist in the understanding alone. For, suppose it exists in the understanding alone: then it can be conceived to exist in reality; which is greater.

Therefore, if that than which nothing greater can be conceived exists in the understanding alone, the very being than which nothing greater can be conceived is one than which a greater can be conceived. But obviously this is impossible. Hence, there is no doubt that there exists a being than which nothing greater can be conceived, and it exists both in the understanding and in reality.

CHAPTER 3

God cannot be conceived not to exist—God is that, than which nothing greater can be conceived—That which can be conceived not to exist is not God.

And it assuredly exists so truly that it cannot be conceived not to exist. For, it is possible to conceive of a being which cannot be conceived not to exist; and this is greater than one which can be conceived not to exist. Hence, if that than which nothing greater can be conceived can be conceived not to exist, it is not that than which nothing greater can be conceived. But this is an irreconcilable contradiction. There is, then, so truly a being than which nothing greater can be conceived to exist, that it cannot even be conceived not to exist; and this being thou art, O Lord, our God.

So truly, therefore, dost thou exist, O Lord, my God, that thou canst not be conceived not to exist; and rightly. For, if a mind could conceive of a being better than thee, the creature would rise above the Creator; and this is most absurd. And, indeed, whatever else there is, except thee alone, can be conceived not to exist. To thee alone, therefore, it belongs to exist more truly than all other beings, and hence in a higher degree than all others. For, whatever else exists does not exist so truly, and hence in a less degree it belongs to it to exist. Why, then, has the fool said in his heart, there is no God

. . . since it is so evident, to a rational mind, that thou dost exist in the highest degree of all? Why, except that he is dull and a fool?

CHAPTER 4

> Hence the fool has said in his heart which cannot be conceived—A thing
> may be conceived in two ways: (1) when the word signifying it is con-
> ceived; (2) when the thing itself is understood as far as the word goes,
> God cannot be conceived not to exist; in reality he cannot.

But how has the fool said in his heart what he could not conceive; or how is it that he could not conceive what he said in his heart? Since it is the same to say in the heart, and to conceive.

But, if really, nay, since really, he both conceived, because he said in his heart, and did not say in his heart, because he could not conceive, there is more than one way in which a thing is said in the heart or conceived. For, in one sense, an object is conceived when the word signifying it is conceived; and in another, when the very entity which the object is, is understood.

In the former sense, then God can be conceived not to exist; but in the latter, not at all. For no one who understands what fire and water are can conceive fire to be water, in accordance with the nature of the facts themselves, although this is possible according to the words. So, then, no one who understands what God is can conceive that God does not exist; although he says these words in his heart, either without any, or with some, foreign signification. For, God is that than which a greater cannot be conceived. And he who thoroughly understands this assuredly understands that this being so truly exists, that not even in concept can it be non-existent. Therefore, he who understands that God so exists cannot conceive that he does not exist.

I thank thee, gracious Lord, I thank thee; because what I formerly believed by thy bounty, I now so understand by thine illumination, that if I were unwilling to believe that thou dost exist, I should not be able not to understand this to be true.

4.3

The Cosmological Argument

St. Thomas Aquinas

Objection 1. It seems that God does not exist; because if one of two contraries be infinite, the other would be altogether destroyed. But the name *God* means that He is infinite goodness. If, therefore, God existed, there would be no evil discoverable; but there is evil in the world. Therefore God does not exist.

Obj. 2. Further, it is superfluous to suppose that what can be accounted for by a few principles has been produced by many. But it seems that everything we see in the world can be accounted for by other principles, supposing God did not exist. For all natural things can be reduced to one principle, which is nature; and all voluntary things can be reduced to one principle, which is human reason or will. Therefore there is no need to suppose God's existence.

On the Contrary, It is said in the person of God: *I am Who am* (*Exod.* iii. 14).

I answer that, The existence of God can be proved in five ways.

The first and more manifest way is the argument from motion. It is certain, and evident to our senses, that in the world some things are in motion. Now whatever is moved is moved by another, for nothing can be moved except it is in potentiality to that towards which it is moved; whereas a thing moves inasmuch as it is in actuality. For motion is nothing else than the reduction of something from potentiality to actuality. But nothing can be reduced from potentiality to actuality, except by something in a state of actuality. Thus that which is actually hot, as fire, makes wood, which is potentially hot, to be actually hot, and thereby moves and changes it. Now it is not possible that the same thing should be at once in actuality and potentiality in the same respect, but only in different respects. For what is actually hot cannot simultaneously be potentially hot; but it is simultaneously potentially cold. It is

From *The Basic Writings of St. Thomas Aquinas,* edited and annotated with an introduction by Anton C. Pegis, Vol. I, pp. 21–23. Copyright © by Random House, Inc., 1945.

therefore impossible that in the same respect and in the same way a thing should be both mover and moved, *i.e.,* that it should move itself. Therefore, whatever is moved must be moved by another. If that by which it is moved be itself moved, then this also must needs be moved by another, and that by another again. But this cannot go on to infinity, because then there would be no first mover, and, consequently, no other mover, seeing that subsequent movers move only inasmuch as they are moved by the first mover; as the staff moves only because it is moved by the hand. Therefore it is necessary to arrive at a first mover, moved by no other; and this everyone understands to be God.

The second way is from the nature of efficient cause. In the world of sensible things we find there is an order of efficient causes. There is no case known (neither is it, indeed, possible) in which a thing is found to be the efficient cause of itself; for so it would be prior to itself, which is impossible. Now in efficient causes it is not possible to go on to infinity, because in all efficient causes following in order, the first is the cause of the intermediate cause, and the intermediate is the cause of the ultimate cause, whether the intermediate cause be several, or one only. Now to take away the cause is to take away the effect. Therefore, if there be no first cause among efficient causes, there will be no ultimate, nor any intermediate, cause. But if in efficient causes it is possible to go on to infinity, there will be no first efficient cause, neither will there be an ultimate effect, nor any intermediate efficient causes; all of which is plainly false. Therefore it is necessary to admit a first efficient cause, to which everyone gives the name of God.

The third way is taken from possibility and necessity, and runs thus. We find in nature things that are possible to be and not to be, since they are found to be generated, and to be corrupted, and consequently, it is possible for them to be and not to be. But it is impossible for these always to exist, for that which cannot be at some time is not. Therefore, if everything cannot be, then at one time there was nothing in existence. Now if this were true, even now there would be nothing in existence, because that which does not exist begins to exist only through something already existing. Therefore, if at one time nothing was in existence, it would have been impossible for anything to have begun to exist; and thus even now nothing would be in existence—which is absurd. Therefore, not all beings are merely possible but there must exist something the existence of which is necessary. But every necessary thing either has its necessity caused by another, or not. Now it is impossible to go on to infinity in necessary things which have their necessity caused by another, as has been already proved in regard to efficient causes. Therefore we cannot but admit the existence of some being having of itself its own necessity, and not receiving it from another, but rather causing in others their necessity. This all men speak of as God.

The fourth way is taken from the gradation to be found in things. Among beings there are some more and some less good, true, noble, and the like. But *more* and *less* are predicated of different things according as they resemble in their different ways something which is the maximum, as a thing is said to be hotter according as it more nearly resembles that which is hottest; so that there is something which is truest, something best, something noblest, and, consequently, something which is most being, for those things that are greatest in truth are greatest in being, as it is written in [Aristotle's] *Metaphysics* ii. Now the maximum in any genus is the cause of all in that genus, as fire, which is the maximum of heat, is the cause of all hot things, as is said in the same book. Therefore there must also be some thing which is to all beings the cause of their being, goodness, and every other perfection; and this we call God.

The fifth way is taken from the governance of the world. We see that things which lack knowledge, such as natural bodies, act for an end, and this is evident from their acting always, or nearly always, in the same way, so as to obtain the best result. Hence it is plain that they achieve their end, not fortuitously, but designedly. Now whatever lacks knowledge cannot move towards an end, unless it be directed by some being endowed with knowledge and intelligence; as the arrow is directed by the archer. Therefore some intelligent being exists by whom all natural things are directed to their end: and this being we call God.

Reply Obj. 1. As Augustine says: *Since God is the highest good, He would not allow any evil to exist in His works; unless His omnipotence and goodness were such as to bring good even out of evil.* This is part of the infinite goodness of God, that He should allow evil to exist, and out of it produce good.

Reply Obj. 2. Since nature works for a determinate end under the direction of a higher agent, whatever is done by nature must be traced back to God as to its first cause. So likewise whatever is done voluntarily must be traced back to some higher cause other than human reason and will, since these can change and fail; for all things that are changeable and capable of defect must be traced back to an immovable and self-necessary first principle, as has been shown.

4.4

On Spontaneity and A Discussion of Death

Wang Ch'ung

ON SPONTANEITY

When the material forces (*ch'i*) of Heaven and Earth come together, all things are spontaneously produced, just as when the vital forces (*ch'i*) of husband and wife unite, children are naturally born. Among the things thus produced, blood creatures are conscious of hunger and cold. Seeing that the five grains are edible, they obtain and eat them. And seeing that silk and hemp can be worn, they obtain and wear them. Some say that Heaven produces the five grains in order to feed man and produces silk and hemp in order to clothe man. This is to say that Heaven becomes a farmer or a mulberry girl for the sake of man. This is contrary to spontaneity. Therefore their ideas are suspect and should not be followed.

Let us discuss these concepts according to Taoism. Heaven (*T'ien*, Nature) gives forth and distributes material force universally into all things. Grains overcome hunger and silk and hemp save people from cold. Consequently people eat grains and wear clothing of silk and hemp. Now, that Heaven does not purposely produce the five grains and silk and hemp in order to feed and clothe man is very much like the fact that there are calamities and strange transformations but not for the purpose of reprimanding man. Things are spontaneously produced and man eats them and wears them,

---

and material forces spontaneously change [in strange ways] and people are afraid of them. To talk otherwise may be agreeable to the minds of people. But if lucky influences from Heaven are intentional, where would spontaneity be, and where would non-action (*wu-wei*) be found?

How do we [know] that Heaven is spontaneous? Because It has neither mouth nor eyes. Those who engage in [purposive] action are something like those with mouth and eyes. The mouth desires to eat and the eyes desire to see. When something is desired inside, that desire is expressed outside, and the mouth and eyes seek for that thing, considering it an advantage to have it. This is the activity of desire. Now that there is no desire in the mouth or the eyes, there is no demand for things. What is any [intentional] act for?

How do we know that Heaven has neither mouth nor eyes? We know it from Earth. The body of Earth is made up of dirt, and dirt of course has neither mouth nor eyes. Heaven and Earth are like husband and wife. Since the body of the Earth has neither mouth nor eyes, we know that Heaven also has neither mouth nor eyes. If Heaven consists of a body, it should be similar to that of the Earth. If Heaven consists of vital force, it would be clouds and fog. How can things like clouds and fog have a mouth or an eye?

Someone says: Everything that moves is from the beginning engaged in action. It moves because it has desires. Since it moves, it is engaged in action. Now, the activities of Heaven are similar to those of man. How can we say that it takes no action?

I reply: The activities of Heaven consist in the giving forth and distributing of the material force. As the body moves, the material force issues forth, and things are then produced. It is like the fact that as one's vital force is moved, his body moves, the vital force issues forth, and a child is produced. When man gives forth and distributes his vital force, it is not for the purpose of producing a child. As the vital force is distributed, a child is born spontaneously. Heaven moves without the desire to produce things and yet things are produced of themselves. That is spontaneity. When material force is given forth and distributed without the purpose of producing things and yet things are produced of themselves, that is non-action. What do we mean when we say that Heaven is spontaneous and takes no action? It is material force. It is tranquil, without desire, and is engaged in neither action nor business.

When the Taoists talk about spontaneity, they do not know how to recite facts to prove their theory or practice. That is why their doctrine of spontaneity has not yet found credence. However, in spite of spontaneity, there must also be activity to help. Ploughing, tilling, weeding, and sowing in the spring are human activities. After the grains have entered the soil, they grow by day and night. It is not something man can do. If someone tries to do it, that would be a way to spoil them. A man of Sung was sorry that his corn was not growing. He went and pulled them up. The next day it dried up and died.[1] Those who take action to be spontaneous are like the man of Sung.

Someone asks: Man is born from Heaven and Earth. Since Heaven and Earth take no action and since man is endowed with the nature of Heaven [and Earth]; he should take no action either. And yet he does take action. Why?

I reply: A person who is rich and pure in perfect virtue is endowed with a large quantity of vital force and is therefore able to approximate Heaven in being spontaneous and taking no action. Those who are endowed with little vital force do not follow moral principles and do not resemble Heaven and Earth. They are therefore called unworthy. By that is meant that they are not similar to Heaven and Earth. Since they do not resemble Heaven and Earth, they do not belong to the same class as sages and worthies and therefore take action.

Heaven and Earth are like a furnace. Their work is creation. Since the endowment of the vital force is not the same in all cases, how can all be worthy? . . .

The Way of Heaven is to take no action. Therefore in the spring it does not act to start life, in summer it does not act to help grow, in autumn it does not act to bring maturity, and in winter it does not act to store up. When the material force of yang comes forth itself, things naturally come to life and grow. When the material force of yin arises of itself, things naturally mature and are stored up. When we draw water from wells or breach water over a dam in order to irrigate fields and gardens, things will also grow. But if rain falls like torrents, soaking through all stalks, leaves, and roots, in an amount equivalent to that in a pond, who would prefer drawing water from wells or breaching water over a dam? Therefore to act without acting is great. Originally no result is sought, and yet results are achieved originally no fame is sought, and yet fame is attained. Great indeed is the achievement and fame of abundant rain. Yet Heaven and Earth do not act for them. When the material forces are united in harmony, the rain gathers of itself. . . .

A DISCUSSION OF DEATH

People say that when men die they become ghosts with consciousness and the power to harm others. If we try to test this theory by comparing men with other creatures, however, we find that men do not become ghosts, nor do they have consciousness or power to harm. . . . Man lives because of his vital force (*ch'i*) and when he dies this vital force is extinguished. The vital force is able to function because of the blood system, but when a man dies the blood system ceases to operate. With this the vital force is extinguished and the body decays and turns to clay. What is there to become a ghost then? If a man is without ears or eyes he lacks faculties of consciousness. Hence men who are dumb and blind are like grass or trees. But when the vital force has left a man it is a far more serious matter than simply being without ears or eyes. . . . The vital force produces man just as water becomes ice. As water freezes into ice, so the vital force coagulates to form man. When ice melts it becomes water and when a man dies he becomes spirit again. He is called spirit just as ice which has melted changes its name to water. People see that the name has changed, but they then assert that spirit has consciousness and can assume a form and harm others, but there is no basis for this assertion.

People see ghosts which in form appear like living men. Precisely because they appear in this form, we know that they cannot be the spirits of the dead. How can we prove this? Take a sack and fill it with millet or rice. When the millet or rice has been put into it, the sack will be full and sturdy and will stand up in clear view so that people looking at it from a distance can tell that it is a sack of millet or rice. Why? Because the shape of the sack bespeaks the contents. But if the sack has a hole in it and all the millet or rice runs out then the sack collapses in a heap and people looking from a distance can no longer see it. The spirit of man is stored up in his bodily form like the millet or rice in the sack. When he dies and his body decays, his vital force disperses like the grain running out of the sack. When the grain has run out, the sack no longer retains its shape. Then when the spirit of man has dispersed and appeared, how could there still be a body to be seen by others?

Since the beginning of Heaven and earth and the age of the sage rulers until now there have been millions of people who died of old age or were cut off in their prime. The number of men living today is nowhere near that of the dead. If men become ghosts when they die, then when we go walking we ought to see a ghost at every step. If men see ghosts when they are about to die then they ought to see millions of them crowding the hall, filling the courtyards, and jamming the streets, and not just one or two of them. . . . It is the nature of Heaven and earth that, though new fires can be kindled, one cannot rekindle a fire that has burned out, and though new human beings can be born, one cannot bring back the dead. . . . Now people say that ghosts are the spirits of the dead. If this were true, then when men see them they ought to appear completely naked and not clothed in robes and sashes. Why? Because clothes have no spirits. When a man dies they all rot away along with his bodily form, so how could he put them on again?

If dead men cannot become ghosts, then they also cannot have consciousness. How do we prove this? By the fact that before a man is born he has no consciousness. Before a man is born he exists in the midst of primal force (*yüan-ch'i*), and after he dies he returns again to this primal force. The primal force is vast and indistinct and the human force exists within it. Before a man is born he has no consciousness, so when he dies and returns to this original unconscious state how could he still have consciousness? The reason a man is intelligent and understanding is that he possesses the forces of the five virtues [humanity, righteousness, decorum, wisdom, and faith]. The reason he possesses these is that he has within him the five organs [heart, liver, stomach, lungs, and kidneys]. If these five organs are unimpaired, a man has understanding, but if they are diseased, then he becomes vague and confused and behaves like a fool or an idiot. When a man dies, the five organs rot away and the five virtues no longer have any place to reside. Both the seat and the faculty of understanding are destroyed. The body must await the vital force before it is complete, and the vital force must await the body before it can have consciousness. Nowhere is there a fire that burns all by itself. How then could there be a spirit with consciousness existing without a body?

Confucius buried his mother at Fang. Later there was a heavy rain and the grave mound collapsed. When Confucius heard of this he wept bitterly and said: "The ancients did not repair graves," and he never repaired it. If the dead had consciousness then they would surely be angry that people did not repair their graves, and Confucius, realizing this, would accordingly have repaired the grave in order to please his mother's spirit. But he did not repair it. With the enlightenment of a sage he understood that the dead have no consciousness.

NOTE

1. Referring to the story in *Mencius,* 2A: 2.

4.5

The Conception of God in Islam

The Qur'ān

PART 1

I, 1-7.

In the name of Allah, the Merciful, the Compassionate.
Praise be to Allah, Lord of mankind,
The Merciful, the Compassionate,
Master of the Day of Judgment.
Thee do we worship, and to Thee do we turn for help.
Guide us in the straight path,
The path of those to whom Thou hast been gracious,
Not that of those with whom Thou art angered, nor of those
who go astray.

II, 255/256

Allah there is no deity save Him, the Living, the Self-subsistent. Slumber takes Him not, nor sleep. His is whatever is in the heavens and whatever is on earth. Who is it will intercede with Him save by His leave? He knows what is before them and what is behind them, whereas they comprehend naught of His knowledge save what He wills. Wide stretches His Throne over the heavens and the earth, yet to guard them both wearies Him not, for He is the High, the Mighty.

Part 1 from *Islam: Muhammad and His Religions,* edited by Arthur Jeffrey, pp. 86–89. Copyright © by The Library of Liberal Arts, 1958; Part 2 from Jamāl ad-Dīn al-Qāsimī's, *Maw' izat al-Mu'minīn min Imyā 'Ulūm ad-Dīn based* on al-Ghazāli's *Revivication of the Religious Sciences, Ibid.,* pp. 90–92.

CXII, 1-3.

"The fact is, Allah is One; Allah is the Eternal. He did not beget and He was not begotten, and no one has ever been His peer."

XXIV, 34-46/45.

1. Allah is the light of the heavens and the earth. The similitude of His light is that of a niche in which is a lamp, the lamp is in a glass, the glass is as it were a pearly star, lit from a blessed olive tree, neither eastern nor western, whose oil would well nigh light up though untouched by fire. It is a light upon a light. Allah guides to His light whom He will, and Allah strikes out parables for men, and Allah knows everything. In Houses (i.e., temples) which Allah has given permission to be erected, in them His name is remembered, glory being given to Him therein in the mornings and in the evenings, by men whom neither commerce nor bargaining divert from the remembrance of Allah, from observing prayer and paying the legal alms (*zakāt*), who fear a Day on which both hearts and sight will be disturbed.

[This is] that Allah may reward them for the best of what they have done, and increase His bounty to them, for Allah makes provision for whom He will without taking account. But those who have disbelieved, their works are like a desert mirage which the thirsty traveler thinks is water until, when he comes to it, he finds that it is nothing, but he finds Allah there beside him, Who pays him his account in full, and Allah is quick at reckoning accounts. Or [their works are] like darkness on a swollen sea where a wave covers him from above, a wave above which is a cloud, black darknesses one above another, [so that] when he stretches forth his hand he can barely see it. The one to whom Allah gives no light, for him there is no light.

Seest thou not that whosoever is in the heavens and the earth gives glory to Allah? Even the birds of the flocks each knows assuredly its prayer and its [form of] giving glory, and Allah is aware of what they do. Allah's is the kingdom of the heavens and the earth, and to Allah is the journey back. Seest thou not that Allah drives along a cloud, then unites it with another, then makes it a heap, so that you see the rain coming forth from its midst? He also sends down from heaven mountainous clouds in which is hail, wherewith He smiles whom He wills and turns it away from whom He wills. The flashing of His lightning almost takes away the sight Allah makes day and night interchange. In that surely there is a lesson for those who can see. Allah has created every beast from water. Some of them go on their bellies, some go on two legs, and some go on four. Allah creates what He wills. Verily, Allah has power over everything. We assuredly have sent down evidential signs, and Allah guides whom He wills to a straight path.

LIX, 22-24.

He is Allah, other than whom there is no deity; the One who knows both the hidden and the evident. He is the Merciful, the Compassionate. He is Allah, other than whom there is no deity, the King, the Most Holy One, the Peacemaker, the Faithful, the Guardian, the Sublime, the Mighty, the Proud. Glory be to Allah, [who is far] from what they associate [with Him]. He is Allah, the Creator, the Maker, the Fashioner. His are the most beautiful names. To Him gives glory whatsoever is in the heavens and the earth, for He is the Sublime, the wise. . . .

XIII, 2-4.

[It is] Allah who raised up the heavens without pillars that ye can see. Then He seated Himself on the Throne and brought into service the sun and the moon, each of which runs to a fixed term. He arranges the affair, setting out the signs distinctly, that maybe ye will be convinced of the meeting with your Lord. He it is who stretched out the earth and set on it mountain masses and rivers. Also He placed in it two pairs of all kinds of fruits. He makes the night obscure the day. Surely in that are signs for a people who take thought. And in the earth are plots set next to one another, and gardens of grapevines, cultivated fields, palm trees both clustered and unclustered, watered by a single source of water. Yet we give preference to some over others in [the matter of] food. Surely in that are signs to a people who have intelligence.

LXIV, 1-4

Whatsoever is in the heavens and whatsoever is on earth gives glory to Allah. His is the sovereignty and His is the praise, and He is powerful over everything. He it is who created you. Some of you are unbelievers, and some are believers, but Allah is observant of what ye are doing. He created the heavens truly, and the earth. He not only fashioned you but excellent did He make your forms and to Him is the journey back. He knows whatever is in the heavens and the earth. He knows what ye keep secret and what ye make known. Indeed, Allah knows about the inmost things of the breasts.

LVIII, 7/8

Hast thou not seen that Allah knows whatever is in the heavens and whatever is on earth? No three are ever in private conference but He is the fourth of them, nor five but He is their sixth, nor [any number] lower than that or higher, but He is with them wherever they may be. Then on the Day of Resurrection He will announce to them what they were doing, for Allah, Indeed, knows about everything.

PART 2

What Muslims believe about the essential nature of the High and Holy One is that He is One God who has no partner. He is from everlasting, having none prior to Him, and He will continue endlessly to exist, having none come after Him. He is eternal, having no ending, continuing without ever being cut off, One who has not ceased and will not cease to be. He is to be described by the attributes of Majesty. For Him there is prescribed no consummation or disjunction by the ceasing of perpetuity or the expiration of fixed terms. Nay, rather (LVII, 3): "He is the First and the Last, the Outward and the Inward, and He knows all things." Yet He is not a body that has been formed, nor does He resemble any created thing, nor any created thing resemble Him, Space does not encompass Him, nor do the earths[1] and the heavens contain Him, although He is seated on the Throne in that manner of which He speaks and in that sense which He means,[2] He is above the Throne and the heavens, above everything. and yet also beneath the lowest reaches of the watery abyss.[3] His being above does not make Him nearer the Throne and the heavens nor further the earth and the watery abyss. Nay, rather He is many stages higher than the Throne or the heavens, as He is many stages beyond the earth and the watery abyss, yet in spite of this He is near to every existing thing. He is nearer to man than his jugular vein (L, 16/15), though His being near does not resemble bodily nearness, just as His essential being does not resemble the essential being of bodily things, He does not come to rest in anything, just as nothing comes to rest in Him. High exalted is He from being included in any space, just as He is far removed from being limited by any time. Nay, indeed, He was before He created time and space, and He is now as He was.

He is known by the intelligence to be existing in His essential being. As such essential being He will be perceived by the sight in the Lasting Abode,[4] as an act of grace on His part and a kindness to the righteous, in some sort a perfecting of His bounties by letting them look upon His noble face. And He—exalted be He—is living, powerful, mighty, overcoming, free from all shortcomings and any inability. "Slumber takes Him not nor Sleep" (II, 255/256), and no passing away, no death ever comes upon Him. None but He can create and invent, for He stands uniquely alone in producing and innovating. He knows everything that is knowable, is aware of all that is taking place from the lowest depths of the earths to the highest reaches of the heavens, so that not an atom's weight of anything either on earth or in heaven exists apart from His knowledge. He is aware of the crawling of a black ant upon a hard stone in the darkness of the night, and He perceives the movement of each mote in the atmosphere. "He knows the secret and the most hidden thing" (XX, 7/6). He is acquainted with the promptings of men's consciences, with the movements of their fancies, with their most deeply concealed secrets, [knowing all this] with a knowledge that is from of old and is to eternity, for He will not cease having this attribute forever and ever.

He—exalted be He—is the One who wills that existing things be, who manages the things that come to pass, so that no affair happens in the world visible or the world Invisible[5] except by His determining, His decree, His decision, His will, so that what He wills is, and what He did not will is not, and there is no one who may resist His command or make a change in His decision. He—exalted be He—both hears and sees (XXII, 61/60). There is nothing that may be heard, however faint, that escapes His hearing, and nothing that may be seen, however minute, that is hidden from His vision. Distance does not dim His hearing, nor does darkness hinder His vision, yet His hearing and His seeing have no resemblance to the hearing and seeing of creatures, just as His essential being has no resemblance to that of creatures. He also—exalted be He—speaks, both to bid and to forbid, to promise and to threaten. The Qur'ān, the Torah, the Evangel, and the Psalter are Scriptures of His which He sent down to His messengers—on whom be peace. He also—exalted be He—spoke to Moses with that speech which is an attribute of His essence and not a created thing He created. The *Qur'ān* is Allah's speech, not a created thing that may perish, nor an attribute of any created thing so that it should be exhausted.

Now He—exalted be He—[is unique in the sense] that there is beside Him no existing thing save that which came into being by His act, proceeding from His equity in the finest and most perfect, in the most complete and equitable way. He is wise in all His actions, just in all His decrees. Every thing apart from Him, whether men or jinn or angels, whether heaven or earth, whether animal or plant or mineral, whether perceived by the mind or by the senses, is a new creation which He produced by His power, being brought out from nonexistence and produced as a created thing when it had been no thing. Since He was existing in eternity He was alone, and there was no other with Him. Then He brought forth the creation after that, as a demonstration of His power, a fulfillment of that which He had previously willed, and a verification of the word that He had spoken in eternity. It was not that He had any need for it or was in want of it, for it is of favor that He creates and produces and undertakes things, not out of necessity, and it is as a service that He grants favors and not because He must. So it is He who is the One who grants favors and benefactions, blessings and grace.

NOTES

1. Plural because there are seven earths as there are seven heavens.

2. This is the famous problem of the *istiwā* which so exercised Muslim theologians. Some seven times in the *Qur'ān* it is stated that Allah *istiwā* on the Throne. which, if used of some earthly monarch, would mean that he "sat upon the throne."

3. *Ath-tharā* in the old cosmology is what is below the lowest depths. Sūra XX. 6/5 says: "To Him belongs what is in the heavens, what is on earth, what is between them both, and what is below the *tharā*."

4. Dār al-Qarār is one of the names of Paradise, so this is a reference to the Muslim doctrine of the beatific vision.

5. *Mulḥ Wa malakūt,* words which both mean "kingdom," but refer more particularly to the kingdom of things seen and the kingdom of things unseen.

4.6

Reality Omnipresent

Sri Aurobindo

If one knows Him as Brahman the Non-Being, he becomes merely the non-existent. If one knows that Brahman Is, then is he known as the real in existence.

Taittiriya Upaniṣad[1]

Since, then, we admit both the claim of the pure Spirit to manifest in us its absolute freedom and the claim of universal Matter to be the mould and condition of our manifestation, we have to find a truth that can entirely reconcile these antagonists and can give to both their due portion in Life and their due justification in Thought, amercing neither of its rights, denying in neither the sovereign truth from which even its errors, even the exclusiveness of its exaggerations draw so constant a strength. For wherever there is an extreme statement that makes such a powerful appeal to the human mind, we may be sure that we are standing in the presence of no mere error, superstition or hallucination, but of some sovereign fact disguised which demands our fealty and will avenge itself if denied or excluded. Herein lies the difficulty of a satisfying solution and the source of that lack of finality which pursues all mere compromises between Spirit and Matter. A compromise is a bargain, a transaction of interests between two conflicting powers; it is not a true reconciliation. True reconciliation proceeds always by a mutual comprehension leading to some sort of intimate oneness. It is therefore through the utmost possible unification of Spirit and Matter that we shall best arrive at their reconciling truth and so at some strongest foundation for a reconciling practice in the inner life of the individual and his outer existence.

We have found already in the cosmic consciousness a meeting place where Matter becomes real to Spirit, Spirit becomes real to Matter. For in the cosmic consciousness Mind and Life are intermediaries and no longer, as they seem in the ordinary egoistic mentality, agents of separation, fomenters of an artificial quarrel between the positive and negative principles of the same unknowable Reality. Attaining to the cosmic consciousness Mind, illuminated by a knowledge that perceives at once the truth of Unity and the truth of Multiplicity and seizes on the formulae of their interaction, finds its own discords at once explained and reconciled by the divine Harmony; satisfied, it consents to become the agent of that supreme union between God and Life towards which we tend. Matter reveals itself to the realising thought and to the subtilised senses as the figure and body of Spirit,—Spirit in its self-formative extension. Spirit reveals itself through the same consenting agents as the soul, the truth, the essence of Matter. Both admit and confess each other as divine, real and essentially one. Mind and Life are disclosed in that illumination as at once figures and instruments of the supreme Conscious Being by which It extends and houses Itself in material form and in that form unveils Itself to Its multiple centres of consciousness. Mind attains its self-fulfillment when it becomes a pure mirror of the Truth of Being which expresses itself in the symbols of the universe; Life, when it consciously lends its energies to the perfect self-figuration of the Divine in ever-new forms and activities of the universal existence.

In the light of this conception we can perceive the possibility of a divine life for man in the world which will at once justify Science by disclosing a living sense and intelligible aim for the cosmic and the terrestrial evolution and realise by the transfiguration of the human soul into the divine the great ideal dream of all high religions.

But what then of that silent Self, inactive, pure, self-existent, self-enjoying, which presented itself to us as the abiding justification of the ascetic? Here also harmony and not irreconcilable opposition must be the illuminative truth. The silent and the active Brahman are not different, opposite and irreconcilable entities, the one denying, the other affirming a cosmic illusion; they are one Brahman in two aspects, positive and negative, and each is necessary to the other. It is out of this Silence that the Word which creates the worlds forever proceeds; for the Word expresses that which is self-hidden in the Silence. It is an eternal passivity which makes possible the perfect freedom and omnipotence of an eternal divine activity in innumerable cosmic systems. For the becomings of that activity derive their energies and their illimitable potency of variation and harmony from the impartial support of the immutable Being, its consent to this infinite fecundity of its own dynamic Nature.

Man, too, becomes perfect only when he has found within himself that absolute calm and passivity of the Brahman and supports by it with the same divine tolerance and the same divine bliss a free and inexhaustible activity. Those who have thus possessed the calm within can perceive always welling out from its silence the perennial supply of the energies that work in the universe. It is not, therefore, the truth of the Silence to say that it is in its nature a rejection of the cosmic activity. The apparent incompatibility of the two states is an error of the limited Mind which, accustomed to trenchant oppositions of affirmation and denial and passing suddenly from one pole to the other, is unable to conceive of a comprehensive consciousness vast and strong enough to include both in a simultaneous embrace. The Silence does not reject the world; it sustains it. Or rather it supports with an equal impartiality the activity and the withdrawal from the activity and approves also the reconciliation by which the soul remains free and still even while it lends itself to all action.

But, still, there is the absolute withdrawal, there is the Non-Being. Out of the Non-Being, says the ancient Scripture, Being appeared.[2] Then into the Non-Being it must surely sink again. If the infinite indiscriminate Existence permits all possibilities of discrimination and multiple realisation, does not the Non-Being at least, as primal state and sole constant reality, negate and reject all possibility of a real universe? The Nihil of certain Buddhist schools would then be the true ascetic solution; the Self, like the ego, would be only an ideative formation by an illusory phenomenal consciousness.

But again we find that we are being misled by words, deceived by the trenchant oppositions of our limited mentality with its fond reliance on verbal distinctions as if they perfectly represented ultimate truths and its rendering of our supramental experiences in the sense of those intolerant distinctions. Non-Being is only a word. When we examine the fact it represents, we can no longer be sure that absolute non-existence has any better chance than the infinite Self of being more than an ideative formation of the mind. We really mean by this Nothing something beyond the last term to which we can reduce our purest conception and our most abstract or subtle experience of actual being as we know or conceive it while in this universe. This Nothing then is merely a something beyond positive conception. We erect a fiction of nothingness in order to overpass, by the method of total exclusion, all that we can know and consciously are. Actually when we examine closely the Nihil of certain philosophies, we begin to perceive that it is a zero which is All or an indefinable Infinite which appears to the mind a blank, because mind grasps only finite constructions, but is in fact the only true Existence.[3]

And when we say that out of Non-Being Being appeared, we perceive that we are speaking in terms of Time about that which is beyond Time. For what was that portentous date in the history of eternal Nothing on which Being was born out of it or when will come that other date equally formidable on which an unreal all will relapse into the perpetual void? Sat and Asat, if they have both to be affirmed, must be conceived as if they obtained simultaneously. They permit each other even though they refuse to mingle. Both, since we must speak in terms of Time, are eternal. And who shall persuade eternal Being that it does not really exist and only eternal Non-Being is? In such a negation of all experience how shall we find the solution that explains all experience?

Pure Being is the affirmation by the Unknowable of Itself as the free base of all cosmic existence. We give the name of Non-Being to a contrary affirmation of Its freedom from all cosmic existence,—freedom, that is to say, from all positive terms of actual existence which consciousness in the universe can formulate to itself, even from the most abstract, even from the most transcendent. It does not deny them as a real expression of Itself, but It denies Its limitation by all expression or any expression whatsoever. The Non-Being permits the Being, even as the Silence permits the Activity. By this simultaneous negation and affirmation, not mutually destructive, but complementary to each other like all contraries, the simultaneous awareness of conscious Self-being as a reality and the Unknowable beyond as the same Reality becomes realisable to the awakened human soul. Thus was it possible for the Buddha to attain the state of Nirvana and yet act puissantly in the world, impersonal in his inner consciousness, in his action the most powerful personality that we know of as having lived and produced results upon earth.

When we ponder on these things, we begin to perceive how feeble in their self-assertive violence and how confusing in their misleading distinctness are the words that we use. We begin also to perceive that the limitations we impose on the Brahman arise from a narrowness of experience in the individual mind which concentrates itself on one aspect of the Unknowable and proceeds forthwith to deny or disparage all the rest. We tend always to translate too rigidly what we can conceive or know of the Absolute into the terms of our own particular relativity. We affirm the One and Identical by passionately discriminating and asserting the egoism of our own opinions and partial experiences against the opinions and partial experiences of others. It is wiser to wait, to learn, to grow, and, since we are obliged for the sake of our self-perfection to speak of these things which no human speech can express, to search for the widest, the most flexible, the most catholic affirmation possible and found on it the largest and most comprehensive harmony.

We recognise, then, that it is possible for the consciousness in the individual to enter into a state in which relative existence appears to be dissolved and even Self seems to be an inadequate conception. It is possible to pass into a Silence beyond the Silence. But this is not the whole of our ultimate experience, nor the single and all-excluding truth. For we find that this Nirvana, this self-extinction, while it gives an absolute peace and freedom to the soul within is yet consistent in practice with a desireless but effective action without. This possibility of an entire motionless impersonality and void

Calm within doing outwardly the works of the eternal verities, Love, Truth and Righteousness, was perhaps the real gist of the Buddha's teachings— this superiority to ego and to the chain of personal workings and to the iden- tification with mutable form and idea, not the petty ideal of an escape from the trouble and suffering of the physical birth. In any case, as the perfect man would combine in himself the silence and the activity, so also would the completely conscious soul reach back to the absolute freedom of the Non-Being without therefore losing its hold on Existence and the universe. It would thus reproduce in itself perpetually the eternal miracle of the divine Existence, in the universe, yet always beyond it and even, as it were, beyond itself. The opposite experience could only be a concentration of mentality in the individual upon Non-existence with the result of an oblivion and per- sonal withdrawal from a cosmic activity still and always proceeding in the consciousness of the Eternal Being.

Thus, after reconciling Spirit and Matter in the cosmic consciousness, we perceive the reconciliation, in the transcendental consciousness, of the final assertion of all and its negation. We discover that all affirmations are asser- tions of status or activity in the Unknowable; all the corresponding negations are assertions of Its freedom both from and in that status or activity. The Un- knowable is Something to us supreme, wonderful and ineffable which con- tinually formulates Itself to our consciousness and continually escapes from the formulation It has made. This it does not as some malicious spirit or freakish magician leading us from falsehood to greater falsehood and so to a final negation of all things, but as even here the Wise beyond our wisdom guiding us from reality to ever profounder and vaster reality until we find the profoundest and vastest of which we are capable. An omnipresent reality is the Brahman, not an omnipresent cause of persistent illusions.

If we thus accept a positive basis for our harmony—and on what other can harmony be founded?—the various conceptual formulations of the Un- knowable, each of them representing a truth beyond conception, must be understood as far as possible in their relation to each other and in their ef- fect upon life, not separately, not exclusively, not so affirmed as to destroy or unduly diminish all other affirmations. The real Monism, the true Ad- waita, is that which admits all things as the one Brahman and does not seek to bisect Its existence into two incompatible entities, an eternal Truth and an eternal Falsehood, Brahman and not-Brahman, Self and not-Self, a real Self and an unreal, yet perpetual Maya. If it be true that the Self alone exists, it must be also true that all is the Self. And if this Self, God or Brahman is no helpless state, no bounded power, no limited personality, but the self-con- scient All, there must be some good and inherent reason in it for the mani- festation, to discover which we must proceed on the hypothesis of some po- tency, some wisdom, some truth of being in all that is manifested. The discord and apparent evil of the world must in their sphere be admitted, but not accepted as our conquerors. The deepest instinct of humanity seeks always and seeks wisely wisdom as the last word of the universal manifestation, not an eternal mockery and illusion,—a secret and finally triumphant good, not an all-creative and invincible evil,—an ultimate victory and fulfillment, not the disappointed recoil of the soul from its great adventure.

For we cannot suppose that the sole Entity is compelled by some thing outside or other than Itself, since no such thing exists. Nor can we suppose that It submits unwillingly to something partial within Itself which is hostile to its whole Being, denied by It and yet too strong for It; for this would be only to erect in other language the same contradiction of an All and something other than the All. Even if we say that the universe exists merely because the Self in its absolute impartiality tolerates all things alike, viewing with indifference all actualities and all possibilities, yet is there something that wills the manifestation and supports it, and this cannot be something other than the All. Brahman is indivisible in all things and whatever is willed in the world has been ultimately willed by the Brahman. It is only our relative consciousness, alarmed or baffled by the phenomena of evil, ignorance and pain in the cosmos, that seeks to deliver the Brahman from responsibility for Itself and its workings by erecting some opposite principle, Maya or Mara, conscious Devil or self-existent principle of evil. There is one Lord and Self and the many are only His representations and becomings.

If then the world is a dream or an illusion or a mistake, it is a dream originated and willed by the Self in its totality and not only originated and willed, but supported and perpetually entertained. Morever, it is a dream existing in a Reality and the stuff of which it is made is that Reality, for Brahman must be the material of the world as well as its base and continent. If the gold of which the vessel is made is real, how shall we suppose that the vessel itself is a mirage? We see that these words, dream, illusion, are tricks of speech, habits of our relative consciousness; they represent a certain truth, even a great truth, but they also misrepresent it. Just as Non-Being turns out to be other than mere nullity, so the cosmic Dream turns out to be other than mere phantasm and hallucination of the mind. Phenomenon is not phantasm; phenomenon is the substantial form of a Truth.

We start, then, with the conception of an omnipresent Reality of which neither the Non-Being at the one end nor the universe at the other are negations that annul; they are rather different states of the Reality, obverse and reverse affirmations. The highest experience of this Reality in the universe shows it to be not only a conscious Existence, but a supreme Intelligence and Force and a self-existent Bliss; and beyond the universe it is still some other unknowable existence, some utter and ineffable Bliss. Therefore we are justified in supposing that even the dualities of the universe, when interpreted not as now by our sensational and partial conceptions, but by our liberated intelligence and experience, will be also resolved into those highest terms. While we still labour under the stress of the dualities, this perception must no doubt constantly support itself on an act of faith, but a faith which the highest Reason, the widest and most patient reflection do not deny, but rather affirm. This creed is given, indeed, to humanity to support it on its journey, until it arrives at a stage of development when faith will be turned into knowledge and perfect experience and Wisdom will be justified of her works.

NOTES

1. II.6.

2. In the beginning all this was the Non-Being. It was thence that Being was born.—*Taittiriya Upaniṣad.* II.7.

3. Another Upaniṣad rejects the birth of being out of Non-Being as an impossibility; Being, it says, can only be born from Being. But if we take Non-Being in the sense, not of an inexistent Nihil but of an x which exceeds our idea or experience of existence,—a sense applicable to the Absolute Brahman of the Adwaita as well as the Void or Zero of the Buddhists, the impossibility disappears, for That may very well be the source of being, whether by a conceptual or formative *Māyā* or a manifestation or creation out of itself.

4.7

Zen Enlightenment

Kaiten Nukariya

1. *Enlightenment Is beyond Description and Analysis.*—In the foregoing chapters we have had several occasions to refer to the central problem of Zen or Enlightenment, whose content it is futile to explain or analyze. We must not explain or analyze it, because by doing so we cannot but mislead the reader. We can as well represent Enlightenment by means of explanation or analysis as we do personality by snapshots or by anatomical operations. As our inner life, directly experienced within us, is anything but the shape of the head, or the features of the face, or the posture of the body, so Enlightenment experienced by Zennists at the moment of their highest Samādhi[1] is anything but the psychological analysis of mental process, or the epistemological explanation of cognition, or the philosophical generalization of concepts. Enlightenment can be realized only by the Enlightened, and baffles every attempt to describe it, even by the Enlightened themselves. The effort of the confused to guess at Enlightenment is often likened by the Zennists to the effort of the blind who feel an elephant to know what it looks like. Some of them who happen to feel the trunk would declare it is like a rope, but those who happen to feel the belly would declare it is like a huge drum; while those who happen to feel the feet would declare it is like the trunk of a tree. But none of these conjectures can approach the living elephant.

2. *Enlightenment Implies an Insight into the Nature of Self.*—We cannot pass over, however, this weighty problem without saying a word. We shall try in this chapter to present Enlightenment before the reader in a roundabout way, just as the painter gives the fragmentary sketches of a beautiful

From *Anthology of Zen,* Edited by William A. Briggs, pp. 122–40. Copyright © by Evergreen Books Ltd., London 1961.

city, being unable to give even a bird's-eye view of it. Enlightenment, first of all, implies an insight into the nature of Self. It is an emancipation of mind from illusion concerning Self. All kinds of sin take root deep in the misconception of Self, and putting forth the branches of lust, anger, and folly, throw dark shadows on life. To extirpate this misconception Buddhism[2] strongly denies the existence of the individual soul as conceived by common sense—that is, that unchanging spiritual entity provided with sight, hearing, touch, smell, feeling, thought, imagination, aspiration, etc., which survives the body. It teaches us that there is no such thing as soul, and that the notion of soul is a gross illusion. It treats of body as a temporal and material form of life doomed to be destroyed by death and reduced to its elements again. It maintains that mind is also a temporal spiritual form of life, behind which there is no immutable soul.

An illusory mind tends either to regard body as Self and to yearn after its material interests, or to believe mind dependent on soul as Ego. Those who are given to sensual pleasures, consciously or unconsciously, hold body to be the Self, and remain the lifelong slave to the objects of sense. Those who regard mind as dependent on soul as the Self, on the other hand, undervalue body as a mere tool with which the soul works, and are inclined to denounce life as if unworthy of living. We must not undervalue body, nor must we overestimate mind. There is no mind isolated from body, nor is there any body separated from mind. Every activity of mind produces chemical and physiological changes in the nerve-centers, in the organs, and eventually in the whole body; while every activity of body is sure to bring out the corresponding change in the mental function, and eventually in the whole personality. We have the inward experience of sorrow when we have simultaneously the outward appearance of tears and of pallor; when we have the outward appearance of the fiery eyes and short breath, we have simultaneously the inward feeling of anger. Thus body is mind observed outwardly in its relation to the senses; mind is body inwardly experienced in its relation to introspection. Who can draw a strict line of demarcation between mind and body? We should admit, so far as our present knowledge is concerned, that mind, the intangible, has been formed to don a garment of matter in order to become an intelligible existence at all; matter, the solid, has faded under examination into formlessness, as that of mind. Zen believes in the identification of mind and body, as Dōgen[3] says: "Body is identical with mind; appearance and reality are one and the same thing."

Bergson denies the identification of mind and body, saying:[4] "It (experience) shows us the interdependence of the mental and the physical, the necessity of a certain cerebral substratum for the psychical state—nothing more. From the fact that the two things are mutually dependent, it does not follow that they are equivalent. Because a certain screw is necessary for a certain machine, because the machine works when the screw is there and stops when the screw is taken away, we do not say that the screw is the equivalent of the machine." Bergson's simile of a screw and a machine is quite inadequate to show the interdependence of mind and body, because the screw does cause the machine to work, but the machine does not cause the screw to work; so that their relation is not interdependence. On the contrary, body causes mind to work, and at the same time mind causes body to work; so that their relation is perfectly interdependent, and the relation is not that of an addition of mind to body, or of body to mind, as the screw is added to the machine. Bergson must have compared the workings of the machine with mind, and the machine itself with body, if he wanted to show the real fact. Moreover, he is not right in asserting that "from the fact that two things are mutually dependent, it does not follow that they are equivalent," because there are several kinds of interdependence, in some of which two things can be equivalent. For instance, bricks, mutually dependent in their forming an arch, cannot be equivalent one with another; but water and waves, being mutually dependent, can be identified. In like manner fire and heat, air and wind, a machine and its working, mind and body.[5]

3. *The Irrationality of the Belief of Immortality.*—Occidental minds believe in a mysterious entity under the name of soul, just as Indian thinkers believe in the so-called subtle body entirely distinct from the gross body of flesh and blood. Soul, according to this belief, is an active principle that unites body and mind so as to form an harmonious whole of mental as well as bodily activities. And it acts through the instrumentality of the mind and body in the present life, and enjoys an eternal life beyond the grave. It is on this soul that individual immortality is based. It is immortal Self.

Now, to say nothing of the origin of soul, this long-entertained belief is hardly good for anything. In the first place, it throws no light upon the relation of mind and body, because soul is an empty name for the unity of mind and body, and serves to explain nothing. On the contrary, it adds another mystery to the already mysterious relationships between matter and spirit. Secondly, soul should be conceived as a psychical individual, subject to spacial determinations; but since it has to be deprived by death of its body which individualizes it, it will cease to be individuality after death, to the disappointment of the believer. How could you think anything purely spiritual and formless existing without blending together with other things? Thirdly, it fails to gratify the desire, cherished by the believer, of enjoying eternal life, because soul has to lose its body, the sole important medium through which it may enjoy life. Fourthly, soul is taken as a subject matter to receive in the future life the reward or the punishment from God for our actions in this life; but the very idea of eternal punishment is inconsistent with the boundless love of God. Fifthly, it is beyond all doubt that soul is conceived as an entity, which unifies various mental faculties and exists as the foundation of individual personality. But the existence of such soul is quite incompatible with the well-known pathological fact that it is possible for the individual to have double or treble or multiple personalities. Thus the belief in the existence of soul conceived by the common sense turns out not only to be irrational, but a useless encumbrance on the religious mind. Therefore Zen declares that there is no such thing as soul, and that mind and body are one. Hwui Chung (Ye-chu), a famous disciple of the Sixth Patriarch in China, to quote an example, one day asked a monk: "Where did you come from?" "I came, sir, from the South," replied the man. "What doctrine do the masters of the South teach?" asked Hwui Chung again. "They teach, sir, that body is mortal, but mind is immortal," was the answer. "That," said the master, "is the heterodox doctrine of the Ātman!" "How do you, sir," questioned the monk, "teach about that?" "I teach that the body and mind are one," was the reply.[6]

Fiske[7] in his argument against materialism, blames the denial of immortality, saying: "The materialistic assumption that there is no such state of things, and that the life of the soul ends accordingly with the life of the body, is perhaps the most colossal instance of baseless assumption that is known to the history of philosophy." But we can say with equal force that the common-sense assumption that the life of the soul continues beyond the grave is, perhaps, the most colossal instance of baseless assumption that is known to the history of thought, because, there being no scientific evidences that give countenance to the assumption, even the spiritualists themselves hesitate to assert the existence of a ghost or soul. Again he says:[8] "With this illegitimate hypothesis of annihilation the materialist transgresses the bounds of experience quite as widely as the poet who sings of the New Jerusalem with its river of life and its street of gold. Scientifically speaking, there is not a particle of evidence for either view." This is as much as to say there is not a particle of evidence, scientifically speaking, for the common-sense view of soul, because the poet's description of the New Jerusalem is nothing but the result of the common-sense belief of immortality.

4. *The Examination of the Notion of Self.*—The belief in immortality is based on the strong instinct of self-preservation that calls forth an insatiable longing for longevity. It is another form of egoism, one of the relics of our brute forefathers. We must bear in mind that this illusion of the individual Self is the foundation on which every form of immorality has its being. I challenge my readers to find in the whole history of mankind any crime not based on egoism. Evil-doers have been as a rule pleasure-hunters, money-seekers, seekers after self-interests, characterized by lust, folly, and cruelty. Has there been any one who committed theft that he might further the interests of his villagers? Has there been any paramour who disgraced himself that he might help his neighbors? Has there been any traitor who performed the ignoble conduct to promote the welfare of his own country or society at large?

To get Enlightened, therefore, we have to correct, first of all, our notions concerning Self. Individual body and mind are not the only important constituents of Self. There are many other indispensable elements in the notion of Self. For instance, I have come into existence as another form of my parents. I am theirs, and may justly be called the reincarnation of them. And again, my father is another form of his parents; my mother of hers; his and her parents of theirs; and *ad infinitum*. In brief, all my forefathers live and have their being in me. I cannot help, therefore, thinking that my physical state is the result of the sum total of my good and bad actions in the past lives I led in the persons of my forefathers, and of the influence I received therein;[9] and that my psychical state is the result of that which I received, felt, imagined, conceived, experienced, and thought in my past existences in the persons of my ancestors.

Besides this, my brothers, my sisters, my neighbors—nay, all my fellow-men and fellow-women—are no other than the reincarnation of their parents and forefathers, who are also mine. The same blood invigorated the king as well as the beggar; the same nerve energized the white as well as the black men; the same consciousness vitalized the wise as well as the unwise. Impossible it is to conceive myself independent of my fellow-men and fellow-women, for they are mine and I am theirs—that is, I live and move in them, and they live and move in me.

It is bare nonsense to say that I go to school, not to be educated as a member of society, but simply to gratify my individual desire for knowledge; or that I make a fortune, not to lead the life of a well-to-do in society, but to satisfy my individual money-loving instinct; or that I seek after truth, neither to do good to my contemporaries nor to the future generations, but only for my individual curiosity; or that I live neither to live with my family nor with my friends nor with anyone else, but to live my individual life. It is as gross absurdity to say that I am an individual absolutely independent of society as to say that I am a husband with no wife, or I am a son to no parents. Whatever I do directly or indirectly I contribute to the common fortune of man; whatever anyone else does directly or indirectly determines my fate. Therefore we must realize that our Selves necessarily include other members of the community, while other members' Selves necessarily comprehend us.

5. *Nature Is the Mother of All Things.*—Furthermore, man has come into existence out of Nature. He is her child. She provided him food, raiment, and shelter. She nourishes him, strengthens him, and vitalizes him. At the same time she disciplines, punishes, and instructs him. His body is of her own formation, his knowledge is of her own laws, and his activities are the responses to her own addresses to him. Modern civilization is said by some to be the conquest of man over Nature; but, in fact, it is his faithful obedience to her. "Bacon truly said," says Eucken[10] "that to rule nature man must first serve her. He forgot to add that, as her ruler, he is still destined to go on

serving her." She can never be attacked by any being unless he acts in strict conformity to her laws. To accomplish anything against her law is as impossible as to catch fishes in a forest, or to make bread of rock. How many species of animals have perished owing to their inability to follow her steps! How many immense fortunes have been lost in vain from man's ignorance of her order! How many human beings disappeared on earth from their disobedience to her unbending will! She is, nevertheless, true to those who obey her rules. Has not science proved that she is truthful? Has not art found that she is beautiful? Has not philosophy announced that she is spiritual? Has not religion proclaimed that she is good? At all events, she is the mother of all beings. She lives in all things and they live in her. All that she possesses is theirs, and all that they want she supplies. Her life is the same vitality that stirs all sentient beings. Chwang Tsz[11] (So-shi) is right when he says: "Heaven, Earth, and I were produced together, and all things and I are one." And again: "If all things be regarded with love, Heaven and Earth are one with me." Sang Chao (Sō-Jō) also says: "Heaven and Earth are of the same root as we. All things in the world are of one substance with me."[12]

6. *Real Self.*—If there be no individual soul either in mind or body, where does personality lie? What is Real Self? How does it differ from soul? Self is living entity, not immutable like soul, but mutable and ever-changing life, which is body when observed by senses, and which is mind when experienced by introspection. It is not an entity lying behind mind and body, but life existent as the union of body and mind. It existed in our forefathers in the past, is existing in the present, and will exist in the future generations. It also discloses itself to some measure in vegetables and animals, and shadows itself forth in organic nature. It is Cosmic life and Cosmic spirit, and at the same time individual life and individual spirit. It is one and the same life which embraces men and nature. It is the self-existent, creative, universal principle that moves on from eternity to eternity. As such it is called Mind or Self by Zennists. Pan Shan (Ban-zan) says: "The moon of mind comprehends all the universe in its light." A man asked Chang Sha (Chō-sha): "How can you turn the phenomenal universe into Self?" "How can you turn Self into the phenomenal universe?" returned the master.

When we get the insight into this Self, we are able to have the open sesame to the mysteries of the universe, because to know the nature of a drop of water is to know the nature of the river, the lake, and the ocean—nay, even of vapor, mist, and cloud; in other words, to get an insight into individual life is the key to the secret of Universal Life. We must not confine Self within the poor little person called body. That is the root of the poorest and most miserable egoism. We should expand that egoism into family-egoism, then into nation-egoism, then into race-egoism, then into human-egoism, then into living-being-egoism, and lastly into universe-egoism, which is not egoism at all. Thus we deny the immortality of soul as conceived by common sense, but assume immortality

of the Great Soul, which animates, vitalizes, and spiritualizes all sentient beings. It is Hīnayāna Buddhism that first denied the existence of Atman or Self
so emphatically inculcated in the Upaniṣads, and paved the way for the general conception of Universal Self, with the eulogies of which almost every
page of Mahāyāna books is filled.

7. *The Awakening of the Innermost Wisdom*.—Having set ourselves free
from the misconception of Self, next we must awaken our innermost wisdom, pure and divine, called the Mind of Buddha,[13] or Bodhi,[14] or Prajñā[15] by
Zen masters. It is the divine light, the inner heaven, the key to all moral
treasures, the center of thought and consciousness, the source of all influence and power, the seat of kindness, justice, sympathy, impartial love, humanity, and mercy, the measure of all things. When this innermost wisdom
is fully awakened, we are able to realize that each and every one of us is
identical in spirit, in essence, in nature with the universal life or Buddha, that
each ever lives face to face with Buddha, that each is beset by the abundant
grace of the Blessed One, that He arouses his moral nature, that He opens
his spiritual eyes, that He unfolds his new capacity, that He appoints his mission, and that life is not an ocean of birth, disease, old age, and death, nor
the vale of tears, but the holy temple of Buddha, the Pure Land,[16] where he
can enjoy the bliss of Nirvana.

Then our minds go through an entire revolution. We are no more troubled
by anger and hatred, no more bitten by envy and ambition, no more stung
by sorrow and chagrin, no more overwhelmed by melancholy and despair.
Not that we become passionless or simply intellectual, but that we have purified passions, which instead of troubling us, inspire us with noble aspirations, such as anger and hatred against injustice, cruelty, and dishonesty,
sorrow and lamentation for human frailty, mirth and joy for the welfare of
fellow-beings, pity and sympathy for suffering creatures. The same change
purifies our intellect. Scepticism and sophistry give way to firm conviction;
criticism and hypothesis to right judgment; and inference and argument to
realization.

What we merely observed before we now touch with heart as well. What
we knew in relation of difference before we now understand in relation of
unity as well. How things happen was our chief concern before, but now we
consider as well how much value they have. What was outside us before
now comes within us. What was dead and indifferent before grows now
alive and lovable to us. What was insignificant and empty before now becomes important, and has profound meaning. Wherever we go we find
beauty; whomever we meet we find good; whatever we get we receive with
gratitude. This is the reason why the Zennists not only regarded all their fellow-beings as their benefactors, but felt gratitude even toward fuel and
water. The present writer knows a contemporary Zennist who would not
drink even a cup of water without first making a salutation to it. Such an at-

titude of Zen toward things may well be illustrated by the following example: Sueh Fung (Sep-pō) and Kin Shan (Kin-zan), once traveling through a
mountainous district, saw a leaf of the rape floating down the stream.
Thereon Kin Shan said: "Let us go up, dear brother, along the stream that we
may find a sage living up on the mountain. I hope we shall find a good
teacher in him." "No," replied Sueh Fung, "for he cannot be a sage who
wastes even a leaf of the rape. He will be no good teacher for us."

8. *Zen Is Not Nihilistic.*—Zen judged from ancient Zen masters' aphorisms may seem, at the first sight, to be idealistic in an extreme form, as they
say: "Mind is Buddha" or, "Buddha is Mind," or, "There is nothing outside
mind," or, "Three worlds are of but one mind." And it may also appear to be
nihilistic, as they say: "There has been nothing since all eternity," "By illusion you see the castle of the Three Worlds; by Enlightenment you see but
emptiness in ten directions."[17] In reality, however, Zen[18] is neither idealistic
nor nihilistic. Zen makes use of the nihilistic idea of Hīnayāna Buddhism,
and calls its students' attention to the change and evanescence of life and of
the world, first to destroy the error of immutation, next to dispel the attachment to the sensual objects.

It is a misleading tendency of our intellect to conceive things as if they
were immutable and constant. It often leaves changing and concrete individual objects out of consideration, and lays stress on the general, abstract,
unchanging aspect of things. It is inclined to be given to generalization and
abstraction. It often looks not at this thing or at that thing, but at things in
general. It loves to think not of a good thing nor of a bad thing, but of bad
and good in the abstract. This intellectual tendency hardens and petrifies the
living and growing world, and leads us to take the universe as a thing dead,
inert, and standing still. This error of immutation can be corrected by the
doctrine of Transience taught by Hīnayāna Buddhism. But as medicine taken
in an undue quantity turns into poison, so the doctrine of Transience drove
the Hīnayānists to the suicidal conclusion of nihilism. A well-known scholar
and believer of Zen, Kwei Fung (Kei-hō) says in his refutation of nihilism:[19]

"If mind as well as external objects be unreal, who is it that knows they
are so? Again, if there be nothing real in the universe, what is it that
causes unreal objects to appear? We stand witness to the fact that there is
no one of the unreal things on earth that is not made to appear by something real. If there be no water of unchanging fluidity, how can there be
the unreal and temporary forms of waves? If there be no unchanging mirror, bright and clean, how can there be the various images, unreal and
temporary, reflected in it? If mind as well as external objects be nothing
at all, no one can tell what it is that causes these unreal appearances.
Therefore this doctrine (of the unreality of all things) can never clearly
disclose spiritual Reality. So that *Mahābheri-hārakaparivarta-sūtra* says:
"All the sutras that teach the unreality of things belong to the imperfect

doctrine" (of the Shakya Muni). *Mahāprajñā-pāramitā-sūtra* says: "The doctrine of unreality is the entrance-gate of Mahāyāna."

9. *Zen and Idealism.*—Next Zen makes use of Idealism as explained by the Dharmalaksana School of Mahāyāna Buddhism.[20] For instance, the Fourth Patriarch says: "Hundreds and thousands of laws originate with mind. Innumerable mysterious virtues proceed from the mental source." Niu Teu (Go-zu) also says: "When mind arises, various things arise; when mind ceases to exist, various things cease to exist." Tsao Shan (Sō-zan) carried the point so far that he cried out, on hearing the bell: "It hurts, it pains." Then an attendant of his asked: "What is the matter?" "It is my mind," said he, "that is struck."[21]

We acknowledge the truth of the following considerations: There exists no color, nor sound, nor odor in the objective world, but there are the vibrations of ether, or the undulations of the air, or the stimuli of the sensory nerves of smell. Color is nothing but the translation of the stimuli into sensation by the optical nerves, so also sounds by the auditory, and odors by the smelling. Therefore nothing exists objectively exactly as it is perceived by the senses, but all are subjective. Take electricity, for example: it appears as light when perceived through the eye; it appears as sound when perceived through the ear; it appears as taste when perceived through the tongue; but electricity in reality is not light, nor sound, nor taste. Similarly, the mountain is not high nor low; the river is not deep nor shallow; the house is not large nor small; the day is not long nor short; but they seem so through comparison. It is not objective reality that displays the phenomenal universe before us, but it is our mind that plays an important part. Suppose that we have but one sense organ, the eye, then the whole universe should consist of colors only. If we suppose we were endowed with the sixth sense, which entirely contradicts our five senses, then the whole world would be otherwise. Besides, it is our reason that finds the law of cause and effect in the objective world, that discovered the law of uniformity in Nature, and that discloses scientific laws in the universe so as to form a cosmos. Some scholars maintain that we cannot think of non-existence of space, even if we can leave out all objects in it; nor can we doubt the existence of time, for the existence of mind itself presupposes time. Their very argument, however, proves the subjectivity of time and space, because, if they were objective, we should be able to think them non-existent, as we do with other external objects. Even space and time, therefore, are no more than subjective.

10. *Idealism Is a Potent Medicine for Self-Created Mental Disease.*—Insofar as Buddhist idealism refers to the world of sense, insofar as it does not assume that to be known is identical with to be, insofar as it does not assert that the phenomenal universe is a dream and a vision, we may admit it as true. On the one hand, it serves us as a purifier of our hearts polluted with materialistic desires, and uplifts us above the plain of sensualism; on the

other hand, it destroys superstitions which as a rule arise from ignorance and want of the idealistic conception of things.

It is a lamentable fact that every country is full of such superstitious people as described by one of the New Thought writers: "Tens of thousands of women in this country believe that if two people look in a mirror at the same time, or if one thanks the other for a pin, or if one gives a knife or a sharp instrument to a friend, it will break up friendship. If a young lady is presented with a thimble, she will be an old maid. Some people think that after leaving a house it is unlucky to go back after any article which has been forgotten, and if one is obliged to do so, one should sit down in a chair before going out again; that if a broom touches a person while someone is sweeping, bad luck will follow; and that it is unlucky to change one's place at a table. A man took an opal to a New York jeweler and asked him to buy it. He said that it had brought him nothing but bad luck, that since it had come into his possession he had failed in business, that there had been much sickness in his family, and all sorts of misfortune had befallen him. He refused to keep the cursed thing any longer. The jeweler examined the stone, and found that it was not an opal after all, but an imitation."

Idealism is a most potent medicine for these self-created mental diseases. It will successfully drive away devils and spirits that frequent ignorant minds, just as Jesus did in the old days. Zen makes use of moral idealism to extirpate, root and branch, all such idle dreams and phantasmagoria of illusion and opens the way to Enlightenment.

11. *Idealistic Scepticism Concerning Objective Reality.*—But extreme Idealism identifies "to be" with "to be known," and assumes all phenomena to be ideas as illustrated in *Mahāyāna-vidyāmātra-siddhi-tridasa-śāstra*[22] and *Vidyśmātra-vincati-śāstra*[23] by Vasubandhu. Then it necessarily parts company with Zen, which believes in Universal Life existing in everything instead of behind it. Idealism shows us its dark side in three sceptic views: (1) scepticism respecting objective reality; (2) scepticism respecting religion; (3) scepticism respecting morality. First it assumes that things exist insofar as they are known by us. It is as a matter of course that if a tree exists at all, it is known as having a trunk long or short, branches large or small, leaves green or yellow, flowers yellow or purple, etc., all of which are ideas. But it does not imply in the least that "to be known" is equivalent to "to be existent." Rather we should say that to be known presupposes to be existent, for we cannot know anything non-existent, even if we admit that the axioms of logic subsist. Again, a tree may stand as ideas to a knower, but it can stand at the same time as a shelter in relation to some birds, as food in relation to some insects, as a world in relation to some minute worms, as a kindred organism to other vegetables. How could you say that its relation to a knower is the only and fundamental relation for the existence of the tree? The disappearance of its knower no more affects the tree

than of its feeder; nor the appearance of its knower affects the tree any more than that of kindred vegetables.

Extreme idealism erroneously concludes that what is really existent, or what is directly proved to be existent, is only our sensations, ideas, thoughts; that the external world is nothing but the images reflected on the mirror of the mind, and that therefore objective reality of things is doubtful—nay, more, they are unreal, illusory, and dreams. If so, we can no longer distinguish the real from the visionary; the waking from the dreaming; the sane from the insane; the true from the untrue. Whether life is real or an empty dream, we are at a loss to understand.

12. *Idealistic Scepticism Concerning Religion and Morality.*—Similarly, it is the case with religion and morality. If we admit extreme idealism as true, there can be nothing objectively real. God is little more than a mental image. He must be a creature of mind instead of a Creator. He has no objective reality. He is when we think He is. He is not when we think He is not. He is at the mercy of our thought. How much more unreal the world must be, which is supposed to have been created by an unreal God! Providence, salvation, and divine grace—what are they? A bare dream dreamed in a dream!

What is morality, then? It is subjective. It has no objective validity. A moral conduct highly valued by our fathers is now held to be immoral by us. Immoral acts now strongly denounced by us may be regarded as moral by our posterity. Good deeds of the savage are not necessarily good in the eyes of the civilized, nor are evil acts of the Orientals necessarily evil before the face of the Occidentals. It follows, then, that there is no definite standard of morality in any place at any time.

If morality be merely subjective, and there be no objective standard, how can you distinguish evil from good? How can you single out angels from among devils? Was not Socrates a criminal? Was not Jesus also a criminal? How could you know Him to be a Divine man different from other criminals who were crucified with Him? What you honor may I not denounce as disgrace? What you hold as duty may I not condemn as sin? Every form of idealism is doomed, after all, to end in such confusion and scepticism. We cannot embrace radical idealism, which holds these threefold sceptical views in her womb.

13. *An Illusion Concerning Appearance and Reality.*—To get Enlightened we must next dispel an illusion respecting appearance and reality. According to certain religionists, all the phenomena of the universe are to succumb to change. Worldly things one and all are evanescent. They are nought in the long run. Snow-capped mountains may sink into the bottom of the deep, while the sands in the fathomless ocean may soar into the azure sky at some time or other. Blooming flowers are destined to fade and to bloom again in the next year. So destined are growing trees, rising generations, prospering nations, glowing suns, moons, and stars. This, they would say, is

only the case with phenomena or appearances, but not with reality. Growth and decay, birth and death, rise and fall, all these are the ebb and flow of appearances in the ocean of reality, which is always the same. Flowers may fade and be reduced to dust, yet out of that dust come flowers. Trees may die out, yet they are reproduced somewhere else. The time may come when the earth will become a dead sphere quite unsuitable for human habitation, and the whole of mankind will perish; yet who knows whether another earth may not be produced as man's home? The sun might have its beginning and end, stars, moon, theirs as well; yet an infinite universe would have no beginning nor end.

Again, they say, mutation is of the world of sense or phenomenal appearances, but not of reality. The former are the phases of the latter shown to our senses. Accordingly they are always limited and modified by the mirror in which they are reflected. On this account appearances are subject to limitations, while reality is limitless. And it follows that the former are imperfect, while the latter is perfect; that the former is transient, while the latter is eternal; that the former is relative, while the latter is absolute; that the former is worldly, while the latter is holy; that the former is knowable, while the latter is unknowable.

These considerations naturally lead us to an assertion that the world of appearances is valueless, as it is limited, short-lived, imperfect, painful, sinful, hopeless, and miserable; while the realm of reality is to be aspired for, as it is eternal, perfect, comfortable, full of hope, joy, and peace—hence the eternal divorce of appearance and reality. Such a view of life tends to make one minimize the value of man, to neglect the present existence, and to yearn after the future.

Some religionists tell us that we men are helpless, sinful, hopeless, and miserable creatures. Worldly riches, temporal honors, and social positions—nay, even sublimities and beauties of the present existence, are to be ignored and despised. We have no need of caring for those things that pass away in a twinkling moment. We must prepare for the future life which is eternal. We must accumulate wealth for that existence. We must endeavor to hold rank in it. We must aspire for the sublimity and beauty and glory of that realm.

14. *Where Does the Root of the Illusion Lie?*—Now let us examine where illusion lies hidden from the view of these religionists. It lies deeply rooted in the misconstruction of reality, grows up in the illusive ideas of appearances, and throws its dark shadow on life. The most fundamental error lies in their construing reality as something unknowable existing behind appearances.

According to their opinion, all that we know, or perceive, or feel, or imagine about the world, is appearances or phenomena, but not reality itself. Appearances are "things known as," but not "things as they are." Thing-in-itself, or reality, lies behind appearances permanently beyond our ken. This is probably the most profound metaphysical pit into which philosophical minds have ever fallen in their way of speculation. Things appear, they would say, as we see them through our limited Senses; but they must present entirely different aspects to those that differ from ours, just as the vibration of ether appears to us as colors, yet it presents quite different aspects to the color-blind or to the pur-blind. The phenomenal universe is what appears to the human mind, and in case our mental constitution undergoes change, it would be completely otherwise.

This argument, however, is far from proving that the reality is unknowable, or that it lies hidden behind appearances or presentations. Take, for instance, a reality which appears as a ray of the sun. When it goes through a pane of glass it appears to be colorless, but it exhibits a beautiful spectrum when it passes through a prism. Therefore you assume that a reality appearing as the rays of the sun is neither colorless nor colored in itself, since these appearances are wholly due to the difference that obtains between the pane of glass and the prism.

We contend, however, that the fact does not prove the existence of the reality named the sun's ray beyond or behind the white light, nor its existence beyond or behind the spectrum. It is evident that the reality exists in white light, and that it is known as the white light when it goes through a pane of glass; and that the same reality exists in the spectrum, and is known as the spectrum when it goes through the prism. The reality is known as the white light on the one hand, and as the spectrum on the other. It is not unknowable, but knowable.

Suppose that one and the same reality exhibits one aspect when it stands in relation to another object; two aspects when it stands in relation to two different objects; three aspects when it stands in relation to three different objects. The reality of one aspect never proves the unreality of another aspect, for all these three aspects can be equally real. A tree appears to us as a vegetable; it appears to some birds as a shelter; and it appears to some worms as a food. The reality of its aspect as a vegetable never proves the unreality of its aspect as food, nor does the reality of its aspect as food disprove the reality of its aspect as shelter. The real tree does not exist beyond or behind the vegetable. We can rely upon its reality, and make use of it to a fruitful result. At the same time, the birds can rely on its reality as a shelter, and build their nests in it; the worms, too, can rely on its reality as food, and eat it to their satisfaction. A reality which appears to me as my wife must appear to my son as his mother, and never as his wife. But the same real woman is in the wife and in the mother; neither is unreal.

15. *Thing-in-Itself Means Thing-Knowerless.*—How, then, did philosophers come to consider reality to be unknowable and hidden behind or beyond appearances? They investigated all the possible presentations in dif-

ferent relationships, and put them all aside as appearances, and brooded on the thing-in-itself, shut out from all possible relationship, and declared it unknowable. Thing-in-itself means thing cut off from all possible relationships. To put it in another way: thing-in-itself means thing deprived of its relation to its knower—that is to say, thing knowerless. So that to declare thing-in-itself unknowable is as much as to declare thing-unknowable unknowable; there is no doubt about it, but what does it prove?

Deprive yourself of all the possible relationships, and see what you are. Suppose you are not a son to your parents, nor the husband to your wife, nor the father to your children, nor a relative to your kindred, nor a friend to your acquaintances, nor a teacher to your students, nor a citizen to your country, nor an individual member to your society, nor a creature to your God, then you get you-in-yourself. Now ask yourself, what is you-in-yourself? You can never answer the question. It is unknowable, just because it is cut off from all knowable relations. Can you thus prove that you-in-yourself exists beyond or behind you?

In like manner our universe appears to us human beings as the phenomenal world or presentation. It might appear to other creatures of a different mental constitution as something else. We cannot ascertain how it might seem to Devas, to Asuras, to angels, and to the Almighty, if there be such beings. However different it might seem to these beings, it does not imply that the phenomenal world is unreal, nor that the realm of reality is unknowable.

"Water," the Indian tradition has it, "seems to man as a drink, as emerald to Devas, as bloody pus to Pretas, as houses to fishes." Water is not a whit less real because of its seeming as houses to fishes, and fishes' houses are not less real because of its seeming as emerald to Devas. There is nothing that proves the unreality of it. It is a gross illusion to conceive reality as transcendental to appearances. Reality exists as appearances, and appearances are reality known to human beings. You cannot separate appearances from reality, and hold out the latter as the object of aspiration at the cost of the former. You must acknowledge that the so-called realm of reality which you aspire after, and which you seek for outside or behind the phenomenal universe, exists here on earth. Let Zen teachers tell you that "the world of birth and death is the realm of Nirvāṇa"; "the earth is the pure land of Buddha."

• • •

18. *All the Worlds in Ten Directions Are Buddha's Holy Land.*—Suffice it to say for the present it is the law of Universal Life that manifoldness is in unity, and unity is in manifoldness; difference is in agreement, and agreement in difference; confliction is in harmony, and harmony in confliction; parts are in the whole, and the whole is in parts; constancy is in change, and

change in constancy; good is in bad, and bad in good; integration is in dis-integration, and disintegration is in integration; peace is in disturbance, and disturbance in peace. We can find something celestial among the earthly. We can notice something glorious in the midst of the base and degenerated.

"There are nettles everywhere, but are not smooth, green grasses more common still?" Can you recognize something awe-inspiring in the rise and fall of nations? Can you not recognize something undisturbed and peaceful among disturbance and trouble? Has not even grass some meaning? Does not even a stone tell the mystery of Life? Does not the immutable Jaw of good hold sway over human affairs after all, as Tennyson says—

> I can but trust that good shall fall
> At last—far off—at last, to all.

Has not each of us a light within him, whatever degrees of luster there may be? Was Washington in the wrong when he said: "Labor to keep alive in your heart that little spark of celestial fire called conscience."

We are sure that we can realize the celestial bliss in this very world, if we keep alive the Enlightened Consciousness, of which Bodhidharma and his followers showed the example. "All the worlds in ten directions are Bud-dha's Holy Lands!" That Land of Bliss and Glory exists above us, under us, around us, within us, without us, if we open our eyes to see. "Nirvāṇa is in life itself," if we enjoy it with admiration and love. "Life and death are the life of Buddha," says Dōgen. Everywhere the Elysian gates stand open, if we do not shut them up by ourselves. Shall we starve ourselves refusing to accept the rich bounty which the Blessed Life offers to us? Shall we perish in the darkness of scepticism, shutting our eyes to the light of Tathāgata? Shall we suffer from innumerable pains in the self-created hell where remorse, jeal-ousy, and hatred feed the fire of anger? Let us pray to Buddha, not in word only, but in the deed of generosity and tolerance, in the character noble and loving, and in the personality sublime and good. Let us pray to Buddha to save us from the hell of greed and folly, to deliver us from the thralldom of temptation. Let us "enter the Holy of Holies in admiration and wonder."

NOTES

1. Abstract Contemplation, which the Zennists distinguish from Samādhi, practised by the Brahmins. The author of 'An Outline of Buddhist Sects' points out the distinc-tion, saying: "'Contemplation of outside religionists is practised with the heterodox view that the lower worlds (the worlds for men, beasts, etc.) are disgusting, but the upper worlds (the worlds for Devas) are desirable; Contemplation of common peo-ple (ordinary lay believers of Buddhism) is practised with the belief in the law of Karma, and also with disgust (for the lower worlds) and desire (for the upper worlds);

Contemplation of Hīnayāna is practised with an insight into the truth of Anātman (non-soul); Contemplation of Mahāyāna is practised with an insight of Unreality of Ātman (soul) as well as of Dharma (thing); Contemplation of the highest perfection is practised with the view that Mind is pure in its nature, it is endowed with unpolluted wisdom, free from passion, and it is no other than Buddha himself."

2. Both Mahāyāna and Hīnayāna Buddhism teach the doctrine of Anātman, or Non-self. It is the denial of soul as conceived by common-sense, and of Ātman as conceived by Indian heterodox thinkers. Some Mahāyānists believe in the existence of real Self instead of individual self, as we see in *Mahāparinirvāṇa-sūtra,* whose author says: "There is real self in non-self." It is worthy of note that the Hīnayānists set forth Purity, Pleasure, Ātman, and Eternity, as the four great misconceptions about life, while the same author regards them as the four great attributes of Nirvāṇa itself.

3. The master strongly condemns the immortality of the soul as the heterodox doctrine in his *Shō-bō-gen-zō.* The same argument is found in *Mu-chū-mon-dō,* by Koku-hi.

4. *Creative Evolution,* pp. 354, 355.

5. Bergson, arguing against the dependence of the mind on brain, says: "That there is a close connection between a state of consciousness and the brain we do not dispute. But there is also a close connection between a coat and the nail on which it hangs, for if the nail is pulled out, the coat will fall to the ground. Shall we say, then, that the shape of the nail gave the shape of the coat, or in any way corresponds to it? No more are we entitled to conclude, because the psychical fact is hung on to a cerebral state, that there is any parallelism between the two series, psychical and physiological." We have to ask, in what respects does the interrelation between mind and body resemble the relation between a coat and a nail?

6. For further explanation, see *Shō-bō-gen-zō* and *Mu-chū-mon-dō.*

7. *The Destiny of Man,* p. 110.

8. *The Destiny of Man,* pp. 110, 111.

9. This is the law of Karma.

10. Eucken's *Philosophy of Life,* by W. II. Royce Gibbon, p. 51.

11. Chwang Tsz, vol. i, p. 20.

12. This is a favorite subject of discussion by Zennists.

13. Zen is often called the Sect of Buddha-mind, as it lays stress on the awakening of the Mind of Buddha. The words 'the Mind of Buddha' were taken from a passage in *Lankāvatāra-sūtra.*

14. That knowledge by which one becomes enlightened.

15. Supreme wisdom.

16. Sukhavātū, or the land of bliss.

17. These words were repeatedly uttered by Chinese and Japanese Zennists in all ages. Chwen Hih (Fu-dai-shi) expressed this very idea in his Sin Wang Ming (Shin-ō-mei) at the time of Bodhidharma.

18. The Rin-zai teachers mostly make use of the doctrine of unreality of all things, as taught in *Prajñā-pāramitā-sūtras.* We have to note that there are some differences between the Mahāyāna doctrine of unreality and the Hīnayāna doctrine of unreality.

19. See the appendix, chap. ii, "The Mahāyāna Doctrine of Nihilism."

20. Appendix, chap. ii, "The Mahāyāna Doctrine of Dharmalaksana."

21. Zen-rin-rui-shū.

22. A philosophical work on Buddhist Idealism by Vasubandhu, translated into Chinese by Hiuen Tsang in A.D. 648. There exists a famous commentary on it, compiled by Dharmapāla, translated into Chinese by Hiuen Tsang in A.D. 659. See Nanjō's Catalogue, Nos. 1197 and 1125.

23. A simpler work on Idealism, translated into Chinese by Hiuen Tsang in A.D. 661. See Nanjō's Catalogue, Nos. 1238, 1239, and 1240.

STUDY QUESTIONS

1. Discuss the ontological argument for the existence of God. Do you agree with Anselm that it proves the existence of God?
2. What is Gaunilo's criticism of the argument? Do you agree with Gaunilo? Argue pro or con.
3. Is it possible for us to distinguish in thought between (i) a being that exists only in our concept, and (ii) a being that exists in our concept and reality? Do you agree or disagree? Defend your position.
4. Is a being that exists in our concept *and* in reality superior to an otherwise identical being existing in concept only? Argue pro or con.
5. In your opinion, is the ontological argument a sound argument? If so, why so? If not, why not?
6. What are the five ways in which Aquinas claims that the existence of God can be proven?
7. Has Aquinas proved the existence of God? Why or why not? Do you see the value of these arguments? Argue for your position.
8. Out of the five ways that Aquinas discusses, which way seems most defensible and why?
9. Compare and contrast ontological and cosmological arguments. Which argument appeals to you more and why?
10. Select a proof for the existence of God and outline it clearly. Does the proof you have selected prove the existence of God? If it does, discuss some of the strongest objections to the proof and why they do not constitute good reasons for rejecting the proof. If it does not, discuss some of the strongest reasons for accepting the proof and why they do not constitute good reasons for the acceptance of the proof.
11. Discuss the main tenets of the Islāmic conception of God.
12. Discuss key ideas of Aurobindo's "Omnipresent Reality."
13. Do you agree with Aurobindo that both being and non-being are different states of one omnipresent reality? Give reasons for your answer.
14. Sri Aurobindo characterizes the reality as conscious existence, supreme intelligence, and self-existent bliss. Explain what Aurobindo means by these characterizations.
15. Compare and contrast western, Islāmic, and Hindu conceptions of God. Discuss the unique feature of each of these religions.
16. Discuss the Zennist conception of enlightenment.
17. Both the Zennists and the Hindus maintain that enlightenment implies an insight into the self. Compare and contrast the two.
18. Summarize the main points of Wang Ch'ung's thesis that the soul after death does not assume any conscious form.

19. Discuss Wang Ch'ung's notion of the spontaneity of the natural order. Outline the method of reasoning he uses to substantiate his naturalism.
20. Do you agree with Wang Ch'ung's thesis that natural is without any consciousness or purpose? Argue for or against.

SUGGESTIONS FOR FURTHER READING

The Mind of Light by Sri Aurobindo, introduction by Robert A. McDermott (New York: E. P. Dutton & Co., 1971), is an excellent, though brief, introduction to Aurobindo's thought.

The Life Divine, The Synthesis of Yoga, and *The Human Cycle* are Aurobindo's most important writings. They are available in various editions.

The Ontological Argument by Jonathan Barnes (London: Macmillan, 1972) is a good general discussion of the argument.

Sounds of Valley Streams: Enlightenment in Dōgen's Zen: Translation of Nine Essays from Shōbōgenzō edited by Francis H. Cook (Albany: State University of New York Press, 1988), is an excellent collection of translations.

Thomas Aquinas by F.C. Copleston (New York: Barnes & Noble, 1977) is an excellent introduction to the philosophy of Aquinas.

The Cosmological Argument from Plato to Leibnitz by William Craig (New York: Barnes & Noble, 1980) is a good survey of the history of the argument.

Islam: The Straight Faith by J.L. Esposito (New York: Oxford University Press, 1990) is a clear and lively account of Islamic religion.

Classical and Contemporary Readings in the Philosophy of Religion, 4th edition, edited by John Hick, is an excellent anthology with introductory remarks on major issues in philosophy of religion.

Arguments for the Existence of God by John Hick (London: Macmillan, 1971) is a clearly written and insightful examination of the traditional arguments for the existence of God.

Islam: Muhammed and His Religion edited by Arthur Jeffery (Indianapolis: The Bobbs-Merrill Company, Inc., 1958), contains a good selection of writings from traditional Islam.

An Introduction to the Philosophy of Sri Aurobindo, 2nd ed., by S.K. Maitra (Benares: Benares Hindu University, 1945) is a brief and concise introduction to Sri Aurobindo's philosophy.

Students interested in comparative philosophy might wish to consult *The Meeting of the East and the West in Sri Aurobindo's Philosophy,* by S.K. Maitra (Pondicherry: Sri Aurobindo Ashram, 1956).

The Existence of God by Wallace Matson (Ithaca, NY: Cornell University Press, 1965) is a cogently argued attack on the traditional arguments.

The Ontological Argument from St. Anselm to Contemporary Philosophers by Alvin Plantinga (Garden City, NY: Doubleday, 1965) contains a good survey of the history of the argument.

The Cosmological Argument by William Rowe (Princeton, NJ: Princeton University Press, 1975) is a thorough and penetrating study of the classic formulations of the argument.

The Existence of God by Richard Swinburne (Oxford: Clarendon Press, 1979) is perhaps the most sustained defense of the traditional arguments.

A Short History of Chinese Philosophy by Fung Yu-lan (New York: Macmillan Publishing Co., 1960), is an excellent account of the development of Chinese philosophy. It is a shorter version of the two-volume work by Fung entitled *A History of Chinese Philosophy* (Princeton: Princeton University Press, 1959–60), a comprehensive and authoritative survey of Chinese philosophy.

Part 5

Philosophical Anthropology

5.1

Introduction: What Is the Nature of Human Beings?

The preceding three parts of this book are concerned with three important areas of human experience: knowledge, morals, and religious experience. Underlying each there is the question concerning the nature of human beings, of the being who knows, acts, and relates to the sacred. Philosophical theories about the three areas of experience implicitly presuppose but sometimes also explicitly make use of, and in other cases even contribute to, a philosophical anthropology, i.e., a philosophical theory about the nature of humans. Therefore, in an important sense, all philosophy—arguably with the sole exception of metaphysics—is thinking about human nature. But if philosophical thinking itself is an activity of humans, and is not a contingent concern but necessary to the nature of humans, then philosophical thinking about humans, about knowledge, morals, and religion itself defines an essential possibility of human nature.

And yet it is with regard to this theme that philosophical traditions show marked differences amongst themselves. Again, as is to be expected, none of these traditions is homogenous; rather each admits of a great deal of internal diversity, sometimes reaching out to what, on a superficial view, may look like its other.

However, before surveying some of these differences, it would be better to introduce the key philosophical terms as well as questions pertaining to the theme of this section. The ordinary term defining the theme has been "man," but this term, with its male sexist meaning and implications, is better replaced by the more neutral "human being." There are also two other, more philosophical terms which sometimes are made to do the job of an overall designation of the topic: "self" and "person." Each of these signifies a certain aspect of the human being. Thus "self" stands for what is the unchanging, invariant, essence of a human; it is always someone's ("mine," "yours," "hers". . .). It suggests an identity, as though my self remains the same—no matter what changes I go through. The word "person" possibly has its origin in legal thinking, meaning one who has legal rights (and also duties), and so, necessarily, is a member of a community; a person is also capable of performing voluntary actions, and ascribing intentional states to oneself ("I hope," I desire," "I believe"). The idea of "person" also seems to imply a certain invariance—but, to be sure, less rigid and more flexible than the "self." Philosophical theories as well as traditions are more concerned with one of these rather than the other, and sometimes they do not clearly distinguish between the two.

Some of the major questions philosophers have asked about human nature are these: What constitutes the identity of the self, and of the person? How is the self related to the body? What is the relation of a person to the mind and the body? How is a human individual related to other humans and to society? Extending this question beyond the realm of humans, one can ask: how is a human related to the universe? Furthermore, is the human individual an irreducible entity? Again, what constitutes the defining character of a human being? Is it rationality? Is it self-consciousness? Is it intentional action? Or, does it lie in social praxis? There is also the ethico-religious question: is human nature rigid or flexible, capable of self-development and limitless expansion, or is it demarcated by rigid limits? Is the person inherently good (evil being a mere appearance), or inherently evil, or a mixture of both good and evil? Or, is human nature neither good nor evil? Keeping these questions in mind, let us take a quick look at the major philosophical traditions represented in the essays included in the present anthology.

The Chinese tradition, especially the Confucian, is represented in the piece by Mencius. Mencius's fundamental thesis that human nature is basically good was a departure from what Confucius had explicitly taught, but may be said to be consistent with it. It is more likely that for Confucius—as for Aristotle—human nature is neither "good" (unlike Mencius) nor "bad" (unlike Hsun Tzu). At the same time, as Tu Wei-Ming has more recently emphasized, the Confucian human nature is not a static essence, but consists in the capacity for self-development through learning to be human. While it is true that the self in Confucius's view is a center of relationships, it needs to be emphasized that Confucianism emphasized self-cultivation and self-transcendence.

When Mencius says that human nature is good, he may be taken to mean that human nature is intrinsically capable of goodness, that humans are capable of perfection through their own effort. The seeds of all of the Confucian virtues are embedded in human nature: the spontaneous feeling of pity and sympathy, the spontaneous feeling of defense of others, the spontaneous feeling of shame and the spontaneous feeling of approval or disapproval of others' actions. This innate goodness can be realized through self cultivation leading to oneness with heaven and earth.

As contrasted with the Chinese understanding of human nature, both the Islāmic and the Christian understandings of it are determined by their theistic positions. In this volume, the Islāmic philosophy of human nature is presented in an essay by Ismaʿīl Fārūqī. Creation of humans is taken as serving a purpose, and this purpose is nothing other than realization in space and time of moral law. In this sense, a human is a bridge linking the moral law and spatio-temporal nature. Only through human beings may moral values be realized—as Nicolai Hartmann held. Human being is the carrier of values; the world is the material and the theater of value-realization.

Kantian philosophy conceptualizes the best of the protestant Christian philosophy of human nature. Kant also recognized a similar purposiveness in human nature. But his position, in this regard, has an internal complexity which is due to his alertness to various scientific and spiritual demands. As an avowed Newtonian, he believed that nature is strictly ruled by causal laws, and yet he recognized that biological nature demands recognition of a certain purposiveness. He squarely faced the fact that even though man is a product of nature, human reason prescribes laws a priori to nature and moral laws to itself. Nature has so willed man that his actions, especially moral actions, shall go beyond "the mechanical ordering of his animal existence," and also that the goal of his life is not satisfaction of his natural desires, but rather a perfection which he can create for himself through his own reason. This leads Kant to recognize that a human being is simultaneously a member of two realms: the realm of nature ruled by blind necessity, and the realm of "kingdom of ends" where he is the lawgiver for his own will. The ultimate goal of the world then is the bringing forth of human nature as morally self-legislative. The world, though mechanically necessary, exhibits this purposiveness.

A child of his own age, the age of Enlightenment, Kant believed in the power of human reason to *critique* all beliefs and dogmas, and also in the progress of human society. The two essays included in this volume dwell on these two issues. In the essay "What is Enlightenment?" Kant gives a classic description: "Enlightenment is man's emergence from his self incurred immaturity." By "immaturity," he means man's inability to use his own reason without someone else's guidance. But as a realist, he distinguishes between the *public* use of reason and the *private* use of it. With regard to the former—i.e., the use of reason in addressing the reading public—he defended unlimited power of reason; but in private use—that is to say, in discharging his duties attaching to a civil or ecclesiastical office—he recognizes that the use of reason needs to be restricted.

Believing as he did in progress, he realized that we have still a long way to go; and if he were alive today he would still say the same thing. But he had to face the question of whether the human race was continually improving. Clearly, he rejects the view that the human race is continually deteriorating (a view which he calls moral terrorism), as also the view (called by him "eudaimonism") that mankind is continuously improving. There is a third possibility which is also rejected by him—the view, namely, that there is a kind of stalemate, a continuous alteration, but no eventual progress and no retrogression. Rejecting these views, Kant argues that the question as to whether the human race is progressing or not cannot be answered on the basis of purely empirical evidence. And yet, he draws from the French Revolution the lesson that the human race has a moral tendency, a moral disposition, towards developing a form of civil constitution as it sees fit, and to avoid wars that have a negative effect on moral progress. This tendency for self-improvement, he insists, could not have been predicted on the basis of past experiences, but he seems to be confident that he could predict from this event—namely, the French Revolution—that humankind would continue progressing toward the goal of "a constitution in harmony with the natural rights of man." Since he was aware of the weakness of the human will, Kant eventually relies upon a higher wisdom (which he calls Providence) to assure us of success of our efforts toward this goal.

Kant's views about human nature are generally regarded as being rationalistic, inasmuch as Kant ascribed to human reason a priori knowledge of nature, and a priori legislation of moral laws. But aware as he was of the presence of "radical evil" in human nature, Kant's total view was a combination of rationality and irrationality in a human being who, on his view, was eventually finite. This finitude of human existence came to the forefront in the thought of Martin Heidegger.

Heidegger uses the technical word "*Dasein*" (or there-being) for the mode of being of humans. He rejects the classical Western understanding of human nature in terms of the Cartesian dualism of body and soul, as also the Kantian understanding of it in terms of the subject of cognition and of willing. The fundamental mode of being of the human, i.e., the *Dasein,* is not captured by those familiar philosophical terms such as soul, subject, consciousness, spirit or the person, the self, and the ego. The *Dasein* is not a thing that is present-at-hand. In its most basic, ontological dimension, the *Dasein* is Being-in-the world and Being-with-others. Heidegger then proceeds to undertake an analysis of Being-in-the-world in terms of *Sorge* or care, and in terms of temporality as being-toward-death. Confronted with the necessary possibility of death as an absolute end of itself, *Dasein*, in a resolute conscience, achieves authentic existence. But, forgetful of this temporality, it becomes the "they," the self of everyday *Dasein*. Human existence oscillates between these two poles of authenticity and inauthenticity.

Contemporary Eastern thought about human nature is represented in the chapter from the Nobel prize–winning Indian poet Rabindranath Tagore's Hibbert lectures entitled "The Religion of Man," and in the concluding chapter on "Self in Japanese Culture" by the anthropologist Takie Sugiyama Lebra.

Tagore presents a modern version of the Upaniṣadic thesis that the true self of a finite individual is the universal spirit called "*ātman*" which the poet calls "Man" (with a capital "M"). In his view, the great truth that the ancient sages of India realized and proclaimed is the harmony between the individual and the universal. Separating man from nature is like dividing the bud from the blossom, we then become merely human, not man-in-the-universe. When Heidegger spoke of "being-in-the-world" as a further unanalyzable structure, he thought of the world as a finite system of references referring back to *Dasein's* temporal project. For Tagore, the universe is infinite, and so also is the human spirit. The spirit for him is feeling—at its innermost, the feeling of love. The goal of human existence is to self-consciously realize this feeling within and the feeling that pervades the universe. This movement is expressed in the movement of human knowledge, morality, and art. For example, to live the life of goodness is to live the life of all. The Indian poet ends the chapter with recalling Lao Tzu and reflecting on the Japanese sense of beauty: in both he finds anticipation of what he calls the "Religion of Man."

But what is the Japanese understanding of the Self? Lebra distinguishes between several layers of self in the Japanese cultural context, of which the last, i.e., the boundless self, which merges with the rest of the world, and which is beyond the subject-object dualism, comes close to Tagore's vision of the unity of the self and nature. But whereas Tagore considers this universal spirit to be positive fullness of love, Lebra ascribes to the Japanese conception features such as emptiness, mindlessness, and nothingness. This "boundless self" stands at the end of a series of conceptions of the self: the interactional, socially constituted, variable and multiple self, and a less relative, more stable, inner self, or the world of pure subjectivity. Lebra finds these three conceptions not exclusive, but partially overlapping layers and mutually complementary, and goes on to show how the concept of "purity" runs through all three. In many respects, this account of the Japanese conception of the self may actually bring it closer to the Indian conception.

5.2

Human Nature

Mencius

BOOK 2 – PART A

6. Mencius said, "No man is devoid of a heart sensitive to the suffering of others. Such a sensitive heart was possessed by the Former Kings and this manifested itself in compassionate government. With such a sensitive heart behind compassionate government, it was as easy to rule the Empire as rolling it on your palm.

"My reason for saying that no man is devoid of a heart sensitive to the suffering of others is this. Suppose a man were, all of a sudden, to see a young child on the verge of falling into a well. He would certainly be moved to compassion, not because he wanted to get in the good graces of the parents, nor because he wished to win the praise of his fellow villagers or friends, nor yet because he disliked the cry of the child. From this it can be seen that whoever is devoid of the heart of compassion is not human, whoever is devoid of the heart of shame is not human, whoever is devoid of the heart of courtesy and modesty is not human, and whoever is devoid of the heart of right and wrong is not human. The heart of compassion is the germ of benevolence; the heart of shame, of dutifulness; the heart of courtesy and modesty, of observance of the rites; the heart of right and wrong, of wisdom. Man has these four germs just as he has four limbs. For a man possessing these four germs to deny his own potentialities is for him to cripple himself; for him to deny the potentialities of his prince is for him to cripple his prince If a man is able to develop all these four germs that he possesses, it will be like a fire starting up or a spring coming through. When these are fully de-

---

veloped, he can tend the whole realm within the Four Seas, but if he fails to develop them, he will not be able even to serve his parents."

7. Mencius said, "Is the maker of arrows really more unfeeling than the maker of armour? He is afraid lest he should fail to harm people, whereas the maker of armour is afraid lest he should fail to protect them. The case is similar with the sorcerer-doctor and the coffin-maker. For this reason one cannot be too careful in the choice of one's calling."

Confucius said, "The best neighbourhood is where benevolence is to be found. Not to live in such a neighbourhood when one has the choice cannot by any means be considered wise."[1] Benevolence is the high honour bestowed by Heaven and the peaceful abode of man. Not to be benevolent when nothing stands in the way is to show a lack of wisdom. A man neither benevolent nor wise, devoid of courtesy and dutifulness, is a slave. A slave ashamed of serving is like a maker of bows ashamed of making bows, or a maker of arrows ashamed of making arrows. If one is ashamed, there is no better remedy than to practise benevolence. Benevolence is like archery: an archer makes sure his stance is correct before letting fly the arrow, and if he fails to hit the mark, he does not hold it against his victor. He simply seeks the cause within himself."

BOOK 4 – PART A

27. Mencius said, "The content of benevolence is the serving of one's parents; the content of dutifulness is obedience to one's elder brothers; the content of wisdom is to understand these two and to hold fast to them; the content of the rites is the regulation and adornment of them; the content of music is the joy that comes of delighting in them. When joy arises how can one stop it? And when one cannot stop it, then one begins to dance with one's feet and wave one's arms without knowing it.

BOOK 4 – PART B

12. Mencius said, "A great man is one who retains the heart of a new-born babe."

19. Mencius said, "Slight is the difference between man and the brutes. The common man loses this distinguishing feature, while the gentleman retains it. Shun understood the way of things and had a keen insight into human relationships. He followed the path of morality. He did not just put morality into practice."

26. Mencius said, "In the theories about human nature put forth by the world there is nothing else other than resort to precedents. The primary

thing in any resort to precedents is ease of explanation. What one dislikes in clever men is their tortuosity. If clever men could act as Yü did in guiding the flood waters, then there would be nothing to dislike in them. Yü guided the water by imposing nothing on it that was against its natural tendency. If clever men can also do this, then great indeed will their cleverness be. In spite of the height of the heavens and the distance of the heavenly bodies, if one seeks out former instances, one can calculate the solstices of a thousand years hence without stirring from one's seat."

BOOK 6 – PART A

1. Kao Tzu said, "Human nature is like the *ch'i* willow. Dutifulness is like cups and bowls. To make morality out of human nature is like making cups and bowls out of the willow."

"Can you," said Mencius, "make cups and bowls by following the nature of the willow? Or must you mutilate the willow before you can make it into cups and bowls? If you have to mutilate the willow to make it into cups and bowls, must you, then, also mutilate a man to make him moral? Surely it will be these words of yours men in the world will follow in bringing disaster upon morality."

2. Kao Tzu said, "Human nature is like whirling water. Give it an outlet in the east and it will flow east; give it an outlet in the west and it will flow west. Human nature does not show any preference for either good or bad just as water does not show any preference for either east or west."

"It certainly is the case," said Mencius, "that water does not show any preference for either east or west, but does it show the same indifference to high and low? Human nature is good just as water seeks low ground. There is no man who is not good; there is no water that does not flow downwards.

"Now in the case of water, by splashing it one can make it shoot up higher than one's forehead, and by forcing it one can make it stay on a hill. How can that be the nature of water? It is the circumstances being what they are. That man can be made bad shows that his nature is no different from that of water in this respect."

3. Kao Tzu said, "The inborn is what is meant by 'nature.'"[2]

"Is that," said Mencius, "the same as white is what is meant by 'white?'"

"Yes."

"Is the whiteness of white feathers the same as the whiteness of white snow and the whiteness of white snow the same as the whiteness of white jade?"

"Yes."

"In that case, is the nature of a hound the same as the nature of an ox and the nature of an ox the same as the nature of a man?"

4. Kao Tzu said, "Appetite for food and sex is nature. Benevolence is internal, not external; rightness is external, not internal."

"Why do you say," said Mencius, "that benevolence is internal and rightness is external?"

"That man there is old and I treat him as elder. He owes nothing of his elderliness to me, just as in treating him as white because he is white I only do so because of his whiteness which is external to me. That is why I call it external."

"The case of rightness is different from that of whiteness. 'Treating as white' is the same whether one is treating a horse as white or a man as white. But I wonder if you would think that 'treating as old' is the same whether one is treating a horse as old or a man as elder? Furthermore, is it the one who is old that is dutiful, or is it the one who treats him as elder that is dutiful?"

"My brother I love, but the brother of a man from Ch'in I do not love. This means that the explanation lies in me. Hence I call it internal. Treating an elder of a man from Ch'u as elder is no different from treating an elder of my own family as elder. This means that the explanation lies in their elderliness. Hence I call it external."

"My enjoyment of the roast provided by a man from Ch'in is no different from my enjoyment of my own roast. Even with inanimate things we can find cases similar to the one under discussion. Are we, then, to say that there is something external even in the enjoyment of roast?"

5. Meng Chi-tzu asked Kung-tu Tzu, "Why do you say that rightness is internal?"

"It is the respect in me that is being put into effect. That is why I say it is internal."

"If a man from your village is a year older than your eldest brother, which do you respect?"

"My brother."

"In filling their cups with wine, which do you give precedence to?"

"The man from my village."

"The one you respect is the former; the one you treat as elder is the latter. This shows that it is in fact external, not internal."

Kung-tu Tzu was unable to find an answer and gave an account of the discussion to Mencius.

Mencius said, "[Ask him,] 'Which do you respect, your uncle or your younger brother?' He will say, 'My uncle.' 'When your younger brother is impersonating an ancestor at a sacrifice, then which do you respect?' He will say, 'My younger brother.' You ask him, 'What has happened to your respect for your uncle?' He will say, 'It is because of the position my younger brother occupies.' You can then say, '[In the case of the man from my village] it is also because of the position he occupies. Normal respect is due to my elder brother; temporary respect is due to the man from my village.'"

When Meng Chi-tzu heard this, he said, "It is the same respect whether I am respecting my uncle or my younger brother. It is, as I have said, external and does not come from within."

"In winter," said Kung-tu Tzu, "one drinks hot water, in summer cold. Does that mean that even food and drink can be a matter of what is external?"

6. Kung-tu Tzu said, "Kao Tzu said, 'There is neither good nor bad in human nature,' but others say, 'Human nature can become good or it can become bad, and that is why with the rise of King Wen and King Wu the people were given to goodness, while with the rise of King Yü and King Li they were given to cruelty.' Then there are others who say, 'There are those, who are good by nature, and there are those who are bad by nature. For this reason, Hsiang could have Yao as prince, and Shun could have the Blind Man as father, and Ch'i,[3] Viscount of Wei and Prince Pi Kan could have Tchou as nephew as well as sovereign.' Now you say human nature is good. Does this mean that all the others are mistaken?"

"As far as what is genuinely in him is concerned, a man is capable of becoming good," said Mencius. "That is what I mean by good. As for his becoming bad, that is not the fault of his native endowment. The heart of compassion is possessed by all men alike; likewise the heart of shame, the heart of respect, and the heart of right and wrong. The heart of compassion pertains to benevolence, the heart of shame to dutifulness, the heart of respect to the observance of the rites, and the rites, and the heart of right and wrong to wisdom. Benevolence, dutifulness, observance of the rites, and wisdom do not give me a lustre from the outside, they are in me originally. Only this has never dawned on me. That is why it is said, Seek and you will find it; let go and you will lose it." There are cases where one man is twice, five times or countless times better than another man, but this is only because there are people who fail to make the best of their native endowment. The *Book of Odes* says,

> Heaven produces the teeming masses,
> And where there is a thing there is a norm.
> If the people held on to their constant nature,
> They would be drawn to superior virtue.

Confucius commented, "The author of this poem must have had knowledge of the Way. Thus where there is a thing there is a norm, and because the people hold on to their constant nature they are drawn to superior virtue."

8. Mencius said, "There was a time when the trees were luxuriant on the Ox Mountain, but as it is on the outskirts of a great metropolis, the trees are constantly lopped by axes. Is it any wonder that they are no longer fine? With the respite they get in the day and in the night, and the moistening by the rain and dew, there is certainly no lack of new shoots coming out, but

then the cattle and sheep come to graze upon the mountain. That is why it is as bald as it is. People, seeing only its baldness, tend to think that it never had any trees. But can this possibly be the nature of a mountain? Can what is in man be completely lacking in moral inclinations? A man's letting go of his true heart is like the case of the trees and the axes. When the trees are lopped day after day, is it any wonder that they are no longer fine? If, in spite of the respite a man gets in the day and in the night and of the effect of the morning air on him, scarcely any of his likes and dislikes resemble those of other men, it is because what he does in the course of the day once again dissipates what he has gained. If this dissipation happens repeatedly, then the influence of the air in the night will no longer be able to preserve what was originally in him, and when that happens, the man is not far removed from an animal. Others, seeing his resemblance to an animal, will be led to think that he never had any native endowment. But can that be what a man is genuinely like? Hence, given the right nourishment there is nothing that will not grow, while deprived of it there is nothing that will not wither away." Confucius said, "Hold on to it and it will remain; let go of it and it will disappear. One never knows the time it comes or goes, neither does one know the direction. It is perhaps to the heart this refers."

9. Mencius said, "Do not be puzzled by the King's lack of wisdom. Even a plant that grows most readily will not survive if it is placed in the sun for one day and exposed to the cold for ten. It is very rarely that I have an opportunity of seeing the King, and as soon as I leave, those who expose him to the cold arrive on the scene. What can I do with the few new shoots that come out? Now take *yi*,[4] which is only an art of little consequence. Yet if one does not give one's whole mind to it, one will never master it. Yi Ch'iu is the best player in the whole country. Get him to teach two people to play, one of whom concentrates his mind on the game and listens only to what Yi Ch'iu has to say, while the other, though he listens, not accept when it was a matter of life and death. I now accept for the sake of the gratitude my needy acquaintances will show me. Is there no way of putting a stop to this? This way of thinking is known as losing one's original heart."

11. Mencius said, "Benevolence is the heart of man, and rightness his road. Sad it is indeed when a man gives up the right road instead of following it and allows his heart to stray without enough sense to go after it. When his chickens and dogs stray, he has sense enough to go after them, but not when his heart strays.[5] The sole concern of learning is to go after this strayed heart. That is all."

15. Kung-tu Tzu asked, "Though equally human, why are some men greater than others?"

"He who is guided by the interests of the parts of his person that are of greater importance is a great man; he who is guided by the interests of the parts of his person that are of smaller importance is a small man."

"Though equally human, why are some men guided one way and others guided another way?"

"The organs of hearing and sight are unable to think and can be misled by external things. When one thing acts on another, all it does is to attract it. The organ of the heart can think. But it will find the answer only if it does think; otherwise, it will not find the answer. This is what Heaven has given me. If one makes one's stand on what is of greater importance in the first instance, what is of smaller importance cannot displace it. In this way, one cannot but be a great man."

BOOK 6 – PART B

1. A man from Jen asked Wu-lu Tzu, "Which is more important, the rites or food?"

"The rites."

"Which is more important, the rites or sex?"

"The rites."

"Suppose you would starve to death if you insisted on the observance of the rites, but would manage to get something to eat if you did not. Would you still insist on their observance? Again, suppose you would not get a wife if you insisted on the observance of *ch'in ying,*[6] but would get one if you did not. Would you still insist on its observance?"

Wu-lu Tzu was unable to answer. The following day he went to Tsou and gave an account of the discussion to Mencius.

"What difficulty is there," said Mencius, "in answering this? If you bring the tips to the same level without measuring the difference in the bases, you can make a piece of wood an inch long reach a greater height than a tall building. In saying that gold is heavier than feathers, surely one is not referring to the amount of gold in a clasp and a whole cartload of feathers? If you compare a case where food is important with a case where the rite is inconsequential, then the greater importance of food is not the only absurd conclusion you can draw. Similarly with sex. Go and reply to the questioner in this way, suppose you would manage to get something to eat if you took the food from your elder brother by twisting his arm, but would not get it if you did not. Would you twist his arm? Again, suppose you would get a wife if you climbed over the wall of your neighbour on the east side and dragged away the daughter of the house by force, but would not if you did not. Would you drag her away by force?"

4. Sung K'eng was on his way to Ch'u. Mencius, meeting him at Shih Ch'iu, asked him, "Where are you going, sir?"

"I heard that hostilities had broken out between Ch'in and Ch'u. I am going to see the king of Ch'u and try to persuade him to bring an end to them. If I fail to find favour with the king of Ch'u I shall go to see the king of Ch'in and try to persuade him instead. I hope I shall have success with one or other of the two kings."

"I do not wish to know the details, but may I ask about the gist of your argument? How are you going to persuade the kings?"

"I shall explain to them the unprofitability of war."

"Your purpose is lofty indeed, but your slogan is wrong. If you place profit before the kings of Ch'in and Ch'u, and they call off their armies because they are drawn to profit, then it means that the soldiers in their armies retire because they are drawn to profit. If a subject, in serving his prince, cherished the profit motive, and a son, in serving his father, and a younger brother, in serving his elder brother, did likewise, then it would mean that in their mutual relations, prince and subject, father and son, elder brother and younger brother, all cherished the profit motive to the total exclusion of morality. The prince of such a state is sure to perish. If, on the other hand, you placed morality before the kings of Ch'in and Ch'u and they called off their armies because they were drawn to morality, then it would mean that the soldiers in their armies retired because they were drawn to morality. If a subject, in serving his prince, cherished morality, and a son, in serving his father, and a younger brother, in serving his elder brother, did likewise, then it would mean that in their mutual relations, prince and subject, father and son, elder brother and younger brother, all cherished morality to the exclusion of profit. The prince of such a state is sure to become a true King. What is the point of mentioning the word 'profit'?"

BOOK 7 – PART A

1. Mencius said, "For a man to give full realization to his heart is for him to understand his own nature, and a man who knows his own nature will know Heaven. By retaining his heart and nurturing his nature he is serving Heaven. Whether he is going to die young or to live to a ripe old age makes no difference to his steadfastness of purpose. It is through awaiting whatever is to befall him with a perfected character that he stands firm on his proper Destiny."

4. Mencius said, "All the ten thousand things are there in me. There is no greater joy for me than to find, on self-examination, that I am true to myself. Try your best to treat others as you would wish to be treated yourself, and you will find that this is the shortest way to benevolence."

9. Mencius said to Sung Kou-chien, "You are fond of travelling from state to state, offering advice. I shall tell you how this should be done. You should be content whether your worth is recognized by others or not."

"What must a man be before he can be content?"

"If he reveres virtue and delights in rightness, he can be content. Hence a Gentleman never abandons rightness in adversity, nor does he depart from the Way in success. By not abandoning rightness in adversity, he finds delight in himself; by not departing from the Way in success, he remains an example the people can look up to. Men of antiquity made the people feel the effect of their bounty when they realized their ambition, and, when they failed to realize their ambition, were at least able to show the world an exemplary character. In obscurity a man makes perfect his own person, but in prominence he makes perfect the whole Empire as well."

21. Mencius said, "An extensive territory and a huge population are things a gentleman desires, but what he delights in lies elsewhere. To stand in the centre of the Empire and bring peace to the people within the Four Seas is what a gentleman delights in, but that which he follows as his nature lies elsewhere. That which a gentleman follows as his nature is not added to when he holds sway over the Empire, nor is it detracted from when he is reduced to straitened circumstances. This is because he knows his allotted station. That which a gentleman follows as his nature, that is to say, benevolence, rightness, the rites and wisdom, is rooted in his heart, and manifests itself in his face, giving it a sleek appearance. It also shows in his back and extends to his limbs, rendering their message intelligible without words."

30. Mencius said, "Yao and Shun had it as their nature. T'ang and King Wu embodied it. The Five Leaders of the feudal lords borrowed it.[7] But if a man borrows a thing and keeps it long enough, how can one be sure that it will not become truly his?"

BOOK 7 – PART B

31. Mencius said, "For every man there are things he cannot bear. To extend this to what he can bear is benevolence.[8] For every man there are things he is not willing to do. To extend this to what he is willing to do is rightness. If a man can extend to the full his natural aversion to harming others, then there will be an overabundance of benevolence. If a man can extend his dislike for boring holes and climbing over walls, then there will be an overabundance of rightness. If a man can extend his unwillingness to suffer the actual humiliation of being addressed as 'thou' and 'thee', then wherever he goes he will not do anything that is not right.

To speak to a Gentleman who cannot be spoken to is to use speech as a bait; on the other hand, not to speak to one who could be spoken to is to use silence as a bait.[9] In either case, the action is of the same kind as that of boring holes and climbing over walls."

32. Mencius said, "Words near at hand but with far-reaching import are good words. The way of holding on to the essential while giving it wide ap-

plication is a good way. The words of a gentleman never go as far as below the sash, yet in them is to be found the Way. What the gentleman holds on to is the cultivation of his own character, yet this brings order to the Empire. The trouble with people is that they leave their own fields to weed the fields of others. They are exacting towards others but indulgent towards themselves."

33. Mencius said, "Yao and Shun had it as their nature; T'ang and King Wu returned to it.[10] To be in accord with the rites in every movement is the highest of virtue. When one mourns sorrowfully over the dead it is not to impress the living. When one follows unswervingly the path of virtue it is not to win advancement. When one invariably keeps one's word it is not to establish the rectitude of one's actions. A gentleman merely follows the norm and awaits his destiny."

NOTES

1. cf. the *Analects of Confucius*, IV. I.

2. In *sheng chih wei hsing* ("the inborn is what is meant by 'nature'"), the two words *"sheng"* and *"hsing"* though slightly different in pronunciation, were probably written by the same character in Mencius's time. This would make the statement at least taulological in written form and so parallel to *"pai chih wei pai"* ("white is what is meant by 'white'").

3. According to the *Shi chi* (Records of the Historian) (1607) the Viscount of Wei was an elder brother of Tchou, and son of a concubine of low rank. For this reason, it has been pointed out that the description of having Tchou as nephew applies only to Pi Kan. Cf. the coupling of the name of Chi with that of Yü in IV. B. 29.

4. The ancient name for the game of *wei ch'i*, better known in the West by the name *go* which is simply the Japanese pronunciation of the Chinese word *ch'i*. This game is also mentioned in IV. B. 30.

5. As quoted in the *Han shih wai chuan* 4/27, this goes on as follows: "Does he think less of his heart than of his chickens and dogs? This is an extreme case of failure to see that one thing is the same in kind as another. How sad! In the end such a man is sure only to perish." This further passage must have dropped out of the present text by accident.

6. This is the part of the marriage rites where the groom goes to the home of the bride to fetch her.

7. Cf. 11. A. 3. The "it" here would seem to refer to benevolence.

8. Cf. VII. B. I.

9. Cf. the *Analects of Confucius*, XV. 8.

10. Cf. VII. A. 30. The "it" here must also be referring to benevolence.

5.3

The Nature of Man in Islām

Isma'īl Rāgī al Fārūqī

In Islām, the world was not created in vain; and neither was man. The purpose for which man was created is the realization of a divine trust which neither heaven and earth nor the angels were capable of realizing. This trust is the realization in space and time of God's desire. God's will being realized in nature by necessity, through the workings of natural law, His desire awaited the arrival of man who can realize value morally, that is, freely. Because only man may do so under the open possibility of realizing as well as denying and violating the divine command a pre[re]quisite without which no realization of value would be moral—man is a cosmic bridge through whom the moral law, as God's eminent desire, may be fulfilled in space-time. The content of divine desire is the highest and final good. It is a pattern into which every part of creation—above all man's own self—ought to be molded. The moral order of the cosmos is precisely one where the man who realized the pattern is blessed and given his due reward, and he who fails is damned and awarded his due punishment. Salvation then is a man's own work. Any other kind of salvation must either deny man's moral freedom and responsibility or expose him to demonization or apotheosis. Man is built of body and soul, each of which is perfectly equipped for its task, the latter to discover the divine pattern and to will it, the former to be instrument, material carrier, and theater for its realization.

The Islāmic imperative is twofold: personal and societal; and it consists of duties to God and duties to man. This notwithstanding, every duty Islām has enjoined aims at the self as well as at the other selves, and it is aimed at once at the service of God as well as of man. None may be exclusively the one or the other. The confession of faith (*shahādah*) (as solemn acknowledgment of the Islāmic imperative and commitment to its cause), the supreme act of worship (*salāt*) (as devotion to God and His will), sharing one's wealth with one's fellows (*zakāt*), fasting (*sawm*) (as self-discipline and commiseration), and, lastly, pilgrimage (*ḥajj*) (as self-identification with Islāmic history and personal and societal stock-taking) constitute "The Five Pillars" or the institutionalized minimum expected of the Muslim in his life on earth. If he is to do more, the Muslim is expected first, to realize the personal values in himself, then to enter into all the processes of history in space-time, whether in the persons of others or in the group life of human societies everywhere, and there to alter the course of every casual chain for the better to bring them to a realization of the divine pattern. His ideal is the felicitous life of the universal brotherhood under the moral law, to whose fate his fate is inextricably attached, not as a passive object of history but rather, as history's active subject, as the second master of creation.

A. SCRIPTURAL: MAN'S PERFECTED NATURE AND COSMIC STATUS; THE ISLĀMIC IMPERATIVE

1. Man: God's Vicegerent on Earth

And when your Lord said to the angels, "I shall create a vicegerent for Myself on earth," they answered, "Will You plant therein a being who sheds blood and works evil, while we perennially worship You and praise You?" God answered, "I know better; and you do not." (Qur'ān or Koran, 2:30) We have offered Our trust to heaven and earth and mountain, but they feared and withdrew from undertaking it. Man, however, came forward and assumed it. (33:72) Say: It is God Who established you as His vicegerents on earth and raised some of you higher than others and of different ranks, that, with all that He had endowed you, you may excel one another in the deed. (6:166) O men who believe, if you turn back from your religion . . . if you will not go forth to fight in God's cause, to obey His command, to realize the divine pattern, He will inflict upon you a painful punishment and will choose in your stead a people other than you who will not be irresponsive like you, who will love Him and whom He will love . . . who will strive in His cause fearful of nothing. (5:55; 9:40) O God, You have not created all this in vain. (3:191) We have not created heaven and earth and all that is between in idle sport. . . . Rather, that truth and goodness may be hurled against falsehood and evil; that the latter may be crushed and disappear. (21:16) Teach and remind (man, O Muḥammad) for teaching does benefit the believers that I have not created man and *jinn* (spiritual beings between angels and men) except to serve Me. (51: 55–56) God has covenanted away paradise to the believers for what they spend of their lives and property in His cause; . . . a true covenant proclaimed in the *Torah,* the *Evangel* and the Qur'ān. Who is truer to his covenant than God? Look forward therefore to the consummation of this covenant in which you have entered. (9:111) Every man, We have entrusted with his own destiny. On the Day of Judgment, We shall enroll for him the record of his own deeds and say, "Read it yourself! And you be the judge thereof." (17:13–14)

2. His Perfected Nature

We have created man out of a substance of clay. We then transformed him into a small organism, and this we have made into a clot, then into a tissue, and then into bones. We covered the bones with flesh. Then We caused him to become a new creature. Blessed is God, the best Creator. . . . Who created everything at its best. . . . Who well-formed man and breathed into him of His own spirit, Who gave man his hearing, his sight, and his faculties of knowledge. (23:12–14; 32:9) It is He Who creates you out of clay . . . brings you out as a child, causes you to grow to full maturity, then to grow old, some to die sooner, others to reach an appointed time, that you may consider. O men! Fear your Lord, Who created you all of one soul, Who created woman therefrom, as well as all the men and women that ever lived. (40:67; 4:1) It is He Who created you all out of one man, Who created out of him his female partner, that he may find rest in her. (7:189) O men! We have created you from male and female, constituted you into diverse peoples and nations that you may know and cooperate with one another. The best among you in the eye of God is the most pious, the most virtuous. (49:13) We have created man to strive and to struggle. . . . Have We not given him his eyes, his tongue and lips, and shown him the two ways of good and evil? (90:4–10) Man was created impatient; he panics at the fall of evil and proudly withdraws unto himself at the fall of good; except those who steadfastly pray, who recognize the right of the destitute and deprived, who believe in the Day of Judgment . . . who maintain their chastity remain true to their trust and covenant and fulfill their testimony. (70:19–33)

3. His Cosmic Status

We commanded the angels to submit and to serve Adam, and they complied except Iblīs (or Satan), who refused and took to pride. . . . We told Adam and his spouse to live in Paradise, to eat happily of its fruits except that tree, which would make them unrighteous. Satan caused them to slip and drove them out of their state. We said, "Go forth, some of your enemies of others, and inhabit the earth for a limited time." Adam then received a revelation in words from his Lord. He repented and was forgiven. God always listens to the repentant voice. (2:34–37)

God said to the angels, "I am about to create man . . . and when I complete his fashioning and breathe into him of My spirit, submit yourselves to him. All the angels did submit except Iblīs who refused . . . and incurred eternal damnation. (15:28–35) And having taught Adam all the names (i.e., natures) of things, God asked the angels to tell the names. . . . They replied, "Glory to You! We have no knowledge other than what you taught us." . . . God then asked Adam, and Adam told the names. (2:31–33) We have favored the sons of man, provided transportation for them on land and sea, granted them the good things of the world and many significant privileges which We did not accord to many of Our other creatures. (17:70) Do you not realize that God has made what is in heaven and on earth subservient to you, and has accorded to you blessings hidden and apparent? . . . that He has made even the sun and the moon subservient to you? (31:20–29) God has made the sea subservient to you, that you may set sail through it and seek His bounty . . . every thing in heaven and earth He made subservient to you. (45:12) He made the rivers subservient to you, the constantly rising and setting sun and moon, the alternating night and day and He granted to you everything which you have asked of Him. Were you to count His favors, you would find them innumerable. (14:32–34)

4. The Islāmic Imperative

a. The Five Pillars or the Institutionalized Minimum

(1) *Confession (shabādab)*. God witnesses that there is no god but He; that He is righteous; that none is God but He, the Wise and Omnipotent; and so do the angels and men of knowledge. (3:18) God Himself witnesses to the veracity of what has been revealed to you, O Muḥammad. For that was revealed in His full knowledge. And so do the angels witness. (4:165) Say: We believe in God, in that which was revealed among us, in that which was revealed to Ibrahim (Abraham), Isma'īl (Ishmael), Ishaq (Isaac), Ya'qūb (Jacob), and his children, in what was revealed to Mūsā (Moses), Īsā (Jesus), and all the prophets. We make no difference between them. To God we submit ourselves. (2:136)

(2) *Prayer (ṣalāt)*. Establish the prayers. Command your people to hold the prayers. . . . Those truly believe in Our revelation who fall to the ground in worshipful prostration whenever the revelation is remembered to them, and humbly praise their Lord. (29:45; 20:132; 32:15) Proclaim good tidings . . . to those who establish the prayers . . . whenever We establish their authority in the world. Felicitous are the believers who hold the prayers and

do so reverently. . . . Prayer forbids evil and debauchery. (22:3441; 23:1–2; 29:45) O you who believe! When you ready yourselves for prayer, wash your faces and arms to the elbows, wipe your heads and your feet to the ankles. In case you are impure, then bathe yourselves; and if sick, on a journey, or you have answered a call of nature or touched women and you find no water, then take clean sand and wipe your hands and faces clean therewith. God does not wish to make things difficult for you but only to help you become clean and to complete His favor unto you. (5:7) Do not come to prayer while in a state of drunkenness, but refrain until you can clearly cognize what you recite. (4:43) Woe to those who are in a state of distraction while they pray, to those who feign piety. (107:4) Do not raise your voice in prayer, nor make it inaudible but follow a mean between the two ways. (17:110) And when you travel over the earth, or fear that the unbelievers may attack you by surprise, it is not blameworthy for you to shorten your prayers. (4:101) When the call to prayer is made on Friday, hurry thereto and put away your business. That is better for you. . . . But when the prayer is done, strike out into the world and seek God's bounty. (62:9–10) Righteousness does not consist in turning your faces east or west (i.e., merely in prayer). Rather, it consists of faith in God, in the Day of Judgment, in His angels, Books, and prophets, in giving lovingly of one's wealth to relative and orphan, to the destitute, the deprived, and the wayfarer, in spending freely for ransoming the slave. It consists in the payment of *zakāt,* fulfillment of trusts and covenants made, in firmness through misfortune and adversity. . . . Such men as do these things are the righteous (2:177)

(3)*Sharing of wealth* (*zakāt*). Establish the prayers and pay the *zakāt.* (2:43) My servants are those who . . . give of what We have provided them. (14:31) You will not achieve righteousness unless you give of that which you cherish. (3:92) Give to the relative, the destitute, and the wayfarer, to each his due. But do not squander your wealth away. Those who do are brothers of Satan. . . . Do not hold your hand so tight as to choke thereby, nor extend it all the way and thus become destitute yourself. (17: 26–30) A kind speech and forgiveness are better than charity followed by harm. . . . Do not nullify your charity by showing off your generosity or by allowing injury to follow it. (2:263)

(4) *Fasting* (*ṣawn*) O you who believe! Fasting is ordained for you, as it was ordained for those who went before you, that you may become virtuous. Fasting is for a set number of days. However, those who are sick or on a journey should make up the days later on; or, if they can afford it, by feeding a destitute man. To volunteer in this however is better, and to fast is better still. . . . God wants your well-being, not your discomfort. . . . Go to your women eat and drink until dawn, when the white thread is discernible from the black, then complete your fast until night. (2:183)

(5) Pilgrimage (*ḥaij*). And we have made the House of God a place of assembly and a place of safety for the people. Make then of the house Ibrahim built a place of prayer for We entrusted it to Ibrahim and to lsma'il before you, to keep it pure and open for pilgrimage and prayer. (2:125) The first house to be built for man's worship of God is the blessed house in lsakkah (i.e., Makkah or Mecca), a guidance for mankind. It is man's duty to God to make the Pilgrimage to the house if such is in his Power. (3:96–97) Pilgrimage is during months well-known. Whoever undertakes it shall avoid all obscenity, all wickedness, and all wrangling. (2:197)

b. Moral Freedom and Responsibility

Whoever wills to believe, or to disbelieve, does so of his own accord. (18:29) God does not require of any person except that of which he is capable. (23:62) God does not change the situation of any group of men until they transform their own selves. (13:11) Do not ask anyone to bear the burden of another. (17:15) God commits no injustice to anyone. It is to themselves that men are unjust. Say: O men, the truth has come to you from your Lord. Whoever accepts this guidance does so to his own merit and whoever errs does so to his own demerit. . . . Teach the Qur'ān, that man may learn that it is by his own deeds that he delivers himself to ruin. . . . Whatever man has earned, he will certainly be given. (10:44; 6:70; 53:40)

c. Ethical Striving

God Comrnands that justice be done, that man should act in charity and contribute to the welfare of the relative. He forbids adultery, wickedness, and rebellion. . . . Fulfill the covenant of God, now that you have entered therein, and do not repudiate your solemn promises of which you made God guarantor. . . . Do not take your oaths as means of deceiving one another. . . . Do not sell away God's covenant. That which is with God is better for you, if you only know. What you have is temporary; what God has is eternal. . . . Whether man or woman, whoever does the good in faith, We shall cause him or her to live a good life rewarding him or her with better rewards than he or she had deserved. (16:90–97) Your Lord commands . . . kindness to parents. . . . Do not show them any sign of disrespect however small and do not speak harshly to them but kindly. Humble yourself to them in love and pray: May God have mercy on them as they nursed me when young. . . . Even if you have to avoid them on account of your fulfillment of God's call, give them a kind and compassionate explanation. . . . Do not kill any man—that is God's prohibition—except after due process of law. Whoever is killed unjustly, to his heir a right of revenge is established. But he may not kill wantonly, for his right shall be recognized. Do not touch the wealth of the orphan unless it be to increase it, until the orphan comes of age. Be true to your covenants, for to covenant is a serious and responsible affair. Fill the measure when you measure, and weigh with the true weight; that is better and more rewarding. Do not pursue that of which you have no knowledge; and remember that your hearing, sight, and heart, as cognitive faculties, were given to you for a responsible function. Do not walk around with impudence and false pride for you will never be a match either to earth or to mountain. (17:23–37) Those believers are felicitous who refrain from gossip . . . and guard their chastity except against their spouses. (23:1–6) The servants of the Merciful are those who tread softly on this earth who say "Peace" when the ignorant contend with them . . . who repent, believe, and do the good. God forgives their past misdeeds and counts their good deeds. They are those who never give a false oath; who pass the gossip of men gently by, who do not fall blindly and overhastily over their Lord's revelations when these are brought to their mind. (25:63–74) Those who believe and rely on their Lord . . . are those who forgive the trespasses of others even in anger . . . and resist victoriously the temptations of evil and rebellion. Punishment for an injury is an equal injury but whoever forgives and reconciles has his merit with God. God does not love the unjust, and whoever avenges the injustice he suffered does so legitimately. Lawlessness is on the side of those who act unjustly, who inflict injuries on the people without right. Theirs will be a painful suffering in the hereafter. Nonetheless, those who bear patiently and forgive are truly endowed with greatness. (42:3643) Tell My servants that they should always stand by the kindlier alternative. (17:53) Never will the good deed be the equivalent of an evil one. Respond, therefore, always with the better deed and you will find that your enemy immediately becomes your closest friend. Only the patient are capable of this, and they are of great fortune. (41: 34–35) Let no people speak contemptuously of another people, or woman of another woman. . . . Do not tease one another with offensive nicknames and titles; that is unbecoming of you after you have entered the faith. Avoid indulgence in doubt or suspicion, for even a little of it is a crime. Do not spy on one another. Do not speak ill of one another in the person's absence. (49:11–12) Do not turn the other cheek in abjection, and do not take to false pride. . . . Observe prayer, enjoin the good and forbid evil and endure with patience whatever may befall you. To do so belongs to great character. Let your walk be serious, and your voice be gentle. Remember the ugliest voice is that of the donkey because it is the loudest. (31:17–18) God will surely bring victory to those who . . . if established on earth will hold the prayers, pay the *zakāt*, enjoin the good and forbid evil. (22:39–41) Let there be of you a people who enjoin the good and forbid the doing of evil. Such people are the felicitous. (3:104)

B. CIVILIZATIONAL: ISLĀMIC VALUES, WORLDLINESS, AND OTHERWORLDLINESS; ISLĀMIC FELICITY

1. Morality as the Meaning of Human Existence

If man moves from contemplation of the beauty of the cosmos, expression of his gratitude for being placed therein, for his capacity to penetrate it with his mind and to enjoy it, to the consideration of his place as man in that cosmos, then will he be seized with the majesty of divine perfection and his will to moral perfection will begin to stir. While his tongue invokes and praises God, his heart will ponder, in fear and in hope, that "O God! Surely You have not created all this in vain. Glory be to you!" (Qur'ān, 3:191) Thus, those who combine thought with remembrance express their achievement of the two virtues, their synthesis of the two requisites, in the thought that God has not created all the heavenly and earthly bodies in vain, that He has not completed and perfected them all, as it were in sport. His transcendence and glory demand that we think of Him as standing above vanity and sport, as assigning to every creature its proper nature, role, and place in the cosmos. For He does not undo what He has done, and He Himself is eternal. As creatures in the cosmos, we too could not have been created in vain; nor could our presence in creation come finally to nought. Our bodies may disintegrate and our parts may dissolve after death. But that is merely the corruption of the corruptible in us. "Your holy face," we may say to God in praise and gratitude, "that which remains in us of Your eternal knowledge (that is, our human soul as subject of knowledge of the divine) will by Your power come back for another life, just as You have brought it the first time in this life on earth. Then will you divide men into those whose earthly life was one of true guidance and those whose life was one of error and misguidance; the former to enter paradise for their works and Your grace, the others to enter hell for their works and Your justice. . . .

That God has not created the cosmos in vain means that the greatness, perfection, and sublimity of everything therein could not have been meant merely to run their short course and pass into eternal oblivion. Man, who was endowed with a mind capable of perceiving this truth and appreciating this sublimity and whose predilection for this knows no bounds, could not have been created merely for this brief span between two eternal "nothings." Rather, man was so endowed and perfected that he may live an eternal life, a life in which each receives the reward of his deeds. (Muḥammad Rashīd Riḍā [d. 1935], *Tafsīr al* Qur'ān al Karim [Exegesis of the Holy Qur'ān], vol. 4, pp. 299–301)

2. Man as Carrier, as Material, and as Theater of Value Realization

Know, that all men are instances of manliness . . . that manliness is synonymous with being naturally capable of ethical action . . . and, hence, with being God's vicegerent on earth. That is the element common to all humanity.

Know, O Brother, that man's imperfect soul has been attached to his imperfect body that the soul's virtues may be realized, that its potentialities of goodness and felicity may be fulfilled, just as the revelation of God's existence, mercy, grace, beneficence, providence, and wise government are impossible without His creation of this great, well-ordered cosmos and all that it contains.

What is the purpose of the instincts built into man's nature? It is to stir the person to seek what benefits his body and to avoid what injures it, to discover and to learn the deeds and habits which lead to its advantage and disadvantage.

Know . . . that since man is composed of the four elements (Earth, Water, Air, and Fire), and these give him his four temperaments (respectively, the hard, the cold, the humid, and the fiery), the wise and praise worthy Creator made his activities and affairs to correspond to these innate elements, that he may be helped by them to achieve the objective of each. Thus we find that some of his deeds are innate; others are psychic and voluntary; others are of the nature and thought and intellect; and others are political and pertain to the law. Know . . . that nature is a servant to the animal soul and precedes it, that the animal soul is servant to reason and precedes it, that reason is servant of *al Nāmūs* (the Law) and precedes it. For, after nature has implanted a habit and ingrained it in a person, the soul deliberately stirs it into activity and enables it to achieve its objective. Here, reason comes with its deliberation and criticism to guide the soul and help it to realize itself through the satisfaction of these habits. Then the law, with its commandments, rectifies and redresses these pursuits so that when an instinct realizes itself as it ought, under the circumstances that it ought, and for the purpose that it ought, it would be good and otherwise evil; that when man allows and pursues such realization as he ought, under the circumstances that he ought and for the purpose that he ought, he would be virtuous and praiseworthy, and otherwise vicious and blameworthy; and that when man's choice and volition are the result of rational deliberation and critique, then he is wise, philosophic, and virtuous and otherwise ignorant, plebeian, and crude, and that when man's deeds, volition, choice, and thought are commanded by the law, and performed as they ought, then he would be rewarded and praised and otherwise punished and blamed.

Know . . . that in ordering the various souls of man (i.e., the elemental, vegetal, animal, rational, etc.), God linked them together so that the higher may assist the lower to realize itself as well as to rise to the higher rank. Thus, the vegetal soul stands in an order lower than the animal which it serves; the human, speaking soul stands in an order lower than the rational, wisdom-seeking soul which it serves; the rational soul in an order lower than the law-pursuing soul which it serves; and, finally, the law-pursuing soul stands under the Divine Essence which it serves.

I considered, investigated, thought, and re-examined. Then I found the true meaning of Satan and of his numerous soldiers, of their enmity and evil inspiration to man. Satan and his host are nothing but internal forces, innate and hence "hidden" powers, built into mankind. They are the immoral pursuits, the blameful habits perpetuated since youth and enhanced by ignorance, by accumulated false opinions and repeated evil and shameless deeds. They are the commonplace passions gone berserk and excessive, usually attributed to the irascible animal soul.

Furthermore, I found that all the virtuous deeds and moral acts are those which proceed from the rational, speaking soul on account of its true opinion and perfect convictions. But I found that such opinions, convictions, and all the habits which realize them proceed from an ethos of the soul acquired and developed by learning and thinking and such just temperaments as are innate to the rational nature of man. . . . Then I understood the saying of the Prophet on his victorious return from the battlefield, "Now we have returned from the lesser struggle to the greater one" [i.e., from the struggle against the external, conspicuous enemy to one internal to and hidden within man].

. . . Thus I learned that if I sought my Lord's help, rolled up my sleeves, exerted myself, and opposed the passions of my irascible and animal soul and warred against all those enemies within which run counter to the purposes and principles of my rational soul, I would vanquish them with His power. Then, commanding them as my servants and slaves, I would put them to work at the service of my rational soul and enable her to perform her good deeds and moral acts, to proclaim its true knowledge and certain convictions and to fulfill its beauteous ethos.

But then . . . looking deep within myself, . . . I found my nature composed of various, mutually conflicting elements, of firebrand passions imbedded in sulphuric bodies . . . whose flames are inextinguishable—like the huge waves of the sea that sweep everything before them; hunger bestirs eternally to make me fall on its object like a starved wolf; the fire of my ambition and anger would fain consume the world, that of my pride regards myself as the best of all and mankind as my slaves and agents whose necessary and sole duty is to obey me. . . . Its desire to recreation makes of myself a mad, drunken god; its love of praise, the most virtuous and worthiest of all; its passion for vengeance weighs on it like a tremendous mountain. . . . Looking closer at this self of mine, I have found that it is all raging flames and inextinguishable fire, perpetual fighting and war between irreconcilable elements, incurable disease, unabatable anxiety, struggle incessant—except in death. (Ikhwān al Safā wa Khillan al Safā [The Brethren of Purity and Friends of Fidelity, anonymous encyclopaedists and philosophers of the eleventh and twelfth centuries], *Rasā' il Ikhwān al Ṣafā* [Epistles of *khwān al Ṣafā*], vol. 2, pp. 306, 318–320; vol. 3, pp. 364–369)

There is no man in the whole world, from its beginning to its end, who approves of anxiety and calls it good, and who does not seek to dissipate it. When I understood this general principle well, it appeared as if I had come by God's guidance upon a wonderful discovery. I then began to search for the way to banish anxiety, which is the objective of all men whether ignorant or refined, noble or ignoble. I found it only in the total orientation to God through works conducive to Paradise. (Ibn Ḥazm, *Kitāb al Akhlāq al Siyar fi Mudāwāt al Nufūs* [Book of ethics and conduct for the curing of souls], pp. 10–11).

Passion, or man's inclination by nature to that which accords with him, was created in man on account of its necessity for survival. Were it not for his passion for food, drink, and sex, man would have neither eaten, drunk, nor procreated himself. Passion moves him to seek that which he desires, just as antipathy moves him to remove that which he avers. By itself, therefore, neither passion nor its Opposite is to be either commended or condemned. What is so is the excessive satisfaction of either. Most men, however, are excessivists in this regard. They pursue their passion or antipathy for objects of desire and aversion beyond the legitimate point of useful advantage for their persons as wholes. That is why passion is more often condemned than praised. . . . Only few men are so just in their natures as to use their passions appropriately. (Ibn al Qayyim al Jawziyyah, *Rawḍat al Muḥibbin wa Nuzhat al Mushtāquīn* [Garden of the loving and recreation of the longing], pp. 321, 463–479).

5.4

"What Is Enlightenment?"[1]

Immanuel Kant

Enlightenment is man's emergence from his self-incurred immaturity. Immaturity is the inability to use one's own understanding without the guidance of another. This immaturity is *self-incurred* if its cause is not lack of understanding, but lack of resolution and courage to use it without the guidance of another. The motto of enlightenment is therefore: *Sapere aude!*[2] Have courage to use your *own* understanding!

Laziness and cowardice are the reasons why such a large proportion of men, even when nature has long emancipated them from alien guidance (*naturaliter maiorennes*),[3] nevertheless gladly remain immature for life. For the same reasons, it is all too easy for others to set themselves up as their guardians. It is so convenient to be immature! If I have a book to have understanding in place of me, a spiritual adviser to have a conscience for me, a doctor to judge my diet for me, and so on, I need not make any efforts at all. I need not think, so long as I can pay; others will soon enough take the tiresome job over for me. The guardians who have kindly taken upon themselves the work of supervision will soon see to it that by far the largest part of mankind (including the entire fair sex) should consider the step forward to maturity not only as difficult but also as highly dangerous. Having first infatuated their domesticated animals, and carefully prevented the docile creatures from daring to take a single step without the leading-strings to which they are tied, they next show them the danger which threatens them if they try to walk unaided. Now this danger is not in fact so very great, for they would certainly learn to walk eventually after a few falls. But an example of this kind is intimidating, and usually frightens them off from further attempts.

Thus it is difficult for each separate individual to work his way out of the immaturity which has become almost second nature to him. He has even grown fond of it and is really incapable for the time being of using his own understanding, because he was never allowed to make the attempt. Dogmas and formulas, those mechanical instruments for rational use (or rather misuse) of his natural endowments, are the ball and chain of his permanent immaturity. And if anyone did throw them off, he would still be uncertain about jumping over even the narrowest of trenches, for he would be unaccustomed to free movement of this kind. Thus only a few, by cultivating their own minds, have succeeded in freeing themselves from immaturity and in continuing boldly on their way.

There is more chance of an entire public enlightening itself. This is indeed almost inevitable, if only the public concerned is left in freedom. For there will always be a few who think for themselves, even among those appointed as guardians of the common mass. Such guardians, once they have themselves thrown off the yoke of immaturity, will disseminate the spirit of rational respect for personal value and for the duty of all men to think for themselves. The remarkable thing about this is that if the public, which was previously put under this yoke by the guardians, is suitably stirred up by some of the latter who are incapable of enlightenment, it may subsequently compel the guardians themselves to remain under the yoke. For it is very harmful to propagate prejudices, because they finally avenge themselves on the very people who first encouraged them (or whose predecessors did so). Thus a public can only achieve enlightenment slowly. A revolution may well put an end to autocratic despotism and to rapacious or power-seeking oppression, but it will never produce a true reform in ways of thinking. Instead, new prejudices, like the ones they replaced, will serve as a leash to control the great unthinking mass.

For enlightenment of this kind, all that is needed is *freedom*. And the freedom in question is the most innocuous form of all—freedom to make *public use* of one's reason in all matters. But I hear on all sides the cry: *Don't argue!* The officer says: Don't argue, get on parade! The tax-official: Don't argue, pay! The clergyman: Don't argue, believe! (Only one ruler in the world says: *Argue* as much as you like and about whatever you like, *but obey!*[4] All this means restrictions on freedom everywhere. But which sort of restriction prevents enlightenment, and which, instead of hindering it, can actually promote it? I reply: The *public* use of man's reason must always be free, and it alone can bring about enlightenment among men; the *private use* of reason may quite often be very narrowly restricted, however, without undue hindrance to the progress of enlightenment. But by the public use of one's own reason I mean that use which anyone may make of it *as a man of learning* addressing the entire *reading public*. What I term the private use of reason is that which a person may make of it in a particular *civil* post or office with which he is entrusted.

Now in some affairs which affect the interests of the commonwealth, we require a certain mechanism whereby some members of the commonwealth must behave purely passively, so that they may, by an artificial common agreement, be employed by the government for public ends (or at least deterred from vitiating them). It is, of course, impermissible to argue in such cases; obedience is imperative. But in so far as this or that individual who acts as part of the machine also considers himself as a member of a complete commonwealth or even of cosmopolitan society, and thence as a man of learning who may through his writings address a public in the truest sense of the word, he may indeed argue without harming the affairs in which he is employed for some of the time in a passive capacity. Thus it would be very harmful if an officer receiving an order from his superiors were to quibble openly, while on duty, about the appropriateness or usefulness of the order in question. He must simply obey. But he cannot reasonably be banned from making observations as a man of learning on the errors in the military service, and from submitting these to his public for judgement. The citizen cannot refuse to pay the taxes imposed upon him; presumptuous criticisms of such taxes, where someone is called upon to pay them, may be punished as an outrage which could lead to general insubordination. Nonetheless, the same citizen does not contravene his civil obligations if, as a learned individual, he publicly voices his thoughts on the impropriety or even injustice of such fiscal measures. In the same way, a clergyman is bound to instruct his pupils and his congregation in accordance with the doctrines of the church he serves, for he was employed by it on that condition. But as a scholar, he is completely free as well as obliged to impart to the public all his carefully considered, well-intentioned thoughts on the mistaken aspects of those doctrines, and to offer suggestions for a better arrangement of religious and ecclesiastical affairs. And there is nothing in this which need trouble the conscience. For what he teaches in pursuit of his duties as an active servant of the church is presented by him as something which he is not empowered to teach at his own discretion, but which he is employed to expound in a prescribed manner and in someone else's name. He will say: Our church teaches this or that, and these are the arguments it uses. He then extracts as much practical value as possible for his congregation from precepts to which he would not himself subscribe with full conviction, but which he can nevertheless undertake to expound, since it is not in fact wholly impossible that they may contain truth. At all events, nothing opposed to the essence of religion is present in such doctrines. For if the clergyman thought he could find anything of this sort in them, he would not be able to carry out his official duties in good conscience, and would have to resign. Thus the use which someone employed as a teacher makes of his reason in the presence of his congregation is purely *private,* since a congregation, however large it is, is never any more than a domestic gathering. In view of this, he is not and cannot be free as a priest, since he is acting on a commission imposed from outside. Conversely, as a scholar addressing the real public (i.e. the world at large) through his writings, the clergyman making *public use* of his reason enjoys unlimited freedom to use his own reason and to speak in his own person. For to maintain that the guardians of the people in spiritual matters should themselves be immature, is an absurdity which amounts to making absurdities permanent.

But should not a society of clergymen, for example an ecclesiastical synod or a venerable presbytery (as the Dutch call it), be entitled to commit itself by oath to a certain unalterable set of doctrines, in order to secure for all time a constant guardianship over each of its members, and through them over the people? I reply that this is quite impossible. A contract of this kind, concluded with a view to preventing all further enlightenment of mankind forever, is absolutely null and void, even if it is ratified by the supreme power, by Imperial Diets and the most solemn peace treaties. One age cannot enter into an alliance on oath to put the next age in a position where it would be impossible for it to extend and correct its knowledge, particularly on such important matters, or to make any progress whatsoever in enlightenment. This would be a crime against human nature, whose original destiny lies precisely in such progress. Later generations are thus perfectly entitled to dismiss these agreements as unauthorised and criminal. To test whether any particular measure can be agreed upon as a law for a people, we need only ask whether a people could well impose such a law upon itself. This might well be possible for a specified short period as a means of introducing a certain order, pending, as it were, a better solution. This would also mean that each citizen, particularly the clergyman, would be given a free hand as a scholar to comment publicly, i.e. in his writings, on the inadequacies of current institutions. Meanwhile, the newly established order would continue to exist, until public insight into the nature of such matters had progressed and proved itself to the point where, by general consent (if not unanimously), a proposal could be submitted to the crown. This would seek to protect the congregations who had, for instance, agreed to alter their religious establishment in accordance with their own notions of what higher insight is, but it would not try to obstruct those who wanted to let things remain as before. But it is absolutely impermissible to agree, even for a single lifetime, to a permanent religious constitution which no-one might publicly question. For this would virtually nullify a phase in man's upward progress, thus making it fruitless and even detrimental to subsequent generations. A man may for his own person, and even then only for a limited period, postpone enlightening himself in matters he ought to know about. But to renounce such enlightenment completely, whether for his own person or even more so for later generations, means violating and trampling underfoot the sacred rights of mankind. But something which a people may not even impose upon itself can still less be imposed on it by a monarch; for his legislative authority depends precisely upon his uniting the collective will of the people in his own. So long as he sees to it that all true or imagined improvements are compatible with the civil order, he can otherwise leave his subjects to do whatever they find necessary for their salvation, which is none of his business. But it is his business to stop anyone forcibly hindering others from working as best they can to define and promote their salvation. It indeed detracts from his majesty if he interferes in these affairs by subjecting the writings in which his subjects attempt to clarify their religious ideas to governmental supervision. This applies if he does so acting upon his own exalted opinions—in which case he exposes himself to the reproach: *Caesar non est supra Grammaticos*[5]—but much more so if he demeans his high authority so far as to support the spiritual despotism of a few tyrants within his state against the rest of his subjects.

If it is now asked whether we at present live in an *enlightened* age, the answer is: No, but we do live in an age of *enlightenment*. As things are at present, we still have a long way to go before men as a whole can be in a position (or can even be put into a position) of using their own understanding confidently and well in religious matters, without outside guidance. But we do have distinct indications that the way is now being cleared for them to work freely in this direction, and that the obstacles to universal enlightenment, to man's emergence from his self-incurred immaturity, are gradually becoming fewer. In this respect our age is the age of enlightenment, the century of *Frederick*.[6]

A prince who does not regard it as beneath him to say that he considers it his duty, in religious matters, not to prescribe anything to his people, but to allow them complete freedom, a prince who thus even declines to accept the presumptuous title of *tolerant,* is himself enlightened. He deserves to be praised by a grateful present and posterity as the man who first liberated mankind from immaturity (as far as government is concerned), and who left all men free to use their own reason in all matters of conscience. Under his rule, ecclesiastical dignitaries, notwithstanding their official duties, may in their capacity as scholars freely and publicly submit to the judgement of the world their verdicts and opinions, even if these deviate here and there from orthodox doctrine. This applies even more to all others who are not restricted by any official duties. This spirit of freedom is also spreading abroad, even where it has to struggle with outward obstacles imposed by governments which misunderstand their own function.

For such governments can now witness a shining example of how freedom may exist without in the least jeopardising public concord and the unity of the commonwealth. Men will of their own accord gradually work their way out of barbarism so long as artificial measures are not deliberately adopted to keep them in it.

I have portrayed *matters of religion* as the focal point of enlightenment, i.e. of man's emergence from his self-incurred immaturity. This is firstly because our rulers have no interest in assuming the role of guardians over their subjects so far as the arts and sciences are concerned, and secondly, because religious immaturity is the most pernicious and dishonourable variety of all. But the attitude of mind of a head of state who favours freedom in the arts and sciences extends even further, for he realises that there is no danger even to his *legislation* if he allows his subjects to make *public* use of their own reason and to put before the public their thoughts on better ways of drawing up laws, even if this entails forthright criticism of the current legislation. We have before us a brilliant example of this kind, in which no monarch has yet surpassed the one to whom we now pay tribute.

But only a ruler who is himself enlightened and has no fear of phantoms, yet who likewise has at hand a well-disciplined and numerous army to guarantee public security, may say what no republic would dare to say: *Argue as much as you like and about whatever you like, but obey!* This reveals to us a strange and unexpected pattern in human affairs (such as we shall always find if we consider them in the widest sense, in which nearly everything is paradoxical). A high degree of civil freedom seems advantageous to a people's *intellectual* freedom, yet it also sets up insuperable barriers to it. Conversely, a lesser degree of civil freedom gives intellectual freedom enough room to expand to its fullest extent. Thus once the germ on which nature has lavished most care—man's inclination and vocation to *think freely*—has developed within this hard shell, it gradually reacts upon the mentality of the people, who thus gradually become increasingly able to *act freely*. Eventually, it even influences the principles of governments, which find that they can themselves profit by treating man, who is *more than a machine*,[7] in a manner appropriate to his dignity.*

Königsberg in Prussia, 30th September, 1784.

* I read today on the 30th September in Büschings[8] *Wöchentliche Nachrichten* of 13th September a notice concerning this month's *Berlinische Monatsschrift*. The notice mentions Mendelssohn's[9] answer to the same question as that which I have answered. I have not yet seen this journal, otherwise I should have held back the above reflections. I let them stand only as a means of finding out by comparison how far the thoughts of two individuals may coincide by chance.

NOTES

1. *Beantwortung der Frage: Was ist Aufklärung?, AA* viii, 33–42. First published in *Berlinische Monatsschrift,* IV (12 December 1784), 481–94. There is a reference in the original edition of the *Berlinische Monatsschrift,* to p. 516 of the number of that journal published on 5 December 1783. This reference is to an essay by the Rev. Zöllner, 'Is it advisable to sanction marriage through religion?'. The relevant passage reads (in translation): *'What is Enlightenment?* The question, which is almost as important as the question *What is truth?,* should be answered before one begins to enlighten others. And yet I have never found it answered anywhere.'

2. Literal translation: 'Dare to be wise'. Horace, *Epodes* 1, 2, 40. Cf. Elizabeth M. Wilkinson and L. A. Willoughby (eds. and trs.), Friedrich Schiller, *On the Aesthetic Education of Man* (Oxford, 1967), LXXIV ff. ; cf. also Franco Venturi, 'Was ist *Aufklärung?* Sapere Aude!', *Rivista Storica Italiana,* LXXI (1959), 119 ff. Venturi traces the use made of this quotation from Horace throughout the centuries. Cf also p. 5.

3. 'Those who have come of age by virtue of nature.'

4. The allusion is to Frederick II (the Great), King of Prussia (1740–86).

5. 'Caesar is not above the grammarians.'

6. Kant here refers, of course, to Frederick the Great.

7. This allusion amounts to a repudiation of Julien Offray de Lamettrie's (1709–51) materialism as expressed in *L' Homme Machine* (1748).

8. Anton Friedrich Büsching (1724–93), professor in the University of Göttingen, theologian and leading geographer of the day, editor of *Wöchentliche Nachrichten von neuen Landkarten, geographischen, statistischen und historischen Büchern.* Kant's reference is to XII, 1784 (Berlin, 1785), 291.

9. Moses Mendelssohn (1729–86), a leading philosopher of the German Enlightenment. The reference is to Mendelssohn's essay 'Über die Frage: Was heisst *Aufklärung?'* ('On the question: What Is Enlightenment?'), *Berlinische Monatsschrift,* IV (9 September 1784), 193–200.

5.5

"Is the Human Race Continually Improving?"

Immanuel Kant

1. WHAT SORT OF KNOWLEDGE ARE WE LOOKING FOR?

What we are seeking to know is a portion of human history. It is not a history of the past, however, but a history of future times, i.e. a *predictive* history. But if it is not discoverable from known laws of nature (as with eclipses of the sun and moon, which can be foretold by natural means) and can only be learnt through additional insight into the future supplied by supernatural revelation, it must be termed *prognosticative or prophetic*.[1] Besides, we are here concerned not with the natural history of mankind (as we should be if we asked, for example, whether new races of man might emerge in future times), but with the *history of civilisation*. And we are not dealing with any *specific* conception of mankind (*singulorum*), but with the *whole* of humanity (*universorum*), united in earthly society and distributed in national groups. All this is implied if we ask whether the human *race* (as a whole) is continually improving.

2. HOW CAN WE ATTAIN SUCH KNOWLEDGE?

We can obtain a prophetic historical narrative of things to come by depicting those events whose a priori possibility suggests that they will in fact happen. But how is it possible to have history a priori? The answer is that it is possible if the prophet himself occasions and *produces* the events he predicts.

It was all very well for the Jewish prophets to foretell that the state to which they belonged would sooner or later suffer not only decline, but also complete dissolution; for they were themselves the architects of their fate. As leaders of the people, they had loaded their constitution with so many ecclesiastical (and thence also civil) burdens that their state became completely unfit to exist in its own right, particularly in its relations with neighbouring nations. Thus the jeremiads of the priests naturally went unheeded, because these same priests stubbornly stuck to their belief in the untenable constitution they had themselves created, so that they were themselves able to foresee the consequences with infallible certainty.

Our politicians, so far as their influence extends, behave in exactly the same way, and they are just as successful in their prophecies. One must take men as they are, they tell us, and not as the world's uninformed pedants or good-natured dreamers fancy that they ought to be. But 'as they are' ought to read 'as we have *made them* by unjust coercion, by treacherous designs which the government is in a good position to carry out.' For that is why they are intransigent and inclined to rebellion, and why regrettable consequences ensue if discipline is relaxed in the slightest. In this way, the prophecy of the supposedly clever statesmen is fulfilled.

Various divines also at times prophesy the complete decline of religion and the imminent appearance of the Antichrist, all the while doing the very things that are best calculated to create the state of affairs they describe. For they are not taking care to impress on the hearts of their congregation moral principles which would directly lead to an improvement. Instead, they see observances and historical beliefs as the essential duties, supposing that these will indirectly produce the same results; but although they may lead to mechanical conformity (as within a civil constitution), they cannot produce conformity in moral attitudes. Nevertheless, these divines complain at the irreligion which they have themselves created, and which they could accordingly have foretold without any special gift of prophecy.

3. SUBDIVISIONS WITHIN THE CONCEPT OF WHAT WE WISH TO KNOW OF THE FUTURE

There are three possible forms which our prophecy might take. The human race is either continually *regressing* and deteriorating, continually *progressing* and improving, or at a permanent *standstill,* in relation to other created beings, at its present level of moral attainment (which is the same as continually revolving in a circle around a fixed point).

The first statement might be designated *moral terrorism,* the second *eudaemonism*[2] (which, if the goal of human progress were already visible from afar, might also be termed *chiliasm,*[3] while the third could be called *abderitism.*[4] For in the latter case, since a genuine standstill is impossible in moral affairs, rises and falls of equal magnitude constantly alternate, in endless fluctuation, and produce no more effect than if the subject of them had remained stationary in one place.

a. The terroristic conception of human history

A process of deterioration in the human race cannot go on indefinitely, for mankind would wear itself out after a certain point had been reached. Consequently, when enormities go on piling up and up and the evils they produce continue to increase, we say: 'It can't get much worse now.' It seems that the day of judgement is at hand, and the pious zealot already dreams of the rebirth of everything and of a world created anew after the present world has been destroyed by fire.

b. The eudaemonistic conception of human history

We may readily agree that the sum total of good and evil of which our nature is capable always remains unchanged, and can neither be augmented nor reduced within any one individual. And how could the quantity of good of which a person is capable possibly be increased? For it would have to be done by his own free agency as a subject, and before he could do it, he would in turn require a greater store of goodness than he already possessed in the first place. After all, no effects can exceed the capacity of their effective cause; and the quantity of goodness in man must therefore remain below a certain level in proportion to the amount of evil with which it is intermixed, so that man cannot work his way beyond a given limit and go on improving further. Thus *eudaemonism*, with its sanguine hopes, appears to be untenable. Its ideas of constant human progress and improvement would seem of little use to a prophetic history of mankind.

c. The hypothesis of abderitism in the human race as a definition of its future history

This point of view probably has the majority of subscribers on its side. To start off swiftly along the way of goodness without persevering on it, and instead, to reverse the plan of progress in order at all costs to avoid being tied to a single aim (even if only from a desire for variety); to construct in order to demolish; to take upon ourselves the hopeless task of rolling the stone of Sisyphus uphill, only to let it roll back down again: such is the industrious folly which characterises our race. In view of all this, it does not so much seem that the principle of evil within the natural character of mankind is amalgamated or fused with that of goodness, but rather that the one is neutralised by the other, with inactivity as the result (or a standstill, as in the case under discussion). This empty activity of backward and forward motion, with good and evil continually alternating, would mean that all the interplay of members of our species on earth ought merely to be regarded as a farce. And in the eyes of reason, this cannot give any higher a value to mankind than to the other animal species, whose interaction takes place at less cost and without any conscious understanding.

4. THE PROBLEM OF PROGRESS CANNOT BE SOLVED DIRECTLY FROM EXPERIENCE

Even if it were found that the human race as a whole had been moving forward and progressing for an indefinitely long time, no one could guarantee that its era of decline was not beginning at that very moment, by virtue of the physical character of our race. And conversely, if it is regressing and deteriorating at an accelerating pace, there are no grounds for giving up hope that we are just about to reach the turning point (*punctum flexus contrarii*) at which our affairs will take a turn for the better, by virtue of the moral character of our race. For we are dealing with freely acting beings to whom one can *dictate* in advance what they *ought* to do, but of whom one cannot *predict* what they actually *will* do, and who are capable, if things go really badly and they experience evils incurred through their own actions, of regarding these evils as a greater incentive to do better than they did in the past. But as the Abbé Coyer[5] says: 'Poor mortals! Nothing is constant among you but inconstancy.'

Perhaps it is because we have chosen the wrong point of view from which to contemplate the course of human affairs that the latter seems so absurd to us. The planets, as seen from the earth, sometimes move backward, sometimes forward, and at other times remain motionless. But seen from the sun—the point of view of reason—they continually follow their regular paths as in the Copernican hypothesis. Yet some thinkers, otherwise not deficient in wisdom, prefer to stick firmly to their own interpretation of phenomena and to the point of view they originally adopted, even at the price of involving themselves to an absurd degree in Tychonic[6] cycles and epicycles. It is our misfortune, however, that we are unable to adopt an absolute point of view when trying to predict free actions. For this, exalted above all human wisdom, would be the point of view of *providence*, which extends even to free human actions. And although man may *see* the latter, he cannot *foresee* them with certainty (a distinction which does not exist in the eyes of the divinity); for while he needs to perceive a connection governed by natural laws before he can foresee anything, he must do without such hints or guidance when dealing with *free* actions in the future.

If it were possible to credit human beings with even a limited will of innate and unvarying goodness, we could certainly predict a general improvement of mankind, for this would involve events which man could himself control. But if man's natural endowments consist of a mixture of evil and goodness in unknown proportions, no one can tell what effects he should expect from his own actions.

5. A PROPHETIC HISTORY OF THE HUMAN RACE MUST NEVERTHELESS START FROM SOME SORT OF EXPERIENCE

In human affairs, there must be some experience or other which, as an event which has actually occurred, might suggest that man has the quality or power of being the *cause* and (since his actions are supposed to be those of a being endowed with freedom) the *author* of his own improvement. But an event can be predicted as the effect of a given cause only when the circumstances which help to shape it actually arise. And while it can well be predicted in general that these circumstances must arise at some time or another (as in calculating probabilities in games of chance), it is impossible to determine whether this will happen during my lifetime, and whether I shall myself experience it and thus be able to confirm the original prediction.

We must therefore search for an event which would indicate that such a cause exists and that it is causally active within the human race, irrespective of the time at which it might actually operate; and it would have to be a cause which allowed us to conclude, as an inevitable consequence of its operation, that mankind is improving. This inference could then be extended to cover the history of former times so as to show that mankind has always been progressing, yet in such a way that the event originally chosen as an example would not in itself be regarded as the cause of progress in the past, but only as a rough indication or *historical sign* (*signum Irememorativum, demonstrativum, prognostikon*). It might then serve to prove the existence of a *tendency* within the human race as a *whole,* considered not as a series of individuals (for this would result in interminable enumerations and calculations) but as a body distributed over the earth in states and national groups.

6. AN OCCURRENCE IN OUR OWN TIMES WHICH PROVES THIS MORAL TENDENCY OF THE HUMAN RACE

The occurrence in question does not involve any of those momentous deeds or misdeeds of men which make small in their eyes what was formerly great or make great what was formerly small, and which cause ancient and illustrious states to vanish as if by magic, and others to arise in their place as if from the bowels of the earth. No, it has nothing to do with all this. We are here concerned only with the attitude of the onlookers as it reveals itself *in public* while the drama of great political changes is taking place: for they openly express universal yet disinterested sympathy for one set of protagonists against their adversaries, even at the risk that their partiality could be of great disadvantage to themselves. Their reaction (because of its universality) proves that mankind as a whole shares a certain character in common, and it also proves (because of its disinterestedness) that man has a moral character, or at least the makings of one. And this does not merely allow us to hope for human improvement; it is already a form of improvement in itself, in so far as its influence is strong enough for the present.

The revolution which we have seen taking place in our own times in a nation of gifted people[7] may succeed, or it may fail. It may be so filled with misery and atrocities that no right-thinking man would ever decide to make the same experiment again at such a price, even if he could hope to carry it out successfully at the second attempt. But I maintain that this revolution has aroused in the hearts and desires of all spectators who are not themselves caught up in it a *sympathy* which borders almost on enthusiasm, although the very utterance of this sympathy was fraught with danger. It cannot therefore have been caused by anything other than a moral disposition within the human race.

The moral cause which is at work here is composed of two elements. Firstly, there is the *right* of every people to give itself a civil constitution of the kind that it sees fit, without interference from other powers. And secondly, once it is accepted that the only intrinsically *rightful* and morally good constitution which a people can have is by its very nature disposed to avoid wars of aggression (i.e. that the only possible constitution is a republican one, at least in its conception),[8] there is the *aim,* which is also a duty, of submitting to those conditions by which war, the source of all evils and moral corruption, can be prevented. If this aim is recognised, the human race, for all its frailty, has a negative guarantee that it will progressively improve or at least that it will not be disturbed in its progress.

All this, along with the *passion* or *enthusiasm* with which men embrace the cause of goodness (although the former cannot be entirely applauded, since all passion as such is blameworthy), gives historical support for the following assertion, which is of considerable anthropological significance: true enthusiasm is always directed exclusively towards the *ideal,* particularly towards that which is purely moral (such as the concept of right), and it cannot be coupled with selfish interests. No pecuniary rewards could inspire the opponents of the revolutionaries with that zeal and greatness of soul which the concept of right could alone produce in them, and even the old military aristocracy's concept of honour (which is analogous to enthusiasm) vanished before the arms[9] of those who had fixed their gaze on the *rights* of the people to which they belonged,[10] and who regarded themselves as its protectors. And then the external public of onlookers sympathised with their exaltation, without the slightest intention of actively participating in their affairs.

7. THE PROPHETIC HISTORY OF MANKIND

In these principles, there must be something *moral* which reason recognises not only as pure, but also (because of its great and epoch-making influence) as something to which the human soul manifestly acknowledges a duty. Moreover, it concerns the human race as a complete association of men (*non singulorum, sed universorum*)[11] for they rejoice with universal and disinterested sympathy at its anticipated success and at all attempts to make it succeed.

The occurrence in question is not, however, a phenomenon of revolution, but (as Erhard[12] puts it) of the *evolution* of a constitution governed by *natural right*. Such a constitution cannot itself be achieved by furious struggles—for civil and foreign wars will destroy whatever *statutory* order has hitherto prevailed—but it does lead us to strive for a constitution which would be incapable of bellicosity, i.e. a republican one. The actual *form of* the desired state might be republican, or alternatively, it might only be republican in its *mode of government,* in that the state would be administered by a single ruler (the monarch) acting by analogy with the laws which a people would give itself in conformity with universal principles of right.

Even without the mind of a seer, I now maintain that I can predict from the aspects and signs of our times that the human race will achieve this end, and that it will henceforth progressively improve without any more total reversals. For a phenomenon of this kind which has taken place in human history *can never be forgotten,* since it has revealed in human nature an aptitude and power for improvement of a kind which no politician could have thought up by examining the course of events in the past. Only nature and freedom, combined within mankind in accordance with principles of right, have enabled us to forecast it; but the precise time at which it will occur must remain indefinite and dependent upon chance.

But even if the intended object behind the occurrence we have described were not to be achieved for the present, or if a people's revolution or constitutional reform were ultimately to fail, or if, after the latter had lasted for a certain time, everything were to be brought back onto its original course (as politicians now claim to prophesy), our own philosophical prediction still loses none of its force. For the occurrence in question is too momentous, too intimately interwoven with the interests of humanity and too widespread in its influence upon all parts of the world for nations not to be reminded of it when favourable circumstances present themselves, and to rise up and make renewed attempts of the same kind as before. After all, since it is such an important concern of the human race, the intended constitution must at some time or another finally reach that degree of stability which the lessons of repeated experience will not fail to instil into the hearts of everyone.

Thus the proposition that the human race has always been progressively improving and will continue to develop in the same way is not just a well-meant saying to be recommended for practical purposes. Whatever unbelievers may say, it is tenable within the most strictly theoretical context. And if one considers not only the events which may happen within a particular nation, but also their repercussions upon all the nations of the earth which might gradually begin to participate in them, a view opens up into the unbounded future. This would not be true, of course, if the first epoch of natural convulsions, which (according to Camper[13] and Blumenbach[14]) engulfed the animal and vegetable kingdoms before the era of man, were to be followed by a second in which the human race were given the same treatment so that other creatures might take the stage instead, etc. For man in turn is a mere trifle in relation to the omnipotence of nature, or rather to its inaccessible highest cause. But if the rulers of man's own species regard him as such and treat him accordingly, either by burdening him like a beast and using him as a mere instrument of their ends, or by setting him up to fight in their disputes and slaughter his fellows, it is not just a trifle but a reversal of the *ultimate purpose* of creation.

8. THE DIFFICULTY OF MAXIMS DIRECTED TOWARDS THE WORLD'S PROGESSIVE IMPROVEMENT AS REGARDS THEIR PUBLICITY

Popular enlightenment is the public instruction of the people upon their duties and rights towards the state to which they belong. Since this concerns only natural rights and rights which can be derived from ordinary common sense, their obvious exponents and interpreters among the people will not be officials appointed by the state, but free teachers of right, i.e. the philosophers. The latter, on account of the very freedom which they allow themselves, are a stumbling-block to the state, whose only wish is to rule; they are accordingly given the appellation of 'enlighteners,' and decried as a menace to the state. And yet they do not address themselves in familiar tones to the *people* (who themselves take little or no notice of them and their writings), but in *respectful* tones to the state, which is thereby implored to take the rightful needs of the people to heart. And if a whole people wishes to present its grievance (*gravamen*), the only way in which this can be done is by publicity. A *ban* on publicity will therefore hinder a nation's progress, even with regard to the least of its claims, the claim for natural rights.

Another thing which is concealed (transparently enough) by legal measures from a certain people is the true nature of its constitution. It would be an affront to the majesty of the people of Great Britain to say that they lived under an *absolute monarchy*. Instead, it is said that their constitution is one which *limits* the will of the monarch through the two houses of parliament, acting as representatives of the people. Yet everyone knows very well that the influence of the monarch upon these representatives is so great and so infallible that the aforesaid houses make no decisions except those which His Majesty wishes and recommends through his minister. Now and again, the latter will certainly recommend decisions wherein he[15] knows and indeed *ensures* that he will meet with contradiction (as with the abolition of the slave trade), simply in order to furnish ostensible proof of parliamentary freedom. But this sort of approach has the insidious effect of discouraging people from looking for the true and rightfully established constitution, for they imagine they have discovered it in an instance which is already before them. Thus a mendacious form of publicity deceives the people with the illusion that the monarchy is *limited*[16] by a law which emanates from them, while their representatives, won over by bribery, secretly subject them to an *absolute monarch*.

All forms of state are based on the idea of a constitution which is compatible with the natural rights of man, so that those who obey the law should also act as a unified body of legislators. And if we accordingly think of the commonwealth in terms of concepts of pure reason, it may be called organised in conformity with it and governed by laws of freedom is an example representing it in the world of experience (*respublica phaenomenon*), and it can only be achieved by a laborious process, after innumerable wars and conflicts. But its constitution, once it has been attained as a whole, is the best qualified of all to keep out war, the destroyer of everything good. Thus it is our duty to enter into a constitution of this kind; and in the meantime, since it will be a considerable time before this takes place, it is the duty of monarchs to govern in a *republican* (not a democratic) manner, even although they may *rule autocratically*. In other words, they should treat the people in accordance with principles akin in spirit to the laws of freedom which a people of mature rational powers would prescribe for itself, even if the people is not literally asked for its consent.

9. WHAT PROFIT WILL THE HUMAN RACE DERIVE FROM PROGRESSIVE IMPROVEMENT?

The profit which will accrue to the human race as it works its way forward will not be an ever increasing quantity of *morality* in its attitudes. Instead, the *legality* of its attitudes will produce an increasing number of actions governed by duty, whatever the particular motive behind these actions may be. In other words, the profit will result from man's good *deeds* as they grow ever more numerous and successful, i.e. from the external phenomena of man's moral nature. For we have only *empirical* data (our experiences) on which to base this prediction—that is, we base it on the physical cause of our actions in so far as they actually take place as phenomena, not on the moral cause which contains the concept of duty as applied to what ought to happen, and which can be determined by processes of pure a priori thinking.

Violence will gradually become less on the part of those in power, and obedience towards the laws will increase. There will no doubt be more charity, less quarrels in legal actions, more reliability in keeping one's word, and so on in the commonwealth, partly from a love of honour, and partly from a lively awareness of where one's own advantage lies; and this will ultimately extend to the external relations between the various peoples, until a cosmopolitan society is created. Such developments do not mean, however, that the basic moral capacity of mankind will increase in the slightest, for this would require a kind of new creation or supernatural influence. For we must not expect too much of human beings in their progressive improvements, or else we shall merit the scorn of those politicians who would gladly treat man's hopes of progress as the fantasies of an overheated mind.[17]

10. WHAT SEQUENCE CAN PROGRESS BE EXPECTED TO FOLLOW?

The answer is: not the usual sequence from *the bottom upwards,* but from *the top downwards.*

To expect that the education of young people in intellectual and moral culture, reinforced by the doctrines of religion, firstly through domestic instruction and then through a series of schools from the lowest to the highest grade, will eventually not only make them good citizens, but will also bring them up to practise a kind of goodness which can continually progress and maintain itself, is a plan which is scarcely likely to achieve the desired success. For on the one hand, the people believe that the expense of educating their children should be met not by them but by the state; and on the other, the state itself (as Büsching[18] laments) has no money left over to pay qualified teachers who will carry out their duties with enthusiasm, since it needs it all for war. But apart from this, the whole mechanism of education as described above will be completely disjointed unless it is designed on the considered plan and intention of the highest authority in the state, then set in motion and constantly maintained in uniform operation thereafter. And this will mean that the state too will reform itself from time to time, pursuing evolution instead of revolution, and will thus make continuous progress. But those responsible for the desired education are also *human beings* who will therefore have to have had a suitable education themselves. And in view of the frailty of human nature and the fortuitous circumstances which can intensify its effects, we can expect man's hopes of progress to be fulfilled only under the positive condition of a higher wisdom (which, if it is invisible to us, is known as providence); and in so far as *human beings* can themselves accomplish anything or anything can be expected of them, it can only be through their negative wisdom in furthering their own ends. In the latter event, they will find themselves compelled to ensure that *war,* the greatest obstacle to morality and the invariable enemy of progress, first becomes gradually more humane, then more infrequent, and finally disappears completely as a mode of aggression. They will thereby enter into a constitution based on genuine principles of right, which is by its very nature capable of constant progress and improvement without forfeiting its strength.

CONCLUSION

A doctor who used to console his patients from day to day with hopes of imminent recovery, telling one that his pulse was better, and others that their faeces or perspiration heralded an improvement, etc., received a visit from one of his friends. 'How are you, my friend, and how is your illness?' was the first question. 'How do you think,' was the reply. *'I am dying of sheer recovery!'*

I do not blame anyone if political evils make him begin to despair of the welfare and progress of mankind. But I have confidence in the heroic medicine to which Hume refers, for it ought to produce a speedy cure. 'When I now see the nations engaged in war,' he says, 'it is as if I witnessed two drunken wretches bludgeoning each other in a china-shop. For it is not just that the injuries they inflict on each other will be long in healing; they will also have to pay for all the damage they have caused.'[19] *Sero sapiunt Phryges.*[20] But the after-pains of the present war[21] will force the political prophet to admit that the human race must soon take a turn for the better, and this turn is now already in sight.

NOTES

1. Those, from pyrhonesses (Prophetic priestesses of the Delphic oracle) to gypsies, who dabble in prophecy with neither knowledge nor honesty, are known as *false prophets.*

2. Eudaemonism usually means the teaching that all human activity is determined by a striving for happiness. . . . Kant does not use it in that sense, however.

3. Originally, the belief that the millennium will be established on earth before the Day of Judgement.

4. After a novel by Christian Martin Wieland, the eighteenth century German writer, called *Geschichte der Abderiten* (*The Story of the Abderites*) (1774–81), in which human follies are satirised. Abdera was a city in ancient Greece whose inhabitants were alleged to be particularly foolish.

5. Gabriel Francois Coyer (1707–82), French Jesuit, author of a *Dissertation sur la difference des anciennes religions* (Paris, 1755).

6. The reference is to Tycho Brahe (1546–1601), Danish astronomer who, in order to refute Copernicus, elaborated an astronomical system of his own, the Tychonic system. He put forward the theory that the sun and the moon rotate around the earth, but that the planets rotate around the sun. His theory was well thought of by many at the time.

7. This is, of course, a reference to the French Revolution.

8. This does not mean, however, that a people which has a monarchic Constitution can thereby claim the right to alter it, or even nurse a secret desire to do so. For a people which occupies extended territories in Europe may feel that monarchy is the only kind of constitution which can enable it to preserve its own existence between powerful neighbours. And if the subjects should complain, not because of their internal government but because of their government's behaviour towards the Citizens of foreign States (for example, if it were to discourage republicanism abroad), this does not prove that the people are dissatisfied with their own Constitution, but rather that they are profoundly attached to it; for it becomes progressively more secure from danger as more of the other nations become republics. Nevertheless, slanderous sycophants, bent on increasing their own importance, have tried to portray this innocuous political gossip as innovationism, Jacobinism and conspiracy, constituting a menace to the state. But there was never the slightest reason for such allegations, particularly in a country more than a hundred miles removed from the scene of the revolution.

9. The reference is to the Wars of the French Revolution.

10. It may be said of such enthusiasm for asserting the rights of man: *posiquam ad arma Vulcania ventum est—mortalis mucro glacies ceu futitlis ictu dissiluit* (Kant misquotes the first words. It should read: *Postquam arma dei ad Vulcania ventum est.* . . . 'Now that he was faced by Vulcan's arms, his mortal blade was shattered by the blow like brittle ice.' Virgil, *Aeneid* XII, 73–41). Why has no ruler ever dared to say openly that he does not recognise any *rights* of the people against himself? Or that the people owe their happiness only to the *beneficence* of a government which confers it upon them, and that any pretensions on the part of the subject that he has rights against the government are absurd or even punishable, since they imply that resistance to authority is permissible? The reason is that any such public declaration

would rouse up all the subjects against the ruler, even although they had been like docile sheep, well fed, powerfully protected and led by a kind and understanding master, and had no lack of welfare to complain of. For beings endowed with freedom cannot be content merely to enjoy the comforts of existence, which may well be provided by others (in this case, by the government); it all depends on the *principle* which governs the provision of such comforts. But welfare does not have any ruling principle, either for the recipient or for the one who provides it, for each individual will define it differently. It depends, in fact, upon the will's *material* aspect, which is empirical and thus incapable of becoming a universal rule. A being endowed with freedom, aware of the advantage he possesses over non-rational animals, can and must therefore follow the *formal* principle of his will and demand for the people to which he belongs nothing short of a government in which the people are co-legislators. In other words, the rights of men who are expected to obey must necessarily come before all considerations of their actual wellbeing, for they are a sacred institution, exalted above all utilitarian values; and no matter how benevolent a government is, it may not tamper with them. These rights, however, always remain an idea which can be fulfilled only on condition that the *means* employed to do so are compatible with morality. This limiting condition must not be overstepped by the people, who may not therefore pursue their rights by revolution, which is at all times unjust. The best way of making a nation content with its constitution is to *rule* autocratically and at the same time to *govern* in a republican manner, i.e. to govern in the spirit of republicanism and by analogy with it.

11. 'Not of individuals, but of mankind as a whole.'

12. Johann Benjamin Erhard (1766–1827), a physician and friend of Kant's, who esteemed Erhard highly. Erhard published several political treatises including an essay *Über das Recht des Volkes zu einer Revolution* (*On the Right of the People to Revolution*) (Jena, 1794), to which Kant alludes here.

13. Petrus Camper (1722–89), a Dutch anatomist. The allusion is to a work published in German translation, *Über den natürlichen Unterschied der Gesichtszüge im Menschen . . .* (ed. A. G. Camper) (Berlin, 1792), §3.

14. Johann Friedrich Blumenbach, Professor of Medicine in the University of Göttingen from 1776. He greatly furthered the study of comparative anatomy. Cf. his *Handbuch der Naturgeschichte* (Göttingen, 1779), p. 44 and pp. 474 ff.

15. This is a reference to George III (1738–1820), King of Great Britain and Ireland (1760–1820).

16. A cause whose nature is not directly perceptible can be discovered through the effect which invariably accompanies it. What is an *absolute* monarch? He is one at whose command war at once begins when he says it shall do so. And conversely, what is a *limited* monarch? He is one who must first ask the people whether or not there is to be a war, and if the people say that there shall be no war, then there will be none. For war is a condition in which *all* the powers of the state must be at the head of state's disposal.

Now the monarch of 'Great Britain' has waged numerous wars without asking the people's consent. This king is therefore an absolute monarch, although he should not be so according to the constitution. But he can always bypass the latter, since he can always be assured, by controlling the various powers of the state, that the people's representatives will agree with him; for he has the authority to award all offices and dignities. This corrupt system, however, must naturally be given no publicity if it is to succeed. It therefore remains under a very transparent veil of secrecy.

17. It is *certainly agreeable* to think up political constitutions which meet the requirements of reason (particularly in matters of right). But it *is foolhardy* to put them forward seriously, and *punishable* to incite the people to do away with the existing constitution. Plato's *Atlantis* (the myth of a city engulfed by the sea, mentioned by Plato in the *Timaeus*), More's *Utopia* (1516, the exact title of this work is *De optima rei publicae statu, deque nova insula Utopia*. It was written by Sir Thomas More (1478–1535), the eminent humanist who was Lord Chancellor of England in 1529–32), Harrington's *Oceana* (a treatise by James Harrington [1611–77], the English political philosopher, who projected the ideal state for England) and Allais' *Severambia* (refers to the Histoire des Seåvarambes [first published in English, London, 1675; Paris, 1677 and 1679], a political novel by Denis Vairasse d'Allais, a French writer of the seventeenth century [translated into German by J. G. Müller as *Geschichte der Sevaramben,* Itzehoe, 1783]), have successively made their appearance, but they have never (with the exception of Cromwell's abortive attempt to establish a despotic republic) been tried out in practice. It is the same with these political creations as with the creation of the world: no-one was present at it, nor could anyone have been present, or else he would have been his own creator. It is a pleasant dream to hope that a political product of the sort we here have in mind will one day be brought to perfection, at however remote a date. But it is not merely *conceivable* that we can continually approach such a state; so long as it can be reconciled with the moral law, it is also the *duty* of the head of state (not of the citizens) to do so.

18. p. 189. Cf. p. 60, n. 8.

19. The likely source for this passage is: 'I must confess, when I see princes and states fighting and quarrelling, amidst their debts, funds, and public mortgages, it always brings to my mind a match of cudgel-playing fought in a China shop.' (Hume, *Of Public Credit, Essays Moral, Political and Literary, ed. cit.* I, 371.) I owe this reference to Professor Lewis Beck White who drew my attention to the fact that he had identified this passage in his edition *Immanuel Kant: On History* (Indianapolis and New York, 1963), p. 124.

20. 'The Phrygians learn wisdom too late' (i.e. they are wise after the event).

21. Presumably this remark refers to the war between France and Austria which was ended by the Treaty of Campo Formio (17 November 1797). It could also refer to the war between France and Prussia which was ended by the Treaty of Basle (5 April 1795). Kant probably wrote this section of the Contest of Faculties some considerable time before its publication (cf. AA VII, 338 ff. for a full discussion of the origin of the treatise by Karl Vorländer).

5.6

The "Who" of Dasein

Martin Heidegger

Historiologically, the aim of the existential analytic can be made plainer by considering Descartes, who is credited with providing the point of departure for modern philosophical inquiry by his discovery of the "*cogito sum*". He investigates the "*ego*", at least within certain limits. On the other hand, he leaves the "*sum*" completely undiscussed, even though it is regarded as no less primordial than the *cogito*. Our analytic raises the onto-logical question of the Being of the "*sum*". Not until the nature of this Being has been determined can we grasp the kind of Being which belongs to *cogitationes*.

At the same time it is of course misleading to exemplify the aim of our analytic historiologically in this way. One of our first tasks will be to prove that if we posit an "I" or subject as that which is proximally given, we shall completely miss the phenomenal content [*Bestand*] of Dasein. *Ontologically,* every idea of *a* "subject"—unless refined by a previous ontological determination of its basic character—still posits the *subjectum* . . . along with it, no matter how vigorous one's ontical protestations against the "soul substance" or the "reification of consciousness". The Thinghood itself which such reification implies must have its ontological origin demonstrated if we are to be in a position to ask what we are to understand *positively* when we think of the unreified *Being* of the subject, the soul, the consciousness, the spirit, the person. All these terms refer to definite phenomenal domains which can be "given form" ["*ausformbare*"]: but they are never used without a notable failure to see the need for inquiring about the Being of the entities thus designated. So we are not being terminologically arbitrary when we avoid these

From *Being and Time* translated by Jobs Macquarrie and Edward Robinson. Copyright © by SCM Prem Ltd., 1962. Reprinted by permission of Harper & Row, Publishers, Inc., pp. 150–53, 163–68. Text edited.

terms—or such expressions as "life" and "man"—in designating those entities which we are ourselves.

AN APPROACH TO THE EXISTENTIAL
QUESTION OF THE "WHO" OF DASEIN

. . . Dasein is an entity which is in each case I myself; its Being is in each case mine. This definition *indicates* an ontologically constitutive state, but it does no more than indicate it. At the same time this tells us *ontically* (though in a rough and ready fashion) that in each case an "I"—not other—is this entity. The question of the "who" answers itself in terms of the "I" itself, the "subject", the "Self". The "who" is what maintains itself as something identical throughout changes in its experiences and ways of behaviour, and which relates itself to this changing multiplicity in so doing. Ontologically we understand it as something which is in each case already constantly present-at-hand, both in and for a closed realm, and which lies at the basis, in a very special sense, as the *subjectum*. As something selfsame in manifold otherness, it has the character of the *Self*. Even if one rejects the "soul substance" and the Thinghood of consciousness, or denies that a person is an object, ontologically one is still positing something whose Being retains the meaning of present-at-hand, whether it does so explicitly or not. Substantiality is the ontological clue for determining which entity is to provide the answer to the question of the "who". Dasein is tacitly conceived in advance as something present-at-hand. This meaning of Being is always implicated in any case where the Being of Dasein has been left indefinite. Yet presence-at-hand is the kind of Being which belongs to entities whose character is not that of Dasein.

The assertion that it is I who in each case Dasein is, is ontically obvious; but this must not mislead us into supposing that the route for an ontological interpretation of what is "given" in this way has thus been unmistakably prescribed. Indeed it remains questionable whether even the mere ontical content of the above assertion does proper justice to the stock of phenomena belonging to everyday Dasein. It could be that the "who" of everyday Dasein just is *not* the "I myself".

But is it not contrary to the rules of all sound method to approach a problematic without sticking to what is given as evident in the area of our theme? And what is more indubitable than the givenness of the "I"? And does not this givenness tell us that if we aim to work this out primordially, we must disregard everything else that is "given"—not only a 'world' that is [*einer seinden "Welt"*], but even the Being of other "I"s? The kind of "giving" we have here is the mere, formal, reflective awareness of the "I"; and perhaps what it gives is indeed evident. This insight even affords access to a phenomenological

problematic in its own right, which has in principle the signification of providing a framework as a "formal phenomenology of consciousness".

In this context of an existential analytic of factical Dasein, the question
arises whether giving the "I" in the way we have mentioned discloses Dasein in its everydayness, if it discloses Dasein at all. Is it then obvious a priori that access to Dasein must be gained only by mere reflective awareness
of the "I" of actions? What if this kind of 'giving-itself' on the part of Dasein
should lead our existential analytic astray and do so, indeed, in a manner
grounded in the Being of Dasein itself? Perhaps when Dasein addresses itself in the way which is closest to itself, it always says "I am this entity", and
in the long run says this loudest when it is 'not' this entity. Dasein is in each
case mine, and this is its constitution; but what if this should be the very reason why, proximally and for the most part, Dasein *is?* What if the afore-
mentioned approach, starting with the givenness of the "I" to Dasein itself,
and with a rather patent self-interpretation of Dasein should lead the existential analytic, as it were, into a pitfall? If that which is accessible by mere
"giving" can be determined, there is presumably an ontological horizon for
determining it; but what if this horizon should remain in principle undeter-
mined? It may well be that it is always ontically correct to say of this entity
that "I" am it. Yet the ontological analytic which makes use of such assertions must make certain reservations about them in principle. The word "I"
is to be understood only in the sense of a non-committal *formal indicator,*
indicating something which may perhaps reveal itself as its "opposite" in
some particular phenomenal context of Being. In that case, the "not-I" is by
no means tantamount to an entity which essentially lacks "I-hood" ["*icheit*"]
but is rather a definite kind of Being which the "I" itself possesses, such as
having lost itself [*Selbstverlorenheit*].

Yet even the the positive interpretation of Dasein which we have so far
given, already forbids us to start with the formal givenness of the "I", if our
purpose is to answer the question of the "who" in a way which is phenomenally adequate. In clarifying Being-in-the-world we have shown that a bare
subject without a world never "is" proximally, nor is it ever given. And so in
the end an isolated "I" without Others is just as far from being proximally
given. If, however, 'the Others' already are *there with us* [*mit da sind*] in
Being-in-the-world, and if this is ascertained phenomenally, even this
should not mislead us into supposing that the ontological structure of what
is thus "given" is obvious, requiring no investigation. Our task is to make visible phenomenally the species to which this Dasein-with in closest everydayness belongs, and to interpret it in a way which is ontologically appropriate.

Just as the ontical obviousness of the Being-in-itself of entities within-the-
world misleads us into the conviction that the meaning of this Being is obvious ontologically, and makes us overlook the phenomenon of the world,

the ontical obviousness of the fact that Dasein is in each case mine, also hides the possibility that the ontological problematic which belongs to it has been led astray. *Proximally* the "who" of Dasein is not only a problem *ontologically;* even *ontically* it remains concealed.

But does this mean that there are no clues whatever for answering the question of the "who" by way of existential analysis? Certainly not. . . . *If the 'I' is an essential characteristic of Dasein, then it is* one *which must be interpreted existentially.* In that case the "Who?" is to be answered only by exhibiting phenomenally a definite kind of Being which Dasein possesses. If in each case Dasein is its Self only in *existing,* then the constancy of the Self no less than the possibility of its "failure to stand by itself" requires that we formulate the question existentially and ontologically as the sole appropriate way of access to its problematic.

But if the Self is conceived "only" as a way of Being of this entity, this seems tantamount to volatilizing the real "core" of Dasein. Any apprehensiveness however which one may have about this gets its nourishment from the perverse assumption that the entity in question has at bottom the kind of Being which belongs to something present-at-hand, even if one is far from attributing to it the solidity of an occurrent corporeal Thing. Yet man's "*substance*" is not spirit as a synthesis of soul and body; it is rather existence.

EVERYDAY BEING-ONE'S-SELF AND THE "THEY"

The *ontologically* relevant result of our analysis of Being-with is the insight that the "subject character" of one's own Dasein and that of Others is to be defined existentially—that is, in terms of certain ways in which one may be. In that with which we concern ourselves environmentally the Others are encountered as what they are; they *are* what they do [*sie sind das, was sie betreiben*].

In one's concern with what one has taken hold of, whether with, for, or against, the Others, there is constant care as to the way one differs from them, whether that difference is merely one that is to be evened out, whether one's own Dasein has lagged behind the Others and wants to catch up in relationship to them, or whether one's Dasein already has some priority over them and sets out to keep them suppressed. The care about this distance between them is disturbing to Being-with-one-another, though this disturbance is one that is hidden from it. If we may express this existentially, such Being-with-one-another has the character of *distantiality* [*Abständigheit*]. The more inconspicuous this kind of Being is to everyday Dasein itself, all the more stubbornly and primordially does it work itself out.

But this distantiality which belongs to Being-with, is such that Dasein, as everyday Being-with-one-another, stands in *subjection* [*Botmässigheit*] to Others. It itself *is* not; its Being has been taken away by the Others. Dasein's everyday possibilities of Being are for the Others to dispose of as they please. These Others, moreover, are not definite Others. On the contrary, any Other can represent them. What is decisive is just that inconspicuous domination by Others which has already been taken over unawares from Dasein as Being-with. One belongs to the Others oneself and enhances their power. The "Others" whom one thus designates in order to cover up the fact of one's belonging to them essentially oneself, are those who proximally and for the most part *"are there"* in every Being-with-one-another. The "who" is not this one, not that one, not oneself [*man selbst*], not some people [*einige*], and not the sum of them all. The "who" is the neuter, the *"they"* [*das Man*].

We have shown earlier how in the environment which lies closest to us, the public "environment" already is ready-to-hand and is also a matter of concern [*mitbesorgt*]. In utilizing public means of transport and in making use of information services such as the newspaper, every Other is like the next. This Being-with-one-another dissolves one's own Dasein completely into the kind of Being of "the Others", in such a way, indeed, that the Others, as distinguishable and explicit, vanish more and more. In this inconspicuousness and unascertainability, the real dictatorship of the "they" is unfolded. We take pleasure and enjoy ourselves as *they* [*das man*] take pleasure; we read, see, and judge about literature and art as *they* see and judge; likewise we shrink back from the "great mass" as they shrink back; we find "shocking" what they find shocking. The "they", which is nothing definite, and which all are, though not as the sum, prescribes the kind of Being of everydayness.

The "they" has its own ways in which to be. That tendency of Being-with which we have called "distantiality" is grounded in the fact that Being-with-one-another concerns itself as such with *averageness,* which is an existential characteristic of the "they". The "they", in its Being, essentially makes an issue of this. Thus the "they" maintains itself factically in the averageness of that which belongs to it, of that which it regards as valid and that which it does not, and of that to which it grants success and that to which it denies it. In this averageness with which it prescribes what can and may be ventured, it keeps watch over everything exceptional that thrusts itself to the lore. Every kind of priority gets noiselessly suppressed. Overnight, everything that is primordial gets glossed over as something that has long been all known. Everything gained by a struggle becomes just something to be manipulated. Every secret loses its force. This care of averageness reveals in turn an essential tendency of Dasein which we call the "levelling down" [*Einebnung*] of all possibilities of Being.

Distantiality, averageness, and levelling down, as ways of Being for the "they", constitute what we know as "publicness" [*die Öffentlichkeit*]. Publicness proximally controls every way in which the world and Dasein get interpreted, and it is always right—not because there is some distinctive and primary relationship-of-Being in which it is related to "Things", or because it avails itself of some transparency on the part of Dasein which it has explicitly appropriated, but because it is insensitive to every difference of level and of genuineness and thus never gets to the "heart of the matter" [*"auf die Sachen"*]. By publicness everything gets obscured, and what has thus been covered up gets passed off as something familiar and accessible to everyone.

The "they" is there alongside everywhere [*ist überall dabei*], but in such a manner that it has always stolen away whenever Dasein presses for a decision. Yet because the "they" presents every judgment and decision as its own, it deprives the particular Dasein of its answerability. The "they" can, as it were, manage to have "them" constantly invoking it. It can be answerable for everything most easily, because it is not someone who needs to vouch for anything. It "was" always the "they" who did it, and yet it can be said that it has been "no one". In Dasein's everydayness the agency through which most things come about is one of which we must say that "it was no one".

Thus the particular Dasein in its everydayness is *disburdened* by the "they". Not only that; by thus disburdening it of its Being, the "they" accommodates Dasein [*kommt . . . dem Dasein entgegen*] if Dasein has any tendency to take things easily and make them easy. And because the "they" constantly accommodates the particular Dasein by disburdening it of its Being, the "they" retains and enhances its stubborn dominion.

Everyone is the other, and no one is himself. The *"they"*, which supplies the answer to the question of the *"who"* of everyday Dasein, is the *"nobody"* to whom every Dasein has already surrendered itself in Being-among-one-other [*Untereinandersein*].

In these characters of Being which we have exhibited everyday Being-among-one-another, distantiality, averageness, levelling down, publicness, the disburdening of one's Being, and accommodation—lies that "constancy" of Dasein which is closest to us. This "constancy" pertains not to the enduring Being-present-at-hand of something, but rather to Dasein's kind of Being as Being-with. Neither the Self of one's own Dasein nor the Self of the Other has as yet found itself or lost itself as long as it is [*seiend*] in the modes we have mentioned. In these modes one's way of Being is that of inauthenticity and failure to stand by one's Self. To be in this way signifies no lessening of Dasein's facticity, just as the "they", as the "nobody", is by no means nothing at all. On the contrary, in this kind of Being, Dasein is an *ens realissimum,* if by "Reality" we understand a Being that has the character of Dasein.

Of course, the "they" is as little present-at-hand as Dasein itself. The more openly the "they" behaves, the harder it is to grasp, and the slier it is, but the less is it nothing at all. If we "see" it ontico-ontologically with an unprejudiced eye, it reveals itself as the "Realest subject" of everydayness. And even if it is not accessible like a stone that is present-at-hand, this is not in the least decisive as to its kind of Being. One may neither decree prematurely that this "they" is "really" nothing, nor profess the opinion that one can interpret this phenomenon ontologically by somehow "explaining" it as what results from taking the Being-present-at-hand-together of several subjects and then fitting them together. On the contrary, in working out concepts of Being one must direct one's course by these phenomena, which cannot be pushed aside.

Furthermore, the "they" is not something like a "universal subject" which is a plurality of subjects have hovering above them. One can come to take it this way only if the Being of such "subjects" is understood as having a character other than that of Dasein, and if these are regarded as cases of a genus of occurrents—cases which are factually present-at-hand. With this approach, the only possibility ontologically is that everything which is not a case of this sort is to be understood in the sense of genus and species. The "they" is not the genus to which the individual Dasein belongs, nor can we come across it in such entities as an abiding characteristic. That even the traditional logic fails us when confronted with these phenomena, is not surprising if we bear in mind that it has its foundation in an ontology of the present-at-hand—an ontology which, moreover, is still a rough one. So no matter in how many ways this logic may be improved and expanded, it cannot in principle be made any more flexible. Such reforms of logic, oriented towards the 'humane sciences', only increase the ontological confusion.

The "they" is an existentiale; and as a primordial phenomenon, it belongs to Dasein's positive constitution. It itself has, in turn, various possibilities of becoming concrete as something characteristic of Dasein [*seiner daseinsmässigen Konkretion*]. The extent to which its dominion becomes compelling and explicit may change in the course of history.

The Self of everyday Dasein is the *they-self,* which we distinguish from the *authentic Self*—that is, from the Self which has been taken hold of in its own way [*eigens ergriffenen*]. As they-self, the particular Dasein has been *dispersed* into the "they", and must first find itself. This dispersal characterizes the "subject" of that kind of Being which we know as concernful absorption in the world we encounter as closest to us. If Dasein is familiar with itself as they-self, this means at the same time that the "they" itself prescribes that way of interpreting the world and Being-in-the-world which lies closest. Dasein is for the sake of the "they" in an everyday manner, and the "they" itself articulates the referential context of significance. When entities are encountered, Dasein's world frees them for a totality of involvements with which the "they" is familiar, and within the limits which have been established with the "they's" averageness. *Proximally,* factical Dasein is in the with-world, which is discovered in an average way. *Proximally,* it is not "I", in the sense of my own Self, that "am", but rather the Others, whose way is that of the "they". In terms *of* the "they", and as the "they", I am "given" proximally to "myself" [*mir "selbst"*]. Proximally, Dasein is "they", and for the most part it remains so. If Dasein discovers the world in its own way [*eigens*] and brings it close, if it discloses to itself its own authentic Being, then this discovery of the "world" and this disclosure of Dasein are always accomplished as a clearing-away of concealments and obscurities, as a breaking up of the disguises with which Dasein bars its own way.

With this interpretation of Being-with and Being-one's-Self in the "they", the question of the "who" of the everydayness of Being-with-one-another is answered. These considerations have at the same time brought us a concrete understanding of the basic constitution of Dasein: Being-in-the-world, in its everydayness and its averageness, has become visible.

From the kind of Being which belongs to the "they"—the kind which is closest—everyday Dasein draws its pre-ontological way of interpreting its Being. In the first instance ontological interpretation follows the tendency to interpret it this way: it understands Dasein in terms of the world and comes across it as an entity within-the-world. But that is not all: even that meaning of Being on the basis of which these "subject" entities [*diese seienden "Subjekte"*] get understood, is one which that ontology of Dasein which is "'closest' to us lets itself present in terms of the world". But because the phenomenon of the world itself gets passed over in this absorption in the world, its place gets taken [*tritt an seine Stelle*] by what is present-at-hand within-the-world, namely, Things. The Being of those entities which *are there with us,* gets conceived as presence-at-hand. Thus by exhibiting the positive phenomenon of the closest everyday Being in-the-world, we have made it possible to get an insight into the reason why an ontological interpretation of this state of Being has been missing. *This very state* of *Being, in its everyday kind of Being, is what proximally misses itself and covers itself up.*

If the Being of everyday Being-with-one-another is already different in principle from pure presence-at-hand—in spite of the fact that it is seemingly close to it ontologically—still less can the Being of the authentic Self be conceived as presence-at-hand. *Authentic Being-one's-self* does not rest upon an exceptional condition of the subject, a condition that has been detached from the "they—*of the "they" as an essential existentiale.*

But in that case there is ontologically a gap separating the selfsameness of the authentically existing Self from the identity of that "I" which maintains itself throughout its manifold Experiences.

5.7

Man's Nature

Rabindranath Tagore

From the time when Man became truly conscious of his own self he also became conscious of a mysterious spirit of unity which found its manifestation
through him in his society. It is a subtle medium of relationship between individuals, which is not for any utilitarian purpose but for its own ultimate
truth, not a sum of arithmetic but a value of life. Somehow Man has felt that
this comprehensive spirit of unity has a divine character which could claim
the sacrifice of all that is individual in him, that in it dwells his highest meaning transcending his limited self; representing his best freedom.

Man's reverential loyalty to this spirit of unity is expressed in his religion;
it is symbolized in the names of his deities. That is why, in the beginning, his
gods were tribal gods, even gods of the different communities belonging to
the same tribe. With the extension of the consciousness of human unity his
God became revealed to him as one and universal, proving that the truth of
human unity is the truth of Man's God.

In the Sanskrit language, religion goes by the name *dharma,* which in the
derivative meaning implies the principle of relationship that holds us firm,
and in its technical sense means the virtue of a thing, the essential quality of
it; for instance, heat is the essential quality of fire, though in certain of its
stages it may be absent.

Religion consists in the endeavour of men to cultivate and express those
qualities which are inherent in the nature of Man the Eternal, and to have
faith in him. If these qualities were absolutely natural in individuals, religion
could have no purpose. We begin our history with all the original promptings of our brute nature which helps us to fulfill those vital needs of ours that
are immediate. But deeper within us there is a current of tendencies which

From *The Religion of Man,* Chapter X, pp. 89–96. First appeared in 1931.

runs in many ways in a contrary direction, the life current of universal humanity. Religion has its function in reconciling the contradiction, by subordinating the brute nature to what we consider as the truth of Man. This is helped when our faith in the Eternal Man, whom we call by different names and imagine in different images, is made strong. The contradiction between the two natures in us is so great that men have willingly sacrificed their vital needs and courted death in order to express their *dharma,* which represents the truth of the Supreme Man.

The vision of the Supreme Man is realized by our imagination, but not created by our mind. More real than individual men, he surpassed each of us in his permeating personality which is transcendental. The procession of his ideas, following his great purpose, is ever moving across obstructive facts towards the perfected truth. We, the individuals, having our place in his composition, may or may not be in conscious harmony with his purpose, may even put obstacles in his path bringing down our doom upon ourselves. But we gain our true religion when we consciously co-operate with him, finding our exceeding joy through suffering and sacrifice. For through our own love for him we are made conscious of a great love that radiates from his being, who is Mahatma, the Supreme Spirit.

The great Chinese sage, Lao-tze, has said: 'One who may die, but will not perish, has life everlasting.' It means that he lives in the life of the immortal Man. The urging for this life induces men to go through the struggle for a true survival. And it has been said in our scripture: 'Through *adharma* (the negation of *dharma*) man prospers, gains what appears desirable, conquers enemies, but he perishes at the root.' In this saying it is suggested that there is a life which is truer for men than their physical life which is transient.

Our life gains what is called 'value' in those of its aspects which represent eternal humanity in knowledge, in sympathy, in deeds, in character and creative works. And from the beginning of our history we are seeking, often at the cost of everything else, the value for our life and not merely success; in other words, we are trying to realize in ourselves the immortal Man, so that we may die but not perish. This is the meaning of the utterance in the Upanishad: *Tam vedyam purusham veda, yathā mā vo mrityuh parivyathah'*—'Realize the Person so that thou mayst not suffer from death.'

The meaning of these words is highly paradoxical, and cannot be proved by our senses or our reason, and yet its influence is so strong in men that they have cast away all fear and greed, defied all the instincts that cling to the brute nature, for the sake of acknowledging and preserving a life which belongs to the Eternal Person. It is all the more significant because many of them do not believe in its reality, and yet are ready to fling away for it all that they believe to be final and the only positive fact.

We call this ideal reality 'spiritual.' That word is vague; nevertheless, through the dim light which reaches us across the barriers of physical existence, we seem to have a stronger faith in the spiritual Man than in the physical; and from the dimmest period of his history, Man has a feeling that the apparent facts of existence are not final; that his supreme welfare depends upon his being able to remain in perfect relationship with some great mystery behind the veil, at the threshold of a larger life, which is forever giving him a far higher value than a mere continuation of his physical life in the material world.

Our physical body has its comprehensive reality in the physical world, which may be truly called our universal body, without which our individual body would miss its function. Our physical life realizes its growing meaning through a widening freedom in its relationship with the physical world, and this gives it a greater happiness than the mere pleasure of satisfied needs. We become aware of a profound meaning of our own self at the consciousness of some ideal of perfection, some truth beautiful or majestic which gives us an inner sense of completeness, a heightened sense of our own reality. This strengthens man's faith, effective even if indefinite—his faith in an objective ideal of perfection comprehending the human world. His vision of it has been beautiful or distorted, luminous or obscure, according to the stages of development that his consciousness has attained. But whatever may be the name and nature of his religious creed, man's ideal of human perfection has been based upon a bond of unity running through individuals culminating in a supreme Being who represents the eternal in human personality. In his civilization the perfect expression of this idea produces the wealth of truth which is for the revelation of Man and not merely for the success of life. But when this creative ideal which is *dharma* gives place to some overmastering passion in a large body of men civilization bursts out in an explosive flame, like a star that has lighted its own funeral pyre of boisterous brilliancy.

When I was a child I had the freedom to make my own toys out of trifles and create my own games from imagination. In my happiness my playmates had their full share, in fact the complete enjoyment of my games depended upon their taking part in them. One day, in this paradise of our childhood, entered the temptation from the market world of the adult. A toy brought from an English shop was given to one of our companions; it was perfect, it was big and wonderfully lifelike. He became proud of the toy and less mindful of the game; he kept that expensive thing carefully away from us, glorying in his exclusive possession of it, feeling himself superior to his playmates whose toys were cheap. I am sure if he could use the modern language of history he would say that he was more civilized than ourselves to the extent of his owning that ridiculously perfect toy.

One thing he failed to realize in his excitement—a fact which at the moment seemed to him insignificant—that this temptation obscured something a great deal more perfect than his toy, the revelation of the perfect child which ever dwells in the heart of man, in other words, the *dharma* of the child. The toy merely expressed his wealth but not himself, not the child's creative spirit, not the child's generous joy in his play, his identification of himself with others who were his compeers in his play world. Civilization is to express Man's *dharma* and not merely his cleverness, power and possession.

Once there was an occasion for me to motor down to Calcutta from a place a hundred miles away. Something wrong with the mechanism made it necessary for us to have a repeated supply of water almost every half-hour. At the first village where we were compelled to stop, we asked the help of a man to find water for us. It proved quite a task for him, but when we offered him his reward, poor though he was, he refused to accept it. In fifteen other villages the same thing happened. In a hot country, where travellers constantly need water and where the water supply grows scanty in summer, the villagers consider it their duty to offer water to those who need it. They could easily make a business out of it, following the inexorable law of demand and supply. But the ideal which they consider to be their *dharma* has become one with their life. They do not claim any personal merit for possessing it.

Lao-tze, speaking about the man who is truly good, says: 'He quickens but owns not. He acts but claims not. Merit he accomplishes but dwells not in it. Since he does not dwell in it; it will never leave him.' That which is outside ourselves we can sell; but that which is one with our being we cannot sell. This complete assimilation of truth belongs to the paradise of perfection; it lies beyond the purgatory of self-consciousness. To have reached it proves a long process of civilization.

To be able to take a considerable amount of trouble in order to supply water to a passing stranger and yet never to claim merit or reward for it seems absurdly and negligibly simple compared with the capacity to produce an amazing number of things per minute. A millionaire tourist, ready to corner the food market and grow rich by driving the whole world to the brink of starvation, is sure to feel too superior to notice this simple thing while rushing through our villages at sixty miles an hour.

Yes, it is simple, as simple as it is for a gentleman to be a gentle man; but that simplicity is the product of centuries of culture. That simplicity is difficult of imitation. In a few years' time, it might be possible for me to learn how to make holes in thousands of needles simultaneously by turning a wheel, but to be absolutely simple in one's hospitality to one's enemy, or to a stranger, requires generations of training. Simplicity takes no account of its own value, claims no wages, and therefore those who are enamoured of power do not realize that simplicity of spiritual expression is the highest product of civilization.

A process of disintegration can kill this rare fruit of a higher life, as a whole race of birds possessing some rare beauty can be made extinct by the vulgar power of avarice which has civilized weapons. This fact was clearly proved to me when I found that the only place where a price was expected for the water given to us was a suburb of Calcutta, where life was richer, the water supply easier and more abundant and where progress flowed in numerous channels in all directions. It shows that a harmony of character which the people once had was lost—the harmony with the inner self which is greater in its universality than the self that gives prominence to its personal needs. The latter loses its feeling of beauty and generosity in its calculation of profit; for there it represents exclusively itself and not the universal Man.

There is an utterance in the *Atharva Veda,* wherein appears the question as to who it was that gave Man his music. Birds repeat their single notes, or a very simple combination of them, but Man builds his world of music and establishes ever new rhythmic relationships of notes. These reveal to him a universal mystery of creation which cannot be described. They bring to him the inner rhythm that transmutes facts into truth. They give him pleasure not merely for his sense of hearing, but for his deeper being, which gains satisfaction in the ideal of perfect unity. Somehow man feels that truth finds its body in such perfection; and when he seeks for his own best revelation he seeks a medium which has the harmonious unity, as has music. Our impulse to give expression to Universal Man produces arts and literature. They in their cadence of lines, colours, movements, words, thoughts, express vastly more than what they appear to be on the surface. They open the windows of our mind to the eternal reality of man. They are the superfluity of wealth of which we claim our common inheritance whatever may be the country and time to which we belong; for they are inspired by the universal mind. And not merely in his arts, but in his own behaviour, the individual must for his excellence give emphasis to an ideal which has some value of truth that ideally belongs to all men. In other words, he should create a music of expression in his conduct and surroundings which makes him represent the supreme Personality. And civilization is the creation of the race, its expression of the Universal Man.

When I first visited Japan I had the opportunity of observing where the two parts of the human sphere strongly contrasted; one, on which grew up the ancient continents of social ideal, standards of beauty, codes of personal behaviour; and the other part, the fluid element, the perpetual current that carried wealth to its shores from all parts of the world. In half a century's time Japan has been able to make her own the mighty spirit of progress which suddenly burst upon her one morning in a storm of insult and menace. China also has had her rousing, when her self-respect was being knocked to pieces through series of helpless years, and I am sure she also will master before long the instrument which hurt her to the quick. But the ideals that imparted life and body to Japanese civilization had been nourished in the reverent hopes of countless generations through ages which were not primarily occupied in an incessant hunt for opportunities. They had those large tracts of leisure in them which are necessary for the blossoming of Life's beauty and the ripening of her wisdom.

On the one hand we can look upon the modern factories in Japan with their numerous mechanical organizations and engines of production and destruction of the latest type. On the other hand, against them we may see some fragile vase, some small piece of silk, some architecture of sublime simplicity, some perfect lyric of bodily movement. We may also notice the Japanese expression of courtesy daily extracting from them a considerable amount of time and trouble. All these have come not from an intense consciousness of the value of reality which takes time for its fullness. What Japan reveals in her skilful manipulation of telegraphic wires and railway lines, of machines for manufacturing things and for killing men, is more or less similar to what we see in other countries which have similar opportunity for training. But in her art of living, her pictures, her code of conduct, the various forms of beauty which her religious and social ideals assume, Japan expresses her own personality, her *dharma,* which, in order to be of any worth, must be unique and at the same time represent Man of the Everlasting Life.

Lao-tze has said: 'Not knowing the eternal causes passions to rise; and that is evil.' He has also said: 'Let us die, and yet not perish.' For we die when we lose our physical life, we perish when we miss our humanity. And humanity is the *dharma* of human beings.

What is evident in this world is the endless procession of moving things; but what is to be realized is the supreme human Truth by which the human world is permeated.

We must never forget today that a mere movement is not valuable in itself, that it may be a sign of a dangerous form of inertia. We must be reminded that a great upheaval of spirit, a universal realization of true dignity of man once caused by Buddha's teachings in India, started a movement for centuries which produced illumination of literature, art, science and numerous efforts of public beneficence. This was a moment whose motive force was not some additional accession of knowledge or power or urging of some overwhelming passion. It was an inspiration for freedom, the freedom which enables us to realize *dharma,* the truth of Eternal Man.

Lao-tze in one of his utterances has said: 'Those who have virtue (*dharma*) attend to their obligations; those who have no virtue attend to their claims.' Progress which is not related to an inner *dharma,* but to an attraction which is external, seeks to satisfy our endless claims. But civilization, which is an ideal, gives us the abundant power to renounce which is the power that realizes the infinite and inspires creation.

This great Chinese sage has said: 'To increase life is called a blessing.' For the increase of life realizes the eternal life and yet does not transcend the limits of life's unity. The mountain pine grows tall and great, its every inch maintains the rhythm of an inner balance, and therefore even in its seeming extravagance it has the reticent grace of self-control. The tree and its productions belong to the same vital system of cadence; the timber, the flowers, leaves and fruits are one with the tree; their exuberance is not a malady of exaggeration, but a blessing.

5.8

Self in Japanese Culture

Takie Sugiyama Lebra

In recent years the concept of "personality" has been discredited in academic discussion, if not in common speech, as too Western-biased, and, particularly in anthropology, as trapped in the tarnished image of the culture-and-personality school. In its stead has emerged the "self" as a more trendy, popular subject of debate involving universalism and relativism, etics and emics (Schweder and Levine 1984, Marsella et al. 1985, White and Kirkpatrick 1985). This essay takes as its point of departure the universalistic thesis on self which is credited to G. H. Mead (1934) and Hallowell (1955). The most essential feature of self, according to these and other scholars, is self-awareness, which is variously worded such as reflexivity, self-objectification, self as an object to itself, self as at once subject and object, "I" and "me," and so on. The same thesis postulates that self-awareness is generated and fostered through self–other interaction on the one hand and the symbolic processing of information on the other. Put another way, self-awareness as a universal feature of self is a product of social participation and cultural representation. To the extent that social and cultural diversity in the human world is inevitable, the quality and content of self-awareness as well as the boundary condition of self are destined to vary from one social-cultural group to the next. The paradox is obvious: universalism and relativism, far from being mutually exclusive, entail each other. A discovery of cultural variations in self-awareness does not disprove but rather confirms the above-stated universalistic thesis on self. My essay is intended, therefore to contribute to understanding the generic features of self by presenting a Japanese variety.[1]

Based upon long years of life as a native Japanese and of research experience as a marginal Japanese, I propose to organize the infinitely variable selves into three dimensions, and these are labeled "the interactional self," "the inner self," and "the boundless self." While defining and elaborating each of these, I attempt to show how one dimension links up to or flows into another.

THE INTERACTIONAL SELF

The interactional self refers to the awareness of self as defined, sustained, enhanced, or blemished through social interaction. This label may sound redundant insofar as all selves are a product of social interaction as stated earlier, and for this reason this dimension of self may be found most commonly across cultural groups. But I am referring here to the particular sense of immediacy of self–other interaction and relationship underlying self-awareness. Self here is "socially contextualized" (Shweder and Levine 1984), and critically interdependent with others in a high degree of awareness. Of all phases of the interactional self, two polar orientations are singled out here: presentational and empathetic.

The presentational self

The presentational self involves the surface layer of self, metaphorically localized on the person's face, visible or exposed to others either in actuality or imagination. The person's self-awareness is sharpened as the object of attention, inspection, and appraisal by others around. This self-awareness is labeled "kao," "mentsu," "taimen," "menboku," "teisai," "sekentei." These terms might be translated as honor, self-esteem, dignity, reputation, and the like, but such translations do not fully convey the self's sensitivity to interactional immediacy and vulnerability entailed in the Japanese terms.

The presentational self is upheld by the presenter's performance which ranges from routine behavior to status attainment, from enactment of protocols to prominent achievement, from conformity to distinction. What obsesses Japanese today is performance in career making, which is preceded by educational achievements as irrevocably scored by the prestige rank of the school admitted to. The housewife's self is affected by vicarious sharing of her husband's promotion or demotion in his career, or her son's success or failure in entrance examinations.

Self's performance (or appearance) is only a part of the presentational self. Others play an equally indispensable part. First, others are significant as an actual or potential audience, watching self's performance approvingly or disapprovingly. Self here consists of continuous reflexivity between performance by self and sanctions by the audience.

Goffman's (1959) dramaturgical analogy fits in well with the above situation, except that the performance–audience relationship in the Japanese social drama is not limited to face-to-face interaction. While still accompanied by a sense of immediacy, the Japanese self, or face here, is often addressed to the world of audience not in immediate presence here and now. This world of audience is called *seken,* and the face-sensitive self addressed to the *seken* is identified as *sekentei.* The close relationship between the *seken* and face is indicated by common expressions like "unable to face the seken" (*seken ni kao muke ga dekina*) or "have no face to meet the seken" (*seken ni awaseru kao ga nai*).

The *seken* constituency varies in accordance to where self happens to stand, and in which direction it faces. It may include one's kindred (outside the immediate family), neighbors, schoolmates, colleagues, clientele, or a large, ill-defined aggregate of people, known and unknown to self. In this sense, the *seken-sekentei* relationship offers another example in line with Bachnik's (1986) interpretation of Japanese self and other as indexical (not referential) of spatial/temporal distance with self as the zero point of the coordinates.

While the *seken* has something in common with the Western concept of "reference group" (Inoue 1977), or with "the generalized other" of Mead, I identify it as the generalized audience or jury surrounding the self in an inescapable way. Two features of the *seken* make the self especially vulnerable to its sanction. In parallel with the "face"-focused self, the *seken-other is* equipped with its own "eyes," "ears," and "mouth," watching, hearing, and gossiping about the self. This body metaphor contributes to the sense of immediacy and inescapability of the *seken*'s presence. On the other hand, the *seken* itself is immediately invisible and ill-defined and thus can make the self defenseless.

A person or action is described in relation to the *seken,* such as *seken-nami* (conformative to *seken* standard, or ordinary), *seken-banare* (incongruent with *seken* convention, or eccentric), *seken-shirazu* (unaware of *seken* rules, or naive), and so on. Inoue (1977: 31) speculates that Japanese have traditionally held "seken-nami" as their goal to attain. Even today, my female informants, if unmarried in their late twenties or older, tend to confess that they are eager to marry, not because they really want spouses but because their *sekentei* hurts ("sekentei ga warui"). They wish, in other words, to appear *seken-nami.*

Self as an actor in the social theater needs not only audience but producers, co-actors, and stage staff. Others here play a co-presentational role in protecting or hurting the presentational self. The face-focused self thus depends for its welfare on others' treatment, politeness, hospitality, and so on. A man who takes his presentational self seriously depends upon his wife's cooperation, when the couple are exposed to outsiders, for example, in host–guest interaction, for sustaining his self as the head of the house. The wife may speak respectfully to her husband, appear modest and compliant with him, quite unlike her usual self. Likewise, an organizer of ceremonies like weddings and funerals pays great attention to the proper rank-ordering of attendants in seat arrangements, order of speakers, order of incense burning, etc., so that every face may be sustained or at least no face smeared.

There is a third role to be played by others. The social standing of one's face is rated in comparison with that of another's, and thus two or more faces may become competitive. Under the seniority rule of Japanese bureaucracy, the same-year entrants are expected to be promoted simultaneously as rank peers, but the pyramidal structure of a bureaucracy necessitates some of the peers to outrank others at certain points of their careers. It is this possibility of being passed by one's peers, or worse yet by a junior entrant, that mid-career employees fear most. Paradoxically, the seniority rule, which should function to minimize internal competition, in fact throws peers into ferocious competition and leaves losers totally demoralized. The losers in career competitions are face-losers in the eyes of their families, friends, or *seken* as a whole. Without considering this aspect of work careers, what is known as Japanese workaholism cannot be fully understood. It is for the same reason that the employee, with no prospect of further promotion, is transferred elsewhere or encouraged to retire prematurely and find another job. In short, the presentational self is keenly aware of other as a rival as well.

The presentational self can vary in its expression between two extremes: aggressive and defensive, assertive and inhibited, exhibitive and modest. In private conversation with a congenial other, it is not uncommon for a Japanese speaker, particularly male, to brag about his success and accomplishments, expecting the listener to respond with praise. But under other circumstances, the same speaker is likely to present an inhibited, humble self in reflection of his keen awareness of those others cast in three roles—audience, co-actor or staging personnel, and competitor—at whose mercy his self stands. In public, the Japanese person tends to play up self-effacement and modesty.

The above depiction of Japanese self as presentational reinforces Benedict's (1946) characterization of Japanese in terms of a shame complex, but does so only partially and conditionally. As my analysis unfolds, Benedict's position will be reversed.

The empathetic self

Empirically continuous with, but conceptually distinct from the presentational self is the intimacy-seeking, empathetic self, the second orientation of the interactional self. Involved here is the awareness of self as an insider of a group or network, or as a partner to a relationship. Though not necessarily actualized, the ideal relationship among members is characterized in terms of love, trust, fellowship, support, cooperation, solidarity, interdependence, sociability, and so on. Others surrounding self here are recognized more as *miuchi* (fellow insiders, tied together in actual or figurative kinship) in contrast to *tanin* (outsiders, known and unknown to self, lacking kinship ties). The above-discussed *seken* as the generalized audience for the presentational self is felt to consist largely of *tanin*.

The empathetic self feels attached or bonded to other, as between intimate friends, fellow members of a group, parent and child, leader and follower, master and disciple, patron and client, *sempai* (senior) and *kōhai* (junior), and so on. The ultimate state of this orientation is a feeling of fusion, synergy, or interchangeability of self and other. In the Japanese figures of speech, self–other substitution often appears as in "becoming a surrogate of my mother" (*haha ni narikawaru*), "I apologize as a surrogate of my son" (*musuko ni narikawatte owabi shimasu*).[2] The Japanese idiom, in other words, can load self and other with "surrogate other" and "surrogate self," respectively. It is because of the possibility of such self–other substitution not only in speech but in practice that Japanese often find it necessary to underline the true, non-substitutive self as *honnin* in distinction from *dainin* or *kawari* (surrogate). This aspect of self has been elaborated elsewhere (Lebra 1989).

Empathy is expected to be mutual. Not only does the self feel bonded and empathetic to other but seeks empathy from other. Again in personal conversation, a Japanese speaker reveals reasons for the listener to feel sorry for him, such as being a victim of someone's unfair treatment. Empathy thus ties in with *amae,* the desire for being indulged. The self, in seeking empathy, may stimulate empathetic feelings in other through *amae* behavior, and other in turn may respond with empathetic indulgence, *amayakasu.*

Like the presentational self, the empathetic self, too, is a universal element of self. Difference may lie in the central location of bonding. While middle-class Americans, for example, tend to locate the bonded self within the family, Japanese spread it to wider society, particularly in a group of intimate peers (Salamon 1974) such as former classmates, or an office group within a company (Rohlen 1975). Further, for Americans, sexual bonding seems essential to the well-being of the empathetic self, and therefore, within the family, it is conjugal ties that claim priority. For Japanese, sexuality plays a less crucial role, and the strongest bond within the family is that of parent, mother in particular, and child. Thus, conjugal estrangement does not necessarily result in a family break-up as it would in America. It may be hypothesized, then, that intimacy seeking among Americans is more concentrated within a family, and further condensed in a sexual pair, whereas it is more dispersed and generalized among Japanese. Insofar as intimacy translates into bodily touching, Barnlund's (1975) finding is interesting in this context.

Based upon the responses from samples of college students, Barnlund found out that more American students touch their parents in more areas of the body than the Japanese. Further, in touching a friend, the American respondents showed a stark contrast between the same-sex and opposite-sex friend as target persons, the latter being much more touchable in all regions of the body. The Japanese did not reveal so much difference between the two kinds of friends. This finding, however, should not be taken as evidence of Japanese being more isolated than Americans are: intimacy or solidarity can take many forms, e.g., co-drinking, co-dining, without necessarily touching, and Japanese are likely, as stated above, to disperse intimate feelings over wider circles which are not included in Barnlund's research.

The bonded self does not always come into awareness as something positive. To the extent that a social bond is sustained by each participant's share of dedication or responsibility, the emotional, social, or economic cost may be felt to outweigh the benefit. In a reciprocal relationship usually involved in such tight consociation, a sense of obligatory *giri* may come to override that of sentimental attachment, *ninjō*. Nevertheless, the intimacy-seeking self is not easily abandoned partly because isolation is a worse alternative but also because it is locked with the presentational self, as will be explained below.

The presentational and empathetic dimensions of self are in opposition in that the former presupposes social or psychological distance between self and other to the point of self-defense and other-avoidance while the latter minimizes such distance. The main commodity in self-presentation is esteem but empathetic ties are constructed on the basis of mutual attachment. If the faulty self-presentation brings shame, the loss of the empathetic self means loneliness. All these differences notwithstanding, the empathetic self flows into the presentational self. Being isolated, being excluded from a group, lacking a friend whose support one can count on or who counts on one's support—all these can result in one's loss of face vis-à-vis the ubiquitous audience. Some of my elderly informants expect to be looked after by their daughters or daughters-in-law, however unwillingly on both sides. The family care of the aged, which superficially may indicate a strong bonding between generations, in fact turns out to involve the presentational self to be kept up in good standing: the elderly "abandoned" into a nursing home, as well as the children abandoning them, would have their *sekentei* damaged. This is why some Japanese, including my informants, consider the childless elderly more fortunate since they are shame-free to enter care homes. Giving and receiving a gift as a symbol of friendship may be also in the same bind in that giving is a performance to live up to one's reputation as much as receiving is a proof of one's honor being sustained. I speculate that the self-presentational function makes gift exchange so compulsive.

The above examples presuppose a triad: self (e.g., gift-giver), other in direct interaction with self (gift-receiver), and a third as audience (*seken*). But the last two are not always distinct. The self–other distance may decrease and increase between the same partners to interaction. One and the same other moves over toward self to create an empathetic rapport, and moves away from self to become an audience, stage manipulator, or even rival confronting the presentational self. A group of inseparable neighbor women usually support one another but also, behind the scenes, may compete with one another over their husbands' promising or faltering careers, and their children's school performances. Co-workers who work side by side every day and spend after-work hours together at a bar, may not be free from rivalry and jealousy. Father and son, co-residing, may feel close to each other until a flood of end-of-year gifts (*seibo*) are delivered home, as in a story taken from a TV home drama series, "Jikan desu yo." All the gifts turn out to be addressed to the son, a section chief of a company, from his subordinates, but none to the senior man and head of the house who is a family shop operator. The father's crushed presentational self is now stimulated and held at distance from the son as well as other members of the family.

THE INNER SELF

The interactional self is what occupies Japanese most of the time, and yet they are aware of its basically precarious, vulnerable, relative, unfixed nature. The relativity of the interactional self is best illustrated by the Japanese terms for self and other. The Japanese speaker either uses no term for self or other ("zero form" [Fischer 1964]), or selects certain terms from among many possible ones that are appropriate to the given relationship at a certain time between self and other. In addressing a child, for example, an adult male stranger is likely to call himself "uncle," just as children do in addressing male adults. Likewise, a schoolteacher, speaking to students, calls him/herself "teacher." This speech behavior, called by Suzuki (1986) "empathetic identification," reflects the lack of the exact equivalent of "I" which would serve as the fixed point of self. As long as one stays in the interactional world, multiple and variable self-identification seems necessary. A multiple and variable self like this ultimately boils down to "non-self" as symbolized by the zero form. Self saturated in the interactional world is therefore negatively described by Japanese as *jibun ga nai* (devoid of self), and is advised to retrieve itself, *jibun o torimodosu*.

A more stable self, something like "I," more immune from social relativity, is sought inwardly. The socially, outwardly[3] oriented interactional self is thus compensated for by the inner self. Japanese do divide self into the outer part and inner part. As much as the social world is divided into outside and inside (*soto* versus *uchi*), or front and back (*omote* versus *ura*), and others into outsiders and insiders, so is self divided into the outwardly (socially) involved and the inwardly oriented realms. The two realms make complementary or compensatory oppositions or juxtapositions.[4] It is the inner self that provides a fixed core for self-identity and subjectivity, and forms a potential basis of autonomy from the ever-insatiable demands from the social world. The inner self is also identified as the residence (shrine) of a god that each person is endowed with.

The inner self is symbolically localized in the chest or belly (though the latter will appear more in the third dimension of self to be discussed below), whereas the outer self is focused on the face and mouth which are socially addressed. At the center of the inner self is the *kokoro* which stands for heart, sentiment, spirit, will, or mind. While the outer self is socially circumscribed, the *kokoro* can be free, spontaneous, and even asocial. Further, the *kokoro* claims moral superiority over the outer self in that it is a reservoir of truthfulness and purity, uncontaminated by circumspections and contrivances to which the outer self is subject. This association of the *kokoro* (or inner self) with truthfulness gives rise to the paradoxical notion that the "real" truth is inexpressible. Thus words and speech as means of expression are often regarded as potentially deceptive and false, and silence as indicative of the true *kokoro* (Lebra 1987).

The moral superiority of the inner self partially accounts for the ambivalence the Japanese actor holds towards the interactional self. The face-conscious presentational self, for example, carries a negative tone, and sensitivity to shame is taken as something to be surmounted. Self-revival through religious conversion oftentimes involves a deliberate self-exposure to shame in order to become free from shame sensitivity. Instead, the "true" feelings of guilt stemming from the bottom of the "heart" are elevated in the hierarchy of moral values. Shame and guilt are not a dichotomy as conceived by Benedict, but rather, when applied to Japanese, they occupy different ranks in the moral hierarchy within a culture, guilt outranking shame (Lebra 1983).

The centrality of the inner self in Japanese self-awareness is further indicated by the sentence-completion-test result obtained from urban samples from Korea, Hong Kong, and Japan (Lebra 1986). Japanese respondents, compared with Chinese and Korean counterparts, were found consistently to pay more attention to their state of mind, feeling, and *kokoro*. To complete the sentence fragment "If you are kind to others," nearly half of the Japanese sample referred to the inner satisfaction or joy of the kind actor whereas similar responses were given by about a quarter of the Korean sample, and only 4 percent of the Chinese.

The Japanese inner–outer division of self seems to resemble the Javanese "bifurcate conception of the self, half ungestured feeling and half unfelt gesture" (Geertz 1984: 128). Indeed, the inner part, when coupled with the socially contextualized presentational self, tends to be encapsulated and remain uncommunicated or "ungestured." In this context it is not surprising that Japanese college students, compared with their American counterparts, were found to hold a larger "private" self which is not shared in communication with others, in proportion to the "public" self that is shared (Barnlund 1975).

Communicational inhibition is only one of the possible manifestations, however. The inner–outer division of self is channeled in the following directions as well. First, while this division may be detrimental to communication, Japanese also believe that the inner self, the *kokoro* in particular, is what makes communication possible and complete. One's heart, if strong, pure, and persistent enough, will eventually remove the communication barrier and reach another's heart (*kokoro ga tsujji au*). The truly empathetic self thus emerges in heart-to-heart communication. While the presentational interaction is at the opposite pole from the inner self, the empathetic communication merges with the latter.

Second, the inner self, when dissociated from the outer self, may be directed as an asocial obsession with self-expression or self-actualization through work or sheer perseverance. We find single-minded craftsmen, artists, and other professionals entirely immersed in their own world of work and performance in indifference to their social surroundings. The products of such inner concentration are often described as "loaded with *kokoro*" (*kokoro no komotta*).

Third, the moral emphasis upon the interiority of self leads to "spiritualism" aiming at the triumph of the spirit over the material world, of mind over matter, the heart over technology. It was this spiritualism that was mobilized in wartime Japan to overcome its material and technological handicaps against its Western adversaries. The inner self was a fountain of strength, energy, and perseverance independent of external resources. Today's version of spiritualism functions differently: economically affluent and technologically advanced, Japanese warn themselves against losing the *kokoro* in the midst of material abundance. Products of the most advanced computer technology are advertised in terms of *kokoro*. As noted by Moeran (1986: 73), "the word *kokoro* was the most commonly used word in advertising in Japan during the 1970s." Very recently, an automatic bread maker was invented to become available to housewives, which must have thrown all the professional bakers into identity crisis. A baker, interviewed by a TV reporter, looked unperturbed, saying, "I am not upset, because what counts after all is one's *kokoro*." He meant that his *kokoro* would produce the kind of bread that no machine could. Here, the *kokoro is* meant to counter not only techno-materialism but to preserve individual identity against mechanical standardization.

Lastly, when one is under cross-pressures from inside and outside of self, the inner self may assert itself insofar as its moral superiority is recognized. The imperative of conforming to interactional norms thus may give way to fidelity to one's inner self. "Be faithful to yourself" (*jibun* ni *chūjitsu* ni) becomes a final verdict. Spontaneous, emotional, impulsive acts are thus tolerated, and even illicit love affairs or other deviant acts, if proved to stem from the center of the inner self, are considered to have to take their "natural" courses to a final consummation. The overloaded "private self" thus has a way of releasing itself into public self.

THE BOUNDLESS SELF

The inner self thus comes to join hands with autonomy and freedom from the external world, whether material, social, or cultural. To the extent that it is free from cultural regulations, it is closer to nature than is the interactional self. And yet we have also noted that the inner self is a locus of spiritualism to transcend the natural basis of existence, and in this sense it is purely cultural. The bipolarity of the inner self along the nature–culture continuum is a corollary of the fact that the inner self is contained within the self boundary. Further, the *kokoro is* believed to manifest itself in *katachi* (outer form), and the latter in turn to shape the former. Freedom associated with the inner self is not without a ceiling. In order to attain unlimited freedom, one must be free from the self boundary itself and become a boundless self, the third dimension of self.

The notion of the boundless self, though this is my term, is embedded in the Buddhist version of transcendentalism. It is tapped from time to time particularly when one faces a need of fundamental self-reorientation. The boundless self entails disengagements from the shackling world of dichotomies, dichotomies between subject and object, self and other, inner and outer realms, existence and non-existence, life and death, sacred and profane, good and bad, and so on. The self as the subject or imposer of such dichotomies through thinking, willing, feeling, or evaluating, then, must be overcome. Self-awareness must be freed from the subject–object differentiation.[5]

With no resistance, self is supposed to merge with the rest of the world. Merging means a twofold process: on the one hand, self becomes part of the objective world or nature; and on the other, self absorbs the outer world into itself. These processes are two aspects of the same coin. Suzuki, in his popular writings (1955), finds the essence of all religions, including Christianity, in the absolute "passivity" or non-resistance without which nothing really can enter the self. With passivity, self becomes an unlimited receptor or reflector of the "true" nature.

In self–other relationship, we have characterized the interactional self as relative, multiple, and variable in accordance to where and how self stands vis-à-vis other; a less relative, more stable, fixed self is captured in the encapsulated inner self—the world of pure subjectivity. Now, in the boundless self, relativity is overcome by the mutual embracement of self and other, subject and object. Far from being actively assertive, self is supposed to be absolutely passive and receptive, and passivity entails the state of being empty. The ultimate self then is equated, paradoxically, with the empty self, non-self, non-thinking, mindless, or nothingness (*muga, mushin, mu,* etc.). Self-awareness itself is to be transcended.

As for body symbolism, the boundless self centers around the belly, *hara* (Lebra 1976), while the center of the inner self is the heart, *kokoro,* although *hara* and *kokoro* are also used interchangeably to mean the inner self. "Having a *hara*" (*hara ga aru*), or "having one's *hara* well-settled" (*hara no suwatta*), refers to the mental stability not upset by small matters. "Having a big *hara*" (*haraga okii*) implies a mental capacity for absorbing all kinds of troubles instead of being upset and obsessed with them. The *hara* capacity thus seems to correspond to the degree of autonomy from the boundary of self.

To transcend dichotomies involves a negation of order. The world of religion is that in which "you can hit anybody when you want to, kick anybody if you want to, or conversely, you just let yourself fall down when kicked by someone or even let yourself die—it is the world of lawlessness (*muchakucha*). That kind of world, if there could be one, must be recognized as one of indiscretion, one that transcends good and bad" (Suzuki 1955: 27–8). If order is a cultural product, the Buddhist universe is pure nature where chaos predominates. The boundless self, merging with such a universe, represents entropy, so to speak. When applied to time, entropy is translated into *mujō* (evanescence) in which everything in existence is believed to change or perish.

All these ideas around the boundless self may represent a symbolic license of exaggeration which cannot be actualized. Concepts like non-self self, and entropic self may sound simply absurd. Nevertheless, the boundless self, thus conceived, offers an alternative goal or strategy that can be mobilized to disengage one from the socially or inwardly obsessed, or entrapped self.

Still, chaos is an overstatement in need of correction. There is a universal order running through the seeming chaos, and that is the idea of predestination which is expressed in the vernacular as *innen, en, inga, shukumei, unmei.* Self is no free agent to determine its own course of action, but is destined to act this way and that way. The "boundless" self is thus surrendered to this fundamental universal law. In order to become free from this chain of destiny, one must "understand" and accept it. Further, since the boundless self does not recognize the dichotomies of subject and object, good and bad, etc., it does not reject the social order. There seems to be a correspondence between a "Zen person" and a secular (social) person with respect to the significance of relationality (Kasulis 1981). The boundless self does not really "replace" the socially bounded relative self.

CONCLUSION

Three dimensions of self have been examined. These three are by no means mutually exclusive but partially overlapping layers of self which are activated as alternative strategies for self-orientations and reorientations. They are mutually compensatory, complementary, or reinforcing.

Illustrative of the dynamic interrelationship between different dimensions of self are two therapies developed in Japan, well known among medical anthropologists as well as Japan specialists. One is Naikan ("inward-looking") therapy which reorients the client from the interactional to the inner self through a period of isolated, concentrated self-reflection. Its purpose is to arouse and maximize guilt consciousness by "piercing" the innermost of his/ her *kokoro* with a mental drill so that the peak intensity of guilt will serve as a lever for self-transformation. This interiorization does not entail an alienation from the interactional dimension as a whole; rather it means a rededication of self to other through empathetic realization of other's sacrifice for self.

The other is Morita therapy whose motto is "Accept things as they are." The neurotic patient, instead of trying to fight and get rid of his illness, should swallow it as part of self. Here, we can see the therapeutic strategy to lift the self bound by the interactional (presentational in particular) dimension or preoccupied with the inner dimension to the boundless dimension. In this therapy, self and nature or self and illness are to be absorbed into one another. Here, too, social obligations, like other "facts," are to be confronted, accepted, and fulfilled.

The three dimensions are thus interrelated, without excluding one another. Ultimately, these converge in the highest value in Japanese culture, namely, "purity"—a key word embracing a variety of meanings cutting across all three dimensions. Purity refers to the absence of selfish motives which is positively demonstrated by sacrificial self-dedication to others or causes; single-minded endeavors at some project; emotional commitment in oblivion of calculated interest; honesty, sincerity, truthfulness, openness, and so on. In the boundless self, purity is identical with emptiness, non-self, nothingness, an unlimited receptor, or a reflector likened to a spotless mirror.[6] The seemingly "autonomous" inner self thus merges with the self-less self via purity.

In conclusion, I speculate, if I may, that the three dimensions can be aligned in a value hierarchy, the interactional self as the lowest, the boundless self as the highest, the inner self in the middle. Thus, the empathetic self, as closer to the inner self, ranks higher than the presentational. This hierarchy may be applied to the culture–nature continuum that has appeared in the text. It was pointed out that there is a variation in the degree of cultural "regulation" of self. It is the interactional self that is most regulated, and the boundless self least regulated, whereas the inner self is mixed. If freedom from cultural regulation is equated with the state of nature, we can say there is a culture–nature continuum along which the three selves are located. It follows then that the more cultural, the lower in the value hierarchy of selves; the more natural, the higher.

This odd correlation between culture–nature and lower–higher makes sense for Japanese to the extent that they place things natural above things artificial. After all, the more natural, the purer. Nevertheless, it does not accord with our common sense to place the natural self above the cultural self. After all, what is natural is so defined only through a cultural lens. The problem lies in our definition of culture only as regulative of nature, and of nature as free from regulation. If culture is understood as symbolically mediated "meaning," what appears as natural is profoundly cultural. The inner self is just as cultural as the interactional self in this sense. It is less regulated but more loaded with ideational "meaning." If culture is thus redefined, the above hierarchy must be reversed: the boundless self is the most cultural and the interactional self least so. It may be further conjectured that these two components of culture—regulatory and ideational—are mutually compensatory so that the less socially regulated, the more meaningful the self tends to be. In other words, the above hierarchical proposition should be restated: the lower the self, the heavier in regulation, and the higher the self, the richer in meaning. With this restatement, it may be said that the levels of self correspond to stages of mental maturation.

Returning to the initial statement on universalism and relativism, I can offer nothing more than my hunches: the interactional self is more universal and thus cross-culturally accessible, and the boundless self the least so; the meaning-loaded self is more culture-bound (culture in still another sense) than the socially regulated self.

NOTES

1. The everlasting controversy between universalists and relativists, nomotheists and idiographers, seems now to have reached a boiling point in Japanese studies. Relativists, who have portrayed Japan with emphasis upon differences between national cultures, have dominated Japan area studies, and are now under attack from universalists as creating a stereotype of Japan and thereby hindering international

communication. In my view, it is a wrong question to ask whether Japan is unique or no different from other nations. Why should difference and sameness be mutually exclusive, why should we respond with an either–or answer? In fact I do not think that a staunch universalist really believes Japan to be an exact replica of, say, Australia; neither do I find a devout relativist as seeing no speck of similarity between Japan and other countries. The either–or question itself is just another example of logical dichotomy removed from reality. Nevertheless, one must take one stand or another to write about Japan. What stand should be taken is, in my opinion, a pragmatic question. It depends upon the writer's interest or purpose at hand, or upon the kind of audience he/she has in mind. If one's goal is to facilitate international communication, one's approach has to vary depending upon the given audience: addressing the Japanese audience convinced of Japan's uniqueness will have to be quite different from addressing a group of Americans who do not question their way of life as natural and human.

2. Such identity substitution between self and other is greatly played up in some religious sects, as observed in a sect called Gadatsukai. Here "other" may be a god, ancestor, the spirit of the dead, animal spirit, or any other supernatural entity as well as a social other (Lebra 1986).

3. To avoid confusion, it should be noted that Dumont (1985) uses "inward" and "outward" in a sense totally different from the way I use them here. Comparing Western with Indian individualism, Dumont characterizes the former as "inwardly" because Westerners are "individuals-in-the-world," whereas the latter is "outwardly" in that Indians actualize their individualism when out of the world, that is, when they renounce the world. My use of inward is closer, though not identical, to Dumont's outward.

4. The double-sidedness of the Japanese self in terms of *omote* and *ura* (or *tatemae* and *honne* which are used in a sense similar to the other pair of concepts) is analyzed by Doi (1986).

5. Continuity, instead of dichotomy, between self and the object world or mind and matter, is symbolized by common references to external phenomena such as weather in depicting the moods of self. A good, happy, healthy state of self is described as "sunny," "cloudless," while the opposite state is associated with bad weather like "cloudy," "rainy," and so forth (see Tanaka-Matsumi and Marsella 1976 for word association studies on depression).

6. Out of this assemblage of the meanings of purity emerges another key word describing an ideal character of person, and that is *sunao*. Japanese parents use this term when asked what type of person they want their children to be. *Sunao* is, like purity, an admixture of different attributes: obedient but straightforward, pliable but honest, gentle but truthful to self, and so on (for the therapeutic use of this concept, see Murase 1982).

REFERENCES

Bachnik, Jane.1986. Time, Space and Person in Japanese Relationships. *Interpreting Japanese Society: Anthropological Approaches.* JASO Occasional Papers no. 5 (J. Hendry and J. Webber, eds.), Oxford: JASO.

Barnlund, Dean C. 1975. *Public and Private Self in Japan and the United States.* Tokyo: Simul Press.

Benedict, Ruth. 1946. *The Chrysanthemum and the Sword: Patterns of Japanese Culture.* Boston, Mass.: Houghton Mifflin.

Doi, Takeo. 1986. *The Anatomy of Self.* Tokyo: Kodansha.

Dumont, Louis. 1985. A Modified View of Our Origins: The Christian Beginnings of Modern Individualism. *The Category of the Person* (M. Carrithers, S. Collins, and S. Lukes, eds.), Cambridge: Cambridge University Press.

Fischer, John L. 1964. Words for Self and Others in Some Japanese Families. *American Anthropologist* 66: 116–26.

Geertz, Clifford. 1984. From the Native's Point of View: On the Nature of Anthropological Understanding. *Culture Theory: Essays on Mind, Self and Emotion* (R. A. Shweder and R. A. LeVine, eds.), Cambridge: Cambridge University Press.

Goffman, Erving. 1959. *The Presentation of Self in Everyday Life.* Garden City, N.Y.: Doubleday.

Hallowell, A. Irving. 1955. *Culture and Experience.* Philadelphia: University of Pennsylvania Press.

Inoue, Tadashi. 1977. *Sekentei no kōzō* (The structure of *seken*). Tokyo: Nihon Hōsō Shuppan Kyokai.

Kasulis, T. P. 1981. *Zen Action, Zen Person.* Honolulu: University of Hawaii Press.

Lebra, Takie Sugiyama. 1976. *Japanese Patterns of Behavior.* Honolulu: University of Hawaii Press.

1983. Shame and Guilt: A Psychocultural View of the Japanese Self. *Ethos 11:* 192–209.

1986. Compensative Justice and Moral Investment among Japanese, Chinese, and Koreans. *Japanese Culture and Behavior: Selected Readings* (T. S. Lebra and W. P. Lebra, eds.), Honolulu: University of Hawaii Press.

1987. The Cultural Significance of Silence in Japanese Communication. *Multilingua* 6: 343–57.

1989. *Migawari:* The Cultural Idiom of Self–Other Exchange in Japan. Paper presented at the Conference on Perceptions of Self: China, India and Japan, East-West Center Institute of Culture and Communication, Honolulu, August 14–18.

Marsella, Anthony J., DeVos, George, and Hsu, Francis L. K., eds. 1985. *Culture and Self: Asian and Western Perspectives.* New York: Tavistock.

Mead, George Herbert. 1934. *Mind, Self, and Society.* Chicago: University of Chicago Press.

Moeran, Brian. 1986. Individual, Group and *Seishin:* Japan's Internal Cultural Debate. *Japanese Culture and Behavior* (T. S. Lebra and W. P. Lebra, eds.), Honolulu: University of Hawaii Press.

Murase, Takao. 1982. *Sunao:* A Central Value in Japanese Psychotherapy. *Cultural Conceptions of Mental Health and Therapy* (A. J. Marsella and G. McWhite, eds.), Dodrecht: Reidel.

Rohlen, Thomas. 1975. The Company Work Group. *Modern Japanese Organization and Decision Making* (E. F. Vogel, ed.), Berkeley: University of California Press.

Salamon, Sonya. 1974. In the Intimate Arena: Japanese Women and Their Families. Ph.D. dissertation, University of Illinois.

Shweder, Richard A. and Levine, Robert A., eds. 1984. *Culture Theory: Essays on Mind, Self and Emotion.* Cambridge: Cambridge University Press.

Suzuki, Daisetsu. 1955. *Mushin to yu koto* (Reflections on *mushin.* Tokyo: Kadokawa.

Suzuki, Takao. 1986. Language and Behavior in Japan: The Conceptualization of Personal Relations. *Japanese Culture and Behavior* (T. S. Lebra and W. P. Lebra, eds.), Honolulu: University of Hawaii Press.

Tanaka-Matsumi, Junko and Marsella, Anthony J. 1976. Cross-Cultural Variations in the Phenomenological Experience of Depression: Word Association Studies. *Journal of Cross-Cultural Psychology* 7: 389–96.

White, Geoffrey and Kirkpatrick, John, eds. 1985. *Person, Self, and Experience. Exploring Pacific Ethnographies.* Berkeley: University of California Press.

STUDY QUESTIONS

1. Discuss the principal theses of Mencius's conception of human nature.
2. Do you agree with Mencius that human nature is essentially good? Argue for or against it.
3. If you assume that Mencius is correct in his assumption of human nature, how would you account for the evil and violence in the world?
4. Discuss the Islāmic conception of man.
5. Comment on the following passage: "man is a cosmic bridge through whom the moral law, as God's eminent desire, may be fulfilled in space-time."
6. Discuss the five pillars of Islāmic imperatives for man.
7. Discuss Kant's claim that enlightenment "is man's emergence from his self-incurred immaturity."
8. What role does religion play in Kant's conception of enlightenment?
9. Do you agree with Kant that "all that is needed for public enlightenment is freedom"?
10. Summarize the main arguments of Kant's article entitled "Is the Human Race Constantly Progressing?"
11. Do you agree with Kant that "the proposition that the human race has always been progressively improving and will continue to develop in the same way . . . is tenable within the most strictly theoretical context"?
12. Islāmic conception enforces a special relationship between human beings and their creator. Do you find such a conception defensible?
13. Discuss the key points of Tagore's essay entitled "Man's Nature."
14. Discuss the distinction that Tagore makes between man's "brute nature" and "true nature." What role does religion play in reconciling the two natures of human beings?
15. Explain the distinction that Heidegger makes between "one's self" and the "they."
16. Discuss the nature of Heidegger's authentic self.
17. What are the generic features of self in the Japanese culture?
18. Show how the three dimensions of self, viz., the interactional self, the inner self, and the boundless self are interconnected.
19. Lebra argues that the different levels of self correspond to stages of mental maturation. Do you believe that Lebra substantiates her thesis? Argue for your position.
20. This section outlines various conceptions of human nature. What have you learned from these conceptions? Which conception, according to you, has the most insight to give? Explain your reasons clearly.

SUGGESTIONS FOR FURTHER READING

Six Existentialist Thinkers by H.J. Blackham (New York: Grove Press, 1962) gives a fair exposition of Heidegger's philosophy. It is one of the most reliable works on leading existentialist philosophers.

A Tagore Reader edited by Amiya Chakrabarti (New York: The Macmillan Co., 1961), contains a variety of articles on the thoughts of Tagore.

"The Background of the Mencian Theory of Human Nature" by A.C. Graham in Tsing Hua *Journal of Chinese Studies,* n.s. 6, 1–2 (1967): 215–274, puts the basic issues surrounding Mencian conception of human nature in the proper perspective.

The Philosophy of Martin Heidegger by J.L. Mehta (New York: Harper Torchbooks, 1971) is an impressive account of Heidegger's philosophy.

Mencius translated by W.A.C.H. Dobson (Buffalo: University of Toronto Press, 1954), is a reliable and clear work that beginners might wish to consult.

Zen Action and Zen Person by Thomas P. Kasulis (Honolulu: University of Hawaii Press, 1981) discusses what is involved in Zen realization for a Zen person and action in the context of Japanese culture.

Creating the Kingdom of Ends by Christine M. Korsgaard (New York: Cambridge University Press, 1995) gives an excellent overview of Kant while stressing his social and political philosophy.

Rabindranath Tagore and Universal Humanism by Saumyendranath Tagore (Bombay: St. Vacuum Co., 1961) is a clear and concise account of Tagore's thought.

Index

About the Editors

Bina Gupta is professor of philosophy and director of the South Asia Studies Area and Language Center at the University of Missouri. She is also president of the Society for Asian and Comparative Philosophy. She is the author or editor of ten books, among them *Perceiving in Advaita Vedanta: Epistemological Analysis and Interpretation* (1991), *The Disinterested Witness: A Fragment of Advaita Vedanta Phenomenology* (1998), and *Cit* (Consciousness) (forthcoming). She was the recipient of the Faculty Alumnae Anniversary award, an honor given for her teaching and improving the status of women and minorities at the University of Missouri–Columbia.

J. N. Mohanty is professor of philosophy at Temple University and Woodruff Professor of Philosophy and Asian Studies at Emory University–Atlanta. He is a past president of the Indian Philosophical Congress and a member of the Institut Internationale de Philosophie, the Indian Academy of Philosophy, and the board of directors of the Center for Advanced Research in Phenomenology. He is internationally known for his work in Indian philosophy and Western phenomenology and is the author or editor of eight books, including *Transcendental Phenomenology* (1989). He has been awarded the Humbolt forschungspries for 1992 and the Sir William Jones Memorial Gold Medal by the Asiatic Society.